European Universities from the Enlightenment to 1914

European Universities from the Enlightenment to 1914

R. D. ANDERSON

OXFORD
UNIVERSITY PRESS

Great Clarendon Street, Oxford OX2 6DP

Oxford University Press is a department of the University of Oxford.
It furthers the University's objective of excellence in research, scholarship,
and education by publishing worldwide in

Oxford New York

Auckland Bangkok Buenos Aires Cape Town Chennai
Dar es Salaam Delhi Hong Kong Istanbul Karachi Kolkata
Kuala Lumpur Madrid Melbourne Mexico City Mumbai Nairobi
São Paulo Shanghai Taipei Tokyo Toronto

Oxford is a registered trade mark of Oxford University Press
in the UK and in certain other countries

Published in the United States
by Oxford University Press Inc., New York

First published 2004

British Library Cataloguing in Publication Data
Data available

Library of Congress Cataloging in Publication Data
Data applied for

ISBN 0–19–820660–7

1 3 5 7 9 10 8 6 4 2

Typeset by Regent Typesetting, London
Printed in Great Britain
on acid-free paper by
Biddles Ltd,
King's Lynn, Norfolk

Preface

The history of universities has been a lively branch of scholarship since the 1970s, but much of the work on it is specialized and difficult to find. My aim in this book is to introduce the reader to some of the results of this scholarship, and to provide within the context of general European history an interpretative account of developments during the period in which the modern university originated and flourished. Whether this 'modern' university is still the university of today, after the transition to mass higher education which began in the 1960s, is a moot point. But the evolution of the university idea in the nineteenth century, the changing relationships of research and teaching, and the characteristic forms taken by national systems of higher education still have relevance today. To give a synthesis of this kind involves some simplification of both university and general history, and the scholars on whose work I have depended may not always feel that full justice has been given to their ideas. The extensive bibliography, used in conjunction with the footnotes, will allow readers to explore this work for themselves.

The book was originally commissioned by Tony Morris at Oxford University Press, and I am grateful to him and his successor Ruth Parr for their encouragement and patience. The administrative duties which are an inescapable part of modern academic life have delayed its completion, which was eventually greatly helped by a grant of research leave from the Arts and Humanities Research Board in 2001–2. I am also grateful to the University of Edinburgh for further regular entitlements of research leave.

Access to foreign-language books and periodicals was essential, and this book could not have been written without the rich scholarly resources of the University of Edinburgh Library, the National Library of Scotland, and the British Library, supplemented in London by those of the Institute of Historical Research, the University of London Institute of Education, and the German Historical Institute. I owe a special debt to Stuart Wallace, whose enthusiasm for university history and extensive knowledge of it have fuelled many stimulating conversations. Other colleagues and friends who have contributed advice and support over the years include Paul Addison, Tricia Allerston, Richard Aldrich, Laurence Brockliss, Jeremy Crang, Pieter Dhondt, Owen Dudley Edwards, Rosemary Gentleman, John Gooding, Gloria Ketchin, the late Maurice Larkin, Richard Mackenney, Jim McMillan, Lindsay Paterson, Nicholas Phillipson, Helga Robinson-Hammerstein, Sheldon Rothblatt, Jill Stephenson, and the late Don Withrington. For the contents of the book I bear entire responsibility.

R.D.A.

September 2003

Contents

Introduction

'Traditionally,' wrote Roger Chartier and Jacques Revel in 1978, 'the history of European universities has been to a massive extent a medieval, institutional, and intellectual history.'[1] Medieval, because of a fixation with the origins of universities and with an apparent golden age of intellectual fecundity; institutional, because much historical writing was devoted to individual universities, and often written in an uncritical mode stimulated by local pride or by the jubilee and centenary celebrations which became a feature of university life in the nineteenth century. And intellectual, because there is a sense in which the history of a university is the history of the science and scholarship which are produced and taught within it. The sociology of knowledge sees universities as the institutional embodiment of academic ideas, which may divert attention from the university's social functions and lead to the neglect of periods seen as intellectually stagnant. Both the institutional and the intellectual approaches can easily become teleological, judging the past by its contribution to a narrative of evolving truth, or stressing those features which most closely conform to a supposedly unchanging 'idea of the university'.

Chartier and Revel were reporting on how the new social history of the 1960s and 1970s was beginning to renew university history, especially for the early modern period. A pioneering example was the seminar on the history of education directed at Princeton University from 1969 by Lawrence Stone, which was notable both for its methodological approaches and for switching attention from the middle ages.[2] It was the forerunner of several other collective projects, some of which in the 1970s and 1980s were based on elaborate quantitative studies of enrolments and similar data. University history also began to emerge as a subdiscipline with its own institutions and agenda.[3] In 1960, the International Commission for the History of Universities was founded as an offshoot of the International Committee of Historical Sciences, and advanced the subject through a series of international conferences and through the publication of bibliographies. A specialized journal, *History of Universities*, started publication in 1981; today it is officially linked with the International Commission. In 1982, the Conference of European Rectors, the body which represents all European universities, decided to sponsor a collective

[1] R. Chartier and J. Revel, 'Université et société dans l'Europe moderne: position des problèmes', *Revue d'Histoire Moderne et Contemporaine*, 25 (1978), 353.

[2] L. Stone (ed.), *The university in society. I. Oxford and Cambridge from the 14th to the early 19th Century*, and *II. Europe, Scotland, and the United States from the 16th to the 20th century* (Princeton, 1974–5). Cf. F. Ringer, 'Problems in the history of higher education: a review article', *Comparative Studies in Society and History*, 19 (1977), 239–58 (includes comment by Stone); C. E. McClelland, 'A step forward in the study of universities', *Minerva*, 14 (1976), 150–61.

[3] M. M. Compère, *L'Histoire de l'éducation en Europe: essai comparatif sur la façon dont elle s'écrit* (Bern, 1995), 211–14.

history which would study the 'university in society' in order to put contemporary policies and problems into historical perspective. This project produced an early flurry of publications,[4] but being conceived on a large scale it was rather slower to produce its full results. The first of four volumes written collectively by leading scholars appeared in 1992, on the middle ages. The second, on the early modern period, appeared in 1996. The volume on the period 1800–1945, edited by Walter Rüegg, was due for publication in 2004; it is likely to offer new riches, but will perhaps not reduce the value of a preliminary synthesis such as is offered here.

The present book shares the view that 'universities have always been defined, fundamentally, not by reference to some abstract ideal type, but by the clientele which they attracted and the functions which they fulfilled in a given society, by the market and social demand'.[5] To write a university history in intellectual terms is probably beyond any single scholar: the histories of science, medicine, classical scholarship, philosophy, and historiography have themselves become the subject of formidable historical subdisciplines. No attempt is made here to cover these, nor perhaps is enough said about the everyday realities of the classroom and laboratory—subjects which historians are only beginning to tackle. What is offered is a history of universities in society, but also 'in politics', looking at issues such as academic freedom, the relation of universities to the state, and the impact of nationalism, an unavoidable theme in the nineteenth century.

Introducing the first volume of the *History of the university in Europe*, the general editor, the Swiss scholar Walter Rüegg, claimed that 'the university is a European institution; indeed, it is the European institution *par excellence*' and 'the only European institution which has preserved its fundamental patterns and its basic social role and functions over the course of history'. Since the eighteenth century it has been 'the intellectual institution which cultivates and transmits the entire corpus of methodically studied intellectual disciplines', and it has 'formed an academic elite, the ethos of which rests on common European values and which transcends all national boundaries'.[6] No doubt this reflects contemporary political ideals, and in 1992 the end of the iron curtain gave Europeanism a new relevance, though even before that university historians had done more than most scholars to maintain links between east and west, especially with Poland and what was then Czechoslovakia. The present book also tries to be comprehensive in this respect. The author's scope is limited by ignorance of any Slavonic (or Scandinavian) language, but in the case of Russia at least, enough is available in western languages to permit a basic outline. The book is also 'European' in its treatment of Britain,

[4] Including special nos. of the Conference's newsletter *CRE-Information*, 62 (1983), 69 (1985), 72 (1985); special no. of *History of European Ideas*, 8 (1987); L. Jílek (ed.), *Historical compendium of European universities. Répertoire historique des universités européennes* (Geneva, 1984). Cf. W. Frijhoff, 'Universités et société: à propos d'un projet de la Conférence européenne des recteurs', *Histoire de l'Éducation*, 22 (1984), 19–25.

[5] J. Verger, in J. Verger (ed.), *Histoire des universités en France* (Toulouse, 1986), 6.

[6] W. Rüegg, in H. de Ridder-Symoens (ed.), *A history of the university in Europe. I. Universities in the middle ages* (Cambridge, 1992), pp. xix–xx.

which emphasizes continental links and parallels while saying little about the imperial and transatlantic links which were stronger for British universities than for any other European system.

The outbreak of the First World War is an obvious terminating point in university history. The choice of a starting point was more difficult. The tradition has been to regard the turn of the eighteenth and nineteenth centuries, particularly the 'Humboldtian' reform in Germany associated with the foundation of Berlin University in 1810, as the 'most important caesura' in the 800-year-old tradition of the European universities, because it introduced the concept of the fusion of teaching and research.[7] Socially and politically, it marks the beginning of the middle-class university and its association with the forces of liberalism, industrialization, and nationalism. Intellectually, it can be seen as standing for principles of academic freedom, original research, and critical thinking which had been less in evidence in the previous 600 years, but which still define the ideal university today. But even if one accepts the importance of 1800 as a turning-point, neither the earlier reforms of enlightened rulers nor the influence of the French model of higher education, which diverged significantly from the Humboldtian ideal of the integrated university, can be neglected.[8] Along with a preliminary sketch of the *ancien régime*, these subjects provide the first four chapters of the book.

Another 'caesura', it can be argued, comes in the decades around 1870. It was only then that the German model spread widely outside the German cultural sphere. More significantly, it was only then that political, religious, and intellectual changes secured real autonomy for universities and began a period of dynamic expansion. Until then rulers had still tried to use universities to enforce political and religious orthodoxy, and liberal principles struggled to establish themselves. This is the theme of Chapters 5 and 6, and Chapter 7 discusses the curricular developments of this period and their cultural consequences. Chapters 8 and 9 attempt to summarize the social developments and interpretative models which underlie the treatment of individual countries in Chapters 10 to 16. A purely thematic treatment proved impracticable for the age of the nation-state. It is not just that national university systems diverged, but that historians in each country have related university history to a different set of general historical problems: relations between middle-class and aristocratic values in Britain, the nature of the republican state in France, the fate of liberalism in Germany, or the emergence of the intelligentsia in Russia. The role of universities in integrating national elites provides one useful comparative theme. Finally, Chapters 17, 18, and 19 deal with themes which fall predominantly in the post-1870 period: women and universities, the development of student life, and the relation between universities and democracy.

[7] H. Titze, *Datenhandbuch zur deutschen Bildungsgeschichte. I. Hochschulen. 2. Teil: Wachstum und Differenzierung der deutschen Universitäten 1830–1945* (Göttingen, 1995), 15.

[8] Cf. R. D. Anderson, 'Before and after Humboldt: European universities between the eighteenth and the nineteenth centuries', *History of Higher Education Annual*, 20 (2000), 5–14.

1
The *Ancien Régime*

The *History of the university in Europe* makes 1800 the dividing line between its second and third volumes, on the grounds that the date 'marks, in a very general way, the beginning of the decisive though contradictory lines of development which are shared by the universities of the nineteenth century. The orientation of the centrally, governmentally organized educational system, perfected by Napoleon and aimed at immediate social utility, is one of these. The other pattern is that inspired by von Humboldt—research without practical ends and intended to serve the intellectual education of the human race.'[1] This contrast may be too strongly drawn—German universities in the nineteenth century certainly did not neglect 'social utility'—but there can be no doubt that the French and German models were widely seen as rivals or alternatives. The present study lays rather more emphasis than has been customary on Enlightenment rulers as devisers of the centralized, state model which was indeed 'perfected' rather than invented by Napoleon, and which has continued to mould university development to the present day. Laurence Brockliss, as we shall see, stresses the continuing efficiency of the eighteenth-century universities in educating the elite and transmitting knowledge, but in a valuable survey of European universities between 1789 and 1850 nevertheless considers that the reforming attempts of enlightened rulers were generally unsuccessful in the face of entrenched conservatism, that 'as the nineteenth century dawned, the university looked a doomed species', and that 'the institution ultimately survived on the Continent because the Germans invented the research university'.[2] This is a perfectly plausible view, given the fate of so many traditional institutions at the hands of the French revolution and Napoleon. The idea that universities faced an existential crisis was a contemporary one, and specialized colleges without the corporate complications of universities were already developing as an alternative. But it is also arguable that eighteenth-century rulers responded to this crisis by rejuvenating the university model, and that a direct line leads from their policies of secularization and centralization to the similar policies of Napoleon, and then to the Humboldtian model by way of reaction against French dominance. State systems of the Napoleonic kind did not lose their attractions in the nineteenth century, and the French separation of education in

[1] W. Rüegg, in H. de Ridder-Symoens (ed.), *A history of the university in Europe. I. Universities in the middle ages* (Cambridge, 1992), p. xxiv.

[2] L. Brockliss, 'The European university in the age of revolution 1789–1850', in M. G. Brock and M. C. Curthoys (eds.), *The history of the University of Oxford. VI. Nineteenth-century Oxford, Part 1* (Oxford, 1997), 87–9, 100, 103.

vocational schools from research in specialized institutes seemed as valid to many as the German ideas of the unity of knowledge and humane education through original research. By the later nineteenth century it was widely accepted that research was the university's prime mission, but the balance between teaching, research, specialization, and general liberal education has never ceased to be disputed.

'Can we still speak, in 1800, of a European university?' asked Willem Frijhoff.[3] The university might be the most European of institutions, but centuries of divergence had strained the universal framework to its limits, modified by national political and social differences, and above all by the impact of the Reformation. The purpose of this chapter is not to summarize the rich scholarly findings of the Ridder-Symoens volume, but to describe some of the fundamental institutional features of the early modern universities in order to identify the deficiencies against which reformers were reacting, and to consider whether the traditional picture of decay and inefficiency is correct. The chapter has four main sections. First, it will look at the general framework of institutions, and particularly at the impact of the Jesuit order in Catholic Europe and at the changing relationship, for which they were partly responsible, between universities, colleges, and 'secondary' schools (a useful anachronism, though the term comes from France in the 1790s). Second, it will briefly summarize the work of historians on university enrolments, which shows that decline was the predominant note in the eighteenth century. Third, the social function of the universities will be examined. This is perhaps the aspect where continuity between *ancien régime* and nineteenth century was greatest. Finally, although no attempt is made at a complete survey of the universities' intellectual life, it is worth asking whether this was as stagnant and pedagogically hollow as was traditionally thought. On this question, as on social functions, particular attention will be given to France, where new scholarship has partly revised negative judgements deriving from the Enlightenment.

Universities still had recognizable common features in the eighteenth century, and retained a common terminology despite innumerable variations and exceptions. They were corporate bodies, supervised by church and state, though with considerable autonomy from both. Their professors were scholars charged with the transmission of knowledge and with the formation of the 'learned' professions—the church, law, and medicine. The universities had the privilege of awarding degree qualifications, which were usually a requirement for exercising those professions. The arts or philosophical faculty gave a preparatory general education for the three professional faculties, and the four faculties were still the standard pattern for new foundations. Institutionally, the most striking divergences were in the growth of residential colleges in certain countries, and in the evolution of the arts faculty.

The Reformation and the Catholic reform which followed it inevitably disrupted the European character of university life, including the international movement of

[3] W. Frijhoff, 'Graduation and careers', in H. de Ridder-Symoens (ed.), *A history of the university in Europe. II. Universities in early modern Europe (1500–1800)* (Cambridge, 1996), 415.

scholars and students. But it also stimulated the foundation or revival of universities, as rulers gave priority to the enforcement of religious orthodoxy and the production of a loyal and efficient clergy. In most respects, Protestant and Catholic universities continued to pursue the same kind of learning, modified in the sixteenth century by the infusion of classical humanism, but still based on the body of knowledge and interpretation inherited from Aristotle through the filter of medieval scholasticism. Latin was still the common language of scholarship, and university teachers were part of an early modern 'republic of letters' which crossed national and confessional boundaries. In Protestant universities canon law, which had sometimes formed a separate faculty from 'civil' law, generally disappeared, but faculties of theology assumed a new importance as the Protestant emphasis on the Bible and preaching demanded a ministry trained in scholarship and rhetoric. In the Catholic world, on the other hand, the Council of Trent made the seminaries, controlled directly by bishops, the preferred place for clerical education. Seminaries might be linked to the faculties of theology, and degrees remained essential for the higher clergy, but they also turned out many priests, especially those serving rural parishes, who had a very limited intellectual grounding.

After the Reformation, religion and political loyalty became inseparable, and it was the secular authorities which held final control. The effects of the Reformation are difficult to disentangle from the emergence and consolidation of the princely or monarchical state, with its new need for trained bureaucrats, and the two movements combined to make the sixteenth and early seventeenth centuries a period of university expansion. Religious rivalry was especially marked in Germany, where the principle of 'cuius regio, eius religio', first established in 1555 and reasserted in 1648 after the Thirty Years War, allowed each ruler to prescribe a single state religion. In both Protestant and Catholic areas, the characteristic form became the *Landesuniversität*, or territorial university, firmly under the thumb of the prince. State universities of this kind were also established, as new creations or by overhauling old ones, by the Lutheran monarchs of Scandinavia. A similar pattern is discernible in England, where the monarchy supervised and purged the two universities of Oxford and Cambridge to ensure that they observed Anglican orthodoxy. In Scotland, the politico-religious conflicts of the seventeenth century caused even more turbulence, until the final establishment of presbyterianism after the revolution of 1688, followed by legislative union with England in 1707. In Ireland, the University of Dublin (more commonly called Trinity College) was established as a bastion of Protestantism in 1592 and remained exclusively Anglican. Some German rulers were Calvinist rather than Lutheran, and Calvinism also produced a distinctive form of urban university or 'academy'. In Switzerland and Holland, both lacking a strong central monarchy, the universities were characteristically controlled by the patrician elites of the cities, who also provided inbred dynasties of professors.[4] The Dutch example was especially notable: the University of Leiden was founded in 1575 as part of the national revolt against Spanish rule, and since the new Dutch state retained a significant Catholic minority its universities

[4] P. A. Vandermeersch, 'Teachers', in Ridder-Symoens, *History of the university. II.* 227–9.

were among the few in Europe which admitted students of different confessions. This spirit of tolerance contributed to their intellectual vigour, and made Leiden and Utrecht internationally influential in the seventeenth and early eighteenth centuries.

While Protestant rulers controlled their national churches, Catholic universities were marked by the supranational influence of the Jesuit order, which specialized in humanist, philosophical, and scientific education, though law and medicine generally remained outside its control. Jesuit dominance of the universities became almost complete in Catholic Germany, the Habsburg dominions, and Poland. With other religious orders, they also controlled the education of adolescents in humanist colleges throughout Catholic Europe, and this had significant consequences for the structure of elite education. The Jesuits preferred to shift general humanist and philosophical education out of the arts faculties into the final years of the college curriculum, weakening the traditional four-faculty university; this was most marked in France, especially in Paris, where the work of the arts faculty was entirely taken over by the numerous colleges. Rulers often favoured this shift, thinking that young men were best kept in their native districts under a stricter discipline than universities provided, and in some cases small and weak universities were demoted to college status. Conversely, religious orders might turn colleges into quasi-universities by adding philosophy and theology at the end of the curriculum. As demand built up, these could be promoted to full university status. Thus the line between schools and universities was blurred, and the age at which students moved from one to the other was still not fixed. This pattern was not confined to Catholic countries—the 'illustrious' schools of Holland and northern Germany had the same sort of advanced classes—but it was especially marked in the Jesuit-dominated areas of east-central and eastern Europe like Bohemia and Moravia, Poland, Silesia, and Hungary, where there were few towns large enough to support a traditional university.[5] The universities of Cracow and Prague were of medieval origin, and remained important. But there were none further east—and none at all in Orthodox countries until Moscow University was founded in 1755.

In the Catholic west, Jesuit dominance was nowhere as complete as in Germany. In the southern Netherlands, controlled by Austria after 1714, the university of Louvain was kept out of their hands. In France, the Jesuit position was a strong one, but always contested by rival orders like the Oratorians, and curbed by the Gallican tradition, which insisted on the autonomy of the French church from Rome under the control of the monarchy, and which was generally supported by lay opinion, including the powerful and privileged judicial bodies, the Parlements. In Italy, political fragmentation both supported a multiplicity of universities and prevented any uniform pattern from emerging. The Papal States, the temporal dominions of the Pope, included a number of historic universities headed by the oldest of all, Bologna. Others were influenced directly or indirectly by the Austrian Habsburgs (Pavia in Lombardy, Pisa in Tuscany), while Naples and Sicily were ruled by a branch of the Spanish Bourbons. Some of the smaller Italian universities were

[5] W. Frijhoff, 'Patterns', ibid. 52–6.

controlled by municipalities or local bishops. Spain had even more universities, some of them very small. This was a legacy of Spain's power and wealth in the sixteenth century, and an expression of the strong local and regional individuality which survived despite a centralized monarchy. The Spanish universities were fervently Catholic, and dominated more than most by religious orders—but here the Jesuits had strong rivals, notably the Dominicans, and their quarrelsomeness was notorious and damaging.

Universities were an expression of the partnership between church and state characteristic of the *ancien régime*. They also reflected the particularism and corporate privilege of that society, and were embedded in local networks of kinship and patronage. Governments rarely exercised direct bureaucratic control, or supported the universities from state revenues. Even when universities were founded or reformed, the state tended to provide a permanent endowment of land or property: Uppsala, for example, was generously enough endowed in the 1620s to survive until the mid-nineteenth century without calling on state support,[6] and Oxford and Cambridge lived on endowments and fees until the 1920s. Sweden and Britain, however, were countries which remained outside the Napoleonic embrace: elsewhere secularization and confiscation after 1789 were to sweep away the mixture of endowed lands, urban property, ecclesiastical sinecures, tithes, and rights to levy taxes on which most universities relied to pay salaries, maintain buildings, and support poor students, leaving them dependent instead on the state and on student fees. Independent revenues had been the basis both of universities' corporate autonomy and of the intellectual lethargy and social unresponsiveness of which contemporary critics often complained. Many early modern universities had lost any international and even national role, and served purely local interests. Professors might be idle and corrupt, and were appointed in ways which put family and local influence before intellectual eminence. Students were a disorderly and unwelcome element in urban society, and the mechanisms designed to seek out and promote talent were no longer effective. These were among the problems or abuses which reformers identified.

In France the colleges which had been attached to the university since the middle ages, originally as a way of recruiting poorer students into the church, merged into urban secondary education. In Paris and other university towns, the arts faculty still existed and awarded degrees, but lost its distinct professorate, and the leading colleges in non-university towns could also give higher instruction. A different development was that in England, where the colleges remained within, and virtually supplanted, the universities. The colleges attracted wealthy donors, sometimes including monarchs, whose endowments solidified into permanent power, and their wealth overshadowed that of the universities. As early as the sixteenth century, the colleges became the focus of teaching at 'Oxbridge',[7] and the

[6] H. de Ridder-Symoens, 'Management and resources', in Ridder-Symoens, *History of the university. II.* 187.

[7] A convenient collective term for the two English universities, first used by the nineteenth-century novelist W. M. Thackeray.

traditional university exercises and examinations began to decay. Colleges were valued for their disciplinary control, and membership of one became compulsory. Scholarships founded for poor students, usually linked with particular localities and schools, were diverted to wealthier families, and by the eighteenth century poorer scholars were being squeezed out. One reason was that, while the English universities continued to be recruiting-grounds for the church, the Anglican church itself became so wealthy that its preferments were a prize target for those who pulled the levers of patronage, and a favourite way of supporting the younger sons of the landed class. Another reason was that the schools to which college scholarships were tied had either become aristocratic themselves at an early stage, as with Eton or Winchester, or, like most provincial grammar schools, had fallen into a state of decay which prevented them from recruiting local talent.[8] There were still some boys from poor backgrounds at Oxford and Cambridge, but the general social atmosphere was aristocratic and their way of life had become too expensive for most of the new middle class. As for the 'fellows' of the colleges, the rule that they had to be both clergymen and celibate meant that most of them regarded their college position as a temporary stage while waiting for preferment, not as a professional teaching post. The historian Edward Gibbon found his fourteen months at Oxford 'the most idle and unprofitable of my whole life', and condemned the more complaisant scholarly idleness of the dons, 'steeped in port and prejudice'.[9] Like Byron, who found Cambridge 'sunk in dullness', Gibbon was hardly an impartial witness.[10]

Colleges with some resemblance to the English ones were also found at Louvain, some Italian universities, and in Spain, but these did not usurp the teaching role of the universities.[11] As in England, however, they tended to be taken over by established families at the expense of the poor. In Spain, the *colegios mayores* at Salamanca, Valladolid, and Alcalá had a special position: they were wealthy, aristocratic, and exclusive, but they recruited 'graduates' rather than ordinary students, and their links were with the legal profession and the bureaucracy rather than the church. The *colegios mayores* and the families associated with them established a grip over the higher ranks of officialdom which made them an early target of enlightened reform.[12]

The shift of students from universities to colleges, and the flexibility of the age of transition, complicate the historical study of university enrolments, which has nevertheless attracted much historical attention. Broadly speaking, universities boomed in the sixteenth and early seventeenth century, but stagnated thereafter, in some countries reviving in the later eighteenth century but in others falling into a

[8] S. Rothblatt, *The revolution of the dons: Cambridge and society in Victorian England* (London, 1968), 29–47.

[9] *The autobiography and correspondence of Edward Gibbon, the historian* (London, 1869), 24, 49.

[10] P. Searby, *A history of the University of Cambridge. III. 1750–1870* (Cambridge, 1997), 237.

[11] See generally D. Maffei and H. de Ridder-Symoens (eds.), *I collegi universitari in Europa tra il XIV e il XVIII secolo* (Milan, 1991); R. A. Müller, 'Student education, student life', in Ridder-Symoens, *History of the university. II.* 333–9.

[12] R. L. Kagan, *Students and society in early modern Spain* (Baltimore, 1974).

clear state of decay. Some of the universities created for religious or dynastic purposes proved fragile, and between 1701 and 1790 twenty-nine universities were closed, merged, or cut back to college status; twenty-eight were founded or restored, but these usually arose from specific reforming projects rather than market demand.[13]

The pioneer in the modern study of enrolments was Lawrence Stone. As part of the Princeton project, he published a long essay on Oxford between 1580 and 1910, expanding his earlier work on the two English universities (and the Inns of Court in London, which provided legal education) in the late sixteenth and early seventeenth centuries.[14] According to Stone, that period saw an 'educational revolution' as laymen flocked to qualify for offices and professions. They included the sons of both the landed classes and the urban bourgeoisie, and in the 1630s, Stone estimates, some 2.5 per cent of the male age-cohort was receiving higher education. But numbers peaked around 1640: new families consolidated their position and their social prestige, and English society again became stable and relatively closed. In the universities, decline and stagnation set in, so that in terms of percentage participation 'English higher education did not get back to the level of the 1630s until after the first World War.'[15] At both Oxford and Cambridge, the graph of enrolments declined steadily from the mid-seventeenth to the mid-eighteenth centuries, then began a modest rise, which became a steeper one after 1800; but it was not until the 1860s that the actual number of students regained and passed the seventeenth-century peak.[16]

Stone's striking findings stimulated a collective project, based in Paris, to investigate the data for other countries—France, Germany, Italy, Spain, Poland, and Bohemia.[17] The survival and quality of the matriculation statistics on which such studies are based vary greatly, and there are many technical difficulties in interpreting them. Germany was one of the few countries where it was possible to establish a series of annual, national figures over a sustained period, and indeed this had already been done in 1904 by the statistician Franz Eulenburg. In France, by contrast, records survived only for a few universities and faculties. The overall result of the Paris project was to show that the 'Stone thesis' worked for some countries but not for others.[18] As in England, the decades around 1600 generally did see a new

[13] Frijhoff, 'Patterns', 71, 89.

[14] 'The size and composition of the Oxford student body 1580–1910', in L. Stone (ed.), *The university in society. I. Oxford and Cambridge from the 14th to the early 19th Century* (Princeton, 1975), 3–110; L. Stone, 'The educational revolution in England 1560–1640', *Past and Present*, 28 (1964), 41–80. Cf. Searby, *History of the University of Cambridge*, 60–5.

[15] Stone, 'Educational revolution', 57, 69.

[16] Stone, 'Size and composition', 6, 91–2.

[17] D. Julia, J. Revel, and R. Chartier (eds.), *Les Universités européennes du XVIe au XVIIIe siècle: histoire sociale des populations étudiantes. I. Bohème, Espagne, États italiens, Pays Germaniques, Pologne, Provinces-Unies* (Paris, 1986); D. Julia and J. Revel (eds.), *Les Universités européennes du XVIe au XVIIIe siècle: histoire sociale des populations étudiantes. II. France* (Paris, 1989).

[18] For general views of the project, see R. Chartier and J. Revel, 'Université et société dans l'Europe moderne: position des problèmes', *Revue d'Histoire Moderne et Contemporaine*, 25 (1978), 353–74; R. Chartier, 'Student populations in the eighteenth century', *British Journal for Eighteenth-Century Studies*, 2 (1979), 150–62. See also reviews by H. de Ridder-Symoens in *Histoire de l'Éducation*, 34 (1987), 84–9, and 53 (1992), 65–70; P. Denley, 'University records, social history, and the creation of large databases', *History of Universities*, 8 (1989), 219–29; M. R. di Simone, 'Admission', in Ridder-Symoens,

interest in education among both nobility and bourgeoisie, corresponding to the expansion of posts in the churches and the bureaucracies of the early modern state, followed as in England by saturation and stabilization, though the patterns of decline and the peaks in the graph did not necessarily correspond to the English model. While the boom lasted, the participation ratio, as in England, often reached 2 or even 3 per cent of the age-cohort. By the end of the eighteenth century, it was typically just above or below 1 per cent, as it was to remain for another hundred years.

The eighteenth century was clearly not a period of general or vigorous growth. The Stone pattern (though not the exact chronology) fits Holland, where numbers peaked at the end of the seventeenth century, then declined in the eighteenth,[19] and to some extent Spain, where the golden age was the end of the sixteenth century, followed by continuous decline, but with a significant recovery at the end of the eighteenth century.[20] In Germany, there was a recovery after the Thirty Years War to a peak in the late seventeenth century, followed by relative stability until around 1750, then a marked decline (from nearly 9,000 in the 1740s to under 7,000 in the 1790s), which helps to explain the emphasis of German historians on the post-1800 revival.[21] In Italy, there was an influx of nobles in the sixteenth century, whose later withdrawal led to 'a prolonged period of stagnation and decline'.[22] But elsewhere the Stone pattern did not seem to apply at all. In Portugal, numbers at Coimbra (the country's only university) rose strongly through the eighteenth century, a reminder, as in sixteenth-century Castile, that high levels of participation could reflect the dominance of the church in a traditional society rather than any advanced social pattern.[23] In France, the fragmentary data failed to support the idea of an educational revolution in the sixteenth century, and fluctuations followed no clear pattern. But there was evidence of a strong upturn in the faculties of law and medicine in the late eighteenth century, though this was probably at the expense of theology rather than part of a general rise in student numbers.[24] From an index of

History of the university. II. 285–325; M. M. Compère, *L'Histoire de l'éducation en Europe: essai comparatif sur la façon dont elle s'écrit* (Bern, 1995), 214–22; C. Charle and J. Verger, *Histoire des universités* (Paris, 1994), 40–7.

[19] W. Frijhoff, *La Société néerlandaise et ses gradués 1575–1814: une recherche sérielle sur le statut des intellectuels à partir des registres universitaires* (Amsterdam, 1981), 383; W. Frijhoff, 'Universités et marché de l'emploi dans la République des Provinces-Unies', in Julia, Revel, and Chartier, *Les Universités européennes I*, 205–43.

[20] M. Peset and M. F. Mancebo, 'La population des universités espagnoles au XVIIIe siècle', in Julia, Revel, and Chartier, *Les Universités européennes I*, 187–204. Cf. M. Peset, J. L. Peset, and M. F. Mancebo, 'La población universitaria de Valencia durante el siglo XVIII', *Estudis d'Història Contemporània del País Valencià*, 1 (1979), 7–42; Kagan, *Students and society*, 196–230.

[21] F. Eulenburg, *Die Frequenz der deutschen Universitäten von ihrer Gründung bis zur Gegenwart* (Leipzig, 1904), 131, 164–5; W. Frijhoff, 'Grandeur des nombres et misères des réalités: la courbe de Franz Eulenburg et le débat sur le nombre d'intellectuels en Allemagne 1576–1815', in Julia, Revel, and Chartier, *Les Universités européennes I*, 23–63 (corrects Eulenburg); H. W. Prahl, *Sozialgeschichte des Hochschulwesens* (Munich, 1978), 369–79. Figures relate to post-1871 boundaries.

[22] R. L. Kagan, 'Universities in Italy 1500–1700', in Julia, Revel, and Chartier, *Les Universités européennes I*, 165.

[23] Chartier and Revel, 'Université et société', 369; di Simone, 'Admission', 307.

[24] R. Chartier, M. M. Compère, and D. Julia, *L'Éducation en France du XVIe au XVIIIe siècle* (Paris, 1976), 276.

100 at the end of the seventeenth century, law graduates rose to 126 in the 1750s and 176 in the 1780s.[25] In medicine, there was 'a spectacular growth in the [student] medical population which responded to social demand, and to which the university was forced to adjust'.[26] At Montpellier, the best-documented medical faculty, the curve was rising steadily before 1789.[27]

How are these long-term fluctuations in enrolments to be explained? Stone used the idea of a cyclical 'over-filling' of the professions: when opportunities are expanding, families are attracted to education as a means of social ambition, but once the professions and government offices are filled up, a surplus of unemployed graduates appears, which then becomes a disincentive to university attendance and diverts ambition into other channels.[28] Similar cycles have been identified in the nineteenth century, and in the 1640s as in 1848 unemployed graduates and frustrated or alienated intellectuals were blamed for revolutionary disorder.[29] From Richelieu to the German rulers of the eighteenth century, governments feared the consequences of admitting too many poor boys to the universities, lamented the diversion of talent away from the productive economy, and tried to curb university access.[30] The prevailing stagnation of the universities in the eighteenth century was too lengthy, however, to be explained solely by cycles in the labour market. General explanations include the apparent irrelevance of university teaching, stuck in the mould of the learned professions, to the new practical needs and expanding new occupations of the age, and the rise of alternatives such as colleges of surgery or engineering. The shift of students into secondary colleges narrowed the university age cohort, and this is illustrated by the contrary case of Scotland. Here the universities continued to take their pupils at ages between 14 and 16, often directly from rural schools where Latin was taught, while advanced classical or mathematical education in urban schools was underdeveloped. At the end of the eighteenth century, the five Scottish universities had some 2,850 students, a remarkably high figure for a population of 1.6 million. They also probably remained more open to the poor than in most countries; but the universities were really performing 'secondary' functions, and could be seen as examples of unreformed educational archaism rather than proto-democratic modernity.[31]

Some other phenomena are apparent from the enrolment statistics. One is the

[25] R. Chartier, *The cultural origins of the French revolution* (Durham, NC, 1991), 190.

[26] Julia and Revel, *Les Universités européennes II*, 389. As well as the main chapter on France by Julia and Revel, this vol. contains findings by L. Brockliss also available in his 'Patterns of attendance at the University of Paris 1400–1800', *Historical Journal*, 21 (1978), 503–44. A less favourable view of enrolments in the late 18th century in J. de Viguerie, 'Quelques remarques sur les universités françaises au dix-huitième siècle', *Revue Historique*, 262 (1979), 37.

[27] Chartier, Compère, and Julia, *L'Éducation en France*, 269–73; G. Cholvy (ed.), *Histoire de Montpellier* (Toulouse, 1984), 210–11.

[28] Stone, 'Educational revolution', 75.

[29] M. H. Curtis, 'The alienated intellectuals of early Stuart England', *Past and Present*, 23 (1962), 25–49; R. Chartier, 'Espace social et imaginaire social: les intellectuels frustrés au XVIIe siècle', *Annales*, 37 (1982), 389–400, repr. in Julia, Revel, and Chartier, *Les Universités européennes I*, 245–60.

[30] Cf. Frijhoff, 'Graduation and careers', 393–7.

[31] R. L. Emerson, 'Scottish universities in the eighteenth century 1690–1800', *Studies on Voltaire and the Eighteenth Century*, 167 (1977), 473. The universities were St Andrews, Glasgow, Edinburgh, and the separate King's College and Marischal College at Aberdeen (united only in 1860).

'regionalization' of universities apparent in almost all countries. International student movement became less common, as rulers applied policies of academic mercantilism which required their subjects to study at home, and greater religious tolerance made it less necessary for members of religious minorities to look abroad.[32] Even within the national monarchies, universities came to recruit largely from their own regions and provinces, and only a limited number retained a role in forming the national elite. This geographical retrenchment was found from Poland, where the University of Cracow drew 83 per cent of its students from the local diocese in the eighteenth century, to Italy, where Padua, once a great international university, now served only the Venetian state.[33] The decline of international study was linked with a second phenomenon found in many, but not all, countries (England was one exception): loss of interest in universities on the part of the higher aristocracy. Humanist colleges now had less appeal than military or 'knightly' academies which stressed the courtly virtues and taught accomplishments like fencing, riding, and dancing. Aristocrats interested in careers in the bureaucracy and the church still needed to study law and theology, but they tended to choose from a select group of prestigious universities, to minimize their stay, and not to mingle with their social inferiors. For the northern European aristocracy, it was the Grand Tour to Italy, accompanied by a tutor, which now gave an essential cultural polish. To attract aristocratic students back to the universities, by developing new forms of gentlemanly liberal education, became one of the aims of university reform, most notably perhaps in Germany.[34]

If aristocrats began to boycott the universities, and the poorer students of medieval tradition were being squeezed out, what was the core clientele which remained? This is the subject of the next section of this chapter. Above all, it was those who aimed at the learned professions and the service of the state, and most of the students were themselves drawn from families in the same groups, including the younger sons of the nobility: the primary function of the university was reproducing the elite, with only limited social ascent from strata below. But to speak of the professions in early modern society raises complex questions. In a 'society of orders', the allocation of social position depended on heredity, kinship, and patronage rather than on merit and formal qualifications. Progress in a profession was a process of apprenticeship, social learning, and acceptance by senior members of the guild; it required mastery of a body of learned knowledge, and some testing of its acquisition, but intellectual performance was not the main criterion for success. Arguably the move from apprenticeship modes of professional recruitment towards merit-driven ones was beginning in the eighteenth century, and was encouraged both by the growth of the professions themselves as society became richer and more complex, and by the attempts of governments to create more efficient bureaucracies. But even in the nineteenth century merit coexisted with

[32] H. de Ridder-Symoens, 'Mobility', in Ridder-Symoens, *History of the university. II.* 436–47.

[33] Julia, Revel, and Chartier, *Les Universités européennes I*, 142 (I. Kaniewska), 167 (R. Kagan).

[34] C. E. McClelland, 'The aristocracy and university reform in eighteenth-century Germany', in L. Stone (ed.), *Schooling and society: studies in the history of education* (Baltimore, 1976), 146–73.

older values and with the power of the family as a force for inheriting and transmitting status, prestige, and cultural capital as well as property.

A principal function of university education was thus the endorsement and legitimation of social position. In the words of Ridder-Symoens, 'the first duty of the early modern university was not to form learned men of science, or even professional experts, but rather men who were sociable, cultivated, and conscious of their social and moral worth. Its role was not to promote a new society, but to preserve the social order.'[35] University education gave a much-prized gloss of learning and distinction, if one sometimes tarnished by the university's image as the home of crabbed pedantry. Willem Frijhoff, whose pioneering work on Holland has asked what 'graduation' meant in early modern society, says that 'under the *ancien régime*, a society structured according to the principle of honour or dignity, the university degree was primarily a source of social rights and privileges'.[36] In several countries, including Spain, Italy, and Austria, degrees in law and medicine were controlled by 'doctoral colleges' which gave local elites in these professions an entrenched position in the university and allowed them to decide access to their guild.

The legitimating role of university education applied both to entry into specific professions, and to the broader process by which new arrivals were absorbed into the existing social structure. Families which had risen through commerce, finance, or industry consolidated their social position by buying land and by putting their sons into prestigious professions like law, the classic path by which new wealth was converted into social prestige, office, and eventual landed and noble status. Social mobility through education meant this lateral process of consolidation, as well as the upward movement of the small number of poor boys able to climb the ladder through talent or luck. To generalize beyond this is difficult given the great diversity of European societies. One obvious difference was in the position of the clergy in Catholic and Protestant countries. In both, the theology faculties normally had the highest proportion of poor students. But a married clergy could share the status of the secular professions, establishing traditions of hereditary service and participating in the network of family links which bound gentry, merchant and urban elites. In Catholic countries, university training was the preserve of the ambitious or the privileged. In France, the higher posts in the church carried requirements for degrees in theology or canon law, and to encourage graduation a third of all benefices falling vacant were reserved for university men.[37] But there was a wide gap between the ordinary clergy and the bishops, members of cathedral chapters, and heads of wealthy religious orders, who were almost all noble by birth. As in law, a university degree was an essential but not a sufficient qualification for success. The

[35] Review of Julia, Revel, and Chartier in *Histoire de l'Éducation*, 34 (1987), 89.

[36] Frijhoff, 'Graduation and careers', 366, and cf. 397–415. See also Frijhoff, *La Société néerlandaise*, 63, 67, 287–8, and 'Le rôle des études universitaires dans une société locale: la ville de Zutphen en Gueldre du Moyen-Âge au début du XIXe siècle. Premier bilan d'une recherche', in M. Kulczykowski (ed.), *Les Étudiants: liens sociaux, culture, mœurs du moyen-âge jusqu'au 19e siècle: Vème session scientifique internationale, Cracovie 28–30 mai 1987* (Warsaw, 1991), 87–114.

[37] J. Verger (ed.), *Histoire des universités en France* (Toulouse, 1986), 155–6.

position was similar in Catholic Germany, Italy, and Spain; the largest Spanish universities in the late eighteenth century—Valencia, Valladolid, and Zaragoza—owed much of their prosperity to the theology faculty, and at Coimbra in Portugal canon law was the boom subject.[38]

Statistical information about the social origins of students in the eighteenth century is rare, and usually too scattered to identify trends. It does exist for some of the French provincial law faculties, and suggests that up to three-quarters of the students themselves came from legal or official families. Only a small proportion (3 or 4 per cent at Dijon and Nancy in the 1780s) came from the landed aristocracy, but there was a significant and probably growing percentage of the sons of merchants and, to a lesser extent, artisans (17 per cent for the two together), though numbers from the peasantry were insignificant.[39] The reproductive nature of law training was reinforced by heredity of office, which meant that many young men had posts waiting for them, especially those born into the hereditary purple of the Parlements. University degrees were required by the state for all judicial posts, but could be taken after a practical training gained through working in the courts. Since the 1690s, the rules had adjusted to this situation by relaxing university attendance requirements for those aged over 24, so the degree was put off until then and became a formality.[40] This exemplified both the way in which universities endorsed existing status, and the nature of university examinations at this time. Sometimes they had become meaningless, but they could be a genuine certificate of knowledge and experience, if only loosely linked with university attendance; they were taken when the individual was ready, not as a competitive standard test applied to a cohort of students. Even after solid study, men might go elsewhere to be examined: many French medical students studied at Paris but took their degrees at Montpellier because it was cheaper, and this was a situation abused in several countries by hard-up universities which sold degrees to absentees. It was not surprising if governments lost faith in university certification and began to create their own examinations for their servants.

Even in the French law faculties, there was room for a few sons of artisans or shopkeepers. This was the most exclusive faculty, law being seen in France and other countries as a standard form of liberal education for wealthy or aristocratic young men. It is likely that arts and theology were more open.[41] It may be over-optimistic to say that the universities 'continued to play the social role which had always been theirs: allowing the children of the "simple people" and the petty bourgeoisie to gain access to offices and benefices', but at Douai 20–5 per cent were

[38] Peset and Mancebo, 'La population des universités espagnoles', 199; di Simone, 'Admission', 307.

[39] Chartier, Compère, and Julia, *L'Éducation en France*, 277–82. Cf. Verger, *Histoire des universités*, 182–3; R. L. Kagan, 'Law students and legal careers in eighteenth-century France', *Past and Present*, 68 (1975), 38–72; D. Ligou, 'The University of Dijon in the eighteenth century', *British Journal for Eighteenth-Century Studies*, 3 (1980), 47–58; H. Cocard, 'Professeurs et étudiants de la Faculté des droits d'Angers au XVIIIe siècle', *Annales de Bretagne et des Pays de l'Ouest*, 86 (1979), 39–43.

[40] Verger, *Histoire des universités*, 160, 188; Frijhoff, 'Graduation and careers', 355–63.

[41] Chartier, 'Student populations', 160–1.

described as 'poor'.[42] Secondary education was open to quite a wide range of town-dwellers, and the Jesuits traditionally offered free education—one of the black marks against them in the eyes of conservatives who feared disruption of the social order. In the Paris arts faculty, fees had been abolished in 1719 in return for the allocation to the university of the income from the state's postal service, and out of 5,000 students at Paris in 1789 there were some 1,000 scholarship-holders living in the colleges and 2,000 day students paying no fees.[43] Here as elsewhere, scholarships and free education were not necessarily used by the poor, being exploited by less affluent noble and bourgeois families. But they at least showed that *ancien régime* corporatism did not confine privilege to the wealthy.

The original reason for making universities accessible to the poor was recruitment to the clergy, and this was true in Protestant countries as well. The German universities had no college system, but in both Catholic and Protestant regions there was a tradition of providing free places, scholarships, hostels, and subsidized meals for those aiming at the church. The Catholic priesthood was poorly paid, and Catholic faculties of theology drew their students from a wider social range than other faculties, including peasants. The Protestant pastorate had more prestige and financial rewards, but it remained more open than in England to poorer boys. Students could earn money by tutoring richer students, and after graduating they often started their careers by continuing to teach in wealthy families, which might then use their patronage and influence to find posts for their protégés in the church or education. The poor but ambitious tutor became a familiar figure in German life and literature, a phenomenon explored for Protestant Germany by Anthony La Vopa.[44] Some aspirants to an often overcrowded profession had to fall back on teaching, but others used their initial study of theology as a springboard for more ambitious careers, and some of Germany's most noted intellectuals in the romantic age took this path, including sons of the poor (Kant, Herder, Fichte) as well as those of pastors or officials.[45] There was a very similar cultural pattern in Scotland, whose beneficiaries included James Mill and Thomas Carlyle.[46]

The University of Paris in 1789, it has been said, 'although antiquated, ill-adapted to the literary, philosophical, and theological movement which it obstructed, and to the scientific movement of which it was largely ignorant, giving a traditional, outdated, and obsolete education, still organized on medieval lines incompatible with changing institutions and the progress of ideas and techniques, was never-

[42] Viguerie, 'Quelques remarques', 31. Cf. L. Trénard, *De Douai à Lille . . . une université et son histoire* (Lille, 1978), 62–3.

[43] P. Costabel (ed.), *L'Enseignement classique au XVIIIe siècle: collèges et universités* (Paris, 1986), 134–6; D. Mornet, *Les Origines intellectuelles de la Révolution française 1711–1787* (Paris, 1933), 323.

[44] A. J. La Vopa, *Grace, talent and merit: poor students, clerical careers and professional ideology in eighteenth-century Germany* (Cambridge, 1988).

[45] H. H. Gerth, 'Die Struktursituation der bürgerlichen Intelligenz im ausgehenden 18. Jahrhundert', in U. Herrmann (ed.), *Die Bildung des Bürgers: Die Formierung der bürgerlichen Gesellschaft und die Gebildeten im 18. Jahrhundert* (Weinheim, 1982), 329, 348–9; C. Charle, *Les Intellectuels en Europe au XIXe siècle: essai d'histoire comparée* (Paris, 1996), 65–6.

[46] R. D. Anderson, *Education and the Scottish people 1750–1918* (Oxford, 1995), 20.

theless relatively flourishing and populous'.[47] The 'fantastic inertia' of the French universities' institutional life and their isolation from contemporary culture contrasted paradoxically with the continuing indispensability of their social function.[48] In recent years, however, there has been a partial rehabilitation of the French universities' intellectual record, especially by Brockliss. They were not generally centres of original thought, and their function was to imbue the elite with orthodox views which shored up the authority of church and state.[49] But this task was performed competently and solidly, and modern discoveries were incorporated into their teaching without excessive delay, though always interpreted within a Christian framework.[50] Extending this argument to Europe generally, Brockliss concludes that the evidence is enough to 'discredit the traditional view that during the Renaissance the universities sank into an intellectual torpor from which they were only awakened by the reforms and new foundations of the early nineteenth century', although they had lost their formal monopoly over creative thought.[51]

Brockliss found that in France, outside the law faculties, the examination system retained its vitality, and traditional methods of teaching, based on the exposition of textual authorities accompanied by catechetical questioning, and leading to oral exercises within a formal framework of logical argument, could be very effective in developing analytical skills and powers of expression.[52] Even at Oxford and Cambridge, a less promising case for historical revisionism than the French universities, these methods were used by the colleges to stimulate students with serious intellectual interests. In the long run, they were to be replaced by the lecture, a form of teaching which involved less personal contact with the student, but allowed the professor to expound the results of his research and to give a discursive treatment of general principles suited to changing ideals of liberal education. This was pioneered in the eighteenth century in Holland, north Germany, and Scotland, and was accompanied in the last two cases by a move to teaching in the vernacular. But in France and elsewhere, teaching in Latin generally held its own, even in science and medicine, and had the advantage of internationalism. For Enlightenment critics, Latin was naturally a symbol of the detachment of the universities from the modern world.

There were various criteria by which the modernity of universities could be judged in the eighteenth century. In philosophy, it was the abandonment of Aristotle and the assimilation first of Descartes, then of Locke and Newton: the Jesuits found Newton a sticking-point. In science—which remained a central part of university teaching, contrary to some stereotypes—it was the advance of experimental and observational methods, requiring the purchase of apparatus for lecture

[47] S. Guenée, *Les Universités françaises, des origines à la Révolution: notices historiques sur les universités, studia et académies protestantes* (Paris, 1982), 52.

[48] Julia in Verger, *Histoire des universités*, 194; Julia and Revel, *Les Universités européennes II*, 28, 32.

[49] L. W. B. Brockliss, *French higher education in the seventeenth and eighteenth centuries: a cultural history* (Oxford, 1987), 178–81, 331–4, 445–58.

[50] Brockliss in Verger, *Histoire des universités*, 250–1.

[51] L. Brockliss, 'Curricula', in Ridder-Symoens, *History of the university. II.* 615.

[52] Ibid. 565–9. Cf. Viguerie, 'Quelques remarques', 38–45; Chartier, Compère, and Julia, *L'Éducation en France*, 287–91.

demonstrations and the creation of expensive facilities such as botanic gardens and observatories. In law, it was departing from the exclusive study of Roman or civil law to embrace both national legal systems and the doctrines of natural law derived from seventeenth-century thinkers like Grotius and Pufendorf. It eventually meant adopting the new scholarly discipline of philology, with its far-reaching applications to the study of history, classical texts, and the Bible, and its new culture of scholarship. Few universities did not go some way along these paths, and prodding them to do so was one of the preoccupations of reformers.

According to Frijhoff, 'the major fact of the eighteenth century was the boom in medicine', bringing experimental sciences like chemistry in its train.[53] The great innovation of the period was the development of clinical teaching, which required hospitals where lectures could be accompanied by the demonstration of cases. This was pioneered in a university context at Leiden by Herman Boerhaave, who attracted an international audience, and whose disciples spread the new ideal of medical education to Scotland, Germany, and Austria. The Dutch universities had been internationally influential since the seventeenth century, but this did not long survive Boerhaave's death in 1738. In France, however (as in Spain), the traditional medical faculties were resistant, and the state founded colleges of surgery to bypass them. The hospitals of Paris became the acknowledged leaders in clinical medicine and retained that reputation well into the nineteenth century, but it was not until Napoleon that their teaching was integrated with the medical faculty. The split also reflected a social and professional division found everywhere between physicians who regarded themselves as a learned profession relying for their status on university degrees, and surgeons for whom practical skills learnt by experience were equally important. In England, a university education was considered necessary for the elite of physicians, but Oxford and Cambridge gave no practical medical training. Germany took the lead in integrating the two branches of medicine as part of university reform; at the end of the eighteenth century, much medical education was still given outside universities, but as a whole it was scientifically advanced and based on both theoretical and practical instruction.[54]

Medicine was closer to the radical side of the Enlightenment than other branches of university learning, as a scientific approach to the body encouraged anti-religious and materialist thinking. Otherwise the French universities existed in a separate cultural sphere from the Enlightenment intellectuals, who objected to the universities' concept of knowledge as professional, corporate, controlled, and supportive of authority.[55] However efficient in delivering education and social status, the universities were cutting themselves off from live intellectual forces. They 'retained a kind of neglected grandeur, important for certain professions but lacking social prestige. They were no longer places for the intellectual self-expression of the nation.'[56] In

[53] Frijhoff, 'Graduation and careers', 384, and cf. 401–6.

[54] T. N. Bonner, *Becoming a physician: medical education in Britain, France, Germany and the United States 1750–1945* (New York, 1995), 34–5; Brockliss, 'Curricula', 609–15.

[55] Viguerie, 'Quelques remarques', 49; Verger, *Histoire des universités*, 251.

[56] N. Hammerstein, 'Relations with authority', in Ridder-Symoens, *History of the university. II*. 128.

other countries this gap was narrower, but it was true everywhere that universities were associated with a narrow range of occupations, the learned professions and public office. One symptom of their isolation from modern life was that they tended to be situated in small towns or traditional ecclesiastical and judicial centres, while vibrant commercial cities like Amsterdam, Hamburg, Lyons, and Milan, or even political and administrative capitals like London, Berlin, and Madrid, felt no need for them.[57] The restricted social function of the universities was to persist into the nineteenth century, when their graduates still went largely into the bureaucracy and the professions, they seemed irrelevant to industry and commerce, and they continued to draw their students from professional, landed, or official families, fringed by aristocrats above and socially mobile members of the merchant or petty bourgeois class below. Under the *ancien régime*, this reflected and reproduced a privileged social structure, and this was unlikely to change as long as offices were hereditary or venal, many posts were reserved for those with noble status, and (in eastern Europe) serfdom tied the mass of peasants to the land. It took the French revolution to shift the balance some way towards merit and individual mobility. When rulers turned their attention to university reform, however, they were more concerned with the practical services which universities could provide to the state, and the most significant outcome of the reform period was not a revolution in the universities' social function, for there was no immediate increase in the relation of enrolments to population, but a revolution in attitudes to knowledge which made universities once more the natural institutional focus for its creation as well as its transmission. *Ancien régime* universities had reflected and served their society in their own rather archaic and lumbering way; the crisis of revolution and war was to test them almost to destruction, but they re-emerged to serve the new social, political, intellectual, and cultural structures. Some at least of the foundations for survival were laid before the crisis came, by universities which adapted to enlightened demands, and rulers and national elites who took reform and renewal in hand.

[57] Frijhoff, 'Patterns', 79.

2
Enlightened Reform

Laurence Brockliss concludes his broadly positive judgement of the universities of early modern Europe by pointing out that 'the three great intellectual movements of the period, the Reformation and Counter-Reformation, the Scientific Revolution, and the Enlightenment, all left a permanent mark on European civilization primarily because they became embedded in the cultural consciousness of the social elite'. This only happened because 'members of the elite encountered these movements as they passed through the universities in their formative years', and at least before 1750 'the professorial chair was the vital link in the chain of communication'.[1] Yet universities play remarkably little part in general accounts of the Enlightenment, even by writers who focus on issues of diffusion and see the Enlightenment as a set of cultural habits rather than of abstract ideas.[2] That is partly because many universities were indeed intellectually stagnant, but it also reflects the traditional focus on France as the nerve-centre of the Enlightenment. A wider perspective gives a different picture. There were many countries—Holland, parts of Italy, Scotland, much of Germany—where the leading Enlightenment thinkers were university professors, whose treatises reflected the ideas elaborated in their lectures. While university reform was largely absent in England and France, this was not true of most parts of Europe.

University reform was part of the agenda of enlightened absolutism (the term generally preferred today to 'enlightened despotism'). One of the aims of rulers and their ministers was to modernize the universities' teaching so that new and useful ideas were not neglected. But they also had wider political and cultural aims: to strengthen the territorial state and increase its military and fiscal efficiency, to create a loyal class of bureaucratic servants, to weaken the independent power of the aristocracy and the obstacles to strong government posed by particularism and corporate privilege, and to subordinate the church to the interests of the state. Institutionally, this usually meant an attack on the control of universities by local elites, and an attempt to make the professors themselves loyal servants of the state by controlling appointments and imposing a prescribed curriculum. The ultimate tendency of this policy, perhaps most clearly shown in the Habsburg empire, was a centralized system in which universities were subordinated to a common

[1] L. Brockliss, 'Curricula', in H. de Ridder-Symoens (ed.), *A history of the university in Europe. II. Universities in early modern Europe (1500–1800)* (Cambridge, 1996), 617.

[2] e.g. D. Roche, *La France des Lumières* (Paris, 1993), 387–90; T. Munck, *The Enlightenment: a comparative social history 1721–1794* (London, 2000), 57; H. Bots and F. Waquet, *La République des lettres* (n.p., 1997), 136–7.

institutional pattern and linked with a similarly uniform system of 'secondary' schools. The idea that a nation should have a rational educational system, not just a collection of institutions bequeathed by history, began to crystallize, and in Catholic countries the dissolution of the Jesuit order in the 1760s and 1770s gave a huge impulse to this change.

Since the training of state servants was seen as the core purpose of the university, the reform of law faculties had a high priority, and was linked with the codification of laws which was another characteristic enterprise of enlightened rulers. But the other faculties were not neglected. In the arts or philosophy faculties, scholasticism was generally identified as the obstacle which prevented education from responding to the needs of the age. New chairs were founded and new subjects introduced, and in many cases, especially in Italy, but also in Switzerland, Spain, and Poland, the faculties were split into philosophical and 'mathematical' or 'physical' sections. This reflected a new sense that science was a separate sphere of mental activity, as well as an economically useful one. Science fed in turn into reform of the medical faculties. Medicine took on a new importance because rulers began to be interested in public health as part of the 'enlightened police state', as well as in the military need for surgeons, and public hospitals, sites of the new clinical teaching, were founded by central governments as well as municipalities and charities.

Enlightened rulers also gave universities a central role in their religious policies. The French Enlightenment thinkers were usually deists or sceptics, but elsewhere in Europe the Enlightenment was far from anti-religious: historians have recently stressed the importance of the 'Catholic Enlightenment', and of similar tendencies in Protestant countries to reform religious institutions and provide a new rational basis for piety and morality. Politically, most Catholic rulers asserted the rights of the state in religious matters, against control from Rome and against the grip of the religious orders, and these policies were often supported by allies within the church, particularly the secular clergy. The model was France, where the autonomy of the national church had long been promoted by the monarchy and endorsed by theologians under the name of Gallicanism; university teachers like other churchmen had to subscribe to the Gallican Articles of 1682. In the eighteenth century, this approach spread to other countries under various names—regalianism, Febronianism,[3] or Jansenism—this last term being used in a loose sense, especially in Spain and Italy, as the antonym of Jesuitism, rather than with reference to Jansenism's original spiritual character. The useful functions of the church, especially its parochial ministry, were now emphasized over supposedly parasitic aspects such as monastic life. The parish clergy should teach a rational, moralistic religion, and encourage their flocks to abjure both old superstitions and newer forms of irrational religious zeal. The priest or pastor was envisaged as a state official like any other, an ally of the doctor and the schoolmaster, or indeed the enlightened landowner, in promoting welfare. For this role to be effective, he needed to be trained alongside other professional men. In Protestant countries, the university

[3] Febronius was the pen-name of J. N. von Hontheim, bishop of Trier, who published a tract against papal power in 1763.

theology faculties had generally retained this function. But in Catholic ones, the adoption of this policy meant that the seminaries, inward-looking and controlled by the bishops, should be replaced by or subordinated to faculties staffed by regalian professors of theology and canon law, and that their students should be forced to take university degrees.

Enlightened absolutism was more radical in economic than in social matters, though its modernization of the economy created the preconditions for the transition to a class society. One aim of rulers was to extend the productive capacity of their countries, through agricultural and industrial improvement, and universities had their part to play in this. In Germany, the economic doctrines of 'cameralism' were introduced into the law faculties, and instilled into fledgling bureaucrats. The resources of the country—population, agriculture, industry, trade—were to be surveyed and used productively; these resources included the ruler's subjects, and if they were better educated, better tended by medical men, and better preached to, they would create more wealth for the state. But the cameralist vision was one of social hierarchy and subordination, moving only cautiously away from the traditional view of a society of orders or estates. Certainly, enlightened absolutism wished to break down the privileges of the aristocracy, and the logic of this policy was to form an alliance with the growing bourgeoisie. But in practice most rulers were happy if they could turn the existing nobility into a more loyal and efficient group by insisting on serious educational qualifications, attracting them back to the universities, and discouraging them from studying abroad. In most of central and eastern Europe the bourgeoisie were thin on the ground—it was this relatively undifferentiated social landscape, compared with the maze of particularist privileges in western Europe, which allowed the assertion of state power in the first place. Rather than allying with a pre-existing bourgeoisie, enlightened absolutism was more notable for creating a new bureaucratic middle class dependent on the state. To the extent that it sought to recruit able men from all backgrounds, there was a move towards a more individualistic, mobile society. But the idea of universities as channels of social mobility did not go much beyond allowing favoured individuals to join the narrow elite.

The aim of attracting the nobility back to the universities was relatively successful in Germany, but in many countries governments admitted partial defeat by creating or adapting special aristocratic institutions to teach law, economics, languages, and other subjects useful to the future official or diplomat. Examples include the Sorø Academy in Denmark, the Reales Estudios de San Isidro in Madrid (taken over by the state from the Jesuits in 1770), the Theresianum in Vienna (1746), the Colegio dos Nobres in Lisbon (1761), and the Collegium Nobilium at Warsaw (1740).[4] Colleges of surgery were another example of alternatives to the university, as were schools of engineering, whether civil or military. The most influential examples were in France: the École des Ponts et Chaussées of 1747, the École des Mines of 1783, the École du Génie at Mézières of 1748. Equivalents were to be found in many countries, and unlike the colleges of surgery, which were later integrated

[4] M. R. di Simone, 'Admission', in Ridder-Symoens, *History of the university*, 321–4.

into the medical faculties, they survived to become the basis of an alternative higher education sector in the nineteenth century.

One of the first states to undertake a reform based on coherent enlightened principles was Piedmont, where the reform of Turin University in 1729 by Victor Amedeus II was part of a broader policy designed to challenge the power of the Jesuits, the nobility, and local elites which characterized baroque Italy. To assert the control of the state over the Italian universities meant targeting the doctoral colleges and their grip over professional qualifications, the power of municipalities, and the surviving remains of medieval student self-government. Piedmont showed the way by rejuvenating the professorate, bringing able men from other parts of Italy and even from France, and introducing new and socially useful subjects. Above all, the state wanted to form a professional and bureaucratic class which would be loyal to the ruler and serve his wider political, social, and economic reforms.[5] This was characteristic of all reform under the aegis of enlightened absolutism, and Piedmont demonstrated some other aspects which became typical. First, the university was seen as the apex of an educational system, with a single bureaucratic body—the Magistrato della Riforma—at its head. To promote education throughout the country, the state sought to build a network of colleges in rivalry with the Jesuits, and to use the university for training their teachers. Piedmont was the first state, it has been claimed, to take up the challenge of planning 'continuity between secondary and university education'.[6] It was also a pioneer in introducing some element of meritocracy in recruiting its officials. The Collegio delle Province created as part of Turin University in 1729 was designed to recruit talent from every part of the kingdom, offering its students scholarships and lodging as well as additional instruction. As was typical of the *ancien régime*, the scholarships tended to fall into the hands of local patrons rather than recruiting impartially, but the college was to produce a significant part of the Piedmontese elite.[7] While bureaucratic priorities gave primacy to law, as did the traditional habits of the Italian elite, the Piedmontese reformers also used the scholarships to steer students into more useful professions. Between 1730 and 1798, Turin University produced 4,619 graduates in law, 1,973 in medicine, and 1,390 in theology—the last figure reflecting the state's regalian policies.[8]

Enlightened religious reform only had its full effect on education once rulers decided to suppress the Jesuit order, a policy which began in Portugal in 1759 and was applied progressively in other Catholic states, until Pope Clement XIV agreed

[5] D. Carpanetto and G. Ricuperati, *Italy in the age of reason 1685–1789* (London, 1987), 91–3; G. Ricuperati, 'L'Università di Torino nel Settecento: ipotesi di ricerca e primi risultati', *Quaderni Storici*, 8 (1973), 575–98; G. Ricuperati and M. Roggero, 'Educational policies in eighteenth-century Italy', *Studies on Voltaire and the Eighteenth Century*, 167 (1977), 223–69; P. del Negro, 'Il principe e l'università in Italia dal XV secolo all'università napoleonica', in G. P. Brizzi and A. Varni (eds.), *L'università in Italia fra età moderna e contemporanea: aspetti e momenti* (Bologna, 1991), 11–27.

[6] Ricuperati and Roggero, 'Educational policies', 235.

[7] M. Roggero, *Il sapere e la virtù: stato, università e professioni nel Piemonte tra settecento ed ottocento* (Turin, 1987); cf. M. Roggero, 'I collegi universitari in età moderna', in Brizzi and Varni, *L'università in Italia*, 130–1.

[8] Roggero, *Il sapere e la virtù*, 119.

to general disbandment in 1773. Meanwhile the initiative in the early eighteenth century passed to Protestant Germany. Here the creation of a state bureaucracy, defined by its educational qualifications and coming to form a socially if not legally distinct estate in society, was to go further than in other countries. The University of Halle, founded in 1694 by the expanding Prussian state, was inspired by a newly coherent vision of the university's mission. It was intended to break with Lutheran orthodoxy and teach religion in the interests of the state; in practice it became a stronghold of the movement of spiritual renewal known as pietism, and the philosopher Christian Wolff, who used the heritage of Leibniz to create the moderate Christian rationalism characteristic of the early Enlightenment in Germany and neighbouring countries, was eventually forced to leave. But his influence, and that of the law professor Christian Thomasius, made Halle a model for other German universities, as well as a nursery of Prussian bureaucrats trained in natural law and cameralism.[9]

More innovatory was the new university of Göttingen, founded in 1737 by the elector of Hanover, who was also George II of Great Britain, but showed no great reforming zeal in that country. The University of Göttingen was largely the work of his minister Gerlach von Münchhausen, with the support of the noble estates. Its novelty lay not so much in what was taught—though the British link did make it a channel for the transmission to Germany of the ideas of Adam Smith, and of liberal thinking generally—as in the unusual freedom allowed to the professors. Münchhausen was determined to attract 'famous and excellent men' from all over Germany, and did so by promising intellectual freedom as well as status and high salaries. At Göttingen the professors were free from close religious supervision, and their prime responsibility was to advance knowledge and carry out original research. In subsequent years they made pioneering contributions to history and to philology, the critical study of language and classical texts, which was to occupy a central place in nineteenth-century university culture. Its great exponent at Gottingen was F. A. Wolf, and his transfer to Halle in 1783 introduced neohumanism to Prussia.[10] Göttingen probably did more than any university in Europe to create 'a system of knowledge no longer based on theology, church history, canon law and Roman law, but on history, geography, statistics, economics—the sciences of the state'.[11] These intellectual emphases reflected the idea that the philosophy faculty, with its lectures in German, was a centre of liberal education in its own right, not just an antechamber to law or theology; there was a deliberate and successful attempt to attract aristocrats from all over Germany, which included the provision of congenial living conditions and instruction in useful and gentlemanly accomplishments such as modern languages.[12] The appeal to a national market in

[9] A. Schindling, *Bildung und Wissenschaft in der frühen Neuzeit 1650–1800* (Munich, 1994), 38–40.

[10] H. H. Gerth, 'Die Struktursituation der bürgerlichen Intelligenz im ausgehenden 18. Jahrhundert', in U. Herrmann (ed.), *'Die Bildung des Bürgers': Die Formierung der bürgerlichen Gesellschaft und die Gebildeten im 18. Jahrhundert* (Weinheim, 1982), 341.

[11] Carpanetto and Ricuperati, *Italy in the age of reason*, 280.

[12] C. E. McClelland, 'The aristocracy and university reform in eighteenth-century Germany', in L. Stone (ed.), *Schooling and society: studies in the history of education* (Baltimore, 1976), 146–73.

the recruitment of both students and professors was a significant reaction against the regionalist spirit of the German *Landesuniversität*.[13] Another notable feature of Göttingen was the absence of any permanent financial endowment, making the university directly dependent on the state.

These innovations caught the eye of other rulers in Germany, Catholic as well as Protestant. Catholic rulers included the bishops or archbishops of ecclesiastical principalities, who were usually drawn from the high aristocracy and shared the ideals of secular rulers, including the desire for a better-trained bureaucracy and impatience with the conservatism of the Jesuits. Ecclesiastical rulers made the universities of Mainz, radically overhauled in 1784, and Würzburg important centres of enlightenment, and the Archbishop of Cologne founded a new university at Bonn in 1777 to bypass the decayed university at Cologne itself.[14] The importance of university reform in the 'Catholic Enlightenment' has been emphasized by Notker Hammerstein, who has shown how the Protestant model spread to the German Catholic universities and from there to Austria; Hammerstein especially stresses the influence of Thomasius's teaching at Halle on the German-speaking world, both for its intellectual approach to law, and in shaping the ideal of general liberal education later developed at Göttingen.[15]

Another Protestant foundation, Erlangen in 1743, also followed reform principles, but was the work of a minor ruler. University reform did not greatly interest the most important of the Protestant enlightened rulers, Frederick II of Prussia (1740–86), though he reinstated Wolff at Halle; Prussia was important nevertheless for three related developments. One was the systematic introduction of examinations, mainly in law, for entry to the civil service; modern bureaucracy, based on rationalism and specialized qualifications, owed much to the Prussian state. The examination system was later extended to professional qualifications for medicine, teaching, and the church, emphasizing the role of the state as the arbiter of merit. The second development was regulation of the relationship between schools and universities. Humanistic schools had developed over the years under various forms of control, but the state now encouraged their coalescence into a common pattern of 'gymnasiums'. In 1788 the *Abitur* was introduced as a standard school-leaving examination, distinguishing school from university education; it was not yet compulsory for university entry, but that was the logic which was to

[13] P. Moraw, 'Aspekte und Dimensionen älterer deutscher Universitätsgeschichte', in P. Moraw and V. Press (eds.), *Academia Gissensis: Beiträge zur älteren Giessener Universitätsgeschichte* (Marburg, 1982), 14.

[14] T. Blanning, *Reform and revolution in Mainz 1743–1803* (Cambridge, 1974), 166–72; A. Schindling, 'Die Julius-Universität im Zeitalter der Aufklärung', in P. Baumgart (ed.), *Vierhundert Jahre Universität Würzburg: Eine Festschrift* (Neustadt an der Aisch, 1982), 77–127.

[15] See especially N. Hammerstein, *Ius und Historie: Ein Beitrag zur Geschichte des historischen Denkens an deutschen Universitäten im späten 17. und im 18. Jahrhundert* (Göttingen, 1972); *Aufklärung und katholisches Reich: Untersuchungen zur Universitätsreform und Politik katholischer Territorien des Heiligen Römischen Reichs deutscher Nation im 18. Jahrhundert* (Berlin, 1977); 'Zur Geschichte und Bedeutung der Universitäten im Heiligen Römischen Reich deutscher Nation', *Historische Zeitschrift*, 241 (1985), 287–328; *Res publica litteraria: Ausgewählte Aufsätze zur frühneuzeitlichen Bildungs-, Wissenschafts- und Universitätsgeschichte* (Berlin, 2000). Hammerstein's work is accessible in English in his chapters in Ridder-Symoens, *History of the university*.

follow later.[16] And thirdly, the Prussian legal code of 1794 defined schools and universities as institutions of the state, creating a bias against private or religious initiatives which marked German thinking throughout the nineteenth century.

From Germany the wave of reform reached the Habsburg Empire during the reigns of Maria Theresa (1740–80) and Joseph II (1780–90). Joseph II at first reigned jointly with his mother, but after assuming sole power he pushed reform in more radical directions. The Habsburg reforms were important for their geographical reach. Apart from Austria itself, the Habsburgs controlled Hungary, in a traditional alliance with the landowning magnates, and the universities of Prague, Pavia, Freiburg in south-western Germany, and Louvain in the Netherlands. In no European country in the eighteenth century, Grete Klingenstein has said, did university reform have such radical consequences.[17] There were a number of reasons for this: Jesuit domination had been so strong that the dissolution of the order in 1773 forced the state to step into their shoes; the universities had a greater monopoly of intellectual life than further west, with few academies, clubs, societies, or journals to support an independent educated public; and outside the Netherlands, the corporate and local privileges which obstructed reform elsewhere were weak. The Habsburgs were able to construct a uniform and centralized educational system unprecedented for a large state, and unsurpassed until Napoleon. Their reforms were a paradigm of what enlightened rulers sought to achieve.

Reform of Vienna University began under Maria Theresa in the 1750s, guided by the Dutch physician Gerard van Swieten, who had come from Leiden to be the Empress's medical adviser. The expulsion of the Jesuits allowed a thorough revision of teaching in the arts faculties, and led to a network of gymnasiums controlled and financed directly by the state, one of the first of the kind in Europe. When Joseph came to power, he carried out a radical revision of the university map, allowing only one university in each political division of his realms, and imposing strict uniformity. Vienna and Prague survived, but in 1782 the smaller universities at Graz, Innsbruck, and Olmütz in Moravia were downgraded to 'lyceums', restricted to teaching arts and theology. A new university was created from a Jesuit college at Lemberg (Lwów in Polish), for the Galician territories acquired in the partitions of Poland. In Hungary, the former Jesuit university of Nagyszombat had already been moved to Budapest in 1777, and under a national scheme of educational reform it was fed by five 'academies' giving two years of preliminary higher education.[18] But Joseph aroused the fierce opposition of the Hungarian political class by insisting in

[16] R. S. Turner, 'The *Bildungsbürgertum* and the learned professions in Prussia 1770–1830: the origins of a class', *Histoire Sociale-Social History*, 13 (1980), 129–31.

[17] G. Klingenstein, 'Universitätsfragen in der österreichischen Monarchie um 1800' in R. G. Plaschka and K. Mack (eds.), *Wegenetz europäischen Geistes: Wissenschaftszentren und geistige Wechselbeziehungen zwischen Mittel- und Südosteuropa vom Ende des 18. Jahrhunderts bis zum Ersten Weltkrieg* (Vienna, 1983), 82.

[18] M. Czáky, 'Von der Ratio educationis zur Educatio nationalis: Die ungarische Bildungspolitik zur Zeit der Spätaufklärung und des Frühliberalismus', in G. Klingenstein and others (eds.), *Bildung, Politik und Gesellschaft: Studien zur Geschichte des europäischen Bildungswesens vom 16. bis zum 20. Jahrhundert* (Vienna, 1978), 205–38.

1784 that all universities in the main body of the empire (though not Pavia and Louvain) were to teach in German. The aim was to produce a single, culturally assimilated service class, but it was part of a general overriding of constitutional rights, in Hungary and elsewhere, which made Joseph's last years turbulent ones. Although it was Latin rather than Magyar which German replaced, patriotic reaction to Joseph's policies helped to stimulate demand for use of the national vernacular.

These reforms had their progressive side. The curriculum was revised, archaic practices were swept away, new chairs were founded (and sometimes given to professors from north Germany), and the universities were well funded and equipped. The General Hospital built at Vienna in 1784 gave the city a long-lasting leadership in medical education. But the state also stressed conformity and control, exercised through an all-powerful bureaucratic body, the Studienhofkommission. The state paid its professors good salaries, but in return it insisted on political loyalty and it closely supervised teaching. Professors had to follow the standard curriculum, and lecture from prescribed textbooks; Maria Theresa appointed 'directors of studies' in each faculty, to report on the conduct and discipline of both students and professors. This was far from the spirit of Göttingen. The main author of the post-1773 reforms, the Vienna law professor K. A. von Martini, had relatively liberal views; he spoke of catching up with the Protestant universities, and was credited with the desire to make the outlying University of Freiburg a 'Catholic Göttingen'.[19] But from 1781 to 1791 the Studienhofkommission was headed by van Swieten's son Gottfried, who saw no use for learning or scientific originality unless they were useful to the state. The function of universities was to transmit necessary knowledge, not to encourage speculation. In this he reflected the anti-intellectual views of Joseph, who is supposed to have declared that 'we need no learned men, only efficient civil servants'.[20] Thus although German models were imitated in the early years, Austria soon abandoned, until after 1848, the ideas of intellectual freedom and criticism already seen in northern Germany as characteristic of the modern university.[21] The universities of the Enlightenment were not necessarily enlightened universities.

Habsburg officials used the term *Nationalerziehung*—'national education'—to describe their policies. But this was not nationalism in the nineteenth-century sense, rather the reverse: a 'state patriotism' which sought to create supra-national loyalty to the dynastic state among peoples of diverse languages and cultures. The

[19] N. Hammerstein, 'Besonderheiten der österreichischen Universitäts- und Wissenschaftsreform zur Zeit Maria Theresias und Josephs II.', in R. G. Plaschka and G. Klingenstein (eds.), *Österreich im Europa der Aufklärung: Kontinuität und Zäsur in Europa zur Zeit Maria Theresias und Josephs II.* (Vienna, 1985), 787; C. Thienen-Adlerflycht, 'Wandlungen des österreichischen Studiensystems im Übergang vom 18. zum 19. Jahrhundert', in *Student und Hochschule im 19. Jahrhundert: Studien und Materialen* (Göttingen, 1975), 37.

[20] Thienen-Adlerflycht, 'Wandlungen', 29. Probably apocryphal, but expresses the gist of the fuller quotation in Hammerstein, *Aufklärung und katholisches Reich*, 197.

[21] G. Klingenstein, 'Despotismus und Wissenschaft: Zur Kritik norddeutscher Aufklärer an der österreichischen Universität 1750–1790', in F. Engel-Janosi, G. Klingenstein, and H. Lutz (eds.), *Formen der europäischen Aufklärung: Untersuchungen zur Situation von Christentum, Bildung und Wissenschaft im 18. Jahrhundert* (Vienna, 1976), 126–57; Hammerstein, *Aufklärung und katholisches Reich*, 184, 197–201.

ruler would work sincerely for the welfare of the people; in return the people would become active citizens rather than passive subjects, performing their allotted duties in a strictly hierarchical society. Enlightened rulers sought to regulate from above every aspect of social relations, yet it was significant, and new, that the language of 'citizens' and the 'nation' was already being used. Part of the Habsburg scheme was a serious attempt to give basic education to the whole population and create mass literacy.[22] The encouragement of social mobility, however, was not part of the plan: each class was to be educated for the duties of its station, an attitude typical of the Enlightenment in general, and of German cameralism in particular. Cameralist thinkers were obsessed with the 'balance' between classes, and fears that education beyond the basics would encourage poor boys to leave the land. Joseph II and Gottfried van Swieten drove down numbers in the gymnasiums, so restricting university entry, by raising fees.[23] Yet there was a limited element of meritocracy in the reforms, in that the government wanted the best men as its servants, regardless of their background, and in practice many students—Klingenstein even says the bulk of them—were drawn from the middle and lower bourgeoisie.[24]

She sees, indeed, a link between this social outcome and the authoritarian nature of the teaching. The Göttingen model was socially exclusive because professors depended on charging fees, and sought wealthier pupils by giving private classes, in which they could freely develop their ideas. In Austria, fees were low and education was based solely on the public lectures with their fixed content. The Austrian universities were not as successful as some German ones in attracting back an aristocratic clientele, but they achieved their specific purpose of creating a modern bureaucracy supporting an active state. Precisely because students came from families with no inherited social status or privilege, university education itself enjoyed great prestige. Klingenstein argues that the Habsburgs thus created a pattern which was characteristic of all central Europe. Evidence from Hungary suggests that there, too, many students were from the peasantry and lower middle class, and that the Josephine reform, by reaching outside the traditional privileged ranks, laid the foundation of the modern intelligentsia.[25] Outside the Habsburg empire, noble dominance had given way to a similar clientele at Cracow, which became, it has been claimed, 'an institution essentially forming intellectuals of plebeian origin'.[26] But in Poland, as in Hungary and Bohemia, the survival of serfdom was incompatible with a free market in talent.

[22] H. M. Scott, 'Reform in the Habsburg monarchy 1740–90', in H. M. Scott (ed.), *Enlightened absolutism: reform and reformers in later eighteenth-century Europe* (Basingstoke, 1990), 172–7.

[23] G. Klingenstein, 'Akademikerüberschuss als soziales Problem im aufgeklärten Absolutismus: Bemerkungen über eine Rede Josephs von Sonnenfels' aus dem Jahre 1771', in Klingenstein and others, *Bildung, Politik und Gesellschaft*, 165–204.

[24] Klingenstein, 'Despotismus und Wissenschaft', 149–55. Cf. Scott, *Enlightened absolutism*, 52.

[25] K. Vörös, 'Les débuts de la formation de l'intelligentsia moderne et son émancipation politique en Hongrie entre 1790 et 1848', in J. Le Goff and B. Köpeczi (eds.), *Intellectuels français, intellectuels hongrois, XIIIe–XXe siècles* (Budapest, 1985), 191–8.

[26] I. Kaniewska, 'La conjoncture étudiante de l'Université de Cracovie aux XVIIe et XVIIIe siècles', in D. Julia, J. Revel, and R. Chartier (eds.), *Les Universités européennes du XVIe au XVIIIe siècle: histoire sociale des populations étudiantes. I. Bohème, Espagne, États italiens, Pays Germaniques, Pologne, Provinces-Unies* (Paris, 1986), 144.

A final component of Joseph's policies was religion. In 1781 he introduced his Toleration Edict, which extended certain civil rights to religious minorities throughout the empire—Protestant, Orthodox, and Jewish.[27] The universities were now open to individuals of different faiths, and this survived Joseph's reign. One motive was again to recruit the best men regardless of background, but another was to discourage study abroad: the many Protestant nobles in Hungary, in particular, had a long tradition of studying in Germany, Switzerland, Holland, and Scotland, and had been a channel for the import of modern ideas. Like many eighteenth-century rulers, Maria Theresa and Joseph took a mercantilist view of education, seeing study abroad as a drain on the economy, and Joseph eventually confined bureaucratic posts to graduates of the Austrian universities. Moreover, tolerance was not intended to undermine the universities' Catholic character as institutions. Rather they were to be instruments of a reformed Catholicism subordinate to the state. Joseph went further than any other ruler in pursuing regalian policies, here dubbed 'josephinism', and various aspects of church reform were pushed through in defiance of the papacy.

Professors of theology and canon law were expected to teach josephinist doctrines, and to give practical pastoral and ethical teaching. Most controversially, Joseph attacked the position of the bishops' seminaries, and forced all clerical students to confront modern ideas, and to rub shoulders with their lay contemporaries, in 'general seminaries' linked to the universities. The policy was first tried at Pavia, and was forced on the bishops by Gottfried van Swieten in Austria. But at Louvain it sparked off serious protests, and along with Joseph's attempt to transfer the non-theological faculties from Louvain to Brussels it helped to provoke the general Belgian rising in defence of traditional liberties in 1789.[28] Austrian rule was thrown off until 1792, then permanently in 1795 when Belgium was conquered by France. From 1792 onwards Austria was almost permanently at war with France, and the association of enlightened reform with the French revolution meant that Joseph's successors abandoned many of his policies. Austrian 'Jacobins', persecuted for their political sympathies in the 1790s, turned out to include many students and graduates. But the fundamental university reforms survived, and were indeed continued in the 1800s, though in the authoritarian, centralized tradition: Lemberg, for example, was demoted to a lyceum in 1803. It was not until the revolutions of 1848 that the Austrian universities were forced to break with the patterns established between 1770 and 1790.

In the 1770s, the Austrian regime carried out reforms of the University of Pavia which made it the cultural centre of Lombardy and intellectually one of the best universities in Italy. But there was to be strict uniformity and state control; the doctoral colleges and other organs of local autonomy were abolished, and

[27] D. Kosáry, 'Intellectuels et élite culturelle en Hongrie au XVIIIe siècle', in Le Goff and Köpeczi, *Intellectuels français, intellectuels hongrois*, 143–54.

[28] E. Wangermann, *Aufklärung und staatsbürgerliche Erziehung: Gottfried van Swieten als Reformator des österreichischen Unterrichtswesens 1781–1791* (Vienna, 1978), 31–41, 72–5; W. W. Davis, *Joseph II: an imperial reformer for the Austrian Netherlands* (The Hague, 1974), 185–8, 217–19, 246.

curriculum and discipline were modelled rigidly on Vienna.[29] This example had more influence elsewhere in Italy than the earlier reform at Turin, which had not been followed up, and the dissolution of the Jesuits encouraged other Italian rulers to attempt reforms on the approved lines, with the support of 'jansenist' Catholics. Examples included Pisa in Tuscany, Parma, and Modena,[30] all under strong Habsburg influence, and Naples, whose Bourbon ruler was to become Charles III of Spain, though there was little change at Bologna or Padua, under Papal and Venetian control respectively. Italy became a centre of the Catholic Enlightenment, and university professors took an active part in public debate and acted as government advisers; they included Antonio Genovesi, who was given the chair of 'commerce and mechanics' founded at Naples in 1754.[31] The Italian universities were open to modern scientific subjects, and readier than most to admit into the academic fold various practical specialities, including engineering, architecture, pharmacy, agriculture, and midwifery (where the universities certified women, but did not themselves organize instruction). Yet despite these signs of innovation, historians agree that there was no real transformation of the Italian universities: it needed the shock of French conquest to destroy the old structures of privilege, intense localism, and intellectual lethargy.[32]

The same might be said of Spain, despite more consistent attempts at national reform. It could not be said of Portugal, which saw one of the most far-reaching and ruthlessly authoritarian reforms at Coimbra in 1772. This was the work of the royal minister Pombal, who had been able to study Habsburg policy at first hand as ambassador to Vienna. The expulsion of the Jesuits led to the closure of their rival university at Evora, and Coimbra came under the full control of the state, with the Junta de Providência as its bureaucratic arm. The faculties of theology and canon law were modernized to teach regalist doctrines, there were new faculties of mathematics and natural philosophy (i.e. science), the plan of studies made general education compulsory before entering the higher faculties, a complete set of new buildings was constructed, and the university was backed up by a network of state secondary schools. While the university turned out priests, doctors, and above all loyal bureaucrats, other needs were met by a college of commerce for the sons of businessmen. The Portuguese case showed how genuine intellectual reform could be combined with a complete lack of political freedom, and with the enforcement of the state's version of Catholic orthodoxy. Coimbra was also an example of a single national university forming virtually the whole of a country's elite; indeed, it also formed the elite of Brazil, for unlike the Spanish the Portuguese did not found

29 Ricuperati and Roggero, 'Educational policies', 240–2.

30 S. Woolf, *A history of Italy 1700–1860: the social constraints of political change* (London, 1979), 104, 108–9; for Parma, Carpanetto and Ricuperati, *Italy in the age of reason*, 191; for Modena, S. Bucci, *La scuola italiana nell'età napoleonica: il sistema educativo e scolastico francese nel Regno d'Italia* (Rome, 1976), 107–25.

31 Carpanetto and Ricuperati, *Italy in the age of reason*, 254.

32 Del Negro, 'Il principe', 23–6, and A. Santoni Rugiu, 'Da lettore a professore', in Brizzi and Varni, *L'università in Italia*, 165–218; P. Schiera, 'Die italienische Universität im Zeichen der Aufklärung: fehlende Institution in einem reformerischen Zeitalter', in N. Hammerstein (ed.), *Universitäten und Aufklärung* (Göttingen, 1995), 221–42.

universities in their American dominions, and Coimbra was to retain its monopoly even after Brazil became independent in the nineteenth century.

As reforming rector of Coimbra, Pombal appointed the Brazilian-born Francisco de Lemos, who combined the post with the bishopric of the town. In 1777, using words which many enlightened ministers would have echoed, he reflected on the purpose of universities:

One should not look on the university as an isolated body, concerned only with its own affairs as is ordinarily the case, but as a body at the heart of the state, which through its scholars creates and diffuses the enlightenment of wisdom to all parts of the monarchy, to animate, and revitalize all branches of the public administration, and to promote the happiness of man. The more one analyses this idea, the more relationships one discovers between the university and the state: the more one sees the mutual dependency of these two bodies one on the other, and that science cannot flourish in the university without at the same time the state flourishing, improving and perfecting itself.[33]

Lemos lost office when Pombal fell out of favour, but returned as rector in 1799 and stayed there until 1821.

The construction of a strong state, the modernization of the economy, and the animation of intellectual life also appealed to reformers in Spain, but the obstacles to reform were strongly entrenched. Although Spain was a centralized state, local loyalties were reflected in municipal control and in the power of professional elites. As in Italy, there were some large universities with national pretensions (but few international links), alongside many small ones which resisted abolition. Twenty-two institutions claimed the title of university; in 1786 there were about 11,000 students, but two-thirds of them were in the six large universities of Salamanca, Valladolid, Valencia, Zaragoza, Santiago, and Cervera.[34] Above all, the Spanish universities were dominated by the religious orders. All reformers saw the dead hand of 'scholasticism' as the main intellectual obstacle to be tackled, but the church was also blamed for encouraging poor boys to join the swollen ranks of the clergy instead of staying on the land or entering useful occupations. Economic and political regeneration, in a country which felt acutely its decline as a European power, was a major incentive to reform. Yet even the most zealous reformers rejected the anti-religious views of the French Enlightenment. Catholicism was seen as central to Spain's national identity, and reform was intended to purify religion under the supervision of the state; it was usually carried out with the support of 'jansenist' academics. As a result, while institutional reform was serious and quite effective, governments proved reluctant to open the universities to the full force of European intellectual progress. The Inquisition was still active in rooting out heresy, and maintained a rigid censorship which excluded Voltaire, Rousseau, and most other writers of the French Enlightenment.

The monarchy showed its hand early. When the Bourbons replaced the

[33] K. Maxwell, *Pombal, paradox of the Enlightenment* (Cambridge, 1995), 105; cf. K. Maxwell, 'Pombal: the paradox of Enlightenment and despotism', in Scott, *Enlightened absolutism*, 75–118.

[34] M. Peset and J. L. Peset, *La universidad española (siglos XVIII y XIX): despotismo ilustrado y revolución liberal* (Madrid, 1974), 108.

Habsburgs as the ruling dynasty in 1714, the change was resisted by Catalonia, and as a punishment the seven Catalan universities (including Barcelona) were abolished and replaced by a single university in the small town of Cervera. But this was a purely political act. There were also reformers within the universities, and the ideas of Descartes and Newton began a belated penetration. General reform had to await the succession of Charles III in 1759. His ministers and advisers, notably P. R. de Campomanes and G. M. de Jovellanos, saw educational reform as part of a wider effort to regenerate Spain, to promote economic development, and to catch up with 'Europe'. They used the language of patriotism, citizenship, and national unity. The Jesuits were expelled from Spain in 1767, and a university law followed in 1769. In 1771, the *colegios mayores* were reformed in the hope of restoring their original function of helping the poor. But the government did not impose a national plan: each university was to be reformed in turn, by sending a powerful commissioner to revise its statutes and force through changes.

The first to be tackled was Seville, and the reports and actions of the royal delegate, Pablo de Olavide, illustrate the general principles of reform. Spain, he said, was torn by rivalries between different factions—provinces, religious communities, colleges, corporations—and was a body without vigour or energy, in which the love of fatherland was extinguished, with no common idea of the nation. The universities, with their disputes between rival religious orders and interests, were a prime source of this disunity. Olavide attacked the sterility of scholasticism, the neglect of science, the uselessness of traditional law teaching, and the incompetence and absenteeism of professors: if they were not monks, of whom there were too many, they were laymen who saw teaching only as a temporary occupation while waiting for lucrative official posts and judgeships.[35] Noble privileges were attacked, but so was the over-production of graduates. The university, said Olavide, is a public institution designed by the state to form 'the small number of men who have to serve the state, and to enlighten and direct the masses'.[36] His practical reforms included the exclusion of the regular clergy from chairs, the introduction of mathematics and physics to replace scholastic philosophy as prior preparation for professional study, and the renaming of the faculty of 'canons and laws' as the faculty of jurisprudence. 'This scholastic revolution', claimed Olavide, 'will awaken our patriots from the profound lethargy in which the vigour of the Spanish genius lies buried, and entirely shaking off the preoccupations of our archaic system of education, it will rapidly bring the Nation to a state where it can play a greater role than today on the literary stage of Europe.'[37]

The reforms at Seville became the model for those elsewhere, applied through a succession of revised statutes.[38] One of the last to be reformed, in 1786, was Valencia, a university which was growing rapidly, partly because it was especially notable for

[35] F. Aguilar Piñal, *Los comienzos de la crisis universitaria en España: antología de textos del siglo XVIII* (Madrid, 1967), 145–9, 199 ff. Cf. A. Álvarez de Morales, *La ilustración y la reforma de la universidad en la España del siglo XVIII*, 2nd edn. (Madrid, 1979), 56–63.

[36] F. Aguilar Piñal, *La Universidad de Sevilla en el siglo XVIII: estudio sobre la primera reforma universitaria moderna* (Seville, 1969), 230–1.

[37] Ibid. 241.

[38] R. Herr, *The eighteenth-century revolution in Spain* (Princeton, 1958), 163–83.

medical education, partly because it represented a shift, which was to accelerate in later years, away from the old universities of the interior like Salamanca towards the wealthier cities with their demand for lawyers and doctors.[39] Valencia also saw the innovation of a rector who was a permanent official appointed by the state. Yet all these reforms met fierce resistance; the exponents of scholastic philosophy saw no reason to change their ways, and the state never really formed a body of sympathetic professors who could give the changes permanent roots. Olavide's work at Seville was denounced by the Inquisition, and in 1778 he was tried for heresy and confined to a monastery (from which he escaped to France).[40] Charles III's death in 1788 was followed by the French revolution, and in 1793 by war with France, which provoked a strong reaction against modern ideas. In 1794, for example, the chairs of natural law rather reluctantly established since the 1770s—but suspect as the product of Protestant Holland and Germany—were abolished.[41] Yet the reforming current was not completely suppressed, and different factions contended for power. The fate of Jovellanos was symptomatic: he was first dismissed and exiled to Gijón, where he created an Asturian Institute to promote modern ideas on higher education, then recalled for a time as minister, exiled again, and finally arrested in 1801 and imprisoned until 1808.[42] But reforms continued: in 1798 the *colegios mayores* were finally abolished, mainly so that the state could take over their revenues, and in 1807 the government carried out the first uniform national reform. Eleven small universities were abolished, and a standardized curriculum was imposed, based on that of Salamanca.[43] This foreshadowed the centralizing reforms of the nineteenth century. But while Charles III's reforms had the general support of reforming opinion, those of Charles IV stressed orthodoxy and central control, in a way which alienated the disciples of enlightenment; Richard Herr sees in this the origins of the liberal and conservative parties which were later to contest university reform, among much else.[44] In the short term, reform was overtaken by the French occupation of 1808 which proved catastrophic for all Spain's universities. But the Enlightenment reforms, however modest their effects at the time, were to be consciously taken up by nineteenth-century liberals.

Spain showed that even a powerful monarchy might not be able to overcome backwardness and obstruction, especially if it lacked the broad backing which could provide a self-sustaining dynamic. Conversely, effective reform might not need a bureaucratic government if there were active national or local elites bent on political revival or economic modernization. The universities in Holland and Switzerland, for example, were essentially controlled by urban patriciates or local professional men, and could be successfully modernized without the intervention of a central authority; Geneva was notable for its development of

[39] M. Peset and others, *Historia de las universidades valencianas* (Alicante, 1993), 123–5.
[40] Herr, *Eighteenth-century revolution*, 209–10.
[41] Peset and others, *Universidades valencianas*, 141.
[42] Herr, *Eighteenth-century revolution*, 354, 431–2.
[43] Aguilar Piñal, *Los comienzos*, 19–20; Peset and Peset, *La universidad española*, 123–4; J. L. and M. Peset, *Carlos IV y la Universidad de Salamanca* (Madrid, 1983), 259 ff.
[44] Herr, *Eighteenth-century revolution*, 436–8, 443–4.

science.[45] In Sweden, reforms of the University of Uppsala which gave a strong impulse to scientific and practical education were carried out by the noble elite in a period of constitutional rule before the absolutist coup of Gustavus III in 1772.[46] Two other examples, with very different outcomes, were Poland and Scotland. The first partition of Poland in 1772 made national reform seem urgent if the rest of the country was not to be swallowed up by the surrounding empires. Following the suppression of the Jesuits, accepted without enthusiasm in Catholic Poland, the Diet created a Commission for National Education, which lasted until 1794 and has sometimes been seen as the first modern 'ministry' of education. Its national plan in 1783 included the reform of Cracow University, under the Catholic intellectual Hugo Kollantai as rector. His policies reflected the radical, scientific side of the Enlightenment. Reforms earlier in the century had included such standard measures as chairs in natural law and experimental sciences, but now the university was renamed the 'central school', and the faculties were abolished and replaced by two colleges, 'moral' (letters, law, and theology) and 'physical' (science and medicine). Except in theology, teaching was to be in Polish not Latin, and Kollantai filled chairs with Poles who had studied in the west. The Göttingen research ideal was favoured, but the university was also to train secondary teachers and to supervise the lower levels of education, as in Piedmont.[47] The former Jesuit academy at Vilna was reformed on similar lines to serve the Lithuanian part of the kingdom. These reforms represented a sustained effort by the national elite to regenerate the intelligentsia and marshal Poland's cultural forces. Ultimately, of course, they failed. After the final partition of 1796, and the end of the Polish state, Cracow passed to Austria, which reversed the reforms and Germanized the university, while Vilna passed to Russia—though, as we shall see, that was not quite the end of the story.

In Scotland, the legislative union with England in 1707 left religious and educational matters under local control. The British state occasionally financed university chairs in new subjects, particularly medicine, but the real initiative for reform came from landowners, ecclesiastical leaders, and urban elites—at Edinburgh the municipality directly controlled the university and appointed most of the professors; these men saw cultural and economic development as a patriotic cause, compensating for the loss of political autonomy.[48] The philosophical teaching of

[45] M. Heyd, 'The Geneva Academy in the eighteenth century: a Calvinist seminary or a civic university?', in T. Bender (ed.), *The university and the city: from medieval origins to the present* (New York, 1988), 79–99.

[46] S. Lindroth, *A history of Uppsala University 1477–1977* (Stockholm, 1976), 92–102, 114; K. Johannisson, *A life of learning: Uppsala University during five centuries* (Uppsala, 1989), 42–3.

[47] K. Mrozowska, 'Les universités polonaises à l'époque de la Commission de l'Éducation Nationale', in A. Gieysztor and M. Koczerska (eds.), *Universitates studiorum saec. XVII et XIX; études présentées par la Commission Internationale pour l'Histoire des Universités en 1977* (Warsaw, 1982), 7–19; L. Hajdukiewicz and M. Karas, *The Jagiellonian University: traditions—the present—the future* (Cracow, 1978), 46–50.

[48] N. T. Phillipson, 'Culture and society in the 18th century province: the case of Edinburgh and the Scottish Enlightenment', in L. Stone (ed.), *The university in society. II. Europe, Scotland, and the United States from the 16th to the 20th Century* (Princeton, 1974), 407–48, and 'Commerce and culture: Edinburgh, Edinburgh University, and the Scottish Enlightenment', in Bender, *University and the city*, 100–16.

the arts faculties was modernized by introducing lectures in the vernacular which focused on contemporary problems. This form of liberal education supported the work of leading thinkers of the Enlightenment like Adam Smith, Adam Ferguson, and the historian William Robertson—though the greatest of them all, David Hume, was disqualified from a university chair by his religious scepticism. For the universities remained Calvinist, and were the nurseries of the national clergy, though they taught a characteristically enlightened form of Christianity: Robertson combined being Principal of Edinburgh University from 1762 to 1793 with leadership of the dominant 'Moderate' faction in the church,[49] and the 'common sense' philosophy first developed at Aberdeen by Thomas Reid, which sought to combat Hume by showing the compatibility of religion and reason, became orthodoxy in the Scottish universities before having a strong influence in France. The Scottish universities also developed their professional teaching in medicine and law, taking their inspiration from Holland, where many of the Scottish elite had previously studied. The Edinburgh medical school was expanded and modernized in the 1720s, and rapidly became one of the best in Europe, with Glasgow not far behind. As in some other countries like Sweden, the teaching of chemistry and botany, first introduced as annexes to medicine, soon began to contribute also to industrial and agricultural innovation. The Scottish universities thus enjoyed a golden age of intellectual progress, and Scottish cultural identity was not felt to conflict with political allegiance to Britain, a situation which was to continue in the nineteenth century. But the absence of any central state authority meant that many institutional weaknesses went unreformed, and the appointment of professors still depended on all-pervading networks of aristocratic patronage.[50]

Was it a paradox that reform was most far-reaching in the less developed parts of Europe? Not necessarily, when education was seen as a way for states to increase their prosperity and drag their societies into the modern age. But the absence of university reform in England and France, the countries most productive of new ideas and most developed commercially, does need some explanation. It lay partly in the attitudes of the enlightened elite, for whom the clerical character of the universities and their monkish seclusion was a condemnation in itself. For Gibbon, Oxford and Cambridge, 'founded in a dark age of false and barbarous science', were 'still tainted with the vices of their origin'.[51] Gibbon endorsed the view of Adam Smith that endowed income promoted intellectual stagnation, and that the lively universities were those, including the Scottish ones, where professors had to live on their fees and offer students what they demanded.[52] British and French intellectuals

[49] R. B. Sher, *Church and university in the Scottish Enlightenment: the moderate literati of Edinburgh* (Edinburgh, 1985).

[50] R. L. Emerson, 'Scottish universities in the eighteenth century 1690–1800', *Studies on Voltaire and the Eighteenth Century*, 167 (1977), 453–74; R. L. Emerson, *Professors, patronage and politics: the Aberdeen universities in the eighteenth century* (Aberdeen, 1992).

[51] *The autobiography and correspondence of Edward Gibbon, the historian* (London, 1869), 25.

[52] A. Smith, *An inquiry into the nature and causes of the wealth of nations*, World's Classics edn. (London, 1904), ii. 393–409.

were inclined to think that the true intellectual forum was the city, where 'the members of this larger university, if I may so call it, catch manners as they rise, study life, not logic, and have the world for correspondents'.[53] Thus the Irish writer Oliver Goldsmith, in a survey of the state of 'polite learning' in Europe in 1759, which found the worst universities to be those on 'the old scholastic establishment' such as Prague, Louvain, and Padua, and the best those which interacted with urban life, such as Edinburgh, Leiden, Göttingen, and Geneva.

Even in Holland, where according to Frijhoff scientific and intellectual life was centred in the universities more than in almost any other country, by the eighteenth century leadership had passed to Amsterdam and the other maritime towns, while the old universities, their golden age in the past, continued to act as a diploma factory reproducing the official and legal elite. Holland thus had 'two intelligentsias', traditional and modern, inside and outside the universities.[54] This was all the more so in England, where the universities were remote from the capital. In this dynamic commercial society, what counted was the intellectual life of London, the world of literature, the press, the Inns of Court, coffee-houses, scientific societies, and salons. And for similar reasons, French intellectuals could write off as a hopeless case the large university situated in the centre of their capital city.

The English, French, and Dutch examples raise the question of the relationship between the bourgeoisie, the Enlightenment, and the universities. Recent historians of France, as part of the reaction against the class-based interpretation of the 1789 revolution, have questioned the notion that the Enlightenment was an expression of specifically bourgeois values. They have stressed that nobility and bourgeoisie were already coming together before 1789, on the basis of common values of which a shared culture was part, and that the long-term outcome of the revolution and its consolidation by Napoleon was the creation of a new elite fusing new and old, whose bourgeois elements were tied to public service and property rather than commerce or industry. This implies more continuity between the colleges and universities of the *ancien régime* and those of the nineteenth century than was traditionally recognized. German historians, on the other hand, have continued to associate the Enlightenment with the emergence of a 'public sphere' or 'civil society', in which a new educated class found its historic role. According to Norbert Elias, a pioneer of this approach, the university was 'the social centre most important in fashioning and disseminating the German middle-class culture . . . The German university was, in a sense, the middle-class counterweight to the court.'[55] This is probably to exaggerate universities' independence from the state, and Jürgen Habermas, in his work on the public sphere, while agreeing that German professors

[53] *Collected works of Oliver Goldsmith*, ed. A. Friedman, vol. 1 (Oxford, 1966), 332.

[54] W. Frijhoff, *La Société néerlandaise et ses gradués 1575–1814: une recherche sérielle sur le statut des intellectuels à partir des registres universitaires* (Amsterdam, 1981), 23–4, 287–8. Cf. W. Frijhoff, 'Université et marché de l'emploi dans la République des Provinces-Unies', in Julia, Revel, and Chartier (eds.), *Les Universités européennes*, 220.

[55] N. Elias, *The civilizing process: the history of manners* (Oxford, n.d.), 24.

made their contribution to wider intellectual life, does not give universities a central role in his scheme.[56]

Perhaps the key to interpreting this question is the degree of social differentiation, which meant ultimately of economic development. In western Europe, the complexity of traditional society and the progress of commercialization meant that reform of universities met many obstacles, but also seemed less urgent given the alternative channels for education, intellectual progress, and social modernization. The bourgeoisie was large and growing, but did not call on their governments to reform institutions which seemed old-fashioned and marginal. At the other pole, in eastern and southern Europe, the middle class was not large enough to dictate policy. Reforming rulers and ministers did not pay particular attention to its needs, could carry out reform with a strong hand (though not always successfully, as in Spain), and were more concerned with turning the aristocracy and the minor gentry into an effective service class. But there were also intermediate areas, such as northern Italy and western Germany, where urbanization and social development meant that a significant middle class coexisted with reforming absolutism, and here there was scope for an alliance. University reform served the interests of both parties: the price of the alliance for the rulers was to concede a measure of university autonomy; for the bourgeoisie, that it became subordinate to the state and developed predominantly as a class of bureaucrats and public servants whose status came primarily from education—the class known in Germany as the *Bildungsbürgertum.*

This chapter has focused on rulers as agents of change. There were enough common features in their reform plans to constitute an Enlightenment model of university reform which was to be permanently influential. The kind of centralized system developed in Austria-Hungary was a decisive step in the growth of state responsibility for education, stimulated in all Catholic countries by the demise of the Jesuits. This was to prove irreversible. It was also a decisive step in secularization, though for the time being that did not mean the rejection of religion, but rather its subordination to state concerns. Governments might no longer be obsessed with religious conformity, as in the age of the Reformation and early absolutism, but they still saw religion as essential to social and moral cohesion, and wished universities to teach some kind of state-approved orthodoxy. This lasted well into the nineteenth century. If the Enlightenment is thought of in Voltairean terms, as a critical challenge to religious ways of thinking and to intellectual authority of all kinds, the universities were seldom part of it. But outside France, in both Protestant and Catholic countries, a reformed and rational religion was in fact more characteristic of the Enlightenment.

Many universities were reformed and rejuvenated in the eighteenth century, in southern as well as northern Europe, but many others were not. In the two most powerful and wealthy states, Britain and France, little had been done in the way of reform. In Germany, Spain, and Italy there remained many small, struggling

[56] J. Habermas, *The structural transformation of the public sphere* (Cambridge, 1989), 23–5.

institutions, and sometimes they gave up the struggle and died. Much university teaching was intellectually obsolete and dubiously relevant to current social needs. It was not certain, therefore, that the future of the institution was secure. It was put in doubt by the French revolution, which swept away the French universities and threatened to transform European society on French lines by military force. Yet it was the revolution and the reaction to it which eventually restored a degree of uniformity and coherence to European universities, and made them instruments of the forces of nationalism, liberalism, and bourgeois interest which shaped the nineteenth century. And when French influence was at its height, it turned out that many features of Napoleon's policies—utilitarian, centralizing, and authoritarian—recalled those introduced before him by enlightened rulers.

3

France from the Enlightenment to the Napoleonic University

The thinkers of the French Enlightenment generally believed that education should be based on science, or at least on a rational hierarchy of subjects ordered by utility. In his article on 'Colleges' in the *Encyclopaedia*, published in 1753, d'Alembert denounced the uselessness of traditional teaching based on scholastic philosophy and classics.[1] Both criticism and attempts at reform in the late eighteenth century focused on the colleges, with their blend of secondary and higher education, rather than on the professional faculties, a focus reinforced by the dissolution of the Jesuits, which occurred in France in 1762. They ran more than a hundred colleges, but these were only a third of the total, and a royal decree of 1763 was able to replace them by calling on other religious orders and municipal initiative without extending the role of the central state. Since Jesuit influence in the universities was weak outside the arts faculties, there was no urgent pressure for broader university reform, and there was only a vague reference to future action in the 1763 decree.[2] There were two significant changes: in Paris, twenty-seven small arts colleges were abolished, consolidating teaching in ten larger ones, and bringing scholarship-holders together in the former Jesuit college (and future lycée) of Louis-le-Grand;[3] and in 1766 the state set up the *agrégation*, a competitive examination to encourage the recruitment of secular college teachers. This was an early example of meritocracy, and in the nineteenth century it was to become a key mechanism of higher education.[4]

Until the end of the reign of Louis XIV in 1715 the French monarchy had intervened actively in university affairs, especially by trying to tighten up the examination requirements for public posts.[5] But thereafter its initiative seemed paralysed. The failure of the French monarchy to carry out the kind of centralizing reform found in central and eastern Europe was among the general causes of revolution in 1789, and explanations must be sought in the political sphere. They included the

[1] Extracts in D. Julia, 'Une réforme impossible: le changement de cursus dans la France du 18e siècle', *Actes de la Recherche en Sciences Sociales*, 47–8 (1983), 53–76. Cf. M. M. Compère (ed.), *Du collège au lycée (1500–1850): généalogie de l'enseignement secondaire français* (Paris, 1985), 169–73.

[2] J. Morange and J. F. Chassaing, *Le Mouvement de réforme de l'enseignement en France 1760–1798* (Paris, 1974), 57.

[3] H. Chisick, 'Bourses d'études et mobilité sociale en France à la veille de la Révolution: bourses et boursiers du college Louis-le-Grand (1762–1789), *Annales*, 30 (1975), 1562–84.

[4] A. Chervel, *Histoire de l'agrégation: contribution à l'histoire de la culture scolaire* (Paris, 1993), 15–29.

[5] J. Verger (ed.), *Histoire des universités en France* (Toulouse, 1986), 154 ff.

feeling that royal power itself was bound up with the preservation of the corporate and religious structures which the universities typified, and that monarchical legitimacy and orthodox Catholicism had a common enemy in the Enlightenment. The Gallican compromise was maintained, but 'josephinist' initiatives taken under Louis XVI such as the reform of monasticism and the granting of limited rights to Protestants did not extend to education. The vacuum of ideas was partly filled by the Parlements, the chief organs of elite opinion in France, and in the aftermath of 1762 they produced a number of schemes for university reform, often envisaging a national system of secular education. The report of Rolland d'Erceville for the Parlement of Paris in 1768 was unusual among these schemes for incorporating the views of reformers within the university itself.[6] The provincial Parlement of Grenoble wanted to abolish the two decayed universities of Valence and Orange in order to create a law school at Grenoble.[7] But this could not prevail against local obstructionism, and these schemes could only have succeeded with vigorous backing from the monarchy. In fact the Parlements were critics and rivals of royal power. Louis XV attempted to crush them in 1771, and though they were restored by Louis XVI in 1774 their educational reform plans were a victim of this power struggle.

When the 1789 revolution started its overhaul of French institutions, some of the universities put forward their own reforming ideas.[8] But any prospect of moderate reform disappeared once the revolutionaries got into their stride. In the long run, the most significant development was the idea embodied in the Declaration of the Rights of Man that offices should be open to all citizens according to merit and without distinction of birth. A society in which nobility and bourgeoisie were distinguished by legal privileges was to be replaced by one with a common elite whose social position depended on competition in an open labour market, which meant in practice one where wealth and property bought education along with other forms of privilege, but where at least there were no formal barriers in the way of individual mobility. In principle, a modern educational system, identifying and promoting talent and giving the new elite a common set of values, should be at the heart of an open society of this kind. In practice, the French revolution swept away what existed without providing any replacement. A majority of the elected Third Estate, which became the core of the National Assembly, were lawyers or officials, and themselves graduates of universities and humanist colleges. Perhaps their experience gave them an animus against the traditional system, and in some interpretations the revolution was another example of frustrated and under-employed intellectuals, their numbers swollen by the expansion of the law faculties on the eve of the revolution, taking their revenge on the system which had blocked their progress.[9] However that may be, this educated elite was instinctively hostile to

[6] R. R. Palmer, 'The old regime origins of the Napoleonic educational structure', in E. Hinrichs and others, *Vom Ancien Régime zur Französischen Revolution: Forschungen und Perspektiven* (Göttingen, 1978), 323.

[7] Morange and Chassaing, *Le Mouvement de réforme*, 74.

[8] Palmer, 'Old regime origins', 328–9.

[9] F. Ponteil, *Histoire de l'enseignement en France: les grandes étapes 1789–1964* (Paris, 1966), 46; R. Chartier, *The cultural origins of the French revolution* (Durham, NC, 1991), 187–92.

privilege, local particularism, and corporate rights, all of which the old universities seemed to embody, and deeply influenced by the anticlerical views of Voltaire and other Enlightenment writers. The enemy soon became anything which recalled the dominance of the church. The universities suffered from the confiscation of church property and endowments in 1789, the imposition of an oath of loyalty to the constitution in 1790 (provoking large-scale resignations and emigration of the clergy), and the abolition of guilds and corporations in 1791. Some sort of university life survived for a few years, but in September 1793 (by which time the revolution was in its most radical phase, and suspicious of any intermediate bodies which came between the state and the citizen) the twenty-two French universities were formally abolished. 'Free nations', said the militant Jacobin Gabriel Bouquier in December 1793, 'do not need a caste of speculative savants, whose minds are constantly wandering, by obscure paths, in the land of dreams and chimeras.'[10] They did need lawyers and doctors, but for a time hostility to privilege and to anything resembling closed guilds led to the removal of qualification requirements so that any citizens could practise these professions. This was soon reversed, however: three 'schools of health' at Paris, Strasbourg, and Montpellier were set up in 1794, and although the law faculties were not restored for the time being, private enterprise moved in to fill the gap.

Even before the revolution, Enlightenment thinkers associated with the *Encyclopaedia* had begun to propose radical schemes of national education which might produce active citizens and serve the public welfare. They included Diderot's proposals for a university in Russia, submitted to Catherine II in 1775, but not published at the time.[11] After 1789, when attention began to turn to reconstruction, a further series of reports and plans appeared, and it was striking that none sought to resurrect the traditional university format, or even to use the name. The revolution in the ordering of knowledge, and a new faith in the usefulness of science and in specialized training, made their religious and philosophical basis seem obsolete and their corporate organization unnecessary. In his plan of 1791, Talleyrand allowed for three stages of education. At the highest level, there would be regional 'special schools' to train lawyers, doctors, military officers, and the clergy, with a single 'national institute' in Paris devoted to the advancement of knowledge by the intellectual elite. In 1792 the marquis de Condorcet drew up the report of the education committee of the Legislative Assembly. Condorcet's plan provided for five stages of education, the fourth of which was constituted by nine lycées, roughly equivalent to the old universities. They would be limited to the small number of men who needed a higher education for the professions, including schoolteaching, but would cover a broad range of subjects, ancient and modern. Above the lycées would be a 'national society' similar to Talleyrand's institute, with the additional

[10] Cited by B. Baczko in F. Furet and M. Ozouf (eds.), *Dictionnaire critique de la Révolution française: institutions et creations* (Paris, 1992), 290.

[11] L. Brockliss, 'The European university in the age of revolution 1789–1850', in M. G. Brock and M. C. Curthoys (eds.), *The history of the University of Oxford. VI. Nineteenth-century Oxford, Part 1* (Oxford, 1997), 866–7; R. Niklaus, 'Le *Plan d'une université* de Diderot et le plan d'instruction publique de Condorcet mis en regard', *Diderot Studies*, 24 (1991), 105–19.

duty of supervising the whole national system and appointing the professors of the lycées.[12] Condorcet's plan was overtaken by political events, and he died, probably by his own hand, in the prisons of the Terror. But his report was of permanent significance, and widely read abroad. It was based on Condorcet's general philosophy of progress and freedom, and he was the key bridging figure between the radical late Enlightenment and the scientific positivism of the nineteenth century.

It was only after the overthrow of Robespierre and the expulsion of foreign invaders in 1794 that the Convention undertook serious educational innovation. The absence of secondary education was now an urgent problem: most colleges had collapsed with the confiscation of church property and the abolition of religious orders. They were replaced in 1795 by a network of 'central schools'. In principle there was one in each of the ninety or so departments through which France was now administered, and they were often housed in the old college buildings. But in matters of curriculum they made a complete break with tradition: teaching was based on science and modern subjects, and students could choose freely rather than having to follow a fixed order. Intellectually, the central schools verged on higher education, but it was the adolescent age-group which they served; their over-ambitious aims, and the absence of any religious education, limited their appeal to middle-class families. Of the other changes made in the mid-1790s, two were especially important. First, scientific institutions were established in Paris devoted to research rather than teaching. At their head was the Institut, the National Institute of Arts and Sciences (1795), a central body on Talleyrand/Condorcet lines, with three 'classes'—physical and mathematical sciences, moral and political science, and literature and fine arts. Napoleon's later reorganization of the Institute revived and incorporated the two national academies of the *ancien régime*, the Académie Française and the Academy of Sciences. Other institutions in Paris inherited from the *ancien régime* and now reorganized included the Museum of Natural History and the Collège de France. The latter, founded as the Collège Royal in the sixteenth century, has survived all political fluctuations as a centre of research and original thought. Its professors were drawn from the most eminent men in all disciplines, and gave lectures which were open to all. These bodies, and others, contributed to a flowering of French science, and of certain branches of scholarship such as oriental languages, under Napoleon and in the early decades of the nineteenth century. But none of them had regular bodies of students.

The second innovation, in 1794, was the École Polytechnique, an elite school teaching mathematics, physics, and chemistry, which prepared pupils for various military careers and for the state's specialized schools (inherited from the monarchy) of mining and civil engineering. Under Napoleon, the Polytechnique took on a strong military character, and its students wore a glamorous uniform. Its most significant feature from the start was that it was recruited by a difficult competitive examination, requiring high levels of mathematics. It was thus based on the pure principle of meritocracy, and was the first of what in the twentieth century became known as the *grandes écoles*, a sector of competitive, specialized schools

[12] Ponteil, *Histoire de l'enseignement*, 53–64.

quite separate from the general, open university faculties. Under its first director Gaspard Monge, the school began to develop a technocratic belief in social transformation through the application of science to engineering and industry. It has been described as the most brilliant and durable of the revolution's educational achievements.[13]

Thus when Napoleon took power as First Consul in 1799, there had been some pragmatic reconstruction, but not of universities. His first priority, as for reformers ever since 1762, was secondary education, to provide France with civilian officials and military officers and to consolidate the appeal to the propertied middle class which was at the heart of his political project. In 1802, the central schools were replaced by lycées: the term was used in a different sense from Condorcet, and in a very different intellectual spirit. The new lycées abandoned the broad modern curriculum of the central schools, and returned to the classical, humanist ideals of the *ancien régime*, with a stiffening of mathematics. Freedom of choice gave way to a rigid and uniform curriculum. The state lycées were elite schools, though below them a wider network of secondary colleges was also recognized, run by municipal councils, the church, or private individuals, but all subject to state permission and control. This was the so-called educational 'monopoly' of Napoleon, which has to be seen in the context of his religious policy, designed to heal the wounds in French society opened by the revolution. There was a limited restoration of religion, but the fundamental secularization of education was not to be reversed. Under the Concordat of 1801 negotiated with the Pope, and the subsequent Organic Articles of 1802, the Catholic church became a state church, with its clergy paid by the state, but with strict controls on the activities of religious orders, and with no return to the exclusion of Protestants and Jews from civil rights. Napoleon was prepared to leave the education of the masses, such as it was, to the church, and to consign middle-class girls to convent schools. But the education of the male elite was to be secular and state-supervised.

To make this effective, and to guard against a return of clerical influence, Napoleon decided that the state needed its own teaching corporation, a secular version of the old religious orders. The outcome was the French 'University', embodied in a decree of 1806 and a definitive law of 1808. The University consisted of the whole body of teachers in secondary schools and in the faculties which were now also reconstituted. In its early years it had considerable financial autonomy and was headed by a 'grand master', though after Napoleon it was to evolve into a more orthodox bureaucracy headed by the minister of public instruction. This use of the term University, and of the related adjective *universitaire*, can be confusing, and 'universities' as individual institutions were not to reappear formally until 1896. As well as corporate identity, the University provided a regional administrative structure through which the various institutions could be controlled from Paris. An early plan by Napoleon's adviser Antoine de Fourcroy in 1806 envisaged seven

[13] F. Mayeur, *De la Révolution à l'école républicaine*, Histoire générale de l'enseignement et de l'éducation en France, ed. L. H. Parias, vol. 3 (Paris, 1981), 83.

'divisions or universities', two of them in the wider French Empire at Brussels and Turin.[14] In the end, the regional divisions were called 'academies', and they were relatively small, usually covering half a dozen departments. At their head was a rector: the title was borrowed from traditional university terminology, but the Napoleonic rector was a centrally appointed official, not an academic, and he was responsible for the whole educational system within his academy. Napoleon is generally thought to have copied this structure from Piedmont, though there were contemporary parallels too in Poland, which he may have noticed when reordering that part of Europe in 1807.

Napoleon had already reorganized medical education in 1803, retaining the three schools of health of 1794, and legal education in 1804, creating nine schools of law which were to focus on the legal codes which were another of his achievements. A rigid system of qualifications and state certification now dominated professional education.[15] In 1808, these schools reverted to the old name of faculties, and were joined by new faculties of arts, science, and theology; the independent status of science reflected the continuing heritage of the Enlightenment. With some exceptions like Lyons, the faculties were established in former university towns rather than modern regional capitals—at Aix-en-Provence rather than Marseilles, Douai rather than Lille. Yet even when a town had several faculties, there was no organic connection between them, and thus no revival of universities as local corporate bodies. Outside Paris, only the law and medical faculties had significant numbers of students, for the lycées already provided as much general education as most students needed. The lycées prepared boys for the baccalaureate, and the baccalaureate led directly into the professional faculties. The creation of the baccalaureate in 1809 was itself a significant innovation: it soon became an essential qualification for a wide range of state posts, and a badge of middle-class status. The name was taken from the pre-revolutionary arts faculties, as were the degrees awarded by the faculties (*licence* for graduation, doctorate at the higher level). To give the school-leaving examination the title of a university degree underlined the way in which the lycées had inherited the role of the *ancien régime* colleges. In principle, the old overlapping and confusion was abolished, and a firm line drawn between secondary and higher education: general education should be completed in the lycée, and philosophy was taught there in the final class. This left the new faculties of letters and science little to do, and the only students really interested in the licence were prospective secondary teachers. In practice, the line between lycées and faculties was still blurred: so short of students and resources in the early years were the provincial faculties that many chairs were held by lycée professors, and the main task of the faculties was to conduct the baccalaureate examinations.[16]

To form the new teaching corporation, the 1808 law created the École Normale Supérieure. An earlier École Normale had been founded in 1794 to train elementary

[14] A. Aulard, *Napoléon Ier et le monopole universitaire: origines et fonctionnement de l'Université Impériale* (Paris, 1911), 156.

[15] J. Verger (ed.), *Histoire des universités en France* (Toulouse, 1986), 264–9; A. Prost, *Histoire de l'enseignement en France 1800–1967* (Paris, 1968), 225–6.

[16] Verger, *Histoire des universités*, 272–3.

teachers, but this was short-lived. The new school was to produce lycée teachers, and to prepare for the *agrégation*, which was now also refurbished; it offered free education to all its students, and like the Polytechnique it recruited by open competition from all over France. Success in these examinations soon became a special target for the lycées, and the school's prestige attracted an intellectual elite. The École Normale provided a path, if a very narrow one, for poor boys to reach the top. It was also, like the Polytechnique, open to all creeds: one early *normalien* was the Protestant François Guizot, who went on to a chair of history at the Sorbonne and to an illustrious political career, and two Jewish students were admitted in 1813. Guizot was typical of the many students who used teaching as a path into politics or into independent literary, scientific, or philosophical careers. They took with them a distinctive set of intellectual attitudes: the *normalien* spirit of tolerance, rationalism, measured idealism, and literary finesse became a noted component in French intellectual life, usually expressed politically in liberalism. These values were strengthened by the intense friendships of a small residential college, and after some political vicissitudes in the early nineteenth century the École Normale was to survive as the spiritual centre of the University, and its ethos continued to bind together lycée and university professors.

In Napoleon's words, the monopoly and teaching corporation were needed so that the state could give direction to the 'public mind' and 'have a means of directing political and moral opinions'.[17] Most of Napoleon's early advisers were drawn from the group of 'ideologues', scientists and intellectuals who represented Enlightenment rationalism, chastened by the experiences of the revolution: unlike the libertarian Condorcet, they favoured a strong state. But when Napoleon appointed a grand master of the university, he chose a far more conservative figure, Fontanes, who was sympathetic to Catholicism and to traditional literary culture. So were many of his officials, and moderate priests, or former priests and monks who had renounced their orders after the revolution, found a safe haven as teachers or administrators.[18] For while Napoleon was determined to exclude the church from direct control of education, he also saw religion as an instrument of political reconciliation and social order. The official philosophy of the University, expounded by Pierre-Paul Royer-Collard at the Sorbonne, drew on the Scottish common-sense school to express a deist 'spiritualism' or 'eclecticism' which claimed to be respectful of all creeds while avoiding the dogmas of revealed religion.[19] Moreover, the 1808 law provided for five faculties of Catholic theology, whose professors had to accept the Gallican Articles of 1682. Since the Pope never accepted the validity of these faculties, they did not train the clergy as originally intended, and the bishops' seminaries retained their independence. The state's Protestant theology faculties were more successful: these were at Strasbourg for Lutherans, moved to Paris in 1870, and at Geneva for Calvinists, moved to Montauban in 1814. Thus Napoleon's religious policies were Gallican and even

[17] Aulard, *Napoléon Ier*, 161.

[18] Ibid. 206 ff.; Ponteil, *Histoire de l'enseignement*, 128–35.

[19] A. Tuilier, *Histoire de l'Université de Paris et de la Sorbonne. II. De Louis XIV à la crise de 1968* (Paris, 1994), 277–8.

josephinist, and had little in common with the anticlericalism of the revolution or of the later Republican tradition.

Napoleon's spokesmen justified the 'monopoly' by claiming (with considerable historical justification) that he was only continuing the work of the monarchy, and that the secularization of education was a natural outcome of the growth of the modern state. 'The University has the monopoly of education, much as the courts have the monopoly of justice, and the army has the monopoly of public violence', said Royer-Collard in 1817.[20] Speaking at the opening session of the Paris faculties in 1811, Fontanes hailed Napoleon as a second founder of the French University. 'A great monarch has created from the debris of the old universities and religious orders a single teaching body.' For this he had founded the École Normale, and his intention was that the teaching corporation 'should give to all the establishments of education a single spirit, a uniform way of working and invariable rules'.[21]

In the same speech, Fontanes explained the difference between the literary and scientific faculties. 'The sciences have a progressive tendency. They advance from discovery to discovery, with the aid of constantly improved methods and experience. The more up-to-date they are, the more certitude and authority they have.' In literature, on the other hand, standards were unchanging over the centuries, and the faculty's duty was to transmit this cultural heritage.[22] This expressed clearly enough the reality of Napoleon's cultural policy. He was prepared to crush intellectual freedom when it touched on political or social questions, and it was characteristic that when he reorganized the Institute, he abolished the section of moral and political science, which had been a stronghold of the idéologues. But Napoleon saw science as an unpolitical activity at the service of the state, and science and medicine were generously funded, not least because of their military value. Most scientists were attached to the special institutions in Paris, or to the Polytechnique, and research was largely divorced from teaching. As for literary education, although not perhaps as unchanging as Fontanes' speech implied, it returned to the emphasis on rhetoric and elegant expression which had acquired deep roots in French culture through the humanism of the Jesuits and other religious orders, rather than absorbing the new German science of philology. The lycée, the baccalaureate, faculty lectures, the École Normale, the *agrégation*, even the doctorate, repeated the same approach at different levels, rather than moving from factual teaching towards original research.[23]

The law faculties regained the position in the education of the elite which they had held under the *ancien régime*, and shaped the officials, landowners, and notables through whom Napoleon ruled his empire. They were also to have a strong international appeal to political liberals because of the modern, rational spirit of the French codes, even if intellectually their teaching was narrowly positivist and neglected the philosophical or historical context of law. Napoleon preserved the

[20] Tuilier, *Histoire de l'Université de Paris*, 292.

[21] Cited in Aulard, *Napoléon Ier*, 342.

[22] Ibid. 341.

[23] Verger, *Histoire des universités*, 273. Cf. L. Liard, *L'Enseignement supérieur en France 1789–1893* (Paris, 1888–94), ii. 110.

'career open to talents', and his regime rested on consolidation of the social achievements of the revolution, offering careers and solid professional advantages to the new elite, and re-establishing national unity by drawing selectively on past traditions. He was willing to accept support from any quarter, including the old nobility, if they transferred their loyalty to him, and historians have generally seen a fusion of elites as the outcome of the revolutionary and Napoleonic era. The price of membership was loyalty to the dynasty, the acceptance of modernity, and the repudiation of clerical influence. This was the 'single spirit' which the University was to instil: in Victor Karady's words, 'the idea of the monopoly was dictated by the social purpose planned by the emperor for the new system. As it was a question of giving a coherent ideological socialization to future elites, in accordance with the interests of the state, it was necessary for this socializing role to be reserved exclusively to the body entrusted with it.'[24] And in Napoleon's own well-known words, 'there can be no stable political State, if there is no teaching body with fixed principles. Unless people learn from childhood upwards whether they should be republican or monarchist, Catholic or irreligious, etc., etc., the State will not form a nation. It will rest on vague and uncertain foundations, constantly exposed to disorder and change.'[25]

This state-building policy was closer to the *Nationalerziehung* of the Habsburgs than to the nationalism of the French revolution, based on active civic participation, or to the ethnically based, organic nationalism which was emerging in Germany. For Napoleon's empire transcended national identities, and so did the elite whose services Napoleon hoped to attract. Where French rule was secure enough to appeal to new elites seeking emancipation from the old feudal structures and to create vested interests among those who benefited from French-inspired reforms, as in Belgium, the Rhineland, or Italy, this policy had some success. In the report which accompanied the founding of the University in 1806, Fourcroy said that 'its spirit will be the same everywhere: at Turin as at Paris, at Brussels or at Mainz, just as at Marseilles or Bordeaux. It will be eminently French, that is to say all will have only one goal, that of forming subjects who are virtuous through religious principles, useful to the state through their talents and their enlightenment, loyal to the government and devoted to its august head from love and from duty.'[26]

As French power expanded over Europe from 1794 onwards, two zones of influence appeared. The first consisted of territories incorporated directly into France: Belgium, the German left bank of the Rhine, Geneva, parts of Italy including Piedmont and Rome, and after 1810 Holland. The second zone was organized first into 'fraternal' republics, later into apanages of the Bonaparte family; this zone included Holland before 1810, the kingdom of Westphalia in Germany, and the 'kingdom of Italy' based on Milan. Where French armies went, French reforms

[24] In Verger, *Histoire des universités*, 269–70.

[25] Cited in Prost, *Histoire de l'enseignement*, 41.

[26] Aulard, *Napoléon Ier*, 155.

such as the confiscation of church lands and the dissolution of corporations and religious orders followed. The immediate effects on universities were as disastrous as in France: Louvain, for example, disappeared in 1797. But under Napoleon's rule the picture became more complex. In the zone absorbed directly into France, the administrative mechanism of the University was applied. The surviving universities were disaggregated into faculties, but were able to retain much of their identity despite the change of terminology. Local men remained in charge, and were prepared to work with the French. At Geneva, the expansion of science, the introduction of medicine, and the national role given to the Calvinist theology faculty were real gains for the university, although here as elsewhere political and financial oppression accompanied reform.[27] In Belgium, Louvain was replaced by faculties at Brussels and Liège. In the Rhineland, however, the balance was negative: the universities at Mainz, Cologne, Bonn, and Trier were abolished in 1798, permanently reducing the tally of German Catholic universities, and the only replacements were single faculties of medicine at Mainz and law at Koblenz. Where French rule was less direct, universities usually fared better. In Holland two small universities, Franeker and Harderwijk, were abolished in 1811 after the absorption into France, but the others (Leiden, Utrecht, and Groningen) survived.

It was in Italy that French influence was most constructive: 'in the Napoleonic period the Italian university became in every case one of the most effective flywheels of the regime, and completed its metamorphosis into an ideological apparatus of the state.'[28] There was continuity of ideas between enlightened reformers in the late eighteenth century, the Italian 'Jacobins' who saw French rule as an opportunity for reform in the 1790s, and the rather more conservative members of local elites who ran the universities under Napoleon. Italian liberals, it has been argued, welcomed Napoleon's 'authoritarian brand of modernization' to shelter them from clerical and aristocratic reaction.[29] Other historians, however, have seen the acceptance of office under Napoleon more as a way of sheltering local cultural traditions from the French.[30] Everywhere there was administrative reorganization to match the French pattern, often accompanied by educational innovation. This was the case, in the areas directly annexed to France, at Turin, Genoa, Pisa, and Parma.[31] In the kingdom of Italy, which eventually extended to Venice and the northern parts of

[27] C. Borgeaud, *Histoire de l'Universite de Genève: l'Académie de Calvin dans l'Université de Napoléon 1798–1814* (Geneva, 1909), 109–13, 127, 221; M. Marcacci, *Histoire de l'Université de Genève 1559–1986* (Geneva, 1987), 67–8.

[28] P. del Negro, 'Il principe e l'università in Italia dal XV secolo all'età napoleonica', in G. P. Brizzi and A. Varni (eds.), *L'università in Italia fra età moderna e contemporanea: aspetti e momenti* (Bologna, 1991), 27.

[29] J. A. Davis, 'Cultures of interdiction: the politics of censorship in Italy from Napoleon to the Restoration', in D. Laven and L. Riall (eds.), *Napoleon's legacy: problems of government in Restoration Europe* (Oxford, 2000), 244.

[30] M. Broers, *Europe under Napoleon 1799–1815* (London, 1996), 133.

[31] D. Outram, 'Military empire, political collaboration, and cultural consensus: the *Université Impériale* reappraised, the case of the University of Turin', *History of Universities*, 7 (1988), 287–303; D. Outram, 'Education and politics in Piedmont 1796–1814', *Historical Journal*, 19 (1976), 611–33; R. Boudard, *L'Organisation de l'université et de l'enseignement secondaire dans l'Académie impériale de Gênes entre 1805 et 1814* (Paris: Mouton, 1962).

the Papal States, several smaller universities were downgraded to lycées in a programme of rationalization, but the larger ones at Pavia, Padua, and Bologna survived. Various engineering and technical schools were also bequeathed by French rule, as was the Scuola Normale Superiore at Pisa, modelled on the École Normale, which flourished for a few years before 1815 and was later revived to serve a united Italy.

When the empire was at its height in 1812, there were twenty-seven 'academies' in France proper, and eight in the annexed parts of Italy, Belgium, and the Rhineland. The various faculties had 8,859 students—4,034 in law, 1,929 in medicine, 596 in theology, 1,841 in letters, and 459 in science.[32] These figures compare with an estimate for France alone in 1789 of 3,500 in law, 620 in medicine, 3,000–4,000 in theology, and 5,000 in arts.[33] The experience of French rule, extending in some cases over twenty years, meant that French principles of secularization and French ideas about scientific and legal education left a permanent legacy. In assessing the character of the Napoleonic model, several points may be made. The first is that there was real continuity both with the old French universities (for example, in the relationship between lycées and faculties) and with the previous history of intervention by the monarchy. The second is that many features of Napoleon's policy were typical of enlightened absolutism—a national administrative framework, appointment of professors by the state, an emphasis on utility and the training of bureaucrats, the subordination of religion to state interests. As in other fields, Napoleon can be seen as carrying out the enlightened policies which the French monarchy had been unable or unwilling to undertake, a failure which helped to precipitate the revolution, yet which the revolution itself lacked the time and resources to remedy. But it had made a start, and a third point is that Napoleon's policies were essentially pragmatic, not the result of any theoretical master plan. For the most part, he took over existing creations, fitted them into a new and logical structure, and imbued them with a dynamic which ensured their survival through all the ensuing regimes. But even such fundamental features of the new model as the concentration of general education in the lycées and the dualist division between faculties and specialized schools and institutes were the result of the sequence in which changes had taken place in the 1790s before Napoleon himself came to power, and some key institutions like the Polytechnique and the Collège de France were never integrated into the University framework.

Napoleon's system has been criticized from various points of view. From around 1830, the monopoly was the target of champions of 'freedom of teaching', mostly Catholics who wanted to set up rival institutions. The monopoly was relaxed for secondary schools in 1850, but for universities only in 1875, and then very partially: the state's control of professional qualifications was fiercely defended. The most celebrated attack was by Hippolyte Taine, in his widely read *Les Origines de la France contemporaine*. This was a sustained attack on the egalitarianism of the French

[32] Aulard, *Napoléon 1er*, 185, 354–5.

[33] R. Chartier, M. M. Compère, and D. Julia, *L'Éducation en France du XVIe au XVIIIe siècle* (Paris, 1976), 273–6.

revolution, which had made possible Napoleon's despotism and undermined the spirit of liberty and the vitality, diversity, and power of France's national life. The centralized educational system had a special responsibility for these failures: the monopoly destroyed private initiative, the University apparatus was a 'machine', a diploma factory, which stifled individuality and originality, enthroned mediocrity, and prevented the emergence of a true elite. Proper universities should have freedom, local roots, and diversity: in Taine's view, even those of the *ancien régime*, however inefficient, had a potential which the Napoleonic spirit had destroyed.[34] As we shall see, Taine and his disciples had their own prescriptions for regenerating the elite, but this critique, which appealed greatly to conservatives hostile to the Third Republic, was remarkably similar to that of the university reform movement espoused by the Republican leadership itself. In the aftermath of France's defeat by Prussia in 1870–1, the German universities were admired and imitated. But the contrast between French and German models went back to the age of Napoleon himself, and to the reactions of German intellectuals to his conquests.

[34] H. Taine, *Les Origines de la France contemporaine. XI. Le régime moderne*, vol. 3 (Paris, 1926), 250. (The volume covering education appeared after Taine's death in 1893.)

4
Germany and the Humboldtian Model

It became common in the twentieth century to refer to the 'Humboldtian model' of the German university, after Wilhelm von Humboldt, who had a decisive role as a Prussian official in the foundation of the University of Berlin in 1810. But it is clear from recent scholarship that this concept took shape only around 1900, when Humboldt's writings on university reform became known, and that before that his name was seldom cited.[1] Nor was the foundation of Berlin University such a decisive step as has been claimed. The general view today is that the German model of the university, which was later admired and imitated elsewhere, grew up over a long period as a cluster of practices and ideals which did not take their full form until the mid-nineteenth century. Its roots lay in the history of university reform in eighteenth-century Germany, in an intensive debate among German scholars and thinkers, which is reflected in Humboldt's writings even if they remained unpublished, and in the political reaction to Napoleon's domination of Germany and his defeat of Prussia in 1806. It fused together a reshaping of the traditional university form, an ideal of scholarship in which teaching and research fructified each other, a set of academic practices which were held to guarantee academic freedom, a new relationship with the state, and a neohumanist ethos which bound universities and secondary schools. Although its proponents chose to stress the superiority of the new German university to its French equivalent, its underlying social and political functions, in the service of the state and the middle class, were not so different.

The complete destruction of the French universities gave the revolution and Napoleon a blank slate. In Germany, it still seemed natural to take the traditional university as the basis of reform, and the absence of any central political authority made sweeping national plans impossible. At the end of the eighteenth century, there was a common feeling that the universities were in a state of crisis: student numbers were stagnant or falling, many smaller universities were becoming unviable, most universities were mired in archaic corporate privilege, and intellectual vitality existed only patchily. Nevertheless, for Germany as for France, recent scholarship has challenged the old stereotype of stagnation—against which, in traditional historiography, the foundation of Berlin shone out all the more

[1] R. C. Schwinges (ed.), *Humboldt International: Der Export des deutschen Universitätsmodells im 19. und 20. Jahrhundert* (Basel, 2001).

brilliantly. The innovations at Göttingen had inspired intellectual renewal in many quarters, while Prussia had already used examinations to promote educational efficiency in the gymnasium as well as the university.

Among the eighteenth-century developments which were eventually absorbed into the Humboldtian ideal was neohumanism, the study of Greek literature and civilization as a source of moral ideals. It was linked on the one hand with philology, the scholarly study of texts and languages, and on the other with the concept of *Bildung*—which can mean simply 'education', but also signified an ideal of personal self-development through the pursuit of truth. In the older humanist tradition, Latin had been studied for its introduction to history and ethics and its literary qualities, but had also been a working tool of scholarship, and the ancient world was seen as continuous with the modern one and thus able to teach practical lessons. With neohumanism (the term itself dates from the late nineteenth century) ancient Greece was conceived rather as a remote and self-contained world, which inspired through the purity and perfection of its unchanging ideals. The Greeks had achieved a unique blend of rationality and vigour, thought and feeling, and their civilization had reached a peak not achieved by any other people. To study Greece, and to understand it from within, was therefore the profoundest form of education. Greece, according to one Munich academic in 1807, was 'a flowering oasis in the deserts of world history'.[2] Academic neohumanism was linked with the enthusiasm for Greek art and architecture associated with Winckelmann. It was a secular ideal, rejecting traditional Christian ideas of salvation and self-perfection, but soon took on mystic overtones of its own, and its peculiar intensity in Germany led to the idea that German culture had a special insight into ancient Greece, and that no one who had not studied Greek was truly cultured.

The late eighteenth century was also a golden age of German literature, the era of the Weimar court where Goethe and Schiller held sway. The university of the state of Saxe-Weimar was Jena, which in the 1790s enjoyed a period of brilliance and creativity.[3] Goethe took a close interest in it as a princely administrator, Schiller was given a chair of history, and it was an incubator of the idealist philosophy which was another component of the nineteenth-century university tradition. The great philosophical names of the post-Kantian generation, Fichte, Schelling, and Hegel, all taught at Jena, and Humboldt lived there for a time. With its emphasis on the autonomy of the individual and the directing power of the conscience, idealism complemented *Bildung*, and the literary ideals of Weimar, especially the cult of Goethe and Schiller, became fused with classical neohumanism in the intellectual heritage of the German middle class.

Kant himself, from his base at Königsberg, made an important contribution to university reform with his treatise on the 'conflict of faculties' in 1798. The conflict

[2] F. Jacobs, cited in M. Jacob, 'Étude comparative des systèmes universitaires et place des études classiques au 19ème siècle en Allemagne, en Belgique et en France', in M. Bollack and H. Wismann (eds.), *Philologie und Hermeneutik im 19. Jahrhundert. II* (Göttingen, 1983), 136.

[3] T. Pester, *Zwischen Autonomie und Staatsräson: Studien und Beiträge zur allgemeinen deutschen und Jenaer Universitätsgeschichte im Übergang vom 18. zum 19. Jahrhundert* (Jena, 1992); G. Müller and others, *Die Universität Jena: Tradition und Innovation um 1800* (Stuttgart, 2001).

was between the philosophy faculty and the three vocational faculties, law, medicine, and theology. Kant argued that the latter all had the duty of teaching authoritative truth, and that since the state had a direct interest in the training which they provided, it had the right to demand orthodoxy from their professors. The philosophy faculty, on the other hand, should be the home of speculation and intellectual freedom, advancing knowledge and establishing new truths which would eventually feed into specialist teaching. Here, therefore, the state should abstain from intervention. Thus what was traditionally regarded as the 'lower' faculty, the old arts faculty, was now given a higher intellectual mission, reflecting the emancipation of philosophy from dogmatic religion.[4] This new status for the philosophy faculty (which embraced science, literature, and the classics as well as philosophy proper) was to be a key feature of the new German ideal, and contrasted with the way that in France the lycées swallowed up the old arts teaching and devitalized the faculties of letters and science.

The German Enlightenment, which developed in close relationship with Christianity, always contained elements of reaction against the deism and worse of its French counterpart. As German thought evolved towards romanticism, the critique of materialist rationality strengthened. The extension of French dominance into Germany inevitably turned this cultural reaction into a political one, yet not all reactions to the French were negative. When Jacobin France briefly conquered the Rhineland in 1792, the most prominent of the German 'Jacobins', Georg Forster, was the librarian of Mainz University. The permanent annexation of the left bank of the Rhine led to the disappearance of Mainz and several other universities, and greater upheavals followed after 1800 when Napoleon used his military victories to impose large-scale political reorganization. In 1803 the ecclesiastical states were dissolved and their territories, along with those of many smaller political units, were redistributed among France's client states, which included Bavaria and the much-enlarged state of Baden. Many small universities were abolished, others were reorganized; the confines of the old *Landesuniversität* disappeared, and the confessional pattern of 'cuius regio eius religio' was disrupted. Baden now became responsible for two universities, Catholic Freiburg and Protestant Heidelberg, while Bavaria followed a classic absolutist programme which included the downgrading of smaller universities to 'lyceums', and the concentration of efforts on Landshut (a former Jesuit university, moved from Ingolstadt in 1800), Würzburg, in annexed ecclesiastical territory, and Erlangen, a Protestant university in other new Bavarian territory. In the kingdom of Westphalia, the prestige of Göttingen ensured that the traditional university pattern survived. Later nationalist myth gave primacy to Berlin, but in reality there was a complex process of reform in which both French influence and the legacy of enlightened absolutism were strong.[5]

[4] *Kant's Werke*, vol. 7 (Berlin, 1907), 17–20, 27–9. Cf. G. Bien, 'Kants Theorie der Universität und ihr geschichtlicher Ort', *Historische Zeitschrift*, 219 (1974), 551–77; R. Pozzo, 'Kant's *Streit der Fakultäten* and conditions in Königsberg', *History of Universities*, 16/2 (2000), 96–128.

[5] S. Paletschek, 'Verbreitete sich ein "Humboldt'sches Modell" an den deutschen Universitäten im

It was not surprising that political upheaval set off a debate on the nature and fate of universities, or that Prussia was at its centre. After its defeat in 1806, Prussia was occupied, but allowed to retain its own government, and this opened the way for the 'reform era' in which the ministers of Frederick William III overhauled and modernized the country's institutions. The University of Berlin, opened in 1810, was a showpiece of the reformed state. These policies have been called 'defensive modernization', or 'anti-modern modernization': the reformers hoped to unleash the kind of national energies which had made the French armies victorious, but in order ultimately to expel the French, while retaining control in the hands of the traditional elite.[6] It was to be, in the words of the minister Hardenberg, a 'revolution in the good sense' carried out from above to avoid revolution from below. Frederick William himself was reputed to say that 'the state must replace through spiritual strength what it has lost physically'.[7] It would be anachronistic to suppose that the Prussian monarchy was already envisaging the political unification of Germany: the aim was to strengthen the Prussian state. But the new university was certainly seen as an instrument of cultural renewal for the whole of Germany, a harbinger of national universities freed from narrow provincial loyalties.

In 1807–8 Fichte gave a famous set of 'Addresses to the German nation' in Berlin. Fichte had been a professor at Jena until 1799, when his radical and atheist views led to his dismissal. He was appointed to the Berlin philosophy chair, and became the university's first elected rector, though he soon resigned after disagreements with his colleagues. Thus his lectures have always been associated with the foundation of the university, though they did not deal directly with the university question, and his educational ideas, influenced by Pestalozzi, were quite radical: he proposed taking children away from their families and educating them communally. What struck a chord in 1808 was Fichte's impassioned appeal to the educated class, and especially to German youth, to devote themselves to the regeneration of the nation, and his belief that through their national genius for education the Germans were 'called upon to begin the new era as pioneers and models for the rest of mankind'.[8] The political division of Germany, contrasted with its cultural unity formed by language, gave a special duty of leadership to men of learning.

Another famous set of lectures was given at Halle in 1808–9 by the Norwegian-German scholar Henrik Steffens, whose title launched the phrase 'the idea of the university'.[9] Steffens too called on youth to fulfil its national mission. Universities should be above all the 'guardians of the national spirit and the awakeners of inner

19. Jahrhundert?', in Schwinges, *Humboldt International*, 75–104; G. Schubring, 'Spezialschulmodell versus Universitätsmodell: die Institutionalisierung von Forschung', in G. Schubring (ed.), *'Einsamkeit und Freiheit' neu besichtigt: Universitätsreformen und Disziplinenbildung in Preussen als Modell für Wissenschaftspolitik im Europa des 19. Jahrhunderts* (Stuttgart, 1991), 279–80, 288–96; C. E. McClelland, *State, society and university in Germany 1700–1914* (Cambridge, 1980), 102–3, 107–8; W. Speitkamp, 'Staat und Bildung in Deutschland unter dem Einfluss der französischen Revolution', *Historische Zeitschrift*, 250 (1990), 549–78.

6 Schubring, 'Spezialschulmodell', 316.

7 Speitkamp, 'Staat und Bildung', 549, 553.

8 J. G. Fichte, *Addresses to the German nation* (Chicago, 1922), 47.

9 Strictly speaking, 'the idea of universities'.

freedom', and their decay had marched in step with the decay of the nation. At the time of the Reformation, universities like Prague and Wittenberg had been at the centre of national energy and spread their spirit over all Europe. Despite this decay, the core meaning of the university had survived in Germany as it had not in other countries, and universities were ready for revival, under the leadership of the state. 'That the state must support them is self-evident, for its whole higher existence rests on the fact that in them the spirit of free inquiry can reign unhindered.'[10] This view of the state's cultural duty was shared by Humboldt, while Steffens's themes of renewal, organic development, and spiritual unfolding were characteristic of German romantic nationalism.

The question of founding a university at Berlin was also debated in practical terms by Prussian officials and educational experts. There were good reasons for such a foundation: Halle had been lost when Napoleon cut down Prussian territory, so a new centre was needed for training state servants; Berlin already had an Academy, founded in 1711, which was a centre of scientific research; it also had an important hospital, the Charité, which was a natural centre for medical education. Contemporary opinion was divided on whether universities were best sited in small towns which could be sanctuaries of learning, or in cities where they could be part of a more lively intellectual scene, but the cities tended to win this debate, with Paris as an obvious model. Even so, the Prussian reformers were divided over whether to adopt the traditional university form, with its somewhat discredited image of corporate decay. In the event, it was Humboldt himself who made the vital decisions, as head of the educational section of the administration for a year in 1809–10. The new university had the traditional four faculties, and the philosophy faculty was to have unprecedented prestige; there was a deliberate attempt to attract the best German talent by paying high salaries.

Humboldt was a strong exponent of neohumanist *Bildung*. 'I have long been convinced that the only way mankind can ceaselessly move forward is by inoculating the Germans with the Greek spirit', he wrote in 1807, and at the end of his life he reflected that 'I consider the true aim of our life here on earth to be, not happiness, but the cultivation to the full of the talents with which we have been endowed.'[11] He also said that 'the idea of disciplined intellectual activity, embodied in institutions, is the most valuable element of the moral culture of the nation. These intellectual institutions have as their task the cultivation of science and scholarship [*Wissenschaft*] in the deepest and broadest sense.'[12] In the twentieth century, the 'Humboldtian' ideal has often been interpreted as meaning that research is the primordial purpose of the university, and teaching its ancillary. But

[10] Steffens in E. Anrich, *Die Idee der deutschen Universität: Die fünf Grundschriften aus der Zeit ihrer Neubegründung durch klassischen Idealismus und romantischen Realismus* (Darmstadt, 1956), 347, 352. This is a useful anthology of key texts; a similar collection in French is L. Ferry and others (eds.), *Philosophies de l'université: l'idéalisme allemand et la question de l'université. Textes de Schelling, Fichte, Schleiermacher, Humboldt, Hegel* (Paris, 1979); and on the early years of Berlin, W. Weischedel (ed.), *Idee und Wirklichkeit einer Universität: Dokumente zur Geschichte der Friedrich-Wilhelms-Universität zu Berlin* (Berlin, 1960).

[11] P. R. Sweet, *Wilhelm von Humboldt: a biography* (Columbus, Ohio, 1978–80), i. 51, 280.

[12] Texts in English in *Minerva*, 8 (1970), 242–3.

this was not Humboldt's conception. He did indeed speak of cultivating science and scholarship 'for their own sake', but the central concept was 'the unity of teaching and research'. Research and *Bildung* were indissolubly linked. Teachers must also be researchers, because *Bildung* places the search for truth and understanding, not professional training or the routine absorption of knowledge, at the centre of general, liberal education. The philosophy faculty was the crucial stage between the gymnasium, which taught established truths and the linguistic and other skills necessary for higher study, and the professional faculties which were seen, following Kant, as the legitimate home of state-prescribed training. In the philosophy faculty every student should be engaged, at however modest a level, in some kind of original work, and it is the function of the teacher to initiate students into the pursuit of truth. 'So the university teacher is no longer a teacher, the student no longer a learner, but the latter carries out research himself, and the professor directs and supports his researches.'[13] This was the origin of the view, orthodox by the twentieth century, that 'the university is a community of scholars and students engaged in the task of seeking truth'.[14]

But the unity of teaching and research worked both ways: professors are to advance knowledge and carry out original work, but it is only through teaching that they can pass their findings on and place them in their broader intellectual context. Humboldt arrived at this view as an almost incidental result of the planning for Berlin. Since Berlin already had an Academy devoted to pure research and learning, did the university also need to carry out these functions? Humboldt argued that it did.

> For free oral expression before listeners . . . surely inspires a man who is accustomed to this type of work as deeply as solitary leisure may inspire another. . . . The course of learning is obviously quicker and livelier at a university where it is constantly rolled around in a large number of energetic, sturdy, and youthful heads. In any event, knowledge as knowledge cannot be properly presented without having it independently and spontaneously accepted, and it would be incomprehensible if a great many discoveries did not stem precisely from such direct interaction. Furthermore the task of teaching at a university is not so time-consuming and difficult that it could be taken as a troublesome interruption of private studies.[15]

As Helmut Schelsky has commented, this last remark showed Humboldt's remoteness from the routines of teaching:

> the 'unconstrained and disinterested' fellowship of the university would probably have been most fully achieved for him, when wealthy, leisured and cultivated men of worldly experience, who wished to dedicate their own lives to intercourse with science and art, spent part of the day in stimulating conversation with each other and with young men who hoped

[13] Humboldt cited in C. Menze, *Die Bildungsreform Wilhelm von Humboldts* (Hanover, 1975), 323.

[14] K. Jaspers, *The idea of the university* (London, 1960), 19.

[15] M. Cowan (ed.), *Humboldt without portfolio: an anthology of the writings of Wilhelm von Humboldt* (Detroit, 1963), 137–8.

to be able to lead a similar existence. This aspect of Humboldt's university idea can be seen as the reverie of cultivated intellectuals of all ages.[16]

Humboldt was, after all, a wealthy aristocrat, who alternated scholarly work on languages with spells of diplomatic service; having returned to Prussia in 1808 after six years as ambassador in Rome, he left again in 1810 for Vienna.

Kant and Humboldt's privileging of the philosophy faculty was part of a general emphasis in German idealist and romantic thought on the 'unity of knowledge'. All aspects of truth were part of a single higher and developing reality, whose inner meaning could be grasped by the trained mind through a form of intuition rather than through positivist analysis. This was the function of *Wissenschaft*—a term notoriously difficult to translate into English, because although the basic equivalent is 'science', that word has a more limited meaning in English: *Wissenschaft* embraces all forms of knowledge and enquiry; to convey this a coupling such as 'science and scholarship' is necessary, but misses the point about unity. Indeed, at the highest level academic *Wissenschaft* was seen as only one aspect of a universal truth of which art, religion, and poetry were other manifestations.[17] Individual *Bildung* was a journey in search of this inner meaning, and for Fichte this made the university a bridge between the human and divine worlds, and 'the most important and most sacred institution which mankind possesses'.[18] These ideas had been developed in a series of lectures on the methods of academic study given at Jena in 1802 by the philosopher Schelling. He stressed that all knowledge 'hung together' because it participated in the Absolute, and that studies which did not recognize this were lifeless. The student entering on academic life was freeing himself from blind belief, and learning to make his own judgements. Students and teachers who did not look beyond narrow specialization in order to grasp the underlying truths were unworthy of the university's mission. The outward form of the university should reflect the coherence and objectivity which the sciences derived from their inner, organic unity.[19]

This meant a single philosophy faculty, and a rejection both of the French division between 'letters' and 'science' which derived from the practical spirit of the Enlightenment, and of the kind of specialization expressed by the Polytechnique and similar engineering schools, or indeed in the German tradition of cameralism. The contrast with France was pointed up by the liberal theologian Schleiermacher, who was to be one of the most influential figures in the new Berlin University. In 1808 he published some 'Occasional thoughts on universities in the German sense'. Universities differed from schools, where pupils learnt basic knowledge and techniques, and from learned academies, devoted to the advancement of knowledge. The university had an essential intermediate role as the place of apprenticeship where the student developed his grasp of scientific method and his independence as

[16] H. Schelsky, *Einsamkeit und Freiheit: Idee und Gestalt der deutschen Universität und ihrer Reformen* (Reinbek bei Hamburg, 1963), 99.

[17] Schelling in Anrich, *Idee der deutschen Universität*, 59.

[18] Weischedel, *Idee und Wirklichkeit*, 232.

[19] Schelling in Anrich, *Idee der deutschen Universität*, 5, 15–18, 32.

an investigator. To awaken this spirit and to initiate men into the unity of knowledge, not to teach elementary facts, was the task of the university teacher. As both Schelling and Schleiermacher pointed out, the universality of knowledge was what had given universities their name.[20] This was historically incorrect, but in any case the contrast between French 'specialization' and German 'unity' became a commonplace.

A further contrast was with the kind of minutely prescribed curriculum characteristic both of Napoleon's University and of most reforms by enlightened rulers, not least in Austria. The German university was to have freedom—freedom of teaching (*Lehrfreiheit*) for the professors, freedom of learning (*Lernfreiheit*) for the students. The idea that professors should be free to pursue knowledge in their own way, and to use their lectures to expound their discoveries, subject to the rules of academic detachment and objectivity, can be traced back to Göttingen. The ideal of *Lernfreiheit* was in some ways more radical. Most educational systems had an ideal of broad, liberal education similar to that of *Bildung*, but usually insisted that this was best achieved by a prescribed mixture of classics, philosophy, and mathematics, taught and examined in the arts or philosophy faculty as a preliminary to the specialized study of the higher faculties. In the new system, this general education was relegated entirely to the gymnasium. Once they reached the university, students should be free to attend whichever lectures they wished in no fixed order, to read extensively, and to form their own cultural and ethical personalities. This was made easier by the way in which, particularly in Prussia, the state had taken over the function of examining students, not only for its own service, but for entry to medicine, law, schoolteaching, and the pastorate. The universities themselves now had no curriculum-related examinations, only the higher doctorate based on the student's individual scientific work.

Along with the union of teaching and research, Humboldt's most famous coupling was *Einsamkeit und Freiheit. Einsamkeit*, literally solitariness or isolation, may be translated as 'the absence of distraction'.[21] Universities must be protected from outside interference if they are to carry out their true task. 'The state must understand that intellectual work will go on infinitely better if it does not intrude.... The state must supply the organizational framework and the resources necessary for the practice of science and scholarship', but must also 'adhere to a deep conviction that if the universities attain their highest ends, they will also realize the state's ends too, and these on a far higher plane'. Humboldt recognized that the state's interests included practical ones as well as the promotion of higher ends like morality and religion, and insisted that 'the right of appointment of university teachers must be reserved exclusively to the state.... The condition of the university is too closely bound up with the direct interest of the state to permit any other arrangement.'[22]

Here too Kant was influential. He had argued that the philosophy faculty, once

[20] Schleiermacher, in Anrich, *Idee der deutschen Universität*, 238–40, 246, 251–2.

[21] *Minerva*, 8 (1970), 243.

[22] Ibid. 244, 246, 249. Cf. Sweet, *Humboldt*, ii. 64.

freed from the pursuit of utility and devoted solely to the pursuit of truth, should be free of state control in a way which could not be expected for the professional faculties; only the university community itself could judge scientific matters. Kant took a parallel view of the freedoms permitted to individual professors. He was a subject of the Hohenzollerns, teaching in the spiritual heart of Prussian monarchism, Königsberg, and he distinguished between 'public' and 'private' reason, though he used these terms in a slightly confusing sense. The professor used his 'public' reason as a man of learning working in the field of his expertise, and here thought and publication must be free. But he was also a citizen who owed his loyalty to the state, and an official charged with the task of educating youth. His activities as an educator, and any opinions which he expressed as a 'private' citizen, were legitimately subject to restrictions imposed by the state.[23] The same idea is found in Schleiermacher: universities must retain autonomy within their proper, scientific sphere, but they and their members are subject to the same restrictions as others in their relation to civil society.[24] This conception of academic freedom as an 'inner', apolitical right compatible with outward obedience to the state drew on the ethos of Lutheranism, as did the Kantian sense of duty and personal responsibility.

In 1811, Fichte inaugurated the new session of Berlin University as rector. At the equivalent ceremony in Paris, Fontanes was glorifying the Emperor. But Fichte glorified academic freedom: 'the true living breath of the university, the heavenly air in which all its fruits can most happily develop and thrive, is without a doubt academic freedom.'[25] The concept of academic freedom has always had two prongs: the autonomy of the university from the state, and the freedom of individuals to study and express their ideas. The political situation in which the new university ideal was forged meant that the emphasis was on the latter. The traditional guarantee of university freedom was corporate privilege, but this was now destroyed or discredited. A greater potential protection was general freedom of thought within the liberal, constitutional state, but Prussia was not much nearer to that ideal than Napoleon's France. The objectivity of *Wissenschaft* and the institutions which embodied it must therefore be the guarantee.

Humboldt and his contemporaries had faith in the state as the defender of public interests above private ones—an ideal which reached its most grandiose expression in Hegel's view of the Prussian state as the bearer of the world spirit working itself out progressively in human history. Prussia was to be a *Kulturstaat* (sometimes translated as the 'ethical state'), whose special glory in the modern world, and whose contribution to the cultural regeneration of Germany, would be the disinterested promotion of science. Humboldt's faith that the state would use its powers wisely, and finance universities generously while abstaining from intervention in their affairs, did not rest so much on constitutional safeguards as on his

[23] Pozzo, 'Kant's *Streit der Fakultäten*', 110–13.

[24] Bien, 'Kants Theorie der Universität'; Schleiermacher in Anrich, *Idee der deutschen Universität*, 272.

[25] Weischedel, *Idee und Wirklichkeit*, 231. Cf. R. A. Muller, 'Vom Ideal zum Verfassungsprinzip: Die Diskussion um die Wissenschaftsfreiheit in der ersten Hälfte des 19. Jahrhunderts', in Schwinges, *Humboldt International*, 349–66; P. Classen, 'Zur Geschichte der "Akademischen Freiheit", vornehmlich im Mittelalter', *Historische Zeitschrift*, 232 (1981), 529–53.

instinctive feeling as a member of the cultivated Prussian elite that his values were widely shared.[26] The idea of the *Kulturstaat* was supported by the German bureaucracy's view of itself as a guardian of the public interest standing above social classes.

The nineteenth-century German universities retained their corporate identity, rather than being simply state organs, and some relics of the past such as exemption from local judicial authority survived for a time. But following the Napoleonic stripping of endowments the universities had little independent income, and the German tradition that universities were founded and sustained by rulers meant there was no challenge to the right of the state to appoint professors. Instead, *Wissenschaft* was to control the use of that right, through a set of interlocking rules and customs which had been developing in the late eighteenth century and reached their final form only after 1815. *Wissenschaft* provided an objective test of ability, protected by professionalism and disciplinary standards. No person could teach in a university without possessing the *Habilitation* or *venia legendi*, which was granted by the universities themselves on evidence of serious scholarly achievement beyond the doctorate. The system was standardized at Berlin in 1816.[27] Once a man had passed this stage, he was free to offer lectures in the university as a lecturer or *Privatdozent*, collecting his own fees from those students who chose to attend. *Lernfreiheit* and the detachment of teaching from examinations were essential to the working of this system. The state could appoint anyone to a chair if he possessed the *venia legendi*, but in practice service as a *Privatdozent* became an almost obligatory stage in which teachers developed their academic credentials. The advantages claimed for the *Privatdozent* system were that it created a free market in knowledge, that it allowed new specialities to be developed as professorial monopolies tied to rigid curricula did not, and that it created a pool of talent from which future professors could be drawn. It also had disadvantages. The *Privatdozent* was not a public official and was not paid a salary, and this tended to close academic careers to men without family means. First they had to support themselves while working for the *Habilitation*, then take their chances once authorized to teach; if successful, they could earn a living from student fees, but this in turn meant that fees had to be relatively high, which made university education more exclusive.

When it came to appointing professors, it became the custom for the relevant faculty to put forward a list of names from which the state would choose. Governments could and often did ignore these lists, but they could not appoint candidates without a *Habilitation*. Thus the academics effectively controlled admission to their guild, in a new form of corporatism. A further consequence was the development of an academic market which embraced the whole German-speaking world, breaking down the localism of the universities, and of a career structure which involved progressive calls from smaller and less prestigious universities to the higher levels of a hierarchy whose apex was Berlin. Competition, both within the universities

[26] Cf. McClelland, *State, society and university*, 141, 144.

[27] A. Busch, *Die Geschichte der Privatdozenten: Eine soziologische Studie zur grossbetrieblichen Entwicklung der deutschen Universitäten* (Stuttgart, 1959), 21–3.

between professors and *Privatdozenten*, and among candidates for chairs, was a powerful stimulus to intellectual progress, and the academic world was one where merit and hard work, not birth or privilege, brought the glittering prizes. 'The realm of the sciences', said Schelling, 'is no democracy, still less an ochlocracy, but an aristocracy in the noblest sense. The Best shall rule.'[28]

Moreover, it was normal practice for faculties to elect their deans, and for the university senate, the collective body of professors, to elect the rector, usually for a year at a time. This autonomy was much prized, and complete control of the academic work of the university by its full or 'ordinary' professors was itself an innovation. No voice was given to other academic staff (including 'extraordinary' professors as well as the *Privatdozenten*), to students, to the graduates who retained rights in some other countries, including England, or to local municipal elites. The new German university had a direct relationship with the state, and its professors were state servants. But there was real autonomy compared with France, where professors, deans, and rectors were all appointed directly by the state. A doctorate was indeed legally required in France, but this was a much less demanding exercise than the *Habilitation*, and could be granted if necessary after the appointment had been decided.

The complex of changes for which Berlin stands as a symbol formed a distinctive and powerful university model, but judgement of them is complicated by the 'Humboldt myth'. The cult of Humboldt at the end of the nineteenth century stressed the disinterested ideals of *Bildung* and scholarship as a reaction to such contemporary trends as the specialization of knowledge, the expansion of enrolments beyond the old educated elite, and the intrusion of vocational and utilitarian pressures.[29] The cult had a similar role in West Germany in the 1950s and 1960s, in reaction to the rise of the mass university (Newman's writings had the same critical-nostalgic function in Britain and America), and as part of the post-Hitler search for a usable past of unblemished cultural values. The Prussian aristocrat also became an unlikely hero of the German Democratic Republic. It was the communist regime in 1949 which renamed the former Friedrich-Wilhelm University of Berlin after Wilhelm von Humboldt and his brother, the scientist Alexander. Humboldt was given a positive place in official marxist historiography, as the East German regime sought to present itself as the heir of the nationalist and progressive forces of the reform era. The bourgeoisie had then been the carrier of those forces, and Humboldt's concept of humanism had been a universal value with the potential to emancipate the whole people. Necessarily limited in its application in absolutist and bourgeois conditions, the ideal was fulfilled under socialism.[30] It was left to

[28] Anrich, *Idee der deutschen Universität*, 23.

[29] M. G. Ash (ed.), *Mythos Humboldt: Vergangenheit und Zukunft der deutschen Universitäten* (Vienna, 1999), 13; C. Charle, 'Les universités germaniques du mythe fondateur à l'histoire sociale', in C. Charle (ed.), *Les Universités germaniques, XIXe–XXe siècles*, special no. of *Histoire de l'Éducation*, 62 (1994), 10–12; Schubring, 'Spezialschulmodell', 309; McClelland, *State, society and university*, 265–6.

[30] W. Hartke and H. Maskolat (eds.), *Wilhelm von Humboldt: Erbe—Gegenwart—Zukunft* (Halle, 1967), 7.

West German iconoclasts to argue that neohumanism was not progressive at all, but an instrument of the neo-feudal Prussian state, or to point out that the utopian rhetoric of Humboldt and Fichte never had much relation to the practical realities of careers and qualifications.[31]

It is not wrong to say that Humboldt's ideal was one which transcended social class. Contemporaries did not use the term neohumanism, but they spoke of 'general human education', which was to apply at all social levels.[32] In Prussia as in Austria, the term *Nationalerziehung* was used to indicate how education should create solidarity between citizens and between the citizen and the state.[33] But if every type of education should be humane in its own way, there was to be the same gulf as elsewhere between the education of the elite and that of the masses. The gymnasium was to be the portal to the university, and its curriculum was essentially classical. Gymnasium and university together were the domain of the *Bildungsbürgertum*, and the mark of its special status in German society. Just as the Napoleonic model owed its power to the entrenchment of the post-revolutionary bourgeoisie in the bureaucracy and the professions, so the Humboldtian model was successful above all because it expressed the interests of this class and caught the tide of its expansion in alliance with the state.

Perhaps one should not speak of the *Bildungsbürgertum* as a 'class', for they were only one segment of the bourgeoisie, and one distinguished by its close connection with the state and its adoption of leisured, 'aristocratic' values. German historians normally distinguish between *Bildung* and *Besitz* as separate upper-bourgeois segments. *Bildung* owed its status to university education, and comprised members of the intellectual professions, headed by the Protestant clergy and the university professors themselves, as well as bureaucrats; *Besitz*, or property, comprised industrialists and merchants. According to C. E. McClelland, 'in important respects, neohumanism was an elite bourgeois ideology directed against a common bourgeois value system', and 'the leisured, vaguely aristocratic ethos of self-development via the pursuit of scholarship had little in common with the practical and hard-headed thinking patterns of the commercial bourgeoisie, let alone those of the artisans and peasants'.[34] The relationship between different segments of the elite will be returned to in Chapter 9.

The success of neohumanism has also been interpreted as a transition to modernity in the educated professions, whereby the 'learned' class of the *ancien régime* were able to transform themselves into a modern, meritocratic professional class by developing *Wissenschaft* as a universal value-system. Thus the *Bildungsbürgertum* was not a new phenomenon created by the Humboldtian reforms, but an old class which used the reforms to disentangle itself from corporatism and

[31] e.g. B. Gafert, *Höhere Bildung als Antiaufklärung: Entstehung und Bedeutung des preussischen Gymnasiums* (Frankfurt, 1979); Menze, *Bildungsreform*, 326–7, 429.

[32] Sweet, *Humboldt*, ii. 36.

[33] K. E. Jeismann, 'Preussische Bildungspolitik vom ausgehenden 18. bis zur Mitte des 19. Jahrhunderts: Thesen und Probleme', in U. Arnold (ed.), *Zur Bildungs- und Schulgeschichte Preussens* (Lüneburg, 1988), 24.

[34] McClelland, *State, society and university*, 114, 121.

establish a new status based on endorsement by state examinations. This interpretation is especially associated with Steven Turner, who concluded that the new *Bildungsbürgertum* was 'an intelligentsia based on . . . preferred access to a state-controlled educational structure and the social and professional licensing which passage through that structure conferred'.[35] Within this broader picture, Turner has further argued that the professionalization of philology and the establishment of a neohumanist monopoly at secondary school level were strategies which assured the status of the professors themselves, and gave them an indispensable role as guardians of 'the cultural bond uniting Germany's educated elite'.[36] Lenore O'Boyle, who put forward a similar argument, pointed out that this cultural role was all the more valued by the many professors who came from relatively modest backgrounds, including the sons of pastors who had now turned to secular learning, for whom neohumanism might become a substitute religion.[37]

Like the broader fusion of aristocratic and bourgeois elements, the professionalization of academic knowledge was not confined to Germany. Fichte and Schleiermacher were reacting to French domination, and criticism of French specialization was part of a wider contrast of German 'culture' with the alleged material, mechanistic, and superficial characteristics of French 'civilization', which continued through the nineteenth century and reached its crude climax in the propaganda of the First World War. But recent historians, notably Gert Schubring, have stressed how much the French and German models had in common, and how they evolved in parallel. The 'unity of knowledge' and of teaching and research were already to be found in the reform plans of Talleyrand and Condorcet, which influenced Fichte, and the Polytechnique and the École Normale did combine teaching and research.[38] As we have seen, there was more continuity between Napoleon and the *ancien régime*, and a stronger corporate element in his University, than German critics recognized.

Both Napoleon's reforms and the foundation of Berlin were the work of authoritarian or neo-absolutist governments, in alliance with a middle class which looked to the state for employment. The *Bildungsbürgertum* was a distinctive German phenomenon, but its adoption of 'aristocratic' values was not so different from the ideology of the new service class in France, or of the upper middle classes in Britain. The parallels were especially close at the level of secondary education, where the emphasis on classics was a common European phenomenon. The lycée and the gymnasium were both devoted to the general liberal education of the elite, and both

35 R. S. Turner, 'The *Bildungsbürgertum* and the learned professions in Prussia 1770–1830: the origins of a class', *Histoire Sociale-Social History*, 13 (1980), 135.

36 R. S. Turner, 'Historicism, *Kritik*, and the Prussian professoriate, 1790 to 1840', in Bollack and Wismann, *Philologie und Hermeneutik*, 476. Cf. R. S. Turner, 'University reformers and professorial scholarship in Germany 1760–1806', in L. Stone (ed.), *The university in society. II. Europe, Scotland, and the United States from the 16th to the 20th century* (Princeton, 1974), 495–531.

37 L. O'Boyle, 'Klassische Bildung und soziale Struktur in Deutschland zwischen 1800 und 1848', *Historische Zeitschrift*, 207 (1968), 592–4; L. O'Boyle, 'Learning for its own sake: the German university as nineteenth-century model', *Comparative Studies in Society and History*, 25 (1983), 8–10.

38 Schubring, 'Spezialschulmodell', 288–96.

embodied a sharp division between secondary and higher education, with the baccalaureate or *Abitur* as the dividing line and the mark of bourgeois status, an innovation which spread later to other countries. In both France and Germany, too, the training of secondary teachers was a basic function of higher education. The German philosophy faculty was to develop as a centre of *Bildung* and a powerhouse of original work, as the French faculties of letters and science certainly did not. Yet in Germany as in France, the specialized law and medical faculties were the ones which attracted the majority of students.

For whatever the propagandists of *Bildung* might claim, the average German student was more interested in gaining qualifications than in embarking on a spiritual journey. Complaints about *Brotstudenten* —students who were only interested in earning their bread—were endemic.[39] As early as 1789, they were being denounced by Schiller in his inaugural lecture at Jena.[40] *Lernfreiheit* was a reality, and the free movement of students from one university to another during their careers remained unique to Germany. Yet the fact that examinations were run in Germany by the state rather than the university hardly made them less important; university professors sat on the examining commissions, and the examination requirements inevitably had a strong influence on the choice of courses. Even the doctoral degree awarded by the universities, though supposedly purely 'scientific', became part of the career structure in law and medicine. Moreover, for all the talk of the unity of knowledge, practical subjects like engineering were taught outside the university structure just as they were in France; specialized schools of various kinds were inherited from the eighteenth century, and were later to form the basis of a separate sector of technical higher education analogous to the French *grandes écoles*. It was normal in all countries for business families to patronize these institutions, and corresponding types of secondary school: the distinction between *Bildung* and *Besitz*, often emphasized as a distinguishing feature of German society, had its equivalents elsewhere.

Many of the differences between France and Germany arose naturally from their different political situations. France was a unified nation-state, Germany was not, and centralized institutions like the École Normale or the Polytechnique could not have an exact equivalent. The survival of the university structure in Germany, and of traditions of academic autonomy, reflected the impact of eighteenth-century reform and the absence of indigenous revolutionary upheaval. One result was a real difference in the French and German religious positions. The German universities, Protestant and Catholic, retained their theology faculties, and Berlin was also given one, although not all the reformers had wanted this. Dogmatic teaching did not seem to fit with the idea of free scientific enquiry. Yet philosophical idealism was not atheistic or anti-religious; it fulfilled a similar role to the spiritualist philosophy propounded by Royer-Collard, and was later to be synthesized with it by Victor Cousin. In practice German idealism proved quite compatible with Protestantism, and the coexistence of philosophy and theology faculties was a stimulus to philological and historical scholarship of a kind which France lacked. The apparent

39 McClelland, *State, society and university*, 110, 118.

40 Schelsky, *Einsamkeit und Freiheit*, 77.

absence in the German universities of religious conflicts also enhanced their appeal in other Protestant countries, notably Britain, where a similar harmony was lacking, whereas the aggressively secularizing policies of Napoleon appealed to liberals in Catholic countries confronting the power of the church.

'In the end', thought McClelland, 'the high ideals of Fichte, Humboldt, and the other neohumanists did not prevail. Their ideas left a certain residue in the University of Berlin . . . and a vast impression on the rhetoric of all German universities—indeed, on the entire modern ideology of higher education everywhere.'[41] This is why description of the Humboldtian university as an ideal type remains necessary: it constituted a powerful and attractive institutional invention, served as a basis for debate and polemic later in the century, and provided German academics with a source of intellectual inspiration. It came to be contrasted very explicitly with the Napoleonic tradition of centralization and specialization, as we shall see in the cases of Spain and Italy, and inspired university reform in France itself. The two ideals were shaped by the specific political and social circumstances of their countries, but both were reacting to the same long-term pressures—secularization, the recognition of education as the business of the state, the decisive shift away from a society of orders based on hereditary privilege, the desire to shape an elite for the emerging nation-state, and the professional needs of the middle classes. Both models proved internationally attractive, the German one because its central features—university autonomy, the union of teaching and research, disinterested pursuit of knowledge, the creative power of the *Kulturstaat*—seemed responsible for impressive intellectual achievements. But the French model had its own attractions, both for bourgeoisies who could envy its meritocratic principles, and for modernizing states which could admire the power of its centralized machinery, its efficiency in producing a technocratic elite, and its commitment to scientific, secular ideology. Besides, after 1815 cultural freedom was compromised in Germany by political reaction. It was France, and those liberal states influenced by French and British political culture, which offered more practical freedom, while Germany and Austria saw a continuation of the Napoleonic police state under the domination of Metternich.

[41] McClelland, *State, society and university*, 127, and cf. 142.

5

Students, Professors, and Politics

'What is a student?', asked the Uppsala poet Johan Nybom in 1848. 'He is the living expression of a nation's noblest youth. He carries his country's future germinating in his breast.'[1] The years before the revolutions of 1848 were unique in the role which students, and professors, played in politics. They had not done so during the events of the French revolution, but conditions after Napoleon's overthrow made them spokesmen for the developing forces of liberalism and nationalism. The demand for parliamentary constitutions and freedom of expression was linked with the question of academic freedom, and in Germany and Italy the universities developed a sense of cultural unity which led naturally to political nationalism. These were essentially bourgeois causes in western and central Europe, and students were acting as the younger bourgeois generation; when left-wing politics became more radical and popular, as was the case after 1830, the commitment of the majority of students began to wane, and in 1848 the majority rallied to the defence of order and property against social revolution.

The Vienna peace settlement of 1815 redrew the map of Europe in ways intended to restrain French power and entrench conservative monarchies. France returned to its pre-1792 boundaries, and Napoleon's University lost its outlying academies. On France's northern frontier, Belgium became part of a new Kingdom of the Netherlands. In Germany, much of the former Kingdom of Westphalia was attached to Prussia, which thus became a major power on the Rhine. The other territorial amalgamations carried out under Napoleon's hegemony remained, and there were now just thirty-nine German states, grouped in a new German Confederation, which had no executive government, but a Diet of state representatives at Frankfurt which could pass binding laws on common matters. It included the German (and Czech) parts of the Austrian empire, and through it the Austrian chancellor Clemens von Metternich was able to dominate German affairs until his downfall in 1848. One of his aims was to stifle any movement towards greater German unity, based on the kind of dynamic popular nationalism which the French revolution had unleashed to such disastrous effect. Austria was also the preponderant power in Italy. Lombardy and Venetia, with their universities at Pavia and Padua, were directly ruled by the Habsburgs, and the power of the minor Italian rulers was backed up, in the last resort, by the Austrian army.

In France, the Bourbon dynasty was restored, and the Restoration regime of 1815–30, though a constitutional one with a parliamentary system and limited civil

[1] S. Lindroth, *A history of Uppsala University 1477–1977* (Stockholm, 1976), 188.

liberties, saw Catholicism as a pillar of the state—the 'alliance of throne and altar'. Hostility to the French revolution and all it stood for, through the restoration of traditional authorities, was the keynote of policy throughout Europe. In Metternich's thinking, the danger to order came from within the middle classes: their agitation threatened to unsettle the natural loyalty of the peasant masses to their monarchs, but could be dealt with by a policy of strict repression. Outside Britain and France, there were few states with written constitutions, liberty of expression, or the freedom to form political organizations. In such an atmosphere universities, as strongholds of idealistic middle-class youth and troublesome liberal intellectuals, became objects of intense official suspicion and supervision. The lodgings, recreations, reading, and religious observance of students, and even their vacation activities, were closely monitored. Daniel Beauvois sees this arising from 'an anti-student psychosis . . . inspired by an instinctive and hyper-reactive [*épidermique*] prejudice against everything emanating from youthful spontaneity and constitutional liberalism'.[2]

Yet in many ways the rhetoric of restoration was misleading. There could be no real return to the *ancien régime*, and the 'neo-absolutist' governments of the period found the centralized mechanisms of state control bequeathed by enlightened reformers and Napoleon too convenient to abandon. The middle classes, if largely excluded from political power, were an economic and social force which could not be ignored.[3] In most parts of Europe the core of the bourgeoisie was still the professions and the bureaucracy rather than industry and commerce, which made universities and secondary schools all the more significant. Governments needed the trained officials which they produced. As for the alliance of throne and altar, the churches did not regain the independence of the *ancien régime*, and states kept control of them as an instrument of government and order. In Italy, universities were generally restored to their pre-Napoleonic form, and even the Papal States saw a typical neo-absolutist reform in 1824: the universities were divided into two grades, with only Rome and Bologna in the first grade; five were retained in the second grade, but several small ones were closed down.[4] While the Jesuits were re-established in secondary schools, there was no return to the church's old role in universities. In Catholic central Europe, josephinist policies largely remained in force. In Prussia, the Lutheran and Calvinist churches were forcibly combined in a new state church in 1817, and the country acquired a large Catholic population in the west, to add to the existing Polish Catholic one in the east. In France, Napoleon's Concordat was maintained, including civil rights for the Protestant and Jewish minorities. Even if religious conformity was still demanded from professors and students, as it usually was, the European university had become a fundamentally secular institution. The exception was England, where Oxford and Cambridge

[2] D. Beauvois, *Lumières et société en Europe de l'Est: l'Université de Vilna et les écoles polonaises de l'Empire russe (1803–32)* (Lille, 1977), 389.

[3] D. Laven and L. Riall (eds.), *Napoleon's legacy: problems of government in Restoration Europe* (Oxford, 2000), 7.

[4] A. Gemelli and S. Vismara, *La riforma degli studi universitari negli Stati Pontifici (1816–1824)* (Milan, 1933), 261 ff.

remained Anglican monopolies, but this was an exception which proved the rule, resulting from Britain's immunity from French conquest, and was soon to come under challenge.

Another partial exception was Austria, which had been occupied at times by Napoleon but never forced to reform its institutions. Some of the former lyceums were restored to full university status—Lemberg in 1817, Innsbruck in 1826, Graz in 1827—but the system remained dominated by the University of Vienna, which retained both its strongly Catholic character and such survivals as the doctoral colleges. Official circles were hostile to the Berlin model on political grounds, and the aim of forming an educated elite loyal to the Habsburg dynasty was carried over from the times of Maria Theresa and Joseph; study abroad was banned. The Emperor Francis I gained some notoriety in 1821 by pronouncing that 'I do not need savants, but good honest subjects'—but he was only echoing a similar statement by Joseph II.[5] Also carried over from Joseph II was insistence on German as the language of culture and administration. While the development of popular education required the use of vernaculars, and concessions to them were grudgingly made in secondary schools, they were firmly resisted at university level. Prague and Lemberg remained German universities, with only minor concessions made to Slav feeling such as chairs in Slav languages. The same policy was enforced at Budapest: linguistic tensions had formerly been avoided by the use of Latin, but teaching in Magyar now became a demand of the Hungarian elite, which (as in Poland) was still based on the nobility and gentry rather than the small middle class, and was strongly conscious of the nation's historic constitutional rights. The Magyarization of the university was to be an important issue in 1848.

Student enrolments rose sharply in most countries between 1815 and the early 1830s, but then stagnated until 1848 and after (see Chapter 8). There were few new foundations, but some universities were remodelled, revived, or moved for political reasons. In 1818 Prussia revived the university at Bonn suppressed by the French in 1798, and made it a model university to consolidate control of its new Rhenish territories, while in 1811 the feeble university of Frankfurt-on-Oder was abolished and merged with the former Jesuit university of Breslau to form a new and important university, and a bastion of Germanness in semi-Polish Silesia, at Breslau. One significant change everywhere was a shift of the university population towards large cities. Napoleon's reforms had left Paris overwhelmingly dominant within France, and in England the first university foundation in London appeared in 1828. Berlin rapidly became the largest university in Germany, regularly attracting 15 per cent of all German students, followed closely by the other big-city universities, Munich and Leipzig.[6] The University of Munich itself was created in 1826 by transferring the main Bavarian university from Landshut to the capital. This was

[5] S. Preglau-Hämmerle, *Die politische und soziale Funktion der österreichischen Universität: Von den Anfangen bis zur Gegenwart* (Innsbruck, 1986), 93.

[6] H. Titze, *Datenhandbuch zur deutschen Bildungsgeschichte. I. Hochschulen. 2. Teil: Wachstum und Differenzierung der deutschen Universitäten 1830–1945* (Göttingen, 1995), 31–2 (percentage for post-1871 Germany).

part of a successful bid by King Ludwig I to make Munich a city of art and culture, and an impressive Renaissance palace was built for the university in the replanned city. Such moves were a feature of the age. The University of Alcalá was moved to Madrid, abortively in 1822 and finally in 1845, and immediately became the largest Spanish university. In Finland, which was transferred from Swedish rule to the Russian empire in 1809, the old University at Åbo (modern Turku) was moved in 1828 to the new administrative centre of Helsinki, where it occupied a neoclassical palace facing the cathedral and the Senate.[7] There was a similar ensemble in Oslo, though in Sweden the transfer of Uppsala to Stockholm was much debated but eventually rejected. Berlin provided the architectural model for such developments, being installed from the start in a former royal palace on Unter den Linden in the heart of the government quarter. These buildings demonstrated the alliance of state and university, but the urbanization of the university also created problems for conservative states through the presence in the capital of a critical intelligentsia and a potentially turbulent student body.

Nowhere was this more true than in the most centralized system of all, the French. Since the faculties of letters and science had few regular students, and there were only two provincial medical faculties, at Montpellier and Strasbourg, most students in the provinces were studying law, and as in most countries law students tended to come from wealthier families than others and to be politically conservative. The largest provincial law faculty was at Toulouse, which had 600 or more students in the 1830s.[8] But two-thirds of all French students were in Paris. Jean-Claude Caron has estimated that Paris had 5,000 students in 1830 (of whom nearly 4,000 were in the law faculty); numbers reached a peak of around 7,500 in 1835, fell in the early 1840s, and rose again to over 5,000 in 1848—when Berlin had about 1,500.[9] Paris had far more students than any other European city, except perhaps Vienna, and its famous scholars and scientists attracted many foreigners, making it 'the university capital of Europe' in the years before 1848, and a magnet for foreign students given France's relative political freedom. The students of the École Normale Supérieure and the École Polytechnique were boarders subject to strict discipline (military discipline in the latter case), but most of the 'jeunesse des écoles', as they were collectively called, were not natives of Paris and were thus emancipated from their families, living like Balzac's archetypal young man from the provinces, Eugène de Rastignac, in the lodgings and cheap hotels which clustered in the Latin Quarter on the left bank. The key institutions of student sociability were cafés, theatres, and dance-halls, and students shared a bohemian lifestyle with other footloose young men—lawyers, artists and musicians, writers and journalists, or budding politicians trying to establish their careers in the

[7] M. Klinge, *Eine nordische Universität: die Universität Helsinki 1640–1990* (Helsinki, 1992), 286–8.

[8] J. M. Burney, *Toulouse et son université: facultés et étudiants dans la France provinciale du 19e siècle* (Paris, 1988), 152.

[9] J. C. Caron, *Générations romantiques: les étudiants de Paris et le Quartier Latin (1814–1851)* (Paris, 1991), 37, 51; J. C. Caron, 'Paris, capitale universitaire de l'Europe (1815–1848)', in J. Schriewer, E. Keiner, and C. Charle (eds.), *Sozialer Raum und akademische Kulturen: A la recherche de l'espace universitaire européen. Studien zur europäischen Hochschul- und Wissenschaftsgeschichte im 19. und 20. Jahrhundert: Études sur l'enseignement supérieur aux XIXe et XXe siècles* (Frankfurt, 1993), 439–54.

capital. No doubt this lifestyle has been romanticized, and there were many students who led irreproachably boring and hard-working lives. But, although many university towns had traditional student quarters, and the authorities sometimes insisted (as at Berlin in the early years) on controlling where students lived as a matter of police supervision, the Latin Quarter had no real equivalent elsewhere. Conditions there were conducive to action in the street, whether on political grounds, over purely student grievances, or simply in the form of alcohol-fuelled rowdyism. A tradition of protest and violence was established in this period which lasted until 1914 and beyond.

French professors as well as students had an important political role. The faculties of letters and science might have few students working for degrees, but they had professors whose lectures could attract enthusiastic crowds, both from the student body and from the general public. Chairs at the Sorbonne[10] or the Collège de France were held by some controversial figures; the Parisian intellectual guru is a figure of long standing, and academic chairs became political tribunes for the liberal intelligentsia, as important as the press or parliament in moulding opinion. For what Alan Spitzer has described as the French 'generation of 1820', the greatest guru was the philosopher Victor Cousin. Cousin was at the École Normale in 1810–14, and first taught at the Sorbonne in 1815 at the age of 23. As the son of a Paris artisan, he was 'the first great athlete of the meritocracy'.[11] His 'eclectic' philosophical system added elements of German idealism to the philosophy of Royer-Collard, and affirmed the rational basis of belief in the existence of God, the immortality of the soul, and the absolute criteria of truth, beauty, and virtue.[12] It was not a radical message by the standards of the Enlightenment, and the 'doctrinaire' liberalism of Cousin and Guizot soon turned conservative. But Cousin was a charismatic lecturer, and gave the young intellectual elite a manifesto for renewal, a sense of the tasks which awaited them in post-revolutionary society, and an idealistic substitute for the dogmatic Christianity which now seemed to have been dethroned.

Spitzer's study shows the importance of the generation factor, as he is able to trace the close links between specific individuals and groups who first met each other in the educational institutions of Paris, and went on to careers in teaching, journalism, or politics. The sense of a new generation has often been central to student consciousness, and there were particular reasons for it around 1815–20. After a period of unprecedented upheaval, young men were cut off from their elders' experiences of revolution and war, yet brought up in an atmosphere of change and idealism which was now denied an outlet. Youth as a concept, and the contrast between the idealism of the new generation and the cynicism of the old establishment, were recurring themes in the mentalities of the time, and the cultural climate of romanticism favoured collective emotional experiences and

[10] The term originally applied to the theology faculty. In the 19th century the faculties of letters and science were housed in the same building, and the use of the word was extended to cover these.

[11] A. B. Spitzer, *The French generation of 1820* (Princeton, 1987), 76.

[12] Ibid., 20–1, 75; A. Tuilier, *Histoire de l'Université de Paris et de la Sorbonne. II. De Louis XIV à la crise de 1968* (Paris, 1994), 295.

intense male friendships. For the German poet E. M. Arndt, youth was an existence of 'poetic freedom and equality, a life sufficient unto itself, in command of itself, without coercion and without sin, in which the unbounded extent of the spiritual world is laid open'.[13] Writers and artists were seen as prophets of a new age, and intellectual creativity was surrounded by a special mystique. German idealist philosophy, with its semi-religious doctrine of the spirit unfolding in harmony with the progress of history, was well calculated to appeal to this mood, as were ideas like those of the French millenarian thinker Saint-Simon, who prophesied a new industrial age to be led by a technocratic elite. Saint-Simon died in 1820, but his doctrines were incorporated into the positivism of Auguste Comte. Saint-Simonism had a special appeal at the Polytechnique, whose graduates went on both to participate in the revolution of 1830, and to construct France's railways, ports, and other public works. A historian of the Polytechnique says that for the post-1815 generation, 'tormented, often in revolt, almost all completely hostile to the Bourbons . . . the École stood for even more: it was a spiritual force, the incarnation for the new age of the revolutionary ideal of progress through science, the nursery of a new elite of scientists and industrialists'.[14] There were also conservative versions of the same impulse, which could make a special appeal to aristocrats in search of a new role, providing a chivalrous or religious vision of moral redemption and national regeneration: the religious revival of the early nineteenth century, in both Catholic and Protestant countries, relied significantly on upper-class youth.

It was in Germany that romantic feeling was most intense, and there that the political organization of students first took shape. Students traditionally had a strong corporate life in the university towns, and various types of organization had appeared by the end of the eighteenth century. There were *Landsmannschaften* which brought together compatriots from specific provinces and countries, and there were semi-secret brotherhoods of a Masonic type, which cultivated Enlightenment ideals of virtue and sentimental friendship.[15] By 1800 the rituals of student sociability—especially drinking and duelling—were becoming crystallized in the 'corps', relatively small and exclusive fraternities. Despite their military trappings—Ruritanian uniforms, sashes, swords, banners, duelling codes—they were ostensibly apolitical, which meant loyalty to the existing governments.[16] But for many reformers, the traditional sociability of students, and its expression in brutal initiation rituals and battles between town and gown, were an embarrassing menace to order, which should be eliminated along with other antiquated privileges such as university justice. Fichte was very hostile to allowing student organizations at Berlin, and this set him against the more tolerant Schleiermacher and led to his

[13] Cited in W. Hardtwig, 'Studentische Mentalität—Politische Jugendbewegung—Nationalismus: Die Anfänge der deutschen Burschenschaft', *Historische Zeitschrift*, 242 (1986), 602.

[14] B. Belhoste and others (eds.), *La Formation polytechnicienne 1794–1994* (Paris, 1994), 17.

[15] W. Hardtwig, 'Studentenschaft und Aufklärung: Landsmannschaften und Studentenorden in Deutschland im 18. Jahrhundert', in É. François (ed.), *Sociabilité et société bourgeoise en France, en Allemagne et en Suisse 1750–1850* (Paris, 1986), 239–60.

[16] G. Gillot, 'Les corporations étudiantes: un archaïsme plein d'avenir (Allemagne-Autriche, 1880–1914)', *Le Mouvement Social*, 120 (1982), 46.

resignation as rector. The traditional forms soon appeared there, and Schleiermacher argued that students' rights of association were one aspect of academic freedom, and could assist the university's task by creating a sense of community.[17]

Soon a new type of student association with political aims was to appear in Germany, the *Burschenschaft* (the name connotes youthful fellowship). To understand the political activism of students at this time, one needs to bear in mind the familiarity of middle-class men with arms and military organization. The volunteer National Guard—part-time soldiers who kept their weapons at home and turned out to defend order—was a feature of the French revolution, and survived in France down to 1848. Imitations of it appeared elsewhere in the course of liberal revolutions and risings, including 'academic legions' or guards formed entirely of students, and sometimes officered by professors. The fragility of a public order in which the citizen armed with a sabre or rifle could successfully challenge the state's gendarmes and soldiers meant that protest could turn easily to dreams of insurrection, and the rituals and oaths which were a common feature of student organizations in this period (and which mirrored the faith of governments in oaths of loyalty and religious tests) made it relatively easy in face of political repression to go underground and to maintain clandestine networks. Secret societies such as the *carbonari* in the 1820s, or Mazzini's 'Young Italy' founded in 1831, frequently involved students, though they seldom remained secret from the police for long.

During the Napoleonic wars, students had often volunteered for service. In Austria, student corps were formed to repel the French invader. In Paris, the students of the Polytechnique turned out to defend the city against the allied invaders in 1814. Above all, German students (and senior gymnasium pupils) volunteered to join the corps formed by Lützow in 1813, which participated in the war of liberation against Napoleon and in the battle of Leipzig in 1813. As with all aspects of the early history of German nationalism, the 1813 episode and the role of students in it later became sanctified and mythologized. It had its own iconography of paintings and engravings, in which bespectacled but armed students take up heroic poses in the German hills and forests. But whatever the value of students' military contribution, there is no doubt that the liberation of Germany created a fervent desire among the younger generation for national renewal and for a new political order, hopes which were dashed by the reactionary settlement of 1815.

The slogan of the *Burschenschaften* was Honour, Freedom, and Fatherland, and they adopted the black-red-gold tricolour which became the symbol of German liberal nationalism. Interpretations of the movement have changed over the years in accordance with contemporary concerns. In the nineteenth century they were celebrated chiefly as harbingers of German unity, and once unification was achieved their initial liberalism faded from the picture; their nationalism appeared in a much darker light after the support which students gave to Nazism.[18] In the

[17] E. Anrich, *Die Idee der deutschen Universität: Die fünf Grundschriften aus der Zeit ihrer Neubegründung durch klassischen Idealismus und romantischen Realismus* (Darmstadt, 1956), 275–9.

[18] e.g. H. Kohn, *Nationalism: its meaning and history* (New York, 1965), 37; G. L. Mosse, *The crisis of German ideology: intellectual origins of the Third Reich* (New York, 1964), 192.

1970s, on the other hand, the *Burschenschaften* were seen as early exponents of student protest, and some historians stressed their left-wing features.[19] More recently they have been interpreted by Wolfgang Hardtwig and others in the context of the 'public sphere' and generational change, as sites of a new bourgeois consciousness, of which both nationalism and the demand for constitutional rights were expressions.[20] Honour, friendship, and fraternity were key concepts for this self-appointed moral elite, because they expressed a new ideal of bourgeois individuality and self-respect, and even duelling, which might appear to be a takeover of aristocratic values, and which some of the *Burschenschaften* rejected, has been seen as one aspect of this.[21]

The *Burschenschaft* movement had its heart in the Protestant universities of central Germany, for although many nationalists were already looking to Prussia for leadership, the Prussian government closely controlled the political activities of its own students. The first *Burschenschaft* was founded at Jena in 1815 by veterans of the 1813 campaign, and the high point of the early movement came in 1817, with the student festival at the Wartburg castle at Eisenach, not far from Jena. Here Luther had taken refuge and worked on his translation of the Bible, and the festival was ostensibly to commemorate the 300th anniversary of the Reformation; it was also the fourth anniversary of the battle of Leipzig, and the atmosphere was markedly anti-French. About 500 attended the demonstration, including some professors. Processions and the singing of hymns and patriotic songs culminated in a bonfire at which various symbols of absolutism and French influence, including a copy of the Napoleonic Code and other books, were cast into the flames. Although this has an unfortunate flavour in the light of the book-burnings of the 1930s, torchlight processions and bonfires were a standard part of the student repertoire throughout northern Europe, as were rural excursions, outdoor festivals, and communal singing. In a period of political repression, traditional or folkloric rituals could be given new meaning as forms of political protest, and the phenomenon recurred in 1848, notably in mass student marches out of the university towns.[22] For the early *Burschenschaft* movement, the patriotic songs and poetry of Ernst Moritz Arndt were popular expressions of the desire for unity, and there were also strong links with the gymnastic movement founded by F. L. Jahn. Jahn's writings were fervently nationalistic (and anti-Semitic), and it was not only in Germany that gymnastics, with their semi-military purpose of promoting physical fitness, were to serve as a youthful incubator of national feeling.

[19] G. Bartol, *Ideologie und studentischer Protest: Untersuchungen zur Entstehung deutscher Studentenbewegungen im 19. und 20. Jahrhundert* (Munich, 1978).

[20] Hardtwig, 'Studentische Mentalität'; W. Hardtwig, 'Sozialverhalten und Wertwandel der jugendlichen Bildungsschicht im Übergang zur bürgerlichen Gesellschaft (17.–19. Jahrhundert)', *Vierteljahrschrift für Sozial- und Wirtschaftsgeschichte*, 73 (1986), 305–35. Cf. R. S. Elkar, 'Young Germans and Young Germany: some remarks on the history of German youth in the late eighteenth and in the first half of the nineteenth century', in M. Roseman (ed.), *Generations in conflict: youth revolt and generation formation in Germany 1770–1968* (Cambridge, 1995), 69–91.

[21] U. Frevert, 'Honour and middle-class cultures: the history of the duel in England and Germany', in J. Kocka and A. Mitchell (eds.), *Bourgeois society in nineteenth-century Europe* (Oxford, 1993), 207–40.

[22] H. Thielbeer, *Universität und Politik in der deutschen Revolution von 1848* (Bonn, 1983), 36–8 (Göttingen), 50–8 (Heidelberg).

In 1818 a general German *Burschenschaft* was formed to unite the efforts of individual universities. Its programme expounded the need for a national, liberal state—and at this stage nationalism and liberalism went together. The aristocrat Heinrich von Gagern, a student at Jena, explained the aims of the *Burschenschaften* to his father:

Love of Fatherland is their guiding principle. Their purpose is to make a better future for the Fatherland, each as best he can, to spread national consciousness, or to use the much ridiculed and maligned Germanic expression, more folkishness, and to work for better constitutions. . . . above all, we want Germany to be considered *one* land and the German people *one* people. In the forms of our student comradeship we show how we want to approach this as nearly as possible in the real world. Regional fraternities are forbidden, and we live in a German comradeship, one people in spirit, as we want it for all Germany in reality.[23]

From the start there were divisions within the *Burschenschaft* movement, both social and political, and official tolerance of its activities came to an abrupt end in 1819, when the playwright Kotzebue, who had been revealed as a Russian police agent, was murdered by Carl Sand, a former student. This gave Metternich the excuse he needed to clamp down on the universities. The Karlsbad decrees of 1819, approved by German rulers while taking the waters at the eponymous Bohemian spa, became part of the law of the German Confederation. All student organizations were forbidden, and individuals defying the law were to be banned from public office; states were obliged to appoint a curator or 'plenipotentiary' in each university to watch over professors and students; professors with subversive views were to be dismissed; and there were to be blacklists, with a central police commission at Mainz, so that radicals could not move to other universities. Prussia regularly forbade its citizens to study at suspect universities in southern Germany and elsewhere. The more liberal states, like Baden and Württemberg, were reluctantly forced into line.[24] One result of this persecution of 'demagogues', which made no distinction between moderate liberals and radical democrats, was a wave of political exiles, but even countries like Switzerland did not necessarily provide a refuge, as Metternich was able to put diplomatic pressure on their authorities. Only a handful of committed radicals kept secret student links alive.[25]

The same repressive atmosphere ruled in France and elsewhere, making the 1820s a bleak period of European university history. The restored Bourbons maintained the institutions which they had inherited from Napoleon, but it soon became clear that only complete political submission was acceptable. In a provincial city like Toulouse, the authorities could minutely supervise students' private lives.[26] This was impossible in Paris, but even the most trivial political incident was 'met with harsh reprisals and anticipated by a rigid and niggling discipline', more

[23] Cited in M. Walker (ed.), *Metternich's Europe* (New York, 1968), 45–7.

[24] R. Müth, *Studentische Emanzipation und staatliche Repression: Die politische Bewegung der Tübinger Studenten im Vormärz, insbesonders von 1825 bis 1837* (Tübingen, 1977), 23–5, 36–41, 204–5.

[25] Lutz, R. R., 'The German revolutionary student movement 1819–1833', *Central European History*, 4 (1971), 215–41.

[26] Burney, *Toulouse et son université*, 203 ff.

appropriate, says Spitzer, to 'a training depot of the Foreign Legion. . . . the paranoid surveillance of the student corps helped to create what it was intended to forestall'.[27] Protests frequently led to the suspension of schools and faculties, and the expulsion of supposed ringleaders. The Polytechnique was closed temporarily in 1816 as a nest of liberalism and Bonapartism, one of the student victims being Auguste Comte. In 1817 the law faculty at Rennes was suspended, and professors and students only readmitted if they subscribed to 'sound principles'. In 1820 the assassination of the duc de Berry, the heir to the French throne, though not the work of a student, led to a general political reaction. A law restricting the already very narrow franchise provoked political riots led by students, one of whom was shot dead, after which a decree of 1820, not repealed until 1883, forbade any sort of student organization. Among other disciplinary actions, in 1821 the law faculty at Grenoble was closed for three years, and in 1822 the medical faculty at Paris was thoroughly purged, eleven teachers being dismissed. Between 1822 and 1828 the grand master of the University was bishop Frayssinous, who struggled to impose Catholic and royalist orthodoxy: the lectures of Cousin and Guizot were suspended until 1828, and the University's spiritual centre, the École Normale, was closed down in 1822, and reopened only partially and under a different name in 1826.[28]

In Italy too, the dominance of the political order by Austria led to reaction, which intensified after liberal risings in 1820–1 which included student participation. At Naples a temporarily successful revolution in 1820 was followed by heavy-handed repression. Four professors were dismissed, all degrees awarded during the liberal period were declared invalid, university autonomy was removed, and the university subjected directly to the minister of public instruction, who was a bishop.[29] The universities under direct Austrian rule, Pavia and Padua, were more generously funded than under Napoleon, but the intellectual atmosphere was stagnant and repressive: both curricula and disciplinary control over professors and students were assimilated strictly to the Austrian pattern, the only concession being teaching in Italian. Many of the professors held office under both Napoleon and the Habsburgs, and were subserviently loyal to both. There were a few exceptions: one Pavia law professor, Adeodato Ressi, was condemned to life imprisonment for his sympathies with the liberal risings, and died in prison.[30] The students were more politically active at Pavia than at Padua, but most student incidents arose from brawls with townsmen and soldiers rather than politics, though in 1821 Pavia students joined the insurrection at Turin as part of a 'battalion of Minerva'.[31] When the Emperor Francis visited Pavia in 1825, there was much demonstration of official

[27] Spitzer, *French generation of 1820*, 37, 41.

[28] Ibid. 43–8; Tuilier, *Université de Paris*, 309 ff. A comprehensive account is in Caron, *Générations romantiques*.

[29] F. Torraca and others, *Storia della Università di Napoli* (Naples, 1924), 574–6.

[30] I. Ciprandi, 'L'Università di Pavia nell'età della Restaurazione', in I. Ciprandi and others, *Problemi scolastici ed educativi nella Lombardia del primo ottocento. 2. L'istruzione superiore* (Milan, 1978), 265–9.

[31] Ibid. 265–9, 282–4; D. Laven, 'Liberals or libertines? Staff, students, and government policy at the University of Padua 1814–1835', *History of Universities*, 11 (1992), 123–64.

loyalty, but a few days later two students were shot dead after disturbances which began with a police ban on bathing in the river Ticino.[32] There were to be further disturbances in Italy in 1830–1, but no real change until 1848.

At Pavia, students in the 1820s were expected to go to mass every Sunday, and to confess and take communion at least six times a year.[33] The use of religion for police purposes was also characteristic of reaction in the Iberian peninsula, a part of Europe outside Metternich's grasp, where liberal risings in 1820 succeeded for a time. The liberal governments in both Spain and Portugal gave a special priority to university policy. The Spanish liberals introduced a comprehensive reform scheme in 1821, based on the Napoleonic principles of centralization (see Chapter 14). But the liberal regime was suppressed in 1823, with the help of a French army, and repression followed. It was not until the 1840s that political change allowed the liberal programme to be brought forward again. It was a similar story in Portugal, where the liberal revolution in 1820 led to a thorough reform of the University of Coimbra, largely reversed after political reaction in 1823.[34] In Spain, the anti-liberal regulations of 1824 included a series of oaths: to the doctrine of the Immaculate Conception (a special national cult: this oath was traditional), to teach and defend the rights of the crown against the church, and not to belong or ever have belonged to a secret society. In order to matriculate, students had to produce certificates of good conduct from their parish priest and local civil authority; priests were placed on university disciplinary tribunals; and there were night rounds to catch students attending theatres and cafés. Religious attendance was compulsory, and there was to be vigilance over local bookshops and student reading.[35] Under such a regime, the Spanish universities became 'a mere skeleton, a hollow ghost of the past'.[36] They were closed altogether for a time after the July revolution in France, for fear of liberal ideas spreading.

Students at Coimbra were still required to wear academic dress, and other features of these social and religious restrictions recall those in force at Oxford and Cambridge. But the political situation was not comparable. In England, students were members of the class which already held political power, and saw their university years as a training in public life. Individual dissidents might be disciplined, usually for religious rather than political reasons, but in the 1820s the Oxford and Cambridge 'Unions' established their right to debate political questions in parliamentary form, to the surprise of foreign observers. The non-residential and more democratically recruited Scottish universities saw little student political activism, though there was both traditional rowdyism and some agitation on questions of

[32] Ciprandi, 'L'Università di Pavia', 305, 310–11.

[33] Ibid. 299.

[34] L. A. de Oliveira Ramos, 'Rénovation du corps enseignant de l'Université de Coimbra à l'aube du libéralisme (1820–1823)', in A. Romano (ed.), *Università in Europa. Le istituzioni universitarie dal medio evo ai nostri giorni: strutture, organizzazione, funzionamento* (Messina, 1995), 501–9.

[35] *Historia de la educación en España. II. De las Cortes de Cádiz a la revolución de 1868*, 2nd edn. (Madrid, 1985), 95, 111–15.

[36] M. Peset and J. L. Peset, *La universidad española (siglos XVIII y XIX): despotismo ilustrado y revolución liberal* (Madrid, 1974), 142.

university reform.[37] Thus important political changes in Britain, like the Reform Act of 1832 which extended the vote to a large part of the middle class, took place without university participation.

On the Continent, the political ice began to crack in 1830, in France, Belgium, and Poland. The fall of the Restoration regime in France, and its replacement by the July monarchy of Louis-Philippe, brought to power many of the academic leaders of liberalism, including Guizot, Cousin, and Abel Villemain, all of whom were to serve as ministers of education in the 1830s and 1840s. The Orleanist monarchy rested on a very narrow social base, with a property-based franchise more restricted than that in Britain after 1832, but its values reflected those of the upper-middle-class, property-owning elite rather than those of the older nobility, and it was a regime in ideological harmony with the University, symbolized in 1830 by the reopening of the École Normale. Orleanist liberalism, satisfied with the limited freedoms which had been achieved, was soon challenged by radical republicanism advocating universal male suffrage, a movement speaking for the 'people' but mainly led by bourgeois intellectuals. The July monarchy soon showed its conservative side, and activist students were involved in numerous demonstrations, disturbances, violent incidents, and political trials; they joined in the characteristic urban means of protests—funerals, banquets, demonstrations at statues of popular figures, visits to the homes of unpopular living ones. As early as 1832, 5,000 students were said to be present at the funeral of the left-wing general Lamarque, which led to a near-insurrection, an event incorporated into Victor Hugo's *Les Misérables*.[38] When repression followed such incidents, some joined conspiratorial secret societies, but this dangerous mode of action attracted only a radical minority, and it offered little real threat to the regime.

The most dramatic events of 1830 were in Poland. Napoleon had created an autonomous Grand Duchy of Warsaw, which allowed some of the national aspirations of the 1790s to be revived, but the Congress of Vienna restored the partitions, and all three powers of the victorious Holy Alliance had an interest in oppressing the Poles. In Austrian Galicia, there was only the German-speaking university of Lemberg, and in Prussian-ruled Posen there was no university or any prospect of the Poles obtaining one. After a period of germanization under Austrian rule, the university of Cracow enjoyed a brief revival under the Grand Duchy; in 1815 Cracow became an autonomous free city, but the close supervision of the three powers kept the university from playing a wider role in Polish life. To its north, however, the 'Congress Kingdom' of Poland came under the rule of the Russian Tsar Alexander I, but with some constitutional rights, including education in the Polish language. A new university was opened at Warsaw in 1817 incorporating the French-style law and medical schools founded under the Grand Duchy. More important for Polish culture was the University of Vilna (today

[37] R. D. Anderson, *Education and opportunity in Victorian Scotland: schools and universities* (Oxford, 1983), 37.

[38] Caron, *Générations romantiques*, 341–5.

Vilnius in Lithuania), which was in Russia proper rather than the Congress Kingdom. This was allowed to function as a Catholic, Polish-speaking university, under its 'curator', the aristocrat Adam Czartoryski, who was an advocate of Polish–Russian co-operation and trusted by Alexander. There was a brief flowering of romantic literary culture, and the Vilna episode was treasured by later Polish nationalists because the national poet Adam Mickiewicz was a student there. The students at Vilna shared in the political awakening of central Europe and in the enthusiasm for German philosophy, and a secret organization called the 'philomaths' cultivated ideals of comradeship. This soon aroused the suspicion of the authorities, who acted in 1824. Czartoryski was dismissed, and replaced by the reactionary Novosiltsov, who held a similar post at Cracow. Trials and expulsions followed.

The replacement of Alexander I by the reactionary Nicholas I in 1825 darkened the picture further, and political tensions built up until a national insurrection broke out in Warsaw in 1830. Students flocked to the national cause, and contributed academic legions to the military campaigns which followed.[39] The Poles were comprehensively defeated, with disastrous cultural consequences. Both Warsaw and Vilna universities were closed down, the latter permanently. Their collections and libraries were shipped to St Petersburg, and Poles in search of higher education had to use Russian universities, including a new one founded in 1834 at Kiev, under safe Russian control in Ukraine. All manifestations of Polish culture were repressed, leading the historian of Vilna in this period to describe its closure in 1832 as 'cultural genocide'.[40] The only remaining Polish-speaking university was Cracow, where students were increasingly active in the 1840s, though the professors were conservative and pro-Austrian. In 1846 the Poles in Galicia rose against Austrian rule, and the Cracow students joined in. But the revolt was crushed, the city of Cracow was annexed to the Habsburg empire, and repression in the university included a policy of Germanization to bring it into line with Austrian norms.[41]

One byproduct of the 1830 defeat was a massive emigration of Poles to western Europe, where they gave a great stimulus to radical movements and made Polish freedom an emotional cause of the left. Many of the Polish intelligentsia found academic posts in France (where Cousin as minister of education created a chair at the Collège de France for Mickiewicz), in Brussels (refuge for a time of the historian Joachim Lelewel, who had been dismissed from Vilna in 1824 and was Polish minister of education in 1830–1), in Switzerland, or in London, where the two university colleges founded at this time provided some convenient berths for Continental exiles. In the 1840s there were 8,000 Poles in Paris alone, and German

[39] M. Wawrykowa, *'Für eure und unsere Freiheit': Studentenschaft und junge Intelligenz in Ost- und Mitteleuropa in der ersten Hälfte des 19. Jahrhunderts* (Stuttgart, 1985), 97–110.

[40] Beauvois, *Lumières et société*, 911.

[41] L. Hajdukiewicz and M. Karas, *The Jagiellonian University: traditions—the present—the future* (Cracow, 1978), 51–4; C. Bobinska, 'Les générations d'étudiants en tant que groupes sociaux', in M. Kulczykowski (ed.), *Les Étudiants: liens sociaux, culture, mœurs du moyen-âge jusqu'au 19e siècle: Vème session scientifique internationale, Cracovie 28–30 mai 1987* (Warsaw, 1991), 135–45.

and Italian exiles swelled the numbers further. As Christophe Charle has pointed out, this phenomenon, and international sympathy between student movements, made the concept of a 'Europe of the intelligence' part of the outlook of the intelligentsia everywhere.[42] Another expression of it was the philhellene movement in support of Greek independence, which had a special appeal in university circles; committees were set up, funds raised, petitions organized, and volunteers recruited—techniques which could then be applied to other liberal causes.

The events of 1830 renewed political stirrings in Italy and Germany. In Germany, there were disturbances in various centres but no revolutions. The *Burschenschaften* were emboldened to resume national meetings in 1831,[43] and a giant liberal demonstration at Hambach in the Palatinate in 1832 included a large contingent of students, mainly from the south-west. This phase culminated in a bungled attempt at insurrection at Frankfurt in 1833, led by a handful of radical students. The consequence was a new federal decree banning student organizations in 1834, and a crackdown on dissent which was harsher than that after 1819, with mass trials and long prison sentences. In Prussia, 165 students were condemned in 1836 to life imprisonment for political activities, and thirty-nine to death, though the latter sentences were commuted. In Württemberg, always rather more civilized, students arrested after 1833 also spent long years in prison, but were allowed to sit their examinations inside.[44] There were now significant signs that students were not always on the left. At Leipzig in 1830, professors and students had joined armed patrols to defend 'order' on behalf of the government, and in Württemberg in 1831 a 500-strong 'student guard' turned out to help suppress a rising of artisans and winegrowers.[45] The average student probably had little sympathy with the bureaucratic, reactionary state, but when political conflict went beyond constitutionalism, his underlying allegiance was to the propertied bourgeois order. As in France, moderates and radicals were separating off, and those who committed themselves to radical politics also broke with the philosophical mainstream, and embraced 'materialism' and the 'left' or 'young' Hegelianism associated with Ludwig Feuerbach. To be an activist or to make contact with secret societies and working-class movements required special commitment: it risked exclusion from a professional career, exile, long confinement in fortresses and prisons, and sometimes death, though usually when troops fired on demonstrations rather than on the scaffold. Once the immediate crisis of the 1830s was over, the authorities generally tolerated non-political organizations like the corps, but the underground *Burschenschaft* movement itself divided between moderate and radical wings. When it eventually re-emerged into legality, which was not fully until the 1860s, it had lost its early political radicalism, and differed little from the corps.

Moderate liberalism embraced professors as well as students, and some became

42 C. Charle, *Les Intellectuels en Europe au XIXe siecle: essai d'histoire comparée* (Paris, 1996), 109–10, 113.

43 Müth, *Studentische Emanzipation*, 140.

44 Ibid. 190–1.

45 Ibid. 96–9, and cf. 218–19.

members of the parliaments which existed in states like Baden. Professors like Karl von Rotteck at Freiburg were important liberal publicists, but Rotteck was dismissed in 1832, and at Würzburg in 1833 the Bavarian government sacked ten professors for 'ultraliberal tendencies'.[46] More famous were the 'Göttingen Seven', dismissed by the Hanover government in 1837 after the dynastic separation from Britain led to a constitutional reaction. The dismissal of professors was itself nothing exceptional. Governments regarded them as public officials whose duty was to uphold the political and religious order, and liberals were as ready as conservatives to remove professors when they had the chance. The Göttingen affair became a *cause célèbre* partly because of the fame and liberal reputation of the university itself, partly because Hanover had begun to develop as a constitutional state, partly because of the eminence of the professors. The repression of moderate liberals showed the narrow basis of consent on which governments rested before 1848. The student body, after all, consisted to a large extent of the state's future servants. The militants of one generation became the political leaders, sometimes the crusty conservatives, of the next. Their demands should have been easily satisfied, and it has been argued that the eventual crumbling of Metternich's system was due as much to the irritation of the educated middle classes with constant petty interference in local, everyday freedoms as to deeper discontents. Universities shared the general reactions of the urban bourgeoisie.[47]

In Austria, little was heard from university liberals or radicals. Joseph II's policies of religious toleration were maintained as a matter of individual rights, but in official teaching strict religious as well as political orthodoxy was enforced: the teaching of Kant and modern idealist philosophy was banned, and in 1821 the Prague philosopher Bernhard Bolzano was dismissed for teaching an unorthodox version of Catholicism.[48] Directors of studies were maintained as in Maria Theresa's day, and the report of the director for the Graz law faculty in 1836 shows the government's ideal: he was able to report his

> gratifying conviction that the conduct of the professors inside and outside their lectures is dignified, their moral conduct is not only blameless but really distinguished, and serves as a good example to the students, that the professors in their lectures stick to the prescribed textbooks, where these exist, and that the students observe the regulations and diligently attend at lectures and at university worship. The students conduct themselves on average irreproachably; there are no illegal disturbances, but everywhere order and peace, which allows one to hope for a happy outcome in respect of their moral and intellectual education.[49]

The restrictions of the Metternichian police state underlined the link between

[46] P. Baumgart and others, *Wider Zopf und Philisterey: Deutsche Studenten zwischen Reformzeit und Revolution (1800–1850)* (Würzburg, 1985), 18.

[47] Thielbeer, *Universität und Politik*, 235; M. John, 'The Napoleonic legacy and problems of restoration in central Europe: the German Confederation', in Laven and Riall, *Napoleon's legacy*, 93.

[48] R. Okey, *The Habsburg Monarchy, c. 1765–1918: from enlightenment to eclipse* (London, 2001), 100; J. J. Sheehan, *German history 1770–1866* (Oxford, 1989), 357.

[49] K. Ebert, *Die Grazer Juristenfakultät im Vormärz: Rechtswissenschaft und Rechtslehre an der Grazer Hochschule zwischen 1810 und 1848* (Graz, 1969), 108.

academic freedom and the broader liberal agenda, and made the freedom of universities a constitutional issue in 1848.

In France, the stifling alliance of the high intelligentsia with the regime alienated the younger generation, and the failure of the government led by Guizot to recognize the political claims of the expanding educated middle class was a prime cause of the revolution of 1848. History repeated itself in the 1840s as a new generation of left-wing and anticlerical lecturers, notably Mickiewicz, the philosopher Edgar Quinet, and the historian Jules Michelet, first enthused their student audiences, then found themselves banned. The dismissal of Michelet in January 1848, followed by protest demonstrations and a petition to the Chamber, contributed to the mounting agitation which overthrew Louis-Philippe in February. The new Second Republic's minister of education, Hippolyte Carnot, suspended Guizot from his chair at the Sorbonne, but restored Michelet and Quinet to the Collège de France. They had become icons of academic freedom, and their return in 1848, to student acclamation, was immortalized in a painting installed in the rebuilt Sorbonne in 1906.[50]

During the turbulent events of 1848, the Latin Quarter was a centre of street fighting and demonstrations, political clubs met at the Sorbonne, and there was a student battalion of the National Guard.[51] Yet students did not play the leading part in these events; the *Polytechniciens*, prominent in 1830, turned out again in their uniforms, but took a largely non-political role in maintaining order. Student enthusiasm for the revolution dissipated as class conflict became more acute. Tension between the relatively conservative parliament returned by a mass electorate of peasants in April and the Paris working class culminated in the major rising of June 1848 and its savage suppression. Of over 11,000 people arrested after the 'June days', only forty-two were described as students, and thirty of them were released immediately.[52] For students were in the last resort 'bourgeois in the making',[53] and the 1848 revolution was a moment of truth for student radicalism. It ended the period when the middle classes were in the vanguard of progress. Political and intellectual liberty might still have to be defended against authoritarian rule, as the French were soon to rediscover, but any hint of social revolution found most students on the side of order.

Events in 1848 in Germany and Austria involved the universities more directly than in France. The agitation which led up to the fall of Metternich in March 1848 included a petition by the Vienna professors and students for Berlin-style freedom of teaching and learning, as well as for broader civil liberties. When a liberal government was appointed by the Emperor, the first act of the new education minister, Franz von Sommaruga, was to address the students in the university Aula (ceremonial hall): 'We want to create a firm and lasting structure, similar to those flourishing universities in Germany which we recognize as the models of thorough

[50] J. Bonnerot, *La Sorbonne: sa vie, son role, son œuvre à travers les siècles* (Paris, 1927), 68.

[51] Caron, *Générations romantiques*, 373 ff.

[52] J. G. Gallaher, *The students of Paris and the revolution of 1848* (Carbondale, Ill., 1980), 100; R. Price, *The French Second Republic: a social history* (London, 1972), 165.

[53] Caron, *Générations romantiques*, 225.

scientific training. Freedom of teaching and learning, subject to no other limits than those of constitutional legality, will be its foundation.'[54] Nowhere more than in Austria were academic issues at the centre of political demands in 1848, and the government's promises survived the political reaction which later crushed the Viennese revolution. But far from returning to their lectures, the students at Vienna formed an Academic Legion which remained under arms (and under the German tricolour) and played an important part in political events. Estimates of its size vary, but there were at least 4,000, and recent graduates and other hangers-on were involved as well as current students. The Vienna students became 'European heroes', and found time to send delegates to a fraternal banquet in Paris.[55] In October 1848, when Vienna saw a working-class rising analogous to June in Paris, some of them remained on the left, and were to be found fighting the last forlorn battles of 1848–9 in Hungary or Dresden. As elsewhere, the fundamental allegiance of the Vienna students was liberal rather than radical, but their unusual militancy may have reflected their relatively broad social origins, as well as pent-up frustration over the disciplinary controls on collective life, the continuing clerical dominance within the university, and the narrow and compulsory philosophy curriculum.[56] Elsewhere in the Habsburg empire—in Prague, Budapest, or Milan—students were also active on the street, but with nationalist as well as liberal motives.

The appointment of liberal governments in response to popular pressure early in 1848 took place throughout Germany, though the academic response varied from state to state. In Halle, for example, the traditions of Lutheran pietism made the university politically conservative, whereas in Protestant Tübingen and Catholic Freiburg theology students were among the most radical. In Berlin, some students took part in the initial street-fighting, and as at Vienna the new minister of education, count Schwerin, came to the university Aula to pledge reform.[57] But unlike in Vienna, most students were won over by these concessions. Radicals in Berlin were a small minority, and there was little resistance when Frederick William IV later re-established royal authority. Nevertheless, the initial political changes paved the way for the Frankfurt Parliament, which was elected to discuss the question of unification and elaborate an all-German constitution. It included representatives from the German-speaking parts of the Habsburg empire, and it had to make a choice between the 'great German' (*grossdeutsch*) solution to the German problem, which would include the Austrian territories and maintain Austrian hegemony, and the 'small German' (*kleindeutsch*) one, which would exclude the Austrian territories and inevitably be dominated by Prussia. The Parliament chose the latter,

[54] Preglau-Hämmerle, *Die politische und soziale Funktion*, 96. Cf. T. Maisel, *Alma Mater auf den Barrikaden* (Vienna, 1998), 43–4.

[55] D. Langewiesche, 'Studenten in den europäischen Revolutionen von 1848', *Jahrbuch für Universitätsgeschichte*, 2 (1999), 40, 44–5; P. Robertson, *Revolutions of 1848: a social history* (New York, 1960), 206–36; Gallaher, *Students of Paris*, 91–2.

[56] G. Stimmer, 'Die Mythologisierung der Revolution von 1848 als Modell einer Studentenrevolution', in *Student und Hochschule im 19. Jahrhundert: Studien und Materialen* (Göttingen, 1975), 243–302.

[57] Thielbeer, *Universität und Politik*, 93–4 (general source for most of this section).

and drew up a constitution providing for Prussian headship. This never came into force, but was none the less significant, for it included a clause on freedom of science and teaching ('Die Wissenschaft und ihre Lehre ist frei'), which was also to appear in the more conservative constitution which Frederick William granted within Prussia in 1850, and in the subsequent constitutions of a united Germany.[58] The attention given to the issue reflected the composition of the Frankfurt Assembly. It has sometimes been called the 'parliament of professors'—what more needed to be said to explain its political incapacity? In fact only forty-nine of the 810 members were professors,[59] though they included some important liberal figures who continued to be politically prominent. In any case, the delegates at Frankfurt were predominantly drawn from the university-educated classes (87 per cent) and represented the *Burschenschaft* generation of 1815; 150–60 were old *Burschenschaft* members, and the President of the Assembly was Heinrich von Gagern.[60] The long-banned black-red-gold colours re-emerged as those of the new German state which the liberals hoped to establish. They failed, leaving the way open for Bismarck's solution through blood and iron, a turn of events which had significant consequences for the relation of the academic world to the state.

The 1848 revolutions (like the events of 1968) were cultural as well as political, and until reaction set in there was a messianic atmosphere. Structures of authority in the family, the workplace, and the school were questioned as much as in the state. This led to a series of all-German university conferences, including representatives from Austria.[61] They included a conference of teachers arranged by the university authorities at Jena in September 1848, which first aired the grievances of the 'extraordinary' professors and *Privatdozenten*; the more radical of the latter had already taken part in a conference of 'young scholars' dominated by the left Hegelians. Welcoming the delegates at Jena, the rector saw the conference as 'the splendid blossoming of the newly awakened united life of our people, of our German national consciousness'.[62] The Prussian government boycotted Jena, but arranged its own professorial conference in 1849. On the student side, there were two conferences at Eisenach (evoking the Wartburg demonstration) in spring and autumn 1848. Their purpose was to draw up a programme for the new government which was expected to emerge from Frankfurt, based on the concept of universities as national institutions no longer tied to the particularist states. Other aims included the abolition of university jurisdiction and student participation in university government and in the appointment of professors.[63] But the first Eisenach

[58] R. A. Müller, 'Vom Ideal zum Verfassungsprinzip: Die Diskussion um die Wissenschaftsfreiheit in der ersten Hälfte des 19. Jahrhunderts', in R. C. Schwinges (ed.), *Humboldt International: Der Export des deutschen Universitätsmodells im 19. und 20. Jahrhundert* (Basel, 2001), 361–6.

[59] R. vom Bruch, *Wissenschaft, Politik und öffentliche Meinung: Gelehrtenpolitik im Wilhelminischen Deutschland (1890–1914)* (Husum, 1980), 59.

[60] Charle, *Intellectuels en Europe*, 129–30; Bartol, *Ideologie und studentischer Protest*, 75.

[61] Thielbeer, *Universität und Politik*, 163 ff. Cf. E. J. C. Hahn, 'The junior faculty in "revolt": reform plans for Berlin University in 1848', *American Historical Review*, 82 (1977), 875–95.

[62] Thielbeer, *Universität und Politik*, 187.

[63] H. H. Brandt, 'Universität und Studenten in Deutschland zwischen alteuropäischer und moderner Welt', in Baumgart and others, *Wider Zopf und Philisterey*, 51–3.

conference revealed deep divisions between conservatives and radicals, and the second 'student parliament' represented only the latter. One of them was Carl Schurz, from Bonn, who reported to the radical press that 'the whole Congress is full of democratic spirit, and well understands the distinctive strength which is guaranteed by its popular character and by the love of the people'.[64] These proved no defence against the suppression of the democratic movement. Schurz, like other radical students, fought in the armed risings in Baden in 1849 which were the last convulsion of the revolution, and then went into exile; he ended up in America, where he became a Civil War general and politician. There was another last-ditch rising in 1849 in Leipzig, where the historian Theodor Mommsen was one of several professors who 'called the citizens to resistance and gave arms out to the students', earning himself prosecution and exile.[65] The events of 1848–9 also saw the first public appearance, as students, of some later leaders of German socialism such as Wilhelm Liebknecht and Ferdinand Lassalle.

In France, the defeat of the June rising was followed by the persecution of left-wing ideas of all kinds, and the considerable electoral success of the 'democratic socialists' in 1849 stirred up fears of red revolution. Conservatives turned to religion as a bulwark of order, and the Falloux law of 1850 encouraged the opening of Catholic schools and gave the clergy an enlarged role in the administration of education. The law had long-term indirect effects for higher education as it allowed Catholic secondary schools, including those of the Jesuits, to compete on equal terms with the state's lycées and colleges. Repression at university level came after the *coup d'état* of December 1851, by which Louis-Napoleon, elected President of the Republic in December 1848, established a personal dictatorship, which he turned into a hereditary Second Empire in 1852. The new minister of education, Hippolyte Fortoul, was himself an academic, a provincial professor of French literature, but was willing to act as an agent of repression. It can be argued that his policies protected the University against even cruder oppression, and the Gallican aspect of the Bonapartist tradition limited the extent of Catholicization: there was no abandonment of the state's monopoly of higher education. But Fortoul was remembered as a reactionary in the University's folk memory and in the history written by republican scholars, which saw the Empire as barely legitimate because of its foundation in the *coup d'état*. Fortoul's attitudes seemed to embody a general anti-intellectualism, expressed in the mutilation of philosophy teaching and in new restrictions imposed on the École Normale. The older generation of liberal academics was shunted aside, and many younger ones driven out. Michelet, Quinet, and Mickiewicz disappeared again, this time along with Cousin. All teachers had to subscribe an oath of loyalty to Louis-Napoleon, and many preferred to resign. Jules Simon, Cousin's substitute at the Sorbonne, announced in his lecture class that he had voted No in the plebiscite following the coup, and was dismissed (he was to return as minister for education after Napoleon's downfall). But many academics shared the general bourgeois relief at the restoration of order

[64] M. Braubach, *Bonner Professoren und Studenten in den Revolutionsjahren 1848/49* (Cologne, 1967), 153.

[65] Thielbeer, *Universität und Politik*, 29.

and accepted the new regime, and since plebiscites gave Napoleon massive popular endorsement, he could afford for the time being to ignore the complaints of liberal intellectuals.

There was a similar reaction in Italy. At Naples, the suppression of the revolution and the return of the Bourbons led to the dismissal of eleven professors and their replacement by loyal mediocrities. There followed a 'squalid period with innumerable episodes of violence against the students, who were supervised ever more closely'. They were required to join religious fraternities, and to show certificates of attendance at mass. The university was put under the special protection of St Thomas Aquinas, and professors had to wear a medal at their neck with an image of the saint on one side and the king on the other.[66] Sicilians were forbidden to study on the mainland, and at Catania the authorities sent an instruction in 1852 requiring professors, students, and employees to shave off any beards: 'considering that beards are no longer in fashion, and that to wear them when they are not common usage recalls disastrous memories, it is necessary that all those who wish to appear of good morals should remove this sign from their faces'.[67] This was not an aberration. Fortoul had issued a similar circular earlier in 1852, which declared that 'now that calm is returning to men's minds and order to society, it is important that the last traces of anarchy should disappear'.[68] This provoked much ridicule, but actually showed a keen awareness of the importance of political symbolism. In the early days of the *Burschenschaft* movement, patriotic students had adopted an 'old German' costume, and long hair, pipes, and special headgear continued to mark students off from other citizens. Visiting Pavia in 1816, Stendhal noted that students had a 'disdainful, savage, taciturn look, made even more bellicose by a huge mass of black hair covering a good part of their faces'.[69] The beard became an abiding symbol of 1848, to which radicals remained faithful in a clean-shaven era, until its day of fashion came round again.

What might happen where liberal and radical advances were not reversed by counter-revolution is shown by the example of Switzerland. In 1815 Switzerland had one university, Basel, and three 'academies'—Bern, Geneva, and Lausanne. They were closely tied to the patrician elites of these cities, and at first a reactionary and narrowly Protestant atmosphere prevailed. But in the 1830s most of the Swiss cantons saw a political takeover by liberals, usually associated with an extension of the vote to the countryside. Secularization and expansion of the universities was part of the liberal programme: Bern was raised to university status (1834), and a new university was founded at Zurich (1833); its charter was the first to incorporate the principle of academic freedom ('akademische Lehr- und Lernfreiheit').[70] The Swiss universities became a refuge for political exiles from Germany, Italy, and elsewhere. But relations with the urban elite remained close, there was much switching

[66] Torraca and others, *Storia della Università di Napoli*, 582–3.
[67] A. Broccoli, *Educazione e politica nel mezzogiorno d'Italia (1767–1860)* (Florence, 1968), 186.
[68] R. D. Anderson, *Education in France 1848–1870* (Oxford, 1975), 55.
[69] Ciprandi, 'Università di Pavia', 303.
[70] Müller, 'Vom Ideal zum Verfassungsprinzip', 361.

between university chairs and positions of power, and this liberalism was of a restricted Orleanist type. At Geneva, the university gained autonomy under a German-style reorganization in 1835, but it 'rested more on the community of social and ideological interests which tied the political oligarchy to the leaders of the Academy than on a real philosophy of university work'.[71]

This elitism came under attack in Geneva from radicals led by James Fazy, a former *carbonaro* who had studied in Paris and had published a denunciation of 'gerontocracy' in France in 1828.[72] He was especially critical of the traditional law faculties. In 1846, following the introduction of universal male suffrage in 1842, the radicals came to power, and in 1848 they purged the university and dismissed half a dozen professors. The reforms included close state control to replace the autonomy granted in 1835, the banning of clergymen from secular chairs, the appointment of political exiles as professors, and free evening classes to bring the university closer to the 'people'. Fazy was in power in Geneva, with a brief interval, until 1861, and after his political retirement got himself appointed as professor of 'legislation and constitutional history'. These upheavals freed the university from its old patrician complacency, but also severely demoralized it, and stability did not return until further reforms in 1872. There was a similar trajectory of events at Lausanne.[73]

Fazy's programme was characteristic of the contemporary leftist view that universities were strongholds of bourgeois privilege. University autonomy was suspect, and direct state control seemed to follow logically from democratic principles.[74] The law faculties were a particular target because they enabled the upper middle class to retain their grip on the bureaucratic levers of the state. Meritocracy had turned into mystification through examinations: as Marx put it, the examination 'is nothing else but the *bureaucratic baptism of knowledge*, the official recognition of the transubstantiation of profane knowledge into sacred knowledge'.[75] It was significant that the only real higher education reform of the French Second Republic was a National School of Administration which was meant to apply the competitive principle to the bureaucracy and break the stranglehold of the law faculties. This school was soon abolished, and during its short life it took most of its students from the usual privileged strata, proving that such policies could 'only marginally offset the confidence, prestige and wealth of society's traditionally dominant groups'.[76] But the idea that political or economic 'science' should challenge the monopoly of law remained on radical agendas.

[71] M. Marcacci, *Histoire de l'Université de Genève 1559–1986* (Geneva, 1987), 82.

[72] Spitzer, *French generation of 1820*, 230.

[73] Marcacci, *Université de Genève*, 84 ff.; P. F. Geisendorf, *L'Université de Genève 1559–1959: quatre siècles d'histoire* (Geneva, 1959), 230 ff.; A. Delessert, *L'Université au défi: une histoire sociale de l'Université de Lausanne* (Lausanne, 1991), 45–54.

[74] Marcacci, *Université de Genève*, 102–3.

[75] 'Critique of Hegel's doctrine of the state' (1843), in K. Marx, *Early writings*, ed. L. Colletti (Harmondsworth, 1975), 112; cf. Preglau-Hämmerle, *Die politische und soziale Funktion*, 139.

[76] V. Wright, 'L'École nationale d'administration de 1848–1849: un échec révélateur', *Revue Historique*, 255 (1976), 21–42; H. Machin and V. Wright, 'Les élèves de l'École nationale d'administration de 1848–1849', *Revue d'Histoire Moderne et Contemporaine*, 36 (1989), 605–39; R. J. Smith, 'The students of the École d'Administration 1848–9', *History of Education*, 16 (1987), 245 (for quotation).

The 1848 revolutions raised questions of elitism and of the university's mission to the people which were to become significant in the twentieth century. In the short term, they were more important as a turning-point in the relation of universities to politics. A new period of reaction followed, but when this was lifted the landscape had changed. When student activity revived in Germany, it was in the transformed context of a Germany united by Bismarck on very different lines from those of 1848. In the 1815–48 period, liberalism had often united professors and students against repression and censorship, but in the later nineteenth century professors generally renounced active political commitment in the confidence that the freedom of science and scholarship were protected by constitutional rights or political custom. Students' communal life could now develop without political implications, and when activists turned to politics it was as often on the right as the left (see Chapter 18). The crisis of 1848 underlined the bourgeois nature of the student body. The other lesson of the 1815–48 period was that, although often presenting an uninspiring picture of stagnant numbers and stifling intellectual conformity, universities had become an indispensable part of the machinery which produced the social elite. No government, however conservative, seriously tried to undo the changes of the Napoleonic period. They did try to make universities a bulwark of religious as well as political loyalty, but that too was to be undermined by the progress of European thought and the logic of liberal beliefs.

6

Universities, Religion, and the Liberal State

Although by the early nineteenth century universities were essentially secular institutions, in the sense that the state rather than the church was the directing authority, religion had by no means lost its importance. Restoration governments used it as an instrument of discipline, and even when not enforcing a single confessional orthodoxy found it difficult to separate religious and political ideologies. Liberals rejected religious dogma and were hostile to clericalism, yet, like Napoleon and the enlightened rulers before him, they were reluctant to abandon the idea that the state should inculcate an official religious creed, or at least a philosophy with strong elements of deism and idealism, to guarantee the morality and the higher cultural aspirations of young members of the elite. Few thought that university education could be divorced from some kind of religious or ethical ideals; 'materialism' was seen as a threat to those ideals, and the separation of religion and science was not a simple matter.

In Catholic countries especially, 'liberalism' referred as much to a belief in free thought and tolerance as to political constitutionalism. Liberals saw freedom of thought as the product of a struggle which dated back through the Enlightenment, the Reformation, and the Renaissance to the first emergence of the secular spirit in the middle ages. Throughout the story, the churches, and religious dogma, had been the great obstructive force; Galileo had become the symbol of this conflict as a martyr of modern science. Universities might once have been part of the ideological apparatus of the church, but their secularization under the aegis of the state was a permanent gain for reason, and the state had become the defender of intellectual freedom. In France after 1801, and increasingly in other countries, the rights of religious minorities were embodied in law, and protecting them was also the duty of the state. One practical implication was the question of religious tests imposed on professors or students. In many Protestant countries, professors of secular subjects as well as theologians were often still clergymen in the early nineteenth century, and the emergence of a fully secular academic profession was a slow business. Few went as far as the Geneva radicals in banning clergymen altogether from secular teaching—even in France there were priests in some university chairs—but the contentious reform of the English universities showed how this question could be tied up with the identity and mission of a university.

Freedom of conscience was an important liberal principle, but liberals acknowledged that 'freedom of education' (*liberté d'enseignement* in French) was another basic right deriving from it, and from the right of families to determine the values taught to their children. But in practice this freedom was interpreted restrictively, and conditioned by class and gender. Liberals were prepared to entrust the education of the masses to religious bodies, which gave the best guarantees of moral indoctrination, and to leave the education of middle-class girls to private enterprise or religious orders. Universities and the secondary education of boys, however, were generally seen as a state responsibility; rival schools might be tolerated alongside the public sector, but only within a framework of state regulation. In particular, the state generally retained the power to award the school-leaving qualifications which were vital for entry to most professions and public services as well as the universities, and the right to approve those establishments which might call themselves universities and award degrees. In France, Spain, and Italy liberals maintained highly centralized systems of state education, for in this field the identification of liberalism with laissez-faire or market principles does not apply.[1] Humboldt published a classic treatise on the limits of state intervention which was admired by liberals like John Stuart Mill, yet saw the *Kulturstaat* as a necessary and creative force. Universities were a state concern because they maintained the scientific level of the professions on which a modern state depended, embodied the principles of free thought and progress, and created unity and common values among the elite of the nation-state.

The right of the churches to re-establish a stake in higher education, or to retain their power within it where this still existed, was thus a contentious issue, and led in some cases to the foundation of Catholic universities under the control of the church authorities. Liberals thought religious authority and freedom of thought incompatible, a problem raised even within state universities when they possessed faculties of theology. This was a minor issue in France, Spain, or Italy, where these faculties were generally not used by the Catholic church for the education of its priests, and were eventually abolished by liberal governments. It was a greater issue in Catholic Germany and Austria, in Protestant Germany, and in Switzerland, Holland, and Scotland, where the theology faculties retained their educational role and their intellectual vitality. If professors were appointed by the state, what should be the role of churches in the appointing process? Given that the purpose of the faculty was to train ministers in the doctrines of their church, what was to be done with professors who taught heretical doctrines, or who lost their religious faith? What should be the relation of faculties to disputes within the churches, notably to the various movements of evangelicalism or spiritual renewal characteristic of the Protestant churches in the early nineteenth century? Religious factionalism was often a vexed issue in university appointments in Switzerland, and in Scotland in 1843 the dramatic 'Disruption' of the established church led to the resignation of theology professors who joined the new Free Church, and the creation of a parallel set of 'free' colleges.

[1] P. Pilbeam, *The middle classes in Europe 1789–1914: France, Germany, Italy and Russia* (Basingstoke, 1990), 236.

The Disruption, like the Oxford Movement in England which sought to rediscover the Catholic roots of the Anglican church, showed the vitality of contemporary religious life and the political importance of debates on church–state relations. In France, supporters of 'liberal Catholicism' in the 1830s and 1840s, while attacking the monopoly of the University and demanding freedom of teaching, also sought Catholic reconciliation with the spirit of the age, and students were to be found among the audience of the charismatic Dominican preacher Henri Lacordaire, among the followers of the apostle of democratic Christianity Félicité de Lamennais, and in the more conservative and paternalistic 'social Catholic' movement which called earnest young men to study the problems of poverty in an industrial society and to practise Christian charity. Such movements, however, fell foul of the increasing ultramontanism of the Catholic church, and of the anti-liberal and anti-modern views developed by Pius IX in the 1850s and 1860s. The Syllabus of Errors of 1864, with its direct attack on liberalism and freedom of thought, contributed to a polarization of views—expressed in the new terms clerical and anticlerical—which made the religious synthesis of philosophers like Cousin unviable, and ultimately pushed universities towards complete secularization. A moderate liberalism prepared to respect the rights of the church gave way to a more militant, positivist anticlericalism.

The willingness of the church to embrace conservatism and defence of the propertied order—under the Restoration, in 1848, and then again in the reactionary atmosphere of the 1850s—gave a strong political impulse to anticlericalism. But there were also more profound forces, with roots in the universities, undermining the position of Christianity. One was the application of philological techniques to oriental and biblical studies. To criticize and interpret the Bible like any other text inherited from antiquity seemed to deny Christianity's claim to revealed truth. The *cause célèbre* here was the publication of the *Life of Jesus* by the German scholar David Strauss in 1835. This so-called 'higher criticism', together with advances in geology and natural history, undermined such historical or scientific authority as the Bible retained well before the publication of Darwin's *Origin of Species* in 1859. A second force was metaphysical: both the Young Hegelians in Germany and the positivist followers of Comte in France saw religion as a human creation, and an intermediate stage in the evolution of thought towards the triumph of reason. For many scientists, positivism meant no more than a belief in impartial methods of investigation, but it could be the basis of an aggressive materialism which denied the existence of the soul and of free will. This had its roots in some of the French thinkers of the later Enlightenment, such as La Mettrie, and in the nineteenth century it was especially strong in medical faculties. The physician Ludwig Büchner's *Force and Matter* of 1855, which cost him his job at Tübingen University, became the bible of materialism for a new generation. It was Carl Vogt, a German exile of 1848 who became a professor at Geneva, who had said in 1847 that 'thought is to the brain more or less what bile is to the liver and urine to the kidneys'.[2] Later,

[2] M. Marcacci, *Histoire de l'Université de Genève 1559–1986* (Geneva, 1987), 112.

like Büchner, he became a champion of Darwin. But even in liberal Switzerland there was tension between freedom of thought and an essentially conservative and religious bourgeoisie. Vogt's colleague Jules Barni, an exile from Napoleon III, caused scandal by including Servetus (burnt by Calvin for heresy in 1553) among the 'martyrs of liberty',[3] while at Zurich the appointment of Strauss to a chair in 1839 caused a major political crisis and his enforced resignation.

Although many of the philosophical and scholarly challenges came from Germany, German universities were largely free of religious conflicts, at least until the *Kulturkampf* of the 1870s. The monopoly of the state in higher education was unquestioned, and the churches continued to use the theology faculties for training priests and pastors. Although the universities had a clear confessional character, and tests for professors survived in some places for a time, the Humboldtian spirit of free enquiry protected freedom of scholarship even in theology. There were generally no religious tests for students, one sign of which was that Jews had begun to attend German universities in the later eighteenth century, and continued to do so. This relative harmony can perhaps be attributed to a long experience of co-existence between Catholics and Protestants, which sometimes took institutional form as 'parity'—the duplication of teaching on confessional lines. When Prussia refounded the universities of Breslau and Bonn, they were given both Protestant and Catholic theology faculties, and this was also the policy at Tübingen in Württemberg. Parity sometimes extended into the appointment of separate professors to '*Weltanschauung*' chairs in subjects like history and philosophy where Catholic and Protestant world-views might differ. Parity seemed the solution in religiously mixed areas; elsewhere religious divisions were manageable because in Germany they were regional, whereas in France or Belgium the national elite was divided vertically on ideological lines.

The German concept of academic freedom was concerned with the autonomy of state-run universities, and intellectual freedom within them, but the French term *liberté d'enseignement*, and its equivalents in Italian and Spanish, referred more to the right to challenge the state's monopoly of higher education and open rival institutions. It was a right most likely to be claimed by the Catholic church, but could also be used by individuals and private bodies, and nowhere in continental Europe applied it more fully than Belgium. After the incorporation of Belgium into the kingdom of the Netherlands in 1815, King William I introduced a highly centralized university policy as a instrument of long-term 'nation forming'.[4] Catholic Belgium, where the educated bourgeoisie spoke French even where the popular language was Flemish, was subjected to the same policies as mainly Protestant Holland. The Napoleonic experiment with a university centre at Brussels was abolished, and Louvain was restored as one of three state universities, with others at Liège and Ghent. The language issue was partly neutralized by continuing to teach in Latin,

[3] Ibid. 96–7.

[4] J. Roelevink, '"Eenen eik, die hondert jahre behoefde, om groot te worden": Koning Willem I en de universiteiten van het Verenigd Koninkrijk', in C. A. Tamse and E. Witte (eds.), *Staats- en Natievorming in Willem I's Koninkrijk (1815–1830)* (Brussels, 1992), 286–309.

but Belgian Catholics were alienated by William's religious policies, which recalled those of Joseph II; from 1825, in response to Catholic families sending their sons to study in France, the Belgian universities and state appointments were closed to those educated abroad, and all seminarists were again forced to attend a common 'philosophical college' at Louvain.[5] The 1830 revolution combined linguistic, national, and religious issues, but Catholics and liberals made common cause around freedom of education, enshrined as a basic right in the constitution of the new Belgian state, which was of a classic liberal kind based on a restricted franchise and rule by the educated bourgeoisie.

The initial instinct of the liberals was to abandon the state universities altogether and rely solely on private enterprise; Dutch and other foreign professors were dismissed (twenty-six of them at Liège),[6] and Louvain and some faculties at Liège and Ghent were closed down. The Catholic church took advantage of the new freedom to open its own university at Malines (Mechelen) in 1834, and at its opening ceremony the rector declared that 'as Catholics, we must welcome all doctrines emanating from the Holy See, and repudiate contrary doctrines with all our soul'. The prospect of clerical dominance of higher education now alarmed the liberals, who opened their own Free University at Brussels with municipal support. Here the rector's opening address, also in 1834, stated that 'the purely human sciences, however imperfect or truncated they may be, must remain entirely independent of Catholicism'.[7] The state now stepped in to moderate this warfare, and the result was the university law of 1835. Ghent and Liège had their future secured as state universities, with religious neutrality; the Catholic University moved from Malines to Louvain, taking over the premises of the medieval university and so claiming to be its rightful successor; and all four universities were to teach to a rigidly prescribed common programme linked to the state's examination requirements. French was the language of instruction in all, which was not at that time controversial. The real innovation of the 1835 law was its device for reconciling religious diversity with the retention of state control over the award of degrees: a central 'jury' or examining board, appointed by the government, and on which (from 1849) all four universities were equally represented. This compromise lasted until 1876, when the universities were given their own degree-awarding powers, though still tied to a common programme laid down by the state.[8] A central examining jury remained after 1876 for initiatives outside the framework of the four universities, such as the Institut Saint-Louis, which started at Malines in 1838 and moved to Brussels in 1858, providing the elements of a Catholic higher education for upper-middle-class students, most of whom went on to a university law faculty. Like Louvain, it drew largely from the numerous Catholic secondary schools.[9]

[5] V. Mallinson, *Power and politics in Belgian education 1815 to 1961* (London, 1963), 15–16; E. H. Kossmann, *The Low Countries 1780–1940* (Oxford, 1978), 128–9.

[6] R. Lejeune and J. Stiennon (eds.), *La Wallonie, le pays et les hommes: lettres—arts—culture. IV. Compléments* (Brussels, 1981), 259.

[7] Mallinson, *Power and politics*, 40–1.

[8] Ibid. 42, 81.

[9] G. Braive, *Histoire des Facultés Universitaires Saint-Louis: des origines à 1918* (Brussels, 1985).

The adoption of educational freedom in Belgium stimulated intellectual diversity, but far from leading to a period of harmonious development, it inaugurated one of the bitterest series of educational conflicts to be found anywhere, especially over primary schools, where the establishment of universal literacy was seriously retarded (there was no compulsory schooling until 1914). As in France, liberalism developed under the influence of positivist doctrines into a militantly secular anticlerical or *laïque* movement, devoted to the principles of free thought and to the state's religious neutrality, and it was the Free University at Brussels which became and remained throughout the twentieth century the stronghold of *laïcité*. A corresponding intransigence was manifest on the Catholic side: the existence of Louvain did not prevent Catholics from attacking the supposed impiety of the state universities, and Pius IX made it clear in a letter to the Belgian bishops in 1856 that outside Catholic orthodoxy there could be no sound education, and that intellectual freedom led directly to immorality and anarchy.[10] In practice, there was some common ground between the two sides. On the one hand, Louvain saw its function as training the Catholic elite for public life rather than teaching dogma, and became something of a haven for liberal Catholics, while the Jesuits had a rival establishment at Namur.[11] On the other, the Free University espoused a spiritualist philosophy of the Cousin type, which claimed to be reconcilable with Catholicism. This led in the 1890s to further conflict when, for both philosophical and political reasons, including a row over a 'materialist' doctoral thesis, a radical New University of Brussels broke away, able in its turn to benefit from Belgium's pluralist legal framework. The continuing significance of religious issues was also shown by the creation of a Free University at Amsterdam in 1880, in this case as a Calvinist refuge from secularism, and of a university for Swiss Catholics at Fribourg in 1889, though this was a state university run by the canton, not independent like Louvain.[12]

Belgium was a Catholic country with an ideological split between Catholics and liberals, like Italy and France. In the British Isles, the problem was the conflict between religious diversity and the claims of established churches. The direct role of the state in university affairs was very limited, yet university questions often preoccupied statesmen and required the intervention of parliament. The United Kingdom, after the abolition of the Irish parliament in 1801, comprised three political units under a single government—England and Wales, Scotland, and Ireland. Each had an established church, Presbyterian in Scotland, Anglican elsewhere, and a distinctive educational system. From the university point of view,

[10] Mallinson, *Power and politics*, 65–6; Braive, *Facultés Universitaires*, 289–91.

[11] G. Massaux, 'L'Université de Louvain dans la société et dans l'Église d'hier et de demain', *CRE-Information*, 39 (1977), 27–40.

[12] A. Uyttebrouck, 'L'Université Libre de Bruxelles et l'enseignement privé non confessionnel', in H. Hasquin (ed.), *Histoire de la laïcité, principalement en Belgique et en France* (Brussels, 1979), 208–10; W. Van Rooy, 'L'agitation étudiante et la fondation de l'Université Nouvelle en 1894', *Revue Belge d'Histoire Contemporaine*, 7 (1976), 197–241; U. Im Hof, 'Die schweizerischen Varianten der kleindeutschen Universität: Zum Problem der ausländischen Einflüsse auf das schweizerische Hochschulwesens im 19. Jahrhundert', in *Festgabe Hans von Greyerz zum sechzigsten Geburtstag* (Bern, 1969), 611–12.

Scotland had fewest problems. The Disruption in 1843 created rival faculties of theology, but had no real implications for secular learning. Religious tests for students had already fallen into disuse, and the requirement for non-theological professors to be members of the established church was abolished in 1853. A further general reform of the universities followed in 1858. There were occasional disputes in Scotland as elsewhere over the philosophical views of professors, but the atmosphere of the universities was essentially secular within a broad framework of Christian culture; the rights of religious minorities were not an issue.

The position in England was very different. The established Church of England was challenged by the various Dissenting or Nonconformist churches, which (to simplify a complex socio-cultural geography) were especially strong in northern England, and were associated with the assertion of middle-class interests. Laws of 1828–9 removed the remaining restrictions on the civil rights of Nonconformists and Catholics (Jews had to wait until 1858), and the extension of the electorate in 1832 put an end to the 'confessional state'. Governments, often dominated by liberals after this date, could no longer make policies which ignored minority rights. This greatly complicated the history of primary education, but the education of the elite was considered to need less direct state intervention, and Oxford and Cambridge were financially independent. They had a central position in national life, yet remained Anglican in almost every respect. Although they did not have theology faculties in the usual sense, training the Anglican clergy was their main professional function. The colleges to which all students had to belong were religious corporations, the fellows who provided the teaching were generally required to be clergymen, and students had to declare their allegiance to the Church of England, on matriculation at Oxford, before graduation at Cambridge. Nonconformists were effectively excluded; some went to Scotland, others used the 'dissenting academies' founded in the eighteenth century, which combined secondary and some higher education. But the dissenting academies failed to develop into alternative universities, and reformers increasingly demanded that the wealth and power of the ancient universities should be put to more efficient national use. The Anglicans, for their part, were determined not to surrender without a struggle one of the areas of life which they still controlled, and saw the two universities as integral to the church's life.

University reform was not only a religious issue, for Oxford and Cambridge also failed to provide a modern, useful curriculum or to meet the professional needs of the growing middle class. Another obvious gap was the absence of any university in London, and it was this which led to the first move by reformers. The 'University of London' founded in 1828 was the work of utilitarians and Nonconformists, and was deliberately secular, as well as following both Scottish and German models to provide a wide range of subjects taught through professors and lectures. This 'godless' college was fiercely attacked by Anglicans, who founded a rival, King's College, in 1831. But neither of the London colleges could award degrees. This was a privilege which only the state could give, and the situation was resolved by creating a new University of London in 1836; the 1828 foundation was renamed University College.

The state financed the University of London and appointed the members of its Senate. It was a purely examining body, and was thus very similar to the Belgian 'central jury' of 1835, which was devised to meet a similar problem and must have acted as a model.[13] Under the 1836 legislation, colleges anywhere in Britain could affiliate to London University and their students could obtain London degrees. From 1858, when the University gained more autonomy from the state, though it still remained an examining university with no teaching, individuals could obtain degrees without needing a college affiliation. This gave a general stimulus to higher education whatever its institutional context, while still serving the original function of neutrality between religious denominations; the foundation of London University is evidence that there was more state intervention in universities in Britain than is often thought, as is the state's active role in Irish university policy.[14]

The Irish university question was to prove one of the more intractable aspects of Ireland's relations with Britain.[15] The University of Dublin (or Trinity College) was founded in 1592, and was an Anglican institution in a predominantly Catholic country. It served the Protestant landowning and professional classes, as well as training the clergy of the Church of Ireland. Protestants in Ireland also included a large Presbyterian minority, concentrated in the north. At Trinity College, religious tests for students were abolished in 1793, but they were retained for the professors and fellows, and the ethos of the college was still strongly Anglican. Thus neither Catholics nor Presbyterians had effective access to higher education, at a time when a Catholic middle class was beginning to appear and when industrial development in the north was making Belfast a vigorous rival of Dublin. The state, for its part, was anxious to mould an elite loyal to the British connection and to give the Catholic population an education free of clerical control.[16] The result was the foundation in 1845 of three secular Queen's Colleges, in Belfast, Cork, and Galway, financed by the state. In 1850 these became constituent colleges of the federal Queen's University, an examining university on the London pattern. Presbyterians had no objection to secular education, and the college at Belfast was relatively successful. But the Irish Catholic hierarchy condemned the Queen's Colleges in 1850, and forbade Catholics to attend them; the foundations at Cork and Galway languished. Everywhere in Europe at this time, the Catholic church rejected any separation of education and religion, but in Ireland this created a deadlock because general British opinion was hostile to the state funding any denominational Catholic university. The hope that a common university education could reconcile the different Irish communities was probably doomed anyway in the aftermath of the Famine, and in the long run

13 Though there is only scanty evidence for this in F. M. G. Willson, *Our Minerva: the men and politics of the University of London, 1836–1858* (London, 1995), 79.

14 S. Rothblatt, 'London: a metropolitan university?', in T. Bender (ed.), *The university and the city: from medieval origins to the present* (New York, 1988), 119–49.

15 S. M. Parkes, 'Higher education 1793–1908', in W. E. Vaughan (ed.), *A new history of Ireland. VI. Ireland under the Union: II, 1870–1921* (Oxford, 1996), 539–70.

16 T. W. Moody and J. C. Beckett, *Queen's, Belfast 1845–1949: the history of a university* (London, 1959), 1.

the university question reinforced the identification of Catholicism with Irish nationalism.

The Queen's University system also left unsolved the problem of Dublin. The Irish bishops decided to found a Catholic university there, and invited the celebrated English Catholic convert and former Oxford academic J. H. Newman to become its rector. If the Queen's University had parallels via London with the Belgian law of 1835, the Catholic University of Ireland was partly inspired by Louvain. It was for the Catholic University, which opened in 1854, that Newman gave the set of lectures later published as *The idea of a university*. Newman's ambitious ideals rather outran the modest demands of the Irish Catholic elite (he resigned in 1858), and the university remained small, without the power to award degrees. In 1869, as part of an attempt to win over Irish opinion by W. E. Gladstone's Liberal government, the Anglican church was disestablished, following which Gladstone sought a national university structure for Ireland which would somehow satisfy all religious interests, but his Irish university bill of 1873 was rejected by the bishops and defeated in parliament. In this debate, Continental examples were cited both by Gladstone, who was familiar with German ideas about parity and *Weltanschauung* chairs, and by intellectuals interested in the general principles involved, such as John Stuart Mill and Matthew Arnold.[17]

Mill wanted to maintain the secularist principle of the Queen's Colleges, while Arnold favoured state support for a Catholic university in order to take it out of clerical control. The eventual outcome was a compromise with the existing religious divisions. Although the remaining religious restrictions at Trinity College were removed in 1873, this failed to win over the Irish hierarchy, who now extended the ban on Catholic attendance to the college (a godless university being worse than an Anglican one). In 1879, there was a new settlement, excluding Trinity College, which lasted for thirty years: the old Queen's University was turned into the Royal University of Ireland, still an examining body only, but one which, like the London University of 1858, was not confined to members of affiliated institutions, and so allowed Catholics to gain degrees whatever their place of education. The final step came in 1908. The Royal University was replaced by the National University of Ireland, which included the colleges at Cork and Galway and University College, Dublin (as the Catholic University had been renamed in 1882). Trinity College was left unchanged, and Queen's College at Belfast became independent as Queen's University. All three were formally secular universities, but in practice each reflected one of the three main religious cultures in Ireland. This tripartism marked the failure of attempts to create a genuinely national university, and foreshadowed the partition of Ireland after the First World War.[18] It was an example of how a

[17] B. A. Rapple, 'Matthew Arnold on the Irish university question', *History of Education*, 23 (1994), 1–15; B. L. Kinzer, 'John Stuart Mill and the Irish university question', *Victorian Studies*, 31 (1987–8), 59–77.

[18] T. W. Moody, 'The Irish university question of the nineteenth century', *History*, 43 (1958), 109; H. Robinson-Hammerstein, 'The Irish nation and university education in the nineteenth century', in M. Norrback and K. Ranki (eds.), *University and nation: the university and the making of the nation in northern Europe in the 19th and 20th centuries* (Helsinki, 1996), 153–63.

segmented system could reflect the existence of different communities whose identity was still based fundamentally on religion, though intersected by issues of nationalism, ethnicity, and social class.

Of all European countries, France was the most noted for the conflict between church and state and for antagonism between Catholicism and modern society. The wounds caused by the French revolution had never fully healed; Napoleon had restored the Catholic church, but with limits on its educational rights which nineteenth-century Catholics never really accepted. Even in the 1820s under Frayssinous, the essential features of Napoleon's work, including the state's monopoly of higher education, survived. After the July revolution, however, Catholics launched an attack in the name of liberty of teaching. The campaign was led by liberal Catholics, notably the layman Count Montalembert and Bishop Félix Dupanloup. Their belief that the church should adapt to the modern world, and that a liberal state should allow freedom for religious education, was sincere enough, but the situation was complicated when the liberal Catholic movement was itself condemned by the Pope in 1832, and attacks on the Napoleonic University and its secular spirit were increasingly linked with intransigence and ultramontanism, provoking a strong defence of the state by Orleanist politicians. Behind this dispute lay social divisions. The French nobility, frustrated by the feeling that it was a natural governing class deprived of its rightful role, came to define itself by its hostility to 1789 and its loyalty to Catholicism; aristocrats and wealthy bourgeois who shared their values boycotted the state's lycées and sent their sons to Catholic schools, which had been allowed to expand under the Restoration. The July monarchy threatened to intensify state control over this sector, and the demand for freedom for secondary schools was at the heart of the Catholic campaign. A particular target was Victor Cousin, who now had an all-powerful influence on philosophy appointments in schools and faculties, and used it against the many priests appointed under the Restoration and in favour of his own disciples. There was no immediate demand for Catholic higher education, but as in Belgium the existence of a strong Catholic secondary sector was likely to create such a demand, to feed upper-class students with Catholic and anti-liberal values into the state's own faculties, and to perpetuate ideological division among the elite.

That at least was the fear of the Orleanist politicians, representing a bourgeoisie which looked to the revolution as the guarantee of its own property and privileges and of the career open to talent. There is a striking continuity between the arguments used by Napoleon's officials and these liberals. Even so moderate and anglophile a liberal as Guizot firmly defended the teaching role of the state.[19] The dispute came to a climax in 1844 when a bill to extend the freedom of Catholic schools was debated in parliament. In a remarkable series of speeches, Cousin argued that the right to teach was not a natural right, but a power of the state, as guardian of the interests of society and of the nation. The French state was heir to centuries of secularization, and the revolution had completed the work of national

[19] F. Guizot, *Mémoires pour servir à l'histoire de mon temps*, vol. 3 (Paris, 1860), 14–17.

unity which the monarchy had begun. Talleyrand's report in 1791 proposed a single organization to replace the individual universities, but it was Napoleon, the modern Charlemagne, who carried this historic project through. Modern society is based on common citizenship, and citizens must be 'imbued with the same civil spirit': thus 'the unity of our schools expresses and confirms the unity of the country'. At their apex was the École Normale, which was 'the image of the university, as the university is the image of France'. Cousin pointed to the danger of 'two forms of education contrary in their essence, one clerical and at bottom jesuitical, the other lay and secular. That creates two generations separated from each other from childhood, with opposite principles instilled into them at an early stage, and one day perhaps enemies' who would engage in 'religious civil wars'.[20] This fear of a divided elite was to be a constant in French official policy, notably restated in a speech by the moderate Republican Waldeck-Rousseau in 1900, when France was indeed split ideologically by the Dreyfus Affair.

Two concepts of liberalism were thus in contention: liberal Catholics claiming Belgian-style liberty, and Orleanists for whom liberalism meant defending the secular spirit against the revival of Catholic domination. Neither version was particularly tolerant of diversity, as was to be seen after the 1848 revolution, when fears of social revolution gave the Catholics a temporary victory. The republican constitution of 1848 provided for freedom of education—but only on conditions prescribed by the state and under its supervision. After the suppression of the June rising and the election of Louis-Napoleon as president, the Catholic party was powerful enough to get most of what it wanted in the *loi Falloux*. But part of its deal with the politicians, led by the Orleanist Thiers, was that the faculties and state control of the baccalaureate should remain untouched. There followed Louis-Napoleon's *coup d'état* and the establishment of the Second Empire. The Empire relied in its early years on the political support of Catholics, and remained deferential to religion, provided that it accepted subordination to the public interest. There were even negotiations in the 1850s for canonical recognition of the Catholic theology faculties, and the dean of the Paris faculty appointed in 1853, Mgr. Maret, upheld the Gallican tradition and revivified the faculty's teaching, though with little general Catholic support.[21] In 1859–60, however, Napoleon III's backing for Italian unification alienated the Catholic party from the regime, which itself became increasingly anticlerical. In 1863 Napoleon appointed Victor Duruy, a former lycée history teacher, as minister of education, and he was to prove an important university reformer.

In the 1860s, Catholics again challenged the state monopoly, and this time they demanded freedom for Catholic higher education. Duruy believed in free thought and was instinctively anticlerical, but he was also hostile to materialist philosophy,

[20] V. Cousin, *Défense de l'Université et de la philosophie: discours prononcés à la Chambre des Pairs dans la discussion de la loi sur l'instruction secondaire (avril et mai 1844)* (Paris, 1845), 55, 69, 323. On the 1844 debate, cf. A. J. Tudesq, *Les Grands Notables en France (1840–1849): étude historique d'une psychologie sociale* (Paris, 1964), ii. 695 ff.

[21] A. Tuilier, *Histoire de l'Université de Paris et de la Sorbonne. II. De Louis XIV à la crise de 1968* (Paris, 1994), 369–71.

and tried both to conciliate a conservative Emperor and to protect the University against its critics. He took over one *cause célèbre* from his predecessor: Ernest Renan, author of a *Life of Jesus* (1863) based like Strauss's on philological and historical scholarship, had been appointed to a chair of comparative linguistics at the Collège de France, but then suspended for denying the divinity of Christ. Duruy endorsed the dismissal, but struck a blow for free thought by appointing a Jewish scholar to the vacant post. Duruy also disciplined French students who attended a free thought congress at Liège in 1865 (see Chapter 18), and in 1867 he acted against students at the École Normale who had congratulated the critic Sainte-Beuve on a speech in the Senate attacking censorship; the director of the school and his deputy, who was Louis Pasteur, were dismissed.[22] In 1868, Duruy annulled a thesis in the Paris medical faculty entitled 'A medical-psychological study of human free will'.[23] Paris was the headquarters of medical materialism (whereas Montpellier remained faithful to 'vitalism') and it was this which drew the strongest Catholic fire, and fuelled the demand for Catholic universities. Doctors were seen as missionaries of atheism: 'it is through higher education that impiety arrives in the hamlets', declared Dupanloup.[24]

In 1867, encouraged by Rome, Catholics organized a petition denouncing materialism in the faculties and demanding freedom in higher education, and in 1868 the issue was debated in the Senate. Duruy himself was sympathetic, on general liberal grounds, and because competition would help to reinvigorate the state system. The assault on the 'clerical party', then a new term, was again led by Sainte-Beuve. He claimed to speak for an 'immense diocese' greater than that of any bishop, composed of freethinkers who subscribed to many philosophies but were united by a belief in science and free enquiry.[25] Sainte-Beuve was not the only one to accuse Catholics of seeking privileges for themselves rather than true scientific freedom, and in the aftermath of the Syllabus of Errors the readiness of Catholic spokesmen to resort to denunciation rather than argument, and to equate all critical views with atheism, seemed to confirm their fears. The important practical issue, however, was the power to grant degrees, which no government was willing to surrender.

Duruy was dismissed following clerical gains in the 1869 elections, and a bill to liberalize higher education was prepared in 1870 by a commission under Guizot. After France's defeat in the Franco-Prussian war, the political climate changed again. The Third Republic was proclaimed in 1870, but the National Assembly elected in 1871 had a conservative majority, predominantly royalist and favourable to Catholic claims. The result was the law of 1875 which allowed the setting up of 'free' faculties ('free' was the usual word in France for the Catholic sector of education) subject to certain standards of equipment and staffing, including professors with doctorates; where there were three faculties, they could be called a university—

[22] R. D. Anderson, *Education in France 1848–1870* (Oxford, 1975), 230.

[23] Tuilier, *Université de Paris*, ii. 380.

[24] Anderson, *Education in France*, 236–7.

[25] Speech of 19 May 1868, in C. A. Sainte-Beuve, *Premiers lundis*, vol. 3 (Paris, 1875), 281–2. Cf. *L'Enseignement supérieur devant le Sénat* (Paris, 1868).

as was not yet the case in the state system. For awarding degrees, there were to be mixed juries on Belgian lines, with state and Catholic representatives. The Catholics moved swiftly, and universities were established at Paris, Angers, Lille, Lyons, and Toulouse. These were regions where the church had support from the nobility and *bien pensant* bourgeoisie, and finance came from wealthy donors rather than congregational collections. At Lille, a gift of 1,000 francs would earn the title of 'founder', but donors who endowed a chair for 100,000 francs were rewarded not only by their name being attached to the chair, but with a perpetual daily mass in their name as long as the university lasted.[26] The clientele aimed at was the lay elite trained in the Catholic secondary schools which had expanded so successfully since 1850, rather than prospective priests, and law proved the most popular faculty.[27] Ironically, given the origins of the movement, the creation of a Catholic medical faculty at Paris was ruled out by the cost of medical teaching and the accompanying laboratories and clinics. Only Lille was able to raise the necessary resources, and the government responded aggressively by creating its own new medical faculty in the city in 1875, as it created a new law faculty at Lyons. In 1887 the existing faculties at Douai were also transferred to Lille, part of the struggle, said a local newspaper, 'against clericalism which has built at Lille its most formidable citadel'.[28]

The Catholic faculties were founded at a time when the Vatican Council had exacerbated the division between liberals and ultramontanes. The more zealous of the latter saw the new system as part of a war for the soul of France between Catholicism and positivism, and republicans were hardly reassured by scenes such as that at Angers, when the newly appointed professors knelt before the bishops to swear obedience to Catholic doctrines.[29] Yet many of the bishops, including the archbishop of Paris, were lukewarm supporters of institutions which challenged their own seminaries. Paris did not acquire a theology faculty until 1878, and it was not granted canonical institution until 1889, due partly to resistance to the Vatican-favoured revival of Thomism. In any case, the favourable political situation of 1875 soon disappeared. By 1880 the anticlerical Republicans were firmly in control. The new minister of education, Jules Ferry, was an exponent of positivist ideology. In the last days of the Empire, he had delivered a notable speech on equality in education, identifying the Catholic church as the enemy of science and progress.[30] Ferry is most famous for the laws which introduced free, compulsory, and secular primary education, but they were preceded by a package of reforms in 1880 which included the banning of Jesuit colleges, the creation of state lycées for girls, and a new law on higher education. Under the 1880 law, the Catholic faculties could no longer use the term 'university'; those in Paris were renamed the Institut Catholique. The mixed juries were abolished, and degrees were to be awarded exclusively by state examiners. In 1885, reflecting the new policy of state neutrality

[26] P. H. Prelot, *Naissance de l'enseignement supérieur libre: la loi du 12 juillet 1875* (Paris, n.d.), 80.

[27] *Institut Catholique de Paris: le livre du centenaire 1875–1975* (Paris, 1975), 38–9, 44–5.

[28] Cited in L. Trénard, *De Douai à Lille . . . une université et son histoire* (Lille, 1978), 86–7.

[29] Prelot, *Naissance*, 67.

[30] L. Legrand, *L'Influence du positivisme dans l'œuvre scolaire de Jules Ferry: les origines de la laïcité* (Paris, 1961), 217–37.

in religious matters and the triumph of Roman authority in the church, the state's faculties of Catholic theology were abolished, though the Protestant ones lasted until the abolition of the Concordat in 1905.

The Third Republic, despite its evident anti-Catholic bias, allowed a real freedom in higher education which the older generation of liberals had refused. But the survival of the Catholic faculties was at a modest level: by the 1900s Paris had settled to a regular student body of 600–700.[31] The faculties helped to raise the intellectual standards of the French clergy, but could not tempt more than a minority of Catholic families to abandon the state schools of medicine or law, with their guarantees of quality and employment, or to abjure entry to the Polytechnique and other specialist schools—in preparing for which Catholic schools, especially the Jesuit colleges, had proved very successful. Catholic secondary schools continued to have a strong social appeal, despite legal harassment by the Third Republic, but the moral atmosphere which parents prized in the education of adolescents seemed less necessary at the university level. Thus despite the pretension of both clerical and anticlerical parties to impose their values as national ones, there was in practice a mingling at the highest level of the elite, as the rich and well-born submitted to the rigours of meritocracy.

The issues raised in the conflicts over church–state relations and 'materialism' were hardly unimportant ones. Were church and state to be allies or rivals in determining a society's ethical values? What common beliefs were necessary to hold together the elite of a modern nation-state? Religious truth apart, did it make sense to exclude from universities the cultural wealth of Christian traditions? What was the nature of the truth which universities pursued, and in seeking to form the whole man could they exclude man's divine dimension? Science might seek to establish immutable laws in the natural world, but traditionalists thought that to deny free will in human affairs and to posit determinism was to undermine the basis of morality. None the less, the shift away from religious to secular and positivist ways of thinking was irreversible, and the 1860s and 1870s were probably the turning-point, the impact of Darwinism being an important factor. Religion receded to the intellectual sidelines, and many of the speakers in the debate in the French Senate in 1868 argued that the religious and philosophical views of professors were irrelevant as long as they left them outside the classroom.

That had not been the case in earlier decades. After the Restoration, most governments had an instrumental view both of university education and of religion. Universities were organs of the state, designed to train its servants and to inculcate loyalty, and professors were expected to toe the religious and political line or face dismissal. Governments might simply enforce an established religion, or might impose a state-dominated form of Catholicism in the style of Joseph II and Napoleon, or support a syncretic deist philosophy like that of Cousin. But intellectual polarization was making these compromises unviable. On the one hand, liberal and ultramontane Catholics united in rejecting state authority in religious matters

[31] *Institut Catholique*, 406.

and official pseudo-religions. On the other, idealism no longer needed to clothe itself in religious forms—or rather, perhaps, alternative religions appeared in the shape of scientific positivism, socialism, and nationalism. By the 1870s, most scholars thought that religion was a matter of private belief, and that objective truth was attainable by the application of agreed scientific methods. The religious conflicts of the period were important because they forced intellectuals and governments to accept pluralism of values, coexistence instead of conformity. This evolution combined with the progress of liberal constitutionalism to create solid conditions for intellectual freedom and university autonomy.

7
Curriculum and Culture

It is acknowledged on all hands that the *Gymnasien* are the best in the world, and that the universities are completely successful in producing the highest scholarship and the greatest scientific attainments. The system of higher instruction has given to Prussia, and to the rest of Germany along with her, the foremost place in the investigation of truth; and all other civilized nations are indebted to her for a great deal of the stimulus which they receive in the prosecution of scholarship and science.[1]

This encomium from a Scottish academic came in 1874, at a time when Prussia's prestige had been reinforced by military victories over Austria in 1866 and France in 1871, and reflected a view by then shared throughout Europe. Academics were impressed and excited by the intellectual achievements of Germany, and admired the high status of professors and the autonomy and generous state support which her universities seemed to enjoy. Statesmen and the general public were impressed by the dividends which investment in higher education seemed to pay in industrial and military power, and by the 1860s the British and French governments were commissioning expert reports on Germany's scientific and technical education. For those struggling to hold together newly united nations, or to create national consciousness among a people seeking emancipation, the German universities had a special appeal, and they retained a lingering glamour from the prestige of German philosophy, art, and literature in the age of romanticism. The adoption of the German model of the university was not straightforward, and imitators tended to select only those features which suited their purpose. But there was no doubt of the achievements of German *Wissenschaft*, or of the spur which freedom of teaching had given to original thought and discovery. In classical and linguistic studies, in Protestant theology, in history and the historical study of law, in the natural sciences, and in the application of science to medicine, Germany seemed to lead Europe, and became a Mecca for young scientists and scholars from all over Europe, who then took the gospel home (Donaldson had studied at Berlin). Even for those who did not travel, the ability to read books and learned journals in German was essential.

But what exactly was to be imitated? By the time it attracted foreign attention, the original ideal of *Bildung* held by Humboldt and his contemporaries, like all such ideals always rather remote from everyday reality, had been modified by the growth of disciplinary specialization.[2] Thus the German model stood both for the latest

[1] J. Donaldson, *Lectures on the history of education in Prussia and England* (Edinburgh, 1874), 7.

[2] R. S. Turner, 'The Prussian universities and the concept of research', *Internationales Archiv für Sozialgeschichte der Deutschen Literatur*, 5 (1980), 68–93.

disciplinary advances in science and scholarship, and for a continuing ideal of *Bildung* and individual ethical formation, and these strands were intertwined and in mutual tension. By the 1860s and 1870s specialization and the concept of the research-driven university had advanced far enough to provoke a strong critique, which broadened out into reflections on the relation of university culture to the new forces of democracy, mass culture, and state power. The gloomiest of these reflections were by Friedrich Nietzsche, but Ernest Renan in France and Matthew Arnold in England illustrate the same concerns.

'The assumption that advanced education needed to be specialized, and that specialized study was necessary for a professional career, was the basis of the transformation of higher education in the nineteenth century', wrote the historian of science Joseph Ben-David.[3] The various aspects of academic professionalization are familiar: the concentration of scientific work in the universities, the exclusion of the amateur, the doctoral thesis, the scholarly journal, the disciplinary association, the national or international conference, an open market for appointments determined by objective scholarly criteria. At the heart of professionalization were the mechanisms of training and appointment. The German structure of *Habilitation*, faculty nomination of candidates for chairs, and appointment from a national pool had parallels in other state systems where impartial competition (*concours*) was meant to replace appointment on political or religious lines. Serious candidates were trained in scientific methods by leading scholars, setting up a master–pupil relationship over the generations which gave great power to the professors as patrons. The key institution now developed in Germany was the seminar, institute, or teaching laboratory, where students met under professorial direction in small groups and prepared an original project which would eventually be turned into a doctoral thesis.

Seminars supplemented lectures, which were well suited to a system whose fundamental aim was liberal education, but not to one which demanded original work and specialized guidance. In Germany, Holland, and Scotland in the eighteenth century, public lectures had been supplemented by private classes given by the professors, and seminars and laboratories could be seen as a revival and modernization of this type of teaching, making it available to all, and tempering the anonymity and the professorial 'wall of monologue' which were weaknesses of the lecture system.[4] The German seminar became established first in philology, then in the 1820s and 1830s in history and other humane subjects, and only after 1830 in science (where the term 'institute' was preferred). Seminar and laboratory teaching was at first confined to an elite of disciples, and it was only in the 1880s, even in Germany, that it became part of most students' experience.[5] Throughout Europe, the lecture remained the commonest form of teaching, supplemented by the student's private reading and preparation for examinations. The professor typically

[3] J. Ben-David, *Centers of learning: Britain, France, Germany, United States* (New York, 1977), 29.

[4] W. Otterspeer, *De wiekslag van hun geest: de Leidse Universiteit in de negentiende eeuw* (The Hague, 1992), 577 (English summary).

[5] See for example S. Paletschek, *Die permanente Erfindung einer Tradition: Die Universität Tübingen im Kaiserreich und in der Weimarer Republik* (Stuttgart, 2001), 424, 521.

gave two lecture courses, at introductory and more advanced levels, and directed a seminar or institute; by the end of the century, there was a new demand for assistants to provide supplementary teaching, supervise laboratory work, or mark assignments in the large lecture courses, and the growth of this junior staff, which could not rely on eventually reaching professorial status like the traditional *Privatdozent*, caused tensions within the academic profession.

In Germany, *Lernfreiheit* meant that students made their own choice of lectures and seminars, and this applied even to subjects with a fixed body of material such as law and medicine. For the mass of *Brotstudenten*, vocational considerations prevailed, and most students in the philosophy faculties were either following courses which would help with their legal, medical, or theological studies, or training to be secondary teachers. The leisured student concerned only to pursue the truth, moving from one university to another in order to study under the most famous professors, did exist, but was hardly typical. More common was the idea that whatever one's ultimate destination, the university was a chance to broaden one's mind through the free availability of lectures in philosophy, literature, or (an early speciality in Germany) the history of art. A year or a semester in Berlin or Munich to sample the theatres, museums, and galleries formed part of many itineraries, and some universities such as Munich and Heidelberg, with agreeable climates and scenery, had a special attraction during the summer semester. German student mobility was a reality, and helped to mould a common national identity, but it was not imitated in other countries.

The primacy of the philological seminar in Germany was related to the philosophy faculty's main vocational role, training secondary teachers, and when extended to other subjects the system continued to give gymnasium and university teachers a shared scientific culture. In the humanities, it encouraged a form of teaching based chiefly on the study and interpretation of texts, and this influenced the specialized development of philosophy, history, biblical and oriental studies, and the nascent social sciences. Through philology the old neohumanism developed into a broader but more professionalized 'science of antiquity'. Classical specialists felt they had a superior status, and their arrogance could be resented by other scholars. And the more the classical world was studied scientifically, the more the idealistic picture of the Greeks, as timeless exponents of truth, beauty, and virtue, as an exemplary civilization and a source of permanent values, was undermined; studies of Greek religion, for example, hardly confirmed Winckelmann or Humboldt's ideal of calm, noble rationality. The famous Greek scholar Wilamowitz-Moellendorf, who dominated classical studies in Germany in the years before 1914, was to admit that 'the ancient world as a unity and an ideal is gone: scholarship itself has destroyed those beliefs'.[6] A persisting tension arose between the high educational claims of neohumanism and a technical scholarship which often seemed arid and pedantic. The prestige of classical studies was also challenged

[6] M. Jacob, 'Étude comparative des systèmes universitaires et place des études classiques au 19ème siècle en Allemagne, en Belgique, et en France', in M. Bollack and H. Wismann (eds.), *Philologie und Hermeneutik im 19. Jahrhundert. II* (Göttingen, 1983), 121.

by the rise of history, a subject in which Germany provided the acknowledged masters, and which could claim a central patriotic role in the creation of national consciousness. German philosophy, on the other hand, so influential in the heyday of idealism when it was based on speculative lectures, was less successful in adapting to text-based seminar methods. It became a rather narrow speciality, no longer at the heart of the 'philosophy' faculty, and professional university philosophers made less of a stir than mavericks like Schopenhauer and Nietzsche.

The comparatively late development of science in Germany was partly due to the restrictions of the so-called *Naturphilosophie*, which discouraged experimental, empirical methods. The idea of discovering the hidden connections and unity which lay behind the appearance of nature was fruitful for zoology or botany where science sought to probe the mysteries of consciousness and life, but less suited to sciences like physics and chemistry which depended on quantitative and mechanical approaches. The pioneer of the new sort of chemical laboratory, devoted to training men for research posts in universities and industrial firms, was Justus Liebig, who became professor at Giessen in 1825 at the age of 22. Liebig demonstrated the practical benefits of chemistry for industry and agriculture, and attracted many foreign pupils. Liebig's type of research and training laboratory spread to other German universities, and was general by the 1850s for chemistry and physiology, though only in the 1870s was it adopted for physics, notably by Hermann Helmholtz at Berlin.[7]

There has been much discussion among historians of science about why France lost the predominance in science which it established under Napoleon. Ben-David blamed the rigid centralization of the French system, which discouraged new initiatives and led to stagnation after 1830. The moribund provincial faculties did not attract able researchers or have the resources to help local industries, and the system of specialized schools meant that scientists worked in isolation without the support of a unified scientific community. The German network of universities was more competitive and responsive to local needs, and created a community through the patron–disciple relationship. The *Privatdozent* system encouraged original work outside the framework of established chairs, and the new specialities which they developed were later elevated to full status, giving a permanent dynamic (argues Ben-David) to the growth and differentiation of disciplines.[8] By taking the German form of university organization as the norm, this interpretation rather undervalues the contribution of the Polytechnique and other scientific institutions in Paris, which provided many posts free of the distractions of teaching; centralization could itself be a source of strength and fruitful interaction.[9] However, Ben-

[7] W. V. Farrar, 'Science and the German university system 1790–1850', in M. Crosland (ed.), *The emergence of science in western Europe* (New York, 1976), 179–92; J. J. Sheehan, *German history 1770–1866* (Oxford, 1989), 802–14.

[8] J. Ben-David, *The scientist's role in society: a comparative study* (Englewood Cliffs, NJ, 1971), 88–138. Cf. his 'The rise and decline of France as a scientific centre', *Minerva*, 8 (1970), 160–79, and J. Ben-David and A. Zloczower, 'Universities and academic systems in modern societies', *Archives Européennes de Sociologie*, 3 (1962), 45–84.

[9] M. Crosland, 'The development of a professional career in science in France', in Crosland,

David also argues plausibly that the general social and intellectual climate moved in opposite directions in France and Germany. In France, science was glamorous and progressive under Napoleon, but young men later turned to literature, politics, or social theory. In Germany, the emphasis in *Bildung* on aestheticism and individual self-expression initially discouraged science, but had the long-term effect of concentrating energies on the university system and on the emergence of a competitive, professionalized career structure.[10]

For Ben-David, the fundamental impulse remained an internal, organizational one, rather than the external demands of industry or the state. This approach, which probably works better for medicine with its marked development of subdisciplines than for other branches of science, reflects the competitive and discipline-driven nature of twentieth-century science, and derives from sociological theories, ultimately inspired by Max Weber, which see progressive differentiation as an inherent characteristic of modern organizational systems.[11] Recent work has laid more emphasis on external factors such as the financial support of governments or 'the *ideological* role of natural science as a powerful symbol of modernity, efficacy, control, and social integration, especially for the social groups that were its agents'.[12] New chairs and laboratories did not appear magically when academic logic demanded them. One reason for French retardation was that after 1815 the political regimes were culturally conservative, and it was not until Napoleon III that the promotion of industry again became a state priority. In Germany, the reasons for the greater activity of governments may also be sought in the political sphere. Both Prussia and Baden consciously embraced a policy of using their universities to promote industrial development, using science to reinforce the prestige and strength of the state. Because in Germany intellectual activity was already concentrated in universities rather than academies or specialized schools, new resources were naturally directed to them, and the process became self-reinforcing. It was the active role of the state which impressed foreign observers, who used the German example as a stick to goad their own governments into action.

In France, science faculties were separate from the start, but in Germany there was much resistance to dividing the philosophy faculty, or even to creating separate scientific and 'philological-historical' sections within it. Scientists themselves often

Emergence of science, 139–59. Cf. (broadly supportive of Ben-David) R. Fox, 'Scientific enterprise and the patronage of research in France', *Minerva*, 11 (1973), 442–73.

[10] For discussions, see R. S. Turner, 'The great transition and the social patterns of German science', *Minerva*, 25 (1987), 56–76; E. Crawford, 'Competition and centralisation in German and French science in the nineteenth and early twentieth centuries: the theses of Joseph Ben-David', *Minerva*, 26 (1988), 618–26; R. S. Turner, 'German science, German universities: historiographical perspectives from the 1980s', in G. Schubring (ed.), *'Einsamkeit und Freiheit' neu besichtigt: Universitätsreformen und Disziplinenbildung in Preussen als Modell für Wissenschaftspolitik im Europa des 19. Jahrhunderts* (Stuttgart, 1991), 24–36.

[11] See for example R. Stichweh, 'La structuration des disciplines dans les universités allemandes au XIXe siècle', *Histoire de l'Éducation*, 62 (1994), 55–73, and 'Differenzierung von Schule und Universität im 18. und 19. Jahrhundert', in Schubring, *'Einsamkeit und Freiheit' neu besichtigt*, 38–49. Many German university historians have been influenced by the sociologist of systems Niklas Luhmann.

[12] Turner, 'German science', 33.

pushed for this reform as they hoped it would improve their funding; it was introduced at Tübingen in 1863 and at the new German university founded at Strasbourg after 1871, but most German and Austrian universities retained the single faculty, as a symbol of the unity of knowledge, down to 1914. However, concentration on science faculties or the industrial applications of science should not obscure the importance for scientific development of medicine, where France remained a centre of international attraction. Medical faculties attracted a mass of students in a way that pure science could not—Thomas Bonner estimates that in 1830 Germany had over 6,000 medical students and France 3,500—and sciences like chemistry and botany had originally grown up to serve their practical needs, including those of pharmacy, which in most countries, though not Britain, was a university-trained profession.[13] If clinical study of the hospital patient had been the great innovation of the eighteenth century, in the nineteenth century the new idea was science-based medicine, initially in the form of pathology and physiology, with microbiology developing later. Physiology followed the Liebig laboratory model, and the university rather than the hospital 'reemerged as the favoured site of medical instruction. . . . This fusion of laboratory medicine with the clinic in a university setting' proved the key to future development.[14] Its progress required teaching laboratories; at first these were used by the professor for demonstrations and for training a handful of advanced students, but it soon became accepted that every medical student needed experience at the laboratory bench. This was an expensive requirement, and individual university histories suggest that the 1870s and 1880s were the crucial period when large building programmes were undertaken to provide laboratories, clinics, and institutes; for governments were prepared to spend money on a branch of science with obvious social benefits and dramatic results for human welfare. Scientists like the physiologist Claude Bernard, based at the Collège de France, Pasteur, Rudolf Virchow, and Robert Koch became popular celebrities and objects of national pride.[15]

The importance of medicine is a reminder that the majority of students in most universities were in the vocational faculties. The Humboldtian ideal of combining teaching with research was meant to apply to all faculties, and the philosophy faculty was now seen as existing in parallel with the others, taking the formation of scholars as its own professional task, while also offering its specialities to all interested students. The Humboldtian union of teaching and research was still conceived as an instrument of liberal education: the search for truth would form the character and personality of the individual, and train the judgement and intelligence as a preparation for professional tasks of all kinds. The stress on originality, on the criticism of accepted views, on the establishment of truth through the rigorous examination and evaluation of evidence, all promoted analytical and independent thinking. Every country had its own tradition of liberal or gentlemanly

[13] T. N. Bonner, *Becoming a physician: medical education in Britain, France, Germany and the United States, 1750–1945* (New York, 1995), 159, 164.

[14] Ibid. 288.

[15] C. Charle, *Naissance des 'intellectuels' 1880–1900* (Paris, 1990), 28 ff.

education, and the German version was as powerful as the others.[16] Since university education was about the acquisition of cultural and social status, not just professional training, liberal education remained central to the purpose of the university, as of the humanistic secondary school. But in other national traditions, it took the form of a preliminary education lasting for several years, with a more or less fixed curriculum leading to examinations which had to be passed before entering the professional faculties. If adopted in full, the Humboldtian reform meant abolishing the fixed curriculum and all examinations short of the doctorate (which was only realistic where there was something like the German system of state examinations), and relegating preparatory work to the schools. In southern Germany and Austria, this was what happened, and the 'reception' of the Humboldtian model was completed in the 1850s. In other countries, the key period was the 1870s. The emphasis then was on the concept of *Wissenschaft*, on giving the universities freedom to develop new subjects, and on redefining their purpose as the advancement as well as the diffusion of knowledge, a purpose often explicitly written into new university laws or charters. But on curricular matters, most countries outside Germany's immediate cultural sphere adopted only a weak form of *Lernfreiheit*, moving from highly prescriptive curricula to ones which allowed students to choose between various specialized lines, usually retaining some compulsory core subjects. As with other aspects of university practice, countries did not adopt the German model *en bloc*, but borrowed what seemed useful to them and ignored what did not conform to their own traditions and the values of their elites.[17]

In Bavaria and Austria, there were one or two compulsory years of philosophy before students could enter the professional faculties, years which could be taken in the provincial lyceums as well as the philosophy faculties. In Bavaria, early attempts to introduce the new pattern were reversed in 1833, but finally enforced in 1848–9; the lyceums were reduced to theology colleges. Maximilian II, who became king in 1848, followed this up with a vigorous 'science policy' designed to make Bavaria the dominant German state in cultural matters after Austria and Prussia. Protestant scholars from the north were imported to enforce the new ideas, and there was much resentment at Munich of these 'northern lights'. The eventual outcome was that in the Bavarian state examinations candidates had to prove that they had attended a number of philosophy classes, but now these could be studied concurrently with professional subjects instead of as part of a fixed prior requirement.[18]

In Austria, a similar reform was carried out between 1849 and 1860 by the minister of education Count Thun, whose policies of authoritarian modernization largely met the liberal demands of 1848. Two years of philosophical preparation

[16] C. E. McClelland, *State, society and university in Germany 1700–1914* (Cambridge, 1980), 122–6.

[17] See generally R. M. Schwinges (ed.), *Humboldt International: Der Export des deutschen Universitätsmodells im 19. und 20. Jahrhundert* (Basel, 2001).

[18] R. A. Müller, *Akademische Ausbildung zwischen Staat und Kirche: Das bayerische Lyzealwesen 1773–1849* (Paderborn, 1986), 5–6, 33–4; A. Sing, *Die Wissenschaftspolitik Maximilians II. von Bayern (1848–1864): Nordlichterstreit und gelehrtes Leben in München* (Berlin, 1996); H. Dickerhof, 'Bildung und Ausbildung im Programm der bayerischen Universitäten im 19. Jahrhundert', *Historisches Jahrbuch*, 95 (1975), 142–69; R. S. Turner, 'Universitäten', in K. E. Jeismann and P. Lundgreen (eds.), *Handbuch der deutschen Bildungsgeschichte. III. 1800–1870* (Munich, 1987), 230–1.

were pushed back into the secondary schools, *Lehr-* and *Lernfreiheit* were embraced fully, and such relics of the Austrian past as directors of studies and doctoral colleges were swept away. The 1848 revolutions, though ultimately unsuccessful, had revealed the archaism and rigidity of the Austrian state, and as in Bavaria university reform was intended to strengthen it culturally and economically; here too the policy offended local feeling, as Austrian traditions seemed to be surrendered to Prussian influences. Thun's reforms were also designed to win over the educated elite to Catholic, conservative ideas of neo-absolutism. But this was less successful, and the universities contributed to the growing strength of Austrian liberalism in the 1860s. A clause on academic freedom was included in the Austrian constitution of 1867, and a new university statute in 1873 consolidated the autonomy of the universities; the general effect of these reforms was to turn what had been a somnolent and submissive university system into one of the strongest in Europe.[19]

A second wave of reform extended to Switzerland, Scandinavia, and the Low Countries. In Switzerland (regarded as an 'academic province of Germany') it extended even to the French-speaking universities. At Geneva, a law of 1872 which finally gave the Academy the name of university introduced complete *Lernfreiheit*, and the abolition of compulsory examinations followed in 1886.[20] In Sweden, a country which was deeply influenced by the German ideal of *Bildung*, and which was also described at the time as 'an intellectual province of Germany', university reform in 1852, further modified in the 1870s, nevertheless retained strong elements of the uniform curriculum.[21] In Belgium, the strongly prescriptive law of 1835 was replaced in 1876, when 'at the end of a long campaign, constantly inspired by the German example, the universities regained freedom of scientific research and freedom of methods', though recent work suggests that it was not until after 1890 that the ideal of *Wissenschaft* was really established.[22] Holland also had an important university law in 1876, seen at the time as liberating the universities from close state control and inaugurating a golden age of expansion. The law abolished compulsory preparatory studies 'based on an encyclopaedic, classic, and text-oriented ideal of knowledge', and allowed students to enrol directly in the faculty of their choice. But J. C. M. Wachelder has pointed out that this was not simply an adoption of the German model, but should be placed in the context of a general process of

[19] H. Lentze, *Die Universitätsreform des Ministers Graf Leo Thun-Hohenstein* (Vienna, 1962). Cf. S. Preglau-Hämmerle, *Die politische und soziale Funktion der österreichischen Universität: Von den Anfängen bis zur Gegenwart* (Innsbruck, 1986), 98 ff.; F. Gall, *Alma Mater Rudolphina 1365–1965: Die Wiener Universität und ihre Studenten*, 3rd edn. (Vienna, 1965), 23–5.

[20] U. Im Hof, 'Die schweizerischen Varianten der kleindeutschen Universität: Zum Problem der ausländischen Einflüsse auf das schweizerische Hochschulwesens im 19. Jahrhundert', in *Festgabe Hans von Greyerz zum sechzigsten Geburtstag* (Bern, 1969), 615 (for quotation); P. F. Geisendorf, *L'Université de Genève 1559–1959: quatre siècles d'histoire* (Geneva, 1959), 258–9; M. Marcacci, *Histoire de l'Université de Genève 1559–1986* (Geneva, 1987), 141–2, 154–6.

[21] S. E. Liedman, 'In search of Isis: general education in Germany and Sweden', in S. Rothblatt and B. Wittrock (eds.), *The European and American university since 1800: historical and sociological essays* (Cambridge, 1993), 74–106; S. Lindroth, *A history of Uppsala University 1477–1977* (Stockholm, 1976), 158–69, 190 (for quotation).

[22] Jacob, 'Étude comparative', 117 (for quotation); J. C. M. Wachelder, 'The German university model and its reception in the Netherlands and Belgium', in Schwinges, *Humboldt International*, 201–2.

modernization and differentiation, common to all countries but always taking specific and complex national forms.[23]

Perhaps no country was more attached to the idea of a uniform university curriculum than Britain, though it existed in two versions. Oxford and Cambridge, because they did not give direct professional training, and because many of their students were destined for a life of leisure or public service, remained faithful to an ideal of liberal education based on a few privileged subjects. Classics predominated at Oxford and mathematics at Cambridge, the latter being taught as a form of mental training, not with a view to its applications in science or engineering. In the 1850s the two universities reluctantly admitted new subjects, particularly law, history, and natural science, but it was not until the 1870s that the curriculum was broken down into specialized disciplines. Even then, new subjects were justified on broad educational grounds, and those of obvious vocational value remained suspect. At Oxford, the new curricula included 'Greats', based on classics, ancient history, and philosophy, which symbolized the continuing prestige of classics as a subject for the leadership class.

The alternative tradition of liberal education was an encyclopaedic one in which students were offered a balanced diet of linguistic, scientific, and philosophical subjects. This was characteristic of Scotland, and was also adopted by London University, and consequently by the many institutions which gained access to degrees through its examinations. Most students, even at Oxbridge, had practical, professional aims, but opinion was reluctant to abandon the idea that broader study was essential to a true university education. This was especially clear in Scotland, where a major reform in 1858 imposed a uniform national curriculum, allowing specialization only after a common foundation; this lasted until 1889. In time these British traditions were undermined by the irresistible pressures, both vocational and academic, in favour of specialization, but in the 1860s and 1870s there was a substantial debate, without an exact equivalent in other countries, between the claims of classics and other humane studies and those of the sciences. The demands of modern, utilitarian subjects were put forward with some force by such propagandists as John Stuart Mill, Thomas Huxley, and Herbert Spencer, and it was amid these contending claims that new university colleges were founded in the industrial areas of England.[24] This debate overlapped with one, closely connected with reform at Oxford and Cambridge, over the rival claims of education and research. The Oxbridge ideal had a good deal in common with Humboldt's original concept of *Bildung*, but the new German model of specialized study and the technicalities of philology met a frosty reception, and the defenders of liberal education repudiated the idea that a university's main function was the pursuit of originality. For the Cambridge scientist William Whewell, defending the traditional order in the 1830s and 1840s, the teaching of established truths and the

[23] Ibid. 198; J. C. M. Wachelder, *Universiteit tussen vorming en opleiding: de modernisering van de nederlandse universiteiten in de negentiende eeuw* (Hilversum, 1992), 268 (English summary).

[24] M. Sanderson, *The universities in the nineteenth century* (London, 1975), 115–41.

mental rigour of mathematical study came first.[25] For his equivalent at Oxford, Edward Copleston, the main business of education was to sharpen the mind, for which the classics were an unrivalled instrument.[26] For Edward Pusey, the leading figure of the Oxford Movement after Newman and an admitted conservative, 'the problem and special work of an University, is not how to advance science, not how to make discoveries, not to form new schools of mental philosophy, nor to invent new modes of analysis . . . but to form minds religiously, morally, intellectually, which shall discharge aright whatever duties God, in his Providence, shall appoint to them.'[27]

It was on this tradition, and on his experience in the 1820s as an Oxford tutor at Oriel College under Copleston's headship, that Newman based *The idea of a university*.[28] Newman's book has become a classic in the English-speaking world for its eloquent defence of the university as a place for the pursuit of intellectual excellence and of knowledge as an end in itself. Liberal education was the culture and discipline of the intellect, aimed at perfecting the human personality and giving it mastery over itself. Professional education and other utilitarian concerns had their place, and as head of a new university at Dublin Newman was necessarily concerned with them, but they were subordinate to the university's role in giving individuals the general intellectual and moral qualities which would allow them to serve the wider needs of society.[29] As rector of a Catholic university, Newman also argued for religion as a branch of scientific knowledge and for the ultimate authority of the church, but was no more successful than other Catholic thinkers in reconciling authority and intellectual freedom. More significant was his exposition of the pastoral, collegiate ideal which he brought from Oxford; its emphasis on the personal influence of the teacher, and the ideal of a university which shaped the whole personality rather than just the intellect, preferably in the context of a religious, residential community, was embodied in secularized form in the Oxford and Cambridge of the late nineteenth century, and was to exercise a strong influence on other parts of English education.

Newman's ideal of seeking truth for its own sake, and of the university as an arbiter of universal knowledge, was close to Humboldt's original notion of *Bildung*, but there is no sign that he was directly influenced by him, or by any university

[25] P. Searby, *A history of the University of Cambridge. III. 1750–1870* (Cambridge, 1997), 445–55; P. Williams, 'Passing on the torch: Whewell's philosophy and the principles of English university education', in M. Fisch and S. Schaffer (eds.), *William Whewell: a composite portrait* (Oxford, 1991), 117–47; M. M. Garland, *Cambridge before Darwin: the ideal of a liberal education 1800–1860* (Cambridge, 1980), 39–51.

[26] Sanderson, *Universities in the nineteenth century*, 36–8; M. G. Brock, 'The Oxford of Peel and Gladstone', in M. G. Brock and M. C. Curthoys (eds.), *The history of the University of Oxford. VI. Nineteenth-century Oxford, Part 1* (Oxford, 1997), 12.

[27] Cited (1854) in M. Richter, *The politics of conscience: T. H. Green and his age* (London, 1964), 61.

[28] P. B. Nockles, 'An academic counter-revolution: Newman and Tractarian Oxford's idea of a university', *History of Universities*, 10 (1991), 137–97.

[29] J. H. Newman, *The idea of a university defined and illustrated*, ed. M. J. Svaglic (New York, 1964), 134. Cf. A. D. Culler, *The imperial intellect: a study of Newman's educational ideal* (New Haven, 1955), 212–16; S. Rothblatt, *The modern university and its discontents: the fate of Newman's legacies in Britain and America* (Cambridge, 1997), 12–22.

developments outside Oxford. In turn, Newman himself was not much cited in his own day. Versions of his lectures were published in 1853 and 1859, and the title *The idea of a university* was given to them in 1873. But their real fame came in the twentieth century, and the cult of Newman was weaker in Britain than in twentieth-century America. It is striking that Matthew Arnold, writing in the 1860s, made no reference to Newman's lectures. The two men are often coupled, with the implication that there was a 'Newman–Arnold' ideal of gentlemanly liberal education, usually seen negatively as an anti-modern doctrine which stifled the scientific and entrepreneurial spirit. But Arnold's thought engaged far more closely with contemporary problems.

Arnold was also an Oxford man, the son of the reforming public-school headmaster Thomas Arnold. He was a school inspector, a full-time official in the English educational administration, as well as a poet and literary critic. Arnold was sent on official missions to study Continental education, and his report on *Schools and universities on the Continent* (1868), originally made to a commission studying the reorganization of secondary education, was especially important. His ideas were developed in a broader work of cultural criticism, *Culture and anarchy*, in 1869. Here and elsewhere, he proposed some celebrated theses: the division of the British elite between barbarians (the landed aristocracy) and philistines (the new bourgeoisie: the term was borrowed from German student slang); the over-dominance of Protestant 'Hebraism' in the British mind, and the need to counter-balance it with an infusion of Hellenism; the function of culture in spreading 'sweetness and light', and in teaching 'the best that has been known and said in the world'. Arnold was one of the first to use 'culture' to mean the common national heritage of literary and artistic achievement, and to see mastering it as the mark of the educated classes; the implicit argument was that culture would provide an alternative standard of spiritual values in an age of declining religious faith. Socially, as Britain moved towards greater democracy with the extension of the franchise to most urban workers in 1867, culture would form a bulwark against disorder by training an intellectual aristocracy to provide continuity and stability. This educational ideal, based on an essentially literary definition of culture (though one which admitted modern as well as classical works), was intended as a corrective to what Arnold dubbed 'industrialism', the narrower side of the mercantile, scientific, and technological spirit of Victorian England.

Arnold's cultured elite was a version of the 'clerisy' originally proposed by the poet S. T. Coleridge: a secular intelligentsia to minister to society as the clergy had done in the past.[30] Coleridge was an important channel for German influence on Britain, and both he and Arnold especially admired the *Kulturstaat*, the ethical state, though for Arnold France exemplified this as much as Germany. In his pronouncements on higher education, Arnold appears as a very clear champion of Humboldt's ideals. As epigraph for his 1868 report, he chose a quotation from Humboldt on the need to 'raise the culture of the nation ever higher and higher'

[30] B. Knights, *The idea of the clerisy in the nineteenth century* (Cambridge, 1978).

through schools and universities.[31] Arnold blamed the public schools for detaching the wealthy professional classes from the bulk of the middle class, which was left without true culture, and called (unsuccessfully) for a fully-fledged system of state secondary education to re-establish the unity of the elite by giving a solid intellectual culture on the lines of the lycée or gymnasium. He followed Humboldt in attributing to the secondary school the task of 'a general liberal culture', after which it was 'the function of the university to develop into science the knowledge a boy brings with him from the secondary school'. Currently the universities were 'the weakest part of our whole educational system', and should be regenerated by German '*Lehrfreiheit* and *Lernfreiheit* . . . *Wissenschaft*, science, knowledge systematically pursued and prized in and for itself', for 'it is in science that we have most need to borrow from the German universities'. An examining university like London ignored the need for systematic study under an expert if serious results were to be achieved, and a 'real love for the things of the mind' implanted.[32]

Since the prime aim of education is 'to enable a man *to know himself and the world*', both humanistic and 'real' studies are essential. Despite Arnold's personal predilection for the classics and his critique of utilitarianism, he agreed that a balanced education must include the natural sciences.[33] In Arnold's view reform of Oxbridge was not the first priority, but rather to 'plant faculties in the eight or ten principal seats of population, and let the students follow lectures there from their own homes, or with whatever arrangements for their living they and their parents choose. It would be everything for the great seats of population to be thus made intellectual centres as well as mere places of business; for the want of this at present, Liverpool and Leeds are mere overgrown provincial towns, while Strasbourg and Lyons are European cities.' The resources of Oxbridge should be partly devolved to these provincial centres—an idea which others were pursuing at the time under the name of university extension.[34] All this differentiates Arnold from Newman, and belies his image as an Oxford nostalgist or hater of modernity. His proposals were designed to produce the leadership of an urban, industrial, democratic country by fusing new and old elites, bound together by a rejuvenated high culture and serious intellectual training.[35]

'The French university has no liberty, and the English universities have no science,' said Arnold; 'the German universities have both.'[36] Arnold's admiration for Germany was shared by Renan, whose thinking in the 1860s and 1870s also centred on the need to strengthen the national culture. In France, of course, general education had been relegated to secondary schools since Napoleon; to conform to the

[31] *Schools and universities on the Continent*, The Complete Prose Works of Matthew Arnold, ed. R. H. Super, vol. 4 (Ann Arbor, 1964), 14.

[32] Ibid. 254, 262–4, 318–20.

[33] Ibid. 290–2.

[34] Ibid. 322.

[35] N. Hammerstein, 'Matthew Arnolds Vorschlag einer Reform der englischen Universitäten', in L. Kettenacker and others (eds.), *Studien zur Geschichte Englands und der deutsch-britischen Beziehungen: Festschrift für Paul Kluke* (Munich, 1981), 103–29.

[36] *Schools and universities*, 264.

German model, the need was rather to restore serious scientific work, and serious students, to the faculties of letters and science. But despite their weakness, a distinctive ideal of liberal education ran through French higher education; it was shared by secondary and university teachers, and embodied in the traditions of the baccalaureate, the École Normale, and the *agrégation*. Three features may be picked out: the centrality of the classics, an emphasis on performance rather than scholarship, and a continued assertion of the separation of teaching and research. Although the classics were part of a common European culture, in the nineteenth century they also took on national forms. If German neohumanism made a fetish of the Greeks, the British gave at least equal weight to the Romans, seen as precursors of their civic culture and imperial mission. In France, Latin rather than Greek was at the heart of the classical ideal, for the obvious reason that French was a romance language. French and Latin literature were studied together, in schools and faculties, and the great French writers of the seventeenth century were seen as modern classics; this was an inheritance on which university and Catholic teachers could agree. By studying Latin, we are French twice over, said A. A. Cournot, the philosopher and mathematician who was also one of Napoleon III's educational officials.[37] French literary culture differed both from Germany, where the academic study of German language and literature was often seen as challenging rather than complementing the dominance of the classical philologists, and from Britain, where English literature struggled to establish its academic credentials, especially at Oxbridge.

An essential part of literary study in France was rhetoric, and the system gave a high valuation to elegance in written and oral expression. Professors were used to addressing general as well as scholarly audiences, in the Collège de France as well as the faculties, and the key institution of the *agrégation* was essentially a test of rhetorical performance, with no research requirement. This emphasis in French culture could be traced back to the *ancien régime* and the influence of the Jesuits. It was also linked by contemporaries with the needs of a constitutional state in which educated men needed to perform in public bodies and persuade their fellow-citizens. In the new era of 'public opinion', the press and the platform were the key to power, and law faculties were instruments of general as well as technical education. According to Count Salvandy, minister of education in 1838, 'the study of law is no longer just a required preparation for certain professions, as it was once, it has become a necessary element of education for anyone who aspires to serve his country usefully in civil careers.'[38] In France as in other Latin countries, liberal education tended to mean a legal education, and legalist modes of thinking became part of the value system of the elite.

But the rhetorical bias worked against the serious pursuit of research. French academic culture stressed 'success at the lectern' rather than in the library or

[37] A. Cournot, *Des institutions d'instruction publique en France*, Œuvres complètes, vol. 7 (Paris, 1977), 65.

[38] Cited in J. C. Caron, *Générations romantiques: les étudiants de Paris et le Quartier Latin (1814–1851)* (Paris, 1991), 44.

laboratory.[39] Napoleon's reforms had located research mainly in specialized institutes, and there was a positive hostility to seeing the faculties as anything but teaching bodies. Contrasting the national Institut and the École Normale, Cousin declared that 'to the Institut is entrusted the advancement and progress of all branches of human knowledge; to the University, the propagation of those which have arrived at that degree of certainty and practical utility which allow them to be taught in the name of the state'. *Normaliens* should learn that the University is not merely a scientific body, but shares the tasks of the magistrature and the priesthood.[40] For the French clerisy, then, imparting orthodox knowledge was more important than advancing its frontiers. The political atmosphere of the Second Empire hardly discouraged this idea: as one official put it, 'the proper mission of universities is to teach the most undisputed parts of human knowledge; it is not to encourage the inventive spirit, nor to propagate discoveries that are not fully verified'.[41]

The Empire also saw the progress of a reform movement which criticized the French academic tradition as superficial and rhetorical, contrasting it with the seriousness of German scholarship; this was often coupled with an Arnoldian feeling that culture must be strengthened against the insidious pressures of industry and democracy. In 1854, as rector of Lyons, Cournot was lamenting that 'amidst the pleasures of civilization, in the presence of the marvellous triumphs of science and industry, the modern world is threatened with invasion by a barbarism of a new kind. . . . The time seems past when one studied for the simple love of study or through respect for inherited traditions. Now one studies to pass an examination, to have a degree, and finally to have a job.' In 1856, he further denounced 'specialization' (treated as a neologism): if it triumphed, the essential 'idea of a university' would be destroyed.[42] The need to preserve disinterested culture became a further argument, along with the defence of national unity and the secular spirit, for state control of higher education.

In articles and speeches of the 1860s, Renan contrasted the serious spirit of German scholarship, especially in his own field of philology, with the superficial, rhetorical teaching and intellectual nullity of the French faculties. Another theme, and a parallel with Arnold, was the need to revive the intellectual life of the provinces, though in France this meant not founding new faculties but cutting down their number to concentrate effort in a few big centres. In 1871, after France's defeat by Prussia, Renan published reflections on the 'intellectual and moral reform of France' which placed the university question in a wider critique of France's weaknesses, attributed by Renan mainly to the levelling effects of egalitarian democracy

[39] R. Fox, 'Scientific enterprise and the patronage of research in France', *Minerva*, 11 (1973), 453.

[40] J. C. Chevalier, 'Victor Cousin et l'enseignement supérieur', in *Au bonheur des mots: mélanges en l'honneur de Gérald Antoine* (Nancy, 1984), 489. Cf. R. D. Anderson, 'Before and after Humboldt: European universities between the eighteenth and the nineteenth centuries', *History of Higher Education Annual*, 20 (2000), 11.

[41] C. Jourdain (1857), cited in R. D. Anderson, *Education in France 1848–1870* (Oxford, 1975), 229. Cf. Jacob, 'Étude comparative', 108–12.

[42] Speeches reprinted in Cournot, *Des institutions d'instruction publique*, 317, 325–7.

and the enervation caused by Bonapartist centralization. 'High culture', he had written in 1864, was essentially aristocratic and required the support of the state.[43] National regeneration would now require the constitution of a new elite, in which the old aristocracy of birth would be reinforced by a new aristocracy of intellect. For this a thorough reform of French education on decentralized, German lines was needed, and it was in higher education that action was most urgent. Reformed universities would put solid science and reason at the head of society and correct the weaknesses of French cultural life.[44] Renan's reaction to the French defeat and his critique of centralization had much in common with Taine, but he was also a prophet, as we shall see in Chapter 12, of the official movement which transformed the universities under the Third Republic.

Arnold and Renan both saw 'culture' as an instrument which could be used to regenerate their societies. A more pessimistic view was taken by the art historian Jacob Burckhardt and by Friedrich Nietzsche, who both surveyed the scene from the University of Basel. The distinctive cultural landscape of Basel has been described by Carl Schorske and Lionel Gossman.[45] It escaped the liberal convulsions of other Swiss cities in the early nineteenth century; the university was small, and retained a close connection with the city's cosmopolitan merchant class, which valued traditional classical culture. Chairs were filled over many generations by patrician dynasties, and Burckhardt belonged to one of them: his father was first minister at the cathedral, but his family had provided forty professors.[46] In Gossman's view, this milieu encouraged Burckhardt to conduct a lifelong battle in defence of the 'old culture of Europe' against the forces which were destroying it: mass politics and industrialism, the meretriciousness of contemporary bourgeois culture, and the subordination of German cultural values to academic specialization and boastful nationalism.

These were also leading themes for Nietzsche, who was not a native of Basel but became professor of Greek in 1869 at the age of 24. In 1872 he delivered a set of public lectures on 'the future of our educational institutions', and developed his thoughts further in his *Untimely meditations*.[47] While Arnold and Renan looked to the state for salvation, and put their faith in the wider cultivation of science and culture, Nietzsche saw the state as the enemy of true culture, because it reduced it to examination routines, and sought to universalize what was aristocratic by nature.[48]

[43] *Œuvres complètes de Ernest Renan*, ed. H. Psichari, vol. 1 (Paris, 1947), 69, 73.

[44] Ibid. 395–8. Cf. P. Bourdieu, 'Systems of education and systems of thought', in M. F. D. Young (ed.), *Knowledge and control: new directions for the sociology of education* (London, 1971), 201–7.

[45] C. E. Schorske, 'Science as vocation in Burckhardt's Basel', in T. Bender (ed.), *The university and the city: from medieval origins to the present* (New York, 1988), 198–209; N. Bouvier, G. Craig, and L. Gossman, *Geneva, Zurich, Basel: history, culture and national identity* (Princeton, 1994); L. Gossman, *Basel in the age of Burckhardt: a study in unseasonable ideas* (Chicago, 2000). Cf. E. Bonjour, *Die Universität Basel von den Anfängen bis zur Gegenwart 1460–1960* (Basel, 1960), 384, 637.

[46] Schorske, 'Science as vocation', 206.

[47] F. Nietzsche, *Untimely meditations*, ed. D. Breazeale (Cambridge, 1997). Cf. W. H. Bruford, *The German tradition of self-cultivation: 'Bildung' from Humboldt to Thomas Mann* (Cambridge, 1975), 164 ff.

[48] F. Nietzsche, *On the future of our educational institutions. Homer and classical philology*, Complete Works, vol. 6 (Edinburgh, 1909), 12–13, 34, 54, 74, 85, 92.

For the philistine German bourgeoisie, 'culture' had become a matter of lifestyle and social prestige, and things were hardly better in the academic profession, dominated now by careerism and money-making, not by a disinterested love of learning. Useless erudition had replaced true insight, and the decline of the classics foreshadowed a new barbarism. Similar criticisms had already been expressed in trenchantly aphoristic form by Schopenhauer in 1851, and in both cases had something to do with rejection of the author's work by the academic establishment.[49] Nietzsche was attacking the complacency of the German university system at a time when its prestige was unprecedentedly high. In a sense, he was calling for a return to the original ideals of *Bildung*, but proposing institutional reforms was not his style, and his vision was essentially of the scholar as a solitary intellectual aristocrat, detached from the vulgar conditions of everyday life, a genius to whom searchers after truth had a duty to defer.

These prophets identified some of the fundamental shifts of the 1860s and 1870s. One particular target of Burckhardt and Nietzsche, and of Renan in his critique of France, was the superficiality of contemporary bourgeois culture as expressed in the press, the theatre, and literature; criticism of commercial mass culture was to become a staple of academic conservatives. The masses were only just making their weight felt, but the extension of the franchise and of literacy, and the consequent power of democracy, aroused fears which could be countered by strengthening the intellectual aristocracy. Education at all levels was to become an instrument of social integration in the new age of nation-states. And finally, university enrolments, which had been stagnant since the 1830s, now began to rise. The business classes were taking a new interest in higher education, and universities were subject to new social pressures and utilitarian demands.

[49] A. Schopenhauer, *Parerga and paralipomena: short philosophical essays* (Oxford, 1974), ii. 479–90.

8

Enrolments and Social Patterns

According to the scientist Jean-Baptiste Dumas, a reforming official under the Second Empire,

> alongside the wealth represented by landed property and transferable stocks, a new form of wealth has been established and developed: that whose capital consists in a solid and practical education, whose symbols and title-deeds are the degrees and diplomas which are its sanction and its reward. . . . Knowledge becomes then at all levels . . . a form of wealth and property of fixed value.[1]

Dumas was anticipating Pierre Bourdieu's influential concept of cultural or symbolic capital, which is in turn linked with Bourdieu's view that educational systems tend to reproduce the relations of wealth and power from generation to generation. Bourdieu's early work (with Jean-Claude Passeron) focused on the twentieth century, and showed the advantage of the 'inheritors' (*héritiers*) over the 'scholarship-holders' (*boursiers*) in the supposedly democratic French system.[2] Students from families already familiar with the cultural traditions and rituals embodied in elite education had an advantage over those from outside the magic circle, who could only use the system on condition of internalizing its values. Bourdieu and Passeron studied 'the specifically pedagogic mechanisms through which the School contributes towards reproducing the structure of relations between the classes by reproducing the unequal class distribution of cultural capital'.[3] In later work, Bourdieu studied particular French elites and showed how cultural capital interacted with social and economic capital in trans-generational family strategies which differed (for example) among the professional groups associated with the various *grandes écoles*. As under the *ancien régime*, education could be a symbolic confirmation of social standing and prestige gained by other means. Christophe Charle has followed a similar line in his 'prosopographical' approach to university history, which looks closely at defined samples of elite members. These studies have the virtue of directing attention away from the supply of higher education to the demand for it and the functions which it served, and towards the complex nature of bourgeois elites in the nineteenth century, questions which will be discussed at more length in the next chapter.

Empirical and comparative work on nineteenth-century elite education is still

[1] Cited (1861) in R. D. Anderson, *Education in France 1848–1870* (Oxford, 1975), 11.

[2] P. Bourdieu and J. C. Passeron, *Les Héritiers: les étudiants et la culture* (Paris, 1964). The contrast originates with A. Thibaudet, *La République des professeurs* (Paris, 1927).

[3] P. Bourdieu and J. C. Passeron, *Reproduction in education, society and culture* (London, 1977), 188.

dominated by the work of Fritz Ringer, who published his *Education and society in modern Europe* in 1979.[4] This was mainly a comparison of France and Germany, with some material on Britain, and it covered secondary as well as higher education: this is essential, since the boundaries between the two shifted as the 'Humboldtian' division between general culture and specialized study became standard, and access to universities was increasingly regulated by the need to pass school-leaving examinations. The social composition of the student body came to depend on how open secondary schools were to different social classes. Recent work suggests that these schools served quite a wide middle-class range, but had little organic connection with primary or popular education: education for the masses, even when it became compulsory, was in a separate compartment, with no ladder which talented individuals could climb. Primary teachers were themselves normally products of the primary system, and did not attend secondary schools or universities. Widespread literacy and availability of schools might indirectly create a set of values favourable to higher education, as in Germany or Scotland, but it was also possible, as in Italy, Spain, or above all Russia, for sophisticated university systems to coexist with widespread illiteracy.

For Ringer, as for many commentators, a striking feature of elite education was the time-lag or incongruence between the demands of a modernizing, industrializing society and the response of a system which remained attached to traditional and aristocratic values, symbolized by the dominance of the classics. He suggested a three-stage chronology. The 'early industrial phase' lasted from the eighteenth to the middle of the nineteenth century. In this phase, there was 'little connection between higher education and economic life. . . . The system catered to the landowning classes, and it prepared future clergymen, lawyers, doctors, and secondary teachers.' Despite the element of modernization and meritocracy introduced by the needs of bureaucracies, 'there was a clear conflict between the traditional academic culture—that of the preindustrial elites—and the emerging business civilization'.[5] The second phase was the 'high industrial' one, lasting from the 1860s to around 1930. In this phase, more modern types of higher education appeared, serving the needs of commerce and technology, but they almost always had inferior prestige, leading to a dualism or tension within the educational system which was not resolved until the 'late industrial' phase after 1930. Increasing differentiation, particularly in schools, allowed the traditional institutions to carry on much as before, perhaps indeed to shed a broader, 'comprehensive' clientele and to take on a more narrowly elite character. The long-term movement over all three phases was for the bond between education and society to become tighter, as factors

[4] F. Ringer, *Education and society in modern Europe* (London, 1979). A foretaste was F. Ringer, 'The education of elites in modern Europe', *History of Education Quarterly*, 18 (1978), 159–72. Significant discussions were W. Frijhoff, 'Sur l'utilité d'une histoire comparée des systèmes éducatifs nationaux', *Histoire de l'Education*, 13 (1981), 29–44; P. Lundgreen, 'Bildung und Besitz: Einheit oder Inkongruenz in der europäischen Sozialgeschichte? Kritische Auseinandersetzung mit einer These von Fritz Ringer', *Geschichte und Gesellschaft*, 7 (1981), 262–75; and reviews by R. Fox in *Minerva*, 18 (1980), 164–70, C. R. Day in *History of Education Quarterly*, 22 (1982), 379–85.

[5] Ringer, *Education and society*, 2–3.

like patronage and kinship (though not wealth) faded out of the picture, and as the state strengthened its control of universities and schools.

A rather similar chronology to Ringer's was proposed by Hartmut Kaelble, focusing on the issue of educational opportunity rather than incongruence of values. He suggests a first 'era of charity opportunities' in which (as for Ringer) education was not directly linked to economic development, and the demand for higher education was very limited. There was some mobility from below into the church and the bureaucracy, and 'an uncoordinated charity system for low income students did exist, sustained by churches, small private foundations, individual notables, family connections, and university members'. Following a pattern familiar before 1789, this 'could produce a relatively high proportion of students from families below the middle classes, such as master artisans, dependent artisans, traditional white collar employees, and farmers'. But in the 'era of competitive opportunities', the links between education and industrialization intensified. University graduation became a 'gateway to well-paid and prestigious positions' and one of the transmitters of social status, though still not as important as property and family. In this more competitive situation, social mobility could not be left to the hazards of charity, and access to higher education through schools became more systematized and more socially restricted. Such expansion in opportunities as took place benefited mainly the lower middle rather than the working classes. Kaelble sees this phase lasting at least until 1914, after which it was to give way to the era of 'welfare opportunities'.[6] The long-term movement was towards a system which was stratified, tied to social class, and responsive to economic demands.

For measuring the conformity of particular systems to broader comparative patterns, Ringer suggested three criteria which have been widely adopted by other historians: *inclusiveness*, measured by student enrolments; *progressiveness*, measured by the degree to which schools or universities were open to families from the middle or lower social strata; and *segmentation* or 'tracking', which refers to the differentiation between institutions.[7] These issues were explored further in a collaborative work, influenced by Bourdieu, in which the systematization and segmentation of secondary and higher education were discussed for Germany, France, and England.[8] The contributors included Ringer, and also Detlef Müller, whose work on secondary education in Germany suggested a progressive restriction of opportunity. Müller challenged the orthodox view of the neohumanistic gymnasium in the early nineteenth century. Far from being confined to a narrow elite, it was a multi-functional school in which university preparation was a minority interest. Various types of school grew up in a pragmatic way without clear

[6] H. Kaelble, 'Educational opportunities and government policies in Europe in the period of industrialization', in P. Flora and A. J. Heidenheimer (eds.), *The development of welfare states in Europe and America* (New Brunswick, NJ, 1981), 242–3.

[7] Ringer, *Education and society*, 22–31; Ringer has revisited the first two themes: 'Patterns of access to the modern European universities: rates of enrollment', *History of Higher Education Annual*, 14 (1994), 101–25, and 'Patterns of access to the modern European universities: the social origins of students', *History of Higher Education Annual*, 15 (1995), 127–42.

[8] D. K. Müller, F. Ringer, and B. Simon (eds.), *The rise of the modern educational system: structural change and social reproduction 1870–1920* (Cambridge, 1987).

social boundaries between them. It was only in the last decades of the nineteenth century, as part of a conservative response to overcrowding, the so-called 'qualifications crisis', that schools were sorted into a clear hierarchy.[9] Segmentation in Wilhelmine Germany meant preserving the socially exclusive character of the gymnasium, and hence of university education, by diverting demand into modern and socially inferior alternatives.

Ringer and Kaelble would both see the 1860s and 1870s as the key period for transition from their first to their second phase, and the significance of these decades as a turning-point in political and religious change has already been suggested. It was also the time when university enrolments began to rise after a long stagnation, and another collaborative work of the 1980s, edited by Konrad Jarausch, compared the growth, differentiation, and 'social opening' of universities in Germany, England, Russia, and the United States (but not France) between 1860 and 1930. Summarizing a set of complex findings, Jarausch saw a 'seismic shift' (originally Lawrence Stone's phrase) from the elite university to the 'middle-class university' of modern times; the decisive changes had already occurred before 1914.[10] Among the many forces driving this shift were growing population, urbanization, the progress of science, the greater need of industry for experts and managers, the expansion of state bureaucracies, the growth of a white-collar bourgeoisie able to afford more advanced education, the idea that higher education was for women as well as men, and the modernization and improvement of secondary schools, including the opening of universities to students with modern as well as classical diplomas—in 1900 in Germany, in 1902 in France, in both cases against much conservative opposition.[11] Even in the traditional professions, attendance requirements became more onerous, forcing students to stay longer—the standard medical curriculum had risen from four to five years by the end of the century, and in Germany the length of study had risen steadily, to six or seven years in reality in medicine by the 1900s, and five years in philosophy, leisurely national habits which were to persist.[12] But perhaps the broadest explanation was the progress of professionalization and the expansion of graduate careers.

The nineteenth century, it has been said, was the 'century of the professions'.[13] But

[9] D. Muller, *Sozialstruktur und Schulsystem: Aspekte zum Strukturwandel des Schulwesens im 19. Jahrhundert* (Göttingen, 1977). In English, D. Müller, 'The qualifications crisis and school reform in late nineteenth-century Germany', *History of Education*, 9 (1980), 315–31, and his chapter in Müller, Ringer, and Simon, *Rise of the Modern Educational System.*

[10] K. H. Jarausch (ed.), *The transformation of higher learning 1860–1930: expansion, diversification, social opening, and professionalization in England, Germany, Russia, and the United States* (Chicago, 1983), 10, 26.

[11] C. E. McClelland, 'Structural change and social reproduction in German universities 1870–1920', *History of Education*, 15 (1986), 185.

[12] T. N. Bonner, *Becoming a physician: medical education in Britain, France, Germany and the United States, 1750–1945* (New York, 1995), 287; M. Mechow, *Berliner Studenten 1810–1914* (Berlin, 1975), 80.

[13] H. Siegrist (ed.), *Bürgerliche Berufe: Zur Sozialgeschichte der freien und akademischen Berufe im internationalen Vergleich* (Göttingen, 1988), 42. The literature on professionalization is large: work especially relevant to universities includes W. Conze and J. Kocka (eds.), *Bildungsbürgertum im 19. Jahrhundert. Teil I. Bildungssystem und Professionalisierung in internationalen Vergleichen* (Stuttgart, 1985); P. Lundgreen, 'Akademiker und "Professionen" in Deutschland', *Historische Zeitschrift*, 254

their history differed significantly between countries. In Germany and central Europe, the professions had emerged under the wing of the state, and overlapped with a bureaucracy which was itself professionalized at an early stage. Here states followed the lead of Prussia by recruiting through state examinations rather than relying on university certification, and this was extended to professions like medicine, teaching, and the church. In France, and in countries which followed its model like Spain and Italy, the state delegated the examining process to the universities, but prescribed the curriculum and qualifications in rigid detail. In these countries, there was more space between the bureaucracy and the 'free' professions, which were regulated by the state but enjoyed some self-government and operated in the market. In France, for example, advocates and other lawyers in private practice were a powerful independent force, and significant participants in political life, whereas in Germany most lawyers began their careers with a state appointment. A third model was the British one, in which informal methods of training and 'learning on the job' retained their appeal, and the state was slow to assume the role of regulator.

The nineteenth century saw both a tightening up of qualifications in the existing learned professions, and the development of professional ambitions in such new vocational fields as engineering, architecture, veterinary medicine, dentistry, pharmacy, and schoolteaching. The familiar characteristics of professionalization included the adoption of objective, universalist criteria based on formal education and examinations, emphasis on a body of knowledge with a strong enough theoretical content to justify university training, and a monopoly for professional bodies which controlled entry and elaborated codes of professional behaviour. These moves were designed to reinforce social prestige as well as expertise, and to assert the liberal or gentlemanly status of the profession, which often meant insisting on a classical education as a prior requirement to professional training—the medical profession, despite its basis in science, was particularly conservative on this point. The effect could be to raise social barriers and make the professions more exclusive than before. 'The study of medicine is becoming a monopoly of the wealthy', complained one German professor in 1896.[14]

Medicine was the profession whose training was most internationally uniform, whereas law reflected national intellectual traditions and political cultures. In Germany and countries influenced by it, law had a virtual monopoly of recruitment to the civil service, and attracted large numbers of students for that reason. In France, Italy, and many other countries, law was a favourite form of general education for members of the elite whatever their career intentions, and usually the largest university faculty. In Britain, by contrast, law was seen purely as a qualification for practitioners, and law faculties had a very limited role in universities where they existed at all. In the third of the learned professions, the church, the differences between Catholic and Protestant countries remained significant. In

(1992), 657–70; essays by R. Torstendahl and M. Burrage in S. Rothblatt and B. Wittrock (eds.), *The European and American university since 1800: historical and sociological essays* (Cambridge, 1993).

[14] Bonner, *Becoming a physician*, 310, and cf. 347.

France, Spain, and Italy the training of priests was lost to the universities, and faculties of theology were eventually abolished. In Catholic Germany, the faculties were notable for recruiting their students from the peasantry and lower middle class, which was good for social mobility but bad for the social status of the priesthood. In Protestant Germany, pastors retained their high status as members of the *Bildungsbürgertum*, and were mostly recruited from it, though a minority were sons of schoolteachers or minor officials.[15] Before 1848, this was still an 'overcrowded' profession which had a strong attraction for the intellectually able, but while other career opportunities expanded (teaching was a secular equivalent) the demand for clerics had reached its ceiling. However, a married clergy made the parsonage, manse, or *Pfarrhaus* a reservoir of cultural capital and a powerhouse of educational ambition, and it is likely that in Protestant countries clerical families produced more university students proportionately than any other occupation.

We may now return to the question of university enrolments. Statistics can be found both for individual universities and for countries as a whole, but there are many difficulties in compiling and interpreting them. Their significance depended on which institutions were included, the average length of attendance, how students were defined, what allowance was made for part-time attendance, the presence of foreign students, and the impact of student migration, domestic or international. Figures become more reliable from the 1860s onwards, when bureaucratic reports and statistical surveys began to reflect the growing interest of governments in the issue. For many countries, figures are only available sporadically, but annual series exist for Germany, and have been intensively studied.[16] There is also reasonably reliable serial evidence for Austria, Belgium, and Holland, but there are no national statistics for France until 1876, and in Britain evidence is firmer for Scotland than for England.[17] Over the long term, European universities do not seem to have expanded much between the end of the eighteenth century and the 1860s or 1870s, but then began a steady rise which in many cases continued until 1914.

The German evidence shows striking growth in the post-1815 period, reaching a peak in the early 1830s, but then a sharp fall followed by a period of stagnation which lasted until the late 1860s. Sources agree that there were just under 8,000 students in the 1780s, but by 1830 there were 15,870. Numbers then fell to 11,930 in 1835, and remained within a few hundred of 12,000 before rising to 13,885 in 1865, though by that date there were also 2,000 students in Technical High Schools. But even if the two sectors are taken together, the growth of higher education barely kept pace with the rise in Germany's population, and it was not until the 1870s that the universities

[15] O. Janz, 'Zwischen Amt und Profession: Die evangelische Pfarrerschaft im 19. Jahrhundert', in Siegrist, *Bürgerliche Berufe*, 181.

[16] Earlier sources for Germany are discussed in Chapter 1. For the 19th century, the standard source is now H. Titze, *Datenhandbuch zur deutschen Bildungsgeschichte. I. Hochschulen*, 2 parts (Göttingen, 1987–95). There are useful summaries for the post-1870 period, also covering Austria and Switzerland, in B. vom Brocke and P. Krüger (eds.), *Hochschulpolitik im Föderalismus: Die Protokolle der Hochschulkonferenzen der deutschen Bundesstaaten und Österreich 1898 bis 1918* (Berlin, 1994), 421–36.

[17] For France, Ringer, *Education and society*, 335–41. For England, R. Lowe, 'The expansion of higher education in England', in Jarausch, *Transformation*, 37–56.

regained the 1830 level.[18] It is unlikely that other countries saw such a large expansion compared with the *ancien régime*, but the pattern of a peak around 1830 followed by decline and slow recovery may have been typical. At Oxford and Cambridge, matriculations rose steeply from 1800 to around 1820, then remained on a plateau until the 1850s, when (coinciding with the beginnings of reform) expansion resumed strongly.[19] In Scotland there were perhaps 4,250 students in 1826, but only 3,399 when regular annual statistics began in 1861—still more than in England, which had a population ten times as great but only 3,385 students.[20] In Holland, there were 786 students in 1820, and 1,527 in 1835, but totals thereafter were mostly between 1,200 and 1,400 until growth resumed, as in Germany, in the 1870s.[21] In Belgium, on the other hand, there was a dip in the early 1830s, but steady growth thereafter.[22] These fluctuations may have something to do with relations between the economic cycle and recruitment to the professions, or with changes in the political climate. But declining enrolments could also result from the expansion of secondary schools and the transfer of teaching to them. In Austria, reform in 1848–9 transferred two years of preparatory teaching from the philosophy faculty to the gymnasium, with a corresponding rise in the university entry age. The effect on university enrolments was striking: there were 10,369 students in 1830 and 11,566 in 1835, but by 1850 there were only 5,697, and this level persisted until the 1860s, rising only to 6,720 by 1865. At Vienna, there may have been 5,258 students in 1844–5, of whom 2,823 were in the philosophy faculty, but by 1850 numbers were down to 2,444.[23]

There was no country in which student enrolments did not expand between 1870 and the eve of the First World War, usually three- or fourfold. In Germany, numbers in the universities rose from 15,359 in 1872 to 54,999 in 1911. If other forms of higher education are included, predominantly the Technical High Schools, the totals were 20,576 in 1872 and 70,280 in 1911. In France they rose from 11,204 in 1876 to 42,037 in 1911, in England from 5,530 in 1871 to 26,432 in 1911, in Austria from 8,532 in 1870 to 28,098 in 1910, in Holland from 1,240 in 1870 to 4,863 in 1910, in Belgium from 2,521 in 1870 to 8,157 in 1912.[24] The 1870s and 1880s were generally a period of

[18] Titze, *Datenhandbuch*, Part 1, 27–8.

[19] L. Stone (ed.), *The university in society. I. Oxford and Cambridge from the 14th to the early 19th Century* (Princeton, 1975), 6, 91.

[20] R. D. Anderson, *Education and opportunity in Victorian Scotland: schools and universities* (Oxford, 1983), 346–51; Lowe, 'Expansion', 45.

[21] N. L. Dodde, *Het Nederlandse onderwijs verandert* (Muiderberg, 1983), 50, 52.

[22] J. Art, 'Les *Rapports triennaux sur l'état de l'enseignement supérieur*: un arrière-fond pour des recherches ultérieures sur l'histoire des élites belges entre 1814 et 1914', *Revue Belge d'Histoire Contemporaine*, 17 (1986), 207–9.

[23] J. Hochgerner, *Studium und Wissenschaftsentwicklung im Habsburgerreich: Studentengeschichte seit der Gründung der Universität Wien bis zum Ersten Weltkrieg* (Vienna, 1983), 215–21: overall totals for 'Austria' as distinct from Hungary, i.e. the western part of the empire, but excluding Lombardy-Venetia. Vienna figure for 1844–5 in J. C. Caron, 'Paris, capitale universitaire de l'Europe (1815–1848)', in J. Schriewer, E. Keiner, and C. Charle (eds.), *Sozialer Raum und akademische Kulturen: A la recherche de l'espace universitaire européen* (Frankfurt, 1993), 442–3.

[24] Brocke and Krüger, *Hochschulpolitik*, 431 (Germany), 425 (Austria); G. Weisz, *The emergence of modern universities in France 1863–1914* (Princeton, 1983), 236; Jarausch, *Transformation*, 45 (incorrectly summarized and attributed to 'Britain' on p. 13); Dodde, *Nederlandse onderwijs*, 52; Art, '*Rapports*

rapid expansion, but in some countries it then levelled off, while in others it continued, notably in Germany, where numbers in 1914 reached 60,234 in the universities alone, 75,271 in all higher education.[25] The significance of this expansion differed between countries. In France and England, there was an element of 'catching up', reflected in the development of provincial universities, but in Scotland, with its precocious university development, numbers less than doubled, from 3,984 students in 1871 to 5,924 in 1911.[26] In Russia, the numbers in higher education (universities and technical education) rose from 8,750 in 1859 to 127,000 in 1914, but the ratio of students to population remained below that in the west.[27] By the later nineteenth century, the presence of foreign students could have a serious distorting effect, notably in Switzerland, where there were 3,152 students in 1891 and 7,686 in 1914, but where no fewer than 35 per cent and 63 per cent at those dates were foreigners, including an exceptional number of women.[28] In all countries, indeed, the admission of women was an important cause of rising enrolments, though there were few where they formed more than 10 per cent of the total even in 1914.

This growth in numbers has to be seen against a rising general population, the rate of which differed between countries. Between 1870 and 1910, the population of Germany rose from 41 to 65 milllion, but of France only from 36 to 39 million. The simplest index for national comparisons, often used at the time, is to relate student enrolments to total population. More satisfactory is to estimate the percentage of the relevant male age-cohort attending a university. Here the difficulty lies in defining the appropriate age-group and the notional length of a university education, but Kaelble has made estimates for a number of countries, which can be supplemented from other sources. From these it appears that around 1870 the typical proportion was 0.5 per cent. This was achieved in France, Germany, and Italy. Countries with participation above this rate included Scotland (1.4), Spain (0.9), Austria and Belgium (0.7), and Sweden and Norway (0.5 or 0.7 according to the source used), while those below it included England (0.3), Hungary and Portugal (0.2), and Russia (0.14 in 1859, 0.17 in 1880). The number of universities, and hence ease of geographical access, seems to have been a factor in encouraging enrolments, as well as the degree of urbanization and economic development. By the eve of the First World War, the norm had risen from 0.5 to 1.2 or 1.3 per cent. Estimates for Germany range from 1.3 to 1.6, for France from 1.2 to 1.7, for England up to 1.3. Countries approximating to the norm included Belgium, Holland, Italy, Finland, and Spain; those above it, Austria (1.7) and Scotland (1.9); those below, Hungary (0.8), Russia (0.8), Portugal (0.2), and the Scandinavian countries

triennaux', 211. Cf. J. Ben-David, 'The growth of the professions and the class system', in R. Bendix and S. M. Lipset (eds.), *Class, status, and power: social stratification in comparative perspective*, 2nd edn. (London, 1967), 463.

25 Brocke and Krüger, *Hochschulpolitik*, 431.

26 R. D. Anderson, 'Education and society in modern Scotland: a comparative perspective', *History of Education Quarterly*, 25 (1985), 467.

27 P. L. Alston, 'The dynamics of educational expansion in Russia', in Jarausch, *Transformation*, 107.

28 Brocke and Krüger, *Hochschulpolitik*, 425.

(Sweden 0.9, Norway 0.8, Denmark 0.4). The real extent of university education thus approximately doubled between the 1860s and 1914.[29]

Can this fairly be described as a 'seismic shift'? Even a cohort figure of 1.2 or 1.3 per cent seems very low, and suggests that universities still catered for a narrow elite. Nor was the recruitment of secondary schools much wider: the percentage of the cohort, male and female, attending secondary schools in Prussia and France in 1911 was 3.2 and 2.6 respectively, but many of these left early, and those reaching the *Abitur* or baccalaureate stage were 1.2 in Prussia and 1.1 in France respectively—representing about 9,100 and 7,200 individuals annually.[30] These low figures present something of a historical puzzle: on the one hand the middle class defined by social historians was substantially larger than this; on the other, data about the social origins of students show that quite a broad range of classes was represented within the universities. One possible answer is that higher education, and advanced secondary schooling, were of interest to only a fraction of the middle class, those who were interested in their specific function of preparing for the professions and public service. Françoise Mayeur thinks that in France the business class long remained uninterested in secondary education, and that 'the baccalaureate took a very long time to become the mark of the bourgeoisie, as it undoubtedly was by the eve of 1914'.[31] Even then, education was far from being the universal mechanism for allocating social position which it has since become. Most middle-class children in the nineteenth century had a short and practical education, and as long as the working classes had an even shorter one, or none at all, this served the need for social differentiation. Only when popular education became more developed did the search for qualifications become a middle-class imperative. Therefore in the nineteenth century the elite educational system did not reproduce the elite power structure directly, but was skewed to specific forms of reproduction and mobility where cultural capital gave some advantage over birth and wealth.

Universities were perennially accused of producing too many qualified men for the posts available, so creating a dissatisfied 'intellectual proletariat'. That term was invented in 1851 by the conservative German publicist Wilhelm Riehl, but complaints about overcrowding were rife in the 1830s and 1840s, and the 1848 revolutions could be conveniently blamed on alienated intellectuals. Frustrated in their career ambitions, such men took out their discontent in demagogic journalism and political agitation.[32] This idea became a standard part of conservative rhetoric, but

[29] The main sources are Ringer, 'Patterns of access . . . rates of enrollment', 111; Kaelble, 'Educational opportunities', 247; Jarausch, *Transformation*, 16, 107 (Russia). For France (1876), Ringer, *Education and Society*, 335. Cf. C. Charle and J. Verger, *Histoire des universités* (Paris, 1994), 120–2; P. Windolf, *Expansion and structural change: higher education in Germany, the United States, and Japan 1870–1990* (Boulder, Colo., 1997), 259–62. It is not always clear how women students have been allowed for in these calculations.

[30] Ringer, *Education and society*, 272, 316.

[31] F. Mayeur, *De la Révolution à l'école républicaine*, Histoire générale de l'enseignement et de l'éducation en France, ed. L. H. Parias, vol. 3 (Paris, 1981), 103.

[32] L. O'Boyle, 'The problem of an excess of educated men in western Europe 1800–1850', *Journal of Modern History*, 42 (1970), 471–95; cf. R. Chartier, 'Espace et imaginaire social: les "intellectuels aliénés",

the reality was more complex. In the case of France, Alan Spitzer argues that there was no shortage of official and professional posts in the Restoration period, even though 'the great career factory of the Napoleonic university system had just begun to spew out the first eager cohorts of the meritocracy'.[33] The theory works better for the revolutions of 1830, when the peak in university numbers occurred, than for 1848, though a frustrated intelligentsia of recent graduates, the under-employed lawyer and the demagogic journalist, were certainly recognizable figures on the political and social scene. Career blockage might be due to individual failings, but it was more satisfying to blame it on the system or on the iron grip of gerontocracy, and perceptions could be as important as reality.

Hartmut Titze gives perceptions an important role in his attempt to find a cyclical pattern in university enrolments, and in the shifting balance between the different professional faculties. He argued that when a profession appeared relatively open, it sucked students into it, leading after a regular interval to overcrowding, which then deterred students and diverted them into other occupations. During phases of expansion, faculties attracted students from a variety of backgrounds, but in phases of contraction there was greater self-recruitment—the sons of lawyers, doctors, or pastors had family advantages in a shrinking market. Titze claimed that in Germany regular enrolment cycles can be identified over nearly 200 years, from the mid-eighteenth century to the Weimar republic, and his data seem to support this claim.[34] In the nature of the theory, the cycles varied for each faculty as the relative attractiveness of the different professions shifted, but it does not provide an explanation for long-term changes in university recruitment, though the stagnation of German enrolments from the mid-1830s seems to fit the pattern. It is also probable that there were cyclical shifts between university and non-university careers: during periods of economic expansion there may be more opportunities in commerce and industry than in the professions, whereas the latter provide a refuge when the economy slumps; this would result in an inverse relationship between economic growth and university enrolments. Some tentative attempts have been made to apply cyclical concepts to other countries,[35] but Titze's work depended on conditions which only Germany fully satisfies: reliable long-term enrolment statistics, a fairly stable university structure, and a close relationship between university qualifications and the flow into the professions.[36]

Complaints about the intellectual proletariat indicated strains and imbalances in the reproductive role of universities, but not necessarily any widening of their social

XVIIe–XIXe siècles', in J. Le Goff and B. Köpeczi (eds.), *Objet et méthodes de l'histoire de la culture* (Paris, 1982), 85–97.

[33] A. B. Spitzer, *The French generation of 1820* (Princeton, 1987), 227.

[34] H. Titze, 'Die zyklische Überproduktion von Akademikern im 19. und 20. Jahrhundert', *Geschichte und Gesellschaft*, 10 (1984), 92–121. See also by Titze, 'Enrollment expansion and academic overcrowding in Germany', in Jarausch, *Transformation*, 57–88; 'Überfüllungskrisen in akademischen Karrieren: eine Zyklustheorie', *Zeitschrift für Pädagogik*, 27 (1981), 187–224; 'Expansion universitaire et sélection scolaire: bilan d'une controverse biséculaire', in C. Charle (ed.), *Les Universités germaniques, XIXe–XXe siècles*, special no. of *Histoire de l'Éducation*, 62 (1994), 31–54.

[35] e.g. W. Otterspeer, *De wiekslag van hun geest: de Leidse Universiteit in de negentiende eeuw* (The Hague, 1992), 578–9.

[36] Ringer, 'Patterns of access . . . rates of enrollment', 102–3.

intake. How far was university education 'progressive', and how far did it promote social mobility? Pushed to its limit, Bourdieu's theory would imply a closed circle of generational reproduction, but this was clearly not the case. In a society with an expanding middle class, there was always room for new blood from below, subject to the expanding and contracting cycles identified by Titze, and there were also permanent opportunities within the structure of the educational system for individuals to climb the social ladder. If the sons of artisans or clerks, however few, became lawyers, doctors, or state officials, then some social mobility was taking place. In practice, it often took place in stages: poorer students aimed first at the church or schoolteaching, which could provide a living as soon as examinations had been passed, unlike the bureaucracy or law, where there was usually a long period of minimal income which needed continuing family support. The academic profession itself followed the latter pattern with the *Privatdozent* system. Medicine came somewhere between: it was easy to set up in practice, but not so easy to make a living, or to get access to salaried hospital appointments. Thus the social character of the faculties varied, law normally being the most exclusive, and theology the least.

Data on the social origins of students are always patchy, and the problems of defining occupations make comparison difficult; the terms used in different languages often corresponded to different conceptualizations of the social structure, and it is difficult to compare like with like in complex and rapidly changing societies.[37] In Germany, for example, it has been usual to draw a sharp distinction between *Bildung*, the university-educated class, and *Besitz* ('possession' or property), the wealthy industrial and commercial class. Elsewhere, the lines which divided the 'business class' or 'economic elite' from other groups, and the different levels of wealth and property within that class, are often difficult to discern. As with most statistics, those for Germany are the fullest, and one thing which they show clearly is that even in the 1900s university education was virtually closed to the working class. Annual statistics for Prussia, amply confirmed from other sources, show that students whose fathers were workers were hardly more than 0.5 per cent at any time between 1886 and 1914.[38] According to the industrialist Walther Rathenau, 'glass walls are raised on all sides, transparent but unclimbable. On the far side lie freedom, self-determination, wealth, and power. The keys to the forbidden land are called education and fortune, and both are hereditary.'[39] And Friedrich Paulsen in the 1900s thought that although 'in Germany, more than in the western countries, student bodies are recruited from all the strata of society', yet 'a large and growing section of the population, the new workingman's class, is not represented at the universities at all'. The egalitarianism of the old German ideal had disappeared, he thought, and snobbery and social exclusiveness were rife among students and professors.[40]

[37] See generally Ringer, 'Patterns of access . . . social origins'.

[38] Titze, *Datenhandbuch*, 240–1.

[39] Cited in K. E. Jeismann, *Das Preussische Gymnasium in Staat und Gesellschaft. II. Höhere Bildung zwischen Reform und Reaktion 1817–1859* (Stuttgart, 1996), 19.

[40] F. Paulsen, *The German universities and university study* (London, 1906), 125–6.

In Germany and elsewhere, the barriers faced by the new working class were both cultural and financial. Kaelble and Detlef Müller seem justified in arguing that, while older forms of charitable aid declined, scholarship systems which would systematically seek out and promote talent still lay in the future. Without these, and without some opening up of secondary schools, the road was barred to the working class. Paulsen estimated the cost of a university education at 1,200–1,500 marks per annum; this was equivalent to 1,500–1,875 francs or £60–75, and these seem valid estimates for France and Britain. In the British case, the cost of a civic or Scottish university was perhaps a little lower than this, though at Oxford and Cambridge it was more like £200.[41] But even the lower figure corresponded to the whole annual income of all but the most skilled workers. If the working class remained excluded, the lower middle or intermediate class might not be. German usage calls this group the *Mittelstand*, and distinguishes usefully between the old *Mittelstand* of artisans, craftworkers, and peasants and the new, white-collar *Mittelstand* which expanded rapidly at the end of the nineteenth century—clerks, shop assistants, minor officials, schoolteachers, and the like. If they lived at home, attended the local university, and took advantage of traditional sources of financial aid, members of these groups might achieve a university education. In Germany and Austria, poorer students were helped by residences (of a far more Spartan kind than Oxbridge colleges), 'free tables', and the reduction or remission of fees. At Vienna, a sample of 933 students in 1848 showed that 543 paid no fees at all, and only forty-two paid the full rate; 356 (38 per cent) were the sons of artisans or minor officials.[42] But much depended on the nature of secondary schooling: the lycée, gymnasium, and their equivalents were intellectually exclusive, at least in principle, and they charged high fees; but they were usually situated in towns, they were accessible to day pupils, and their public character made them open to all citizens regardless of class or confession. Many students embarked on the classical curriculum without expecting to finish it, and only those with enough money or cultural capital could rely on going further. Yet the initial openness of the schools could awaken new ambitions, and there was the chance of a talented but poor pupil being noticed and given some kind of financial help. The absence of schools of this kind in England was what critics like Arnold deplored.

The German data on students' social origins suggest a three-part chronology: stagnation down to 1870 when the universities remained dominated by the *Bildungsbürgertum* whose reproduction they guaranteed; a first wave of expansion in the 1870s and 1880s marked by an influx of students from the business class, a process dubbed 'plutocratization' by contemporaries; and a second wave in the 1900s which saw buoyant recruitment from the *Mittelstand*, which retained its proportionate position in an expanding system. For the early nineteenth century, a

[41] R. D. Anderson, 'Universities and elites in modern Britain', *History of Universities*, 10 (1991), 236; S. Rothblatt, *The revolution of the dons: Cambridge and society in Victorian England* (London, 1968), 65–75.

[42] G. Stimmer, 'Die Mythologisierung der Revolution von 1848 als Modell einer Studentenrevolution', in *Student und Hochschule im 19. Jahrhundert: Studien und Materialen* (Göttingen, 1975), 293.

fairly consistent pattern emerges from figures for individual universities analysed by Ringer and Jarausch.[43] Over 40 per cent of the students, and sometimes over 50 per cent, were drawn from the bureaucracy and the professions. Nobles also used the universities, but some were more fashionable than others—over the period 1777–1867, Göttingen and Heidelberg had 14 and 13 per cent respectively, but Kiel only 6 per cent.[44] In this period, the sons of wealthy industrialists and merchants accounted for 15–20 per cent at most. Thus taken together, at least 70 per cent came from the wealthy or privileged classes, and most of them would be the sons of university graduates. Of the remaining 30 per cent, virtually none were the sons of unskilled workers, whether rural or urban. Some were the sons of skilled artisans, but more often of minor officials, clerks, and shopkeepers.

In the 1870s a clear shift began, and the percentage from the *Bildungsbürgertum* fell to about a third. Their places were taken partly by the business class, partly by more sons of minor officials. A sample covering Berlin, Bonn, Leipzig, and students from Württemberg shows that in the 1860s 42 per cent of the students still came from the professional or official classes and 23 per cent from *Besitz*; but the share of *Bildung* then declined steadily to 30 per cent on the eve of 1914, and that of *Besitz* rose to 38 per cent in the 1890s and was still 36 per cent in the 1910s. The *Mittelstand* consistently represented about a third, but students from the lower classes were a fraction of 1 per cent.[45] The universities in this sample were probably more bourgeois than others: figures for all universities in Prussia suggest that by 1911 *Bildung* had fallen to 21 per cent, while the *Mittelstand* rose to over half.[46] This large lower-middle-class presence has impressed historians, who see it as evidence for the vitality of Wilhelmine society, while also being a source of social tensions and conservative political reactions. The lower middle class, says Jarausch, 'became the numerically dominant student group in the last years of the Second Empire. The adaptation of artisans and peasants to high industrialization was more successful than has often been assumed'; thus the attempt to limit social mobility by the segmentation of secondary education, which was a response to the first wave of expansion, was perhaps less successful than Ringer and Müller claimed.[47] Hans-Ulrich Wehler agrees with Jarausch on this point, but while Jarausch stresses the decline in the *Bildungsbürgertum*'s position, Wehler considers that, by retaining 20 per cent of the places, given their small share of the total population, this group had

[43] Ringer, *Education and Society*, 301–5; K. Jarausch, 'Die neuhumanistische Universität und die bürgerliche Gesellschaft 1800–1870: Eine quantitative Untersuchung zur Sozialstruktur der Studentenschaften deutscher Universitäten', *Darstellungen und Quellen zur Geschichte der deutschen Einheitsbewegung im neunzehnten und zwanzigsten Jahrhundert*, 11 (1981), 32–44; discussed together in Ringer, 'Patterns of access . . . social origins', 130–4. Cf. K. Jarausch, *Deutsche Studenten 1800–1970* (Frankfurt, 1984), 24–34.

[44] Jarausch, 'Die neuhumanistische Universität', 39.

[45] K. Jarausch, 'The social transformation of the university: the case of Prussia 1865–1914', *Journal of Social History*, 12 (1978–9), 625; K. Jarausch, *Students, society and politics in Imperial Germany: the rise of academic illiberalism* (Princeton, 1982), 125.

[46] K. H. Jarausch, 'Frequenz und Struktur: Zur Sozialgeschichte der Studenten im Kaiserreich', in P. Baumgart (ed.), *Bildungspolitik in Preussen zur Zeit des Kaiserreichs* (Stuttgart, 1980) 138–42, 144. Cf. Ringer, 'Patterns of access . . . social origins', 131; Windolf, *Expansion and structural change*, 47–50.

[47] Jarausch, 'Social transformation', 627; 'Frequenz und Struktur', 130–1.

been 'astonishingly effective in defending access to the traditional graduate career paths and therewith to highly prized cultural and social capital'.[48] As McClelland puts it, the expansion of recruitment broke down the closed circle of elite membership, but did not necessarily disturb 'the ability of the traditional elites to "reproduce" their own social standing in their children'.[49] One symptom of this was that expansion was concentrated in the philosophy faculties, the gates of the more privileged law and medical faculties being better guarded. Between 1890 and 1910, students in philosophy (including science) more than trebled—from 7,809 to 27,736—while those in law grew by 61 per cent and in medicine by 24 per cent. In 1890, 27 per cent of students were in philosophy, but 52 per cent in 1910, when law and medicine accounted for 20 per cent each, and theology for a mere 8 per cent.[50] Since the philosophy faculty led to no specific career except teaching, contemporaries may have been justified in worrying about the social effects of this expansion, though the war was to mop up surplus manpower, and a real crisis of graduate employment came only in the 1920s.

The presence of lower-middle-class students was a notable feature of the German universities, but when less than 2 per cent of the national age-cohort attended a university these students could be a significant proportion of the student body while being a tiny minority of their own class. When statistics for students' social origins are complete enough to be compared with national censuses, it is possible to work out what percentage of a particular occupational group became students, and to calculate the ratio between a group's share in the university population and its share in the general population (an 'opportunity' or 'selectivity' ratio). John Craig has done this for Germany, and the results confirm the continuing dominance of the *Bildungsbürgertum*. In Prussia in 1911, for example, 32 per cent of sons in this group went to university, compared with only 3 per cent for the entrepreneurial class and old *Mittelstand* together, 6.5 per cent for the new *Mittelstand*, and 0.25 per cent for the working classes. The *Bildungsbürgertum* had nineteen times the share of the student population which they would have had if all groups had been equally represented, compared with 1.9 for the entrepreneurial class and old *Mittelstand*: in other words, the former were ten times more likely to go to the university than the latter, confirming the limited appeal of university education even within the bourgeoisie.[51] Opportunity ratios have also been calculated for Scotland in the 1860s, and show a similar over-representation of the professional classes. A clergyman's son was a hundred times more likely to go to the university than a miner's.[52]

[48] H. U. Wehler, *Deutsche Gesellschaftsgeschichte. III. Von der 'Deutschen Doppelrevolution' bis zum Beginn des Ersten Weltkrieges 1849–1914* (Munich, 1995), 1214–15.

[49] C. E. McClelland, 'Structural change and social reproduction in German universities 1870–1920', *History of Education*, 15 (1986), 178.

[50] Jarausch, *Students, society and politics*, 136. Cf. R. S. Turner, 'Universitäten', in K. E. Jeismann and P. Lundgreen (eds.), *Handbuch der deutschen Bildungsgeschichte. III. 1800–1870: Von der Neuordnung Deutschlands bis zur Gründung des Deutschen Reiches* (Munich, 1987), 230.

[51] J. E. Craig, 'Higher education and social mobility in Germany', in Jarausch, *Transformation*, 219–44. Cf. Kaelble, 'Educational opportunities', 251, 254.

[52] Anderson, *Education and opportunity*, 152.

France resembled Germany in combining bourgeois privilege with limited opportunities for the white-collar middle class. Minor state officials, including the growing army of elementary schoolteachers, or those who had served their country in the army, were often rewarded with state patronage and scholarships for their children. Secondary schools were urban and relatively accessible, and statistics for the 1860s show pupils coming from quite a wide social range.[53] But direct evidence about the social origins of university students is sparse, and almost confined to the *grandes écoles*. The Polytechnique, in Terry Shinn's words, was a bastion of bourgeois hegemony in the early nineteenth century, but his analysis of its matriculation registers shows that the clientele did change later. In 1815–29, the percentage from the landed classes, the liberal professions, and high officials was 62. It was still 61 in 1848–79, but then fell to 31 in 1880–1914. Sons of industrialists and merchants were only 9 per cent in 1815–29, but rose to 17 per cent in 1848–79 and 23 per cent in 1880–1914. The remainder of the students came from the ranks of middling and minor officials, army officers, and artisans and shopkeepers. Students from the 'popular classes' were invisible before 1879, but rose to 10 per cent in 1880–1914.[54] There was thus some democratization, due largely to scholarships, but more striking was the new interest shown by the business class, as the school became less military and began to supply engineers to private business. This was also reflected in the appearance of new engineering schools such as the École Centrale, which appealed more directly to the industrialists and merchants who provided 35 per cent of its students between its foundation in 1830 and 1900.[55]

The École Normale, which charged no fees and which had become a target for the cleverest students of all classes, had a different social profile. Among the science students there between 1808 and 1879, only 39 per cent came from the landowning, professional, or higher business classes, with 23 per cent from the middling professional, managerial, or official ranks; 22 per cent were the sons of craftsmen and small businessmen, and 16 per cent of workers, clerks, and farmers, a group hardly represented at all at the Polytechnique in that period.[56] After 1870, the École

[53] P. Harrigan, *Mobility, elites, and education in French society of the Second Empire* (Waterloo, Ont., 1980). Cf. R. D. Anderson, 'Secondary education in mid nineteenth-century France: some social aspects', *Past and Present*, 53 (1971), 121–46, and 'New light on French secondary education in the nineteenth century', *Social History*, 7 (1982), 147–65.

[54] T. Shinn, *Savoir scientifique et pouvoir social: l'École Polytechnique 1794–1914* (Paris, 1980), 182, 185. Other figures, compatible but not identical, in A. Daumard, 'Les élèves de l'École Polytechnique de 1815 à 1848', *Revue d'Histoire Moderne et Contemporaine*, 5 (1958), 227; M. Bradley, 'Scientific education for a new society: the École Polytechnique 1795–1830', *History of Education*, 5 (1976), 11–24; C. Charle, *Les Élites de la République (1880–1900)* (Paris, 1987), 49–53.

[55] M. Lévy-Leboyer, 'Innovation and business strategies in nineteenth- and twentieth-century France', in E. C. Carter and others (eds.), *Enterprise and entrepreneurs in nineteenth- and twentieth-century France* (Baltimore, 1976), 108–9. Cf. Kaelble, 'Educational opportunities', 253; J. H. Weiss, *The making of technological man: the social origins of French engineering education* (Cambridge, Mass., 1982), 72, 77.

[56] C. Zwerling, 'The emergence of the École Normale Supérieure as a centre of scientific education in the nineteenth century', in R. Fox and G. Weisz (eds.), *The organization of science and technology in France 1808–1914* (Cambridge, 1980), 50–8. Cf. V. Karady, 'Scientists and class structure: social recruitment of students at the Parisian Ecole Normale Superieure in the nineteenth century', *History of Education*, 8 (1979), 99–108; V. Karady, 'Normaliens et autres enseignants à la Belle Époque: note sur

Normale broadened its middle-class recruitment without becoming significantly more democratic: there were fewer from business, and more from the middle official and white-collar ranks, and especially from schoolteaching, whose ethos the school represented as the Polytechnique did that of the technocrats.[57] In Ringer's words, 'they represented diametrically opposed models of the relationship between knowledge and society; they were the poles of an antithesis at the heart of French culture'. And Craig Zwerling concludes that 'the Polytechnique tended to recruit more students from the upper levels of the bourgeoisie, from those families that were closest to economic and political power, whereas the Normale tended to recruit from the lower levels of the bourgeoisie where education offered a means of upward mobility'.[58] But both drew their students disproportionately from Paris, and despite some well-known individual cases, students from genuinely poor backgrounds remained uncommon even at the Normale.

In France, traditions of social mobility through education especially favoured the urban middling and lower middle class, and by 1914 they had established their presence in elite institutions. The expansion of the faculties, with open rather than competitive entry, and supported under the Third Republic by state scholarships, must have had similar social effects, and the revival of the provincial faculties, including the promotion of specialities relevant to local industries, probably made higher education more attractive to the business class. Solid evidence is lacking, and one piece which does exist shows a different sort of change: at the law faculty of Toulouse, the percentage of landowners among parents was 50 per cent in the 1840s, and 41 per cent in 1883, but had fallen to 22 per cent in 1910. The main beneficiaries were the liberal professions, who rose from 30 per cent in 1883 to 41 in 1910; the percentage from the lower middle class rose modestly from 2.5 to 10 per cent, but the business class actually declined from 14 to 10 per cent. Law faculties were the most exclusive part of the French system, and this was a broadening of middle-class patronage at the expense of the more traditional elite. It resembled in that respect what happened at Oxford and Cambridge.[59]

In England, the picture was complicated by greater segmentation than in Germany or France. The middle classes were offered new opportunities for higher education in London from the 1820s, but it was not until after 1870 that a network of provincial universities developed. Oxford and Cambridge remained expensive, and continued to take most of their students from the landed, professional, and wealthy bourgeois classes. The new universities were substantially cheaper, being local and non-residential, and were more adaptable than Oxbridge to new vocational demands. While Oxford and Cambridge drew a majority of their students from the expensive public schools, the new universities developed in tandem with new or

l'origine sociale et la réussite dans une profession intellectuelle', *Revue Française de Sociologie*, 13 (1972), 35–58.

[57] R. J. Smith, *The École Normale Supérieure and the Third Republic* (Albany, NY, 1982), 30–45.

[58] Ringer, *Education and society*, 174; Zwerling, 'Emergence', 58.

[59] J. M. Burney, *Toulouse et son université: facultés et étudiants dans la France provinciale du 19e siècle* (Toulouse, 1988), 163–71.

reformed urban secondary schools, which were reorganized by the state in 1902. When this happened, a more serious effort was made than in France or Germany to provide scholarships for working-class students. Unfortunately, the data for students' social origins in the newer universities are very fragmentary, but there are some indications that by 1914 working-class students were beginning to appear in England, and even more in Wales. Otherwise the new universities probably had a mix of a familiar type from professional, business, and lower-middle-class families, but with the wealthier or more ambitious elements creamed off by Oxbridge.[60]

For Oxford and Cambridge themselves, the social data are fuller. They show that these universities were always more middle-class than aristocratic, and when they expanded after 1870 this became more marked. At Cambridge in the period 1800–49, 31 per cent of parents were landowners, 32 per cent clergy, 16 per cent lawyers or doctors, and probably no more than 6 per cent from business. In the period 1850–99, landowners fell to 19 per cent, but the proportions from the clergy and from law and medicine changed little, at 31 and 19 per cent respectively, while those from business rose to 15 per cent.[61] At Oxford, the pattern seems similar. In 1861 the proportion from the clergy reached 'an all-time peak' of 31 per cent. It was still 28 per cent in 1870, but down to 17 per cent by 1910. Between 1870 and 1910, parents in the landed and leisured class fell from 40 to 15 per cent, professionals other than the clergy rose from 21 to 31 per cent, and businessmen and industrialists rose from 7 to 21 per cent. There were some sons of shopkeepers and clerks (2 per cent in 1870, 9 per cent in 1910), and by 1910 there was a handful of working-class students from the new grammar schools. Lawrence Stone sees in these patterns a successful adaptation to social needs, as the traditional patrons, the clergy and the landed class, were 'swamped by a great tide of students from the new middle classes, professional, commercial, industrial, and white collar'.[62] Surely there is some exaggeration here: the influx from business families (following a similar move into the public schools) was significant, but compared with Germany the lower-middle-class presence was small. Oxford and Cambridge remained faithful to a broadly professional mission.[63]

It was very different in Scotland, where high rates of enrolment corresponded to an unusual degree of progressiveness. The universities prepared effectively for all three traditional professions, and thus had a strong middle-class appeal. Being situated in the cities (apart from the small university at St Andrews), and being

[60] Anderson, 'Universities and elites', 234–40.

[61] H. Jenkins and D. C. Jones, 'Social class of Cambridge University alumni of the 18th and 19th centuries', *British Journal of Sociology*, 1 (1950), 99. Other data in S. Rothblatt, *The revolution of the dons: Cambridge and society in Victorian England* (London, 1968), 280–4; C. N. L. Brooke, *A history of the University of Cambridge. IV. 1870–1990* (Cambridge, 1993), 249–52, 601–3.

[62] L. Stone (ed.), *The university in society. I. Oxford and Cambridge from the 14th to the early 19th Century* (Princeton, 1975), 66–7, 103. Other data in M. C. Curthoys and J. Howarth, 'Origins and destinations: the social mobility of Oxford men and women', in M. G. Brock and M. Curthoys (eds.), *The history of the University of Oxford. VII. Nineteenth-century Oxford, Part 2* (Oxford, 2000), 578; D. I. Greenstein, 'The junior members 1900–1990: a profile', in B. Harrison (ed.), *The History of the University of Oxford. VIII. The twentieth century* (Oxford, 1994), 56.

[63] G. Sutherland, 'Education', in F. M. L. Thompson (ed.), *The Cambridge social history of Britain 1750–1950. III. Social agencies and institutions* (Cambridge, 1990), 157–8.

non-residential and cheap, they were accessible to a wide range of urban society, while also keeping alive their links with parish schools throughout Scotland: an 'uncoordinated charity system' of the kind described by Kaelble was still in place to encourage boys from poor or rural backgrounds, many of whom still aimed at the church. Even in the eighteenth century, the universities were open to new urban demands. In Glasgow between 1740 and 1839, 44 per cent of the students came from industrial and commercial backgrounds, and of these a third were 'working class'.[64] This openness to the sons of artisans and skilled workers (though far less to the really poor) continued through the nineteenth century. In the 1860s, inquiries in all four Scottish universities showed that 33 per cent of the students came from professional families, 16 per cent from the economic bourgeoisie, 15 per cent from agriculture (mostly tenant farmers), 6 per cent from the urban lower middle class, and 23 per cent from the working class. The fact that professionals formed the largest group was in line with German or French norms, but the presence of so many working-class students was probably unique.[65] It was encouraged by the absence of entrance qualifications, a low age of entry, and the teaching of Latin in local schools. Later Scotland moved to the common European pattern of secondary schooling to 17 or 18, and a Leaving Certificate, the equivalent of the baccalaureate, was introduced in 1888. By 1900 the remodelling of the school structure was complete. But contrary to some predictions at the time, and some interpretations since, this did not reduce access to the universities. Scholarships were available, and the Scottish-American millionaire Andrew Carnegie set up a trust in 1900 which paid the university fees of all deserving Scottish students. At Glasgow University in 1910, 26 per cent of the male students were the sons of professional men, and 25 per cent of businessmen, but 20 per cent came from the small bourgeoisie, and 24 per cent were working class, mostly the sons of artisans and skilled workers.[66] Unusually full data are also available for Aberdeen, where comparison of students' social origins with their career destinations provides evidence for a phenomenon common throughout Europe, the channelling of poorer students into schoolteaching or the church.[67]

The social character of the Scottish universities was reflected in the composition of their professorate, the final point to be considered in this chapter. Throughout the nineteenth century, with very little change over time, 57–8 per cent came from the professional classes, including 20 per cent from the clergy, and 17 per cent from the economic bourgeoisie. The rest were the sons of farmers, the lower middle class, or (8–9 per cent) the working class.[68] National data for England are not available, but at Oxford the dons reflected the university's own more limited recruitment: in 1881–1900, 79 per cent came from what Engel calls the 'gentleman class', though

[64] W. M. Mathew, 'The origins and occupations of Glasgow students 1740–1839', *Past and Present*, 33 (1966), 74–94.

[65] Anderson, *Education and opportunity*, 148–53.

[66] Ibid. 308–18.

[67] R. D. Anderson, *The student community at Aberdeen 1860–1939* (Aberdeen, 1988), 138–40.

[68] R. D. Anderson, 'Scottish university professors 1800–1939: profile of an elite', *Scottish Economic and Social History*, 7 (1987), 46–50.

with a shift compared to earlier years from the clergy to the professional and business groups.[69] The academic profession in all countries was less accessible to the poor than schoolteaching or the church because of the long preparation required before a career could be established and a reasonable income earned. It was only towards the end of the century that salaried posts below the professorial level appeared and provided something like a career structure. In France, university teachers of all kinds rose from about 570 in 1865 to 2,200 in 1919.[70] They shared the general characteristics of the liberal professions, with a bias to recruitment from the official and educational sectors.[71] In Germany, expansion of the profession caused particular strains, as we shall see in Chapter 10, because professorial chairs did not expand at the same rate, cutting off the traditional promotion prospects of the *Privatdozenten.* The German academic profession (of all ranks) rose from 1,504 in 1873 to 3,838 in 1910, and it seems to have been affected much more directly than in Britain or France by the changing composition of the student body: the percentage from the *Bildungsbürgertum* was 70 in 1873, but fell to 52 in 1910. They were replaced by men from both the business class and the *Mittelstand,* despite the economic obstacles which the latter faced: Ringer comments on the 'extraordinary commitment to social mobility through learning in this very interesting group'.[72]

Professors formed a small profession, but an important one, because of their national uniformity. In most countries they were civil servants, with common salary scales, disciplinary procedures, methods of appointment, and hierarchical attitudes.[73] In France and in Austria, promotion to Paris or Vienna was the pinnacle of an academic career. When Spain and Italy centralized their university systems, this meant destroying local links and turning the professorate into a bureaucratic service. In Germany, professors were employees of the individual states, but mobility throughout the German-speaking world was established even before the Humboldtian reforms, and professors became spokesmen for the national cause. Even in Britain, while Oxford and Cambridge usually appointed from their own ranks, they also supplied a large number of professors to new universities elsewhere, helping to spread a common ethos, and a national market in academic jobs was established. The academic profession, therefore, was one of the means by which universities served the cause of national integration.

[69] A. J. Engel, *From clergyman to don: the rise of the academic profession in nineteenth-century Oxford* (Oxford, 1983), 287.

[70] G. Weisz, *The emergence of modern universities in France 1863–1914* (Princeton, 1983), 316.

[71] C. Charle, 'Le champ universitaire parisien à la fin du 19e siècle', *Actes de la Recherche en Sciences Sociales,* 47–8 (1983), 78, and generally C. Charle, *La République des universitaires 1870–1940* (Paris, 1994).

[72] F. Ringer, 'A sociography of German academics 1863–1938', *Central European History,* 25 (1992), 266–9.

[73] Cf. C. Charle, *Les Intellectuels en Europe au XIXe siècle: essai d'histoire comparée* (Paris, 1996), 207–20.

9
The Formation of Elites

Modern theorists of nationalism have stressed the role of education and culture in integrating the modern nation and providing it with an elite. Ernest Gellner argued that in industrial societies the legitimacy of the political order depends on a common culture shared by rulers and ruled, with a continuum between the 'high culture' of the elites and the popular culture of the masses. In traditional societies, where authority does not depend on consent, ethnic groups and communities can lead separate lives, but modern ones cannot work without cultural homogeneity, which usually means a common language. An essential feature, therefore, is a national educational system run by the state, which forms

> a pyramid at whose base there are primary schools, staffed by teachers trained at secondary schools, staffed by university-trained teachers, led by the products of advanced graduate schools. . . . At the base of the modern social order stands not the executioner but the professor. . . . The monopoly of legitimate education is now more important, more central than is the monopoly of legitimate violence.

Universities are the home of high culture, without which a viable national identity cannot exist. 'A high culture pervades the whole of society, defines it, and needs to be sustained by the polity. *That* is the secret of nationalism.'[1]

This concept of a national educational system and its role was certainly held by the French revolutionaries and their successors, and by those consciously seeking to create modern nations, such as the liberals of the Cortes of Cadiz or the founders of united Italy. But there are some problems in using Gellner's model to explain nineteenth-century nationalism. Hardly any country had an integrated educational pyramid of the kind he describes: rigid separation between the education of the masses and that of the elite was the norm. Both French and German models stressed the close articulation of secondary schools with universities, and the common values taught in both, but the purpose was to distinguish the elite from the masses rather than to bind them together. Moreover, Gellner's explanation in terms of industrialization does not account for the strong and early identification of education with national emancipation in countries like Greece, Romania, or Finland. Perhaps it is significant that Gellner avoids concrete examples, and illustrates his points by appeal to a generic 'Ruritania'.

Nevertheless, in what Gellner describes as the 'classical Habsburg nationalism' of nations seeking emancipation, the creation of a distinct high culture by nationalist

[1] E. Gellner, *Nations and nationalism* (Oxford, 1983), 18, 34. (It was Joseph de Maistre who said that the executioner is the bond of human association.)

intellectuals and the demand for education in vernacular languages were of central importance. This sort of movement, and the specific problems of the Habsburg Empire, will be discussed in Chapter 15, while the present chapter looks at national integration in the larger states, seeking to give a framework of ideas for the national chapters which follow. In the two great unification movements of the nineteenth century, the German and the Italian, the role of cultural nationalism in paving the way for political unity is familiar, and once it was achieved educational systems were consciously used to consolidate it. But even established states like Britain and France, faced with the stresses of industrialization and mass democracy, and the loss of authority by traditional governing classes, needed an active policy of what E. J. Hobsbawm calls 'state patriotism' and Benedict Anderson 'official nationalism', based on a state language.[2] The use of elementary education to create citizens and promote social stability is familiar to historians, but at all levels, as George Weisz says of France, 'social tensions and political conflicts seemed to demand educational institutions more closely integrated into the state apparatus, and capable of elaborating ideologies which promoted national unity'.[3] In France the Third Republic had to rebuild a nation after military defeat and to establish its own ideological roots. Modern states also needed to override regional and local loyalties within the elite by a common national culture. This had perhaps already been achieved in France by the *ancien régime* monarchy; in Germany and Italy it became an obvious priority; in Britain, the forging of a united kingdom was a conspicuous success in the case of Scottish union after 1707, but the attempt to do the same for Ireland after 1801 was an equally conspicuous failure, directly reflected in university policy. In the early nineteenth century, the old concept of *Nationalerziehung*—state-building by imposing a single language and culture from above—still had some validity. Napoleon followed this kind of cultural imperialism in Italy, and the Habsburgs took it up again after 1815, not finally abandoning it until the 1860s. In the Netherlands, the university policy of William I tried to override linguistic and religious differences to forge a dynastic state, but this collapsed in 1830. By the last decades of the nineteenth century, the successful states were those which inspired the active co-operation of their elites and identified their own authority with the nation and its cultural and historical mission. A state which notably failed to do this was Russia, where the tsarist regime alienated both the Russian intelligentsia trained in the universities and the national minorities which it subjected to cultural russification.

A homogeneous elite might be the ideal, but the reality was seldom so simple. Elites could be divided by their sources of income, by clashing social values, by religious and other ideological conflict, and sometimes by ethnicity. Socially, the basic building blocks in most countries were the landed aristocracy, the public service and

[2] E. J. Hobsbawm, *Nations and nationalism since 1870: programme, myth, reality*, 2nd edn. (Cambridge, 1992), 91–100; B. Anderson, *Imagined communities: reflections on the origin and spread of nationalism*, revised edn. (London, 1991), 83–111.

[3] G. Weisz, 'Le corps professoral de l'enseignement supérieur et l'idéologie de la réforme universitaire en France 1860–1885', *Revue Française de Sociologie*, 18 (1977), 201.

professional bourgeoisie, and the growing business class. The second of these groups was the one most closely associated everywhere with university education, but the use of universities by the others varied between countries and over time, depending partly on the progress of industrial development. Education had a key mediating role in their relationships. Throughout western and central Europe, the nineteenth century saw the emergence of a composite elite based on some kind of compromise or fusion between old and new sources of wealth and prestige, and between landed, professional, and economic bourgeoisies. These questions were at the heart of an international study of the comparative history of European bourgeoisies directed at Bielefeld by Jürgen Kocka from 1986 to 1997.[4]

A natural starting-point for this inquiry was the German *Bildungsbürgertum*, a social group peculiarly identified with university education. Central Europe had, in Kocka's words, 'a very specific educational and university tradition, rooted in the Enlightenment and in neo-humanism, and linked with a very specific bureaucratically-influenced variant of state-formation'. Part of that bureaucratic influence was the close alignment of the professions with the state, leading to a clear gap between the bourgeoisie of *Bildung* and the *Wirtschaftsbürgertum* or economic bourgeoisie, which in Germany 'was much more internally integrated, less fragmented and more clearly separate from both academics and professionals as well as from the nobility than was the case in either England or France'.[5] The contrast between *Bildung* and *Besitz* is a staple of German historical interpretation. So has been the idea of a German 'special path' to modernity (*Sonderweg*), in which Germany failed to follow the Anglo-French model of liberal, capitalist development, an interpretation linked with explanations of Germany's putative responsibility for the outbreak of war in 1914 and of the rise of Nazism. Imperial Germany supposedly saw a 'feudalization' of the bourgeoisie, to which universities contributed both through their general nationalist orientation and through the socializing activities of bodies like the student corps.[6] The *Sonderweg* theory has attracted much discussion, and critics particularly question its sharp contrast between Germany and her western neighbours: the inculcation of 'aristocratic' values through education, and the gap between public-service and economic bourgeoisies, were hardly confined to Germany. In Kocka's view, the 'aristocratic-*haut bourgeois* symbiosis' was more advanced in France or Britain than in Germany, even if 'the core of the *Sonderweg* thesis . . . survives'.[7] Werner Mosse, another Bielefeld participant, was also sceptical about feudalization, arguing that the new composite elite was urban and plutocratic, not landed; its formation had gone

[4] The main results were published in J. Kocka (ed.), *Bürgertum im 19. Jahrhundert: Deutschland im europäischen Vergleich*, 3 vols. (Munich, 1988). A selection in English is J. Kocka and A. Mitchell (eds.), *Bourgeois society in nineteenth-century Europe* (Oxford, 1993). For reviews of the project, see C. Charle, 'A la recherche des bourgeoisies européennes', *Le Mouvement Social*, 153 (1990), 91–7; P. Lundgreen (ed.), *Sozial- und Kulturgeschichte des Bürgertums: Eine Bilanz des Bielefelder Sonderforschungsbereichs (1986–1997)* (Göttingen, 2000).

[5] J. Kocka, 'The European pattern and the German case', in Kocka and Mitchell, *Bourgeois society*, 22, 24.

[6] See for example H. U. Wehler, *The German Empire 1871–1918* (Oxford, 1985), 45, 100 ff.

[7] Kocka, 'European pattern', 26–7, 32.

furthest in Britain, thanks partly to 'common socialization in the universities of Oxford and Cambridge'. E. J. Hobsbawm similarly thought that in Britain the bourgeoisie was the dominant partner, able to 'adapt, modify and use elements from the tradition of the nobility and gentry for middle-class purposes', elements which included their educational traditions.[8]

The contrary view, that the bourgeoisie were indoctrinated with aristocratic values, was pushed furthest by Arno J. Mayer, who extended the *Sonderweg* theory to the whole of Europe. He argued that the traditional elites remained in control down to 1914, when they led Europe into war rather than surrender their privileges; Mayer saw privileged educational institutions and classical culture as bulwarks of this 'persistence of the old regime'. 'Higher education was aligned with the other hegemonic institutions and like them was a solid pillar of the *anciens régimes*. . . . secondary schools and universities were less locomotives of progress than regenerators and conveyors of the preindustrial and prebourgeois cultural heritage that upheld the established order', and 'vehicles for the reproduction of the world-view and learning of the old notables'.[9] It was the economist Joseph Schumpeter, seeking an explanation for imperialism in 1919, who first suggested the persistence of pre-industrial or aristocratic values within bourgeois society, and the idea has links with Fritz Ringer's thesis on incongruence, and with the extensive debate among both French and British historians over whether education was responsible for retarded economic performance by teaching values hostile to entrepreneurship and diverting the sons of the business class away from productive activity. One obvious objection to this theory is that the country which France and Britain were supposedly lagging behind and the exemplar of dazzling economic success, Germany, was also that where classical education was most venerated, where higher technical education had to struggle to establish parity with the old universities, and where according to the *Sonderweg* theory the bourgeoisie were most in thrall to aristocratic values. Without entering into that debate, one can at least acknowledge its value in directing attention to the complexity of the 'bourgeoisie' or the 'elite' and to their internal segmentation.

These relations were further complicated by segmentation within national education systems themselves. One can suggest a fourfold university typology, still influencing national developments in the twenty-first century: single-university, multipolar, centralized, and hierarchical. In smaller countries, including many of the new ones created in the nineteenth century, there might be only one university, with the classic professional faculties. This made for strong integration of the different elements of the elite, often including the national political leadership. A second type was the multipolar university system, characteristic of countries with traditions of regional and civic independence. Germany and Italy were obvious examples, but so on a smaller scale was Holland. In Germany, the development of

[8] W. Mosse, 'Nobility and middle classes in nineteenth-century Europe: a comparative study', in Kocka and Mitchell, *Bourgeois society*, 83; E. J. Hobsbawm, 'The example of the English middle class', ibid. 147.

[9] A. J. Mayer, *The persistence of the old regime: Europe to the Great War* (London, 1981), 253.

the universities as national institutions largely preceded political unity and helped to shape it, but the federal structure of the new German empire and the division between Catholic and Protestant regions continued to protect diversity; in Italy, the need to consolidate unity after 1861 led to a policy of rigid uniformity. Neither Rome nor Berlin could dominate the scene like Paris or Vienna, but in both Germany and Italy there was a broad distinction between a group of large universities with national prestige and others which were small (often very small) and essentially local.

A third type was the French centralized pattern, inherited from the *ancien régime*, and greatly strengthened by Napoleon. The position of Paris in the university system reflected its dominance in politics, administration, and culture. Under the Third Republic, reformers sought to revive the provincial universities, but the effect was a useful increase in the provision of higher education rather than a real change in its centralized character. With the French model one may place Spain, which inherited a multipolar system from the *ancien régime*, but adopted centralization in the nineteenth century in an attempt to create modern national feeling. Spanish policy included a new central university at Madrid, which soon became as dominant as Paris. To bring young men to the capital city for a few years was a very effective way of creating unity among the elite. They might return to their provinces after graduating, but made personal contacts which could last a lifetime, and absorbed the national traditions embodied in the political institutions, the monuments, the theatres and museums, and other forms of what Pierre Nora has called sites of memory (*lieux de mémoire*). In Russia, the twin capitals of Moscow and St Petersburg had the same role for the educated elite of a vast country. In Germany, although Berlin had only some 15 per cent of the student total, the custom of migration meant that a larger proportion experienced life in the capital city, and became familiar with the different regions of the new Reich. Even in Britain, Oxford and Cambridge were national institutions with strong metropolitan links, and university memories were particularly important in creating and sustaining 'British' feeling throughout the far-flung empire. Indeed, if these two universities are taken together, the English system could be seen as the most centralized of all, as was appropriate to one of the oldest and strongest nation-states in Europe, since until the 1820s they had no rivals. When the British university system did expand, the result was a hierarchy of prestige (forming the fourth type of system), though the picture is complicated by the existence of separate university traditions in Scotland and Ireland. In England, the foundation of new universities, taking hold from the 1870s but coinciding with successful reform of the ancient universities, failed to challenge the prestige of the latter or their hold on the topmost elite, so that by 1914 there was a university system with two tiers.

In England, the new civic universities were mostly in industrial cities, and could be seen as a response to new economic needs and as an expression of the utilitarian ideology of the business class; they were open to technical and vocational education of a kind firmly resisted by Oxford and Cambridge. This was another structural aspect which differed between countries. In Germany, there was similar resistance from the traditional universities, and technical education was developed in a regional network of Technical High Schools, which took on a common shape in the 1860s, drawing many of their students from a corresponding modern sector of secondary education (*Realschulen* and their offshoots). It was not until 1899 that they gained most of the privileges of universities (but not the name), and their prestige remained lower. This was a quite different pattern from France, where the Polytechnique was the model for a series of specialized engineering and vocational schools, mostly based in Paris, reflecting and reinforcing the tradition of centralization, and recruiting nationally. These schools had more prestige than the ordinary faculties, the reverse of the German situation, and they left a gap in the provinces. This was partly filled by the science faculties when these were rejuvenated by the Third Republic, and there were parallels with the English civic universities.

The failure of Britain to develop technical institutions with the prestige of the French engineering schools or the German Technical High Schools was seen as a weakness by contemporary champions of science, and partly remedied in the 1900s. In conditions of increased international economic competition after 1870, there was much debate among contemporaries, continued since by historians, about the virtues of these different structures of technical education and their contribution to economic performance. The French schools gave mathematics and engineering high prestige, but were often criticized for their excessive theoretical emphasis, while in Britain the problem seemed to be prejudice on the part of industry against any sort of theoretical approach or formal training. In Belgium and Italy, engineering and other technical subjects were usually taught within the universities or in institutes linked with them. In the sphere of German influence (including Austria, Russia, Holland, and Scandinavia) the German pattern of high-powered but all-purpose technical schools fed by *Realschulen* was normal, though some individual schools had a French-style specialization linked to particular state services. They might also have distinct political missions. The school at Delft, founded in 1842 and renamed Polytechnic in 1863 and Technical High School in 1905, trained officials for the Dutch empire in the East Indies as well as civil engineers for the state.[10] The Zurich Polytechnic, which was regarded as a model of its kind, and which resembled a German Technical High School rather than the Paris Polytechnique, was created in 1855 as a federal institution at a time when the Swiss constitution was being remodelled on more centralized lines. The universities were controlled by the cantons, and mutual jealousies prevented the designation of any of them as a federal university; the Polytechnic therefore became an important symbol of national integration.

Engineering and technical schools did not necessarily have a direct link with economic elites. In France, the traditions of the Polytechnique attracted families in state or military service rather than the business class, and it recruited from the topmost lycées, while at Delft the students came from 'an active upper-middle class'

[10] C. Disco, 'Making the grade in Dutch civil engineering 1780–1920', *Paedagogica Historica*, 30 (1994), 371–410.

which also looked to the state and needed to gain its living by work 'rather than by inheritance or the logic of capital accumulation . . . a class whose fortunes were tied to the process of modernization, including industrialization and state-formation (with all the normative and cultural dispositions this implies)'.[11] In Germany, the Technical High Schools appealed more directly to the business class, and the existence of a modern educational sector vertically divided from the gymnasiums and universities supports Kocka's picture of a self-contained economic bourgeoisie. The expansion of modern schools and the lack of a classical requirement might also encourage students from skilled working-class or artisan strata, and social data for Technical High Schools suggest a more industrial, urban profile than for universities. It can be argued that the German business class valued technical education for its own sake, and that this explained German economic dynamism, particularly compared with Britain, where the absence of such schools either left businessmen without an adequate intellectual grounding, or drove them to defer to the traditional patterns of elite education. But foreign admirers of Germany, who assumed too readily in any case that there was a direct connection between education, science, and economic performance, tended to overlook the lower status of the German technical sector and the growing discontent of its patrons with its lack of parity. It was also the case that while in France engineers from the Polytechnique and elsewhere held key positions in the state and private industry, the graduates of Technical High Schools held subordinate positions, and although industry used them effectively, men with traditional university training in science or law retained the top posts.[12] In Germany and countries which followed its model, virtually all bureaucrats were trained in law, which was not notably more relevant to the needs of an advanced industrial society than the classics or history favoured in Britain.[13]

As the quantitative evidence suggested, universities and classical secondary schools long seemed simply irrelevant to much of the middle class. But the process of professionalization eventually spread, first to engineers, then to industrial experts and managers as corporate organization began to replace family ownership, then to the commercial world, resulting in a new crop of business schools. In a comparative study of business elites at the end of the century (meaning the owners and directors rather than the technicians) Kaelble found an increasing reliance on higher education compared with the period of the industrial revolution, when 'the majority of the business elite had some secondary education but thereafter entered directly into business careers or obtained vocational training and apprenticeships rather than going to universities'. Kaelble found less movement into business from landowning or professional families in Germany than in Britain or France, due to 'the tenacious anti-industrial value system' in Germany. That corrects one stereotype, as does Kaelble's finding that at the end of the nineteenth century business leaders in Germany were less likely to have a higher education (up to 26 per cent)

[11] Disco, 'Making the grade in Dutch civil engineering', 407–8. Cf. T. Shinn, 'Reactionary technologists: the struggle over the École polytechnique 1880–1914', *Minerva*, 22 (1984), 329–45.

[12] R. R. Locke, 'Industrialisierung und Erziehungssystem in Frankreich und Deutschland vor dem 1. Weltkrieg', *Historische Zeitschrift*, 225 (1977), 274–5.

[13] D. Lieven, *The aristocracy in Europe 1815–1914* (New York, 1993), 218.

than in France (around 50 per cent, presumably because of the *grandes écoles*) or Britain (33 per cent).[14]

The importance of professionalization, and hence of the universities, was stressed in Harold Perkin's interpretation of British social history. Like Hobsbawm, Perkin saw the mid-century reform of Oxbridge as essentially the work of the middle class, turning aristocratic institutions to their own use. But the 'entrepreneurial ideal' which prevailed earlier in the century was replaced after about 1880 by the 'professional ideal', which created a society based on 'trained expertise and selection by merit'.[15] As the universities controlled this process, they were transformed 'from a marginal institution, an optional finishing school for young gentlemen and prospective clergymen, into the central power house of modern industrial society'. Perkin saw the 'critical turning point' of this transformation in the early twentieth century.[16] As with Jarausch's 'seismic shift', such a judgement may exaggerate a relatively small expansion in the universities' social function. But Perkin backed it up with a study of over 3,000 elite members, whose results have been described more fully by W. D. Rubinstein. The elites concerned were those over which Oxbridge held sway (bishops, higher civil servants, heads of universities), and they seem to show two things. First, they were drawn from all strata of the middle classes except the lowest, even if before 1914 there were few from the lower-middle or working classes. The service class created by educational reform was drawn only partly from the ranks of wealth and privilege, and Rubinstein argues that the figures show 'the long existence and the key importance of the meritocracy and the pervasiveness of a meritocratic basis of promotion throughout even the highest ranges of the British élite structure'.[17] Secondly, the sample, which includes a selection of top businessmen, suggests that the British bourgeoisie was not highly segmented. Middle-class families, whatever their own form of activity, seem to have regarded the whole range of occupations as open to their sons, and to have made their choices (including the choice not to use a university at all) accordingly.

This makes an interesting comparison with Christophe Charle's study of the elites of the Third Republic between 1880 and 1900, based on a sample of 1,093 holders of top positions.[18] Charle was not concerned only with their social origins,

[14] H. Kaelble, 'Long-term changes in the recruitment of the business elite: Germany compared to the US, Great Britain and France since the industrial revolution', *Journal of Social History*, 13 (1979–80), 407, 416.

[15] H. Perkin, *The rise of professional society: England since 1880* (London, 1989), 155; cf. 366–74, and H. Perkin, *The origins of modern English society 1780–1880* (London, 1969), 298–9, 320.

[16] H. Perkin, 'The pattern of social transformation in England', in K. H. Jarausch (ed.), *The transformation of higher learning 1860–1930: expansion, diversification, social opening, and professionalization in England, Germany, Russia, and the United States* (Chicago, 1983), 207, 217–18.

[17] W. D. Rubinstein, 'Education and the social origins of British elites 1880–1970', *Past and Present*, 112 (1986), 185. Cf. Perkin, *Rise of professional society*, 258–66; H. Perkin, 'The recruitment of elites in British society since 1800', *Journal of Social History*, 12 (1978–9), 222–34; R. D. Anderson, *Universities and elites in Britain since 1800* (London, 1992), 47–58.

[18] C. Charle, *Les Élites de la République (1880–1900)* (Paris, 1987). Developed into a comparative project from 1987: C. Charle, 'The present state of research on the social history of elites and the bourgeoisie: a critical assessment', *Contemporary European History*, 1 (1992), 99–112; C. Charle and

but pursued intensive 'prosopographical' enquiry into individuals, emphasizing the differences between segments of the elite, the part which education played in family strategies, and the ways in which particular forms of education and individual institutions formed the identity of specific groups.[19] The *grandes écoles* were especially important, and Charle's work is connected with that of Bourdieu on the later twentieth century. Bourdieu argued that these schools created a 'state nobility' comparable in its sense of privileged identity to the office-holders of the *ancien régime*.[20] Families identified themselves over the generations with individual schools and with the bureaucratic corps to which they led, and their *esprit de corps* was reinforced by strong alumnus associations, which defended the schools against political intervention, sustained professional networks, and helped to find jobs for new graduates. (This phenomenon was characteristic of engineering and business schools throughout Europe, partly because small schools could have a clearer sense of identity than amorphous universities.) Elites could be distinguished from each other by the importance which they attached to cultural capital as against social capital, and Bourdieu emphasized the broad distinction between economic elites and those tied more to the state and its educational mechanisms, a distinction analogous to that between *Besitz* and *Bildung*. Bourdieu showed how education contributed to the complex pattern of values, mentalities, and lifestyles which constituted the 'habitus' of a social group; also relevant is his theory of intellectual 'fields', which suggests that ideas and knowledge can only be understood within a web of social and cultural meanings and power relationships. The academic field is one of these webs, in which corpuses of knowledge, intellectual traditions, institutions, and elite identities interact. As Ringer has shown, the concept can also be fruitful for cross-national comparisons.[21] These perceptions were not entirely new. The *grandes écoles* have always celebrated their distinct traditions, and Cournot pointed out in 1856 that the faculties of law and medicine too gave their products not just a professional training, but 'a certain cast of mind, the inevitable result of their intellectual formation, and of the influence of the scientific milieu in which they have lived'.[22]

Charle's investigation refined Bourdieu's approach by distinguishing further between groups, concentrating particularly on the academic world and on the history of intellectuals, manipulators *par excellence* of symbolic capital. University intellectuals differed from literary ones, and professors of science, letters, and law

J. Schriewer, 'Pour une histoire prosopographique comparée des universités européennes', in J. Schriewer, E. Keiner, and C. Charle (eds.), *Sozialer Raum und akademische Kulturen: A la recherche de l'espace universitaire européen. Studien zur europäischen Hochschul- und Wissenschaftsgeschichte im 19. und 20. Jahrhundert: Études sur l'enseignement supérieur aux XIXe et XXe siècles* (Frankfurt, 1993), 10–41.

[19] Charle, *Les Élites de la République*, 106–19.

[20] P. Bourdieu, *La Noblesse d'État: grandes écoles et esprit de corps* (Paris, 1989).

[21] P. Bourdieu, 'Intellectual field and creative project' and 'Systems of education and systems of thought', in M. F. D. Young (ed.), *Knowledge and control: new directions for the sociology of education* (London, 1971), 161–207. Cf. F. Ringer, *Fields of knowledge: French academic culture in comparative perspective 1890–1920* (Cambridge, 1992), 1–25.

[22] A. Cournot, *Des institutions d'instruction publique en France*, Œuvres complètes, vol. 7 (Paris, 1977), 325.

from each other.[23] This was the area of professional life in which, in principle, cultural capital should count for more than any other sort, or (to use a different vocabulary) where meritocracy should apply in the purest form, but in practice all sorts of social and cultural factors intervened. Like all the elites studied by Bourdieu and Charle, the University included a strong element of auto-recruitment, and a feature characteristic of France, and probably of other countries too, was generational mobility within the educational system, encouraged by loyalty to its shared values and (in France) to the secular state: the elementary teacher's son became a lycée teacher, his son in turn a university professor. Charle also argues that in the early nineteenth century university intellectuals were drawn from narrower social strata, and were closely integrated with the ruling bourgeois elite, but under the Third Republic broader recruitment meant a more inward-looking academic world, which had its own hierarchies from the École Normale downwards, but was increasingly isolated from the world of real power and social influence; he suggests that the emergence of the new category of intellectuals was a reaction to this sense of isolation and frustration.[24] Even so, in a comparison of the backgrounds of professors at Paris and Berlin, Charle found that more came from the business class in France than in Germany.[25] No simple generalization is possible, but the German university system, with its lack of differentiation between institutions, seems to have supported a correspondingly undifferentiated *Bildungsbürgertum*, despite the survival of state loyalties and religious divisions, but to have reinforced its sense of separation from the business class, whereas in France the segmentation of the educational system created a more complex group of elites, with the business class as well as the 'state nobility' having a stake in the *grandes écoles*.

There was also a long-term chronological dimension. In Germany, the *Bildungsbürgertum* emerged at the end of the eighteenth century in alliance with the state and identified itself both with the reformed educational system and with the creation of a modern nation. It was also allied with the enlightened part of the nobility, which successfully modernized its service role by making its own use of the Humboldtian university.[26] This partial fusion of old and new elites preceded industrialization, and when a capitalist class appeared it was socially separate, and initially uninterested in university education. The unification of Germany led not to liberal dominance, but to a synthesis of monarchy, army, land, and big business, pioneered by Bismarck and consolidated in the Wilhelmine period. According to *Sonderweg* theorists, the university-educated elite sold out to this system. But an alternative interpretation would stress the growth of a vigorous and diverse bourgeoisie, as part of a civil society distinct from the political elite, in which the *Bildungsbürgertum* was less isolated than before; for McClelland, its growing

[23] C. Charle, *La République des universitaires 1870–1940* (Paris, 1994); Charle, *Les Élites de la République*, 226–48.

[24] C. Charle, *Naissance des 'intellectuels' 1880–1900* (Paris, 1990), 12, 67, 229–31.

[25] Ibid. 231–2; Charle, *La République des universitaires*, 102–7.

[26] C. E. McClelland, *State, society and university in Germany 1700–1914* (Cambridge, 1980), 95–8. Cf. W. Speitkamp, 'Staat und Bildung in Deutschland unter dem Einfluss der französischen Revolution', *Historische Zeitschrift*, 250 (1990), 574–5.

integration with the business class was one of the few successful examples of social integration in the German Empire.[27] The two sectors shared the same basic bourgeois values, and their educational experiences also converged: the modern sector of secondary and technical schools acquired most of the privileges of the gymnasiums and universities, conventional university education received an influx from the business bourgeoisie, and this eventually changed the social composition of the professorate itself.

In France, developments followed in some respects an opposite trajectory. A national culture based on Paris had existed since at least the sixteenth century, and on the eve of the French revolution nobility and bourgeoisie seemed to be merging in a common educated class. The revolution then drove a wedge into this unity, between a modern class of notables created by Napoleon's fusion of old and new elites, and an irreconcilable minority of aristocrats and conservative bourgeois for whom religion and a Catholic education, especially at secondary level, were essential ideological markers. Between about 1830 and 1880, the modern-minded notables dominated society and politics, with a close alliance between political power, property, and the academic elite represented by Cousin or Guizot. The Second Empire, though its illiberalism alienated the academics, did not change the fundamental basis of power, but the foundation of the Third Republic brought (according to Charle) a shift from the domination of the notables to a meritocratic model of society.[28] Propertied and business interests reconciled themselves to the new order (as the limited appeal of the Catholic universities showed), and remained powerful; the University and those who identified with it were now more dependent than before on cultural capital and more distinct from other elites. But they were in ideological harmony with the new regime, beneficiaries of its belief in progress through hard work and merit, and confident in their national role. On the right, unreconciled traditionalists sought to modernize their appeal by mobilizing right-wing nationalism, which led to an ideological assault on the 'new Sorbonne' in the 1900s. But this failed to shake the system. Essentially, by 1914 the centre of gravity was on the left in France while in Germany it was on the right, and the academic establishments of the two countries reflected this.

Where does Britain fit in? In the nineteenth century Britain was widely admired for its social stability and political continuity, and the reform of the public schools and the ancient universities gave them the role of reconciling old aristocracy and new wealth, using the standardized ideal of the educated gentleman to assimilate men of diverse origins into a single, nationally-minded class with a strong sense of public duty. The price paid was (in Arnold's terms) a split between the professionalized upper bourgeoisie and the entrepreneurial class, or (in Perkin's) the

[27] C. E. McClelland, 'Structural change and social reproduction in German universities 1870–1920', *History of Education*, 15 (1986), 192–3. Cf. J. Kocka, 'La bourgeoisie dans l'histoire moderne et contemporaine de l'Allemagne: recherches et débats récents', *Le Mouvement Social*, 136 (1986), 17–18, 22; D. Blackbourn and G. Eley, *The peculiarities of German history: bourgeois society and politics in nineteenth-century Germany* (Oxford, 1984), 286–92. For a more sceptical view, H. Kaelble, 'French bourgeoisie and German Bürgertum 1870–1914', in Kocka and Mitchell, *Bourgeois society*, 283–5.

[28] Cf. C. Charle, *A social history of France in the nineteenth century* (Oxford, 1994), 2–3, 211–17.

eventual triumph of the professional ideal, which was also a triumph of metropolitan over provincial values. This was reflected in the structure of the university system as it expanded. Britain never had a strong bureaucracy with specialized corps as in France, but there are parallels nevertheless. The examination system which increasingly dominated recruitment to the public services was consciously based on the French principle of competitive merit; many British families developed Bourdieu-style attachments over the generations to schools, universities, colleges, and branches of state service (in India, for example); and just as French elite studies show a bias towards Parisian origins, so British ones suggest the favoured status of south-eastern England. Above all, the adaptation of Oxford and Cambridge to produce a service class created a group, drawn from the gentry, *rentier*, professional, or business class, which was dependent on intellectual capital for careers, and which had parallels both in France and with the *Bildungsbürgertum*. Hobsbawm makes this point about the economist John Maynard Keynes, son of a Cambridge don but grandson of a gardener; Keynes's Cambridge contemporary and fellow-member of the 'Bloomsbury' set Leonard Woolf, who started his career in the Ceylon civil service, described the class which he had joined, and into which he married, as a

> social class or caste of a remarkable and peculiar kind which established itself as a powerful section of the ruling class in Britain in the nineteenth century. It was an intellectual aristocracy of the middle class, the nearest equivalent in other countries being the French eighteenth century noblesse de robe. The male members of the British aristocracy of intellect went automatically to the best public schools, to Oxford and Cambridge, and then into all the most powerful and respectable professions.[29]

The strong kinship links over the generations within this intellectual aristocracy were emphasized in an essay of 1955 by Noel Annan.[30] There are parallels with Charle's work, but the difference from France or Germany was that the highest elements of all the British elites—political, military, bureaucratic, ecclesiastical, legal, financial, to some extent industrial—shared the same education and consequently the same values, outlook on life, and sense of national identity.[31] This homogeneity and interpenetration of elites may have contributed to the absence of intellectuals as a self-conscious caste in Britain, or to the erosion of economic dynamism, but it testified to the success of universities in the task of national integration.

This chapter has mainly been concerned with the three leading countries of nineteenth-century Europe. One conclusion might be that the differences between them were not fundamental, but variants on common themes, and that by the early twentieth century they were converging. All three were relatively successful in

[29] E. J. Hobsbawm, *The age of empire 1875–1914* (London, 1989), 177; L. Woolf, *An autobiography. I. 1880–1911* (Oxford, 1980), 119.

[30] Repr. in N. Annan, *The dons: mentors, eccentrics and geniuses* (London, 1999), 304–41.

[31] Cf. F. Ringer, 'The education of elites in modern Europe', *History of Education Quarterly*, 18 (1978), 169; F. Ringer, *Education and society in modern Europe* (London, 1979), 241–2.

creating a single national elite on the basis of high culture, but it was never monolithic. In Britain, the elite excluded most of those who could not afford to send their sons to public schools—capital of an old-fashioned sort mattered as well as cultural capital. In France, the militant anticlericalism of the Third Republic ensured that the social divisions of 1789 were kept alive. The German educated elite was probably the most socially comprehensive in recruiting widely from the lower middle class, though not the working class, and was internally less divided than its French equivalent; but the split between education and money remained, even if there was some coalescence by 1914. However, the division between professional or public service elites and economic ones was apparent in all three countries, and was not particularly surprising. Serving the needs of the former was the traditional function of universities, and there was no strong reason for the latter to use them at all. It was only gradually that their interest was aroused by changes in the map of knowledge, in the technical and scientific basis of industry, and in social attitudes, and what happened then depended on the pace of industrialization and on the national peculiarities of the existing institutional structure. In countries where industrialization was less advanced, however, the professional emphasis remained the dominant one. Italy and Spain had a powerful 'humanistic bourgeoisie' opposed to modernization of their universities. In eastern Europe, the professional classes had a more isolated, precarious existence, forming an intelligentsia dependent on the state (or in Russia, unable to come to terms with it). And in the Habsburg Empire and south-eastern Europe, ethnic divisions cut across national elites and stimulated the formation of new ones—which will bring us back in due course to Ernest Gellner.

10

Germany: Academic Golden Age

The Humboldtian model of the university was devised in a pre-industrial and disunited Germany. As organs of national culture, the universities had a leading role in unification, but the ideal of *Bildung* and the influence of the *Bildungsbürgertum* still reflected the older Germany, and by 1914 there had been adaptation rather than fundamental change. Student numbers expanded after 1870 due to the general growth of the middle class, there was an influx of students from business families, and women were belatedly admitted in the 1900s. Some of this expansion was diverted into Technical High Schools, but even in the traditional universities enrolments nearly quadrupled between 1872 and 1914 (see Chapter 8). Nearly all these extra students had to be fitted into the existing universities, as there were only three new foundations: Münster in the Prussian Rhineland in 1902, reinstating a university which had been demoted to a Catholic seminary in 1818; Strasbourg, where the French faculties were replaced after the annexation of Alsace-Lorraine by a showplace German university; and Frankfurt-on-Main, which opened in 1914 as a result of local rather than state initiative. Although pressure on the universities was relieved by the Technical High Schools, internal tensions of various kinds were growing, and exemplified some of the coming problems of all universities in the twentieth century, notably those connected with the rise of large-scale science.

In the German Empire proclaimed in 1871, universities remained the responsibility of the separate state governments. University policy was debated in state parliaments, not the national Reichstag, and there was scope for differences of policy. But it was Prussia which dominated the university scene, as it did the political system. Annexations following Bismarck's wars brought Marburg, Göttingen, and Kiel under Prussian control (from Hesse, Hanover, and Denmark respectively), and in 1914 eleven of the twenty-two universities were Prussian. Prussia also had about half the students: 30,870, of whom 8,024 were at Berlin, 13 per cent of the Reich total.[1] Of the other states, only Bavaria and Baden had more than one university.[2] But the uniformity of academic traditions and habits, professorial career patterns, the popularity of student migration, and the sense that universities had a peculiarly close relationship with the successful process of unification, all meant that the universities were seen as a national system.

[1] B. vom Brocke and P. Krüger (eds.), *Hochschulpolitik im Föderalismus: Die Protokolle der Hochschulkonferenzen der deutschen Bundesstaaten und Österreich 1898 bis 1918* (Berlin, 1994), 424.

[2] The full list in 1914 was as follows. *Prussia*: Berlin, Bonn, Breslau, Frankfurt, Göttingen, Greifswald, Halle, Kiel, Königsberg, Marburg, Münster. *Bavaria*: Erlangen, Munich, Würzburg. *Baden*: Freiburg, Heidelberg. *Saxony*: Leipzig. *Württemberg*: Tübingen. *Hesse*: Giessen. *Mecklenburg-Schwerin*: Rostock. *Saxe-Weimar*: Jena. *Alsace-Lorraine*: Strasbourg.

The strengthening of Prussian dominance was especially associated with Friedrich Althoff, who was the leading figure in the higher education branch of the Prussian ministry of education from 1882, and its director from 1897 to 1907 (he died in 1908). Althoff pursued an active policy of intervention, designed to keep academic standards high and to fortify Germany's cultural prestige. The power of the state was exercised through university budgets and the appointment of professors. The creation of new chairs, institutes, and seminars was an obvious, if expensive, way of encouraging new developments. Influencing appointments to existing chairs was more difficult because of the convention that governments chose from the lists presented by faculties; but they were not obliged to choose the first candidate on the list, and could go outside it altogether. Under Althoff, the convention was often defied. He was notorious for possessing a network of informants and confidants which allowed him to spot promotable talent, and then to bring pressure on faculties to put the right men on their lists. He was able to poach promising professors for Prussia, especially for Berlin, and his influence was felt throughout Germany. He also cultivated contacts in the press, in politics, and at court. Thus the German system acquired some of the centralized, hierarchical character familiar in France or Austria. The 'Althoff system' of secret patronage and bureaucratic intrigue provoked much resentment in the academic profession. One prominent critic was Max Weber, who initially benefited from Althoff's interest, but later moved to Heidelberg, away from his direct influence. 'Every time I left the territory of the Prussian educational administration for that of Baden', Weber said in 1911, 'I had the feeling of coming into clean air.'[3]

Recent historians, however, have taken a more positive view of the achievements of this enlightened bureaucrat. At a time of competition between nation-states, Althoff was able to take a broad view of Germany's needs and of how universities were evolving, and to override the prejudices and rigidities of the academic establishment; his priorities were always intellectual rather than political. Bernhard vom Brocke argues that Althoff managed to preserve the tradition of the liberal *Kulturstaat* at a time of growing political reaction and polarization, to defend the universities against outside intervention, and to uphold the ideals of objective science and freedom of teaching and learning.[4] He also developed a 'cultural policy', continued after his time by chancellor Bethmann-Hollweg, which used the international prestige of German universities as a weapon of foreign policy. Efforts were made to attract more foreign students, especially in competition with Paris. A seminar in oriental languages had been set up by Bismarck in 1887 to support Germany's colonial ambitions, and German classicists and archaeologists were

[3] A. Busch, *Die Geschichte der Privatdozenten: Eine soziologische Studie zur grossbetrieblichen Entwicklung der deutschen Universitäten* (Stuttgart, 1959), 68.

[4] See especially by B. vom Brocke: 'Hochschul- und Wissenschaftspolitik in Preussen und im deutschen Kaiserreich 1882–1907: das "System Althoff"', in P. Baumgart (ed.), *Bildungspolitik in Preussen zur Zeit des Kaiserreichs* (Stuttgart, 1980), 9–118; 'Friedrich Althoff: a great figure in higher education policy in Germany', *Minerva*, 29 (1991), 269–93; B. vom Brocke (ed.), *Wissenschaftsgeschichte und Wissenschaftspolitik im Industriezeitalter: Das 'System Althoff' in historischer Perspektive* (Hildesheim, 1991).

now pressed into service as agents of German influence in Turkey and the Middle East.[5]

By the 1880s German universities had settled into a pattern which was described and justified in standard works like those of Johannes Conrad (1884), Friedrich Paulsen (1884 and later editions), and Wilhelm Lexis (1904), which were translated and widely read abroad. The international prestige of German universities, already high before 1871, was now almost unchallenged, and within Germany itself the primacy of German culture became a focus of national pride and an endless source of complacent satisfaction for the upper middle classes. But the ideal of the German university which foreigners admired (often identified emotionally with their youthful experiences as visitors) naturally diverged from the reality, and internal observers were more conscious of the strains caused by expansion, which were academic as well as political: internal conflicts between disciplines, the problems of the academic profession, and the pressures of vocationalism and specialization. The Humboldtian ideal had always over-idealized the motivation of students, as every generation lamented the presence of *Brotstudenten*, and looked back to a golden age of disinterested scholarship and idealistic *Bildung*. The advance of scientific research added a new dimension to these complaints.

The foundation of seminars and institutes increased the power of the state at the expense of university autonomy. The state allocated the funds and appointed the directors, who were normally the full professors, thus increasing their power within the university and their ability to favour their own disciples, and aggravating a growing crisis in the academic profession as the provision of full chairs failed to catch up with university expansion. The sufferers from this were the *Nicht-ordinarien*, comprising both *Privatdozenten* and 'extraordinary' professors, who were paid a salary (considerably lower than that of full professors) but not admitted to the decision-making academic senate. Although *Privatdozenten* were in principle unsalaried, seminars and laboratories now provided research posts for young aspirants to academic life, but these were untenured, ill-rewarded, and subject to the authoritarian whims of the professors. The regular path from *Habilitation* and *Privatdozent* status to an extraordinary and then to a full chair suffered from blockage. Between 1886 and 1911 the number of students rose by 97 per cent and the number of *Privatdozenten* by 94 per cent, but full professorships only grew by 23 per cent, from 1,015 to 1,247.[6] The average ages for taking the doctorate, achieving *Habilitation*, and obtaining a salaried post rose from 24.4, 27.6, and 33.5 in 1864 to 24.9, 30.9, and 38.2 in 1910.[7]

This problem exercised the regular conferences of German and Austrian university teachers which began in 1907, and which commissioned the statistician

[5] S. L. Marchand, *Down from Olympus: archaeology and philhellenism in Germany 1750–1970* (Princeton, 1996), 188 ff.

[6] A. Busch, 'The vicissitudes of the *Privatdozent*: breakdown and adaptation in the recruitment of the German university teacher', *Minerva*, 1 (1962–3), 319; Busch, *Geschichte der Privatdozenten*, 76–7.

[7] F. Ringer, 'A sociography of German academics 1863–1938', *Central European History*, 25 (1992), 264–5.

Eulenburg to study academic recruitment—his study included a questionnaire, and focused on the waiting time after *Habilitation*.[8] Discontent was also reflected in the foundation of separate associations for extraordinary professors and *Privatdozenten*, which merged in a *Kartell deutscher Nichtordinarier* in 1912.[9] The growth of a junior staff of this kind was actually a common feature of European universities, being a natural result of the growth of specialized research, the proliferation of subdisciplines, and the development of tutorial, laboratory, and clinical teaching to supplement professorial lectures. Nor was the change in balance overwhelming: in 1900 the average German university had 53 full professors, 34 extraordinary professors, and 49 *Privatdozenten*, and even in 1914 there were 1,318 full professors among 3,642 academic staff.[10] But the problem seemed more acute in Germany because of the former high status and independence of the *Privatdozent*, the long wait for promotion with no regular salary, and the absence of new or revived universities (as in France and Britain) to absorb rising talent. For the fortunate, the professorial career retained enormous prestige and social advantages, but the holders of full posts came to seem more and more a closed caste. Survival through the early years favoured those with private means, and men drawn from the classic *Bildungsbürgertum* resented this 'plutocratic' influx.[11] Greater competition for posts also made it easier to exclude those whose political or religious faces did not fit.

If a conflict between generations was one source of academic tension, conflict between and within disciplines was another.[12] The emergence of the social sciences, and of new methods within traditional subjects like history, was an aspect whose political implications will be discussed in the next chapter. Equally striking was the development of the natural sciences, and their claims to a new place in university life. As rector of Berlin in 1892, Rudolf Virchow proclaimed that 'the dominance of neohumanism is broken'.[13] Virchow, professor of pathology at Berlin, was best known as a medical scientist, and was militantly anti-religious, but he was also both a notable archaeologist and a leading liberal politician. He was politically active in 1848, a member of the Prussian parliament in the 1860s, and of the Reichstag between 1880 and 1893. Like the historian Theodor Mommsen, who had a similar political career, he continued to uphold the liberal cause when Bismarck's Germany had turned against it. For him as for others, there was a natural connection between

[8] F. Eulenburg, *Der 'akademische Nachwuchs': Eine Untersuchung über die Lage und die Aufgaben der Extraordinarien und Privatdozenten* (Leipzig, 1908).

[9] J. Ben-David, *The scientist's role in society: a comparative study* (Englewood Cliffs, NJ, 1971), 130.

[10] H. W. Prahl, *Sozialgeschichte des Hochschulwesens* (Munich, 1978), 208–9; Brocke and Krüger, *Hochschulpolitik*, 435.

[11] C. E. McClelland, *State, society and university in Germany 1700–1914* (Cambridge, 1980), 271–2.

[12] Cf. P. Lundgreen, 'Differentiation in German higher education', in K. H. Jarausch (ed.), *The transformation of higher learning 1860–1930: expansion, diversification, social opening, and professionalization in England, Germany, Russia, and the United States* (Chicago, 1983), 149–79.

[13] B. vom Brocke, '"Die Gelehrten": Auf dem Weg zu einer vergleichenden Sozialgeschichte europäischer Bildungssysteme und Bildungseliten im Industriezeitalter', *Annali dell'Istituto Storico Italo-Germanico in Trento*, 10 (1984), 398.

science and progressive politics.[14] He was also interested, as a member of the Berlin city council, in questions of public health, and his career is a reminder that medicine was as important as industry in shaping the development of science and the proliferation of research institutes and laboratories. The Reich Health Office set up in 1876 indicated the growing interest of the state in medical research, especially after Bismarck introduced state-supported health insurance in the 1880s.

The impact of science on the university system can be discussed under three aspects: its development within universities, where it had to contend with prejudices against utilitarian subjects; the growth of a rival system of modern and technical education, at both secondary and higher level, and its struggle for equal status; and the appearance in the early twentieth century of scientific research as an activity which broke free of educational tasks and made heavy demands on public and private resources. Within the universities, the research and training laboratory pioneered by Liebig became the norm in the 1870s and 1880s. In the application of science to industry, Germany was by then considered a model for other countries. This connection owed something to fortunate timing: Germany was industrializing at a time when science was itself in a period of rapid development, and the textile industry which was at the heart of the early industrial revolution demanded more theoretical sophistication just when academic chemistry was in a position to supply it.[15] Initial achievements in the field of dyestuffs laid the foundations of later work in artificial fabrics, explosives, and pharmaceuticals. Along with the development of electrical engineering, this enabled Germany to establish an unchallenged lead in the 'second industrial revolution' of the late nineteenth century. Germany had the first 'educational-industrial complex', which 'both fascinated and alarmed' her neighbours.[16] She seemed to have found the secret of putting science in the service of industry: scientists could identify the key areas for development and train men with an eye to industrial applications, while employers were alert to the need for industrial progress to be based on science and willing to employ university-trained scientists, to subsidize new chairs and institutes, and to commission applied research. The Siemens firm was notable for its support of electrical engineering. At Jena, the fortunes of the university were transformed through the patronage of the Zeiss optical firm, which channelled resources through the Carl Zeiss Foundation from 1889.[17] In the chemical industry, pupils of Liebig had a direct role as the founders of new firms. In Baden, which became an important centre of that industry, the state embarked on a policy of investing in university education to promote industrial development; Heidelberg was one of the universities which set up a separate science faculty, in 1890. In 1910–14 Baden was spending 2.20 marks per head of population on science and learning, compared with 1.48 in Bavaria, 1.34 in

[14] B. A. Boyd, *Rudolf Virchow: the scientist as citizen* (New York, 1991).

[15] P. Lundgreen, 'Education for the science-based industrial state? The case for nineteenth-century Germany', *History of Education*, 13 (1984), 59–67.

[16] R. R. Locke, 'Industrialisierung und Erziehungssystem in Frankreich und Deutschland vor dem 1. Weltkrieg', *Historische Zeitschrift*, 225 (1977), 281.

[17] D. Höroldt, 'Zur wirtschaftliche Bedeutung der Universitäten für ihre Städte', in E. Maschke and J. Sydow (eds.), *Stadt und Hochschule im 19. und 20. Jahrhundert* (Sigmaringen, 1979), 48.

Saxony, and 1.22 in Prussia.[18] In Prussia, following a campaign by the mathematician Felix Klein at Göttingen, new chairs in industrial chemistry were founded in several universities, and at Göttingen itself in the 1890s institutes for applied mathematics and physics were financed with the help of industrialists who also formed a science lobby in the Prussian parliament.[19]

The involvement of universities like Heidelberg, Göttingen, and Jena in applied research showed that there was openness to change, as long as applied science could be seen as an offshoot of pure research. What was much less acceptable was direct training for technical occupations: the German universities set their face against extending the 'learned' professions to include engineering, despite its theoretical basis in mathematics, and most states had created specialized colleges in this field in the eighteenth or early nineteenth centuries. From the 1820s these began to expand their remit, often under the title 'polytechnic'. The first examples were in Austria, at Prague and Vienna, and in 1825 Baden became the German pioneer at Karlsruhe. By 1870 there were also colleges at Munich, Dresden, Stuttgart, Darmstadt, Hanover, and Braunschweig—apart from Munich, all cities without universities. By the 1870s, these colleges were adopting the title of Technical High School, and taking on some of the attributes of universities, such as a faculty structure, academic autonomy, and the pursuit of research. It was only in 1870 that Prussia joined the movement with a foundation at Aachen, and in 1879 several existing institutions in Berlin were brought together in a single school in the suburb of Charlottenburg. Charlottenburg immediately became a leading centre, and (along with the polytechnic at Zurich) a model for other countries. Later Prussian foundations were at Danzig (1904) and Breslau (1910), both intended as bastions of Germanism in parts of Prussia with Polish minorities. The German Technical High Schools came to form a distinct sector of the national higher education system. Engineering in all its forms was at their heart, including architecture as an extension of civil engineering, but they also specialized in chemistry and physics, and began to receive the same type of support from industrialists and from state governments as the university science faculties.

Unlike the École Polytechnique at Paris, the Technical High Schools were open to all qualified candidates, and while the former drew its pupils from the elite lycées, the latter were linked with a separate sector of modern secondary schools, developed and systematized out of various early nineteenth-century initiatives. The basic institution was the *Realschule*, which taught modern subjects (usually with some Latin, as a general cultural subject, but not Greek), and had local roots and vocational links. The *Realschule* curriculum lengthened as demand increased, and a *Realschule Abitur* was introduced in Prussia in 1859. Later the term *Oberrealschule*

[18] F. R. Pfetsch, *Zur Entwicklung der Wissenschaftspolitik in Deutschland 1750–1914* (Berlin, 1974), 52; W. Doerr (ed.), *Semper apertus: Sechshundert Jahre Ruprecht-Karls-Universität Heidelberg 1386–1986 . . . II. Das neunzehnte Jahrhundert* (Berlin, 1985), 17–18.

[19] K. H. Manegold, *Universität, Technische Hochschule und Industrie: Ein Beitrag zur Emanzipation der Technik im 19. Jahrhundert unter besonderer Berücksichtigung der Bestrebungen Felix Kleins* (Berlin, 1970), 85 ff., 157 ff.; N. Andernach, *Der Einfluss der Parteien auf das Hochschulwesen in Preussen 1848–1918* (Göttingen, 1972), 155–6.

was applied to schools with a full curriculum, and another hybrid type, the *Realgymnasium*, combined humanist education with modern alternatives. But these schools had lower prestige than the full gymnasium, and their leaving qualifications did not at first entitle students to university entry. In 1870, students with the *Realschule Abitur* were allowed to matriculate in the philosophy faculty, but the professional faculties remained closed: for doctors and lawyers as for bureaucrats, a full classical education remained an essential indicator of cultivated social status. Pupils from the modern schools could go to the Technical High Schools, but the latter lacked the right to award doctoral degrees (*Promotion*), leading to a campaign for equal status which was fuelled by the status aspirations of the engineering profession.

Debate on this question became politicized in the 1880s and 1890s, as part of the 'qualifications crisis', study of which stimulated the work of Detlef Müller on secondary schools and of Titze on cycles of recruitment, and underlies Ringer's argument that differentiation and segmentation were ways of diverting excess demand while leaving traditional education intact.[20] In a revival of polemic about the intellectual proletariat and the overcrowding of the professions, political conservatives, including Bismarck, claimed that the system was producing too many graduates with traditional qualifications who could not find jobs, and blamed this for the rise of socialism and other evils. The rapid growth of university enrolments in this period was real enough. But while the arguments were partly inspired by social reaction, they were cross-cut by more progressive ones. In government circles, there was impatience with the universities' old-fashioned attitudes, and a fear that Germany's industrial momentum was slowing down and her international competitive position becoming weaker. The Technical High Schools seemed better able to deliver the necessary scientific and technical expertise, and their status should be improved, along with that of the schools which fed into them. Academic conservatives, on the other hand, resisted equal status for modern education, and continued to assert that only the full classical curriculum was suited to the intellectual aristocracy of the nation.

The main debate was over school qualifications: whether the modern versions of the *Abitur* should give full right of entry to the universities. In 1890 the Kaiser took a personal interest in the Prussian 'school conference' called to consider the question, declaring that the time had come to educate young Germans rather than young Greeks and Romans. There was stubborn resistance from those who believed that 'the intellectual general staff must for a long time, for ever . . . still be formed by the school of Greece and Rome', and it was not until a second school conference in 1900 that the universities were fully opened to leavers from any type of secondary school.[21] Meanwhile, the right to award diplomas and doctorates was granted to the

[20] The qualifications crisis gave its name to the collective QUAKRI project of 1977–81, of which Titze's statistical work was a major outcome.

[21] G. Roethe, cited (1906) in K. E. Jeismann, *Das Preussische Gymnasium in Staat und Gesellschaft. II. Höhere Bildung zwischen Reform und Reaktion 1817–1859* (Stuttgart, 1996), 635; J. Albisetti, *Secondary school reform in Imperial Germany* (Princeton, 1983), 140 ff.

Technical High Schools in 1899.[22] This enhanced the prestige of the latter, and of engineers. But if the intention was to divert demand to the technical sector, the policy was a decided failure, for the school reforms set off a recruitment boom in the traditional universities, whose enrolments rose from 33,688 in 1900 to 60,234 in 1914. By 1911 over a quarter of Prussian students came from modern secondary schools.[23] But the Technical High Schools stagnated—full-time students had risen from 4,209 in 1890 to 11,072 in 1900, but were still only 11,451 in 1914, and they had a lower proportion of the total student body in 1914 than in the 1870s, though the expansion of science teaching in the universities meant that the overall proportion studying science and technology remained stable at around a third.[24] As we have seen, expansion in the universities attracted new strata of the middle class, which did little to assuage the fears of conservatives or the career pressures felt by students.

By the 1900s the Technical High Schools also had rivals for the patronage of the bourgeoisie in a new type of higher commercial or business school, an innovation found in all European countries at this time. As with engineers and the Technical High Schools, one motive was to extend professionalization to commercial and managerial careers, thus also raising barriers against those who rose from the ranks.[25] While Technical High Schools were founded and financed by the states, the higher commercial schools usually owed their origin to local elites working through municipalities or chambers of commerce. Leipzig was an early example (1898), and by 1914 there were also schools at Berlin (1906, symbolically sited next to the stock exchange), Cologne, Frankfurt, Königsberg, Mannheim, and Munich, with a total of 2,695 students.[26] Their teaching was based on economics, accountancy, modern languages, and other practical subjects, but they also developed branches of social science which had not found a haven in the universities. The economic historian Werner Sombart, for example, taught at the Berlin school.[27]

Especially significant was the school at Frankfurt, which called itself an 'Academy for Social and Business Sciences'. It was opened in 1901, but the intention from the start was to work for the creation of a university. It also employed many Jewish academics who could not get chairs in universities.[28] Despite the hostility of conservatives to the utilitarianism of business studies, and to the supposed political subversiveness of social science, the Prussian state consented to the creation of the university in 1914, and it opened that autumn after the outbreak of war; the business school became its social science faculty and was to be the home of the 'Frankfurt

[22] The title of 'university' was still denied, which implied inferior status (though *Hochschule* is the generic term for higher education).

[23] P. Windolf, *Expansion and structural change: higher education in Germany, the United States, and Japan 1870–1990* (Boulder, Colo., 1997), 55.

[24] Brocke and Krüger, *Hochschulpolitik*, 424, 427; Prahl, *Sozialgeschichte*, 212–13; Lundgreen, 'Education for the science-based industrial state', 62.

[25] R. Riese, *Die Hochschule auf dem Wege zum wissenschaftlichen Grossbetrieb: Die Universität Heidelberg und das badische Hochschulwesen 1860–1914* (Stuttgart, 1977), 310.

[26] Brocke and Krüger, *Hochschulpolitik*, 430.

[27] K. Tribe, 'Business education at the Mannheim Handelshochschule 1907–1933', *Minerva*, 32 (1994), 167.

[28] G. Kirchgässner, 'Die Gründung der Handelshochschulen Frankfurt und Mannheim als Leistung des Besitz- und Bildungsbürgertums', in Maschke and Sydow, *Stadt und Hochschule*, 137.

school' of social theorists under Weimar. Although formally a state institution, Frankfurt was an innovatory 'foundation' university, similar constitutionally to the civic universities of England, financed locally and with the donors retaining control over appointments. Its creation was part of a wider debate over the need for new and more experimental universities, especially in the large cities, and there were other movements, at Cologne and Hamburg, which achieved their aims after the war.[29] The Frankfurt case also illustrated a new theme of the early twentieth century: the growing unwillingness of the *Kulturstaat* to bear the sole financial burden of science and higher education.

The state originally supported university laboratories and institutes as a necessary offshoot of teaching and academic training. But by 1900 scientific research was becoming an independent activity, which could be carried on just as efficiently, and with greater practical focus, in company laboratories or freestanding research institutes. An early example of the latter was the Reich Physical-Technical Institute of 1887, a standards and testing laboratory, especially for the electrical industry, which was partly financed by Siemens; the Berlin physicist Hermann Helmholtz became its president.[30] Althoff was involved in this, as in most initiatives of the time, and he looked to the United States as his model, learning from the reports of German academic delegations to the international exhibitions at Chicago in 1893 and St Louis in 1904. Althoff was impressed by America's wealthy private universities and munificent donors, and hoped this pattern of patronage might be transported. His thinking was shared by Adolf Harnack, a theologian and academic politician who had much influence in government circles, and whose phrase 'science as big business' (*Wissenschaft als Grossbetrieb*), coined in 1899, passed into general debate.

The culmination of this line of thinking was the foundation in 1911 of the Kaiser-Wilhelm-Gesellschaft (KWG), as a general funding organization for scientific research. Harnack was its first president, and although Althoff was dead by then, the idea owed much to him and to a group of Berlin professors who wanted to develop research independently of teaching, and who lobbied for an equivalent of the Physical-Technical Institute for chemistry. It was linked with another of Althoff's American inspirations, the creation of a campus at Dahlem in the Berlin suburbs, where scientific and medical institutes could expand freely.[31] The KWG was to be only a semi-public institution, for one of its functions was to raise private funds and relieve the state of its burdens. After a great fundraising effort, which exploited the personal support of the Kaiser, it started with an endowment of 6 million marks, and this had reached 12.6 million by 1914. Most of the money came from industrialists and bankers, and was directed towards applied science, especially chemistry. By 1914 some ten Kaiser Wilhelm institutes were operating, including those for physical chemistry at Berlin, directed by Fritz Haber, for coal research at Mülheim,

[29] Riese, *Hochschule*, 322–4.

[30] D. Cahan, *An Institute for an Empire: the Physikalisch-Technische Reichsanstalt 1871–1918* (Cambridge, 1989).

[31] After 1945, when the original University of Berlin fell into the Soviet sector, Dahlem became the site of the Free University.

financed by Ruhr industrialists to develop synthetic products based on coal, and for theoretical physics at Berlin, to which Albert Einstein was called as director. Most of the institutes were in Prussia, and as they and their powerful directors were entirely independent of the universities the latter lost a further part of their influence.[32]

On the eve of 1914, a new partnership between the state, the universities, and industry was beginning to emerge; Max Weber was to say in 1918 that university institutes had become 'state capitalist' enterprises, in which the scientist had become a dependent worker.[33] Since Germany's great-power ambitions were one of the driving forces, the relations between power and intellect, *Macht* and *Geist*, were also close—Haber and his Institute were to lead the development of poison gas as a weapon in the First World War. 'Military prowess and science', said Harnack, 'are the two great pillars of Germany's greatness, and the Prussian state has the duty to ensure the preservation of both.'[34] And according to Paolo Schiera, Althoff 'made a decisive contribution to the international-imperialist glorification from which German science benefited at the turn of the century. A great protector of the universities and, in that respect, the latest exponent of the Humboldtian project, he was also the boldest interpreter of the new tendencies which were ever increasing in the conditions of the age of industrialization.'[35] As the home of Europe's most developed university system, Germany had early experience of the dilemmas of the twentieth century. And if dependence on the state was dangerous, dependence on capitalism had its problems too. As Harnack pointed out, state finance was coupled with a strong tradition of university autonomy. Would other paymasters allow the same freedom?

> Today science in all its branches needs large resources; large resources are in the nature of things only handed over in return for benefits. If the state does not provide them, then the business of science can only become dependent on the views of those who give the money—see America, Rockefeller, Carnegie! Just as in the middle ages we had a science which was entirely tied to the church, since the church gave money and prestige, so there is a danger that henceforth we shall have a science which is party-political and subordinate to high finance or to industry.[36]

Harnack took a less optimistic view of the American example than Althoff, and warned that the nation-state's use of higher education for its own purposes was undermining the internationalism of science.

[32] L. Burchardt, *Wissenschaftspolitik im Wilhelminischen Deutschland: Vorgeschichte, Gründung und Aufbau der Kaiser-Wilhelm-Gesellschaft zur Förderung der Wissenschaften* (Göttingen, 1975); B. vom Brocke and H. Laitko (eds.), *Die Kaiser-Wilhelm-/Max-Planck-Gesellschaft und ihre Institute. Studien zu ihrer Geschichte: Das Harnack-Prinzip* (Berlin, 1996); J. A. Johnson, *The Kaiser's chemists: science and modernization in Imperial Germany* (Chapel Hill, NC, 1990).

[33] 'Science as a vocation', in H. H. Gerth and C. Wright Mills (eds.), *From Max Weber: essays in sociology* (London, 1948), 131.

[34] Cited in F. Ringer, 'The German academic community 1870–1920', *Internationales Archiv für Sozialgeschichte der Deutschen Literatur*, 3 (1978), 122.

[35] P. Schiera, 'Scienza e politica in Germania da Bismarck a Guglielmo II', in G. Corni and P. Schiera (eds.), *Cultura politica e società borghese in Germania fra otto e novecento* (Bologna, 1986), 30–1.

[36] Cited in Busch, *Geschichte der Privatdozenten*, 67–8; cf. A. Harnack, *Aus Wissenschaft und Leben* (Giessen, 1911), i. 13; Ringer, 'German academic community', 123.

Surveying the German universities at the turn of the century, Friedrich Paulsen was mildly critical of some aspects—he thought, for example, that technical education should have been embraced by the universities instead of ceding the field to the Technical High Schools, and was concerned about the lack of opportunities for working-class students; but generally his view was optimistic. He described the German system as one in which the 'controlling purpose' of the university was research, and the training of scholars in seminars was the chief means of education. Research was the prime duty of university staff, and Paulsen defended the research-based *Habilitation* over the French *agrégation*. In defining the aims of university education, he put 'scientific professional knowledge' first, the ability to do independent scientific work second, and 'philosophical culture' third.[37] In his re-evaluation of Althoff's work, Brocke comes to a rather similar conclusion: the ideal of general humanist education, the tasks of professional training, and the new ideal of scientific research had reached a new, fruitful, and lasting synthesis. Education and science were now accepted as a 'fourth factor of production' along with land, capital, and labour.[38] On the positive side, one can also argue that the rise of the Technical High Schools and buoyant university enrolments showed a system successfully meeting the new challenges of an industrial and democratic era. Yet in the 1900s there was a pervasive sense of crisis in the academic world. The Humboldtian balance between teaching and research was felt to be disturbed by big science, the academic profession was losing its status, and in the age of specialization the dream of disinterested *Bildung* seemed distant.[39] These pessimistic judgements came naturally to those who felt their interests and ideals to be threatened, but they also reflected a political culture in which the progress of modernity aroused fears and reactions which seem irrational in the light of Germany's political and intellectual strength.

[37] F. Paulsen, *The German universities and university study* (London, 1906), 165, 306.

[38] Brocke, *Wissenschaftsgeschichte*, 1.

[39] B. vom Brocke, 'Die Entstehung der deutschen Forschungsuniversität, ihre Blüte und Krise um 1900', in R. C. Schwinges (ed.), *Humboldt International: Der Export des deutschen Universitätsmodells im 19. und 20. Jahrhundert* (Basel, 2001), 386 ff.

11

Germany: Political Tensions

If the German universities were a model internationally admired, they also took on national characteristics which allied them with conservative forces in the unified German state. In 1848, professors and students had still been a liberal force, though seldom a radical one. In the 1850s and early 1860s, during the conflicts in Prussia between the elected parliament and the crown, university intellectuals were still mostly on the liberal side. But after Prussia's triumph over Austria in 1866, they followed the general trend of German liberalism in accepting the leadership of the Hohenzollern monarchy. For the historian Gustav Droysen, a member of the Frankfurt parliament in 1848, events had vindicated those who had preached 'the destiny, the power, and the right' of Prussia.[1] Bismarck's policies of blood and iron, which had achieved the nationalist dreams of 1848, won over most of the academic world, and professors became characteristic supporters of the National Liberal party, which was closely identified with the foundation years of the Reich and with the interests of the upper middle class.

In 1870, at the outbreak of the Franco-Prussian war, the rector of Berlin, the scientist Du Bois-Reymond, proclaimed that 'Berlin university, quartered opposite the royal palace, is from its foundation deeds the intellectual bodyguard of the house of Hohenzollern'.[2] Such rhetorical flourishes apart, professors had good reason to be loyal to a state in which their own prestige was high. The German empire was a *Rechtsstaat*, a state ruled by law, and freedom of teaching and learning were embodied in the constitution. Arbitrary dismissals of the 'Göttingen seven' type became unthinkable. But academic freedom had clear boundaries: it was based on the idea that science was objective, and that politics could and should be excluded from the halls of the university. The tradition of *Bildung* included a high-minded contempt for party politics as such, and a belief which went back to Kant, or even Luther, that the inner freedom of the individual was best supported by a strong state and could somehow be separated from political freedom and the rights of citizens. The professor as scholar had freedoms denied to the professor as citizen, and 'politics' was defined to mean dissent, while active and loyal support for the regime was seen as apolitical. Like their counterparts in other countries, German professors espoused the destiny of their nation and believed that it had a special cultural mission. Max Weber, in many respects a liberal and a critic of the regime, was typical in insisting, down to 1914 and beyond, that the 'national power state' was the essential basis for everything of value in German life.[3]

[1] Cited in W. M. Simon, *Germany in the age of Bismarck* (London, 1968), 105.

[2] M. Mechow, *Berliner Studenten 1810–1914* (Berlin, 1975), 74.

[3] Marianne Weber, *Max Weber: a biography* (New York, 1974), 117.

As the life of the empire evolved, especially after the accession of Wilhelm II in 1888, the coexistence of liberal and national traditions became more problematic. Germany's rapid industrialization produced new forms of large-scale capitalism, nationalism was subsumed into *Weltpolitik* and imperialism, and social tensions generated a hostility to socialism which pervaded the political establishment and the educated classes. Professors and students shared the general evolution to the right and towards 'academic illiberalism' (or so argues Konrad Jarausch), while political conservatism combined with reaction against some of the unwelcome academic developments described in the last chapter to turn the academic 'mandarins' (or so argues Fritz Ringer) against the modern world and against progress.[4]

The empire was selective in the values which it identified as national. Politically it was dominated by Prussia, and culturally by Protestantism. The ideal of *Bildung* had always drawn on Protestant roots, and in the triumphalist mood after unification it was common to see a direct line from Luther to Bismarck, from the Reformation to the free thought and science of the nineteenth century. Even when they were freethinkers, as many were, professors of Protestant background remained faithful to their instincts. This was especially significant in the 1870s, when Bismarck sought to consolidate the new state by stirring up opinion against supposed enemies of the Reich. In later years socialists filled that role, but the first target was the Catholic church, which was associated with Austria and the southern states which had taken her side in 1866. This was the *Kulturkampf*, the clash of cultures: it consisted of various legal and administrative measures within Prussia (for religion, like education, remained a state not a Reich responsibility) against the rights and self-government of the Catholic church. As in France and other countries, both Protestants and freethinkers were alarmed by ultramontanism and by episodes like the Syllabus of Errors and the proclamation of Papal infallibility, and they turned to the state as the guarantor of freedom.

The Vatican Council of 1870 had particular repercussions in Germany because it caused a breakaway movement of 'Old Catholics' who rejected Papal authority. They included academics within faculties of Catholic theology, and this raised one of the classic problems of church–state relations: since the function of these faculties was to train for the priesthood, could the church demand the expulsion of professors who defied its authority and held heretical views? Could the state go against the views of the church in making new appointments? The state appointed theology professors through the standard academic procedures, but they required episcopal approval before taking office. The leader of the Old Catholic movement was Ignaz von Döllinger, professor at Munich, whose stance was supported by the Bavarian government. In Prussia, several theology professors at Bonn joined the Old Catholics, and when one of them died the state defied the church authorities by appointing an Old Catholic successor, Moritz Ritter. In the ensuing controversy,

[4] K. Jarausch, *Students, society and politics in Imperial Germany: the rise of academic illiberalism* (Princeton, 1982); F. Ringer, *The decline of the German mandarins: the German academic community 1890–1933* (Cambridge, Mass., 1969). A third essential book for the English reader is C. E. McClelland, *State, society and university in Germany 1700–1914* (Cambridge, 1980).

the government made it clear that it would not appoint professors connected with the Centre Party, the political arm of orthodox Catholicism, because the party was opposed to the fundamental basis of the state. This policy had strong support from liberal academics—but it was a line with dangers to academic freedom, as it could later be turned against socialists, atheists, and other radicals.[5] For their part, Centre politicians revived earlier demands for a Belgian or French-style Catholic university, but the German tradition of state monopoly was too strong for this to have a chance.[6] The general result of the *Kulturkampf* was to strengthen Catholic resistance, and in 1879 the campaign was called off. Old Catholic professors died or retired in due course. Above all, Bismarck now broke his alliance with the liberals, and German politics thenceforward rested on conservative coalitions which usually included the Centre Party. In retrospect, the 1870s appeared as something of a golden age for academic liberals, when they were valued allies of the state. After that, they were more likely to be regarded by the political establishment as potential subversives who needed to be kept under strict political control, and this was the context in which Althoff could be seen as a defender of academic autonomy.

One of Althoff's aims was to remedy the under-representation of Catholics (the so-called 'educational deficit') at both student and professorial level. Napoleon's abolition of universities in the Rhineland had a long-lasting impact, especially when industrialization and migration from the countryside made this a rich and populous area; the revival of the University of Münster in 1902 did something to improve the balance. In the student body, under-representation reflected the more rural character of the Catholic population as well as a feeling that university culture was unsympathetic to Catholic values.[7] In professorial appointments, there was clear prejudice against Catholics, and even in the southern states the determination of governments to appoint the best men regardless of religion, and the intellectual dominance of Berlin and other Protestant universities in the training of scholars, worked against them. In Bavaria, where 71 per cent of the population was Catholic, Protestants still had proportionately more student places than Catholics (5.5 per thousand population, against 3.2), and at Munich in 1896 only fifty-two of the ninety-three professors were Catholics, while at Würzburg—a centre of Catholic theological orthodoxy—the Catholic professors were in a minority, twenty-two out of fifty-two.[8]

Religion was also a problem at the new University of Strasbourg. After the annexation of Alsace-Lorraine (which remained a territory under direct Reich control) a new German university replaced the French faculties. Most of the French staff chose the path of exile, and Strasbourg was turned into a showpiece for the German university ideal, and a classic exercise in nation-building through elite

[5] N. Andernach, *Der Einfluss der Parteien auf das Hochschulwesen in Preussen 1848–1918* (Göttingen, 1972), 40–2, 88–96.

[6] H. Dickerhof, 'Staatliches Bildungsmonopol: Die Idee einer katholischen Universität und die Schulen der katholischen Theologie im 19. Jahrhundert', *Archiv für Kulturgeschichte*, 66 (1984), 175–214.

[7] W. Rösener, 'Das katholische Bildungsdefizit im Deutschen Kaiserreich: ein Erbe der Säkularisation von 1803?', *Historisches Jahrbuch*, 112 (1992), 104–27.

[8] L. Boehm, *Geschichtsdenken, Bildungsgeschichte, Wissenschaftsorganisation: Ausgewählte Aufsätze von Laetitia Boehm anlässlich ihres 65. Geburtstages* (Berlin, 1996), 788.

culture; there were some who hoped that the university might be a bridge between French and German cultures, but the bitterness caused by the annexation ruled this out. Large sums were spent on buildings and equipment (notably on the medical school, already important under the French), able and dynamic professors were attracted by high salaries, and the university was a testing-ground for innovations. Strasbourg had a separate faculty of science, for example, which was only the second in Germany. Althoff cut his teeth as an administrator in the organization of Strasbourg, and himself occupied a law chair there for ten years. The historian Friedrich Meinecke served at Strasbourg in the 1900s, and recalled that the 'colony' of professors planted there retained the 'liberal and passionately national humanism' of a generation before.[9] But this did not necessarily help the purpose of the institution, which was to win over the largely Catholic, French-speaking Alsatian elite to the German cause. No concessions were made on the linguistic front, and although the area was strongly industrial, the university's science remained pure rather than applied.

In 1900, although a third of the Strasbourg students were Catholic, there were only two Catholics among the forty-eight full professors (along with four Jews). Althoff planned to create a Catholic theology faculty to broaden the university's appeal, and when a chair in history fell vacant in 1901, he overrode the faculty to appoint Martin Spahn, manipulating the appointment so that this appeared to be a new chair, when the government had first right of appointment: as at Bonn and Breslau, history was to be a *Weltanschauung* subject with duplicate chairs. The Spahn case created a storm of protest, for although academically well qualified, Spahn was also the son of the leader of the Centre Party. The appointment was widely interpreted as an academic coup carried out through political intrigue, and as a deliberate challenge to the conventions of appointment.[10] The Catholic theology faculty was created in 1902, and in common with other German universities Strasbourg was now widening its social recruitment, which brought in more Catholic students from peasant or lower-middle-class backgrounds. The historian of these developments, John Craig, concludes that by 1914 the university was making some progress in winning over local opinion and putting down deeper roots, so that when the French returned after 1918 regaining support for their own anticlerical ideology did not prove straightforward.[11]

The historian Heinrich von Treitschke said that in Germany 'university professors have gained over a period of time an influence in shaping the customs and views of our people unprecedented in any other country'.[12] Writing in 1922,

[9] M. Nebelin, 'Die Reichsuniversität Strassburg als Modell und Ausgangspunkt der deutschen Hochschulreform', in B. vom Brocke (ed.), *Wissenschaftsgeschichte und Wissenschaftspolitik im Industriezeitalter: Das 'System Althoff' in historischer Perspektive* (Hildesheim, 1991), 68.

[10] J. E. Craig, *Scholarship and nation building: the universities of Strasbourg and Alsatian society 1870–1939* (Chicago, 1984), 145–58; B. vom Brocke, 'Hochschul- und Wissenschaftspolitik in Preussen und im deutschen Kaiserreich 1882–1907: das "System Althoff"', in P. Baumgart (ed.), *Bildungspolitik in Preussen zur Zeit des Kaiserreichs* (Stuttgart, 1980), 100–5.

[11] Craig, *Scholarship and nation building*, 192–4.

[12] H. Flaig, 'The historian as pedagogue of the nation', *History*, 59 (1974), 19.

Meinecke identified three historical stages in their influence. In the early nineteenth century,

> philosophers dominated the academic scene and established the basic notions of a free and nationally united political life. In the second period, historians had a preponderant role fusing idealism with historical experience in the synthesis of classical liberalism. The third period brought economists into the foreground, men who could deal as experts with the new social and economic problems of the German national state.[13]

This schema omits the scientists and technologists of the Wilhelmine era, who identified *Wissenschaft* with Germany's modernity and industrial power. But historians and economists were certainly deeply engaged with political questions. The rediscovery of the German past had been central to the creation of national consciousness since the late eighteenth century, and the 'Prussian school' of historians put their own spin on it, seeing unification on Bismarckian lines as the working out of the Prussian monarchy's historic mission—somewhat crudely in Treitschke, more subtly in the work of the liberal nationalists Droysen and Heinrich von Sybel. This school dominated the professional scene, and alternative versions of history, pro-Austrian or pro-Catholic, fell out of academic favour. The father of modern scientific history, Leopold von Ranke, professor at Berlin for many years, was less nationalistic, but his emphasis on the nation-state and international relations made his disciples fervent supporters of Germany's great-power position and of Wilhelmine Weltpolitik. The emphasis of orthodox German historians on the state and international relations made them resistant to the intrusion of social science on history:

> The distinctive object of historical study was the moral realm of ideas, free will, and purposeful human activity. . . . The supreme institutional manifestation of this moral realm, and hence the proper focus of historical study, was the state, whose development alone provided meaning to the past. . . . The primacy of the state in history corresponded . . . to the supremacy of the state over society, to the role of this institution as the guarantor of order against the social and religious forces that challenged the Bismarckian settlement.[14]

These attitudes, linked with the customary hostility to 'materialism' and its denial of free will, were widely shared.

The career of the unorthodox historian Karl Lamprecht shows the penalties of dissent. Lamprecht started as a protégé of Althoff, but in 1890 he was called to Leipzig, where the university was generously supported by the Saxon government in rivalry with Prussia. In the same year, he published the first volume of a history of Germany which 'destroyed his reputation in the German historical profession'.[15] This was not because of his politics, which were orthodox in the pro-Prussian mode, but because his slapdash scholarly methods and his penchant for generalization and overarching interpretative schemes of 'cultural history' offended the ideal

[13] As summarized by F. Gilbert, 'Political power and academic responsibility: reflections on Friedrich Meinecke's *Drei Generationen Deutscher Gelehrtenpolitik*', in L. Krieger and F. Stern (eds.), *The responsibility of power: historical essays in honor of Hajo Holborn* (London, 1968), 402–3.

[14] R. Chickering, *Karl Lamprecht: a German academic life (1856–1915)* (Atlantic Highlands, NJ, 1993), 34.

[15] Ibid. 122.

of document-based objectivity. Lamprecht went on publishing his history, which was a popular best-seller but boycotted by the academic historians. His work was not reviewed, and his doctoral pupils found it impossible to get posts, so much so that the historical seminar in Leipzig had to be divided, with Lamprecht running his own in 'cultural and universal history'. Boycotting, favouritism, and the sycophancy of young scholars towards their academic patrons showed the dark side of professorial power. But Lamprecht's experience also showed how the devolved system could be a refuge for academic freedom. In his Leipzig citadel, with the support of the Saxon government and of a carefully-cultivated network of politicians, businessmen, and journalists, he was impregnable. He also had the sympathy of colleagues in other disciplines, and was elected rector in 1910–11; he was successful in raising private money, he helped to set up a Saxon version of the Kaiser-Wilhelm-Gesellschaft, and like Althoff he was interested in promoting Germany's interests through a cultural foreign policy.

The conflict of methods among historians (the *Methodenstreit*) was part of a wider redefinition of the relations between academic subjects in the later nineteenth century. Once the idea of the unity of knowledge became untenable, it was usual to distinguish between *Geisteswissenschaften* (the humanities) and *Naturwissenschaften* (natural sciences). It was not difficult to imagine a value-free study of the natural world, once religious explanations were sidelined, but more difficult for the human sciences. Disciplinary objectivity and the scientific approach were meant to be a guarantee of neutrality. But what if the objects of study were the economy, labour, social change, or political activity itself? What were the implications when attempts to understand these phenomena moved from a historical approach which accepted present arrangements as the natural outcome of organic development, to an approach which examined the empirical data of contemporary society and sought scientific laws of society applicable to the future as well as the past? The positivist idea of applying scientific methods to the study of society had always had radical implications, and they were particularly difficult to reconcile with the apolitical stance with which the German professorate now protected its freedom. Moreover, materialism had now taken on the new and politically alarming shape of marxism.[16]

The economists of Meinecke's third phase were the so-called 'socialists of the professorial chair', or *Kathedersozialisten*, who tried to study social problems while avoiding overt political commitment. Their appearance was as much a response to Germany's rapid industrialization as was the evolution of chemistry or physics. According to Adolf Wagner in 1895, 'what the unification question was in the past, the social question is today'.[17] Wagner was a member of the Verein für Sozialpolitik (Association for Social Policy) founded by this school in 1872. The professors involved mostly had a background in economics, but wished to move beyond liberal orthodoxy while repudiating the class-based socialism of the Social

[16] Ibid. 212 ff.

[17] R. vom Bruch, *Wissenschaft, Politik und öffentliche Meinung: Gelehrtenpolitik im Wilhelminischen Deutschland (1890–1914)* (Husum, 1980), 157.

Democrat party (SPD) founded in 1875. In 1910 the association had 760 members.[18] It was an elite organization, including some businessmen and officials as well as professors, and leading figures included Gustav Schmoller, Lujo Brentano, and Max Weber. By basing their theories on empirical scholarly enquiry, so creating a new body of scientific knowledge, they claimed to be expounding a value-free social science. But they advocated social policies such as co-operation, moderate trade-unionism, and state-supported welfare, policies antipathetic to their colleagues who taught classical 'Manchester' economics, to traditionally-minded employers, and to the political right. Yet these doctrines did not challenge the fundamental character of capitalism based on private ownership. Since the Bismarckian-bureaucratic state was also sympathetic to welfare capitalism directed from above, with the hope of integrating workers into the system, the *Kathedersozialisten* could be tolerated. Their main activity was holding congresses and sponsoring publications, and Brentano's biographer comments that 'once political action was regarded as incompatible with scholarship, there remained nothing political for scholars to do but talk, and hope that someone with power would listen'.[19] Schmoller at least was an influential figure who was happy to work within the monarchist–bureaucratic consensus, and did have the ear of the men in power.[20]

There was, however, a complete ban on appointing true socialists to chairs. The SPD's electoral support grew rapidly despite Bismarck's 'anti-socialist law' which was in force between 1878 and 1890. While socialism in other countries attracted many middle-class intellectuals, the strength of the SPD lay in its working-class base, and it espoused orthodox marxist ideology aiming at a working-class revolution. Instead of seeking to tame and accommodate this force, the regime saw socialism as an illegitimate and divisive doctrine, and rightly feared its advocacy of genuine parliamentary democracy. Socialism replaced materialism in Germany as the bogeyman of conservatives. No open supporter of the SPD could be a state official, and this ban was extended to academics. There was a self-reinforcing link between the ban and the fact that very few workers' children ever got to university: the SPD tended to write the universities off as irredeemably bourgeois, or to claim rhetorically that they should be 'republics of the spirit' devoted to intellectual freedom, rather than campaigning to extend equality of opportunity.[21]

Jewish academics also suffered from discrimination, which was sharper than against Catholics, for while the latter suffered from the political balance within the Reich, they were a large minority who could not be regarded as outsiders in German life, and were powerful within their regional strongholds. The Jewish community was small, and had lived a self-contained life until legal emancipation opened up new possibilities, the price of which was the abandonment of tradition and the acceptance of German secular culture and the ideas of the Enlightenment. Some

[18] Bruch, *Wissenschaft, Politik*, 303.

[19] J. J. Sheehan, *The career of Lujo Brentano: a study of liberalism and social reform in Imperial Germany* (Chicago, 1966), 87.

[20] Bruch, *Wissenschaft, Politik*, 415.

[21] Andernach, *Der Einfluss der Parteien*, 188, 192.

Jews had entered universities even in the eighteenth century, especially in medicine.[22] French rule brought legal emancipation, but this gain was temporary. Even 1848 did not bring full civil rights, which were introduced in the North German Confederation in 1869, and extended to the whole of the new empire in 1871. Despite the surviving legal restrictions, the German Jewish community underwent a transformation in the early nineteenth century. Already largely urban, it became predominantly a bourgeois community rather than one of small traders and artisans. As in France, German Jews opted for assimilation or acculturation, and religious practice declined. By the twentieth century, indeed, the Jewish educated class was notable for its patriotism and its devotion to German culture. Yet emancipation proved deceptive, as even after 1871 the Prussian and Reich governments reserved the right to bar Jews from various forms of public service, including the officer corps, the higher bureaucracy, the judiciary, and schoolteaching.[23] This turned Jewish ambitions either into business activities or, as outlets for a university education, into the 'free' professions—medicine (always the most popular faculty for Jewish students), the private practice of law, and less structured intellectual professions like the arts and journalism. University teaching was one of the few branches of public service open to Jews, and was also attractive because it drew on the traditional Jewish emphasis on learning, and conferred social prestige on families which had initially risen in the social scale through business. Most Jewish students, especially those who entered academic careers, were examples of second-generation mobility of this kind, and came from relatively well-off backgrounds.[24]

Thus while Catholics were under-represented in higher education, social and cultural factors had the reverse effect for Jews. The proportion of Jews in the general German population fell from 1.25 per cent in 1871 to 0.95 per cent in 1910. Their presence in the universities was at its strongest in the 1880s and 1890s, then fell as more Catholics and more lower-middle-class students appeared; Jews were about 9 per cent of the student population in Prussia in 1890, falling to 7 per cent in the 1900s. Between 1886 and 1891 in Prussia, relative to the total population of each confession, there were 0.8 students per thousand Protestants, 0.4 Catholics, and 5.7 Jews; by 1911 the figures had risen to 1.3 per thousand for Protestants, 0.9 for Catholics, and 6.6 for Jews.[25] Turning a student presence into academic posts encountered more obstacles. A few Jews had become professors before 1848, but when Disraeli, in his novel *Coningsby* (1844), made his character Sidonia say that Jews 'almost monopolize the professorial chairs of Germany', this was pure fantasy.[26] By the 1860s, however, a remarkable expansion was beginning: the

[22] M. Richarz, *Der Eintritt der Juden in die akademischen Berufe: Jüdische Studenten und Akademiker in Deutschland 1678–1848* (Tübingen, 1974).

[23] D. Vital, *A people apart: a political history of the Jews in Europe 1789–1939* (Oxford, 1999), 268–9.

[24] S. Volkov, 'Soziale Ursachen des Erfolgs in der Wissenschaft: Juden im Kaiserreich', *Historische Zeitschrift*, 245 (1987), 325–6; S. Volkov, 'The "*Verbürgerlichung*" of the Jews as a paradigm', in J. Kocka and A. Mitchell (eds.), *Bourgeois society in nineteenth-century Europe* (Oxford, 1993), 367–91.

[25] G. Michalski, *Der Antisemitismus im deutschen akademischen Leben in der Zeit nach dem I. Weltkrieg* (Frankfurt, 1980), 41; A. Busch, *Die Geschichte der Privatdozenten: Eine soziologische Studie zur grossbetrieblichen Entwicklung der deutschen Universitäten* (Stuttgart, 1959), 159–60.

[26] B. Disraeli, *Coningsby*, Everyman edn. (London, 1911), 208.

percentage of Jews among newly-appointed university staff was 9 per cent in 1864 and 17 per cent in 1880, but it then fell to 12 per cent in 1890 and 8 per cent in the 1900s.[27] This certainly reflected the growth of discrimination. Moreover, although it was relatively easy to become a *Privatdozent*, and even an extraordinary professor, promotion to full Ordinary status was frequently blocked. In 1910 only 2.5 per cent of full professors were Jews; 40 per cent of Christians in the academic profession had reached Ordinary status, but only 26 per cent of baptized Jews and 12 per cent of practising Jews: accepting baptism was a relatively common practice, but did not equalize chances.[28] Jewish candidates had to work harder than others to show their ability, and to wait longer for promotion, if it came at all. Yet for all the undoubted discrimination, the Jewish presence in German intellectual life was one of weight and great distinction.

In the early years, Jews were regarded as a confessional minority, but by the 1880s, when the percentage of Jewish students was at its height, the universities were affected by the politicized, racial anti-Semitism which was a new feature on the European scene. It was stimulated by the immigration of Jewish refugees from Russia, but there were fewer of these in Germany than in France or Britain, and being mostly poor they were not competing for university places. Anti-Semitism was rather a product of the decay of liberalism, and an expression of conservative resentments against various forms of economic change, including the rise of large-scale capitalism and socialism; on the intellectual plane the language of anti-Semitism could draw on the ethnic emphasis which had always been part of German nationalism. Eugen Dühring's pseudo-scientific treatise of 1881 on the 'Jewish question as a racial, moral and cultural question' was particularly influential in the universities, and anti-Semitism attracted virulent support from some students. Most professors did not endorse this, but Treitschke was an exception, and a prominent one as holder of the Berlin history chair and a member of the Reichstag. In 1879, when political anti-Semitism was enjoying a wave of electoral success with Adolph Stöcker's Christian Social Party, Treitschke wrote that educated opinion was declaring 'with one voice that the Jews are our misfortune'. But this scandalized other academics, and produced a rival 'declaration of the notables' in 1880, denouncing anti-Semitism, and signed by the leading liberal professors.[29] Anti-Semitism was to remain a pervasive but low-level element in the general nationalist stance of the majority of professors, but after the 1880s it was of less political importance in Germany than in Russia, Austria, or even France. Anti-Semites called for quotas on Jewish entry to the universities or the professions, but it was never likely that the government would yield to such demands.

The most celebrated academic case of this period, raising significant issues of

[27] F. Ringer, 'A sociography of German academics 1863–1938', *Central European History*, 25 (1992), 273–9; F. Ringer, 'Academics in Germany: German and Jew, some preliminary remarks', *Leo Baeck Institute Year Book*, 36 (1991), 210–11. But note that this covers only a quarter of Ringer's sample of professors, the religion of the rest being unknown.

[28] Busch, *Geschichte der Privatdozenten*, 160–1; Volkov, 'Soziale Ursachen des Erfolgs', 329.

[29] Mechow, *Berliner Studenten*, 86; Treitschke's text in Michalski, *Antisemitismus*, 135; 1880 manifesto in P. G. J. Pulzer, *The rise of political anti-semitism in Germany and Austria* (New York, 1964), 337–8.

academic freedom, combined anti-socialist and anti-Semitic prejudices. Leo Arons was a Jewish *Privatdozent* in physics at Berlin. He was also an active member of the SPD, who spoke regularly at its congresses and meetings. Following right-wing agitation, pressure was put on the Berlin philosophy faculty, whose dean was Schmoller, to withdraw his right to teach (*venia legendi*). The faculty refused to do this, though it warned Arons against importing politics into his teaching, and even Treitschke signed their declaration of protest shortly before his death in 1896. The Kaiser, who frequently intervened personally in university matters, declared that 'this gentleman must be immediately got out of the university. . . . I will not tolerate socialists among my officials.'[30] But as a *Privatdozent*, Arons was not a state employee, which forced the government to push through a special law, the 'lex Arons' of 1898, to bring about his dismissal. The affair became an important political issue, attracting international attention, and Arons had the support of most academics. His dismissal proved to be a unique case: as officials, professors generally had strong legal protection for their tenure—once they were appointed, for the filters of prejudice operated effectively at an earlier stage. But it was notable that Althoff did not exert himself to counter anti-Semitic or anti-socialist prejudice as he did for Catholics, and socialist sympathies would normally prevent or stall an academic career. The sociologist Ferdinand Tönnies had to wait until 1913 before getting a full chair at Kiel at the age of 58, after sympathizing with a Hamburg dock strike in 1897. The political sociologist Robert Michels was refused *Habilitation* at two universities because he was a member of the SPD (and a Jew) and was forced to move to Italy in 1908 to continue his career.[31] Nor was socialism the only contentious issue: the military historian Hans Delbrück, normally conservative and loyal, was prosecuted at the Kaiser's insistence in 1899 for criticizing the policy of Germanization directed by Prussia against its Polish and Danish minorities.

The Michels case particularly disturbed Max Weber, and led him to publish a newspaper article which concluded (with the Spahn case also in mind) that in Germany

> the alleged academic freedom is obviously bound up with the espousal of certain views which are politically acceptable in court circles and in salons, and furthermore with the manifestation of a certain minimum of conformity with ecclesiastical opinion or, at least, a facsimile thereof. *The 'freedom of science' exists in Germany within the limits of political and ecclesiastical acceptability.* Outside these limits, there is none. . . . we should not delude ourselves that we in Germany possess the same freedom of scientific and scholarly teaching which is taken for granted in countries like Italy.[32]

Weber's position on academic freedom, which he also expounded in his post-war

[30] 'Academic freedom then and now: the dismissal of Leo Arons from the University of Berlin', *Minerva*, 18 (1980), 500. This is a useful account of the case with documents. Cf. Andernach, *Der Einfluss der Parteien*, 119–26.

[31] U. Sieg, 'Im Zeichen der Beharrung: Althoffs Wissenschaftspolitik und die deutsche Universitätsphilosophie', in Brocke, *Wissenschaftsgeschichte*, 293–300.

[32] M. Weber, 'The power of the state and the dignity of the academic calling in Imperial Germany: the writings of Max Weber on university problems', *Minerva*, 11 (1973), 587–8 (text of 1908, emphasis in original).

lecture on 'science as a vocation', rested on a strict separation between academic and political roles, and on a concept of value-free science. The professor must keep politics out of the classroom, and make no attempt to influence his students' value choices. Paulsen took a very similar view: though one of the Berlin professors who protested against the dismissal of Arons, he could not bring himself to condemn this in his book. Professors 'cannot and should not engage in politics', and should confine themselves to the realm of theory, protected by academic freedom; yet they must also 'assume a positive relation to the people and the state'.[33] The uneasy patriotism of Paulsen and Weber was alarmed by the tensions between science and power, and by the mounting national rivalries of 'our era, dazzled as it is by power'.[34]

The question of professors' political views has attracted much attention because of the fate of the universities under Hitler. There was widespread acceptance of Nazi racial and national theories, and complicity in the purging of Jewish academics; there was little overt resistance to the destruction of academic freedom. Like the rest of the German establishment, it appears, professors never really accepted the democracy of the Weimar Republic. Should the roots of this be sought in the ideology of the pre-1914 universities? If they are, it is difficult to avoid an element of historical hindsight. One well-established interpretation traces the problem back to Kant and Humboldt, and blames the ideal of *Bildung* for the professors' concentration on inner freedom rather than civic activism, their idolization of *Wissenschaft*, their repudiation of party politics as vulgar and compromising, and their trust in the strong state, which turned into a worship of power.[35] Insistence that political choices were the preserve of the ruler, or by Weber's time of the professional politician, seemed to deny that the scholar was also a citizen with civic responsibilities. Gordon Craig saw the seeds of this as early as the 1790s, when German intellectuals repudiated their earlier support for the French revolution. 'There have been few things more universal and more stubborn than the determination of German intellectuals to have nothing to do with any form of politics, except those undemanding ones that involve supporting the establishment, and few things have contributed more to the tragic course of German history in the modern era.'[36]

One problem with this approach is that it passes over the academic liberalism of the early nineteenth century, and the political careers, extending into the Wilhelmine era, of figures like Mommsen and Virchow, who joined the Progressives or left-wing liberals rather than the National Liberals. It is more convincing to argue that the shift away from liberalism began only in the 1860s, and took some time to develop fully. Some professors, following in the path of Nietzsche, turned to a cultural pessimism which reflected their hostility to mass society and

[33] F. Paulsen, *The German universities and university study* (London, 1906), 105–6, 246, 255.

[34] Ibid. 423.

[35] W. H. Bruford, *The German tradition of self-cultivation: 'Bildung' from Humboldt to Thomas Mann* (Cambridge, 1975).

[36] G. A. Craig, 'Engagement and neutrality in Germany: the case of Georg Forster 1754–94', *Journal of Modern History*, 41 (1969), 15–16. Cf. G. A. Craig, *Germany 1866–1945* (Oxford, 1981), 198–206.

mass culture, and the rise of socialism helped to drive the academic world to the right. In 1969 Fritz Ringer put forward a thesis on *The decline of the mandarins* which attracted much attention.[37] Ringer's book with this title spanned the pre-war and Weimar periods, and looked back from the 1920s to a shift in opinion which began around 1890. The professorate, the 'mandarins', had once seen themselves as spokesmen for the ruling elite, but now felt that their power was slipping away and that they were living in an alien world. The old cultural tradition was threatened from all sides—by the mass of *Brotstudenten* who had no interest in disinterested study, by the extension of university recruitment outside families with academic experience, by the new demand for the admission of women to the sacred precincts, by the end of the classical monopoly in the *Abitur*, by the growth of science and medicine which dethroned philology and history and made their professors a minority. Professors were part of a professional class whose status was dwindling in an expanding capitalist society, and in reaction to the plutocracy and vulgarity of Wilhelmine Germany they cultivated a set of anti-industrial, anti-modern values which paved the way to the acceptance of Hitler.

Ringer's thesis, appearing in the aftermath of the student troubles of 1968, attracted particular attention in the United States, but it did not escape criticism. His exploration of German intellectual history brilliantly expounds some of the mentalities of the time, but (it has been said) the shadow of the Nazis 'hovers over every page',[38] and one may question how representative these attitudes were before 1914. Ringer's mandarins are mainly historians and social scientists, and exclude natural scientists, many of whom had more positive political attitudes and close links with industry, as well as medics, lawyers, and theologians.[39] According to one critic, he leaves out 1,293 of the 1,688 professors in 1910.[40] Ringer himself found that there were moderate 'accommodationists' as well as 'orthodox' conservatives, and only a small minority of extreme nationalists. Critics also questioned Ringer's focus on 1890 as a turning-point, and his claim that until then 'the nonentrepreneurial upper middle class, the mandarin aristocracy of cultivation', for whom the professors were the spokesmen, had been 'the functional ruling class of the nation'.[41] In the age of Bismarck the real power in Germany surely lay with the army, the aristocracy, and big business, and 1848 had already seen the *Bildungsbürgertum* sidelined. The explanatory value of the mandarin thesis can also be questioned from a comparative point of view, for cultural pessimism and hostility to mass

[37] For re-evaluations, see S. E. Liedman, 'Institutions and ideas: mandarins and non-mandarins in the German academic intelligentsia', *Comparative Studies in Society and History*, 28 (1986), 119–44; F. Ringer, 'Differences and cross-national similarities among mandarins', *Comparative Studies in Society and History*, 28 (1986), 145–68; J. Albisetti, '*The Decline of the German Mandarins* after twenty-five years', *History of Education Quarterly*, 34 (1994), 453–65.

[38] K. D. Barkin, 'Fritz K. Ringer's *The decline of the mandarins*', *Journal of Modern History*, 43 (1971), 280.

[39] Cf. J. Harwood, 'Mandarins and outsiders in the German professoriate 1890–1933: a study of the genetics community', *European History Quarterly*, 23 (1993), 485–511.

[40] B. vom Brocke, '"Die Gelehrten": Auf dem Weg zu einer vergleichenden Sozialgeschichte europäischer Bildungssysteme und Bildungseliten im Industriezeitalter', *Annali dell'Istituto Storico Italo-Germanico in Trento*, 10 (1984), 392–3.

[41] Ringer, *Decline*, 38.

society and industrialization were widespread among European intellectuals before 1914.[42] And if some professors felt a sense of crisis, others took a very positive view of contemporary Germany and its scientific and political energies, and for some observers a mood of optimistic self-confidence was characteristic of the universities at the turn of the century.[43] On the surface, Germany appeared to be a stable and successful country whose glittering scientific and cultural achievements were a matter of general pride; it took war, defeat, and economic crisis to bring out the underlying political weaknesses and social tensions.[44]

Recent research, especially by Rüdiger vom Bruch, has questioned the idea that professors repudiated politics. The role of intellectuals in the unification period had been exceptional, and it was natural that once the new state was consolidated politics became the business of professional politicians, while professors found security in the world of objective *Wissenschaft*.[45] There might be fewer professors in the Reichstag (sixteen in 1871, seven in 1912),[46] but they remained active in state parliaments, and if they turned away from general political issues, everyday politics included university and professional questions which became a matter for academic pressure groups. The older generation of liberals disappeared, but professors were now prominent in patriotic and nationalist organizations such as the Navy League of 1894, with its many *Flottenprofessoren*. The historian Dietrich Schäfer, who was both one of the most right-wing professors and one of the very few of working-class origin (as the son of a Bremen dockworker), was one of the founders of its military rival, the *Wehrverein*, in 1912.[47] These organizations tried to build up mass support, and professors were prominent as pamphleteers and lecturers. They were also numerous in the more elitist Pan-German League, which campaigned for territorial expansion and a nationalist foreign policy. Of its 18,184 members in 1901, 5,339 were university professors and lecturers.[48] These activities were to rise to a new peak after the outbreak of war in 1914, when academics inspired by the cause of German culture issued patriotic manifestos and continued to give strong support to the war effort and to annexationist war aims even when the national consensus crumbled. The patriotic orientation of most professors, which was of course seen as apolitical loyalty to Germany's national interests, made them representative spokesmen of the upper middle class generally, and in view of later developments in the twentieth century it is difficult to say that devotion to the capitalist, corporate power-state was less 'modern' than liberalism.

According to Thomas Nipperdey, the allegiance to the state of the typical professor had three components: 'the state was the *Rechtsstaat*, which was the secure liberal inheritance. It was the *Kulturstaat*, which guaranteed the freedom and prosperity of education and science. And the state was the *Nationalstaat*: the

[42] D. Blackbourn and G. Eley, *The peculiarities of German history: bourgeois society and politics in nineteenth-century Germany* (Oxford, 1984), 211–21.

[43] Mechow, *Berliner Studenten*, 95.

[44] See review of Ringer by J. Habermas, *Minerva*, 9 (1971), 422–8.

[45] Andernach, *Einfluss der Parteien*, 181–2.

[46] Bruch, *Wissenschaft, Politik*, 59.

[47] Ibid. 66–92, 206.

[48] Pulzer, *Rise of political anti-semitism*, 281.

permanence, honour, and greatness of the nation and its influence in the world—as everywhere in Europe, that was never subject to doubt.'[49] Once more, Paulsen is a good guide to professorial self-esteem. 'The relation of the state to the university has become one based essentially upon confidence in its independence', he wrote, for 'the freedom of thought, research, and teaching is the jealously guarded palladium of the unwritten constitution of the German people'. In Germany, 'the unity of university education contributes, in a high degree, to impart to the academically educated classes the feeling of unity and solidarity, the feeling of an aristocracy of intellect, an aristocracy which can hold its own against both birth and wealth.... the university, as formerly the clergy, represents both the unity and intellectual leadership of the people.'[50]

Welcoming the new century in 1900, a Marburg professor said that 'two ideals hover over our age... they are called Fatherland and Science. We academic citizens are devoted to both these ideals.' He went on to say that 'the German science of our century signifies the triumph of the German spirit over everything foreign, it is our title of honour, and its workplaces are the German universities'.[51] It was not only in Germany that academics worshipped at the altar of fatherland and science. But in each country they shared in the consensus of the establishment, and in Germany this meant alliance with the conservative state, and a 'negative integration' which identified Catholics, socialists, and Jews as outsiders. The weight of professorial authority came down on the right of politics. In France, on the other hand, a different political history meant a different establishment, a different patriotic consensus, and a different set of outsiders.

[49] T. Nipperdey, *Deutsche Geschichte 1866–1918. I. Arbeitswelt und Bürgergeist* (Munich, 1990), 595.

[50] Paulsen, *German universities*, 75, 227, 432–3.

[51] Theodor Birt, cited in T. Ellwein, *Die deutsche Universität: Vom Mittelalter bis zur Gegenwart*, 2nd edn. (Frankfurt, 1992), 195.

12

France

French higher education underwent a process of sustained reform in the late nineteenth century, which combined the introduction of German ideas of science and research with an attempt to provide the arts and science faculties with a real student body and to regenerate France's provincial universities.[1] This movement was stimulated by Germany's victory over France in 1870–1, and by the subsequent establishment of the Third Republic, whose values associated science and education with democracy, anticlericalism, and nationalism. The Republican reforms saw close co-operation between leading academics, officials, and politicians. But reform was in the air well before 1870.

Antoine Prost's standard history discusses higher education between 1800 and 1880 under the heading 'the long stagnation'. The system established by Napoleon continued with little fundamental change, apart from the vagaries of political oppression. The only solid educational work was done in the faculties of law and medicine; otherwise the provincial faculties vegetated, and professors resorted to lecturing to the general public in the absence of students who might stimulate a more scientific and scholarly approach.[2] But even under the Restoration and July monarchy, men like Guizot and Cousin called for the revival of provincial intellectual life. What was needed, said Cousin, was 'a small number of great centres of study, with eminent professors and numerous students', and when he was minister of education in 1840 he had plans to create a 'Breton university' at Rennes.[3] Effective reform would depend on concentrating resources; but pressure from towns which saw a faculty as a mark of prestige, and the growth of the baccalaureate, for which the university professors acted as examiners, pushed the other way. The Restoration had abolished seventeen of the faculties of letters created by Napoleon, and there were only five outside Paris in 1830, but the July monarchy set up seven new ones, all inevitably small and weak.[4]

The Second Republic produced only the short-lived School of Administration,

[1] Fundamental sources are G. Weisz, *The emergence of modern universities in France 1863–1914* (Princeton, 1983); J. Verger (ed.), *Histoire des universités en France* (Toulouse, 1986), sections by V. Karady; F. Mayeur, *De la Révolution à l'école républicaine*, Histoire générale de l'enseignement et de l'éducation en France, ed. L. H. Parias, vol. 3 (Paris, 1981).

[2] A. Prost, *Histoire de l'enseignement en France 1800–1967* (Paris, 1968), 224–9.

[3] V. Cousin, *Défense de l'Université et de la philosophie: discours prononcés à la Chambre des Pairs dans la discussion de la loi sur l'instruction secondaire (avril et mai 1844)* (Paris, 1845), 256–7.

[4] Verger, *Histoire des universités*, 271–4; L. Trénard, 'Les facultés des lettres sous la monarchie de juillet', in *Actes du 89e Congrès National des Sociétés Savantes. Lyon 1964. Section d'histoire moderne et contemporaine* (Paris, 1965), ii. 669–715.

and the early years of Napoleon III were noted chiefly for political repression. Hippolyte Fortoul acquired a lasting reputation as a reactionary. But though the Second Empire was authoritarian, it was also a modernizing regime which believed in industrial development, and there was potential for reform from above. A close collaborator of Fortoul was the chemist Jean-Baptiste Dumas, who had been a pupil of Liebig, and he presided over a significant attempt to give science equal status in the secondary schools, although this eventually foundered in the face of traditionalist obstruction. In higher education Fortoul, himself a former professor, anticipated some later ideas for strengthening the faculties, such as scholarships for advanced study and full-time training of secondary teachers.[5] He even laid a foundation stone for the rebuilding of the Sorbonne. When the educational administration was reorganized in 1854 on the basis of sixteen regional academies, officials claimed this as a move towards 'the restoration of those provincial universities whose role was so remarkable in a former age'.[6] Fortoul might have become an authoritarian modernizer like his contemporary count Thun, but the Emperor and his ministers were not prepared to support these initiatives with cash, and the new Sorbonne remained unbuilt. Dumas was able to set up a research laboratory in 1855, but the physiologist Claude Bernard, though given a university chair in 1854, had to use a laboratory at the Collège de France. The only significant change in the 1850s was the creation of science faculties in the industrial centres of Lille and Marseilles; Louis Pasteur was made dean of the former, and created links with local industries, before being recalled to Paris as head of the scientific side of the École Normale.[7] Nancy, where local pressure was backed up by the willingness of the municipal council to finance new buildings, also acquired new faculties, of letters and science in 1854, of law in 1864.[8]

Victor Duruy, minister between 1863 and 1869, was a more effective pioneer of reform.[9] His own experience was as a lycée teacher rather than a faculty professor, but his commitment to liberal values did much to restore academic morale. Although his actual achievements were modest, he mobilized public opinion by collecting and publishing data on the inadequacies of French higher education, by sending missions to foreign countries and publishing their reports, and by publicizing the nationalistic view that France had fallen behind Germany in the race for supremacy. The Prussian victory over Austria at Sadowa in 1866 was often described at the time as the 'victory of the Prussian schoolmaster', but Duruy also pushed the idea that it was the victory of German science, and the international exhibition at Paris in 1867 confirmed alarm at the growing superiority of German industry. Duruy bombarded Napoleon III with facts and arguments on these lines. 'I venture to request the Emperor to read this description of the physico-chemical

[5] R. D. Anderson, *Education in France 1848–1870* (Oxford, 1975), 226–31; P. Raphael and M. Gontard, *Un Ministre de l'instruction publique sous l'Empire autoritaire: Hippolyte Fortoul 1851–1856* (Paris, 1975).

[6] A. Cournot, *Des institutions d'instruction publique en France*, Œuvres complètes, vol. 7 (Paris, 1977), 318.

[7] L. Trénard, *De Douai à Lille . . . une université et son histoire* (Lille, 1978), 76–8.

[8] A. Logette, *Histoire de la Faculté de Droit de Nancy (1768–1864–1914)* (Nancy, 1964), 64–88.

[9] Anderson, *Education in France*, 232–9; S. Horvath-Peterson, *Victor Duruy and French education: liberal reform in the Second Empire* (Baton Rouge, La., 1984), 174–211.

laboratory which the Prussians are building at Bonn,' he wrote in 1868. 'It is heart-rending for your minister of education, and menacing for French science.'[10] Once France led the world intellectually, he wrote in public, but now 'the efforts successfully made abroad to renew studies in history and philology, those which are being made everywhere today, in America as in Germany, in Russia as in England, to set up at great expense those arsenals of science called laboratories . . . are a serious threat to one of our most legitimate ambitions'.[11]

As with Fortoul, real resources were not forthcoming, but Duruy was able to create the École Pratique des Hautes Études. This was not a separate institution with a home of its own, but a funding framework through which the state could encourage seminars and laboratories, at first mainly in Paris.[12] It was to become a permanent feature of the French scene, and included a section on 'historical and philological sciences' which reflected the new German scholarship. Duruy also shook up various learned bodies and institutions, and introduced economics teaching into the law faculties. He had ideas for promoting the revival and autonomy of provincial universities which were similar to those of his successors, and he was rightly seen by them as a precursor, but he was more open than Republicans to the idea that state education could benefit from outside competition, either from Catholics, as we have seen, or from independent lecturers. Duruy allowed university premises to be used for 'free courses' aimed at the general public, despite the risk of touching on dangerous political subjects.

France's defeat in 1871 seemed to justify Duruy's forebodings, and set off a mood of national re-examination and renewal, comparable to that in Prussia after 1806. According to Michel Bréal, a classical scholar and one of the many critics of the rhetorical superficiality of French education, 'history shows that after great wars, after lost wars above all, public attention turns towards education'. While French education was still stuck in the routines of the *ancien régime*, in Germany the university was the centre from which the scientific, reflective spirit spread through the whole nation. Only a thoroughgoing reform of the French system, especially the faculties of letters and science, could regenerate France. Educated youth should be able to 'associate the idea of the fatherland with that of a French culture represented by great and flourishing universities', which would 'become centres of patriotism as of science, thus contributing doubly to the greatness of our country. Let us not forget that the definitive victory belongs to whoever represents the highest moral idea.'[13] The idea that Germany owed its victory to superior scholarship as much as to political and military factors made a natural appeal to a generation of French intellectuals who dreamt of playing a similar role.[14]

[10] Anderson, *Education in France*, 233.

[11] *L'Administration de l'instruction publique de 1863 à 1869: ministère de S. E. M. Duruy* (Paris, n.d. [1870]), 644.

[12] J. Rohr, *Victor Duruy, ministre de Napoléon III: essai sur la politique de l'instruction publique au temps de l'Empire libéral* (Paris, 1967), 116–21, 196–200.

[13] M. Bréal, *Quelques mots sur l'instruction publique en France*, 5th edn. (Paris, 1886), 2, 396, 407 (original edn. 1873).

[14] C. Digeon, *La Crise allemande de la pensée française (1870–1914)* (Paris, 1959), 74.

To reconcile patriotism with admiration for German models, French scholars developed a theory (revived during the First World War) of the 'two Germanies', good and bad—the tradition of the militaristic state derived from Hegel was balanced by the tradition of freedom derived from Kant.[15] But for many admirers of German science and culture, Germany's new militarist face brought shock and disillusion, again as in 1914. Academic links with Germany were broken off, and Pasteur returned his Bonn doctorate. Both Renan and the ancient historian N. D. Fustel de Coulanges, forced to leave his chair at Strasbourg, saw their German colleagues' support for the annexation of Alsace-Lorraine as a particular betrayal, and wrote bitterly reproachful letters to Strauss and Mommsen respectively.[16] Fustel shared Renan's view that a new intellectual aristocracy was needed if France was to be regenerated in a democratic age. As we have seen, Renan's pronouncements in the 1860s on the need to strengthen French culture and scholarship, especially in the provinces, made him an important precursor of reform. Pasteur too had campaigned since 1858 to publicize the defects of France's scientific infrastructure, and called for a new emphasis on research and closer links between research and teaching; defeat in 1871, he reflected, was due to France's loss of interest during the last half-century in 'the great tasks of the mind, particularly in the exact sciences'.[17]

This was also the context in which Taine developed his critique of Napoleonic centralization, and he inspired a practical initiative for the renewal of the elite, the École Libre des Sciences Politiques, opened in 1872, and headed by Taine's disciple Émile Boutmy. While the progressive Republican reformers were influenced above all by Germany, Taine shared the admiration of many upper-class conservatives for Britain, and wanted to import into France some of the aristocratic independence and public spirit supposedly learnt in the English public schools and universities. 'Sciences po' remained a private institution until 1945, charged high fees, and was socially exclusive: between 1885 and 1913, 83 per cent of its students came from the upper-middle or professional classes, compared with 58 per cent at the Polytechnique and 50 per cent at the École Normale.[18] According to Boutmy, it would train an elite 'formed of men who by their family situation or special aptitudes had the right to aspire to exercise an influence on the masses in politics, in the service of the state, or in big business'.[19] It aimed at a similar clientele to the Catholic

[15] Ibid. 3, 110. Cf. M. Hanna, *The mobilization of intellect: French scholars and writers during the Great War* (Cambridge, Mass., 1996), 9.

[16] *Œuvres complètes de Ernest Renan*, ed. H. Psichari, vol. 1 (Paris, 1947), 437–62; F. Hartog, *Le XIXe siècle et l'histoire: le cas Fustel de Coulanges* (Paris, 1988), 375–92. Cf. F. Mayeur, 'Fustel de Coulanges et les questions d'enseignement supérieur', *Revue Historique*, 274 (1985), 387–408.

[17] L. Pasteur, *Pour l'avenir de la science française* (Paris, 1947), 63 (a collection of his writings in this period).

[18] R. J. Smith, 'The social origins of students of the École Libre and the Institut d'Études Politiques 1885–1970', *History of Education*, 17 (1988), 234; T. R. Osborne, *A grande école for the grands corps: the recruitment and training of the French administrative élite in the nineteenth century* (New York, 1983), 83–9.

[19] Cited in T. Zeldin, *France 1848–1945. II. Intellect, taste and anxiety* (Oxford, 1977), 343. Cf. P. Favre, 'Les sciences d'État entre déterminisme et libéralisme: Émile Boutmy et la création de l'École libre des sciences politiques', *Revue Française de Sociologie*, 22 (1981), 429–65; Osborne, *A grande école*, 53–9.

universities, but more successfully, as it established a near-monopoly on recruitment to the higher branches of the civil service. Ironically, 'Sciences po' thus became part of the centralized, Parisian, and Napoleonic machinery for channelling the sons of the bourgeoisie into jobs against which Taine had inveighed.[20]

Taine was widely read by conservative critics of the Republic, yet his critique of centralization was remarkably similar to that of the Republican establishment. Republican politicians did not have full control of the state until 1876–7, as the legalization of Catholic universities in 1875 showed, but once in power they focused on reviving the faculties.[21] In 1878, a group of leading academics formed the Society for the Study of Questions of Higher Education, and in 1881 the same group began the *Revue Internationale de l'Enseignement Supérieur*, whose aim (as its title indicated) was to report on developments outside France and the lessons which they held. The intimate links which this group enjoyed with the new political elite ensured the success of their programme. Jules Ferry and his successors as ministers of education pursued a consistent policy of investment in higher education, and a leading light of the reform party, Louis Liard, was head of the higher education division within the ministry from 1884 to 1902, and thereafter rector of the University of Paris. He occupied a position similar to Althoff's, but with much greater direct power, and no need to engage in intrigue, being at the head of a single system controlled and financed from Paris, and not having the German system of faculty lists to constrain appointments.

Liard was also able to control the interpretation of his work by publishing a history of higher education which long remained authoritative, and which spread a negative view of Napoleon's achievements and of conditions in the early nineteenth century. Centralization and bureaucratic control were again condemned, especially for stifling the vigour of provincial universities, as were the absence of serious students in letters and sciences and the separation of research and teaching. The dual system of faculties and specialized schools, however much a natural product of French political conditions, was now thought inferior to the integrated German universities, and the reform movement sought to introduce into France their seriousness, scholarship, and corporate independence. But Liard's admiration for the German fusion of teaching and research led him to play down the educational role of the law and medical faculties and the *grandes écoles*, while focusing on the defects of the faculties of letters and science. It was certainly true that these had few regular students, but this was the case in other countries as well until the Humboldtian model spread outside the German-speaking world in the 1870s. In France as elsewhere, law traditionally had a general educational function, and provincial law faculties like that at Toulouse, with several hundred students, were comparable to universities elsewhere. At Montpellier, the lectures in the faculty of letters were typical in being attended by 'ladies, notables, priests, officers, and the occasional student', and there was no law faculty until 1880, but the importance of

[20] Cf. C. Charle, *La République des universitaires 1870–1940* (Paris, 1994), 437–53.

[21] Verger, *Histoire des universités*, 323–34.

medicine meant that the university had 710 students in 1859.[22] The same was true of the pre-1870 complex of faculties (including medicine and theology) at Strasbourg, which was already influenced by the German example.[23] One result of the lack of continuity and corporate identity in French university history has been an absence of university histories of the kind which abound in Germany, but those which do exist suggest that, behind the façade of Napoleonic uniformity, the faculties did have close connections with local elites and regional cultures.

Nevertheless, French higher education had undeniably suffered from the parsimony of the state, which allowed the loss of its earlier predominance in science, and from the gulf between its essentially liberal ideology and the authoritarianism of the Second Empire. Under the Third Republic, university reform became a priority because education was at the centre of the regime's values; some important politicians, like the physiologist Paul Bert and the chemist Marcellin Berthelot, were scientists. The founding generation of the Republic had an unusually cohesive set of ideas. They saw themselves as the heirs of the French revolution, and put their faith in universal male suffrage. As orthodox economic liberals, they did not believe in radical social reform, but saw education as a unique solvent of social divisions. In his programmatic speech of 1870, Jules Ferry had claimed the authority of Condorcet in pledging himself to work for an egalitarian educational system, but had glided over the implications for the existing class-based arrangements.[24] Once in power (Ferry was minister of education in 1879–81, and again briefly in 1882), though rhetorically committed to equality of opportunity, the Republicans did not break down the barriers between primary and secondary schools. Most social mobility came about, as in the past, through family ambition in the middle ranks of society. Many of the Republicans themselves had risen in this way, and they believed their leadership of the masses was justified because it was based on hard work and merit rather than money or birth. The function of higher education, for them as for the liberals of the 1840s or for Taine, was to produce an intellectual aristocracy, but now this was to be based on science.

Ferry's speech in 1870 was made to an audience of positivists. Many of the Third Republic's leaders subscribed to the doctrines of Auguste Comte and his disciple Émile Littré. The nineteenth century, they thought, was moving into the final phase foreseen by Comte, when mankind would abandon the crutches of religion and metaphysics and rely on the laws revealed by empirical scientific methods. Thus the Republicans had a mystic faith in science as the ally of democracy and progress. According to Liard, universities were the natural homes of science, and science had a 'triple function—intellectual, economic, and social'. Intellectually, it crowned the Republic's educational edifice. Economically, it was a factor of wealth. 'Today science has fully descended from heaven to earth. . . . Invisible currents of transmission link its laboratories to the machinery of modern labour, and it is truly by

[22] G. Cholvy (ed.), *Histoire de Montpellier* (Toulouse, 1984), 342, 348.

[23] G. Livet, *L'Université de Strasbourg de la Révolution française à la guerre de 1870: 'la rencontre avec l'histoire'* (Strasbourg, 1996).

[24] L. Legrand, *L'Influence du positivisme dans l'œuvre scolaire de Jules Ferry: les origines de la laïcité* (Paris, 1961), 217–37.

the strength of science that the strength of a country's industry is now measured.' Finally there were the moral and social effects. 'Many of the most enlightened men of the new regime have understood that it is through science, first among the elite and then filtering down to the masses, that the public spirit, conscious, firm, and coherent, which is indispensable to the Republic and to democracy, will be established.'[25] As George Weisz has pointed out, it was not difficult for academics to equate this concept with their own ideal of objective enquiry and the search for truth, but to suppose that universities could mould their diverse clientele into an integrated elite which was Republican, secular, and loyal to a single concept of the nation's interests was a taller order.[26] The practical implication of positivism for most Republicans was anticlericalism, and although this affected higher education less than other sectors, measures like the closure of Jesuit colleges and the opening of state lycées for girls (both in 1880) had important indirect effects. The secularist character of the regime appealed to academics who had suffered from censorship and suspicion under the Second Empire, and attracted Protestants and Jews, both of which groups were well represented in the professorate and the educational administration; but, conversely, Catholics and those out of sympathy with the Republic's ideals felt unwelcome.

In philosophy, Cousinian eclecticism gave way to neo-Kantianism as the dominant academic school, providing ethical stiffening for Republican ideas of citizenship and duty.[27] Ideological considerations were even more characteristic of academic history, which fused belief in progress and the cult of 1789 into a republican, anticlerical narrative which made historians 'the principal agents of France's patriotic revival'.[28] As in other countries, scientific methods proved quite compatible with a nationalist message; what was unusual about France was the way in which university historians, as part of their patriotic mission, wrote school textbooks and history for the general public. The leading example was Ernest Lavisse, a key member of the reform movement, who was professor of history at the Sorbonne, and director of the École Normale between 1904 and 1919.

One reason for the success of the Third Republic's reforms was that they went with the grain of the academic world's own ambitions. Germany was admired for the status of its professors and the generosity of the *Kulturstaat* as well as for the ideal of *Wissenschaft*, and young scholars were sent there by the state to study the model at source, and to write reports when they returned. They were not blind to German weaknesses, especially overspecialization, and generally took a balanced view of what might be borrowed.[29] The *Privatdozent* system for example, though recommended by various reformers in the 1860s, was thought alien to French traditions;

[25] L. Liard, *L'Enseignement supérieur en France 1789–1893* (Paris, 1888–94), ii. 338, 341–4.

[26] Weisz, *Emergence of modern universities*, 270–314, 373.

[27] Hanna, *Mobilization of intellect*, 33–7; J. L. Fabiani, *Les Philosophes de la République* (Paris, 1988), 22.

[28] W. R. Keylor, *Academy and community: the foundation of the French historical profession* (Cambridge, Mass., 1975), 3.

[29] C. Charle, 'L'élite universitaire française et le système universitaire allemand (1880–1900)', in M. Espagne and M. Werner (eds.), *Transferts: les relations interculturelles dans l'espace franco-allemand (XVIIIe et XIXe siècle)* (Paris, 1988), 345–57; Charle, *La République des universitaires*, 21–59.

but in 1877 the state established salaried research and teaching posts, using the title *maître de conférences*, borrowed from the École Normale. Seminar training was introduced for advanced students, and the doctorate was upgraded. This had previously been an unchallenging exercise—even though a subsidiary thesis had to be written in Latin until 1903: the socialist leader Jean Jaurès, a *normalien* who started his career as a philosophy professor, wrote a Latin thesis in 1891 on the origins of German socialism (*De primis socialismi Germanici lineamentis*). The research doctorate now became the equivalent of the *Habilitation*, a formidable hurdle in an academic career and a guarantee of scientific ability. Since university posts remained scarce, it was common to work as a lycée teacher while completing it: in Germany secondary and higher education had become separate professions, but in France they continued to overlap. Partly for this reason, most university teachers passed through the competitive *agrégation*, and the French traditions of elegant composition, oral performance, and incisive analysis were not abandoned—indeed, they found a new home in the oral examinations for doctoral theses, which were public occasions, as in most countries. The French traditions of liberal education embodied in the lycées, with their mixture of humanist culture, philosophy, and mathematics, expanded into the regenerated faculties.

The Third Republic showed an unprecedented willingness, at least for a time, to spend money on higher education. Chairs and seminars were founded, laboratories were built and equipped, and medical education was brought up to the increasingly expensive standards of the day. The most spectacular achievement was the complete rebuilding of the Sorbonne between 1884 and 1901, one of the largest urban projects of the time. Its importance as a symbol of the Republic was reinforced by an elaborate set of historical and allegorical frescoes in the main lecture-theatres.[30] Such schemes were popular at the time. The new Aula at Oslo built in 1911 acquired a noted set by Edvard Munch, which found the Norwegian master in one of his less gloomy moods, while at Vienna the unconventionality and eroticism of Gustav Klimt's ceiling decorations, supposedly representing the faculties of philosophy, medicine, and law, but failing to endorse the official rationalism of the professors, provoked a major politico-cultural scandal in the early 1900s.[31]

The new Sorbonne also symbolized one of Liard's fundamental ideas, the reconstitution of universities as corporate bodies with a single identity. In 1885 the faculties in each town were given a common 'university council', and in 1893 they gained greater financial independence. In 1896 they were renamed universities, and there was a deliberate effort to claim continuity with their medieval precursors and to arouse local patriotism.[32] The motives for this reform, which had to overcome strong Republican prejudice against decentralizing power from Paris, included competition with the Catholic faculties (themselves forbidden in 1880 to use the university name) and the creation of legal personality so that universities could accept legacies and donations instead of relying solely on the state: like Althoff,

[30] P. Rivé, *La Sorbonne et sa reconstruction* (Lyons, 1987).

[31] C. E. Schorske, *Fin-de-siècle Vienna: politics and culture* (Cambridge, 1981), 226–54.

[32] There were 15: Aix/Marseilles, Besançon, Bordeaux, Caen, Clermont-Ferrand, Dijon, Grenoble, Lille, Lyons, Montpellier, Nancy, Paris, Poitiers, Rennes, Toulouse.

Liard was impressed by the American example. The new universities enjoyed some success in gaining the confidence and financial support of local industrialists. But in other respects, the reform fell short of giving real autonomy. Appointments were still controlled from Paris, rectors remained educational administrators representing the state rather than the professorate, and teaching continued to be minutely regulated by centrally prescribed programmes. Within the new university framework, it was the faculty which remained the practical and emotional focus for most academics, as everyday linguistic usage showed.

More successful was the programme of creating a genuine student body in letters and science, where the main instrument was state scholarships, especially for prospective secondary teachers. These were introduced in 1877 for the first degree, the *licence*, and in 1880 for the *agrégation*, which began to break the stranglehold of the École Normale on this examination; the number of scholarships was initially modest, but they helped stimulate a more general demand.[33] The faculties also benefited from an increasing number of women students, though fewer than might be expected since the girls' lycées of 1880 were not intended to lead to the university, and their teachers were trained apart (see Chapter 17). Enrolment statistics showed dramatic results. National figures for the early nineteenth century are not available, but according to Duruy's enquiries there were 6,649 full-time students in 1855 and 8,467 in 1865. The latter included 4,913 in law and 3,098 in medicine and pharmacy, but only about 100 full-time students in either letters or science, though each had sixteen faculties; in 1865 the *licence* was awarded to only ninety students in letters and 100 in science (thirty-one and forty-eight of them respectively at Paris), and there were only twenty-five doctorates in letters or science (seventeen of them at Paris).[34] Total enrolments then rose to 11,204 in 1876, 16,587 in 1890, and 42,037 in 1914, nearly five times the 1865 figure. In 1876, before the Republic's reforms began, the number of students in letters and science was still only 238 and 293 respectively, but had risen to 6,586 and 7,330 in 1914, though they were still outnumbered by law (16,465) and medicine and pharmacy (11,656). Moreover, the revival of the provincial faculties did not prevent the simultaneous expansion of the University of Paris: 55 per cent of all students were in Paris in 1876, 43 per cent in 1914.[35]

These figures do not include the *grandes écoles*, whose student numbers were small, but whose prestige and influence were great. The Third Republic made no attempt to end the dualism of the French system. The École Normale Supérieure became formally part of the University of Paris in 1903, but this hardly changed its character. There were too many *normaliens* among the university elite and in the political world to allow any change, and the Polytechnique was similarly safeguarded by its former pupils in the administration, the army, and business. The system of *grandes écoles* became entrenched, as did the special classes in the lycées which prepared a schoolboy elite for their entrance examinations. The École

[33] F. Mayeur, 'Naissance de l'étudiant en sciences et en lettres à la fin du XIXe siècle en France', in M. Kulczykowski (ed.), *Les Étudiants: liens sociaux, culture, mœurs du moyen-âge jusqu'au 19e siècle: Vème session scientifique internationale, Cracovie 28–30 mai 1987* (Warsaw, 1991), 160–1.

[34] *Statistique de l'enseignement supérieur 1865–1868* (Paris, 1868), 5–7; Rohr, *Victor Duruy*, 93.

[35] Weisz, *Emergence of modern universities*, 236, 238. Cf. Prost, *Histoire de l'enseignement*, 243.

Centrale, founded in 1830 as an equivalent of the Polytechnique for private business, with a similar emphasis on engineering, had been taken over by the state in 1857.[36] After 1870, there was an expansion of such schools, often founded initially by private interests or municipalities. Examples included the École Supérieure de Physique et de Chimie, founded by the Paris municipal council in 1882 on the urging of a group of leading industrialists, the École Supérieure d'Électricité, founded privately by the electrical engineering profession in 1894, the École des Hautes Études Commerciales, a creation of the Paris Chamber of Commerce in 1881 which remained private, and the state's own École Coloniale (1889) for training colonial administrators.[37] Nearly all such schools were in Paris, reinforcing the capital's dominance.

There was thus no equivalent of the German national network of Technical High Schools, with their non-competitive entry, but the revived science faculties came to fulfil a similar function. George Weisz has shown that many of them were able to establish links with local industry, to raise substantial funds locally, and to do effective applied research. Specialized institutes multiplied, particularly in new fields like the chemical and electrical industries. Nancy, Grenoble, Lyons, Lille, and Toulouse were particularly successful: here 'the institutes trained technicians for industry, engaged in product testing and development, provided laboratory space for local industrialists, and occasionally sponsored sophisticated applied research'.[38] Weisz considers the provincial institutes the most successful of the Third Republic's innovations, but although they proved that French science was responsive and adaptable, their concentration on industrial applications and turning out graduates with practical qualifications worked against research productivity, where the record of the provincial faculties was poor.[39] The Paris faculty of science, on the other hand, largely ignored practical needs and remained devoted to pure research. The best minds continued to gravitate to the capital, and research funding was concentrated there, including private support for independent organizations like the Pasteur Institute (founded in 1888) and funds allocated by the Caisse des Recherches Scientifiques set up by the state in 1901. In the intensified atmosphere of Franco-German rivalry characteristic of the 1900s, French science was able to hold its own. Nobel prizes began in 1901, and by 1914 France had won five

[36] J. H. Weiss, *The making of technological man: the social origins of French engineering education* (Cambridge, Mass., 1982).

[37] T. Shinn, 'Des sciences industrielles aux sciences fondamentales: la mutation de l'École supérieure de physique et de chimie 1882–1970', *Revue Française de Sociologie*, 22 (1981), 167–82; T. Shinn, 'From "corps" to "profession": the emergence and definition of electrical engineering in modern France', in R. Fox and G. Weisz (eds.), *The organization of science and technology in France 1808–1914* (Cambridge, 1980), 198–9; M. Meuleau, *Histoire d'une grande école* (Jouy-en-Josas, 1981).

[38] Weisz, *Emergence of modern universities*, 179, and cf. 371. Cf. H. W. Paul, *From knowledge to power: the rise of the science empire in France 1860–1939* (Cambridge, 1985), 134–79; M. J. Nye, 'The scientific periphery in France: the Faculty of Sciences at Toulouse (1880–1930)', *Minerva*, 13 (1975), 374–403.

[39] T. Shinn, 'The French science faculty system 1808–1914: institutional change and research potential in mathematics and the physical sciences', *Historical Studies in the Physical Sciences*, 10 (1979), 271–332; R. Fox, 'L'attitude des professeurs des facultés des sciences face à l'industrialisation en France entre 1850 et 1914', in C. Charle and R. Ferré (eds.), *Le Personnel de l'enseignement supérieur en France aux XIXe et XXe siècles* (Paris, 1985), 135–49.

awards in physics and chemistry (including the Polish expatriate Marie Curie twice over), while Germany had ten and Britain four.

The expansion of enrolments caused less political tension than in Germany because of a more favourable ideological climate. The foundation of the Third Republic corresponded to a real shift in social power. In Germany, political unification was not accompanied by any social revolution. If anything, the old educated class of professionals and officials lost ground, as rapid industrialization threatened it from both sides—a new moneyed bourgeoisie on one side, the proletariat below. In France, however, the 'end of the notables' favoured the professional and educated classes. In a famous speech in 1872, Léon Gambetta declared that the Republic was the regime of the 'new social strata' of talent and hard work, created by modern economic development. So if Germany had its alienated mandarins, the Third Republic was dubbed the 'Republic of the professors', and there was harmony of values at all levels of education between the Republic and the teachers.

Liard and his colleagues used their powers of patronage in an enlightened manner, respecting academic rather than party-political criteria, but within an ideological consensus which tended to exclude the more Catholic and conservative section of the elite.[40] These powers were highly centralized, and all such systems tend to favour cliques and to give particular power to those leading figures in each discipline who can secure the ear of authority and become patrons. There was nothing new about that, as the influence of Cousin over philosophy chairs had shown, but it gave great advantages to those who shared the official way of thinking, especially if they sought coveted posts in Paris. There is no doubt also that in science and letters graduates of the École Normale formed a powerful network, and tended to monopolize the best posts. In 1910, 80 per cent of professors in the faculty of letters at Paris were *normaliens*, 51 per cent in the provinces.[41] But in science and medicine, the academic patron–client relationships formed in the laboratory and clinic were probably as powerful as political factors, and the overall effects of patronage were palliated by what Weisz has called 'the extraordinary complexity of the French system, with its persistence of variety, and even of a certain disorder below the surface of structures which were strongly centralized'.[42] Faculties, *grandes écoles*, Collège de France, and scientific institutions offered different career paths. The historian Lucien Febvre once described French higher education as 'anglican', by which he meant that it was far more empirical and disparate than at first appeared.[43]

[40] V. Karady, 'Il dualismo del modello di istruzione superiore e la riforma delle facoltà di lettere e di scienze nella Francia di fine ottocento', in I. Porciani (ed.), *L'Università tra Otto e Novecento: i modelli europei e il caso italiano* (Naples, 1994), 69–70.

[41] V. Karady, 'Recherches sur la morphologie du corps universitaire littéraire sous la Troisième République', *Le Mouvement Social*, 96 (1976), 57. Cf. V. Karady, 'L'expansion universitaire et l'évolution des inégalités devant la carrière d'enseignant au début de la IIIe République', *Revue Française de Sociologie*, 14 (1973), 443–70; C. F. Bompaire-Evesque, *Un Débat sur l'Université au temps de la Troisième République: la lutte contre la Nouvelle Sorbonne* (Paris, 1988), 60–5.

[42] G. Weisz, 'L'idéologie républicaine et les sciences sociales: les durkheimiens et la chaire d'histoire d'économie sociale à la Sorbonne', *Revue Française de Sociologie*, 20 (1979), 112.

[43] C. Bouglé (ed.), *Encyclopédie francaise. XV. Éducation et instruction* (Paris, 1939), 5–8.

The clearest discrimination was likely to be against Catholics, as Catholicism was associated politically with anti-republicanism.[44] Militant anticlericalism was less important in higher education than in secondary or primary schools, and there were many practising Catholics in the faculties, and even in the temple of the university spirit, the École Normale; but it was not easy to express views which drew on Catholic or specifically Christian traditions.[45] When the Catholic theology faculties were abolished, for example, a section for 'religious sciences' was added to the École Pratique des Hautes Études—but this meant the study of comparative religion, and of Christianity as a human rather than a divine institution. Protestants and Jews, on the other hand, could identify with the Republican tradition of 1789 which had brought emancipation, and professors with these backgrounds (though often no longer practising their religion) were over-represented, though not excessively: of 120 teachers at the Faculty of Letters of Paris between 1900 and 1913, about fifteen were Protestant and ten Jewish.[46] Though anti-Semitism became politically significant in the 1890s, it was a movement of the right, and prejudice hardly affected academic appointments. Nor was there any equivalent of the German ban on socialists, and by the 1900s it was possible for academics like the literary scholar Gustave Lanson to have links with the marxist socialist party without causing a crisis.

Catholicism, anti-Semitism, and socialism were all components of the Dreyfus Affair, which followed Alfred Dreyfus's conviction for spying for Germany in 1894, and was at its height in 1898–9, polarizing the political and intellectual worlds between critics and defenders of the democratic Republic, for whom Dreyfus's guilt or innocence became a symbol of rival value-systems. One well-known consequence was the emergence of intellectuals as actors on the political stage, committed to causes and making their views known through manifestos and pressure-groups. The noun 'intellectual' was a product of this period, although the phenomenon of the committed writer or philosopher was itself hardly new in France. In the Affair, which notoriously divided French opinion into two camps, right-wing, nationalist, anti-Dreyfusard intellectuals were as prominent as pro-Dreyfus ones, and many of them were active in the corresponding 'leagues'—the Ligue de la Patrie Française and the Ligue des Droits de l'Homme. The more prominent academic intellectuals were generally to be found on the left, along with progressive writers and artists, while the nationalist side had a rather narrower base among literary intellectuals of a conservative cast. There were in fact many moderate anti-Dreyfusards within the University, but they generally rallied to its defence when conservatives launched a highly politicized attack on the 'new Sorbonne' in the aftermath of the Affair. Thus although junior university staff had

[44] Hanna, *Mobilization of intellect*, 39; M. Larkin, *Religion, politics and preferment in France since 1890: La Belle Epoque and its legacy* (Cambridge, 1995), 128–9.

[45] P. Cohen, 'Les élèves catholiques de l'École Normale Supérieure 1906–1914', *Cahiers d'Histoire*, 29 (1984), 33–46.

[46] Bompaire-Evesque, *Le Débat sur l'Université*, 65–6.

many of the same grievances about promotion and incomes as their colleagues in Germany, they were not tempted to join these attacks.[47]

In these events, at least three controversies interlocked.[48] First, a general critique of the University had developed in the 1890s as part of nationalist hostility to the Republic. Second, certain academic subjects were felt to have developed in directions of which conservatives disapproved. Third, France saw an equivalent of the German school debate, culminating in a reform of the baccalaureate in 1902 which opened up the curriculum (and consequently university entry) to modern subjects, but which remained strongly contested. The broader background was one of resentment against educational expansion, materialism, and other manifestations of modernity. But while in Germany these attitudes were adopted by the academic mandarins (or some of them), in France they were mostly held by outsiders who directed them against the academic world, which itself remained broadly loyal to progressive values, and unshaken in its self-confidence. The different political cultures and experiences of the two countries put the centre of gravity in France well to the left. If there was cultural pessimism in Germany, there was cultural optimism in France.[49]

The founders of the Republic were intensely patriotic, and saw higher education as an instrument of national unity. But in the 1890s, nationalism as a political creed moved to the right. One of its exponents was the novelist, political writer, and nationalist deputy Maurice Barrès, who drew on Taine's critique of centralization and egalitarianism. Barrès's novel *Les Déracinés* (1897) sought to show how the abstract, universalist teaching of the lycées and universities 'uprooted' young men from their regional roots and their national traditions. He was one of the first to use the term 'intellectuals', initially in a derogatory sense. By the 1890s this critique chimed with a wider intellectual mood comprising disillusion with rational liberalism and science, fears of 'degeneration', and attraction towards a more instinctive politics. Anti-Semitism served these attitudes all too well, and the Dreyfus Affair was interpreted by the right as showing that France's national values had been undermined by a conspiracy of Jews, Protestants, freemasons, and other anti-national elements. Barrès espoused this interpretation, expounded even more rigorously by Charles Maurras and his Action Française movement, which was to have a strong following among students and to stir up violent agitation in the Latin Quarter throughout the 1900s (see Chapter 18). For the Republican university was a potent symbol of everything the right detested.

There was also resentment that philosophy, history, and the social sciences seemed to be monopolized by schools of thinkers loyal to the Republic. As in other countries, social science aroused political suspicions, and took time to

[47] Bompaire-Evesque, *Le Débat sur l'Université*, 67–8. Charle's work on the University and on intellectuals (see Chapter 9) is also fundamental, and cf. P. Ory and J. F. Sirinelli, *Les Intellectuels en France, de l'Affaire Dreyfus à nos jours* (Paris, 1986), 41–60.

[48] Bompaire-Evesque, *Le Débat sur l'Université*, *passim*, and (including comparisons with Germany) F. Ringer, *Fields of knowledge: French academic culture in comparative perspective 1890–1920* (Cambridge, 1992).

[49] Fabiani, *Les Philosophes de la République*, 127–30.

establish its academic respectability. In France it was the school of Émile Durkheim which achieved this, partly by cultivating academic modes of discourse such as their specialized journal, *L'Année sociologique*, but even more because they were in harmony with the progressive ideology of the Republic.[50] Durkheim himself, whose first appointment at Bordeaux was in pedagogy, before sociology became fully respectable, stressed the role of education, at all levels, in promoting national unity and social cohesion. Rival groups, some of whom were rather closer to the German *Kathedersozialisten*, notably those inspired by the Catholic social thinker Le Play, felt excluded from the official system.[51]

The reform of the baccalaureate in 1902 offended conservatives of a more moderate kind, including traditionalists within the University. Progressive politicians hoped that this reform would rejuvenate meritocratic competition and open higher education to new social strata, as well as reflecting the inevitable progress of science. Against this, conservative academics and literary intellectuals argued that the classics were an essential component of the national spirit embodied in French thought and literature. Loyal Republicans used the long-standing argument about democracy's need for a leadership elite, an 'aristocracy of merit' in the words of the philosopher Alfred Fouillée, and insisted that only liberal culture untainted by practical demands could give them the necessary disinterested qualities. There was no place in the lycées or universities for the utilitarian spirit of the primary schools.[52] The traditionalist case had wide support in Parliament and the press, reflecting the views of the cultivated middle class, who like their equivalents in Germany cherished the idea that classical culture had made them what they were. Even the scientific stronghold, the Polytechnique, was hostile to relaxation of the classical entry requirement.[53] In 1902 the conservatives lost the battle, though the issue recurred when university entry requirements were further relaxed in 1910, opening the universities to some products of the primary system.

The feeling that French culture was being betrayed became a strand in the right-wing attack on the 'new Sorbonne', which was at its height in 1910–11, although the controversy generated more heat than light. *L'Esprit de la Nouvelle Sorbonne* by 'Agathon' (the pseudonym of Henri Massis and Alfred de Tarde: Agathon was a character in Plato's *Symposium*) appeared in 1910. The polemic exploited anti-German feeling to denounce the new scholarly methods, accused of causing a crisis in French culture and killing the national spirit of elegance, finesse, and Cartesian clarity. Historians like Lavisse, literary scholars like Lanson, philosophers, and

[50] V. Karady, 'Stratégies de réussite et modes de faire-valoir de la sociologie chez les durkheimiens', *Revue Française de Sociologie*, 20 (1979), 49–82; Weisz, 'L'idéologie républicaine', 83–112.

[51] On this see also V. Karady, 'Durkheim, les sciences sociales et l'Université: bilan d'un semi-échec', *Revue Française de Sociologie*, 17 (1976), 267–311; T. N. Clark, *Prophets and patrons: the French University and the emergence of the social sciences* (Cambridge, Mass., 1973); T. N. Clark, 'Émile Durkheim and the institutionalization of sociology in the French university system', *Archives Européennes de Sociologie*, 9 (1968), 37–71; S. Lukes, *Émile Durkheim, his life and work: a historical and critical study* (Harmondsworth, 1975), 320–60.

[52] Ringer, *Fields of knowledge*, 155–60.

[53] T. Shinn, 'Reactionary technologists: the struggle over the École polytechnique 1880–1914', *Minerva*, 22 (1984), 332–7.

sociologists were all targeted. In expressing a widespread unease at the aridity of positivism and over-specialization, the critics were making an important point, and traditionalism could make common cause with a younger generation's search for a new idealism amid the complacent conformities of bourgeois society. The 'Agathon' authors and most of their press supporters were on the orthodox Republican right, though the controversy was stoked up by the Action Française, which identified the Sorbonne with the Dreyfusard conspiracy against the national cause. But the attacks failed to dent the confidence of the academic establishment or to shake its broadly progressive commitment.

In 1870, when the two countries had populations of comparable size, France had about 10,000 students and Germany 15,000. The growth of the German universities, especially in the philosophy faculty, had been the exception rather than the norm, and Liard and other reformers were wrong to imply that France was uniquely backward. The adoption of the ideal of *Wissenschaft* followed a similar chronology to that in other countries, including Britain, which also had about 10,000 students in 1870. The social pressures from new strata of the middle class were also similar. The achievements of the Third Republic in modernizing university organization and responding to new needs were impressive, and in relation to population French enrolments had caught up with Germany by 1914. The changes added new facilities to the existing system—provincial universities, the new Sorbonne, the training of secondary teachers, the infrastructure of seminars and laboratories, a growing academic profession—yet they did not transform its structure. Indeed, while France sought to emulate Germany, Germany was moving closer to France with the growth of specialized scientific institutes and the centralizing trends promoted by Althoff. Such characteristics of French higher education as the strength of its vocational *grandes écoles*, the prestige of the law and medical faculties, the dominance of Paris, and the value attributed to rhetorical performance survived robustly into the twentieth century.

13
The British Isles

British universities are sometimes seen as forming a third type alongside the French and German models, marked by the priority given to social training or character formation over intellectual achievement, and by the residential and pastoral ideal.[1] This picture is based on Oxford and Cambridge, and on the gentlemanly ideals developed in the public schools which supplied so many of their students and which helped to give Britain an unusually cohesive and hegemonic elite.[2] The importance of this ideal cannot be denied; it influenced the new foundations of the nineteenth century in Britain itself and in its overseas empire, and pervaded much twentieth-century thinking about the purpose of universities. But concentration on Oxbridge can be misleading. First, this is a specifically English ideal, and historians are now more aware of Britain as a construct of the age of nationalism, in which English, Scottish, and Irish elites were fused together with greater or less success. Each of these three kingdoms had a university system with its own historical roots, and their universities were important in sustaining cultural identities. A fourth nationalism, that of Wales, appeared only in the nineteenth century, and a national university was one of its demands. Even within England, there was a distinction between metropolitan and provincial cultures which religion and education helped to determine.

A second point is that while English peculiarities may be explained by the lack of enlightened or revolutionary reform, allowing Oxford and Cambridge to display medieval features which had been abolished elsewhere, the archaism of these universities should not be exaggerated. They were able to resist reform in the early nineteenth century because they retained deep roots in the political and religious establishment, and when they were reformed between the 1850s and the 1870s they adapted very successfully to the creation of a modern service elite; the pastoral ideal of collegiate teaching was a product of this period rather than an ancient tradition. The timing of this was crucial. The new colleges in London, and others in the English provinces, did not succeed in establishing a rival university model in the

[1] P. Schiera, 'Modelli di università nell'ottocento europeo: problemi di scienza e di potere', in I. Porciani (ed.), *L'Università tra Otto e Novecento: i modelli europei e il caso italiano* (Naples, 1994), 5–34.

[2] Both universities have large-scale recent histories: M. G. Brock and M. C. Curthoys (eds.), *The history of the University of Oxford. VI. Nineteenth-century Oxford, Part 1*, and *VII. . . . Part 2* (Oxford, 1997–2000); P. Searby, *A history of the University of Cambridge. III. 1750–1870* (Cambridge, 1997); C. N. L. Brooke, *A history of the University of Cambridge. IV. 1870–1990* (Cambridge, 1993). Particularly useful for the wider system are V. H. H. Green, *British institutions: the universities* (Harmondsworth, 1969); M. Sanderson, *The universities in the nineteenth century* (London, 1975) (includes documents); M. Sanderson, *The universities and British industry 1850–1970* (London, 1972).

public mind, and by the time this sector began to expand the reform of Oxbridge was well under way. The result, and one of the keys to understanding English higher education, was that expansion and differentiation took a hierarchical form.[3] Broadly speaking, Oxford and Cambridge continued to be national universities producing a rejuvenated elite of a traditional kind and drawing mainly on the public schools, but did not attempt to serve the full range of middle-class needs, while the new civic universities were angled to local demands and catered for rather lower strata of the middle class. They started with a distinctive scientific mission, but as they matured they expanded their arts teaching, and increasingly subscribed to Oxbridge values without being able to challenge Oxbridge on the level of prestige. They recruited mainly from the local schools of various kinds which multiplied after 1870 and which from 1902 formed a state system whose relation to the public schools was similar to that of the new universities to the old. Thus by 1914 the English educational system 'had become segmented at various levels, the better to serve the needs of a differentiated society'.[4]

By then the state was far more directly involved in university policy, even if Britain never had the kind of bureaucratic control experienced on the Continent. With some exceptions (particularly in Scotland) the state did not appoint professors, and there could be no Althoff or Liard. Much was left to local or private initiative, and laissez-faire ideology was strong. Yet the role of the state even in the early nineteenth century should not be underestimated.[5] The creation of the University of London and of the Irish Queen's Colleges were exercises of state power, and new foundations could only grant degrees when authorized by royal charters or acts of parliament. The political culture of nineteenth-century Britain centred on parliament, and legislation followed reports by royal commissions where politicians sat alongside experts; once such reports created a reforming consensus, conservative resistance could be overcome. This was the mode of reform applied in the 1850s both to the Scottish universities and to Oxford and Cambridge, which as corporate bodies connected with the established church were seen as public not private institutions, and where the use or abuse of endowments inherited from the past was regarded as a legitimate subject for public intervention.

[3] R. Lowe, 'Structural change in English higher education 1870–1920', in D. K. Müller, F. Ringer, and B. Simon (eds.), *The rise of the modern educational system: structural change and social reproduction 1870–1920* (Cambridge, 1987), 163–78; R. Lowe, 'The expansion of higher education in England', in K. H. Jarausch (ed.), *The transformation of higher learning 1860–1930: expansion, diversification, social opening, and professionalization in England, Germany, Russia, and the United States* (Chicago, 1983), 37–56; R. Lowe, 'English elite education in the late nineteenth and early twentieth centuries', in W. Conze and J. Kocka (eds.), *Bildungsbürgertum im 19. Jahrhundert. Teil I. Bildungssystem und Professionalisierung in internationalen Vergleichen* (Stuttgart, 1985), 147–62; A. H. Halsey, 'British universities and intellectual life', in A. H. Halsey, J. Floud, and C. A. Anderson (eds.), *Education, economy and society: a reader in the sociology of education* (London, 1961), 502–12.

[4] Lowe, 'Structural change', 177.

[5] S. Rothblatt, 'Historical and comparative remarks on the federal principle in higher education', *History of Education*, 16 (1987), 151–80; S. Rothblatt and M. Trow, 'Government policies and higher education: a comparison of Britain and the United States 1630–1860', in C. Crouch and A. Heath (eds.), *Social research and social reform: essays in honour of A. H. Halsey* (Oxford, 1992), 173–215; S. Rothblatt, 'State and market in British university history', in S. Collini and others (eds.), *Economy, polity and society: British intellectual history 1750–1950* (Cambridge, 2000), 224–42.

From the 1870s, state interest intensified. Royal commissions, often followed by legislation, investigated university education in Scotland, Wales, Ireland, and London; state grants to the new civic universities began in 1889; there was a new public concern for industrial competitiveness, 'national efficiency', and Britain's role as an imperial and world power. A modest start was made in the state funding of scientific and medical research. By 1914, therefore, Britain had the elements of a state university system, organically connected with other sectors of education, and its policy-makers were preoccupied by the same sort of problems as their equivalents in France or Germany, countries often held up as models and competitors.

The early nineteenth century has already been discussed under the rubric of religion, the issue which aroused most political passion at the time. But social issues were also involved. The foundation of the first University of London in 1828 (later University College) expressed the Benthamite ideology of utilitarian knowledge and rational reform; as a non-residential college teaching through lectures, it drew both on the Scottish model and on Humboldt's Berlin. Socially, both University College and its Anglican rival King's College had a large potential market in the middle classes of the capital, and the former was open to dissenters, Catholics, and Jews as the old universities were not. But the new foundations did not discover a great frustrated demand, and if there was now a growing middle class whose weight was becoming felt in politics, university reform was not among their priorities. Even after the Reform Act of 1832, parliamentary attempts to open up Oxford and Cambridge failed, and the first new university in England was another Anglican one—Durham, created in 1834 from the surplus revenues of a wealthy episcopal see. The entrepreneurial classes in the industrial midlands and north as yet showed little interest in creating their own universities as organs of anti-metropolitan culture. Owens College at Manchester opened in 1851, as a strictly non-denominational foundation financed by the bequest of a cotton merchant. But neither Owens nor Durham, or indeed the two colleges in London, prospered. They suffered continual financial crises throughout the 1850s and 1860s, and had great difficulty in attracting students; those who did use them were often only preparing for Oxford or Cambridge entrance, and though the University of London's degrees were after 1858 open to individuals throughout the country the numbers awarded were modest.

There are various explanations for this low demand. The self-confident entrepreneurial class gave priority to empirical knowledge and learning on the job, and few industries had reached a stage where experts with technical and scientific training were needed. Scientific research was mostly conducted by wealthy amateurs, or supported by a small number of privately-financed institutions in London; the professionalization of science in a university context had begun in Scotland in the late eighteenth century, but came late to England. History, philosophy, and literary study were equally unprofessionalized, and supported by the periodical press as much as the universities. Of the two fields of employment which provided Continental universities with most of their students, bureaucracy was underdeveloped, and the liberal professions still relied on a mixture of apprenticeship and formal training which might be given outside the universities. In law, the Inns of Court in London monopolized the admission of barristers, the elite of the English legal profession, and lower practitioners were not required to be graduates. In theology, even the Anglican clergy who attended Oxford and Cambridge—still the destination of half their alumni at mid-century—got a general rather than a professional education, and other denominations had to organize their own theological training. Engineering was a field into which universities were prepared to venture, and chairs were founded in London, Glasgow, Dublin, and Durham around 1840, but practical experience as an apprenticed pupil remained essential, and it was the professional associations which controlled qualification. In medicine, however, a shift towards more theoretical training was beginning, and led to the creation in London and the larger provincial towns of medical schools based on hospitals, whose surgeons and consultants acted as teachers. In the provinces, schools of this kind often became part of the universities founded later. In London, King's and University College opened hospital schools, but they had to compete with others based on more famous charitable hospitals. It was only in Scotland that medical education was already centred in the universities, and most British doctors with degrees were Scottish graduates. But in 1858, legislation on medical qualifications, coupled with the revised London University degree system, marked a decisive shift towards university training. The 1850s also saw the beginnings of civil service reform, replacing patronage or family connections with competitive examinations, which applied to most branches of state service by the 1870s. Examinations and formal qualifications were becoming an unavoidable gateway to middle-class careers.

Nirad Chaudhuri described pre-reform Oxford as 'only the clerical-pedagogic wing of a whole established order', and this powerful link made the older universities resistant to change, especially in their confessional character.[6] The idea that state and church should form one body was restated in 1830 by Coleridge, and his concept of the clerisy, followed up by Arnold and others, shows how reluctant intellectuals were to abandon the idea of a spiritual authority giving society cohesion and guidance. For some who thought in these terms, Anglicanism needed to be tolerant and comprehensive in order to remain a national church, but for others religious renewal required a narrower definition of orthodoxy and loyalty. The Oxford Movement of Pusey and Newman had its roots in protest against secularization of the university and resistance to dilution of its religious character. The fact that Oxford and Cambridge produced most of the Anglican clergy, and educated them alongside the governing class, seemed a strong guarantee of social stability, as did the way in which they assimilated the sons of the industrial and mercantile bourgeoisie, like the future prime ministers Robert Peel and William Gladstone, into the governing class. Defenders of the traditional order might claim that Oxford and Cambridge, however set in their ways, had clear social functions and a defined

[6] N. C. Chaudhuri, *Scholar extraordinary: the life of... Max Müller* (London, 1974), 93.

clientele, and that as long as they continued to give a liberal education and a sense of unity to the nation's governing class, they were far from marginal to its life.

This framework of thinking did not preclude internal reform even before the process began in earnest with the appointment of royal commissions on Oxford and Cambridge in 1850. But the obstacles to a broader modernization were great. Most of the endowed wealth belonged to the colleges, not the university, and the personnel of the university consisted essentially of the college fellows, who shared a spirit of corporate conservatism. There were university professors, who were supposed to engage in the advancement of knowledge, but their lectures had become disconnected from the rest of the teaching and examining system, and many chairs had become sinecures or part-time posts. There were chairs in medicine and law, yet the universities did not give the practical teaching which led to professional qualifications. College fellowships were given to young men as a way of supporting themselves while they trained for a profession, and only became permanent if their holders were ordained as clergymen and remained celibate; a lucrative post in the church followed by marriage was the common aim rather than a lifetime academic career. Only a small number of fellows had teaching as a regular part of their duties, and ambitious students had to employ expensive private coaches, especially at Cambridge, if they were to succeed in examinations. To outsiders, a great deal of wealth and scholarly potential seemed to await liberation for more effective educational purposes, and this was compounded by the exclusion of non-Anglicans and the expensive and wasteful nature of college life. The universities needed to be reclaimed for national purposes from an aristocratic and clerical caste.

Early internal reforms concentrated on strengthening the intellectual level of the elite through an examination system in which ambitious students competed for honours. Examinations and other devices like prizes were used to revive intellectual life within the more progressive colleges, but the important development was at university level. The rigorously mathematical 'tripos' at Cambridge had its roots in the eighteenth century, and was formalized after 1800; examinations in classics of a similar kind followed at Oxford. They were seen as a test of individual achievement rather than a mechanism of professional qualification, though there is evidence that they appealed especially to career-minded middle-class students.[7] University honours soon acquired a high public reputation, and helped to launch political, professional, or literary careers. For those who went in for them, the work prescribed was intense if narrow, and competitive ranking made the experience a stressful one, risking disaster as well as triumph.[8] But many students, especially those who did not have an urgent need to earn their living, were content to spend

[7] H. W. Becher, 'The social origins and post-graduate careers of a Cambridge intellectual elite 1830–1860', *Victorian Studies*, 28 (1984–5), 97–127.

[8] S. Rothblatt, 'The student sub-culture and the examination system in early 19th century Oxbridge', in L. Stone (ed.), *The university in society. I. Oxford and Cambridge from the 14th to the early 19th Century* (Princeton, 1975), 247–303; P. R. Deslandes, 'Competitive examinations and the culture of masculinity in Oxbridge undergraduate life 1850–1920', *History of Education Quarterly*, 42 (2002), 544–78; J. Smith, 'Trinity College annual examinations in the nineteenth century', in J. Smith and C. Stray (eds.), *Teaching and learning in nineteenth-century Cambridge* (Woodbridge, 2001), 122–38.

their university years more easefully and to take a 'pass' degree, a phenomenon which continued down to 1914. Belief in examinations as a stimulus to improvement became an article of faith for Victorian educational reformers, and the Oxbridge system of classified honours eventually spread to all British universities. When the new civil service examinations developed, the principle of meritocracy was tempered by a second principle, that public servants should possess a sense of duty, service, and professionalism, of which the best guarantee was the complex of ethical and social qualities identified with the gentleman. Traditionally, gentlemen were born and not made, but now a way of manufacturing them had been devised: the reformed and expanded system of public schools, whose ethos was shared by the ancient universities into which they fed. Although the civil service examinations were formally open to all, the curriculum deliberately favoured the kind of education in classics, mathematics, or history in which Oxford and Cambridge excelled, and these universities dominated civil service entrance as much as 'Sciences po' in France. The production of a bourgeois service class became their core task, and the basis of their renewed sense of national mission.

If examinations were one way of restoring seriousness to university life, another was moral and religious reform. The public image of undergraduate life was one of aristocratic dissipation, debt, and religious indifference. This needed to be cleaned up, and the costs of a university education lowered, if the universities were to conform to the religious ideals of Victorian society and to attract the middle classes. Newman's ideal of the college as a religious community with close personal relations between teachers and taught was one version of this. Another, with a different religious orientation, was the moral earnestness of Thomas Arnold's public-school ideal, which also particularly affected Oxford. By the 1850s, the arrival of a generation of dons imbued with ideas of change ensured that at both universities there was a core of internal reformers who could work with external pressures and steer them in acceptably moderate directions. Internal reform continued for two or three decades, and was consolidated by act of parliament in 1877. The abolition of religious tests had come earlier—for undergraduates in 1854 (Oxford) and 1856 (Cambridge), but not until 1871 for chairs, fellowships, and scholarships. Religion remained a strong force in the ancient universities, and was even reinforced as new colleges were founded, both by Anglicans who wanted to preserve something of the old atmosphere and by Roman Catholics and Nonconformists for their own adherents. The universities' intellectual life and ideals were now essentially secular, but they continued to preach an ethic of duty and service.

Reform at Oxbridge transformed college fellows from clergymen with their eyes on ecclesiastical advancement to professional teachers committed to lifetime academic careers.[9] There were strong internal reasons for this, as in an age of religious doubt the supply of able young men willing to commit themselves to clerical careers dried up, and the dons themselves were inspired by a new ideal of academic

[9] S. Rothblatt, *The revolution of the dons: Cambridge and society in Victorian England* (London, 1968), 181–247; A. J. Engel, *From clergyman to don: the rise of the academic profession in nineteenth-century Oxford* (Oxford, 1983), *passim*.

professionalism and scientific seriousness.[10] Teaching was now done mainly within the colleges by their fellows, but this outcome was not inevitable. Many critics in the early nineteenth century, especially outsiders influenced by Scotland and Germany, had seen the revival of the professorate—and thus of university rather than college teaching—as the key to reform. By the 1850s, this view was also held by many within the universities, particularly those aware of German scholarly progress. Professors and university departments did become more important, at Cambridge more than Oxford, and especially in science, where the need for laboratories made the college an unsatisfactory teaching unit. But the collegiate or 'tutorial' party was the overall victor in reforming politics. Both universities remained committed to a liberal education as their main purpose, and suspicious of subjects which were primarily vocational or which were thought too factual to provide rigorous mental exercise; the professional ethos of the new-style dons, and their links with the public schools rather than the business world, tended to reinforce this bias.[11] The collegiate teaching which now developed, and which prevailed until 1914 and beyond, gave priority to producing all-rounders with intellectual flexibility and leadership qualities rather than, in the German style, training the next generation of specialists (the Ph.D. was not introduced in Britain until 1919). This ideal had a deep influence on British education generally, not least in the new universities which developed after 1870.

The characteristic form of teaching at Oxford and Cambridge became the individual encounter and discussion based on the student's personal work. It could be argued that this tutorial system was closer to the original Humboldtian ideal than the specialized scholarly training which had evolved in Germany, though it differed in stressing a collective ethos of social responsibility rather than individual self-development.[12] Nor did it emphasize the unity of teaching and research: professors and fellows used lectures to communicate their scientific and scholarly findings, but lectures were not directly linked to the examinations in the way normal elsewhere. The examination system itself continued to develop. From the 1850s new subjects like law, history, natural science, and economics could be taken, but only after completing the traditional classical or mathematical course. In the 1870s, these prior requirements were removed, and Oxford and Cambridge offered a choice of specialized degrees. They also revived serious professional training in law, medicine, and theology. Particularly characteristic, however, were the teaching of classics and history, both of which were consciously angled to the training of a future governing class of politicians, civil servants, and diplomats. In history, the emphasis was on constitutional and diplomatic questions. In classics, Oxford developed the 'Greats' course which combined classical literature with ancient

[10] A. G. L. Haig, 'The church, the universities and learning in later Victorian England', *Historical Journal*, 29 (1986), 187–201.

[11] Rothblatt, *Revolution of the dons*, 86–93.

[12] L. Brockliss, 'The European university in the age of revolution 1789–1850', in Brock and Curthoys, *University of Oxford. VI. . . . Part 1* (Oxford, 1997), 132–3; M. Schalenberg, 'Die Rezeption des deutschen Universitätsmodells in Oxford 1850–1914', in R. Muhs, J. Paulmann, and W. Steinmetz (eds.), *Aneignung und Abwehr: Interkultureller Transfer zwischen Deutschland und Grossbritannien im 19. Jahrhundert* (Bodenheim, 1998), 198–226.

history and ancient and modern philosophy, and a similar combination was available at Cambridge. The teaching of natural science did not have the same ruling-class glamour, but though at Oxford it failed to develop strongly, at Cambridge it was able to draw on the traditional prestige of mathematics, and the Cavendish laboratory founded in the 1870s by an aristocratic donor became a leading international centre of research in physics. In 1900, natural sciences was the largest tripos at Cambridge, followed by classics and mathematics. But at Oxford, classics and history predominated, with roughly equal numbers; law and natural science came next, but a long way behind.[13]

It would be misleading to suppose that Oxbridge and Cambridge only trained the governing elite. Most graduates became clergymen, lawyers, doctors, civil servants, schoolteachers, and to a growing extent managers and businessmen—not only at home but in the British Empire, which now became a vital part of the middle-class career world. This was a service class rather than a ruling class, but its public service ethos was given a new impulse by the neo-Hegelianism which dominated British university philosophy at the end of the century, emphasizing the state as an ethical community and the duties of social solidarity. The new role of the university in training for public service was especially associated with Balliol College at Oxford and its tutor and later head Benjamin Jowett, though many at Oxford deplored Jowett's cult of examination performance and flattery of worldly success. The system was meritocratic in its way, but worked best when students came from cultured and leisured backgrounds, and when similar ideals were instilled in the schools. The obverse of Oxbridge's successful reform was the continuing narrowness of its social recruitment. By comparison with the early nineteenth century, the universities now served a much wider range of the middle class, but they also developed tighter bonds with the public schools, which by the 1860s had fused into a homogeneous system and driven out private rivals, and whose share of entrants to Oxford and Cambridge reached 65–70 per cent by the 1890s.[14] Critics attacked these schools for their conformity, anti-intellectualism, and worship of athleticism, features which spread to the universities along with more positive sides of the gentlemanly ethos. The cult of rowing, football, and cricket was as strong there as in the schools, and was deliberately fostered as a means of creating solidarity within the colleges.[15] Down to 1914, aristocratic idleness and hearty philistinism cohabited at Oxbridge with serious scholarship and academic competition. Their gilded image as aristocratic finishing schools or 'a playground for the sons of the wealthier classes' (as the Bishop Charles Gore said in a House of Lords debate in 1907)[16] was reflected in literary classics like Max Beerbohm's *Zuleika Dobson* (1911), but was

[13] G. W. Roderick and M. D. Stephens (eds.), *Where did we go wrong? Industrial performance, education and the economy in Victorian Britain* (Lewes, 1981), 192–3. Cf. G. W. Roderick and M. D. Stephens, 'Scientific studies at Oxford and Cambridge 1850–1914', *British Journal of Educational Studies*, 24 (1976), 49–65; J. Howarth, '"Oxford for arts": the natural sciences 1880–1914', in Brock and Curthoys, *University of Oxford. VII. . . . Part 2*, 457–97; M. C. Curthoys, 'The examination system', ibid., *Part 1*, 361.

[14] J. R. de S. Honey and M. C. Curthoys, 'Oxford and schooling', in Brock and Curthoys, *University of Oxford. VII. . . . Part 2*, 545–69.

[15] H. S. Jones, 'University and college sport', ibid. 517–43.

[16] J. Howarth, 'The Edwardian reform movement', ibid. 831.

misleading. The real virtue of Oxford and Cambridge was that while it was difficult to enter them except through an expensive public school, since even the scholarships given by colleges favoured those with a public-school preparation, those families which could raise the money were offered a road to secure incomes and status, and sometimes to the very top of British society. Throughout the nineteenth century, a gentlemanly education was a good investment for middle-class families without much capital or influence, and one result of the mid-century reforms was to bring it more within their reach by curbing the worst excesses of the old extravagant lifestyle.

Some, including Jowett, wanted to go further and open the old universities to the talented poor, but this was an aspect of reform which failed. It became possible for students to attend the university without being members of a college, but this did not prove attractive. Real social broadening had to await action by the state to create genuinely public secondary schools with scholarships for university study, and this came only in the 1900s. In the meantime, those who sought a wider social mission turned to university 'extension'. This movement, which started at Cambridge in the 1870s, sent lecturers to carry the university gospel to the larger provincial towns. Regular courses were organized, which sometimes attracted working-class audiences, but were also significant for stimulating the latent demand for higher education for women, and in several towns the interest aroused by extramural work was one of the strands in the foundation of a university college.[17]

Campaigners for a university in Wales in the 1860s pointed out that the advance of popular education required a similar improvement in education for the upper and middle classes, and that 'the demand for educated talent, for scientific acquirements, for engineering skill—in a word, for all the results of a liberal training—is becoming more and more imperative'.[18] Such themes, and the view that universities were a requirement of modern civilization and the key to economic strength in an age of mounting great-power rivalry, became commonplace. The provincial university movement revived, and colleges now took shape in the larger cities—Leeds (1874), Bristol (1874, with a connection through the extension movement with Balliol College), Sheffield (1879), Birmingham (1880), Liverpool (1881), and Nottingham (1881). At Manchester, Owens College was virtually refounded in 1870–1, and sleepy Durham acquired an offshoot in industrial Newcastle when the College of Physical Science was founded in 1871; it had the first British chair of mining. The existing local medical schools were absorbed in due course, and provided students for the science faculties. The civic colleges were the result of local initiative, not of any policy, or even pressure, from the state, and differed in the details of their foundation and ethos. Most colleges in the early years emphasized science and the needs of the local economy. The charter of University College

[17] J. F. C. Harrison, *Learning and living 1790–1960: a study in the history of the English adult education movement* (London, 1961), 219–45.

[18] W. C. Davies and W. L. Jones, *The University of Wales and its constituent colleges* (London, 1905), 74.

Liverpool defined its object as 'to provide such instruction in all the branches of a liberal education as may enable residents in the City of Liverpool and the neighbourhood thereof to qualify for Degrees in Arts, Science, and other subjects . . . and at the same time to give such technical instruction as may be of immediate service to professional and commercial life'.[19] The founding deed of the Mason Science College at Birmingham laid down that its teaching should be 'specially adapted to the practical, mechanical, and artistic requirements of the manufactures and industrial pursuits of the Midland district . . . to the exclusion of mere literary education and instruction'—a phrase intended to differentiate it from secondary education.[20] Industry was also stressed at Leeds, where the original name was the Yorkshire College of Science, and at Sheffield, where it was Firth College in honour of the steel magnate who provided much of the money. But the colleges were never seen as exclusively scientific or technical: the aim was to provide a broad range of training, free of religious discrimination, for a local middle class which could not afford Oxford or Cambridge and did not identify with their metropolitan ethos. They were 'both expressions and agencies of a provincial culture striving for self-assertion', and for the bourgeoisies of Manchester or Liverpool the foundation of a university showed that the great cities of the nineteenth century, like those of the Renaissance, knew how to turn wealth into culture.[21]

The new 'redbrick' colleges (as they are often called from their architectural style) seldom had permanent financial backing from industrial interests: more commonly they were financed by gifts and legacies from wealthy individuals, or groups of philanthropic subscribers like the Unitarians prominent at Liverpool. All the colleges remained local, and were administered by university councils on which businessmen were prominent. In the early years, professors were employees with no security of tenure, and could run into trouble if they showed too much interest in causes like trade unionism and co-operation. There were initial hopes of attracting the sons of the local elites, training them for the tasks of industrial direction, but once Oxford and Cambridge were opened up the wealthy were tempted away. For many years the colleges struggled to find students, and their quest for income from almost any source produced a very miscellaneous student body. The inadequacies of English secondary education before 1902 did not help. Even at Manchester, the strongest of the colleges intellectually, it was not until the 1890s that 'a recognizably university-type clientele had clearly been created'.[22] London University's degrees provided a common standard, but only a minority of students reached this level, and part-time students, evening classes, and quasi-secondary education were more important. At Birmingham, only 123 students took degrees between 1880 and 1898.[23] At Sheffield, evening students were always more numerous, and out of 585 day

[19] T. Kelly, *For advancement of learning: the University of Liverpool 1881–1981* (Liverpool, 1981), 52.

[20] E. Ives, D. Drummond, and L. Schwarz, *The first civic university: Birmingham 1880–1980. An introductory history* (Birmingham, 2000), 12–13.

[21] D. R. Jones, *The origins of civic universities: Manchester, Leeds and Liverpool* (London, 1988), 3 (for quotation), 18, 39, 42. Cf. E. J. Morse, 'English civic universities and the myth of decline', *History of Universities*, 11 (1992), 177–204.

[22] Jones, *Origins*, 154.

[23] Ives, Drummond, and Schwarz, *First civic university*, 58.

students in 1905, 114 were studying for degrees.[24] The colleges were also able to benefit from state grants for technical education, dispensed by a government department in London which also ran a group of technical institutions at South Kensington, including colleges of art, science, and mining, which formed a scientific university in embryo. From 1890 onwards, following pressure from propagandists who claimed that Britain was falling behind in the international industrial race, local elected authorities were encouraged to expand into this field. Some of them channelled funds into the university colleges, others founded separate technical colleges which reached an advanced level; relationships varied, but at Manchester the municipal technical college opened in 1902 became the university's Faculty of Technology in 1905.[25]

The record of the new colleges in providing scientific and technical education has been scrutinized by Michael Sanderson, as part of the debate on Britain's supposed economic retardation. His general conclusion is that the civic universities (including London) 'were a prime expression of the industrial spirit, closely linked with industry, drawing their life-blood finance from it, and pumping back research and students to it'.[26] They showed no antipathy to vocational education, unlike the German universities, and scored notable successes in applied research directly relevant to local industries, when they were asked to undertake it. But many industrialists did not ask, and were reluctant to employ trained scientists and engineers, to see management as a profession, or to accept that empirical methods were no longer adequate. At Nottingham, the hosiery and lacemaking firms which were the city's main employers showed little interest in the college, which differed from the others in being truly civic, getting most of its resources from the city council. For Sanderson, the real problem was 'not . . . anti-industrial attitudes in the universities so much as anti-intellectual, anti-academic attitudes in industry'.[27] This was even more so in commercial education, where universities like Birmingham organized quite elaborate teaching based on subjects like economics and modern languages, but found hardly any response. Other experts have been less impressed than Sanderson by the record of the civic universities, especially when compared with the Technical High Schools. The number of students involved was simply much smaller—in 1914 Germany had 60,000 trained engineers and France 40,000 (about the same level in proportion to their populations), but Britain only 15,000; the intellectual level was low, with doctorates almost unknown, and neither industry, nor the engineering profession, nor a parsimonious state had been persuaded of the key importance of university training.[28]

[24] A. W. Chapman, *The story of a modern university: a history of the University of Sheffield* (London, 1955), 202–4.

[25] E. P. Hennock, 'Technological education in England 1850–1926: the uses of a German model', *History of Education*, 19 (1990), 313–16.

[26] M. Sanderson, 'The English civic universities and the "industrial spirit" 1870–1914', *Historical Research*, 61 (1988), 103. Cf. Sanderson, *Universities and British industry*, 61–120.

[27] Sanderson, 'English civic universities', 102.

[28] G. Ahlström, *Engineers and industrial growth: higher technical education and the engineering profession during the nineteenth and early twentieth centuries. France, Germany, Sweden and England* (London, 1982), 13–14, 81; R. R. Locke, *The end of the practical man: entrepreneurship and higher education in Germany, France, and Great Britain 1880–1940* (Greenwich, Conn., 1984), 48–53.

In the 1890s the English university colleges became more financially secure, and also developed a more balanced curriculum. One reason was that the state allowed them a share in training elementary teachers, which was unusual for European universities. These students were given scholarships, and came from working-class or lower-middle-class backgrounds. The miner's son and future novelist D. H. Lawrence was a student in the day training college at Nottingham in 1906–8, an experience transposed to a female character in his novel *The Rainbow* (1915). Nottingham had an unusually democratic recruitment, and was described as a 'people's university' at the time.[29] In 1902, the reorganization of English secondary schools created a national system, locally administered but with standards prescribed by the state in return for central subsidies. These grammar schools gave classical as well as scientific teaching, allowing their pupils to aspire even to the ancient universities. From 1907, state-subsidized secondary schools had to provide free places for at least a quarter of their pupils. This allowed them to draw on elementary schools, and at the other end of the educational ladder (a popular image of the time) a rather haphazard system of scholarships, from local councils or charitable endowments, allowed a selected few to go on to universities. On the eve of 1914, the Liberal government was considering further extension of equality of opportunity.[30] The new grammar schools also expanded the demand for secondary teachers, male and female, and as in France this provided the arts and science faculties of the university colleges with a solid student body.

Equally significant was the introduction of direct grants to the English university colleges in 1889. These were initially modest, but expanded continually until 1914. They gave security to the existing colleges, and encouraged the formation of new ones: by 1914 the list included colleges at Reading, Southampton, and Exeter, all in southern England rather than the industrial regions. At Liverpool in 1913, 28 per cent of the university's income came from the central state, at Birmingham a third, and these were typical figures; since funds also came from local authorities, students' fees usually provided half or less of the income.[31] State aid also meant some superintendence, through a central committee (given more status in 1906) and a system of reports and inspections. The initiative remained with the universities, but the state sought to channel it in desirable directions. Apart from finance, the main instrument was control of the power to award degrees. As in London and Ireland, examining and federal universities were seen as a way of promoting higher education and maintaining standards in a situation where university development was weak. As the university colleges in northern England reached maturity, they began to demand degree-giving powers, but at first this was only permitted through the federal Victoria University of 1880 which included Manchester, Liverpool, and Leeds. At Birmingham, however, there was agitation for an independent university, supported both financially and politically by the powerful local and national politician Joseph Chamberlain. Birmingham obtained its charter in 1900, and was the

[29] R. D. Anderson, 'Universities and elites in modern Britain', *History of Universities*, 10 (1991), 238–40.

[30] E. Ashby and M. Anderson, *Portrait of Haldane at work on education* (London, 1974), 114–19.

[31] Kelly, *For advancement of learning*, 140; Ives, Drummond, and Schwarz, *First civic university*, 138–9.

first of the civic universities to have independent degree powers, though Chamberlain stressed that Birmingham was not intended to compete with Oxbridge, but to provide for the technical and managerial ranks of industry.[32]

The Birmingham charter was followed by the break-up of the Victoria University: Liverpool and Leeds gained their own charters in 1903 and 1904 respectively, as Sheffield did in 1905 and Bristol in 1909. The grant of these powers was on condition that the universities shed their more elementary work and offered a broad spread of subjects; the charters also extended academic autonomy through features like professorial senates. Colleges which did not meet these criteria remained under the tutelage of the London University degree. While the idea of the research university was still not fully accepted in Britain, there was now certainly a belief that a university differed from a technical college or a vocational school, and should promote the advancement of learning and offer liberal as well as professional education. The new universities moved rather closer to the Oxbridge model, but they did not recruit nationally, and nearly all the students lived at home or in lodgings, not in residential halls. In 1908–9, three-quarters or more of those in the provincial universities, and two-thirds at University College London, came from within thirty miles.[33]

In 1910–11, there were 19,617 students in England, 1,375 in Wales, and 6,736 in Scotland, making a total of 27,728 for Great Britain, of whom 5,654 (20 per cent) were women. The English students included 4,191 at Cambridge, 3,442 at Oxford, and 5,344 in London, spread among nine general colleges (including three for women) and several hospital medical schools. The remaining 6,640 were in eleven provincial universities or university colleges.[34] Oxford and Cambridge were thus by far the largest non-federal universities, and together with London they accounted for two-thirds of all English students, a form of centralization in the 'golden triangle' of south-eastern England comparable to the dominance of Paris in France. The new universities had not displaced the old ones from their leading position in English intellectual, social, and political life.

While these developments were taking place in England, there were others in Scotland, Wales, and Ireland. Scotland was already well provided with universities, and the role of the state in subsidizing and regulating them was long established. As three of Scotland's four large cities already had universities, there was little need for new civic foundations; the fourth, Dundee, acquired a university college in 1883,

[32] Ibid. 98.

[33] A. H. Halsey, 'The changing functions of universities', in Halsey, Floud, and Anderson, *Education, economy and society*, 462.

[34] Official statistics reproduced in J. Howarth and M. C. Curthoys, 'The political economy of women's higher education in late nineteenth and early twentieth-century Britain', *Historical Research*, 60 (1987), 210–11. Because of the difficulty of defining degree-level students in the new universities, sources differ considerably. Apart from Oxford and Cambridge, the institutions were as follows. *London*: Birkbeck, Imperial, King's, Queen Mary, London School of Economics, University College, and for women only Bedford, Royal Holloway, Westfield, plus medical colleges. *Chartered universities*: Birmingham, Bristol, Durham/Newcastle, Leeds, Liverpool, Manchester, Sheffield. *University colleges*: Exeter, Nottingham, Reading, Southampton. *Scotland*: Aberdeen, Edinburgh, Glasgow, St Andrews/Dundee. *Wales*: University of Wales with three colleges.

which soon became affiliated to nearby St Andrews. The established universities underwent substantial reform, especially in legislation of 1858 and 1889, driven essentially by the demand of the Scottish middle classes for improved professional training.[35] A striking feature of this legislation was its emphasis on uniformity, in both constitutions and curriculum, since public opinion saw the universities as a single national system. They retained close ties with Scottish secondary schools, which differed from English ones in being predominantly urban, under public control, and non-residential. Like their Continental counterparts, and unlike the English public schools, they were accessible to the lower as well as the higher strata of the middle class. Secondary education was reorganized and developed, with 1892 as the key date for the introduction of state financing, and as in England this created a new demand for qualified teachers. The reforms put an end to the tradition of university entry at 15 or 16, and the age of entry rose to 17 or 18, but the effects of this on the university curriculum were limited as the Scots retained a strong preference for a preliminary general education before specialization began. Like the English colleges, the Scottish universities played a part in training elementary teachers, but they did not need to seek students through evening classes or sub-degree work. They were also under less pressure to undertake technical education, as the Scottish educational administration encouraged the creation of separate higher technical schools. By the early twentieth century, those in Edinburgh and Glasgow were being described in official rhetoric as 'industrial universities', were undertaking applied research for local industries, and could be compared without exaggeration to the German Technical High Schools.[36] This left the universities to continue producing a mainly professional and public-service elite, which could compete with Oxford and Cambridge graduates in seeking jobs outside Scotland, both in England and in the British Empire. Scotland was a large exporter of ministers of religion, teachers, doctors, and engineers, and the success of Scots in the wider world was probably one reason for the absence of any political nationalism in this period, despite a strong sense of national cultural identity.

Nineteenth-century Wales, like Scotland, was transformed by industrialization, but had no university tradition—its small landed and professional elite usually looked to Oxford. But Wales had become predominantly Nonconformist in religion, and a new sense of cultural identity, with strong rural roots, demanded a higher education which would reflect this while also serving the needs of the expanding middle class. Campaigning led to the foundation of a first college at Aberystwyth in 1872, followed by others at Cardiff (1883) and Bangor (1884), and state grants were given, earlier than in England, in 1882. 'If we are not a nation,' said the Principal of Aberystwyth in 1896, 'it is because we had no Colleges, no University, to create and cherish our intellectual life. With a National University, we shall make ourselves a nation.'[37] As in northern England, a degree-awarding

[35] See generally R. D. Anderson, *Education and opportunity in Victorian Scotland: schools and universities* (Oxford, 1983); J. J. Carter and D. J. Withrington (eds.), *Scottish universities: distinctiveness and diversity* (Edinburgh, 1992).

[36] R. D. Anderson, *Education and the Scottish people 1750–1918* (Oxford, 1995), 274–8.

[37] Cited in R. Anderson, 'The formation of national elites: the British case', in M. Norrback and

federal university seemed the answer, and the University of Wales was set up in 1893. While the Victoria University broke up, the University of Wales survived as an important symbol for a growing cultural nationalism. It aroused wide popular enthusiasm, and developed an ethos of educational democracy similar to that in Scotland.[38] The colleges at Aberystwyth and Bangor were unusual in serving rural areas, and developed a particularly wide student base.[39] Cardiff was more like the English civic universities, though like some of them it attracted only lukewarm interest from the leading local industry, in this case coal.[40] Welsh nationalism was linked with the Welsh language, which was then spoken by about half the population, yet there was no real demand for the new university to be Welsh-speaking, for the Welsh, like the Scots, saw education as a road to success outside Wales and did not challenge the British political structure.

In Wales the university helped to unite a country which was geographically, linguistically, and socially diverse, and in E. J. Hobsbawm's words, 'the national university . . . became for a while the first and *only* national institution of a people whose small country had no administrative or other existence distinct from England'.[41] The same could hardly be said of Ireland, where university education reinforced religious and cultural divisions. University College Dublin (the successor of the Catholic University) became a nursery for nationalist intellectuals, including the founding generation of Irish independence. The schoolmaster and poet Patrick Pearse, one of the martyrs of the Easter rising of 1916, was one of these. A new Catholic middle class was emerging, and the settlement of 1908 largely satisfied its wants by setting up the National University, though its decision to make knowledge of the Irish language a condition of entry was controversial. Trinity College Dublin continued to serve the Protestant elite, who identified with the United Kingdom, and often sought jobs there or in the empire, much like their Scottish counterparts. In the 1890s, two-thirds of its students came from the upper middle classes, and 93 per cent were Protestant, mostly Anglican.[42] In the more industrialized north, Queen's Belfast drew its students from a broader range of classes and denominations, and after 1908 it was more successful in attracting Catholics.[43] Whatever their political and cultural differences, the social functions of the Irish universities had much in common—all had successful medical faculties, for example, whereas law was weak because Ireland followed the English rather than the Scottish pattern of training.

K. Ranki (eds.), *University and nation: the university and the making of the nation in northern Europe in the 19th and 20th centuries* (Helsinki, 1996), 119.

[38] K. O. Morgan, *Rebirth of a nation: Wales 1880–1980* (Oxford, 1981), 106–11.

[39] J. G. Williams, *The University College of North Wales: foundations 1884–1927* (Cardiff, 1985), 214, 289–90; Anderson, 'Universities and elites', 234–5.

[40] G. W. Roderick and D. A. Allsobrook, 'Welsh society and university funding 1860–1914', *Welsh History Review*, 20 (2000), 49–50.

[41] E. J. Hobsbawm, *The age of empire 1875–1914* (London, 1989), 157.

[42] R. B. McDowell and D. A. Webb, *Trinity College Dublin 1592–1952: an academic history* (Cambridge, 1982), 323–5, 507–8.

[43] T. W. Moody and J. C. Beckett, *Queen's, Belfast 1845–1949: the history of a university* (London, 1959), 408–9, 542, 547, 661–3.

University affairs in all four countries of the United Kingdom occupied much political attention from the 1880s onwards, through a succession of commissions of inquiry and acts of parliament, the growth of state grants, and the charters given to the more successful English colleges.[44] Oxford and Cambridge survived without state aid until after the war, but the other parts of the system were all subsidized. This new public concern was seen by some at the time as a natural consequence of the state's responsibility for the lower levels of education, or as a belated catching up with the European norm. One of the main driving forces was a sense of international competition, both economically and politically, particularly with Germany. The so-called national efficiency movement of the 1900s stressed that Britain's human resources needed to be mobilized and trained if she was not to lose her imperial hegemony. Chamberlain, a noted exponent of imperialism, said in 1902 that 'university competition between states is as potent as competition in building battleships, and it is on that ground that our university conditions become of the highest possible national concern'.[45] The involvement of leading politicians was itself significant. Even more active than Chamberlain was Richard Haldane, who was Liberal minister of war between 1905 and 1912, but whose previous public career had focused on university questions. Trained in philosophy at Edinburgh and Göttingen, Haldane was an admirer of German thought and German educational organization—so much so that he was forced to resign office in 1915—and worked for a co-ordinated national system of universities which would combine scientific and educational efficiency.

Other exponents of efficiency included members of the Fabian school of moderate socialism such as Sidney Webb, who guided the technical education policy of the London County Council, and worked with Haldane to recast university education in London. In 1900 London University became a teaching as well as an examining university. The various colleges which had grown up in the capital now became federal constituents, and included two of particular significance. The London School of Economics and Political Science was founded in 1895 by Webb and other Fabians with private funding. As its name indicated, it was partly inspired by the Paris model, but did not resemble it much in practice. The ethos of the London school was that economics and social science should provide an empirical basis for the practice of administration, in the public or private sphere, and it had some affinities with the French or German business schools. The second new institution was Imperial College, founded with state support in 1907. It was essentially an expansion of the existing state colleges in South Kensington, and was intended to be a 'London Charlottenburg', a powerhouse of applied science and technology.

The college's name told its own story, for London was now to be 'a university fit for the metropolis of the Empire'.[46] In this period, the empire was central to the British elite's sense of identity and mission. Unlike most Continental colonial powers, Britain did not set up a special school to train colonial administrators, but

[44] K. Vernon, 'Calling the tune: British universities and the state 1880–1914', *History of Education*, 30 (2001), 251–71.

[45] W. H. G. Armytage, *Civic universities: aspects of a British tradition* (London, 1955), 247.

[46] Ashby and Anderson, *Portrait of Haldane*, 126.

relied on the universities and the competitive examination system to produce men with the necessary qualities of all-round education. Imperial needs influenced academic developments in such varied fields as oriental languages, anthropology, forestry, and tropical medicine. Nor was it simply a matter of training administrators, for even after the establishment of universities in the empire itself (the first Congress of Universities of the British Empire was held in 1912), large numbers of students came to Britain to study medicine and law, both from India and from the white dominions of Canada, Australia, New Zealand, and South Africa. The Rhodes scholarships founded at Oxford in 1902 under the will of the South African mining magnate and politician Cecil Rhodes (for Americans and Germans as well as dominion students) were only the icing on this cake. Even in France, the second largest colonial power, there was no equivalent to the role of the universities in creating a 'greater British' consciousness.[47]

Two other developments before 1914 deserve attention. One is that the state began to give direct financial aid to scientific research, responding to a powerful science lobby. A National Physical Laboratory opened in 1902 was modelled on the Berlin Physical-Technical Institute, and a Medical Research Committee which started work in 1913 was part of the Bismarck-style health insurance system set up in 1911. State intervention in science was to be transformed by the war, but Peter Alter argues that the breakthrough occurred before it, and that Britain was already catching up with Germany.[48] The second innovation was a relaunch of the extension movement, targeted more directly than the earlier one at the working class. The Workers' Educational Association founded in 1903 was independent of the universities, but worked closely with them and developed a system of tutorial classes sharing the spirit of university teaching and often taught by idealistic young academics; there was a notable annual summer school at Oxford. This development reflected a widespread feeling that in a democratic age, with a rising labour movement, the universities needed to connect with the people and to assume new social and civic responsibilities. There were similar stirrings in other countries, as we shall see in Chapter 19, and this was one of the few areas where British examples had a European influence.

By 1914 Britain had four systems of higher education (or three-and-a-half, as the Welsh one did not fully replace dependence on England), which were largely self-contained, though linked by certain aspects of state policy and finance and by the emergence of a national market in academic posts. Within England, Oxford and Cambridge stood apart, cushioned by endowments, making most of their appointments from their own graduates, and still the natural choice for the aristocracy and the wealthy. The provincial universities were now solidly established and had mostly gained academic autonomy through charters, but their income still depended on a good deal of teaching at sub-degree level. They were local in their

[47] R. Symonds, *Oxford and empire: the last lost cause?* (Oxford, 1986); J. D. Hargreaves, *Academe and empire: some overseas connections of Aberdeen University 1860–1970* (Aberdeen, 1994).

[48] P. Alter, *The reluctant patron: science and the state in Britain 1850–1920* (Oxford, 1987), 138–90. Cf. F. R. Pfetsch, *Zur Entwicklung der Wissenschaftspolitik in Deutschland 1750–1914* (Berlin, 1974), 314–47.

recruitment, mostly non-residential, and drew from lower social strata than Oxbridge. But their record in applied research and technical education was generally good, and they could bear comparison with the Technical High Schools, or the French faculties whose growth followed much the same pace. In the 1900s, however, it was in London that the most significant expansion was taking place, and the new teaching university was bidding for a national or international role in educating the elite. In all parts of the British system, science and scholarship had been professionalized, and research was accepted as an essential function of the university. Yet traditions of general education remained strong. At Oxbridge, impressive scholarly achievements were only partly integrated with a teaching ideal which emphasized liberal education and socialization. Perhaps the Scottish universities were closest to the German model, with their professorial teaching, solid student base, and large medical faculties. Many Scottish professors had studied in Germany, and Haldane's pro-German enthusiasms had roots in his student days at Edinburgh. Yet even there, as indeed everywhere in Europe, the reception of the Humboldtian ideal and the union of teaching and research were limited and modified by national conditions and priorities.[49]

[49] S. Wallace, 'The university and national identity: Scottish academics and German universities', in M. Hewitt (ed.), *Scholarship in Victorian Britain* (Leeds, 1998), 14–26; S. Wallace, 'Scottish university men and German universities before 1914', in Muhs, Paulmann, and Steinmetz, *Aneignung und Abwehr*, 227–61.

14

Italy and Spain

Italy and Spain were countries which aspired to catch up with the more advanced parts of Europe, and where liberal elites of an old-fashioned kind based on land and the professions came to dominate political life. In the 1850s and 1860s, these elites created highly centralized university systems of a French type, based on the inheritance of the Enlightenment and the Napoleonic era. This centralization was clearly motivated in Italy by the need to consolidate the national unity achieved in 1861. In Spain, there was a similar desire to overcome fissiparous regional loyalties and to impose ideological unity. But in both countries, the disadvantages of centralization almost immediately provoked a reaction, in which Germany became the idealized model of intellectual freedom. In Italy, there was an almost permanent debate on the 'university question' from the 1860s onwards, encouraged by the close relationship between professors, parliament, and the press. In Spain, the political and academic worlds were less close, and the reform movement took radical, libertarian forms. By the 1900s, more had been achieved in Italy than in Spain: in the former, a relatively prosperous and stable country, the universities were able to achieve considerable intellectual distinction, even if there was little reform of their structure; in Spain, the universities remained underfunded and intellectually stagnant, and defeat by the United States in 1898 created a new sense of crisis among intellectuals. Both countries saw important debates in the 1900s about the relationship between universities and democracy, but real democratic pressures were weak: Italy and Spain had parliamentary systems of a closed kind where power alternated between cliques, and universal male suffrage arrived only in 1912 and 1890 respectively. High illiteracy also limited pressures from below. Thus the elites felt less need than in France or Britain to justify their leadership role as an 'intellectual aristocracy', and the universities were more insulated from challenges to their traditional role.

In Spain, the Napoleonic wars brought only chaos and destruction, but in Italy prolonged French rule left a more positive legacy. Most of the changes in university organization were reversed after 1815, but there was now a more self-conscious bourgeoisie, enriched by the sale of church lands and given new opportunities by the bureaucratic state, for whom higher education, especially in law, was the road to jobs and prestige. Such men, along with liberal nobles like Camillo Cavour, were to be the core of the Risorgimento movement. In the short term, however, the scope for political action was limited. The universities under Austrian rule, Pavia and Padua, though providing a solid range of teaching, made no concessions to north German ideas of freedom and original thinking. According to Irene Ciprandi, the intellectual value of the law and philosophy teaching at Pavia was an 'absolute nullity', and the university turned out submissive bureaucrats, not potential leaders for a united Italy.[1]

Other universities in northern and central Italy were subject to Austrian or Papal control. In Naples, however, although the government was reactionary, the thirst of the bourgeoisie for professional and official posts was strong. The University of Naples had no matriculation requirements, and attracted huge numbers: the Bourbon government tried to choke this off in 1816, and to keep young men in their home provinces, by creating four 'university institutes' at Salerno, Bari, Catanzaro, and Aquila. Another peculiarity of Naples was the growth of private schools, especially in law, to avoid the censorship and conformity of official teaching. The spirit behind this movement was Francesco De Sanctis, who introduced German philosophical idealism into Italy, especially the ideas of Hegel, with effects that lasted until the days of Benedetto Croce in the twentieth century. In 1848, De Sanctis supported constitutional monarchism, and belonged to a reforming commission during the brief period of concessions to liberalism. In 1860, when Garibaldi conquered Sicily and Naples, De Sanctis returned from exile in Zurich and was put in charge of education. He immediately dismissed thirty-four professors from Naples University, replacing them with exiles or men from the private schools.[2] The four provincial institutes were abolished, and there were said to be over 9,000 students at Naples in 1861–2.[3] While reviving intellectually, Naples was now integrated into the national system, losing its links with traditional local culture, and De Sanctis served briefly as the first minister of education of united Italy.[4]

In Italy, unlike Germany, the strength of local traditions and tight political control prevented the universities from acting as harbingers of national unity, though there were other ways for intellectuals to create an Italy of the mind. King Charles Albert of Piedmont said of the series of national scientific congresses which began in 1839 at Pisa, in relatively liberal Tuscany, 'the sciences and arts are only the pretext for these congresses: their real purpose is the Italian revolution.'[5] But he still allowed the congress to meet at Turin in 1846: it met at Naples in 1845 and Venice in 1847, for even the conservative authorities felt they would lose prestige by banning such meetings.[6] Piedmont, which was to take the political lead in unification, remained authoritarian and Catholic down to the 1840s. But in 1847 Charles Albert created a modern ministry of public instruction headed by a layman to replace the Magistrato della Riforma, and an advisory Higher Council for Public Instruction modelled on that in France. Both were carried over into the new Italy. Piedmont

[1] I. Ciprandi, 'L'Università di Pavia nell'età della Restaurazione', in I. Ciprandi and others, *Problemi scolastici ed educativi nella Lombardia del primo ottocento. 2. L'istruzione superiore* (Milan, 1978), 296, and cf. 260, 287–90.

[2] A. Broccoli, *Educazione e politica nel mezzogiorno d'Italia (1767–1860)* (Florence, 1968), 194–7.

[3] A. Pizzitola, 'Gli studenti della nuova Italia', in G. P. Brizzi and A. Varni (eds.), *L'università in Italia fra età moderna e contemporanea: aspetti e momenti* (Bologna, 1991), 141, 147.

[4] F. Torraca and others, *Storia della Università di Napoli* (Naples, 1924), 610.

[5] Cited in C. Charle, *Les Intellectuels en Europe au XIXe siècle: essai d'histoire comparée* (Paris, 1996), 70.

[6] A. Broccoli, *Educazione e politica nel mezzogiorno d'Italia (1767–1860)* (Florence, 1968), 147.

emerged from the revolutions of 1848 as the only Italian state with a parliamentary constitution, and the 1850s saw much discussion of 'liberty of teaching' and of the rival claims of French and German models. This culminated in 1859 in the Casati law which remained the basis of Italian educational legislation until 1923.[7]

The Casati law was passed when Piedmont was about to annex Lombardy during the war against Austria, but the escalating political events of 1860–1 which united Italy, apart from Rome and Venice, extended it like other Piedmontese laws to the whole of the new kingdom. It imposed a uniform framework of state organization, finance, and appointment on all Italian universities, with common qualifications and examinations; secondary schools were also systematized, with the *licenza liceale* as the equivalent of the *Abitur*. The law's definition of the university's purpose was closer to Napoleon than to Humboldt: 'Higher education has as its aim to direct youth, already provided with the necessary general knowledge, into those careers, whether public or private, which need a training in accurate specialized studies, and to maintain and increase scientific and literary culture in the various parts of the State.'[8] The law also permanently fixed the geography of the universities, of which there were twenty-one after 1870.[9] Political realities made it impossible to abolish even the smallest ones, though four were classified as 'free' universities, financed locally rather than directly by the state; but even they could not escape the uniform state curriculum. No new universities were founded, either in Italy's largest industrial city, Milan, or in Florence, the capital between 1861 and 1870; these cities were given a 'scientific and literary academy' and an 'institute of higher studies' respectively, but they did not come to much. The result was a serious imbalance, with fewer universities in the north than in the centre, two in Sardinia and three in Sicily, but still only Naples, with its swollen numbers (4,741 in 1891–2, out of an Italian total of 16,059), for the whole of the southern mainland. In practice, a distinction developed between the ten or so major universities and the smaller ones, with a few hundred students in law and medicine, which were of interest only to the local elites, but cherished by them as symbols of urban and regional cultures.[10]

For the 'humanistic bourgeoisie' saw university culture, much as under the *ancien régime*, as an enhancement of their prestige rather than a simple instrument of professional advancement. At Pavia under the Habsburgs, according to Irene Ciprandi, the Lombard elite looked to the Austrians to revive 'the old concept of

[7] F. Colao, *La libertà di insegnamento e l'autonomia nell'università liberale: norme e progetti per l'istruzione superiore in Italia (1848–1923)* (Milan, 1995), 27, 48–51; F. Colao, 'La libertà d'insegnamento e l'autonomia universitaria nell'università liberale: brevi considerazioni', in A. Romano (ed.), *Università in Europa. Le istituzioni universitarie dal medio evo ai nostri giorni: strutture, organizzazione, funzionamento* (Messina, 1995), 361–3.

[8] A. Colombo, 'Per una storia dei modelli di università (dalla legge Casati all'autonomia degli atenei)', in Brizzi and Varni, *L'università in Italia*, 30.

[9] *State universities*: Bologna, Cagliari, Catania, Genoa, Macerata, Messina, Modena, Naples, Padua, Palermo, Parma, Pavia, Pisa, Rome (from 1870), Sassari, Siena, Turin. *Free universities*: Camerino, Ferrara, Perugia, Urbino.

[10] M. Rossi, *Università e società in Italia alla fine dell'800* (Florence, 1976), 76, 100, 104–5; I. Porciani, 'Lo stato unitario di fronte alla questione dell'università', in I. Porciani (ed.), *L'Università tra Otto e Novecento: i modelli europei e il caso italiano* (Naples, 1994), 164.

culture as the patrimony of the few, valued not only and not so much for its practical utility and its intrinsic value, but rather as a sign of nobility and distinction for those who possessed it'. The professors themselves 'remained anchored, in their hearts, to an aristocratic and restrictive concept of culture'.[11] These attitudes had to be broken down in a united Italy, and the new political elite were determined to create a unitary state on French lines.[12] The Piedmontese statesman Massimo d'Azeglio famously declared that 'we have made Italy, now we must make Italians', and this applied as much to the formation of the governing class of politicians, bureaucrats, and notables as to the masses. Systems which had been distinctive, like those in Tuscany and Naples, were forced to assimilate to the standard pattern.[13] The original law of 1859 sought to balance centralization with elements of German academic autonomy, but political imperatives tended to drive out the latter.[14] For example, Casati allowed private teachers to teach within the universities and collect their own fees, with the corollary that students were free to choose their own curricula, a system based on precedents in Naples as well as Germany. But as minister in 1862 the scientist Carlo Matteucci introduced a uniform scale of fees and salaries and a rigidly prescribed curriculum, which made *Lernfreiheit* unworkable.[15] Also significant was the Scuola Normale Superiore at Pisa, originally founded by the French, and revived by the Tuscan government in 1847; this now became a national institution, comparable to its namesake in Paris, for producing the elite of secondary schoolteachers.[16] In practice, as scholars have recently emphasized, much local diversity survived behind the façade of uniformity: for Marco Meriggi, indeed, 'localistic polycentrism remains the fundamental characteristic of the liberal university'.[17]

Two other ideas dominated this formative period: anticlericalism, and hopes for a social and economic regeneration stimulated by 'science'. Down to 1859 liberals like Cavour, influenced by French liberal Catholics and by Cousin, hoped for a 'free church in a free state' and for a creative relationship with enlightened Catholicism.[18] But the events of 1848–9 turned Pius IX against liberalism and nationalism; in 1860 most of the Pope's temporal dominions, and in 1870 Rome itself, were absorbed into the new state, of which the Papacy now became an implacable enemy. The political class responded in kind. In 1870 the state took over the main university of Rome, the Sapienza (though the Vatican was allowed to retain some colleges teaching theology and philosophy) and in 1872 the university faculties of theology, which

[11] Ciprandi and others, *Problemi scolastici*, 202–3.

[12] M. Moretti and I. Porciani, 'Il sistema universitario tra nazione e città: un campo di tensione', in M. Meriggi and P. Schiera (eds.), *Dalla città alla nazione: borghesie ottocentesche in Italia e in Germania* (Bologna, 1992), 289–306.

[13] Rossi, *Università e società*, 1–3.

[14] S. Polenghi, *La politica universitaria italiana nell'età della destra storica (1848–1876)* (Brescia, 1993), 240 ff.

[15] L. Berlinguer, 'L'autonomia universitaria tra legge Casati e riforma Gentile: prime considerazioni', in M. Ascheri (ed.), *Scritti di storia del diritto offerti dagli allievi a Domenico Maffei* (Padua, 1991), 569.

[16] G. P. Brizzi, 'L'influenza della Scuola Normale Superiore sull' università italiana', in M. P. Musatti (ed.), *Università e collegi: storia e futuro* (Bologna, 1994), 47–56.

[17] Meriggi and Schiera, *Dalla città alla nazione*, 13.

[18] Colao, *La libertà di insegnamento*, 21–2, 27.

had survived previous legislation, were closed down. Political anticlericalism was as strong as in France, and in some ways more dogmatic: there was no question of permitting Catholic universities in Italy, and while French anticlericalism had a strong popular base, in Italy this was one more factor cutting the political elite off from the masses. The state's monopoly of higher education remained a fundamental principle for Italian liberals, who rejected the sort of liberty practised in Belgium. As one jurist pointed out in 1875, the Catholic universities at Louvain and Dublin were 'partisan schools, tools of war, not sanctuaries of science'—and as for Oxford and Cambridge, absence of state control had made them 'citadels of immobility'.[19] The German model was much more appealing because it combined a firm state monopoly with internal autonomy and scientific vigour—and because of its apparently brilliant role in forming a successful nation-state.

The second and more creative factor was the hope of raising Italy to the same economic level as France or Britain by creating a national market and a dynamic elite open to modern scientific ideas. There was the same mystical faith in science as in France, and the need for an 'intellectual Risorgimento' to follow the political one was a standard theme. Introducing his legislation in 1862, Matteucci said that if Italy was to be free and great again, soldiers and railways were not enough: she needed to regain the intellectual level, in letters and science, of her past ages of greatness.[20] Universities were thus a vital national question, and endless political rhetoric described them as laboratories of the national spirit, or the test of a people's civilization.[21] 'On the new ordering of national and academic science', says Ilaria Porciani, 'depended the possibility not just of setting up, but also of psychologically motivating, an elite of scientific and professional experts conscious of constituting the backbone of the nation.'[22] Or, in the words of Floriana Colao, universities were linked with 'the nerve-points of Italian history: relations between the state and the church, between centre and periphery, between science and power, between scientific and cultural renewal and the modernization of the country', making them central to the 'construction and consolidation of the liberal State'.[23]

In 1888, there were lavish celebrations for the eight-hundredth anniversary of the University of Bologna, to which professors and students from all over the world were invited. As often at such events, the date being commemorated was conjectural, and the real purpose was to display the achievements of the new, secular state and to assert continuity with the glories of the medieval past. In the presence of the king, the poet Giosuè Carducci identified the history of the university with that of the Italian people.[24] But behind such celebrations, there were already doubts. Opening the university session at Bologna the next year, the law professor Tullio Martello entitled his speech 'The decadence of the Italian university': the

[19] L. Palma, cited ibid. 163.

[20] Porciani, 'Lo stato unitario', 135.

[21] T. Tomasi and L. Bellatalla, *L'università italiana nell'età liberale (1861–1923)* (Naples, 1988), 32.

[22] Porciani, 'Lo stato unitario', 136.

[23] Colao, *La libertà di insegnamento*, pp. xiii, xvi, and cf. 103.

[24] *Prose di Giosuè Carducci, MDCCCLIX–MCMIII*, 3rd edn. (Bologna, 1907), 1169–90.

Risorgimento had been a revolution from above, and it was the mission of the universities to extend it beyond the elite and to confront the problems of the age, but they were failing to do so.[25]

This sense of disappointment was a keynote of the debate on the university question: unrealistic hopes had been vested in the universities, and they became scapegoats for Italy's failure to become a great political and military power, for reasons such as lack of economic resources, rural poverty and illiteracy, tensions between north and south, and the failure of the political elite to construct a democratic state. The university debate has been well covered by historians.[26] It owed its salience partly to the close overlap between political and academic elites. Leading scientists and scholars frequently entered politics: in 1909 there were seventy-five professors in the Chamber of Deputies and fifty-four in the Senate, and of forty men who served as minister of education between 1861 and 1923, twenty-six were or had been university professors.[27] Reform bills were introduced from time to time, but no real changes were ever made in the structure inherited from Casati and Matteucci. Nowhere in Europe was the contrast between French centralization and German freedom a more passionate subject of debate, but appeals to Germany were more to an idealized myth from the days of Humboldt than to Bismarckian or Wilhelmine realities. The fundamental criticism was that centralization stifled initiative and scientific creativity; reforms should introduce greater financial and administrative autonomy, more say for the universities in the choice of professors, and a true *Privatdozent* system which would allow the separation of teaching and examining and genuine freedom for both professors and students. Examinations and curricula were laid down by the state but were administered by the universities themselves, which meant, the argument ran, that they had become diploma factories rather than centres of original research. The lecture and the examination tied to it were what mattered, and advanced seminars and disinterested study were neglected. Instead of being independent scholars, *liberi docenti* were either subordinates of the all-powerful professors, or the posts were sought by local lawyers, doctors, or engineers simply for the sake of the title, not as a stage in an academic career: in 1910 it was pointed out that while Germany managed with 1,210 *Privatdozenten*, Italy had 2,496.[28] As for the professors, political patronage and the clienteles of powerful academic barons often dictated appointments, and too many were absentees who spent more time following political or literary careers in Rome than on their university duties.

[25] Rossi, *Università e società*, 28–9; Tomasi and Bellatalla, *L'università italiana*, 32–4.

[26] Tomasi and Bellatalla, *L'università italiana*; A. Colombo, 'Per una storia'; F. Colao, *Libertà di insegnamento*; F. Colao, 'La libertà d'insegnamento'; A. La Penna, 'Modello tedesco e modello francese nel dibattito sull'università italiana', in S. Soldani and G. Turi (eds.), *Fare gli italiani: scuola e cultura nell'Italia contemporanea. I. La nascita dello stato nazionale* (Bologna, 1993), 171–212.

[27] M. Moretti, 'L'"Associazione Nazionale fra i Professori Universitari" e la politica universitaria nell'età giolittiana: note ed osservazioni', in Romano, *Università in Europa*, 595; Tomasi and Bellatalla, *L'università italiana*, 96.

[28] M. Moretti, 'La questione universitaria a cinquant'anni dall'unificazione: la Commissione Reale per il riordinamento degli studi superiori e la relazione Ceci', in Porciani, *L'Università tra Otto e Novecento*, 264.

Linked with this criticism of academic structures were similar complaints to those in Germany about the overcrowded professions and the intellectual proletariat. University numbers doubled between 1870 and 1900, from 13,178 to 26,761, but then stabilized.[29] While in Germany there was an influx of the business class, in Italy the under-development of the economy meant that demand was generated more by the expansion of the existing professional and white-collar class. There were fewer alternatives to professional careers, making it difficult to divert this demand away from the universities, and law and medicine remained the chief targets. Thus, according to critics, the universities were turning out 'misfits' without a secure future, while economic and technical posts, or less valued professions like schoolteaching, found it difficult to attract able men.[30] In 1898 there were said to be about 500 posts available annually in both law and medicine, but the universities were producing 1,240 and 940 graduates respectively.[31] It was difficult to change these deep-rooted social habits. In the 1860s, Matthew Arnold found the numbers in letters and science faculties 'utterly insignificant', which he thought a grave weakness as 'the prevalence of the study of letters is a good test of a country's general condition of culture and civilization'.[32] In 1881, there were 4,489 students in law, 3,976 in medicine, and only 426 in letters (which puts Liard's complaints about France in context); by 1913 there were 9,383 in law, 5,342 in medicine, 1,908 in letters, and 1,325 in science.[33] The bourgeoisie which set its heart on a traditional university education was also the main electoral clientele of the men in power, and deputies were protectors of local interests and manipulators of state patronage rather than disinterested legislators. The professionals and intellectuals of the small towns and local capitals were essential intermediaries who 'helped to bind a culturally underdeveloped and divided civil society to a nation state intent on expanding its functions and sources of power'.[34] Antonio Gramsci was only one of many commentators who underlined the contrast between this rural, old-fashioned but tenacious class, with its strongholds in the south, and the modern-minded bourgeoisie of the northern cities.[35] If universities were diploma factories, that was what their customers wanted, and their aim was to gain a share of privilege rather than to dismantle the system; the hankering of professors and other intellectuals for disinterested science and high culture did not cut much ice when social interests were at stake. Nor, indeed, did the idea of opening the universities to lower social strata, and socially the universities, which charged relatively high fees, remained more 'aristocratic' than in Britain or Germany.[36]

[29] A. Cammelli, 'Universities and professions', in M. Malatesta (ed.), *Society and the professions in Italy 1860–1914* (Cambridge, 1995), 74–8.

[30] M. Barbagli, *Educating for unemployment: politics, labor markets, and the school system—Italy, 1859–1973* (New York, 1982), 13–39, 71–101.

[31] Tomasi and Bellatalla, *L'università italiana*, 38; cf. Rossi, *Università e società*, 113.

[32] *Schools and universities on the Continent*, The Complete Prose Works of Matthew Arnold, ed. R. H. Super, vol. 4 (Ann Arbor, 1964), 162.

[33] Tomasi and Bellatalla, *L'università italiana*, 25.

[34] M. Meriggi, 'The Italian *borghesia*', in J. Kocka and A. Mitchell (eds.), *Bourgeois society in nineteenth-century Europe* (Oxford, 1993), 431.

[35] A. Gramsci, *Gli intellettuali e l'organizzazione della cultura* (Rome, 1971), 20–3.

[36] Tomasi and Bellatalla, *L'università italiana*, 30, 94, 98, 218; Rossi, *Università e società*, 76–8.

One possible outlet was emigration, or migration from southern to northern Italy, but frustration at limited career prospects was also expressed in persistent and often violent student riots in the 1890s and 1900s. These reflected the growth of nationalist agitation and of socialism, in a deeply troubled period for Italy, yet political incursions on university autonomy were few. There was no bar to the appointment of socialists or Jews, and security of professorial tenure was strong. Under the Casati law, appointments were made by national competition, which as in France meant ultimately by the minister, but on the advice of the Higher Council for Public Instruction, which nominated selection commissions and also regulated questions of discipline; appointment to the Council reflected political patronage, but from 1881 it included elected university representatives.[37] There were only two significant dismissals, both in 1898. One was of Maffeo Pantaleoni, an economist and sociologist at Naples who criticized the colonial policies which led to Italy's defeat at Adua in Abyssinia in 1896. Threatened with prosecution, he resigned and took refuge in Geneva, though he returned in 1901 as a professor at Rome; he also evolved, like some other critics of the regime, from radicalism to nationalism, later becoming a deputy. The other case was Ettore Ciccotti, dismissed from the Scientific and Literary Academy of Milan for participating in the socialist insurrection of 1898. He too later found another post.[38] Both cases provoked national debate, and the difficulty of making such dismissals was an important safeguard of intellectual freedom, even if it could also encourage professors to neglect their duties.

The professional concerns of academics were reflected in the formation of a national association of professors in 1905, and in 1910 the state set up a commission to try to draw some new conclusions from fifty years of debate on university reform.[39] Its report, written by a *docente* at Rome University, Luigi Ceci, appeared in 1914. Some of its ideas reflected the nationalist spirit of the age: more than ever, it declared, knowledge represents power and wealth, and 'intellectual superiority frequently signifies political and economic supremacy'.[40] One proposal was for a new university at Bari, to promote Italian interests in the Adriatic and Albania. But on university questions proper, as so often in the past, the report turned to the German model and cited the foundation of Berlin in 1810. The solutions to Italy's problems, including student riots, were the familiar ones: state examinations, individual course fees, and genuine *Privatdozenten*. No action was taken, and it was left to Mussolini's minister of education, the philosopher Giovanni Gentile, to break with the Casati system in 1923, underlining how closely it had been tied up with the interests and ideologies of liberalism.

According to a sampling of 1911, 37 per cent of university students' fathers were landowners, 25 per cent from the liberal professions, 12 per cent merchants or industrialists, 16 per cent white-collar workers; only 5 per cent were workers, and 2

[37] M. Moretti and I. Porciani, 'Il reclutamento accademico in Italia: uno sguardo retrospettivo', *Annali di Storia delle Università Italiane*, 1 (1997), 11–39.

[38] Rossi, *Università e società*, 151–4; Tomasi and Bellatalla, *L'università italiana*, 53–4, 143–4.

[39] M. Moretti, 'L' "Associazione Nazionale fra i Professori Universitari" ', 581–600.

[40] Ibid. 297.

per cent farmers, peasants, or farmhands. This was a very traditional pattern, and the title 'landowner' probably concealed many bourgeois who bought small estates for prestige reasons. But the neglect of modern subjects was not quite as great as the universities' critics maintained—3,105 students were studying engineering, and a further 3,227 were in a two-year engineering preparatory course.[41] Italian universities had a practical tradition going back to the Enlightenment, and engineering was a profession enjoying high status and endorsed by university degrees. The Casati law provided for modern as well as classical secondary education: alongside the three-year *ginnasio* followed by the two-year *liceo* was the *scuola tecnica* followed by the *istituto tecnico*, and the diploma of the latter gave admission to the university science faculties. Outside the universities, a number of specialized schools came to be supported by the state. The Technical Institute at Turin grew up in association with the university, from which it only became fully independent in 1906, and prided itself on its theoretical approach. The Higher Technical Institute at Milan, on the other hand, was modelled on Karlsruhe and Zurich.[42] Although a state school from the start (in 1863), the real initiative lay with the local industrialists; it supplied an elite of engineers and managers to Lombard industry, and was particularly strong in mechanical and electrical engineering.[43] There were other higher technical schools at Palermo, Naples, Rome, Padua, and Bologna, but civil engineering generally had the highest status, and links with local industry and applied research, as in the German Technical High Schools and the French provincial science faculties, seem to have been weak.

A final development, outside the state system, was in commercial education. A higher commercial school was founded at Venice in 1868, and others followed at Genoa (1884) and Bari (1886). These schools focused on mercantile needs, and in the 1900s the state recognized their diplomas. More ambitious was the school created at Milan in 1902 by Ferdinando Bocconi, founder of the famous department store later known as La Rinascente.[44] He was supported by the Chamber of Commerce and other like-minded businessmen, whose ambitions went beyond the Lombard capital. There was a parallel with Boutmy and the École Libre des Sciences Politiques, the aim being to create a new type of national elite adapted to the age of international industrial competition. The syllabus was general and rigorous, based on economics as the central subject, with practical studies like law, accountancy, and languages being subordinate. The professors, mostly part-timers from the outside world, included the sociologist Gaetano Mosca, who was strongly influenced by Taine and whose thinking about elites pointed to the need for a new 'aristocracy of knowledge'.[45] Like the Paris school, Bocconi's school remained independent of

[41] Barbagli, *Educating for unemployment*, 127, 135; cf. Tomasi and Bellatalla, *L'università italiana*, 25–6. The total in all subjects was 28,026.

[42] A. Guagnini, 'Higher education and the engineering profession in Italy: the *Scuole* of Milan and Turin 1859–1914', *Minerva*, 26 (1988), 512–48.

[43] *Il centenario del Politecnico di Milano 1863–1963* (Milan, 1964); *Il Politecnico di Milano: una scuola nella formazione della società industriale 1863–1914* (Milan, 1981). (The title Polytechnic dates from 1937.)

[44] The school was named after his son Luigi, a journalist killed at Adua.

[45] D. Musiedlak, *Université privée et formation de la classe dirigeante: l'exemple de l'Université L. Bocconi de Milan (1902–1925)* (Rome, 1990), 155, 161.

the state (until 1925), though it established the right to call itself a university, and its degrees were officially recognized. It charged high fees, yet with the aid of scholarships it managed to recruit its students from all over Italy and to attract a higher proportion from the white-collar classes, and even the upper working class, than did the traditional universities. Between 1906 and 1915, 43 per cent of the students at Bocconi came from those milieux, compared with 36 per cent from the ranks of landowners and industrialists, and 21 per cent from the professional and managerial class.[46] And quite unlike the Paris graduates, most of them made careers in industry and business, not in the public service. The fact that Milan had two colleges for producing a technocratic elite, but no university, underlined the contrast between the dynamic values of the industrial north and the more traditional ones persisting elsewhere and upheld by the national political class.

This class had its counterpart in Spain, where the liberal bourgeoisie was essentially pre-industrial and tied to land and government office. In the nineteenth century the universities were remodelled to serve its needs.[47] Spain was already a unified country, and so had no turning-point compared with 1861 in Italy, but it had deep ideological divisions, and the same need to create a national elite with common values. Here too, therefore, liberalism meant centralization and uniformity. 'For the men of the nineteenth century, liberty might be an ideal for the individual, but institutions, on the other hand, should be fully subordinate and coordinated as part of the unitary organization of the state, down to the minutest details.'[48] Liberals looked back to the Enlightenment, but also to the French example, and it was ironic, in the light of the experiences of 1808–14, that Spain had perhaps the most Napoleonic system outside France.

The reforming impulses of the Enlightenment had been revived on the eve of French rule. In 1807, a common curriculum was prescribed for the first time, and the number of universities was reduced to ten. Under French rule, in conditions of constant warfare, university life in Spain virtually ceased. The government of Joseph Bonaparte was never secure enough to carry out its own plans, which did have some local support from those who favoured reform by a strong state.[49] The universities suffered damage to their revenues and in some cases their buildings. Most of the University of Zaragoza was destroyed, and Valencia lost its library when the city was bombarded by the French in 1812. (Copenhagen University was a similar casualty of British bombardment in 1807.) Resistance to the French took refuge in Cadiz, where the 'Cortes of Cadiz' drew up a liberal constitution in 1812, and laid its own plans for university reconstruction, strongly influenced by Condorcet and by the new idea of an integrated educational system serving the nation rather than simply state interests. When the French were expelled, however,

46 Musiedlak, *Université privée*, 75–6.

47 M. Peset and J. L. Peset, *La universidad española (siglos XVIII y XIX): despotismo ilustrado y revolución liberal* (Madrid, 1974), 393–5.

48 Ibid. 34.

49 M. de Puelles Benítez, 'The influence of political factors on the formation of the Spanish educational system 1809–1814', *Paedagogica Historica*, 28 (1992), 485–510.

the Restoration regime of Ferdinand VII restored the universities in a conservative sense, and political and religious repression predominated over reform.

After the liberal revolution of 1820, the new government looked back both to the Enlightenment and to Cadiz. Its priority was to create a central university at Madrid, by moving the ancient university of Alcalá, and the rest of the system was to be rationalized by providing one university for each province, including one for Catalonia at Barcelona. The rector of the new Madrid University was Manuel José Quintana, the author of the Cadiz reform plans, and in his opening speech in 1822 he declared that it would be at the centre of the nation's intellectual life. 'The Central University is the work of the nation, born with liberty, the product of enlightenment and of the civilization of the centuries.' The dark days of the Inquisition were past, and the light which had dawned in the eighteenth century was spreading: 'the two greatest goods of civilized man are EDUCATION and LIBERTY.'[50] But in 1823 the liberal regime was overthrown, and its changes were reversed. In 1824, the government produced its own legislation, the 'last creation of the *ancien régime*'.[51] As in Restoration France, conservatives were happy to use centralization for their own anti-liberal purposes, and in Spain they saw themselves working in the Enlightenment tradition of authoritarian reform. There was a rigidly uniform curriculum, and the kind of minute surveillance of teaching, religious observance, and discipline characteristic of the 1820s.[52] Despite its reactionary nature, the 1824 plan can be seen as part of a continuous process of accretion of power to the state.

After Ferdinand VII died in 1833, the struggle for power between liberals and conservatives was complicated for decades by military *pronunciamientos* and by the Carlist civil wars, which had both dynastic and regional aspects. This strengthened the desire for a centralized educational system to hold the nation together and maintain Castilian supremacy. Even when the liberals were in power (which was most of the time after 1836) they were themselves divided between 'moderate' and 'progressive' wings, one of the dividing-points being attitudes towards the church. All parties in these struggles expected university professors, as state officials, to support their political projects, and dismissals were common—often followed by restitution a few years later.[53] By 1845 the moderate wing of the liberals had achieved a relatively stable victory, and they enacted the 'Pidal plan' whose basic principles regulated the universities for the rest of our period, taking final form in the Moyano law of 1857.

The most influential figure in the 1840s was Antonio Gil de Zárate, a playwright and political figure who headed the education section in the ministry of the interior

[50] *Historia de la educación en España. II. De las Cortes de Cádiz a la revolución de 1868*, 2nd edn. (Madrid, 1985), 403, 411.

[51] Peset and Peset, *La universidad española*, 139.

[52] *Historia de la educación*, 68–122.

[53] V. M. Montalt, 'Depuraciones y postergaciones en la Universidad de Valencia durante la época isabelina 1833–1874', in *Doctores y escolares: II Congreso internacional de historia de las universidades hispánicas* (Valencia, 1998), ii. 111–21.

(there was no separate ministry of education until 1900). He had been educated in France, and was influenced by the practices of the July monarchy. An advisory Higher Council, for example, was created in 1843, one of several parallels with Italy. Like French liberals, the Spanish moderates wanted a system from which the direct influence of the church was excluded, and thought detailed state control an essential bulwark of secularism; there was to be no freedom for Catholic higher education. Faculties of canon law were abolished in 1842, and the number of theology faculties was cut to five in 1845 (they were closed down for good in 1868). But like the Enlightenment reformers, the liberals also saw the Catholic religion as part of Spanish identity and a force for social stability, and were willing to impose conformity on students and to suppress anti-religious ideas. There was a Concordat with the Papacy in 1851, and subsequent political developments did not lead to any permanent shift to militantly anticlerical policies as in France and Italy.

The University of Barcelona was reopened in 1842, and in 1845 Madrid finally replaced Alcalá. The Pidal plan fixed a pattern of ten universities which thereafter remained unchanged.[54] Some reformers, as in France and Italy, would have liked to reduce the number even more to produce strong intellectual centres. But as the preamble to the Pidal plan complained, everyone was in favour of this until their own university was threatened, when it was discovered to be essential to local social life and cultural prestige.[55] However, Madrid became the Central University and the others were described as 'district' universities, which was only a step away from the French model of a single University. Madrid was the only university entitled to give doctoral degrees, and it rapidly established numerical dominance. Urban universities like Barcelona and Valencia were also large, but once-famous ones like Salamanca, Oviedo, and Valladolid were now backwaters. Madrid was also the seat of a small number of elite schools training engineers for the state, on French lines, which were separate from the universities and bastions of social privilege.[56]

The autonomy of the Spanish universities had once rested on independent revenues, but what was not destroyed in the Napoleonic wars disappeared with the abolition of tithes and confiscation of church property which was another aspect of liberal policy. Most of the scholarships which had formerly helped poor students were also wiped out, and the liberals favoured high fees to maintain social exclusivity. Basic income now came from the state, and an important aspect of the 1845 law was that it turned the professorate into a single, bureaucratic body with a common salary scale and conditions of service. In 1847 there were 276 professors: sixty-one of them were in Madrid, while at the other end of the scale Salamanca had only fifteen and Granada thirteen.[57] Appointments in Spain had traditionally been

[54] Barcelona (formerly at Cervera), Granada, Madrid, Oviedo, Salamanca, Santiago, Seville (with a medical school at Cadiz), Valencia, Valladolid, Zaragoza.

[55] *Historia de la educación*, 203–4.

[56] Peset and Peset, *La universidad española*, 455.

[57] J. L. Guereña, 'El primer escalafón de catedráticos de universidades (1847) y la creación del cuerpo de catedráticos de universidades en España', in *Doctores y escolares*, 245–6. Cf. F. Villacorta Baños, 'Catedráticos y auxiliarios: la formación de los cuerpos burocraticos universitarios (1857–1923)', in J. L. Guereña and E. M. Fell (eds.), *L'Université en Espagne et en Amérique latine du moyen âge a nos jours. II. Enjeux, contenus, images* (Tours, 1998), 151–63.

made by public competition (*oposición*). This continued, but all contests were now held in Madrid under ministerial supervision, and Madrid's monopoly of the doctorate also meant a virtual monopoly of academic talent. A further aspect of centralization was that rectors now became administrators appointed by the state, as in France, not academics elected by the Senate (*claustro*), as in Germany. They were usually not professors, but bureaucrats, priests, or politicians chosen for their loyalty.[58]

The Moyano law of 1857 brought the division between secondary and higher education, ambiguous in previous plans, into line with the Humboldtian model; as in France, the bachelors' degree became the school-leaving examination. The 1857 law also separated the faculty of science from that of 'philosophy and letters'. But with general education relegated to the schools, and the role of philosophy as a preparation for theology removed, neither faculty flourished. Law and medicine became the dominant subjects of study: at Valencia, these faculties accounted for 33 per cent of the students in 1820, 70 per cent in 1839, 89 per cent in 1878.[59] As the Pidal plan put it, legal studies were 'needed for a large number of occupations, and are useful for those who aspire to political life in nations which are subject to a representative regime'.[60] It has been said that 'Spain was the land of advocates and jurists', and the nineteenth century 'an age of advocates'.[61] It was through law that the liberals sought to remodel and modernize their society, and its study was tied up both with the liberal conception of public life, and with the career demands of the dominant bourgeois groups. The dogmatic style of teaching, the rigidly prescribed official curricula and textbooks, and the centrality of examinations all had a strong social rationale, but a deadening intellectual effect.[62] Thus a movement calling for greater freedom and scientific regeneration soon emerged as a counterforce to the liberal legislation.

A key figure in this movement was Julián Sanz del Río, a professor at Madrid, who brought back from his studies in Germany the thought of the otherwise obscure German philosopher, Karl Krause. Krause had died in 1832, and was outside the mainstream of German philosophy. His thought, though deist, had some parallels with Comte's—the other centre of Krausism was that positivist stronghold the Free University of Brussels, and the Spanish Krausists had close links with freemasonry. What made it a significant force in Spain was its passionate faith in education as an instrument of national moral renewal and (a concept recurring in all phases of

[58] Peset and Peset, *La universidad española*, 474–7, 502.

[59] M. Baldó Lacomba, 'El impacto liberal-burgués en la Universidad de Valencia', in *O liberalísmo na peninsula ibérica na primeira metade do século XIX* (Lisbon, 1982), 211; M. Peset and others, *Historia de las universidades valencianas* (Alicante, 1993), i. 170.

[60] *Historia de la educación*, 205.

[61] Peset and Peset, *La universidad española*, 679.

[62] J. M. Hernández Díaz, 'La pedagogía de la universidad liberal: Salamanca (1845–1868)', in Guereña and Fell, *L'Université en Espagne*, 363–78. For the similar role of the university in Portugal, see R. A. de Azevedo, 'L'Université dans la formation des élites portugaises (1834–1870)', in *Higher education and society: historical perspectives. Educación superior y sociedad: perspectivas históricas* (Salamanca, 1985), 36–45.

Spanish university reform) regeneration. Sanz del Río propagated these ideas in the 1860s, when political tensions interacted with liberal opposition to the ultramontanism of Pius IX, and in 1867 he and some of his allies at Madrid were dismissed.[63] This sort of arbitrary action was now becoming unusual, and the affair attracted European attention. Protests helped to bring about the fall of the regime in 1868, followed by a period of radical political experiment. The dissidents returned to their chairs in triumph.

'The revolution of 1868 was impregnated with pedagogic concerns and pretensions', and it inaugurated a unique flowering of libertarian ideas, in which education was seen as the key to social progress.[64] The new regime's political 'federalism' was hostile to the centralized state of the liberals, and the long-term aim was that the state should withdraw from education entirely. Admittedly it was not easy to pass smoothly 'from the most absolute and tyrannical centralization to perfect liberty'.[65] Meanwhile the new plans gave complete freedom to open private institutions, promoted the German *Privatdozent* system, removed the obligations of students to attend courses before taking examinations and of professors to lecture on a fixed curriculum, extended the power to give doctorates to all the universities, tried to introduce more open competition for posts, and gave the universities internal autonomy, including the nomination of rectors.[66] The new rector of Madrid, Fernando de Castro, one of the victims of the 1867 purge, celebrated the principles of liberty and independence. Until now, cut off from the movement of European culture, the Spanish state had seen universities just as a machine for producing officials. 'Exorbitant centralization' had stifled initiative and produced mechanical teaching. 'My presence in this place signifies the end of that regime and the vindication of the professorate.'

> Science, progress, and social reform will all find a new centre in the university, independent in the internal organization of its functions, and declared a neutral arena, in which all schools and all theories can plant their standard. The professor, inviolable in the expression of his thought under the safeguard of his scientific dignity and his moral conscience, will stand for reason, not arbitrary power, for right not force. This consecration of liberty of teaching will be one of the most glorious marks of our present regeneration.[67]

There was much here which reflected German influence, but the libertarianism of the 'generation of 1868' was strongly marked by Spanish conditions, and one commentator has seen it as a re-emergence of the ideas of Condorcet, running underground since the days of the Cortes of Cadiz.[68]

In 1874 the Bourbon monarchy was restored, in a constitutional form based on the rotation of power between cliques. The universities were restored to tight state

[63] R. Carr, *Spain 1808–1939* (Oxford, 1966), 301–4.

[64] Y. Turin, *L'Éducation et l'école en Espagne de 1874 à 1902: libéralisme et tradition* (Paris, 1959), 4.

[65] 1868 decree cited in *Historia de la educación*, 335.

[66] Ibid. 325–34.

[67] Ibid. 520–1.

[68] M. de Puelles Benitez, 'Revolución francesa y educación: su incidencia en la génesis del sistema educativo español', in G. O. Sauter and M. de Puelles Benítez (eds.), *La revolución francesa y su influencia en la educación en España* (Madrid, 1990), 93.

control. The men of 1868 were dismissed from their chairs, but were allowed to return in 1881, and political purges ceased. The universities became rather more open to international influence and more imbued with the scientific spirit. But their general intellectual level remained mediocre. Whereas in Italy the constant hand-wringing of university reformers concealed real scientific achievements, Spain was a poorer and more isolated country. Most strikingly, at a time when university numbers rose sharply in most countries, they stagnated in Spain: there were 16,894 students in 1878–9, 17,733 in 1889–90, 16,277 in 1900–1, and 15,201 in 1909–10 (of whom 5,001 were at Madrid and 2,674 at Barcelona); the 276 professors of 1847 had risen only to 537, with 258 'auxiliaries', in 1911.[69] Most professors were part of the political establishment and its clienteles, and had little motive to challenge the system or to disturb the routines of dogmatic teaching. Nor was there any internal pressure to extend university education beyond the existing elite, and neither technical nor commercial education saw developments like those in Italy. 'Hyper-centralized and arthritic, the university at the beginning of the twentieth century remained very largely a bastion against new ideas, without a real purchase on society.'[70]

Faced with an archaic and somnolent state system, reformers turned to private initiative. In 1876 the Krausists formed the Institución Libre de Enseñanza (ILE), which through its practical creations and publications was to inspire most educational innovations in Spain for the next fifty years, including higher education for women. The core founders were the Madrid professors deprived of their chairs after 1874, including the chief theorist of the movement, Francisco Giner de los Ríos.[71] Giner and his allies would have liked to found a free university on the Brussels model, but this was barred. The ILE stood for a reorientation of Spain towards 'Europe', and for a creative public role for intellectuals; it sought to win over elite opinion, and appealed to those within the universities frustrated and alienated by the official system. It also worked with an old-established elite body, the Ateneo at Madrid, which traced its origins to 1835, and whose public lectures and library had been a rallying-point for upper-class liberals. In 1896 the Ateneo inaugurated a School of Higher Studies to give more systematic courses.[72] While Italian reformers looked mainly to Germany, Spanish ones were also inspired by Belgium and England. The English pattern of university extension was a strong influence on their attempts to revive provincial intellectual life and to spread university education to the people (see Chapter 19). They also had some impact on the official system, especially after Spain's defeat in 1898, which provoked a critical re-examination of all Spain's institutions. A ministry of education was created in 1900, and briefly

[69] Peset and others, *Universidades valencianas*, i. 169; Villacorta Baños, 'Catedráticos y auxiliarios', 156.

[70] J. M. Guereña, 'L'introduction de la sociologie dans l'université espagnole à la fin du XIXe siècle', in Guereña and Fell, *L'Université en Espagne*, 404.

[71] Carr, *Spain*, 469–72.

[72] F. Villacorta Baños, *El Ateneo Científico, Literario y Artístico de Madrid (1885–1912)* (Madrid, 1985), 99 ff.

headed by two ministers, Garcia Alix and Count Romanones, who promoted ideas of university autonomy, though in practice (despite the compulsory retirement of ninety-four inefficient professors) little was done.[73] One isolated victory was the creation of a chair of sociology at Madrid University in 1899, which was given to a 'positivist' scholar; the faculty of law was renamed 'law and social sciences'. The movement was also behind the creation by the state in 1907 of the Junta de Ampliación de Estudios, modelled on Duruy's École Pratique des Hautes Études and intended to stimulate research and international contacts; it had limited success given the general stagnation.[74] A more unusual innovation, reflecting the impact of Taine's views on England, was the opening in 1910 of a university residence at Madrid, which was designed to give intensive training on the Oxbridge model to a new elite; its students in the early 1920s included Salvador Dalí, Federico García Lorca, and Luis Buñuel.

As in Italy, centralization survived because its social function of giving a uniform training to the professional classes, and its political function of holding together the national elite, had not lost their rationale. But the defeat of 1898, and the social tensions arising from the growth of an industrial working class in parts of Spain, provoked a bout of national soul-searching, and called forth a new generation of intellectuals. The 'generation of 1898', as it was later called, was a literary rather than an academic phenomenon, but some of its members held university posts. Miguel de Unamuno, professor of Greek at Salamanca since 1891, had become known as a socialist, though he later rediscovered Catholicism. In 1900 he inaugurated his course with a speech which called on the students to abandon fusty literary traditions and throw themselves into the life of the nation, and to make a new contact with the people. Later in the same year, aged only 36, he was appointed rector of the university by Garcia Alix, and stayed until 1914, battling with the local conservatives. In stagnant Salamanca, promoting regeneration was an uphill struggle.[75] Another member of this generation was the philosopher José Ortega y Gasset, then a professor at Madrid, who wrestled with the problem of how Spain could become part of the mainstream of European culture while remaining true to its own character. Ortega, who also considered himself a socialist, urged his students to take on the idealistic task of national renovation.[76] In 1930, by when he was better known as a Nietzschean defender of true culture against both the masses and academic specialization, he concluded that the university had not transformed society or reached the people because 'only a great reform of our state will make our university effective'.[77]

[73] M. Peset, 'Los origenes de la autonomia universitaria y el proyecto de Garcia-Alix de 1901', in Guereña and Fell, *L'Université en Espagne*, 185–201; Turin, *L'Éducation et l'école*, 384–5.

[74] J. L. Guereña, 'Les institutions du culturel: politiques éducatives', in C. Serrano and S. Salaün (eds.), *1900 en Espagne (essai d'histoire culturelle)* (Bordeaux, 1988), 47–66; L. A. Baratas Díaz, 'La influencia francesa en el proyecto de reforma universitaria español de principios del siglo XX: una analogía incompleta', *Hispania*, 55 (1995), 645–72.

[75] J. C. Rabaté, 'La rentrée universitaire de Miguel de Unamuno dans la presse salmantine (1900)', in Guereña and Fell, *L'Université en Espagne*, 501–13.

[76] R. Wohl, *The generation of 1914* (Cambridge, Mass., 1979), 130–1.

[77] J. Ortega y Gasset, *Mission of the university* (London, 1946), 41.

15

Habsburg and other Nationalisms

'The progress of schools and universities measures that of nationalism,' said E. J. Hobsbawm, 'just as schools and especially universities became its most conscious champions.'[1] In the major nation-states, where high culture helped to integrate elites, the dominance of a single language could generally be taken for granted. But where nationalism took the form of emancipation movements, as in Gellner's 'classical Habsburg nationalism', of which the Czechs are perhaps the leading example, this was usually based on the assertion of linguistic rights and on the restoration or reinvention of a national language, so closely was language tied up with nineteenth-century conceptions of ethnicity and identity. Intellectuals had a central role in these movements, and Miroslav Hroch has provided a systematic account of the 'social preconditions of national revival' which distinguishes usefully between three phases. In Phase A, scholars from the traditional elite create national consciousness by their work as folklorists, linguists who turn peasant dialects into written languages, poets who publish national epics, or historians and literary scholars who rediscover a people's past glories. Many such scholars worked outside the universities, like the Czech historian Frantiszek Palacky, but others held university chairs, and in this phase conservative governments could take a benevolent attitude to activities which were seen as scholarly rather than political, even creating new chairs in vernacular languages and literatures. In Hroch's Phase B, cultural nationalism spreads to a wider constituency of activists, and leads naturally to a demand for national educational institutions, teaching in the newly validated national language, in order to form the cadres of the new nation, actual or potential; in phase C, national consciousness reaches the masses. Hroch's book was particularly concerned with Phase B, and he analysed the social character of the activists, identified by membership of patriotic societies, subscriptions to newspapers, and similar evidence.[2] Though their composition varied according to national conditions, these groups almost invariably included a second-order intelligentsia of clergymen, teachers, lawyers, doctors, or journalists, products of the universities but often based in small towns or the countryside; sometimes current students, for whom the social or gymnastic associations of Germany provided a model, were also members.

Clearly education was essential to the diffusion of nationalism, though secondary schools could be as important as universities, or more so given their wider reach.

[1] E. J. Hobsbawm, *The age of revolution: Europe 1789–1848*, paperback edn. (London, 1977), 167.

[2] M. Hroch, *Social preconditions of national revival in Europe: a comparative analysis of the social composition of patriotic groups among the smaller European nations*, 2nd edn. (New York, 2000).

As the history of nationalism in the Habsburg empire shows, secondary education in vernacular languages was crucial because of its connection with bureaucratic and white-collar jobs. Resistance to linguistic claims in universities might hold out longer, but once minorities had a right to use their language in the schools or the law courts, teachers and lawyers had to speak them too. (Vernaculars had frequently been allowed in theology faculties when they were banned elsewhere, as parish priests were useless if they did not know the language of the peasants.) The consequences of these claims were (in rising order) demands for parallel lectures in vernacular languages (as at Helsinki), for the splitting of existing universities on linguistic lines (as at Prague), for the conversion of universities wholly from one language to another (successful in Austrian Poland, unsuccessful at Ghent in Belgium), and for the creation of completely new universities to express the national will. Where small nations succeeded in establishing their independence, as in Greece or Romania, new universities to produce the national elite usually followed without delay. For, as in Italy, the achievement of national liberty needed to be followed by a process of nation-building in which education and intellectual elites had a fundamental role.

The relationship between language, national identity, and nationalism was never straightforward. National unity was reconciled with linguistic diversity in Switzerland, where the canton system allowed French- and German-speaking universities to coexist. Religion could be as important as language in uniting or dividing peoples. In the British Isles, Ireland presented an example of a political nationalism based on religion rather than language, Scotland an example of a cultural nationalism which had no real linguistic component and very limited political ambitions, while in Wales, in some ways a classic example of small-nation nationalism where patriotic feeling focused on the university, language could be a divisive factor, and like the Scots the Welsh combined cultural nationalism with loyalty to the British state. A general problem was that a successful nation might need a high culture, but not all linguistic or ethnic groups were large enough to support one, and it took time to develop languages to the point where they could express modern scientific or philosophical ideas. It was only in the 1840s that Magyar (Hungarian) was felt to have reached this point.[3] The major languages of culture such as English, French, German, or Russian had great prestige, and gave access to rich cultures and to the national and international intellectual world. In a multinational empire like Austria-Hungary, the nobility and the official or military elite saw speaking German or Hungarian as a mark of dynastic or supra-national loyalty. Other educated families might speak their vernacular at home, or even demand it at the secondary school, but were content to remain bilingual and for university education to be in the language of culture. One mark of a mature national movement was conversion of the educated elite to the vernacular, leading to a linguistic shift of families over generations. Another phenomenon of the same kind was the abandonment of Yiddish by assimilated Jews; they normally adopted the language of the

[3] A. Cser, 'Language and linguistics at the University of Pest in the 19th century', *Jahrbuch für Universitätsgeschichte*, 4 (2001), 49.

country, but this too could involve choices with political implications—German or French in Alsace, Polish or Russian in Russian Poland, German or Czech in Bohemia.[4] A further complication was the significant international migration of students in this period: the intelligentsias of small nations, especially in south-eastern Europe, expected to become fluent in one of the major languages, and continued to study abroad and to value their cosmopolitan links even when universities were established at home. Thus the correspondence between political and social elites and the indigenous educational system was not always as close as Gellner posited.

Before turning to the Habsburg Empire and the Balkans, the classic lands of nationalist conflict, it is worth looking at the cases of Scandinavia and Belgium. In Norway, the foundation of the University of Oslo (then called Christiania) in 1811 came just before the country's transfer in 1814 from Danish rule to a dynastic union with Sweden, but reflected long-standing discontent on the part of an intelligentsia which had formerly been forced to study in Copenhagen. Denmark also suffered from the growth of German nationalism in Schleswig-Holstein, of which Kiel University was a centre, and this issue stimulated a pan-Scandinavian student movement which began in the 1840s and held a series of congresses, but tailed off after 1848 and collapsed when Sweden failed to come to Denmark's aid in the 1864 war which led to Prussian annexation of Schleswig-Holstein.[5] As the sole university in a small country, Oslo developed a close relationship with the country's political as well as its intellectual life.[6] This was also true in a more complicated context in Finland, which passed from Swedish to Russian rule in 1809. The university at Åbo was transferred to Helsinki in 1828. The educated elite in Finland spoke Swedish, while most peasants were ethnically and linguistically Finnish. The rise of Finnish nationalism was a classic case of the rediscovery or invention of national traditions through the study of language and folklore, some of it by scholars within the university like Elias Lönnrot, who turned the Kalevala legends into a national epic. By the 1840s, nationalist intellectuals (the 'Fennomanes') were calling for university teaching in Finnish, and in due course Finnish-speaking chairs appeared.[7] Many students threw themselves into this movement, spending their summers exploring the rural roots of Finnish culture. But the university remained mainly Swedish-speaking until the 1920s, and Finnish nationalism was a movement which overrode the linguistic division. The relationship of cultural and political nationalism was complex. Within the Russian empire, Finland was a grand duchy with genuine constitutional rights, extended by Alexander II in the 1860s, and the university escaped

[4] G. B. Cohen, *Education and middle-class society in Imperial Austria 1848–1918* (West Lafayette, Ind., 1996), 136–7.

[5] S. Lindroth, *A history of Uppsala University 1477–1977* (Stockholm, 1976), 187–8.

[6] Hroch, *Social preconditions*, 33–43; S. Langholm, 'The new nationalism and the new universities: the case of Norway in the early 19th century', in M. Norrback and K. Ranki (eds.), *University and nation: the university and the making of the nation in northern Europe in the 19th and 20th centuries* (Helsinki, 1996), 139–52.

[7] M. Klinge, *Eine nordische Universität: die Universität Helsinki 1640–1990* (Helsinki, 1992), 356–82. Cf. Hroch, *Social preconditions*, 62–75.

the Russification imposed on other minorities like the Poles. In a small country without much urban life outside the capital, the university was central to national identity. The Finnish national anthem was a creation of students in 1848, the university building in the heart of the city was a national monument, and in a country without an aristocracy the university produced virtually all the educated elite; its annual graduation ball was the highlight of the Helsinki social season.[8] For most of the nineteenth century, nationalism developed within a framework of political loyalty, but at the end of the 1890s the regime began a systematic attack on Finnish autonomy, and this stirred up a new anti-Russian nationalism in which the university and its students played a central part—the imposition of Russian conscription being a particularly inflammatory issue. The 1905 revolution led to the extraction of new constitutional concessions, but this turbulent period saw both the rise of a more intransigent Finnish-language movement at the expense of Swedish, and a turning towards Germany, which already enjoyed much intellectual prestige, leading Finnish student volunteers to fight on the German side in the First World War.[9]

Linguistic conflict within a national community also appeared in Belgium. After 1830, all the Belgian universities were entirely francophone, and the educated elite saw French as a badge of culture and social status. A Flemish language movement began in the 1830s, aiming from the start to introduce Dutch courses into the University of Ghent, and ultimately to turn it into a Flemish university. This started as a movement of the intelligentsia, including students and many priests, and later gained wide popular support. But it was bitterly opposed both by the Flemish bourgeoisie and by the Catholic hierarchy, who were equally hostile to the Flemish movement at the Catholic University of Louvain. According to the economist Émile de Laveleye in 1889, 'the upper class, which is the seat and the instrument of intellectual culture, speaks French. The Flemish people—the farmers, workers, and *petit bourgeois*—are thus separated from the ray of civilization.'[10] The dispute was within the Flemish community, not an ethnic conflict between Flemings and Walloons. In fact religious questions were more divisive than linguistic ones in nineteenth-century Belgium. Although Flemish secondary education was permitted from 1883, and the movement had continuing support from student activists, it had achieved only a limited bilingualism at the University of Ghent by 1914.[11] During the war the issue was exploited by the German occupiers, who reopened Ghent as a Flemish-speaking university in 1916. Nearly all of the existing professors refused to collaborate, but others were found to do so, and several hundred students attended, events which inevitably caused bitterness and reprisals after the war.

[8] L. Kolbe, 'The university town as a *lieu de mémoire*: student identity and manifestations at the University of Helsinki 1828–1990', *History of Universities*, 14 (1995–6), 181–200.

[9] Klinge, *Eine nordische Universität*, 497–528, 565 ff.

[10] S. B. Clough, *A history of the Flemish movement in Belgium: a study in nationalism* (New York, 1968), 94, and cf. 151–3, 159–69.

[11] Cf. Hroch, *Social preconditions*, 107–16; L. Vos, 'Nationalism and student movements: conceptual framework and a Flemish case-study', in Norrback and Ranki, *University and nation*, 77–87.

In a recently independent country, a language movement which threatened to divide the elite had difficulty in making headway. In Belgium, no new universities were needed; but in other cases the assertion of one Flemish propagandist that a university was 'the supreme teacher of a nation, the chief organ, the fountain-head of the moral national existence' had more resonance.[12] Greece provides one example. The Greek struggle for independence did not result in the establishment of a Greek state until 1830, and before then Greeks had studied in western Europe, especially in Italy, Pisa being popular because of trading links with Livorno. Greek cultural revival had also found a home in the Ionian Academy at Corfu, opened in 1824 as 'the first Greek university'.[13] The Ionian islands had come under British rule after 1814, and the Academy was financed by a philhellene English nobleman, the earl of Guilford. It was organized like a university, and used the title in its official documents. Its special significance was that modern Greek, not Italian, became the teaching language, and it was able to attract students from the mainland. The Academy suffered from Guilford's death in 1827, but survived until 1864, when the Ionian islands became part of Greece. By then Greece had a national university at Athens, opened in 1837. The country's first king was Bavarian, and when a national system of education was organized it followed Bavarian lines, though Göttingen was also a model for the university. Seven of the original thirty-four professors were German, as was the general character of the system, with an emphasis on philosophy and (not surprisingly) neohumanism.[14] Providing a small country with the bulk of its professional classes, politicians, and writers, the University of Athens performed the classic functions of a national university. But there were also some tensions peculiar to Greece. Nationalists were anxious to assert continuity with classical Greece, and created a literary language which was close to ancient Greek and purified of later accretions. This was the language of higher education, and students had a vested interest in its maintenance. But it was very different from the language spoken by most Greeks, and when attempts were made to reach the people through a more demotic form of the language, this produced violent student riots, in 1901 against a translation of the New Testament, in 1903 against staging Aeschylus in demotic Greek.[15]

Greece gained its independence from Turkish rule earlier than other states in the region. The one with the most developed universities was Romania, which enjoyed some autonomy after 1829 and became effectively independent after the Crimean war. It had two distinct provinces, Moldavia and Wallachia, with their intellectual centres in Iasi and Bucharest respectively. Both towns had 'academies' which could trace their history to the seventeenth century. In the early nineteenth century, the academies developed the teaching of engineering, law, and philosophy, so training

[12] F. van Cauwelaert (1910), cited in E. H. Kossmann, *The Low Countries 1780–1940* (Oxford, 1978), 466.

[13] G. P. Henderson, *The Ionian Academy* (Edinburgh, 1988), p. ix.

[14] S. N. Derwissis, *Die Geschichte des griechischen Bildungswesens in der neueren Zeit mit besonderer Berücksuchtigung der Einflüsse der deutschen Pädagogik* (Frankfurt, 1976), 191, 194.

[15] N. C. Louros, 'L'Université Nationale d'Athènes (1837–1937): repères d'histoire', *CRE-Information*, 68 (1984), 17–18.

an incipient bourgeoisie. But the aristocrats who remained in control down to 1856 were hostile to teaching in the vernacular. The traditional language of culture, in an Orthodox country, was Greek, but the Romanian elite also studied abroad in France or Italy, and French was widely used in Romanian education. There were many Romanian students in Paris in the 1840s; they were active in the 1848 revolution, both there and at home, and this was the only Balkan country affected by that movement, one of whose unfulfilled aims was the creation of a national university system. In 1859 the provinces were united under a constitutional monarchy of classic elitist-liberal type, which proceeded to create such a system, raising the academies to university status, Iasi in 1860 and Bucharest in 1864 as part of a general educational law. It was a sign of French influence that the latter incorporated a 'higher normal school' for training secondary teachers. But there were no medical schools until 1869 (Bucharest) and 1879 (Iasi), and foreign study remained common, especially in Paris, though the German university model also influenced the academic world.[16]

The dean of the Bucharest law faculty, C. Bozianu, became prime minister in 1865, with two other law professors as ministers. This was typical of the prominent part which university professors played in political and intellectual life in new countries. University intellectuals, says Keith Hitchins, took as their 'special province . . . social change and the adaptation of existing institutions to the "spirit of the times". It was they who were mainly responsible for elaborating the theory of the ethnic nation and for devising the strategies of national development.' They saw themselves as the main bearers of western or 'European' ideas.[17] He cites the example of the Juminea, a 'youth' movement founded in 1863 and based on the university of Iasi, which put forward a theory of organic, conservative national development. Many of its members had studied in Germany or France, including its leader Titu Maiorescu, who was rector of Iasi in 1863, and later a professor at Bucharest.[18] One of his successors at Iasi, Constantin Stere, was to be a leader of populist socialism before the First World War. Nor were these the only examples: conservative, liberal, or socialist movements all looked to the universities for leadership. As in southern Europe rather earlier, universities were seen as instruments of modernization and economic development, and they created a new intelligentsia or middle class in what had been largely peasant territories.

Even with a relatively developed university system, Romania continued to send students abroad, especially for higher scientific, legal, or medical studies.[19] Students from eastern and south-eastern Europe were familiar presences in France,

[16] J. Livescu, 'Die Entstehung der rumänischen Universitäten im Zusammenhang der europäischen Kulturbeziehungen (1850–1870)', in R. G. Plaschka and K. Mack (eds.), *Wegenetz europäischen Geistes: Wissenschaftszentren und geistige Wechselbeziehungen zwischen Mittel- und Südosteuropa vom Ende des 18. Jahrhunderts bis zum Ersten Weltkrieg* (Vienna, 1983), 21–35. Cf. J. Sadlak, 'The use and abuse of the university: higher education in Romania 1860–1990', *Minerva*, 29 (1991), 195–225.

[17] K. Hitchins, *Rumania 1866–1947* (Oxford, 1994), 9.

[18] Ibid. 56–61.

[19] L. Nastasa, 'Le rôle des études à l'étranger dans la carrière des professeurs d'université roumains (1878–1944)', in V. Karady and M. Kulczykowski (eds.), *L'Enseignement des élites en Europe centrale (19–20e siècles)* (Cracow, 1999), 149–58.

Germany, Austria, Switzerland, Italy, and Belgium down to 1914, and the host countries were beginning to see them as a way of turning cultural into political influence. Some links were traditional religious ones, as with Hungarian Calvinists who studied in Holland, Switzerland, or Scotland, but the medieval tradition of *peregrinatio*, discouraged by absolute rulers in the eighteenth century, took on new vitality in the nineteenth, and spread western ideas of science, liberalism, and nationalism.[20] The latest urban and western ideas were brought back from Paris, Berlin, or Vienna: Ivo Andric, in his novel of Bosnian life *The bridge over the Drina* (1945) showed how in the little town of Visegrad before 1914 the 'return of the students' each summer began a period of intensive political discussion and activity. Some of these migrating students, especially the Russians and Poles, were political exiles; others were women who travelled abroad because their own universities were still closed (see Chapter 17). But most students from the Balkans would return to leading positions, and were often financed by their governments, who found this more cost-effective than creating their own universities. Serbia, for example, became autonomous in the 1820s, but was a small and poor country. A 'higher school' was founded in 1863 at Belgrade, but did not become a full university until 1905. Students were regularly sent abroad with scholarships, mostly to Germany and Austria, but also to France after 1900 when Serbia's diplomatic allegiances shifted. It has been estimated that 70 per cent of the Serbian intelligentsia were educated abroad.[21] There was the same pattern in Bulgaria, where a higher institution was founded at Sofia in 1888 following independence, but did not achieve full status until 1904.[22] Bulgarians were to be found in force in France, Switzerland, and Belgium: the New University of Brussels was nicknamed the Bulgarian University of Brussels because it attracted so many.[23] Throughout the Balkans, the professional classes had a strongly cosmopolitan character, more so than their western counterparts—but were all the more cut off from the peasant masses.

Student movement took place within the boundaries of the Habsburg Empire as well as internationally, and by 1914 it had four Slav-language universities, at Prague, Cracow, Lwów, and Zagreb.[24] After the suppression of the 1848 revolutions, the Habsburg monarchy returned to a unitary structure in which authoritarian policies were imposed on Austrian and Hungarian universities alike. Defeat in Italy in 1859

[20] See generally Plaschka and Mack, *Wegenetz . . . Wissenschaftszentren*, and R. G. Plaschka and K. Mack (eds.), *Wegenetz europäischen Geistes. II. Universitäten und Studenten: Die Bedeutung studentischer Migrationen in Mittel- und Südosteuropa vom 18. bis zum 20. Jahrhundert* (Munich, 1987).

[21] L. Trgovcevic, 'Serbian intellectuals in foreign universities in the 19th century', in Karady and Kulczykowski, *L'Enseignement des élites*, 159–73.

[22] P. Boyadjieva, 'The social legitimization of an "untimely" institution: the case of the first Bulgarian university', *History of Universities*, 16/1 (2000), 179–96.

[23] A. Despy-Meyer, 'Un laboratoire d'idées: l'Université Nouvelle de Bruxelles (1894–1919)', in G. Kurgan-Van Hentenryk (ed.), *Laboratoires et réseaux de diffusion des idées en Belgique (XIXe–XXe siècles)* (Brussels, 1994), 52.

[24] The complete list by 1914 was: in *Austria*, Vienna, Graz, Innsbruck, Prague, Czernowitz (all German), Cracow, Lwów (Polish), Prague (Czech); in *Hungary*, Budapest, Kolozsvár (Magyar), Zagreb (Croat), plus Technical High Schools at Vienna, Graz, Lwów, Prague (German and Czech), Brno (German and Czech), Budapest.

forced the regime to make liberal concessions, which included making Magyar the language of education at all levels in Hungary, and to restore a measure of parliamentary life. Austria's defeat by Bismarck in 1866 led to the 'compromise' of 1867 which created the 'dual monarchy', and after this there was significant divergence between the nationality policies of the two governments.[25] In Austria (meaning the whole of the western half) the government's policy was to balance off national demands, but concessions to minorities provoked a nationalist backlash from the Germans. From the 1880s, as in France, Italy, and Germany, nationalism turned into a right-wing domestic force, directed against the enemy within, and was particularly strong among students. It included anti-Semitism, and Austrian Jews were torn more than those in Germany between cultural assimilation and the beginnings of a nationalism of their own in the shape of Zionism. Nationalist agitation in Austria was also cross-cut by religious divisions, between freethinkers and clericals, which had a particular impact on the universities. In the Hungarian half of the empire, however, the dominant Magyars, though only about half the population, were determined to maintain their position, refusing to move towards universal suffrage or to concede minority language rights. The exception was Croatia, whose loyalty to the Habsburg cause won it special constitutional status. A Croat-speaking university was founded at Zagreb in 1874. It was preceded by the creation of a 'Yugoslav Academy' in 1867, at whose opening the nationalist historian and priest F. Racki declared that 'today we must either advance in science and acquire all the resources which it offers, or remain the slaves either of Latin science or of Germanic science, and be no more than the instrument of the greatness of neighbouring peoples'. But repudiation of 'Germanic science' brought the penalty of intellectual isolation.[26] The university became a stronghold of Croatian nationalism rather than of the broader South Slav movement favoured by Racki and other intellectuals; it attracted students from neighbouring Bosnia, and in 1895 the students used an imperial visit to mount a spectacular anti-Hungarian demonstration.[27]

Other large minorities in Hungary were the Slovaks, a mainly peasant people whose nationalism remained underdeveloped, and whose intelligentsia tended to look to Prague, and the Romanians in Transylvania, where nationalism was active but no concessions were made, either to the Romanians or to the significant German minority. A new university was founded at Kolozsvár (modern Cluj) in 1872, but it was purely Hungarian-speaking, and designed as a secular counterweight to Catholic dominance at Budapest. Besides, as was common in eastern Europe, there was a linguistic difference between the towns with their merchants and professional men and the countryside, and even in 1910 only 12 per cent of the population of Kolozsvár itself were Romanian.[28] On the eve of 1914 the Hungarians

[25] Cf. G. Otruba, 'Die Universitäten in der Hochschulorganisation der Donau-Monarchie: Nationale Erziehungsstätten im Vielvölkerreich 1850 bis 1914', in *Student und Hochschule im 19. Jahrhundert: Studien und Materialen* (Göttingen, 1975), 75–155.

[26] P. Saly and others (eds.), *Nations et nationalismes en Europe 1848–1914* (Paris, 1996), 52.

[27] M. Glenny, *The Balkans 1804–1999: nationalism, war and the great powers* (London, 1999), 260–1.

[28] Hitchins, *Rumania*, 219.

had agreed to new universities at Debrecen, a Calvinist stronghold, and at Bratislava (Pressburg) in Slovakia, but the latter was aimed at Magyar-speaking Lutherans. For the firm policy of all Hungarian governments was to maintain Magyar as the language of government and culture. The German minority largely accepted this, although German (with Latin) had been the language of Budapest University until 1844, and was imposed again between 1849 and 1867.[29] Hungarian Jews also assimilated to Magyar culture, which was especially significant because, in a largely unindustrialized country whose political culture was dominated by the values of the landed gentry, a high proportion of the bourgeoisie was Jewish. At the University of Budapest, which had about three-quarters of all the students in Hungary, 35 per cent of the students were Jewish in 1910.[30] This reflected Jewish urbanization—Jews were 5 per cent of the population of Hungary, but 23 per cent in Budapest—and led to a dominant Jewish presence in the intelligentsia and the professions: nearly half of all lawyers, doctors, and journalists in Hungary were Jewish.[31] Yet before 1914 anti-Semitism was far less evident than in Vienna, due, it has been argued, to a segmentation of the elite peculiar to Hungary: late economic development meant there was only a small Magyar middle class, and the Magyar elite was not interested in the professions because its gentry traditions were political and military. There was thus a dual structure of ambition and social mobility: the gentry relied on their social qualities and political influence to get official positions, while Jewish families wagered on cultural capital, and on merit and hard work.[32] In 1908–9, only 4 per cent of Hungarian students were the children of landowners, but 46 per cent were those of professional men and civil servants, 30 per cent of artisans and white-collar workers, and 11 per cent of farmers or smallholders.[33] Budapest dominated the system: it was now the fifth largest university in Europe, and had a key role in the process of economic and social modernization which was overtaking east central Europe.

Jozséf Eötvös, the first education minister of post-1867 Hungary, insisted that 'the idea of humanity should be placed above that of the nation.... Science does not belong to particular nations and a single epoch, but is the common treasure of mankind.'[34] In its organization, scientific ideals, and international links, Budapest remained a very 'German' university, and this was true of central Europe generally, until French and even British influences began to seep in at the end of the century. One example was the college founded at Budapest in 1895 in memory of Eötvös by his son the mathematician Loránd Eötvös, when himself minister. This was a

[29] P. Hanák, 'Wandlungen der österreichisch-ungarischen wissenschaftlichen Beziehungen im Laufe des 19. Jahrhunderts', in Plaschka and Mack, *Wegenetz... Wissenschaftszentren*, 344, 349.

[30] G. Otruba, 'Die Nationalitäten- und Sprachenfrage des höheren Schulwesens und der Universitäten als Integrationsproblem der Donaumonarchie (1863–1910)', ibid. 100.

[31] R. Okey, *The Habsburg Monarchy, c. 1765–1918: from enlightenment to eclipse* (London, 2001), 316.

[32] V. Karady, 'Dualité scolaire et dualité sociale dans la formation des élites en Hongrie au début du 20e siècle', in Karady and Kulczykowski, *L'Enseignement des élites*, 121–36; V. Karady, 'Assimilation and schooling: national and denominational minorities in the universities of Budapest around 1900', in G. Ránki (ed.), *Hungary and European civilization* (Budapest, 1989), 285–319.

[33] J. Mazsu, *The social history of the Hungarian intelligentsia 1825–1914* (Boulder, Colo., 1997), 124, 131 (figures appear to exclude Croatia).

[34] Hanák, 'Wandlungen', 350.

residential college modelled on the Paris École Normale, but specializing in mathematics and physics, and also drawing on the English ideal of tutorial teaching. The aim was to produce a broader, modern elite with a European orientation, and it belonged to the same family of innovations as the Bocconi university or the Madrid student residence. In practice, secondary teaching remained the main outlet, and the college had a quite different profile from the university, as a third of the students were sons of university or secondary teachers, and only 6 per cent came from Budapest itself; 48 per cent were Protestant but only 3 per cent were Jewish—the segmentation of educational paths is again apparent.[35]

In the western half of the empire, or 'Cisleithania', the Germans were only about a third of the population, but were determined to defend their cultural dominance, in opposition if need be to the dynasty's policies. The most direct threat came from the Czechs. Prague University had been a bastion of German culture since the seventeenth century, and there was a significant German minority in the city, and a larger one in other parts of Bohemia and Moravia, where in 1910 Czech speakers were less than two-thirds of the population. The growth of Czech national feeling owed as much to historians like Palacky and philologists like Josef Jungmann (though neither of these held university chairs) as to musicians, playwrights, and poets. A chair in Czech language and literature was founded at Prague in 1793, and the growth of Czech secondary education after 1848 produced a new bourgeois intelligentsia and a need for trained teachers. Some Czech-speaking chairs were founded in the 1860s, along with a bilingual Technical High School. Bilingualism proved only a stage on the way to separation, and in 1882 the university was split into separate Czech and German universities, each with its own set of faculties.[36] The Czech university soon became the larger, though the German one retained a high scholarly reputation, and also served the Jewish population, which assimilated to German rather than Czech: in 1910 Jews were 20 per cent of students at the German university, only 2 per cent at the Czech one.[37] At the Czech university, the leading figure was Thomas Masaryk, who became professor of philosophy in 1882, and retained his chair while pursuing a political career which ended as the first president of independent Czechoslovakia. Masaryk's position within Czech nationalism was often controversial, and his advocacy of 'peaceful cultural work' as the way forward rather than political militancy alienated many students.[38] But he had a strong

[35] V. Karady, 'Le Collège Eötvös et l'École Normale Supérieure vers 1900: note comparatiste sur la formation d'intellectuels professionnels', in J. Le Goff and B. Köpeczi (eds.), *Intellectuels français, intellectuels hongrois, XIIIe–XXe siècles* (Budapest, 1985), 235–53; E. F. Donoghue, 'Brief tenure but lasting influence: Baron Roland Eotvos and the Budapest Collegium', *History of Education Society Bulletin*, 63 (1999), 35–9.

[36] G. B. Cohen, 'Education and Czech social structure in the late nineteenth century', in H. Lemberg and others, *Bildungsgeschichte, Bevölkerungsgeschichte, Gesellschaftsgeschichte in den Böhmischen Ländern und in Europa: Festschrift für Jan Havránek zum 60. Geburtstag* (Vienna, 1988), 32–45; M. N. Kuz'min, 'Die Teilung der Prager Hochschulen: Zur Formierung des Tschechischen Schulsystems', in Plaschka and Mack, *Wegenetz . . . Wissenschaftszentren*, 112–23.

[37] Otruba, 'Die Nationalitäten- und Sprachenfrage', 100.

[38] H. J. Skilling, *T. G. Masaryk: against the current 1882–1914* (Basingstoke, 1994), 13–14.

influence on a new generation of leaders, and his teaching was a magnet for Slav students from other parts of the empire, notably Croatia.[39]

The 1882 settlement did not put an end to Czech problems. The Austrian constitution of 1867 gave citizens the right to use the recognized languages of their province in education and for official purposes, and the linguistic requirements for lawyers, teachers, and officials were of acute interest to students. Tensions culminated in 1897 with the 'Badeni decrees' giving equal status to Czech and German in Bohemia, which would have favoured bilingual Czechs over monolingual Germans. They had to be withdrawn after violent opposition by German speakers, including student riots and a protest by 860 professors in Reich Germany.[40] Demands continued for a second Czech university at the Moravian capital, Brno, which the monarchy resisted, though the Technical High School there was split in 1899. Riots on the university question in 1905, in which two students were killed, inspired a patriotic composition by Leos Janáček. German–Czech tension eventually paralysed Austrian parliamentary life, especially after the introduction of universal male suffrage in 1907, which removed the advantages which Germans had formerly gained from their greater wealth and gave minority ethnic groups blocking power.

The other group which benefited from a more liberal language policy after 1867 were the Poles. In 1869 Polish became the language of all education in Galicia, and Cracow and Lwów universities were fully converted from German, becoming refuges of Polish culture at a time when it was oppressed in Russia and Germany. Yet having asserted their own rights, the Polish elite found themselves challenged in turn by second-wave nationalism, as democratization and the spread of education highlighted the ethnic and religious differences between Polish landowners and Ukrainian peasants (usually called Ruthenes at the time). At Lwów, a chair in Ukrainian language and literature was established in 1849, and further Ukrainian-speaking chairs in the 1890s; but although about a quarter of the students at Lwów were Ukrainian, the government refused demands for a separate university, being anxious to retain the political loyalty of the Poles by maintaining their status as master race in Galicia.

Further east, in the territory known as Bukovina, a different policy was followed. Here there was a mixture of peoples and religions. There were Ukrainians, Romanians, Germans, and Jews, but the Ukrainians and Romanians were mainly peasants whose education was undeveloped. In 1875 a German-speaking university was founded at Czernowitz, partly to compensate for the polonization of Cracow and Lwów, and it remained German down to 1914, though there were chairs for the literary study of Romanian and Ukrainian, and these languages were used for teaching in the Orthodox theology faculty.[41] The minister of education who founded the

[39] A. Suppan, 'Bildungspolitische Emanzipation und gesellschaftliche Modernisierung: Die südslavischen Studenten an der tchechischen Universität Prag um die Jahrhundertwende und der Einfluss Professor Masaryks', in Plaschka and Mack, *Wegenetz . . . Wissenschaftszentren*, 303–25.

[40] Okey, *Habsburg Monarchy*, 306–7.

[41] It was transferred to Romania in 1919 (Cernauti), to the Soviet Union in 1945 (Cernovcy), to Ukraine in the 1990s (Chernivtsi), and has thus experienced four language regimes (as has Lwów: German, Polish, Russian, Ukrainian).

university hoped that it would be 'a beachhead of German education in the eastern part of the monarchy', and in an area where other nationalities were too weak to put up a challenge this hope was fulfilled.[42] Although Galicia and Bukovina were among the poorest regions of Europe, their universities presented a pattern of high attendance. Lwów had over 5,000 students in 1914, and Cracow nearly 3,000. Unusually, a significant number of students here came from peasant backgrounds.[43] The percentage of Jewish students in 1910 was 13 at Lwów and Cracow, and 42 at Czernowitz—higher even than at Budapest.[44] These figures were less surprising when one considers the proportion of Jews in the urban populations (30 per cent at Czernowitz). University education in these regions, supported by a relatively dense network of gymnasiums, had clearly become a focus of intense social ambition for a wide social spectrum, and in the absence of industrial development this meant competition for posts in law (normally the largest faculty in all Austrian universities) and in medicine.[45]

Ethnicity, class, and religion intersected in complex ways which reflected the differing stages of development of the Habsburg peoples. The statistics carefully collected by the bureaucrats show that in 1910, for Austria and Hungary together, the peoples over-represented in higher education were the Germans (24 per cent of the population, 30 per cent of students), the Magyars (20 and 23), and the Poles (10 and 18). The Czechs had a strong interest in secondary and higher education, but they were counted together with the Slovaks, and appeared under-represented (17 per cent of population, 12 per cent of students), as were the South Slavs (14 and 7), Ruthenians (8 and 4), and Romanians (6 and 2). These statistics were based on language, so that Jews were counted as Germans, Magyars, or Poles. But separate religious statistics show that Jews, though only 4 per cent of the total population, made up 20 per cent of the students. As in Germany, the Jewish presence was higher in the 1880s and 1890s than in the 1900s, being then overtaken by general bourgeois growth, though Budapest was an exception.[46]

This was the context in which German ethnic nationalism became more aggressive. Down to the 1850s, German was promoted as the official language in all the Austrian universities, and the Germans could feel that they were at home there. But once concessions to other groups were made, the supremacy of German culture seemed

[42] K. Stremayr, cited by R. A. Kann, 'Higher education and politics in the Austrian constitutional monarchy (1867–1918)', in R. A. Kann, *Dynasty, politics, and culture: selected essays* (Highland Lakes, NJ, 1991), 328.

[43] A. Podraza, 'Jugend plebejischer Herkunft an der Jagiellonien Universität im 19. und 20. Jahrhundert', in M. Kulczykowski (ed.), *Les Étudiants: liens sociaux, culture, mœurs du moyen-âge jusqu'au 19e siècle: Vème session scientifique internationale, Cracovie 28–30 mai 1987* (Warsaw, 1991), 179–88.

[44] Otruba, 'Die Nationalitäten- und Sprachenfrage', 100.

[45] G. Stourzh, 'Die Franz-Josephs-Universität in Czernowitz 1875–1918', in Plaschka and Mack, *Wegenetz . . . Wissenschaftszentren*, 54–9; M. Kulczykowski, 'La formation des nouvelles élites juives en Galicie (1878–1918)', in Karady and Kulczykowski, *L'Enseignement des élites*, 79 ff.

[46] Otruba, 'Die Nationalitäten- und Sprachenfrage', 98, 100. Similar figures in J. Hochgerner, *Studium und Wissenschaftsentwicklung im Habsburgerreich: Studentengeschichte seit der Gründung der Universität Wien bis zum Ersten Weltkrieg* (Vienna, 1983), 212–13; Cohen, *Education and middle-class society*, 148, 278.

threatened. This was complicated by religious and political considerations. In the 1850s, under Thun, the state was committed to Catholicism, but the professorate tended to be freethinking, liberal, and believers in science. When the regime was forced to make political concessions after 1860, the liberal party enjoyed its heyday, and there were several professors in the Austrian parliament, the *Reichsrat*.[47] As elsewhere the ultramontanism of Pius IX alienated liberals further from the church, and the universities continued to be 'bastions of bourgeois liberalism'.[48] At Graz in 1865, the rector, a zoologist, caused a scandal by giving a speech in praise of Darwin; the clericals in this strongly Catholic area denounced the 'intrusion of atheism and materialism, which are being smuggled into our Christian Styria in the sheep's clothing of Darwinism'.[49] At Vienna in the same year, fifty-eight professors signed a demand for deconfessionalization and final abolition of the doctoral colleges,[50] and these aims were satisfied by the general education law of 1868, a decisive step in transferring control from church to state, by the abrogation of the 1855 Concordat in 1870, and by the university law of 1873 which completed secularization and guaranteed the academic freedom promised by the 1867 constitution.[51] University theology faculties survived, but their position was now difficult, and at both Graz and Vienna the professors in the secular faculties refused to elect their clerical colleagues as rectors. Austrian professors resembled their German colleagues in their freethinking, but from a Catholic rather than Protestant starting-point: the battle was between anticlericals and clericals. In the 1860s the situation was further complicated by the unification of Germany, which undermined traditional Habsburg patriotism and made many professors, and even more students, look to the new Reich as the home of German culture. The Schiller centenary of 1859 was a landmark in this new German patriotism, and once freedom of organization was permitted in the 1860s Austrian students took over German traditions of corps and *Burschenschaft*. The death of Wagner in 1883 gave another excuse for pro-German demonstrations, and led to the disciplining of students at Vienna.[52]

In 1879 the liberals lost control of the Austrian parliament, and liberalism never regained its dominance. Subsequent conservative governments ruled through playing the nationalities off against each other, the creation of the Czech university at Prague being an example. In these circumstances, German nationalism began to take an extreme form, and the pan-German movement of Georg Schönerer, at its height in the 1880s and 1890s, had much student support. Many professors remained faithful to the old liberalism, others to the dynastic concept of *gross-deutsch* Germandom. But the mainstream of German nationalism abandoned liberalism while remaining anticlerical, and its chief opponent was the Christian Social movement led by Karl Lueger, who had cut his political teeth as a student

[47] Okey, *Habsburg Monarchy*, 205–6.

[48] S. Preglau-Hämmerle, *Die politische und soziale Funktion der österreichischen Universität: Von den Anfängen bis zur Gegenwart* (Innsbruck, 1986), 110.

[49] W. Höflechner, *Die Baumeister des künftigen Glücks: Fragment einer Geschichte des Hochschulwesens in Österreich vom Ausgang des 19. Jahrhunderts bis in das Jahr 1938* (Graz, 1988), 4.

[50] Preglau-Hämmerle, *Die politische und soziale Funktion*, 108.

[51] Cohen, *Education and middle-class society*, 49.

[52] Hochgerner, *Studium und Wissenschaftsentwicklung*, 198.

leader in the 1860s. Lueger's movement was populist, petit-bourgeois, clerical, anti-liberal, and anti-Semitic, and had its strongest support in Vienna, of which Lueger became the all-powerful mayor in 1897. But anti-Semitism was no less characteristic of the pan-German form of nationalism, and was adopted with some zeal by the student organizations. As in Germany, it reflected social fears of an 'intellectual proletariat' and exploited resentment at Jewish success in higher education and the professions, but it was also a surrogate for German fears of Slav dominance.

The Badeni affair in 1897 included serious student riots at Vienna, in which Schönerer's movement was involved, leading to temporary closure of the university. From this time onwards, there was constant tension, as much within the German community as inter-ethnic, which reached a peak in 1907–8. In 1907 Lueger caused much alarm by declaring that the universities were the next institution to be 'reconquered'. Graz, near the frontier between Germans, Slovenes, and Italians, was a particular flashpoint. In 1908 there was the so-called peasant assault (*Bauernsturm*): when the secretary of the local Christian Social party was undergoing his doctoral examination, several hundred peasants led by a *Reichsrat* deputy appeared to 'protect' him with sticks and umbrellas, and to assert the strength of clericalism against the anticlerical students.[53] Innsbruck, also in a strongly Catholic area, was another troubled university. In the 1850s the faculty of theology had been revived and entrusted to the Jesuits. In 1907 Ludwig Wahrmund, professor of canon law, was suspended for a public lecture defending Catholic freedom of thought against Rome. The case raised important issues of academic freedom, and was taken up by Masaryk and others in the *Reichsrat*, but it was Wahrmund's German-national views which led to student protests throughout Austria against his victimization, countered by rival clerical demonstrations and demands for his dismissal. The governor of the Tirol closed the university for a time in 1908, provoking a national wave of student strikes, but the affair ended tamely when Wahrmund accepted a transfer to Prague.[54]

Of wider significance was the affair of the Italian law faculty at Innsbruck. Trieste and the Trentino had remained under Austrian rule when Italy was united, and the Italian minority, though small, was predominantly middle class. But the regime refused demands for a university at Trieste, understandably fearing that it would become a centre of irredentist agitation. Many Italian students crossed the Alps to study at Innsbruck, where lectures in Italian were provided. In 1904 a separate Italian-speaking law faculty was opened, but this provoked violent demonstrations from the German students; the faculty building was destroyed by the mob, there was intervention by troops, and the faculty was closed down after one day, never to reopen. There were further clashes between Italian and German students in 1908, involving revolvers rather than umbrellas, and discontent rumbled on until 1914,

[53] A. Mölzer, 'Zur Grazer Studentengeschichte', in W. Höflechner (ed.), *Beiträge und Materialen zur Geschichte der Wissenschaften in Österreich* (Graz, 1981), 485–6.

[54] F. Gall, *Alma Mater Rudolphina 1365–1965: Die Wiener Universität und ihre Studenten*, 3rd edn. (Vienna, 1965), 187; Kann, 'Higher education and politics', 322–5.

undermining the loyalty of the Italian bourgeoisie and straining diplomatic relations with Italy. The fear of German hostility effectively paralysed any new initiatives in university policy, and the government was unable to respond either to the Italians or to the growing demands from Slovenes for a university at Ljubljana, from Ruthenes for a separate university at Lwów, and from the Germans themselves for a revived Moravian university at Olmütz. This situation reflected the general political paralysis of the Danubian monarchy by 1914.

Nationalist agitation among the German population, particularly among students, had a strong element of anti-Semitism. In the western half of the empire, where Jews were about 3 per cent of the population, and had gained full civil rights in 1867, they were 20 per cent of all students in 1890, falling to 18 per cent in 1910; they were four or five times more likely to become students than Catholics.[55] As in Germany, discrimination made academic careers difficult, particularly promotion to full professorial status, though the government itself was perhaps less prejudiced than in the Reich. Jewish academics, like students, were initially attracted to medicine, and between 1848 and 1900 a tenth of the professors appointed to the Vienna medical faculty were unbaptized Jews, but by 1910, indicating their growing wealth and status aspirations, over half of Austrian Jewish students were studying law.[56] The Jewish community in Vienna was a nineteenth-century creation through immigration from other parts of the empire, and became strongly entrenched in the professions and business. The Jewish population of the city was around 10 per cent, but Jewish students at the university were 33 per cent of the total in 1890, 25 per cent in 1910.[57] This reflected similar percentages in the city's gymnasiums.[58] The position of Jews in Vienna clearly had a connection with the cultural phenomenon of 'Vienna 1900', though historians have disagreed about the nature of the relationship. What is in less doubt is that their position was not an easy one in a city ruled by Karl Lueger and racked by other social and racial tensions. As in Germany itself, assimilated Jews had identified strongly with German culture, and Steven Beller has argued that the abandonment of liberalism by the German-Austrian bourgeoisie left them in a peculiarly isolated position, as an ethnic group in a multinational empire without a language or territory of their own. The 'Waidhofen decrees' of 1896, in which the German-Austrian student organizations declared that Jews were outside the code of honour and refused to meet them in duels, were symptomatic of this betrayal by 'the very group who should have been their closest ally, the German national intelligentsia'.[59]

Competition for scarce professional jobs was one of the motives of anti-Semitism, and Gary Cohen suggests that ethnic competition in general was driving the expansion of higher education in Austria.[60] Student numbers rose from 14,796

[55] Cohen, *Education and middle-class society*, 148, 278. Cf. Hochgerner, *Studium und Wissenschaftsentwicklung*, 212–13.

[56] Cohen, *Education and middle-class society*, 167, 233.

[57] Otruba, 'Die Nationalitäten- und Sprachenfrage', 100. Cf. D. Vital, *A people apart: a political history of the Jews in Europe 1789–1939* (Oxford, 1999), 133–5.

[58] S. Beller, *Vienna and the Jews 1867–1938: a cultural history* (Cambridge, 1989), 43–70.

[59] Ibid. 192.

[60] Cohen, *Education and middle-class society*, 91.

in 1900 to 24,619 in 1914 (8,056 of them at Vienna), and from 5,261 to 10,467 in the Technical High Schools, which acquired doctoral rights in 1901 and were now expanding more successfully than their German equivalents.[61] Unlike Germany, however, growing enrolments did not involve a major social shift, because Austrian universities had always had a strong contingent from the *Mittelstand*. In 1860, only 34 per cent of the students at Vienna University were from the *Bildungsbürgertum*, 14 per cent from *Besitz*, 43 per cent from the *Mittelstand*, and 9 per cent sons of manual workers. By 1910 the equivalent figures were 33, 18, 45, and 4; at the Czech University of Prague, nearly two-thirds of the students were from the lower-middle class.[62] In a country where industrialization was still limited, this social pattern was bound to cause strains, and the contrast between underdevelopment and social ambition was especially strong in Galicia. Whatever the problems of the empire on the eve of 1914, they did not include social or intellectual stagnation, and the Habsburgs presided over a vigorous university scene. They had been unable to use their universities to inspire a loyal, multinational elite which could hold the empire together, but given the unstoppable dynamic of nineteenth-century nationalism that was probably beyond their power.

[61] B. vom Brocke and P. Krüger, *Hochschulpolitik im Föderalismus: Die Protokolle der Hochschulkonferenzen der deutschen Bundesstaaten und Österreich 1898 bis 1918* (Berlin, 1994), 425, 427. Cf. Cohen, *Education and middle-class society*, 56.

[62] Ibid. 280.

16
Russia

Introduced as a western or 'European' innovation, Russian universities had become deeply rooted in Russian life by mid-century, and had thrown up social and cultural forms not easy to classify in western terms. But they never established stable relations with the tsarist state. Throughout Russia's modern history, the educated elite had been cut off from the peasant masses, but the new universities also drove a gulf between them and their rulers, creating the specifically Russian phenomenon of the intelligentsia, and contributing to a crisis in relations between state and society. The universities suffered from alternation between reform and reaction, and political extremism among students was countered by crude if spasmodic repression of a type which had largely disappeared in western Europe, where universities achieved relative autonomy from politics after 1870. A liberal university law of 1863 was followed by a repressive one in 1884, and Russia became an exporter of students seeking greater freedom. Yet there were many paradoxes. Political repression coexisted with policies of modernization from above, and the universities achieved high intellectual and scholarly standards. By 1914 Russia not only had the largest student body in Europe, but also one of the most socially diverse, and the most emancipated set of women students. Like Austria-Hungary, Russia was a multinational empire, but its method of ruling was to enforce Russian culture on all in the attempt to produce a homogeneous elite. This policy had some success with the less developed nationalities, but not with the Poles or the Finns. Even the Russian educated classes were not won over wholeheartedly to the interests of the state, and by 1914 the alienation of the universities was symptomatic of the wider crisis which was to engulf tsardom.

Russia did not share in the old European university tradition with its roots in Latin Christianity and classical humanism. The Russian Orthodox Church had its own traditions of learning, and theological academies at Kiev and Moscow, influenced by the Jesuits, were founded in the seventeenth century.[1] But when Peter the Great and his successors turned to the west for inspiration it was mainly practical, specialized training which they sought. Foreign experts were imported, Russians were sent abroad to gain expertise, and the nobility had their own traditions of foreign travel which often included a spell at a university, especially in Germany. The remodelling of education to produce a trained bureaucracy of the central European type was difficult in Russia because official service, under Peter

[1] W. Frijhoff, 'Patterns', in H. de Ridder-Symoens (ed.), *A history of the university in Europe. II. Universities in early modern Europe (1500–1800)* (Cambridge, 1996), 48, 55–6.

the Great's 'Table of Ranks', was seen as an attribute of nobility, not requiring formal educational qualifications, and open only in its lower ranks to non-nobles. In the longer run this made education attractive as a road to status, but inhibited the development of an autonomous bourgeoisie; the immediate effect was that there was no equivalent of the German *Bildungsbürgertum*, with its investment in education as a value-system.

When Peter founded the St Petersburg Academy of Sciences in 1724, it included a teaching section which is sometimes regarded as Russia's first university, but this did not flourish. In 1755 Moscow University was founded on the model of Halle, with faculties of law, medicine, and philosophy (but not theology). Numbers at Moscow remained very small, however, and subsequent rulers seemed more interested in creating specialized schools on French lines, such as the Corps of Mining Cadets (1773, later Mining Institute), an Institute of Transport Engineers in 1809, and two quasi-universities specifically aimed at the nobility, the Alexander Lyceum at Tsarskoe Selo, later moved to St Petersburg (1811), and the St Petersburg School of Jurisprudence (1838).[2] Along with various military schools, and the St Petersburg Technical Institute of 1828, these competed with the capital city's university, and it was Moscow which developed as the larger university centre.

The creator of the modern Russian university system was Alexander I (1801–25). In later years Alexander turned to mystical religion, but he started off as a reformer in the enlightened, westernizing tradition, spurred to 'defensive modernization' by the political convulsions in the west. His plan, promulgated in 1803 and implemented in 1804, was for the co-ordinated development of education on a district basis, with the university authorities responsible for promoting and inspecting the other levels of education—and also for the censorship of publications. This regional system owed something to the Polish National Education Commission's reforms in 1783, and to Adam Czartoryski's influence on Alexander. There were to be six districts, each headed by a government curator. Four were purely Russian—Moscow, St Petersburg, Kharkov, and Kazan—but Alexander also set up two peripheral universities, Vilna and Dorpat. The history of Vilna, until its suppression in 1832, has already been described. Dorpat (today Tartu in Estonia) had been defunct since 1710, and was now revived to serve the German landowning and merchant community in the Baltic provinces, which provided Russia with many of its high officials. It was German-speaking and Lutheran, and developed on the common German pattern, with an especially strong medical faculty; chairs there became part of the German academic circuit, and Dorpat stood apart from the rest of the Russian system. The Finnish university at Åbo, later transferred to Helsinki, had a separate status altogether because of Finland's autonomous constitution.

Alexander's policies preceded the establishment of the University of Berlin, but were directly influenced by Göttingen.[3] 'French' features included a prescribed curriculum rather than *Lernfreiheit*, examinations conducted by the university

[2] D. Lieven, *The aristocracy in Europe 1815–1914* (New York, 1993), 176–8.

[3] J. T. Flynn, *The university reform of Tsar Alexander I 1802–1835* (Washington, DC, 1988), 7–10, 18–19.

rather than the state, and central bureaucratic control. But the German model provided the idea of corporate autonomy, and this was significant for the future. Under the political supervision of the curator, the professors were to elect their rector and the faculties to nominate professors, and though this autonomy was later suspended for long periods the principle was not forgotten. The German ideal of scientific freedom made a strong impression on the Russian educated class; Berlin became a centre of academic pilgrimage, and in the early nineteenth century the idealist philosophy of Fichte, Schelling, and Hegel captivated the younger generation. It was also significant that the universities did not have theology faculties, so that from the start they had a strongly secular character, open to the doctrines of scientific materialism. The 'mathematical-physical' faculties always attracted far more students than the 'historical-philological' ones. The separation from Orthodoxy meant that on the one hand it was difficult for the regime to use religion for keeping the educated classes in line, as in the west, but on the other, while free-thinking western intellectuals had to grapple with religion as a living force, in Russia it could be dismissed simply as a part of the reactionary state apparatus.

Alexander's reforms included gymnasiums on German lines, which expanded in symbiosis with the universities, closely linked with them in policy-making because they formed the control mechanism for entry. In principle, the 1803 decree provided a ladder of opportunity from the village school to the university, and in the early years the universities had to recruit widely because of the nobility's lack of interest. But basic education remained woefully underdeveloped in Russia, and as in every country a full secondary education was expensive and socially privileged. Alexander's policies included the introduction of civil service examinations on Prussian lines in 1809, and although this was repealed in 1834 it served its purpose of winning over to university education the noble and official class, from which two-thirds of the students were drawn between the 1830s and 1850s.[4] Serfs, who needed special permission to attend a gymnasium, were few and far between. Yet the principle that education was not the 'preserve of the privileged' but should be open to all on merit, which dated from the foundation of Moscow University, 'passed into the life-blood of Russia's educationalists, giving them a bias towards a democratic, open-access system which survived all nineteenth-century attempts to narrow it'.[5] The Russian state, it has been claimed, 'stretched the scholastic framework to include the ambitious poor within the professional service class' and 'offered more concrete educational opportunity to the propertyless and the obscure at the university preparatory level and beyond than did any other major European power'.[6] A tradition was established of remitting fees for poorer students, and supporting them was a charitable cause taken up by the wealthy. The openness of the universities was a radical idea in a state which continued to divide its subjects into legal estates.

In the last years of Alexander I, Enlightenment ideals faded; Napoleon's invasion

[4] S. Brim, *Universität und Studentenbewegung in Russland im Zeitalter der Grossen Reformen 1855–1881* (Frankfurt, 1985), 35, 167.

[5] G. Hosking, *Russia: people and empire 1552–1917* (London, 1997), 127.

[6] P. L. Alston, *Education and the state in tsarist Russia* (Stanford, 1969), 244.

in 1812 revived Russian nationalism, and the mood was reflected in official encouragement of pietistic religion. German philosophy, and even Latin and Greek, came under suspicion as westernizing influences. Thus in its early years the system was very fragile. At first the universities relied heavily on foreign scholars, from Germany or the Slav parts of the Habsburg Empire, and it took a generation for a native professorial class to emerge. Moscow University was mostly destroyed in the 1812 fire (it had only 215 students at the time),[7] and the foundation of St Petersburg University was delayed until 1819. Kharkov and Kazan remained small and inadequate, and all the Russian universities suffered from political repression after 1815, including the dismissal of professors. At Kazan, the reactionary curator M. L. Magnitskii caused havoc in the 1820s, and similar repression almost stifled the new foundation at St Petersburg.[8]

Alexander's death in 1825 was followed by the failure of the Decembrist conspiracy (an aristocratic affair, without the university connections of western liberal insurrections), and his successor Nicholas I was a more straightforward conservative; symptomatic measures were a law of 1827 banning serfs altogether from gymnasiums and universities, and a requirement for all students, as officials in the making, to wear uniforms. The minister of education between 1833 and 1849 was Sergei Uvarov. Recent scholarship has stressed that Uvarov protected the universities from the more reactionary pressures, and even argued that the 1830s and 1840s were a 'golden age' before repression returned in 1848.[9] Uvarov's university law of 1835 preserved the main principles of 1803. Political supervision by the curators intensified, and the ministry was given more power over appointments, but the election of rectors was retained, professors were released from the duties of school inspection and censorship, the quality of the teaching force was strengthened (using Dorpat to train young academics in German methods), and the universities began to give more effective preparation for bureaucratic service. It was in this period that universities became rooted in Russian society, and this was reflected in the growth of numbers, from 2,016 in 1836 to 4,566 in 1848.[10]

In a report to the tsar on Moscow University in 1832, before he became minister, Uvarov said that it faced 'one of the most difficult problems of our time, providing true education, a fundamental necessity of our century, with deep reverence and warm faith in the truly-Russian conservative principles of orthodoxy, autocracy, and nationality', and he stressed 'the necessity to be Russians in the spirit of old while striving for European education, the necessity to unite true faith with higher learning, and with that enlightenment which belongs to all people and all ages'.[11] 'Orthodoxy, autocracy, and nationality' became the slogan of the regime under

[7] Flynn, *University reform*, 33, 35.

[8] Ibid. 90–103, 112.

[9] C. H. Whittaker, *The origins of modern Russian education: an intellectual biography of count Sergei Uvarov, 1786–1855* (De Kalb, Ill., 1984), 92, 152–88. Cf. D. Saunders, *Russia in the age of reaction and reform 1801–1881* (London, 1992), 74–6; Flynn, *University reform*, 181–4.

[10] Alston, *Education and the state*, 36.

[11] Flynn, *University reform*, 219.

Nicholas, and the principle of 'official nationality' identified the state with the dominant 'great Russian' ethnic group and the Russian language. In the 1830s this was manifested in the crushing of Poland, and after Vilna University was closed it was Uvarov who founded the St Vladimir university at Kiev in 1834, designed, in his own words, as 'an intellectual fortress', dedicated to 'suppressing the spirit of a separate Polish nationality and merging it with the general Russian spirit'.[12] Teaching was in Russian, but until the 1860s, when the university was purged because of support for the Polish rising of 1863, about half the students were Polish, reflecting the presence of a Polish landowning class in the western Ukraine.[13] Ukrainian nationalism itself was slow to develop; as a cultural phenomenon it found a home in the university, but political manifestations were outlawed.[14]

When Uvarov spoke of the need to be both Russian and European, he put his finger on a dilemma which was to run through university policy until 1917. A contradiction was appearing between the desire to modernize Russia through science and education, and the danger that intellectual freedom would unleash social and political movements outside the regime's control: 'squaring the circle of educating people without giving them ideas of their own would not be easy'.[15] The question involved such central problems of Russian history as the impact of westernization and the emergence of the intelligentsia, in the sense of an educated class unable to share the values of the regime. The term 'intelligentsia' did not come into use until the 1860s, but the phenomenon had its roots in the 1830s and 1840s. Indeed, the historian of Vilna University has argued that it was foreshadowed there in the 1820s. The Polish gentry who flocked to Vilna, making it the largest university in Russia, were mostly poor and needed qualifications to make a living, but in the absence of a Polish state and in the face of Russian hostility they lacked any natural outlet for their talents. They were a governing class left without anyone to govern, and the result of their search for a new role was the desperate nationalism of 1830.[16]

The Russian intelligentsia did not lack opportunities for serving society and the state, but were alienated by Russia's failure under Nicholas I to move towards the sort of liberal order which might integrate them with the political regime. The German ideal of *Bildung* with its emphasis on individual self-development, and the heady idealism of German philosophy, encouraged utopian rather than practical conceptions of social change. By the 1860s they had given way to a scientific positivism with French or British roots, in Comte and Darwin; the Russian intelligentsia adopted a fervent belief in science, seen as the key to social progress and popular wellbeing, and conceived in an abstract, even mystical, sense as much as a body of useful knowledge. The 'sense of moral obligation to strive for an ideal society that

[12] J. C. McClelland, *Autocrats and academics: education, culture, and society in Tsarist Russia* (Chicago, 1979), 19.

[13] Flynn, *University reform*, 191–2; M. F. Hamm, *Kiev: a portrait 1800–1917* (Princeton, 1993), 64, 76, 224–5.

[14] C. B. Clay, 'Le rôle de l'ethnologie universitaire dans le développement d'une nation ukrainienne dans l'Empire russe 1830–1850', *Histoire de l'Éducation*, 86 (2000), 61–82.

[15] J. Gooding, *Rulers and subjects: government and people in Russia 1801–1991* (London, 1996), 31.

[16] D. Beauvois, *Lumières et société en Europe de l'Est: l'Université de Vilna et les écoles polonaises de l'Empire russe (1803–32)* (Lille, 1977), 322–5, 349–58, 367–71, 375.

was so characteristic of the entire Russian intelligentsia' was shared by professors and students, and reinforced the view that universities had a mission to regenerate the nation. Yet the emergence of the intelligentsia coincided with the consolidation of the universities as an effective instrument for producing an authoritarian but enlightened bureaucracy, and the state had its own near-utopian belief that western standards of education and science could transform society from above.[17] Writers of the time identified a conflict between the older liberal generation and the new materialists or 'nihilists', as depicted in Turgenev's *Fathers and sons* of 1862. Turgenev also coined the term 'superfluous men', for those paralysed by the contrast between the ideals of their university years in Moscow or St Petersburg and the routine of life as an official in a backward provincial town or an estate owner marooned in a sea of peasant ignorance. Most graduates abandoned their youthful militancy and settled down to more or less useful lives, but they remained conscious of their alienation both from the peasant masses and from the political direction of the state.

The mentality of the intelligentsia had roots in the specific conditions of Russian student life, experienced as 'an egalitarian republic at the heart of the most unequal society in Europe'.[18] Most students were poor, even when they came from the gentry, and were far from home. They lived in crowded and often squalid conditions, as depicted in Dostoevsky's *Crime and punishment* (1866). Any sort of formal student organization was banned, but an active life outside the classroom developed instead. Poverty and isolation were countered by co-operative enterprises such as canteens and reading-rooms, and by a proliferation of informal discussion groups and 'circles', where the ideas of foreign and native gurus were debated with passion, and comradeships were forged. By the 1860s, the presence of women on equal terms was a notable feature of these circles. From this atmosphere was born the populist revolutionary movement of the 1870s, and the idea that students were a separate force in Russian society with a distinct moral and patriotic mission was to persist until the end of tsarism.[19]

In 1848 the authorities were determined to insulate Russia from revolutionary contagion. Uvarov was dismissed, and the appointment of rectors and deans was transferred from the universities to the ministry. Attempts were made to limit university intakes by rigid control of admissions and by restricting access to the gymnasiums, and enrolments fell to 3,018 in 1850. But this reaction was relatively short-lived, and they rose again to 4,998 in 1859.[20] Nicholas I died in 1855, in the middle of the Crimean war, and it was Russia's defeat in that war against Britain and France which—as in 1806 in Prussia or 1871 in France—revived the modernizing agenda. 'If our enemies triumph over us,' said Nicholas's last minister of education A. S. Norov, 'it is due solely to the superiority of their education.'[21] The new Tsar

[17] McClelland, *Autocrats and academics*, 22–3, 31, 65 (for quotation), 112–13.

[18] A. Besançon, *Éducation et société en Russie dans le second tiers du XIXe siècle* (Paris, 1974), 54.

[19] Hosking, *Russia*, 263–70. Cf. I. Berlin, *Russian thinkers* (London, 1978), 114–35, 210–37.

[20] Alston, *Education and the state*, 39–40, 45.

[21] Ibid. 44.

Alexander II initiated a series of reforming policies in the 1860s, of which the most fundamental was the abolition of serfdom in 1861.

Political and social restrictions in the universities were now relaxed, and new professors were appointed to reinvigorate them intellectually.[22] The changed atmosphere encouraged students to engage for the first time in political campaigning, but this soon aroused the government's alarm. In 1861, following the appointment of a conservative minister of education, Admiral E. Putiatin, there were rallies, student strikes, and demonstrations in St Petersburg and elsewhere, leading to clashes with troops and police. There followed mass arrests and temporary university closures, but also the replacement of Putiatin and the appointment of a committee of inquiry which prepared a new university law in 1863.[23] The law took a conciliatory line, guided, in Alston's words, by 'the circumstance that with each passing year tsardom became more dependent on the coherence of its educated class to restrain the centrifugal tendencies of its myriad tribes, creeds, races, and peoples'.[24] German practices like *Lernfreiheit* and corporate student organization, advocated by advisers like the leading surgeon N. I. Pirogov, were rejected, but the 1863 law restored some university autonomy, and the universities benefited from other aspects of Alexander's reforms.[25] Censorship was relaxed, reform of the legal system on western lines created new opportunities for lawyers, and the creation of the *zemstvos*, elected local authorities responsible for services like roads, public health, and education, did the same for doctors, teachers, and engineers. Russia still had far fewer professional experts than she needed, and if the Russian intelligentsia felt frustrated, it was not because of any surplus of educated men.[26]

Alexander II was a reformer, but hardly a liberal. Reform was not pushed to the point of abandoning autocratic authority, and the Polish rising of 1863 did much to turn the tsar's mind against further change. In 1866 he was the victim of an attempt on his life by an impoverished nobleman who had been expelled from two universities. As became normal in incidents of this kind, the government made wholesale arrests and mounted show trials, and used the existence of a minority of revolutionary students to turn public opinion against the universities generally.[27] Alexander now appointed as minister of education Dmitri Tolstoi, who combined this post with that of Procurator of the Holy Synod, effectively minister for religion: as under Nicholas I, orthodoxy and nationality were seen as inseparable allies. Tolstoi remained in office until 1880, and enforced an ideology which Alston has called 'westernizing nationalism', based on the 'belief that rigorous enforcement of tested European educational standards was the best means for providing the disorderly empire with the disciplined educated class that might just hold it together as

[22] Saunders, *Russia*, 250–2.

[23] Alston, *Education and the state*, 46–52; Besançon, *Éducation et société*, 131 ff.

[24] Alston, *Education and the state*, 54.

[25] W. L. Mathes, 'N. I. Pirogov and the reform of university government 1856–1866', *Slavic Review*, 31 (1972), 29–51; W. L. Mathes, 'N. I. Pirogov and the university question in the era of the great reform', *Jahrbücher für Geschichte Osteuropas*, NS 36 (1988), 1–14.

[26] Besançon, *Éducation et société*, 74–5.

[27] McClelland, *Autocrats and academics*, 95 ff.

it plunged towards the scientific-industrial future'.[28] The 1863 law was retained, but political dissent, whether from professors or students, was harshly suppressed. Repression was coupled with the enforcement of rigorous academic standards, including a renewed emphasis on Latin and Greek—which had the effect of associating the classics with political reaction and increasing the appeal of science and materialism. Tolstoi's policy aimed at creating loyalty to the Russian state among the elites throughout the empire, a policy reflected both in the Russification policies which followed the suppression of the Polish rising, and in the development of the University of Odessa (founded in 1865) as a beacon for the Slav peoples of the Balkans. These policies can be seen as analogous to the contemporary emphasis in western countries on universities as a means of national integration, and on culture as a unifying and anti-materialist force.

Speaking in 1875, Tolstoi said that 'we make only one distinction among pupils—a distinction on the basis of merit.... Our gymnasia must produce aristocrats, but what kind? Aristocrats of the mind, aristocrats of knowledge, aristocrats of labour. May God grant that we gain more such aristocrats.'[29] His policies represented tsarism's last chance of winning the educated elite over to active co-operation, but failed to do so. Tolstoi was seen as an enemy of intellectual freedom, and was hated as a reactionary. Yet the policies can also be seen as a last manifestation of enlightened reform from above, designed to force Russia out of backwardness. The regime continued to fund the universities generously to European standards, and 'by the 1860s the best Russian universities maintained standards of learning and research comparable to the best anywhere in the world, and the ethos of free scientific enquiry had become a component of the national myth second only to literature'.[30] But in the west universities now had an accepted critical role, and the days when they could be simple instruments of absolutism were past. If elites were to serve as a bridge with the people, they needed to be trusted, but in Russia the enforcement of official ideology took on cruder repressive forms as student opposition grew.

A report by a group of Moscow professors in 1861 said that 'Russian society ... has instilled in the student a high conception of his own worth, a conception which can hardly be found in any other country.... In the eyes of many, the student represents the future hope of Russia.'[31] The student years were an interlude in life when idealism and opposition were in order. In the 1840s and 1850s, the universities had shaped the intelligentsia by creating a frustrated idealism which they carried into adult life. In the 1860s and 1870s, students themselves became a political force, and a generational view of the importance of youth was part of the set of ideals known as populism, strongly influenced by student reading of N. G. Chernyshevskii's *What is to be done?* (1862), and most strikingly displayed in the movement known as 'going down to the people' in 1873–4, when thousands of young men and women

[28] Alston, *Education and the state*, 81–2, and cf. 246.
[29] McClelland, *Autocrats and academics*, 14.
[30] Hosking, *Russia*, 328.
[31] McClelland, *Autocrats and academics*, 59.

dispersed to the villages to spread their ideals and to learn from the peasants' instinctive wisdom.

Politically, populism represented disillusion with western liberalism, and a shift towards socialism, soon evolving into rival forms which included marxism, agrarian socialism of a distinctively Russian kind, and an apocalyptic terrorism which adopted the assassination of political leaders as the only way of bringing the regime to an end. Students, both men and women, were involved in these terrorist attempts, leading to trials and executions in the 1870s and 1880s. The emotional solidarity of Russian student life, and the belief in personal sacrifice and example fostered by its peculiar form of idealism, were a good preparation for the underground work of revolutionary cells. This was an unusual time and place, when to become a full-time 'revolutionary' seemed a career option. In fact, historians have seen 1861 as the high point of student activity in the sense of university-centred political agitation, but the involvement of individual students or young graduates in revolutionary movements, and the broad sympathy for them in student circles, created a permanent bias against the universities in the bureaucratic mind, and an image which could be exploited against them to justify repression.[32]

In 1881 Alexander II was assassinated, and this inaugurated a period of reaction under Alexander III, dominated by K. P. Pobedonostsev, who was Procurator of the Holy Synod and the real mind behind educational policy. He was a former professor of law at Moscow—a reminder that the bureaucrats who directed the autocracy, including technocrats committed to economic modernization like Sergei Witte, minister of finance in the 1890s, were just as much products of the universities as the populists. The policies of Alexander III, and of Nicholas II who succeeded him in 1894, were more narrowly nationalist and less European than under Tolstoi; apart from general political repression, they included social restriction, anti-Semitism, Russification, and an end to initiatives for the higher education of women (see Chapter 17). The centrepiece was the university law of 1884, which replaced that of 1863 and remained in force until 1917. It removed most of the universities' remaining autonomy, and put power in the hands of the ministry. This frustrated the professors, most of whom would have favoured moderate liberalism rather than either reaction or populism, but valued scientific freedom above all. Students were the main target. Uniforms, abolished in 1861, were reintroduced, and students were required to attend the nearest university instead of swelling the radical ranks in Moscow and St Petersburg. It remained impossible to form legal student organizations, and students were subject to close police repression and surveillance. There were periodic outbursts of protest, notably the large-scale student strikes of 1899, but these were usually over specific student grievances and detached from wider political movements. There was a continuing sense of the student community as a separate social body, and the underlying tensions were to find release in the revolution of 1905.

Until the 1880s the openness of the universities and gymnasiums to all social

[32] Besançon, *Éducation et société*, 146, 163.

classes had generally been maintained, as was the tradition of support for poorer students. At Moscow in 1875, 283 of the 1,259 students were government scholars, 337 exempt from fees, and forty had their fees deferred.[33] Open recruitment was part of Tolstoi's conception of an aristocracy of work, and he also encouraged Jewish participation. The 1870s and 1880s saw a surge of numbers in the universities, as in western countries, and a significant change in their social composition. The emancipation of the peasantry had limited direct effects, given the mass illiteracy of the Russian countryside, but there was an influx of the *raznochintsy*, a term which meant people in the middle strata of society, or whose status no longer fitted the legal estate categories. They included the sons of priests (Russia having a married parish clergy), of merchants and small traders, and to some extent of artisans, peasants, and workers. By 1880 the proportion of nobles and officials' sons had fallen from about two-thirds to 47 per cent, with 23 per cent sons of clergy (this proportion soon fell sharply after seminarians were banned from universities), 8 per cent of merchants, and 11 per cent of artisans or craftsmen—but only 3 per cent were the sons of peasants.[34] The rise of the *raznochintsy* has often been linked with that of the intelligentsia and of populism, but the formation of the intelligentsia came when the universities were still dominated by the landowning and official class, whose members (sometimes from families impoverished by the end of serfdom) were probably more likely to lead revolutionary movements than men for whom university education meant a new opportunity for social mobility and security.[35]

The expansion of enrolments alarmed Alexander III's government, which tried to check it by raising fees sharply and controlling access to secondary education. In 1887 it issued the 'cook's circular', so called because it sought to exclude from gymnasiums the 'children of coachmen, menials, cooks, washerwomen, small shopkeepers, and the like. For, excepting occasionally gifted children, it is completely unwarranted for the children of such people to leave their position in life.'[36] The circular helped to discredit official policies in moderate eyes, but it proved ineffective in face of the social pressures generating demand and the continuing need of the state for administrators and experts of all kinds, especially once the policy of industrialization began in the 1890s. The government preferred to divert growth into technical institutes, which were seen as more useful and less politically threatening, and new and well-funded Polytechnics were founded by Witte at Kiev and Warsaw in 1898, and St Petersburg in 1902.[37] One new university also appeared, at Tomsk in Siberia (1888).[38] There was an initial fall in university numbers after

[33] Alston, *Education and the state*, 55. Cf. Besançon, *Éducation et société*, 84–9.

[34] D. R. Brower, 'Social stratification in Russian higher education', in K. H. Jarausch (ed.), *The transformation of higher learning 1860–1930: expansion, diversification, social opening, and professionalization in England, Germany, Russia, and the United States* (Chicago, 1983), 246–50; Brim, *Universität und Studentenbewegung*, 170–1.

[35] Besançon, *Éducation et société*, 83–4. Cf. M. Pushkin, 'The professions and the intelligentsia in nineteenth-century Russia', *University of Birmingham Historical Journal*, 12 (1969–70), 77–9.

[36] Cited in Alston, *Education and the state*, 129.

[37] McClelland, *Autocrats and academics*, 45–6.

[38] The list for the Russian Empire in 1914 was: Dorpat, Helsinki, Kazan, Kharkov, Kiev, Moscow,

1887, but they soon grew again; university enrolments were 11,551 in 1885 (having more than doubled from 5,032 in 1875), 15,180 in 1899, and 21,506 in 1904; they were to reach their peak in 1909 at 38,440.[39] Nor did the tradition of financial aid disappear: at Moscow in 1899, 2,000 of 4,500 students were exempt from fees, and 900 received state scholarships.[40]

In 1887 quotas were placed on the admission of Jewish students to gymnasiums and universities: 10 per cent in the 'Pale of Settlement', 5 per cent elsewhere, and 3 per cent in St Petersburg and Moscow.[41] Since 1804 Jews had been admitted to all levels of education, but there had never been any legal emancipation. The Pale comprised former Polish provinces, and most of the Jewish population lived there, forming about 12 per cent of the population (compared with 3 per cent in the empire as a whole). As in the Habsburg Empire, there was now large-scale migration to the towns, a breakdown of the closed Jewish cultural community, and the development of bourgeois aspirations. With command of the Russian language, secondary education was relatively accessible, after which the universities of Moscow and St Petersburg, and professional jobs in the cities, were the natural targets of ambition. But whereas Vienna developed a large Jewish community in the nineteenth century, the tsarist regime controlled migration to the cities. Only from 1879 were Jewish university graduates even allowed to live outside the Pale, and virtually all forms of state employment were closed. Yet, as experience in Germany and Austria showed, even a quota of 10 per cent fell well below the natural share of higher education which an urbanized and socially mobile Jewish population was likely to achieve. The *numerus clausus* was not only unjust in principle, but part of a wider growth of officially encouraged anti-Semitic prejudice, including occasional violent pogroms in which students suffered along with others. This gravely damaged Russia's international reputation, and encouraged the migration of students abroad. It was also yet another facet of the tsarist regime's inability to gain the confidence of the educated classes, contrasting with Austria, where Jewish loyalty to the Habsburgs was a counter to German nationalism.

The Habsburgs tried to balance off their nationalities, but Alexander III adopted a policy of great-Russian nationalism and linguistic Russification which went well beyond the 'official nationality' policies of Nicholas I and Uvarov. Russification was applied at all levels of Polish education after 1863, alienating both Catholic Poles and Polish-speaking Jews. In Finland, as we have seen, the university escaped a similar fate. But Russification was extended to German-speaking secondary schools in the Baltic provinces, and then to Dorpat University. Russian professors began to replace German ones, and in 1893 the town and the university were renamed Iur'ev. Enrolments fell at first, but the university recovered as the formerly dominant

Odessa, St Petersburg, Saratov (medical faculty only, founded 1909), Tomsk, Warsaw. There were technical institutes at Helsinki, Kharkov, Kiev, Moscow, Novocherkassk, Riga, St Petersburg (several specialized institutes), Warsaw.

[39] P. L. Alston, 'The dynamics of educational expansion in Russia', in Jarausch, *Transformation of higher learning*, 92, 96 (figures exclude Helsinki and Warsaw).

[40] Alston, *Education and the state*, 155.

[41] Ibid. 130.

Baltic Germans were replaced by Jews and others from urban backgrounds, and by Estonians and Latvians from the more prosperous peasantry.[42] The stirrings of nationalism among these minorities were as yet feeble, and the same was true of Central Asia or the Caucasus, where the elites were prepared to accept Russian as the price of admission to a wider culture. In the short term, therefore, Russification seemed to work, and the Romanovs kept the lid on nationalism more effectively than the Habsburgs. But the contrast between the Austrian loyalty of the Habsburg Poles and the bitter gulf between Poles and Russians showed the negative side of this homogenizing policy, and was a recipe for political conflict if there was to be any move towards representative institutions.

Apart from Poland and Finland, the most serious nationalist potential was in Ukraine, since recognition of Ukrainian as a separate language from Russian would shake great-Russian dominance of the empire. It was not Kiev but Lwów that became the centre of Ukrainian nationalism, for though the Habsburgs resisted calls for a separate Ukrainian university, they were not averse to encouraging anti-Russian nationalism. Lwów had a cultural role for Ukrainians similar to that of Cracow for Poles, and it was from his chair there that the historian Michael Hrushevsky, who was to be president of the short-lived Ukrainian republic in 1917–18, laid the scholarly foundations of Ukrainian separatism.

A new Ukrainian university was founded at Odessa in 1865, partly to serve the mainly Russian elite of a developing region, partly to attract Bulgarians and other Slavs from outside the empire; the university also attracted Georgians and Armenians from the Caucasus. The largest minority, however, were Jews—31 per cent of the total in 1886, falling to 19 per cent in 1890 after the introduction of quotas. The percentage of nobles fell from 62 per cent in 1870 to 48 per cent in 1890, by which date 7 per cent were sons of the clergy, 4 per cent of peasants, 4 per cent foreigners, and 37 per cent from the various urban strata.[43] The historian of this episode concludes that the university became 'above all a channel of mobility for the urban population groups', with Jewish students becoming, in classic fashion, doctors, lawyers, and journalists. He also says that at Odessa there was not a 'Ukrainian question' or a 'Jewish question', but a 'Russian question': here as elsewhere, the nature of autocracy blocked the development of a true civil society which would allow the Russian elite to combine professional freedom with loyalty to the regime.[44]

Russification and political repression undermined attempts to attract foreign students, and to use the universities as a weapon of Russian policy in the Balkans. Even Bulgarians and Serbs, despite their cultural and religious sympathies with Russia, preferred to go to France or Switzerland, and those who did come were more likely to take home ideas of populist socialism than of Panslavism. Any influx of foreign students was far outnumbered by the emigration of Russian and Polish

[42] K. Siilivask (ed.), *History of Tartu University 1632–1982* (Tallinn, 1985), 97–8, 141.

[43] G. Hausmann, *Universität und städtische Gesellschaft in Odessa 1865–1917: Soziale und nationale Selsbstorganisation an der Peripherie des Zarenreiches* (Stuttgart, 1998), 181, 183.

[44] Ibid. 507, 510.

students to the west. At Moscow University, there were only 260 foreign students in all between 1906 and 1914, and this included 132 from Russian Poland.[45] But at Cracow and Lwów in 1910 there were 800 Polish-speaking Russian citizens,[46] although the two rival leaders of Polish nationalism in the early twentieth century were both educated at Russian-speaking universities, Jozef Pilsudski at Kharkov and Roman Dmowski at Warsaw. The emigration of women was a particularly striking phenomenon, as opportunities for higher education which appeared in the 1860s were stifled in the 1870s and 1880s. The most famous colonies of Russian students, male and female, were in Switzerland, but they were also to be found in Germany and France, where there were over 2,000 and 3,000 respectively on the eve of 1914; these colonies continued to grow even after the 1905 revolution improved conditions at home, and were a focus both for émigré political activities and for xenophobic and anti-Semitic attacks by right-wing nationalists.[47]

Like the revolutions of 1848, 1905 was a cultural revolution which aroused expectations of change in every sphere. The strikes and demonstrations which temporarily paralysed the tsar's authority had an immediate effect on the universities, which were granted disciplinary autonomy, so barring the police from their premises and making them centres of impassioned debate, involving workers as well as students, almost in the style of 1968. For most of 1905–6 academic activities were suspended. Nicholas II's reluctant concession of a constitution which included an elected duma and a measure of free speech and civil liberty aroused hopes for the permanent restoration of autonomy, organizational freedom for students, and the removal of Jewish quotas. But, as Samuel Kassow has shown, the revolution also exposed divisions in the university community. Students were inevitably supporters of the revolutionary left, but the sympathies of most professors were with the moderate liberals, whose Kadet party was led by one of their number, the historian P. N. Miliukov. During 1905, when spontaneous collective organizations were springing up all round, university staff formed an Academic Union, but dissension between the professors and the more radical junior staff soon appeared, and it did not last long. The professors dreamt of apolitical universities serving the nation through their devotion to science: as the Moscow professors put it in November 1905,

> the university should unite people on the basis of scientific and educational interests and direct them to the service of science and enlightenment. . . . The university can and should, as long as it does not stray from its primary purpose, serve the cause of freedom. By struggling

[45] V. G. Karasev and others, 'Ausländische Studenten aus slawischen Ländern an der Moskauer Universität in der zweiten Hälfte des 19. und Anfang des 20. Jahrhunderts', in R. G. Plaschka and K. Mack (eds.), *Wegenetz europäischen Geistes. II. Universitäten und Studenten: Die Bedeutung studentischer Migrationen in Mittel- und Südosteuropa vom 18. bis zum 20. Jahrhundert* (Munich, 1987), 242.

[46] G. B. Cohen, *Education and middle-class society in Imperial Austria 1848–1918* (West Lafayette, Ind., 1996), 151.

[47] B. vom Brocke and P. Krüger (eds.), *Hochschulpolitik im Föderalismus: Die Protokolle der Hochschulkonferenzen der deutschen Bundesstaaten und Österreich 1898 bis 1918* (Berlin, 1994), 433; C. Weill, 'La "question des étrangers": les étudiants russes en Allemagne 1900–1914', *Le Mouvement Social*, 120 (1982), 77–94; G. Weisz, *The emergence of modern universities in France 1863–1914* (Princeton, 1983), 261.

for the freedom of science and teaching, and for the principle of academic autonomy . . . the university serves the cause of freedom and progress.

But this vision, more appropriate to a western *Rechtsstaat*, left the professors adrift between radical students and an unsympathetic state.[48] Conditions returned to normal from 1906, until in 1910–11 there was a new crisis at Moscow University following student demonstrations sparked off by the funeral of Leo Tolstoi. The government criticized the rector and his two deputies for not enforcing discipline strongly enough, and when they resigned office they were also dismissed from their chairs. This provoked the resignation of more than a third of the teachers—twenty-five professors and seventy-four others—and the ensuing protests led to the expulsion of thousands of students, crippling the university as a centre of learning.[49] Although these troubles did not spread beyond Moscow, they undermined the educated public's belief in the sincerity of reform, as did the refusal to abolish Jewish quotas. The ministers of education of this period acquired a black reputation, and in Kassow's view relations between universities and government were worse than at any time since Nicholas I.[50]

Despite these political problems, university education expanded remarkably on the eve of war. Concessions in 1905 included the admission of students with the diplomas of modern secondary schools, and although women were still not admitted to the universities, separate women's courses were now free to offer a full higher education programme. In 1914 there were about 127,000 higher education students: 35,000 men in universities, 34,000 women in higher courses, and 58,000, mostly men, in specialized institutes. With nearly 10,000 students, Moscow was the third largest university in Europe, after Paris (17,500) and Berlin (14,000). In the universities, the law faculties had 40 per cent of the students, medicine and science about 25 per cent each, and arts the remainder.[51] In 1914, the sons of nobles had fallen to 35 per cent, from 52 per cent in 1900; 23 per cent came from the petty bourgeoisie, 10 per cent were sons of priests, 11 per cent of merchants, and 13 per cent of peasants—up from 5 per cent in 1900.[52] Private universities and courses, usually aimed at a wide audience and without fixed curricula, were also now permitted, and the Shaniavskii University, endowed by a retired general but supported by the Moscow municipality, absorbed many of the professors sacked in 1911.

This dynamism testified to the vitality of Russian life. 'There was no crisis in Russian higher education or in Russian science on the eve of World War I', according to Kassow. 'In both areas Russia had achieved unparalleled strength and diversity. . . . The real problem was the crisis in relations between the universities and the

[48] S. D. Kassow, 'Professionalism among university professors', in H. D. Balzer (ed.), *Russia's missing middle class: the professions in Russian history* (Armonk, NY, 1996), 209. Cf. K. E. Bailes, *Science and Russian culture in an age of revolutions: V. I. Vernadsky and his scientific school 1863–1945* (Bloomington, Ind., 1990), 80–129.

[49] D. Wartenweiler, *Civil society and academic debate in Russia 1905–1914* (Oxford, 1999), 148.

[50] Kassow, 'Professionalism', 198.

[51] Alston, 'Dynamics of educational expansion', 95–9; cf. C. E. Timberlake, 'Higher learning, the state, and the professions in Russia', in Jarausch, *Transformation of higher learning*, 328.

[52] Brower, 'Social stratification', 248; S. D. Kassow, *Students, professors, and the state in Tsarist Russia* (Berkeley, 1989), 409–10.

state', and failure to 'create the basis for a modern concept of citizenship and partnership between civil society and the state'.[53] In most European countries, universities produced officials, technical experts, professional men, and teachers who did not question the legitimacy of their governments, identified their country's interests with those of progress and civilization, and transmitted the nation's values and the myths which constituted its identity to the people as a whole. The Russian autocracy had failed to bring this about; despite the policies of official nationality under Nicholas I and Russification under Alexander III, it had not succeeded in welding its interests to those of the living nation, nor had it taken advantage of the liberal moments in the 1860s and 1905 to build bridges with the educated class which its own university policy had created. The test of war was soon to expose these weaknesses.

[53] Ibid. 344, 388.

17

Women and Universities

The admission of women can be seen as one of the complex of changes which occurred in the decades around 1870, as universities were remodelled to meet a broader range of middle-class demands. It has a context in the history of universities as well as in the history of women. Yet many of the 'social history' approaches to the expansion and diversification of higher education fail to explain this important change. Theories of elites, social mobility, or national integration have little to say about women at a time when they were excluded from elite positions, from almost all branches of state service, and from political rights. They hardly figure, for example, in the studies of elites by Charle or Rubinstein. The theory of professionalization has more relevance, because of women's focus on breaking into medicine, and because of the appearance of female secular schoolteaching as a genuinely new profession. Bourdieu's idea of reproduction may also explain the limits on women's progress, as their education often took forms designed to reproduce rather than transform gender relations.

There were occasional cases in the seventeenth and eighteenth centuries, particularly in Italy, of women being awarded university degrees, or even holding teaching posts, but this was a recognition of individual scholarship and did not involve attendance as a student. Neither the Enlightenment nor the French revolution was sympathetic to this cause, apart from radical thinkers like Condorcet. Women's exclusion from the university reforms of the period reflected a society in which political and public responsibilities were confined to men, usually acting as heads of families, and concepts of liberal education such as *Bildung* were related to men's role as actors in the public sphere. Women were not expected to develop autonomous personalities in the same way, and the Catholic church was at one with the French revolutionaries and their liberal and republican successors in expecting education to prepare women for their tasks as wives and mothers. When feminism first appeared as a European political force in 1848, there was wide agreement that the deficiencies of women's education were one of the barriers to full citizenship, but few concrete demands for entry to higher education. In France, Pauline Roland and the radical newspaper *La Voix des femmes* demanded the opening of all educational opportunities in principle, but were more directly interested in schools.[1] It was in the 1860s—with striking simultaneity in every European country—that admission to universities became an issue. America provided an influential model:

[1] H. Grubitzsch, '"Wissen heisst leben . . .": Der Kampf der Frauen um die Bildung zu Beginn des 19. Jahrhunderts (Frankreich)', in I. Brehmer and others, *Frauen in der Geschichte IV. 'Wissen heisst leben . . .': Beiträge zur Bildungsgeschichte von Frauen im 18. und 19. Jahrhundert* (Düsseldorf, 1983), 195–6.

some European women went there to gain medical qualifications, and many American women came to study in Europe, where the level of research and advanced work was higher, helping to make the idea of women in university classes familiar.

John Stuart Mill's essay *On the subjection of women*, which did not discuss universities specifically, but used the liberal (and Humboldtian) principle of the individual's right to full self-development to argue for complete equality of access to occupations and social functions, was quickly translated and appreciated after its publication in 1869.[2] Within the developing women's movements, the demand for higher education attracted almost universal support—more so than the demand for political rights, for many noted pioneers of women's education remained hostile to women's suffrage. The growth of the demand for university education may be explained in demographic terms, as more unmarried middle-class women needed to find careers, or in terms of the history of gender and the family, as women sought relationships based on intellectual equality. It also reflected wider changes such as the advance of political liberalism and the waning influence of the churches. But other explanations relate more to the evolution of educational systems.

There were common European patterns, but development was conditioned by national political and educational peculiarities. Hence the formal admission of women to universities was staggered over nearly fifty years: in the 1860s in France and Switzerland; in the 1870s in England, Holland, Italy, Denmark, and Sweden; in the 1880s in Belgium and Spain; in the 1890s in Scotland, Austria, and Hungary; and in the 1900s in Germany, with Prussia almost the last to yield in 1908. As a result, the percentage of women in the student body by 1914 also varied, though it was not necessarily highest in the countries with the earliest dates of admission, and progress in Germany was rapid once the barrier was down. The most 'progressive' country was probably Britain, with about 20 per cent, due partly to the universities' share in training elementary teachers. In France it was around 10 per cent, in Germany 7 per cent. Russia saw a remarkably vigorous expansion in the 1900s, reaching a percentage higher than in Britain, but women were not admitted to the established universities. Study abroad was a vital resource for Russian women, and there was a notable international movement of women students, especially to France, Belgium, and Switzerland. Medical education was a particular target, and there are really two chronologies for the growth of women's higher education before 1914: the first phase, beginning in the 1860s, was medical and international, and involved relatively small numbers of women, forced by circumstances into unconventional patterns of study; a second phase, in which women proceeded regularly from secondary schools to universities, within national educational systems, and studied a wide range of subjects in the same way as men, did not really gather force until 1900.

Traditional historiography emphasizes the role of pioneers, whether those who led the campaigns, or those who first broke barriers as students. Such women

[2] e.g. in Italy: M. Raicich, 'Liceo, università, professioni: un percorso difficile', in S. Soldani (ed.), *L'educazione delle donne: scuole e modelli di vita femminile nell'Italia dell'Ottocento* (Milan, 1989), 148.

required courage and ability in the teeth of obstruction and prejudice, but their success depended on wider forces, sometimes on legal accident. In France, it was found that Napoleonic legislation had omitted to specify that university qualifications were for men only, and women were able to take early advantage of this. In Scotland, on the other hand, though this was one of the few countries where mixed education was normal at secondary level, formal entry to the universities had to await 1892 because of legal obstacles. Apart from these quirks, the broader factors which interacted to determine national patterns were religion, the organization of girls' secondary schools, the relationship between the state, the professions, and university qualifications, the structure of the higher education system, and the general political context.

Some contemporaries thought there was a natural connection between Protestantism and women's emancipation. The German feminist Käthe Schirmacher gave this explanation a quasi-racial slant. She put the 'Germanic' countries (Scandinavia and Holland as well as America, Britain, and Germany) at the top of the tree; then the Romance countries, where the movement had to contend with Catholicism; and finally the Slavic countries where 'there is a lack of an ancient, deeply rooted culture like that of western Europe. Everywhere the oriental viewpoint has had its effect on the status of woman.'[3] The late admission of women in Protestant Prussia, and the educational achievements of Russian women, made this explanation unconvincing, but it was true that Catholicism provided an unfavourable environment. In France, Italy, and Spain, religious orders made a vital contribution to girls' secondary education—and one which is only now being given its full recognition by historians—but the Catholic emphasis on the family and motherhood made the church generally hostile to careers for women. No distinctive ideal of Catholic higher education for women was ever developed; the Catholic universities in France did not train women teachers, and the University of Louvain was one of the few which remained exclusively male until after the First World War. On the other hand, most Catholic countries by the 1870s had anticlerical governments, and in France in particular the Republicans deliberately promoted state girls' schools in order to challenge the power of the church over the family realm.

The organization of secondary schools was a further conditioning force. If women were to enter universities, they needed to acquire the baccalaureate, *Abitur*, or other standard qualification, invariably based on the classics. Most of the existing girls' schools, lay as well as religious, had a curriculum designed to train wives and mothers, which excluded Greek and taught mathematics and Latin at an elementary level if at all. The development of more academic schools for girls (or their partial admission to the existing boys' schools) was therefore a prerequisite for the expansion of university entry. Yet many feminist educationists themselves believed that women's mission lay in a separate sphere from men. Much depended on whether girls' schools aimed to prove that women were the intellectual equals of

[3] K. Schirmacher, *The modern women's rights movement: a historical survey* (New York, 1912), 215 (orig. German 1905).

men, or to cultivate womanly values—the positions in Britain and France respectively, with Germany in between. A second determinant was whether the teachers in secular girls' schools were women, which would create a demand for women graduates to staff this new profession. This was the case in England (as distinct from Scotland) and in France, but not in Germany, where male teachers in girls' schools formed a vested interest hostile to women's aspirations. These two factors of school organization form a matrix. Where schools both had an academic curriculum and were taught by women, as in England, the road to the university was most open. Where schools had a women's curriculum and a tradition of male teachers, as in Germany, change was delayed. France, with women teachers but a non-academic curriculum, came between.

Attitudes towards women's secondary education were also influenced by the situation in primary schools. In Catholic countries, the dominance of girls' education by religious orders made opinion suspicious of lay schoolmistresses, and created a prejudice against mixed education even after schools were secularized, notably in France. In Protestant countries, where mixed primary education was more usual, it was still usually thought unacceptable for the education of the middle classes. But the absence of nuns meant that trained women teachers began to replace men in primary schools rather earlier than in secondary ones, and their training (even if it was usually outside the university sector) opened up new opportunities for social mobility. The general pressure towards women's higher education in the 1860s can be explained partly by a time-lag in the professionalization of teachers. In boys' education, lay teachers in the gymnasiums or lycées, trained in the new disciplines of humanist education, replaced monks, private tutors, and entrepreneurial private teachers in the early nineteenth century. Now trained women teachers and academic girls' schools with public status began to replace nuns, governesses, and the private schoolmistresses who had taught girls womanly accomplishments rather than Latin. Or, from another point of view, the institutionalization of education in large, impersonal, hierarchical schools which is characteristic of modern society was now extended to women. Once this sort of girls' secondary education was established, higher education was a logical consequence, though with further time-lags caused by the strength of the domestic ideal and the prejudices deriving from it, and the fact that other professions were not as easily opened to women as teaching, where a female profession could grow up alongside a male one without directly threatening it.

As long as the professions remained closed there was a natural ceiling on the usefulness of a university education. Apart from a few specialized areas such as inspecting factories and schools, bureaucracies were normally closed to women. Women gained entry to the bar in Switzerland in 1899 and France in 1900, but this was unusual, and the connection of law with the civil service generally kept law faculties—the largest faculties in many countries—closed until after the First World War. This was one reason why medicine was the main target of the early pioneers, though other motives included humanitarian idealism and an enthusiasm for science characteristic of the age. But here too conditions varied between countries:

in Britain and France, a university medical degree itself gave the right to practice, even if graduates then found many further obstacles to professional success, especially where prestigious posts in hospitals were concerned.[4] In Germany, however, the state controlled the examination giving access to medical qualifications, and this was not opened to women until 1899. In Germany too the strong tradition of state monopoly barred initiatives outside the universities, whereas in Britain, and in a different way in Russia, it was possible to found independent medical schools.

Questions of this kind have led Ilse Costas, in a rare attempt at comparative synthesis, to apply Bourdieu's theory of reproduction to the gender dimension. Academic education was bound up with the transmission of power, privilege, and wealth. But the resistance met by women's demands depended on the nature and intensity of those links in particular countries.[5] In bureaucratized central Europe, university entry and graduation were linked closely with the right to enter public service, and the professions were regulated by the state. If women were admitted to study law, could the vote be far behind? This occurred both to suffragists, who saw higher education paving the way to the vote, and to their opponents.[6] In Germany, the *Abitur* and university matriculation were blocked to women because they brought legal privileges and state employment rights: hence the paradox that it was possible in Germany for women to take doctorates, university distinctions which gave no legal rights, some years before they were allowed to matriculate and become regular students. Because they saw themselves as the gatekeepers to social status (and for other reasons) German university professors were the fiercest opponents of women's rights, which were eventually forced on them by the state. Countries where the professions were 'free', on the other hand, like Switzerland and Britain, could afford to be more relaxed in opening up university qualifications just because they were not binding on the self-regulating professions, and their expansion did not threaten the 'overcrowding' which was such an obsession in Germany. France had an intermediate position: the professions were state-regulated and entry to them was guarded, but admission to universities was less contentious because the real strongholds of privilege, the *grandes écoles*, remained closed.

In France women's education had traditionally fallen into the province of the church. Even among the liberal or anticlerical middle class, women were expected to remain good Catholics while their husbands became freethinkers—the strong identification of religion with the feminine sphere of life ('sexual dimorphism' is the historian's jargon) was a distinctive feature of French culture. For the state to intervene in girls' education was thus a direct challenge to the church, and it was undertaken in the late 1860s by Victor Duruy. He encouraged the opening of

[4] See for example W. Alexander, *First ladies of medicine: the origins, education and destination of early women medical graduates of Glasgow University* (Glasgow, 1987).

[5] I. Costas, 'Der Kampf um das Frauenstudium im internationalen Vergleich', in A. Schlüter (ed.), *Pionierinnen, Feministinnen, Karrierefrauen? Zur Geschichte des Frauenstudiums in Deutschland* (Pfaffenweiler, 1992), 115–44.

[6] J. Albisetti, *Schooling German girls and women: secondary and higher education in the nineteenth century* (Princeton, 1988), 168–9. Albisetti's book includes comparative material.

voluntary secondary courses for girls, run on secular lines. This provoked a storm of opposition from the church, notably its chief educational expert, Bishop Félix Dupanloup, but in many towns the courses survived throughout the 1870s. Writing in 1866 to the Empress Eugénie (a supporter of the cause), Duruy explained that 'I would not want to make "bluestockings" of them, but the influence of mothers on the education of their sons and on the direction of their ideas is too great not to feel alarmed at seeing women remain strangers to the intellectual life of the modern world.'[7] This policy of improving women's intellectual level within the context of family life and emancipating them from the reactionary influence of the church was taken up by Republicans: though the Third Republic denied women the vote, the middle-class family was now to be an agency of national integration. It was time, said Ferry in 1870, to claim women for the rational realm of science and to establish harmony of values between husbands and wives.[8] In 1880 the state established girls' lycées. The hostility of the church was unabated, and the lycées particularly attracted families who were Protestant, Jewish, or committed to the ideology of the Republican state, while the conservative bourgeoisie continued to use convent schools, so that the girls' lycées never had as many pupils as the boys'.

The new lycées were not intended, as might be supposed, to encourage girls to think of a university education. On the contrary, the Republicans shared the domestic ideology of the Catholics, and were anxious to prove that the lycées did not subvert feminine qualities. They had a distinctive curriculum, which did not include the classics and did not lead to the baccalaureate. Their teachers were recruited through separate *agrégation* examinations, and the whole system remained separate from that for boys. To train the new lay schoolmistresses, a residential school was founded at Sèvres, in the Paris suburbs, well away from the corruptions of the city, as was the college at Fontenay-aux-Roses which trained women teachers for the elementary training colleges—this was higher education of a kind, but typical of the rigid separation of elementary and secondary sectors in France. The director of Sèvres, Julie Favre, was the widow of a prominent Republican politician, and the daughter of a Protestant pastor—elite links of a characteristic kind. Jo Burr Margadant has shown how the communal life of this college, as well as its formal teaching, reinforced its secular but fervently idealistic ethos; as many remarked, it was a kind of lay convent.[9] The lycée teachers it produced were a new element in the professional elite, and as in the male École Normale, they came up from the best of the lycées and returned to the system through the *agrégation*. But the school had little connection with the rest of higher education, whose general extension to women followed different lines.

The first woman took the baccalaureate in 1861; Julie Daubié, like many early women students, was a mature woman already working as a teacher. Admission to some faculties began soon afterwards. The first women entered the Paris medical

[7] Cited in E. Charrier, *L'Évolution intellectuelle feminine* (Paris, 1931), 141.

[8] Cited in A. Prost, *Histoire de l'enseignement en France 1800–1967* (Paris, 1968), 268–9.

[9] J. B. Margadant, *Madame le professeur: women educators in the Third Republic* (Princeton, 1990). For the general context, F. Mayeur, *L'Enseignement secondaire des jeunes filles sous la Troisième République* (Paris, 1977).

faculty in 1868, and the English medical pioneer Elizabeth Garrett took her degree there in 1870. The first Frenchwoman qualified in 1875, but in the early years the great majority of medical students were foreigners, who were particularly attracted by the opening of hospital internships to women in 1885, imposed over the heads of the professors by the Paris municipal council.[10] Of 108 women in the medical faculty in 1886, only seven were French, and in 1903 France had only ninety-five women doctors.[11] The non-medical faculties at Paris did not accept women students until 1880, and the real change came with Liard's university reforms, especially the creation of faculty bursaries. The girls' lycées never relaxed their stance on university entry, but by the 1900s this attitude seemed old-fashioned. As a growing range of occupations for middle-class women appeared, women began to take the baccalaureate after private study, and this became easier after the school reform of 1902 permitted modern alternatives to the classics, though girls were not allowed to prepare for their examinations in boys' lycées as happened in Italy and parts of Germany. In 1902 there were 1,084 women university students, 3 per cent of a total of 30,370; 673 were French and 411 foreign. By 1914 there were 2,547 French and 1,707 foreign women, 6 and 4 per cent respectively of the total of 42,037. Foreigners still outnumbered natives in the medical faculties in 1914 (469 to 400), and most of the French women were now studying letters (1,288) or science (508).[12] The real strongholds of power, the Polytechnique and other engineering schools, and the lycées in Paris where the male intellectual elite competed for the glittering prizes, remained closed. Nor did women make much progress in the academic profession: the only female professor before 1914 (in 1908) was Marie Curie, who was something of a special case as she took over her husband's university laboratory after his death, even then waiting two years for promotion. Curie's earlier career included a period teaching at Sèvres.

The girls' lycées, like the convent schools before them, created a sphere of action for women separate from the male world, but unlike the convents they also stimulated a demand for higher education. Their significance is shown by comparison with other countries of Catholic culture. In Belgium, the state created girls' schools on French lines in 1881, but even more rigidly confined to a domestic curriculum, and limited to three years' teaching. Convent schools continued to dominate the scene, and in 1890 entry requirements for the universities were tightened up, with a rigorous examination in Latin and Greek. Girls who wished to prepare for this had to study in private courses, and it 'brutally restricted the entry of women into the Belgian universities'.[13] There was no real change down to 1914. The universities were opened to women in 1880–2 (apart from Louvain), and foreign students were immediately attracted by their teaching in French and their free intellectual

[10] T. N. Bonner, *To the ends of the earth: women's search for education in medicine* (Cambridge, Mass., 1992), 49–51, 72–3.

[11] Albisetti, *Schooling*, 130; Charrier, *L'Évolution intellectuelle*, 301.

[12] G. Weisz, *The emergence of modern universities in France 1863–1914* (Princeton, 1983), 242, 246.

[13] B. Lacomble-Masereel, *Les Premières Étudiantes à l'Université de Liège: années académiques 1881–1882 à 1919–1920* (Liège, 1980), 105.

atmosphere. But the number of native Belgian students remained small. The total number of all nationalities in 1914 was only 260 (3 per cent), the highest proportion being at the Free University of Brussels, where 359 of the 615 women who attended between 1880 and 1914 were foreign.[14] At Liège over a similar period, 348 of 646 women were foreigners, mostly Russian (241) or Polish (57).[15] Among the Belgian students, the absence of opportunities in secondary teaching meant that few entered the philosophy faculty. Science was the popular choice, and most of the science students were aiming at pharmacy, which was something of a women's speciality in Belgium—seventeen of the twenty-six degrees awarded to Belgian women at Ghent before 1914 were in pharmacy.[16] Pharmacy was a business as well as a profession and could be inherited by daughters. In Catholic countries there was a tradition of nuns dispensing drugs, and a sense that pharmacy fell within women's domestic sphere—after all, said a Liège medical journal in 1892, it was 'un peu une question de cuisine'.[17] The popularity of pharmacy was also a feature in Spain, where otherwise the underdevelopment of women's education reflected a general intellectual stagnation very different from the Belgian case. It was one of the issues taken up by the Institución Libre de Enseñanza, but with very limited effects by 1914.[18]

In Italy, women were legally admitted to universities in 1875, but no system of state girls' schools followed, and as elsewhere it was impossible to enter without the classical leaving certificate. Many of the early graduates were foreigners, or Italian Protestants and Jews, and only the northern universities had significant numbers. Italian governments, though hostile to the church, were more willing than French ones to accept its dominance of women's lives; yet mixed education was acceptable in Italy as it was not in France, and girls were allowed to attend boys' schools to prepare for the university, which they did in significant numbers after 1900. Women were also admitted to the Scuola Normale Superiore at Pisa.[19] They were still barred from law, the main focus of Italian universities, and without secular girls' schools the demand for teachers was limited. But women began to share in the national pursuit of diplomas: in the words of a contemporary observer, 'the daughters of the educated, liberal (but often poor) bourgeoisie are driven by want and conviction to acquire a higher education and to engage in academic callings. The material difficulties are not great.'[20] It has been argued that Italy enjoyed 'the advantages of backwardness', as in the absence of girls' lycées women were forced to compete directly with men, and once they reached the university they were accustomed to

[14] Ibid. 8, 11, 73–4; A. Despy-Meyer and J. Becquevort, *Les Femmes et l'enseignement supérieur: l'Université Libre de Bruxelles de 1880 à 1914* (Brussels, 1980), p. xv.

[15] Lacomble-Masereel, *Les Premières Étudiantes*, 88, 90.

[16] A. M. Simon-Van der Meersch, *De eerste generaties meisjesstudenten aan de Rijksuniversiteit te Gent (1882/1883 tot 1929/1930)* (Ghent, 1982), 85.

[17] Lacomble-Masereel, *Les Premières Étudiantes*, 151–2.

[18] A. Shubert, *A social history of modern Spain* (London, 1990), 37–8; Y. Turin, *L'Éducation et l'école en Espagne de 1874 à 1902: libéralisme et tradition* (Paris, 1959), 273–5.

[19] Raicich, 'Liceo, università, professioni', 147–81. Cf. T. Tomasi and L. Bellatalla, *L'università italiana nell'età liberale (1861–1923)* (Naples, 1988), 156–60.

[20] Schirmacher, *Modern women's rights movement*, 199–200.

jumping the same intellectual barriers.[21] By 1913 there were 4,300 women students, about as many as in France or Germany, and several women had become university teachers.[22] One of them was Maria Montessori, an early medical graduate who obtained a post in a university clinic in 1897, and became a lecturer in anthropology at Rome University in the 1900s.[23]

In a general survey of women's education in nineteenth-century Europe, Françoise Mayeur claims that in England 'few women pursued a higher education before 1914, owing in part to powerful resistance from certain professions, especially medicine, but perhaps also to lack of ambition or to a diversion of women's energies into the suffragist movement'.[24] But this judgement is questionable, and perhaps comes from looking too much at Oxford and Cambridge, which by 1910 accounted for only a fifth of English women students. At the two ancient universities, women were only 9 per cent of the student population, but in the rest of England they made up 20 per cent (the average for Great Britain), in Scotland 24 per cent, and in Wales 35 per cent. These were much higher percentages than in France, partly because male enrolments in France were higher, but even the absolute numbers of women were greater in Britain (5,654) than in France (4,254, of whom only 2,547 were French: the proportion of foreigners in Britain is not known, but was probably small).[25]

One reason for these high figures was that from the 1890s the universities (even Oxford and Cambridge) had a share in training elementary teachers, though these students did not always take full degrees; another British peculiarity, also connected with elementary teacher-training and with 'national efficiency' arguments about women's role in producing healthy families, was the teaching of domestic science, taken up at King's College London and Cardiff. Once girls' grammar schools expanded in the 1900s, training secondary teachers became the main task of the arts and science faculties. Other favourable factors came into play earlier. Since the British state did not lay down secondary school curricula, or claim any monopoly of education, the field was open for experiment and private initiative, and when academic secondary schools for girls appeared in the 1850s most of the pioneers insisted that women needed to prove their equality with men by tackling the full classical and mathematical curriculum. This attitude was carried over into the early days of higher education, notably by Emily Davies, author of *The higher education of women* (1866), who founded what became the first women's college at Cambridge, Girton. Others followed at both Oxford and Cambridge in the 1870s. In some ways, these universities provided a favourable environment: women's colleges could be added to the college structure without disturbing the men's

21 Raicich, 'Liceo, università, professioni', 163–4.

22 Charrier, *L'Évolution intellectuelle*, 189; Albisetti, *Schooling*, 300.

23 V. Babini, 'Science, feminism and education: the early work of Maria Montessori', *History Workshop Journal*, 49 (2000), 45–67.

24 G. Fraisse and M. Perrot (eds.), *A history of women in the west. IV. Emerging feminism from revolution to world war* (Cambridge, Mass., 1993), 234.

25 J. Howarth and M. C. Curthoys, 'The political economy of women's higher education in late nineteenth and early twentieth-century Britain', *Historical Research*, 60 (1987), 210–11; R. D. Anderson, *Universities and elites in Britain since 1800* (London, 1992), 23.

colleges, and the tutorial ideal of personal teaching and character formation harmonized with the genteel family atmosphere which the women's colleges sought to promote.[26] The Oxbridge women's colleges, and similar initiatives which followed in London, had all-female staffs which gave women scholars a sense of community and allowed them to establish careers in a way which hardly existed on the Continent, or indeed in a professorial system like the Scottish one, where there were a few female lecturers before 1914 but no professors.[27] On the other hand, women at Oxford and Cambridge were a minority whose relations with male students were rigidly supervised, and they remained marginal to most university activities. Above all, although women were admitted to the university examinations and soon began to shine in the contest for honours, they were refused degrees at Oxford and Cambridge, until 1920 and 1948 respectively, because this would have given them a share in university decision-making.

Outside Oxford and Cambridge, women established the right to degrees on equal terms, including London degrees from 1877. Committees to promote higher-level lectures for women appeared in the larger cities at the end of the 1860s, and fed into the extension movement and then into the new civic colleges, which were usually open from the start, though at Manchester women had to make do with informal lectures of this kind until the formation of the Victoria University in 1880.[28] An area which remained contested was medicine: the leading medical schools in London and Edinburgh refused to admit women before 1914, and separate schools of medicine for women were set up instead, but in other parts of Scotland and England formal equality was achieved. Medicine was less of a focus for women's aspirations in Britain than in some other countries, with fewer than 500 studying medicine in 1914, probably because of the comparatively wide opportunities in teaching and the interest shown from the start in breaking into traditional elite education.[29]

For the early years of the movement can be placed in the broader context of middle-class educational reform, and there were personal as well as ideological links with the new public schools and with the reforming parties at Oxford and Cambridge. The propagandists for women's education and the principals of women's colleges were often the wives, daughters, or sisters of male dons and other members of the intelligentsia, and were well placed to pull political and social strings.[30] These connections with the elite were typical of the women's education

[26] J. S. Pedersen, 'Enchanting modernity: the invention of tradition at two women's colleges in late nineteenth- and early twentieth-century Cambridge', *History of Universities*, 17 (2001–2), 162–91; M. Vicinus, *Independent women: work and community for single women 1850–1920* (London, 1985), 121 ff.; J. Howarth, '"In Oxford but . . . not of Oxford": the women's colleges', in M. G. Brock and M. C. Curthoys (eds.), *The history of the University of Oxford. VII. Nineteenth-century Oxford, Part 2* (Oxford, 2000), 237–307.

[27] F. Perrone, 'Women academics in England 1870–1930', *History of Universities*, 12 (1993), 339–67.

[28] T. Kelly, *For advancement of learning: the University of Liverpool 1881–1981* (Liverpool, 1981), 35–7; L. Moore, *Bajanellas and semilinas: Aberdeen University and the education of women 1860–1920* (Aberdeen, 1991), 1–36.

[29] Bonner, *To the ends of the earth*, 136–7.

[30] G. Sutherland, 'The movement for the higher education of women: its social and intellectual context in England *c.* 1840–80', in P. J. Waller (ed.), *Politics and social change in modern Britain: essays presented to A. F. Thompson* (Brighton, 1987), 91–116.

movement in all countries, as was the fact that women students tended to come from higher levels of the middle class than men—but less so from the landed aristocracy, who saw no need for advanced education for their daughters, or from the working class, where seeking scholarships, making family sacrifices, and thinking in terms of social mobility encountered even more cultural obstacles than for boys.[31] In Britain, there was often a perceptible difference between women students from the professional classes, prominent in the early years because of the self-confidence given by their family backgrounds, and interested in general culture, and a broader middle-class stratum which arrived after 1900, exploiting the new secondary schools and focused on careers in schoolteaching.[32] If historians of elites need to take more account of women, conversely elite membership, social privilege, and insider status were factors in women's educational success.

When the German feminist Helene Lange visited England in 1888 she was entranced by the stately buildings and gardens of the women's colleges at Cambridge. All this, she reflected, had been achieved by women's own efforts, with the help of sympathetic men.[33] 'With an energy without precedent,' she later wrote, 'the English women went to work. . . . England has witnessed a complete revolution in female education, aided . . . by the fact of its absolute freedom from governmental interference.'[34] This contrasted with 'the all-powerful conservative spirit in old Prussia', the obstructionism which the cause met in Germany, and the legal and bureaucratic obstacles which ruled out private initiatives of the British or American type.[35] Lange published an important pamphlet on girls' secondary schools in 1887. A Progressive (left-wing liberal) in politics, Lange was a dualist feminist, who believed that women had a separate cultural task related to their role as mothers. Ideally, they would develop a distinctive form of higher education; but it was never very clear what this might be, and Lange admitted that Emily Davies's strategy of equality was the only one which would gain women equal respect.

The German movement had started in the 1860s, and also contained more radical figures like Hedwig Dohm, who called both for the vote and for university entry; she published *The scientific emancipation of women* in 1874. But developments in secondary education were slow to create any university demand. Germany possessed 'higher' girls' schools, which had expanded greatly since the 1850s. These were of a secular type, predominantly Protestant, and socially exclusive, being typically attended by the daughters of officials and pastors. Many of the schools had public status, supported by cities and sometimes by states, though they were not a full part of the state apparatus like the boys' gymnasiums. As with the girls' lycées in France, these schools aimed to give a general not a vocational education, and one

[31] For Germany, Albisetti, *Schooling*, 289; for Vienna, M. Tichy, 'Soziale Herkunft, Elternhaus und Vorbildung der Studentinnen', in W. Heindl and M. Tichy (eds.), *'Durch Erkenntnis zu Freiheit und Gluck. . .': Frauen an der Universität Wien (ab 1897)* (Vienna, 1990), 95.

[32] Howarth and Curthoys, 'Political economy', 215–31.

[33] H. Lange, *Lebenserinnerungen* (Berlin, 1930), 162–3.

[34] H. Lange, *Higher education of women in Europe* (New York, 1901), 12 (orig. German 1889).

[35] Lange, *Lebenserinnerungen*, 212.

inspired by family values. Their syllabus excluded the classics, mathematics, and science, and the only career to which they led apart from marriage was teaching; seminars for women were established outside the universities to train teachers, but most of their graduates had to find posts in elementary or private schools. In the higher girls' schools—of which there were probably over 300 by 1887—the teaching posts were mostly held by men, and over 90 per cent still had male directors in the 1890s.[36] The directors formed a powerful lobby for development on existing lines, and the initial aim of feminist campaigners was to open the schools up to women teachers and to improve their intellectual level. Lange's German Women's Teachers' Association was founded in 1890, and in response to this agitation Prussia gave more official recognition to the higher schools and created an examination for women teachers in 1894. Entry to universities was a rather later priority, and feminists like Lange were suspicious of the aridity of philological scholarship and the over-academic curriculum. But if women were to enter professions like medicine, and to establish a claim for university matriculation, they needed the *Abitur*, and this could only be gained by allowing women to follow classes in the boys' gymnasiums, as happened in some states (though not Prussia or Bavaria), or by establishing gymnasiums for girls.

In Germany as elsewhere, lecture courses for women, supported by sympathetic professors, began at the end of the 1860s in the larger towns. Those in Berlin, which started in 1869 at the Victoria Lyceum, a leading higher girls' school, proved the longest-lasting.[37] In the 1860s and 1870s a few women, mostly foreigners, appeared in lecture-rooms as auditors, but this was banned in 1879. Others worked in institutes or laboratories, and were able to gain doctorates. The Russian mathematician Sofia Kovalevskaia was awarded a doctorate at Göttingen in 1874, and after a spell back in Russia became modern Europe's first woman professor, at Stockholm in 1883, this being a new university (1878) prepared to be unconventional. German women interested in medical careers, however, had to seek training in America or Switzerland. German law allowed them to practice, but not to take the state medical examinations. Feminist campaigning flagged in the face of inflexible official attitudes, but revived in the late 1880s, and led to a continuing series of pamphlets, conferences, petitions, and Reichstag debates. Gradually the walls began to crumble, first in the more liberal states. Baden allowed privately-prepared girls to take the *Abitur* in 1891, and Prussia followed suit in 1895. Courses to give this preparation were opened in the major cities, and girls' gymnasiums were founded at Karlsruhe in 1893 and Stuttgart in 1899. In the 1890s university lectures were again opened to women auditors, many of them American. By 1902 Berlin had 611 women auditors, of whom 422 were German, though only 35 held the *Abitur*.[38] The first doctorate awarded to a German woman was at Heidelberg in 1894, but Berlin held out until 1899. The strongest demand was still for medicine, and the key steps were the

[36] Albisetti, *Schooling*, 36–9. This is a general source for what follows. See also J. Albisetti, 'Women and the professions in Imperial Germany', in R. E. Joeres and M. J. Maynes (eds.), *German women in the eighteenth and nineteenth centuries: a social and literary history* (Bloomington, Ind., 1986), 94–109.

[37] Albisetti, *Schooling*, 117–21.

[38] Ibid. 233.

opening of the Reich medical examinations to women holding the *Abitur* in 1899 and the qualifications reform of 1900 which broke the monopoly of Greek, for the modern *Realgymnasium* programme was relatively easy for girls' schools to adopt. The refusal of matriculation now seemed an anomaly. Baden allowed it in 1900, followed by Bavaria in 1903, Württemberg in 1904, Saxony in 1906, and Prussia in 1908. Alsace-Lorraine (i.e. the University of Strasbourg) and conservative Mecklenburg (Rostock) brought up the rear in 1909.[39] The Technical High Schools were also opened up, though very few women studied there. This set of reforms was completed by admitting women into the standard examination for secondary teachers, in 1905 in Prussia, and by a recasting in 1908 of the higher schools for girls, which were renamed Lyceums, allowed to prepare for the *Abitur*, and encouraged to employ women teachers. By 1911 there were thirty-one schools with *Abitur* streams in Prussia, seventy-one in the Reich as a whole—still far fewer than boys' gymnasiums.[40]

The long resistance of Prussia seems surprising for a Protestant, highly industrialized, and in many ways socially progressive state. In elementary education, mixed classes and the feminization of teaching were more advanced than in France. Resistance came above all from the universities themselves, and in the end the state intervened after parliamentary pressure to impose change on a reluctant professorate. Germany was not the only country where women encountered opposition from conservative professors, but here it was peculiarly fierce and irrational.[41] Perhaps the ideal of *Bildung* was inherently patriarchal, with its aim of creating an autonomous personality active in the public sphere. Perhaps traditional student life in Germany, with its duelling and beer-drinking, made it especially difficult to contemplate female students: 'What? a student who can't get drunk?', said the Berlin historian Treitschke, who announced that 'for half a millennium the German universities have been designed for men, and I will not help to destroy them'. According to the medievalist Otto Gierke, 'our universities are men's universities . . . adapted to the male spirit'.[42] For the German upper and middle classes, university life was central to the construction of masculinity, and the intrusion of women created deep insecurities linked both with *fin-de-siècle* ideas about racial and physical degeneration and with the panic about overcrowding, which was at its height just when the women's movement came on the scene. Along with socialists, Jews, and *Brotstudenten*, women were another threat to the dominance of the mandarins and the humanist culture on which their status rested.

Medical professors and students were especially hostile, partly because their profession was the first target, partly because they could wield pseudo-scientific arguments about women's constitutional incapacity for intellectual work, supported by anthropological data. Theodor Bischoff, professor of anatomy at Munich, who weighed 391 male and 253 female brains and found an average difference of 134 grams, published a popular compendium of such arguments in 1872. Another best-

[39] Albisetti, *Schooling*, 204 ff., 238 ff.

[40] Ibid. 280.

[41] T. E. Fischer, *Die Anfänge des Frauenstudiums in Deutschland: Das Beispiel der Universität Kiel* (Trier, 1996), 23–8.

[42] Albisetti, *Schooling*, 200, 228.

seller, in 1900, was by the Leipzig psychiatrist Paul Möbius, who claimed that women's education would 'atrophy the maternal organs' and create 'hateful and useless hermaphrodites'.[43] In response, the women's lobby resorted to defensive arguments like the need for woman doctors to treat women patients; one argument which could not be used in Germany, though it was popular in France, Britain, Russia, and even Austria after it took over Bosnia in 1878, was that Islamic subject peoples needed women doctors acceptable to the female population.

The admission of women, once agreed, was more far-reaching in Germany than elsewhere, as the system contained no protected areas for the male elite like the French *grandes écoles* or Oxbridge colleges. The new demand for women teachers meant, as in other countries, an influx into the philosophy faculty, and numbers there overtook those in medicine. By 1914 there were 2,433 women students in Prussia and 4,056 in Germany (7 per cent of the total).[44] Once foreigners were deducted (about a seventh in Germany) this was comparable to France. Albisetti concludes that Germany was now as advanced in this respect as other countries, and that the campaign had been a 'major victory for German feminism'.[45] Two restrictions remained. State law examinations were closed until after the war; and no women were admitted to the *Habilitation*, and thus to university teaching. At most, a few posts as assistants were available, and in an exceptional case at Bonn in 1908 the zoologist Marie von Linden became head of an institute, but without a professorial title.[46] The woman student had been accepted, thanks largely to the persistent campaigning of the women's movement, but in Germany the woman professor was still a figure difficult to imagine.

The pattern in Austria was very similar to that in Germany. The existence of higher girls' schools with a non-academic curriculum and the hostility of professors delayed change in the same way, though formal university admission came rather earlier, to the philosophy faculties in 1897 and medicine in 1900. (In Hungary both were opened in 1895.) The Romance philologist Elise Richter took the *Habilitation* and became a *Privatdozent* in 1907, but this remained unique; the physicist Lise Meitner started her research career at Vienna, but moved to Berlin in 1907. Both Richter and Meitner were Jewish, and women from religious and ethnic minorities showed the same passion for education as men. When modern secondary schools for girls were recognized, they were sparse in the German areas, but more numerous in Bohemia (where the cause was linked with Czech nationalism) and in Galicia, where Cracow and Lwów each had four.[47] At Vienna

[43] M. Tichy, 'Die geschlechtliche Un-Ordnung: Facetten des Widerstands gegen das Frauenstudium von 1870 bis zur Jahrhundertwende', in Heindl and Tichy, *'Durch Erkenntnis . . .'*, 30, 35–6, 40.

[44] B. vom Brocke and P. Krüger (eds.), *Hochschulpolitik im Föderalismus: Die Protokolle der Hochschulkonferenzen der deutschen Bundesstaaten und Österreich 1898 bis 1918* (Berlin, 1994), 424.

[45] Albisetti, *Schooling*, 305, and cf. 292 ff.

[46] Albisetti, 'Women and the professions', 101.

[47] S. Danielski, 'Der Berufsweg der Lehrerinnen an den höheren Schulen', in M. Forkl and E. Koffmahn (eds.), *Frauenstudium und akademische Frauenarbeit in Österreich* (Vienna, 1968), 75; R. Dutkowa, 'Les lycées de filles à Cracowie (1867–1918)', in V. Karady and M. Kulczykowski (eds.), *L'Enseignement des élites en Europe centrale (19–20e siècles)* (Cracow, 1999), 13. Cf. G. B. Cohen, *Education and middle-class society in Imperial Austria 1848–1918* (West Lafayette, Ind., 1996), 73–5, 189–90, 286–8.

University, where many of the Polish women went, 37 per cent of women philosophy students in 1913 and 59 per cent of medical students were Jewish.[48] By 1914 there were 2,275 women students in Austria, 8 per cent of the total.[49]

In the early years of Alexander II, Russian women seemed on the verge of a breakthrough, helped by the absence of the grip over women's education held by the church in western Catholic countries. In 1858 the state set up a system of girls' gymnasiums, the first of its kind; as in Germany the teachers were male, but the schools were later allowed to teach Latin and Greek. Women seeking higher education were mainly interested in medicine, which could 'combine the desire to serve society with the near-mystical faith in science so characteristic of the 1860s'.[50] There was less resistance than in the west because the medical profession was shorthanded and did not have especially high prestige, and unlike most forms of public service it was open to Jews.[51] Yet the vagaries of Russian policy resulted in most women studying abroad. In 1859 they were briefly admitted to university lectures, but this was banned in 1861. Medical training for women was then available for a time in the academy of military surgery at St Petersburg (the army being one of Russia's more modern-minded institutions), but this too was stopped in 1864, and the university law of 1863, otherwise fairly liberal, failed to address the issue. The late 1860s saw a first exodus of Russian women to Zurich. In 1869 the government allowed higher courses for women outside the university framework, and the Bestuzhev courses in St Petersburg, founded in 1878, were regarded as a 'university for women'.[52] In 1878–9, there were nearly 1,300 women in various courses; like male students they were often quite poor, and lived collectively in squalid lodgings.[53] Women were also readmitted in 1872 to the military academy, where the composer Alexander Borodin taught chemistry and supported their cause; many served at the front in the Russo-Turkish war of 1877–8.[54] But the growth of populist politics in the 1870s, in which women were active participants, aroused the suspicions of the state and meant that the courses were closely watched. The assassination of Alexander II in 1881 put an end to this phase. By 1886 all except the more socially exclusive Bestuzhev courses were closed down, and these had to observe a Jewish quota of 3 per cent.[55] Some medical courses for women were revived in the late 1890s, but from the 1880s until 1905, Russian women generally sought higher education abroad, in Paris, Berlin, Belgium, or Switzerland.

[48] W. Heindl, 'Die konfessionellen Verhältnisse Jüdischer und katholischer Studentinnen', in Heindl and Tichy, *'Durch Erkenntnis . . .'*, 145. Cf. W. Heindl, 'Die Studentinnen der Universität Wien: Zur Entwicklung des Frauenstudiums seit 1897. Eine Projektbeschreibung', in V. Karady and W. Mitter (eds.), *Bildungswesen und Sozialstruktur in Mitteleuropa im 19. und 20. Jahrhundert. Education and social structure in Central Europe in the 19th and 20th centuries* (Cologne, 1990), 259–76.

[49] Brocke and Krüger, *Hochschulpolitik*, 425.

[50] B. A. Engel, 'Women medical students in Russia 1872–1882: reformers or rebels?', *Journal of Social History*, 12 (1978–9), 396.

[51] C. Johanson, *Women's struggle for higher education in Russia 1855–1900* (Kingston, Ont., 1987), 77–9.

[52] B. A. Engel, *Mothers and daughters: women of the intelligentsia in nineteenth-century Russia* (Cambridge, 1983), 61.

[53] Johanson, *Women's struggle*, 63–5.

[54] Bonner, *To the ends of the earth*, 89–93.

[55] Johanson, *Women's struggle*, 99–100.

The political liberalism of the Swiss cities, and the history of their universities as refuges for exiles, paved the way for the admission of women on fully equal terms, at Zurich in 1864, at Bern and Geneva in 1872. The Russian émigré community in Zurich has been much studied because it became a centre of revolutionary political activity, influenced at different times by Bakunin's anarchism and by marxism. It attracted men as well as women, and not all the women students were Russian, since for thirty years the Swiss universities were the only ones open to German-speaking women.[56] When the Russian government banned attendance at Zurich in 1873, there were about 100 Russian women there, and many moved to Bern, Geneva, or Paris rather than returning to Russia. The willingness of these students to travel abroad and live independently belies some of the stereotypes of nineteenth-century women, and once in Switzerland they acquired a reputation for radical lifestyles. They were 'new women' who lived in lodgings, cut their hair short, wore sensible clothes, sported blue-tinted glasses (a recognized symbol of radicalism in Russia), smoked in public and frequented cafés, and, most provocatively of all, believed in comradely relationships with men. In an age of chaperonage and rigid social conventions, the reputation of Russian women students did some harm to the cause in Germany and elsewhere, seeming to prove the standard argument that university education would destroy womanly qualities. These women lived a life apart from staid Swiss society, and when the prudent bourgeoisie of Basel opened their conservative university to women in 1890, they framed the rules in a way which excluded foreigners.[57] Swiss women themselves were slow to make use of the new opportunities.

Nearly all the Russian women in Switzerland studied medicine, though there were exceptions like the Polish revolutionary Rosa Luxemburg, whose doctoral thesis on the industrial development of Poland became the basis of her contributions to marxism; she also met her life partner Leo Jogiches there. The first woman to be awarded a medical doctorate in Europe, at Zurich in 1867, was Nadezhda Suslova, who had gone there after women were forced out of the academy of military surgery. She was the daughter of a serf, which was unusual, for most of the women came from gentry or merchant families, and were of higher social status than those who stayed in Russia.[58] A high proportion were Jewish. One who was not was the revolutionary Vera Figner, who came from a well-off gentry family and travelled to Zurich with her husband (who was soon ditched) and her sister, but was inspired by Suslova's example. In her memoirs she recalled her youth: 'All around was the countryside. Mud, poverty, sickness, ignorance. A golden thread led from Suslova to me, and then led on, a little later, to the countryside and its inhabitants, and later still towards the people, the fatherland, humanity.'[59] This thread led Figner to give up her medical studies and she returned to Russia to work as a nurse

[56] G. Einsele, '"Kein Vaterland": Deutsche Studentinnen im Zürcher Exil (1870–1908)', in Schlüter, *Pionierinnen*, 9–34.

[57] E. Bonjour, *Die Universität Basel von den Anfängen bis zur Gegenwart 1460–1960* (Basel, 1960), 444–54. Cf. Engel, *Mothers and daughters*, 136.

[58] Bonner, *To the ends of the earth*, 33–7, 57.

[59] V. Figner, *Mémoires d'une révolutionnaire* (Paris, 1973), 55–6.

and midwife; involved in the People's Will movement and the murder of Alexander II, she spent twenty-two years in a Tsarist prison, dying in 1942 as a Soviet heroine. The revolutionary activity was unusual, but the desire to serve the people as a doctor or teacher was not, and most students returned to Russia to do so.

The 1905 revolution reopened the question of women's higher education, but did not lead to the direct admission of women to the universities. Its effect was to create a free market, with separate institutes for women, supported from a variety of sources but not by the state. These were universities in all but name, whose graduates were admitted to degree qualifications in 1911, and they multiplied rapidly in provincial cities as well as the capitals; many Russian and Polish women continued to study abroad, but by 1914, as we have seen, there were almost as many women in the Russian institutes as in the male universities, and they were 27 per cent of all students in higher education. The search for medical education, at home and abroad, meant that in 1914 Russia had over 1,600 women doctors, more than the rest of Europe together, making up about a tenth of the medical profession.[60] But tsarism could claim little of the credit, and the Russian case shows that there was no simple correlation between women's emancipation and social and political modernity.

Women's university education was a diverse phenomenon. At one end of the scale were the crop-headed radicals of Zurich, at the other the demure bourgeois students depicted by the historian of Liège University: the Belgian student

> is most often a young woman of 17, coming from a relatively modest family, living in the university town or its surroundings. . . . Her sensible and reasonable tastes have directed her towards pharmacy, which fits quite well into the traditional conception of the feminine role. She has nothing of the English suffragette, or any aggressive feminism. She does not frequent the student cafes, lives with her parents. . . . She is anxious to get her diploma, and is studious and hardworking. Her results are there to prove it, and once qualified she opens a dispensary.[61]

Belgian students tended to come from the lower middle class, as the Catholicism of the upper bourgeoisie prejudiced them against higher education. But a phenomenon noted in other countries by the 1900s was the 'fashionable' student who cared nothing for the sacrifices of the pioneers, and came to the university to enjoy its social life and look for a husband.[62]

The diversity of the student body was a sign of normalization. After about 1900, women's higher education settled into an accepted pattern, and shared many features with its male counterpart: the generally middle-class social profile of

[60] Bonner, *To the ends of the earth*, 78, 82. Cf. C. E. Timberlake, 'Higher learning, the state, and the professions in Russia', in K. H. Jarausch (ed.), *The transformation of higher learning 1860–1930: expansion, diversification, social opening, and professionalization in England, Germany, Russia, and the United States* (Chicago, 1983), 332–3.

[61] Lacomble-Masereel, *Les Premières Étudiantes*, 173, and cf. 130–3.

[62] A. Burchardt, *Blaustrumpf—Modestudentin—Anarchistin? Deutsche und russische Medizinstudentinnen in Berlin 1896–1918* (Stuttgart, 1997), 215; I. Bandhauer-Schöffmann, 'Zum Engagement der österreichischen Frauenvereine für das Frauenstudium', in Heindl and Tichy, *'Durch Erkenntnis . . .'*, 78.

students, the prominence of Jewish students in central and eastern Europe, the contrast between those with leisure and *Brotstudenten*. Numbers still seemed to be expanding on the eve of the war, but were likely to reach a ceiling until more careers were opened up. With some exceptions, like Oxbridge colleges and the French college at Sèvres, where an academic culture 'owned' by women could develop, European countries chose to admit women to the existing universities rather than adopting the American precedent of separate colleges. Egalitarian in principle, it is arguable whether this gave women more real opportunities. Beyond graduation lay professional fields dominated by male elites and by alumni networks, clubs, and professional associations of all kinds: public school and Oxbridge college affiliations in Britain, corps or *Burschenschaft* membership in Germany, contacts formed at the lycée or *grande école* in France. The world of science and scholarship was itself conditioned by male assumptions and difficult to break into, and while admitting women to their portals universities did not feel a corresponding need to change their gendered nature or to adjust their traditional aims or values to female needs.[63] Even while they were students, women generally led separate social lives and were segregated in the classroom: in Belgium they had to follow the professor into the room and sit on the front benches, and there are similar reports from many countries. Women remained latecomers and outsiders in university culture: formal admission was the culmination of one struggle, but the beginning of another.

That women were in universities without being fully of them was to be pointed out forcibly by the modernist writer Virginia Woolf.[64] Woolf was the daughter of Leslie Stephen, a man of letters and former Cambridge don, and her male relatives and social circle were part of the Bloomsbury group with its strong Cambridge connections. But while Woolf's brothers had automatically attended the university, there was no question of her doing so herself. The Stephens were typical of the many cultivated bourgeois families in all countries where the domestic ideal continued to rule, women were not expected to earn a living, and higher education was suspect as creating bluestockings.[65] It was rather lower down the middle-class scale, where economic imperatives were stronger, that these obstacles might be overcome. As in the general study of universities and elites, historians need to turn their attention from supply to demand, to the strategies and mentalities of families, and to ask at what point, and why, it became desirable and acceptable to give daughters as well as sons an academic education. They might conclude that the entry of women to universities owed as much to the changing expectations of families and the resulting collective pressures as to changes in the law or even the efforts of feminist pioneers.

[63] C. Dyhouse, *No distinction of sex? Women in British universities 1870–1939* (London, 1995), 238–46; M. Bosch, *Het geslacht van de wetenschap: vrouwen en hoger onderwijs in Nederland 1878–1948* (Amsterdam, 1994), 583–6 (English summary).

[64] V. Woolf, *A room of one's own. Three guineas*, World's Classics edn. (Oxford, 1992) (texts of 1929, 1938).

[65] A. Schlüter, 'Wissenschaft für die Frauen?—Frauen für die Wissenschaft! Zur Geschichte der ersten Generationen von Frauen in der Wissenschaft', in Brehmer and others, *Frauen in der Geschichte*, 256–7.

18

Student Communities and Student Politics

The life of students is one of the less studied aspects of university history. Whether that history is seen as the history of a community, or of the ways in which the lives of individuals are shaped by institutions, or of the processes of intellectual training and discovery, one would expect to find students at the heart of the story. Yet many university histories are predominantly histories of professors and their scientific and scholarly achievements. 'Students', in the words of Thomas Bonner, 'appear in standard accounts, if at all, only as passive and voiceless participants in an impersonal process.'[1] It is true that the events of '1968', in Europe and America, provoked a flurry of writing on past student politics, and parallels could be drawn between 1968 and 1848. But political militancy was episodic, and the everyday life of students, their social habits and organizations, has generally been studied only at the local level; even then, it is easier to talk about student communal life and organizations than about what really dominated students' lives—the daily routine of lecture-hall, library, laboratory, and evening study.

This should not be a byway of history. Students formed the future elites of their countries, and their university experiences helped to shape national cultural and social values and created influential networks of personal contacts. Students embodied concepts of 'youth' and generational change, and their political activities were often nationally significant; even passive social and political attitudes formed by the student were likely to persist in the adult life of the citizen and the official. Student life became part of the rites of passage of the upper and middle classes, and was particularly important in the nineteenth century in shaping a new bourgeois identity.[2] It became 'an idyllic interlude of freedom and leisure, after escaping from parental authority and the oppressive discipline of the secondary school, and before the regimentation of adult, professional life'.[3] And before the orthodoxies of

[1] T. N. Bonner, *Becoming a physician: medical education in Britain, France, Germany and the United States, 1750–1945* (New York, 1995), 3.

[2] W. Kaschuba, 'German *Bürgerlichkeit* after 1800: culture as symbolic practice', in J. Kocka and A. Mitchell (eds.), *Bourgeois society in nineteenth-century Europe* (Oxford, 1993), 392–422.

[3] R. S. Turner, 'Universitäten', in K. E. Jeismann and P. Lundgreen (eds.), *Handbuch der deutschen Bildungsgeschichte. III. 1800–1870: Von der Neuordnung Deutschlands bis zur Gründung des Deutschen Reiches* (Munich, 1987), 242. For recent work in Germany see R. Müller, *Ideal und Leidenschaft: Sexuelle Sozialisation der akademischen Jugend im Biedermeier* (Berlin, 1999); S. Möller, *Zwischen Wissenschaft und 'Burschenherrlichkeit': Studentische Sozialisation im Deutschen Kaiserreich 1871–1914* (Stuttgart, 2001); M. Stickler, 'Neuerscheinungen zur Studentengeschichte seit 1994: Ein Forschungsbericht über

bourgeois marriage, for the student years were important in constituting masculine identity, and part of the resistance to the admission of women to universities arose because they threatened to destabilize a world where early sexual experiences were gained from unmarriable social inferiors.[4]

The attention of historians (or rather, in many cases, of antiquarians and pious alumni) has focused disproportionately on those forms of student life which attained institutional continuity—colleges at Oxford and Cambridge, *grandes écoles* in France, the corps and *Burschenschaft* movements in Germany. But the generational nature of student life meant that many organizations were short-lived, and the activists who ran them, the editors of newspapers, the heroes of the sports field, the debating hall, or the political demonstration, were by definition untypical of the mass. It is clear that there was no single 'European' pattern of student life.[5] Probably the most universal feature was the social consumption of alcohol. Beyond that, and leaving Russia aside, four broader patterns may be distinguished. First the German one, focused on small, closed organizations, with an intense social life, but rather hostile to co-operation with each other on a university basis. Second, there were other countries in northern Europe which also had strong corporate traditions, and absorbed some German ideas, but maintained a wide range of university-wide activities with open rather than selective membership. General student associations developed in some cases into national organizations. Third was the residential system, where the shaping and socializing force was institutional life itself, not specific student organizations; Oxford and Cambridge were obvious examples, but so were the *grandes écoles*. Private languages, initiation ceremonies, and the influence of former members in acting as pressure and mutual support groups were characteristic of this type. And finally in the 'Latin' countries—France for most students, Spain, Italy—specific student organizations were weak, and students shared in the wider life of the town, centred characteristically on cafés, theatres, and dance-halls. This pattern did not preclude a strong student consciousness, or political militancy. In fact, all four patterns of student life involved relations with the surrounding town or city, sometimes hostile, sometimes co-operative. The small university town, economically dependent on students and obliged to work with the university authorities as the guardians of discipline, was still very common; German students cherished a subculture which set them apart from the 'philistine' townsmen. In the big city, however, students might have their distinctive lodging and leisure quarters, but could also profit from the diversity and anonymity of city life.

The early history of the *Burschenschaft* and similar movements has already been touched on in Chapter 5. Until 1848 and after, that history can be seen mainly in political terms. In Metternichian Europe, the formation of student clubs and

ein bisweilen unterschätztes Arbeitsfeld der Universitätsgeschichte', *Jahrbuch für Universitätsgeschichte*, 4 (2001), 262–70.

4 K. Jarausch, 'Students, sex and politics in Imperial Germany', *Journal of Contemporary History*, 17 (1982), 285–303.

5 Cf. H. S. Jones, 'Student life and sociability 1860–1930: comparative reflections', *History of Universities*, 14 (1995–6), 225–46.

organizations and the expression of collective student views were banned, and the daily life of students was closely supervised by the police. To organize student activities was itself a political act, generally implying a liberal, radical, or nationalist programme. After 1848 there was fresh repression, and it was only when the political atmosphere began to relax in the 1860s that student organizations of a broader kind began to appear. In France the ban on any kind of student organization lasted until the Third Republic, and in Russia until 1905, forcing Russian students to rely on informal social networks and friendships, which could easily take a subversive turn. Elsewhere, engagement in politics now became just one option in a diverse and largely uncontroversial associational life. But whereas down to 1848 student politics were characteristically on the left, students being the vanguard of a middle class still excluded from power, by the end of the century they were more commonly on the right. Dissent from the norms of bourgeois society could now also be expressed through bohemian ways of life, aestheticism, or a search for moral and spiritual renewal rather than through conventional politics.

The expansion of student activities at the end of the nineteenth century also had social functions. Willem Otterspeer, the historian of Leiden University, has argued that the Dutch student community was homogeneous in the early nineteenth century, but came under strain from the 1870s as universities expanded and the student body became more diverse. A gap opened up between richer students who could afford to participate in corporate activities, and poorer ones who did not share their elitist assumptions. New forms of student life helped to assimilate the latter into university values, while the traditional corporate organizations became more conservative and socially exclusive. There was also political polarization as identification with national class politics replaced the liberal consensus.[6] These points are more widely applicable. In Britain, for example, student sport encouraged social bonding, as well as reflecting the wider range of activities which greater wealth, improved communications, and more relaxed social habits were now making possible for middle-class youth generally.

In Germany, governments began to liberalize their attitudes in the 1850s. Even during the days of the Karlsbad decrees, the corps had often been tolerated because of their conservative, monarchist views. Now the *Burschenschaften* also re-emerged, but without their previous political character, apart from pride in their past role as champions of national unity. The two types of organization (and in some places the old *Landsmannschaften*) grew side by side, as did many new sorts of association which followed the same model, creating a bewilderingly complex history.[7] By the end of the century there were Catholic associations, Jewish associations, and 'free'

[6] W. Otterspeer, *De wiekslag van hun geest: de Leidse Universiteit in de negentiende eeuw* (The Hague, 1992), 477 ff., 579 (English summary).

[7] See generally K. Jarausch, *Students, society and politics in Imperial Germany: the rise of academic illiberalism* (Princeton, 1982), 234–332. There is a huge antiquarian and celebratory literature on the subject: an informative modern example is P. Krause, *'O alte Burschenherrlichkeit': Die Studenten und ihr Brauchtum* (Graz, 1980). For a brief scholarly survey, see G. Gillot, 'Les corporations étudiantes: un archaïsme plein d'avenir (Allemagne-Autriche, 1880–1914)', *Le Mouvement Social*, 120 (1982), 45–75.

associations for those who did not want to claim any special allegiance. There were distinctions between colour-bearing associations with uniforms and flags, and non-colour-bearing ones, and within the former between duelling associations and those which disapproved of the practice. Universal customs were singing, often based on special student songbooks, and regular drinking bouts in a favourite tavern, also with their prescribed rituals. The initiation of new members, banquets, committee elections, summer outings, and concerts all made membership almost a full-time activity, and an expensive one, though it was recognized that commitment could be reduced when examinations loomed. Student associations were generally small, with fifteen to thirty members, crossing faculty boundaries. In a large university, there would usually be several dozen, and they did not always work closely together. This weakened any sense of loyalty to the individual university, and just as significant was affiliation to national associations such as the Kösener Senioren-Convents-Verband formed by the traditionalist corps in 1855.

One aristocrat recalling his student days at Bonn in the 1860s admitted that 'towards his profession the corps student learns little, as long as he remains active'; but 'it shapes the man, and he learns a host of things for later life which are not to be found in books, yet which are more important than any school knowledge'. Students of this kind spent a good deal of their time fraternizing with the officers of the local garrison, and a careful choice of regiment could allow them to combine their year of military service with university study.[8] The highly ritualized duel was at the centre of corps life, and some students adopted the military code of honour which led to challenges and genuine combat. Traditionalists claimed that duelling inculcated the values of self-respect, loyalty, and social solidarity, and duelling scars were a badge of honour. To foreign observers the custom seemed a bizarre one. Mark Twain, who used a stay at Heidelberg for his travel book *A tramp abroad* (1880), described rather queasily the real injuries inflicted in duels—finding more humour in another staple of the tourist circuit, the student prison. In 1900, in his *Three men on the bummel*, the English humorist Jerome K. Jerome had a much harsher judgement of the duel, and of student drinking customs.[9] With its picturesque situation and its position on the tourist route through the Rhineland, Heidelberg contributed heavily to the popular image of the German student. It was the setting for Wilhelm Meyer-Förster's novel *Karl Heinrich* (1899), turned first into a successful play, *Alt-Heidelberg*, in 1901, then filmed by D. W. Griffith in 1915, and further adapted as a stage and Hollywood musical as *The Student Prince*.

Where students lived in lodgings in an unfamiliar town, took lunch in cheap cafés, and lacked the comforts of the home or of the private clubs favoured by bourgeois male adults, student organizations met a universal need for friendship and socializing. In Germany they had particular value because of the habit of moving from one university to another between semesters—the corps or *Burschenschaft*

[8] Hugo Count Lerchenfeld-Koefering, cited in T. Ellwein, *Die deutsche Universität: Vom Mittelalter bis zur Gegenwart*, 2nd edn. (Frankfurt, 1992), 217.

[9] M. Twain, *A tramp abroad* (London, 1918), 14–28, 311–15; J. K. Jerome, *Three men in a boat and Three men on the bummel*, Everyman edn. (London, 1957), 330–42.

member could find congenial company wherever he went. They also had a special role in a country which lacked an elite sector of universities: exclusivism was cultivated instead within each university. Members of the traditional corps were usually wealthy, if not aristocratic, and all the organizations chose their members with care. Once admitted, membership was for life, and could play the same kind of networking role as public school and college in Britain, or the ex-pupils' associations of the French engineering and business schools. Memories of youthful comradeship and its physical setting could always arouse emotion. The old members, the *alte Herren*, were well placed to find jobs for their young successors. They often retained a close interest in the life of the association, attended reunions and ceremonies, read newsletters and histories, and helped to pay for the clubhouses which the wealthier associations were building for themselves by the end of the century. All this tended to reinforce social divisions, but even the more exclusive associations had a role in assimilating new wealth into old traditions—or, as critics would have it, in indoctrinating the bourgeoisie with feudal, reactionary, chauvinist values, as happens to the anti-hero of Heinrich Mann's novel *Man of straw* (*Der Untertan*, 1918).

The corps and *Burschenschaften* have tended to overshadow other sorts of student association, and themselves diversified at the end of the nineteenth century. Würzburg, for example, was important in the 1860s for the development of Catholic corporate organizations, which later had their own national federation, and many Jewish organizations also followed the traditional model, complete with beer-drinking rituals and duelling.[10] In German usage these were *Verbindungen*, corporations with closed membership, distinguished from *Vereine* open to all, which tended to come and go in line with student interests and fashions. Musical and gymnastic societies, and associations which maintained student reading-rooms or libraries, appeared at an early stage, and by the 1890s there was a 'pluralization' of student life, with clubs for students of philology, science, mathematics, and medicine as well as for women, foreign students, and those interested in religion, charitable work, or educational missions to the working class.[11] Student journalism was another entrée into adult life. German universities had no officially organized sport, but there was plenty of individual participation in riding, tennis, rowing, gymnastics, and walking. Traditional romantic enthusiasm for mountains and forests found new outlets in climbing and skiing, and German and Austrian students were important in the history of modern Alpinism.

Attempts were also made to found general students' associations to co-ordinate student life, and the university authorities encouraged this so that they could deal with a representative body. At Heidelberg, the non-corporate students formed a

[10] M. Stickler, 'Der Würzburger Bund von 1864: Ein Beitrag zur Frühgeschichte des politischen Katholizismus in Deutschland', in B. Grün and others, *Zwischen Korporation und Konfrontation: Beiträge zur Würzburger Universitäts- und Studentengeschichte* (Cologne, 1999), 239–59; K. H. Pickus, *Constructing modern identities: Jewish university students in Germany 1815–1914* (Detroit, 1999), 81–110.

[11] M. Stickler, 'Zwischen Anpassung und Aufbegehren: Studenten an der Universität Würzburg im 19. Jahrhundert', in Grün and others, *Zwischen Korporation und Konfrontation*, 76–140; M. Biastoch, *Tübinger Studenten im Kaiserreich: Eine sozialgeschichtliche Untersuchung* (Sigmaringen, 1996), 137–69, 268 ff.

Students' Council (*Ausschuss*) in 1881, and in 1885 the corporate bodies joined it; membership became compulsory, and it had a monopoly of official recognition.[12] But at Leipzig it was only in 1910 that a similar body was formed, encouraged by the historian Karl Lamprecht when rector.[13] At most universities general associations failed, and the fissile nature of German student organization also prevented the permanent establishment of any national representative body. The corps and *Burschenschaften* saw themselves as the real representatives of German studenthood, even if numerically they were outnumbered. Jarausch estimated that in 1911 almost exactly half of all university students belonged to an association of some kind, and of these 27,100, about 10,000 (37 per cent) were in the traditional duelling corps and 6,700 (25 per cent) in other colour-bearing associations. Religious, political, scholarly, or sporting associations attracted far fewer.[14]

The German corps and *Burschenschaft* organizations included Austrian members, though in Austria the associations did not appear until political liberalization in the 1860s, and remained controversial as they represented a German-national political stance. Their appearance with banners and uniforms at political demonstrations was often provocative, and rectors tried unsuccessfully to ban these displays of colours. But in Switzerland, the other area of direct German influence, the movement was weaker. Zurich was the main stronghold of the corps and duelling—adopted at the Polytechnic earlier than at the university itself—but elsewhere duelling was generally disapproved of.[15] In Switzerland the universities had closer links than in Germany with civic traditions and local urban elites, and students adopted a pattern of national political organization which had more in common with Scandinavia and Holland than with Germany, where student organizations often had strong political views, or 'apolitical' prejudices, but few direct links with parties or parliamentary life. In Switzerland, students had formed national associations at an early stage, the first being the Zofingerverein of 1819, followed by others of different political persuasions. These were a significant part of the movement to greater national unity, and as was often the case in small countries student associations were a training ground for the political elite.[16] But by the end of the century the advent of democratic politics, religious divisions (as in Holland), and the 'social question' posed by the rise of an industrial working class tended to split representative student organizations on the same lines as national parties.

[12] W. Doerr (ed.), *Semper apertus: Sechshundert Jahre Ruprecht-Karls-Universität Heidelberg 1386–1986 . . . II. Das neunzehnte Jahrhundert* (Berlin, 1985), 26.

[13] R. Chickering, *Karl Lamprecht: a German academic life (1856–1915)* (Atlantic Highlands, NJ, 1993), 377.

[14] Jarausch, *Students, society and politics*, 306–7. Cf. Gillot, 'Les corporations étudiantes', 73; N. Kampe, *Studenten und 'Judenfrage' im Deutschen Kaiserreich: Die Entstehung einer akademischen Trägerschicht des Antisemitismus* (Göttingen, 1988), table opp. p. 116.

[15] U. Im Hof, 'Die schweizerischen Varianten der kleindeutschen Universität: Zum Problem der ausländischen Einflüsse auf das schweizerische Hochschulwesens im 19. Jahrhundert', in *Festgabe Hans von Greyerz zum sechzigsten Geburtstag* (Bern, 1969), 621.

[16] O. Meuwly, *Histoire des sociétés d'étudiants à Lausanne* (Lausanne, 1987), 11.

The northern countries shared the German idea that students should have a distinct corporate identity, and at least some of the German enthusiasm for uniforms, banners, and insignia. The peaked cap, with a distinctively coloured band or top, became a mark of the student in northern and central Europe. But outside Germany organizations were generally open rather than socially selective, and there was a greater sense of common university interest. In Sweden, and at Swedish-influenced Helsinki, regionally based *Landsmannschaften* remained the centre of student life, and by the end of the century they had built impressive clubhouses at both Uppsala and Helsinki. Drinking, singing, and rural excursions were favourite diversions: the Uppsala student choir became famous, and performed internationally. Swedish students were also open to national political and social influences, particularly once industrialization disrupted what had been a rather conservative society. The student society 'Verdandi' was founded at Uppsala in 1882, by a student who later became a liberal prime minister, to discuss social questions and propagandize for reformist solutions, provoking in turn a Patriotic Students' Association in 1889 and the national Heimdal Society for conservative students in 1891, which had a real influence in politics. In 1902, advanced members of the Verdandi at Uppsala formed a social democrat students' organization, 'Laboremus'.[17] There were similar developments in Denmark: Copenhagen had a single Students' Union, which dated from 1820, but from 1882 there was a left-wing rival, which was active in social questions and attempts to reach out to the workers.[18]

Holland had a particularly active student life.[19] As the main universities were not in the largest cities, most students lived in lodgings, and conducted their social life in cafés. The historian Jan Huizinga recalled how at Groningen they strolled to lectures in their slippers and dressing-gowns.[20] There were some uniformed organizations in Holland, but most student associations were open and informal, and linked with a university-wide representative body. At Groningen a union of this kind appeared in 1815, and by the end of the century there was a large common building which was the centre of student activities.[21] Apart from the usual range of interests, Holland had two local specialities. One was rowing, where the university crews produced Olympic competitors; perhaps this is unsurprising in so watery a country, but the fact that the annual aquatic contest between the universities was called the Varsity suggests a direct English influence.[22] The second, dating from the 1820s, was the elaborate pageant or 'masquerade', usually depicting historical events with patriotic overtones. For these, authentic and expensive costumes were devised, on a different level from the fancy dress common at student processions and carnivals in other countries, and the masquerades were popular spectacles, fitting into a strong local tradition of civic pageantry.

[17] S. Lindroth, *A history of Uppsala University 1477–1977* (Stockholm, 1976), 230–3.

[18] S. E. Stybe, *Copenhagen University: 500 years of science and scholarship* (Copenhagen, 1979), 184–5.

[19] A. C. Vrankrijker, *Vier eeuwen nederlandsch studentenleven* (Voorburg, n.d. [*c.*1939]).

[20] J. Huizinga, *Verzamelde werken. VIII. Universiteit, wetenschap en kunst* (Haarlem, 1951), 188.

[21] J. Kingma and others, *Universitair leven in Groningen 1614–1989* (Groningen, 1989), 55–8.

[22] E. W. A. Henssen (ed.), *Het Corps als Koninkrijk: 150 jaar Delftsch Studenten Corps* (Hilversum, 1998), 60.

This may seem far from the inward-looking life of the older English universities, centred on the colleges, with few university-based organizations apart from the Unions, which continued to have close connections with politics and to train their members in parliamentary debate. But collegiate social and sporting life was itself a development of the reform period, designed to discipline students' lives and eliminate the contacts with the raffish side of urban life depicted in an early Oxford novel, *The adventures of Mr Verdant Green* (1853).[23] Outside Oxbridge, both the Scottish universities and the largely non-residential civic colleges in England and Wales developed student life on more Continental lines. In Scotland, the 1880s saw a vigorous development of corporate life, and Edinburgh founded the first Students' Representative Council (SRC) in 1884, apparently modelled on the student Ausschuss at Strasbourg. These bodies spread quickly to the other Scottish universities, and were officially recognized as the voice of student opinion and the umbrella organization for sporting and social associations of all kinds. English influence was reflected in the building of Unions, social and debating centres modelled on the gentleman's club; German influence in the *Scottish students' song book*, jointly produced by the SRCs, which first appeared in 1891 and went through many editions.[24] The new English universities created similar student associations or guilds, but one institution which remained unique to Scotland was the rectorship, a medieval survival rejuvenated in 1858. The rector was a figurehead elected by the students, who was usually a leading political or literary figure. His duties were formal, but the electoral campaigns became a focus both for party-political loyalties and for various forms of ritualized display and rowdyism. As elsewhere, the general purpose of the new corporate life was to initiate students from diverse backgrounds into the forms of bourgeois sociability.

Official efforts to encourage student organizations in France were less successful. For Liard, Lavisse, and the Third Republic reformers, a vigorous corporate life should be part of the revival of university identity. According to Liard, the German student associations fragmented the student body, but French ones would unite it under the slogan 'la science et la patrie'.[25] The last legal restrictions on freedom of organization were removed in 1883, and in 1884 a general Students' Association was founded at Paris with official sponsorship and subsidy. Models already existed at Lille and Nancy, and Toulouse followed suit in 1886. In 1888 Lavisse accompanied a delegation of French students to the jubilee celebrations at Bologna, which were used by Italian student activists to revive the picturesque corporate and 'goliardic' artistic life supposedly typical of the middle ages.[26] Students were invited from all over Europe, and the meeting helped to spread such ideas more widely, though the

[23] M. C. Curthoys and C. J. Day, 'The Oxford of Mr Verdant Green', in M. G. Brock and M. C. Curthoys (eds.), *The history of the University of Oxford. VI. Nineteenth-century Oxford, Part 1* (Oxford, 1997), 268–86.

[24] R. D. Anderson, *The student community at Aberdeen 1860–1939* (Aberdeen, 1988), 32–55.

[25] J. M. Burney, *Toulouse et son université: facultés et étudiants dans la France provinciale du 19e siècle* (Paris, 1988), 248.

[26] *Università di Bologna. Gaudeamus Igitur: studenti e goliardia 1888–1923* (Bologna, 1995).

French also made it an occasion for scoring off the German delegations.[27] The efforts of the French students' associations to become centres of social activity had limited success. Students were reluctant to abandon their traditional freedom, or their participation in the 'legendary Parisian nightlife'. By 1914 fewer than 12 per cent of Paris students had joined the official association, and it was a similar story at Toulouse.[28] Even though the French movement succeeded in establishing a National Union of Students (UNEF) in 1907, it remained marginal to most students' lives, still characteristically centred on the café. The associations suffered from their links with the official establishment, and necessarily stood aside from the passionate political conflicts which were a feature of the 1900s.

Down to 1848 student politics were almost by definition on the left, if liberal rather than radical, and as long as political repression lasted this continued to be the case. The first international congress of students was held at Liège in 1865, and showed both the revival of internationalism (the First Workers' International had been founded the year before) and the movement of student radicals towards socialism and anarchism. Liège was primarily a congress of 'free thought', which made strong positivist and materialist statements under the banner of 'progress through science and freedom'.[29] It was organized by the General Association of Belgian students, which started at Liège in 1860 and became national in 1861. Most of the 1,400 participants were Belgian, including some from Louvain who defied a ban by their university. Prussia also banned attendance, and there were only four Germans. But there were seventy-two French delegates, who used the opportunity to attack Napoleon III, provoking Duruy to expel the ringleaders when they went home. The conference proceedings were in fact hijacked by radicals and revolutionary socialists, including the Frenchman Paul Lafargue, Marx's future son-in-law. Once the main congress was over, the left-wingers moved on to Brussels for their own meeting, which proclaimed an alliance of students and workers. Further congresses (international in name, but in fact mainly Belgian) were held at Brussels in 1867 and Ghent in 1868. A weekly *Journal des Étudiants* was published at Liège in 1866–8, and a Fédération Internationale des Écoles was founded in 1870. There were relations with the First International, but the anarchism of Proudhon had more influence than marxism. When the Paris Commune broke out in 1871, these student activities seemed to justify the view of the French authorities that the rising was the result of an international conspiracy, and it led to wholesale repression, in France and elsewhere, of movements with a socialist tinge.[30]

When socialism revived, the notion of bourgeois students as leaders of the

[27] E. Lavisse, *Études et étudiants* (Paris, 1890), 290, 308.

[28] G. Weisz, 'Associations et manifestations: les étudiants français de la Belle Époque', *Le Mouvement Social*, 120 (1982), 34 (for quotation); Burney, *Toulouse et son université*, 251–74; J. M. Burney, 'Student organization in nineteenth-century France: the example of Toulouse', *History of Education Quarterly*, 25 (1985), 303–23.

[29] Press comment cited in L. E. Halkin, 'Documents et notes sur le Congrès International des Étudiants réuni à Liège en 1865', *Annales d'Histoire Liégoise*, 8 (1964–5), 153.

[30] See generally Halkin, 'Documents', and J. Bartier, 'Étudiants et mouvement révolutionnaire au temps de la Première Internationale: les Congrès de Liège, Bruxelles et Gand', in J. Bartier, *Libéralisme et socialisme au XIXe siècle: études rassemblées et publiées par Guy Cambier* (Brussels, 1981), 177–206.

revolutionary workers did not revive with it. While radical republicanism and anti-clericalism were now more clearly bourgeois, the socialist emphasis was on trade unions and on political parties bidding for the working-class vote, and working-class leaders were generally suspicious of middle-class intellectuals. This was especially true of the German Social Democrats, who made little effort to build up a university following. Young idealists did not find it easy to establish personal contact with the proletariat. The student socialists of the 1880s were less attracted by class politics than by the moderate, reformist socialism represented by the Fabian Society in Britain, or by the romantic individualism of anarchism, which made a special appeal to literary men and artists. But in western Europe students were not prominent in the more violent forms of anarchism, Russian populism having little appeal outside the Slav world.

In France, there was no single socialist party until 1905. The first socialist student organization, the Étudiants Socialistes Révolutionnaires Internationalistes, was founded in 1891 by the orthodox ('guesdist') marxist party, and there was a national congress of student socialists in 1893. There were similar developments in Belgium.[31] Following the foundation of the Second International in 1889, marxism also inspired a series of international student congresses—at Brussels in 1891, Geneva in 1893, and Paris in 1900.[32] Tensions soon arose between different groups (or factional *groupuscules*), and between them and the political leaders who wanted student activity to be subordinate to party interests.[33] From the turn of the century, however, stimulated by the Dreyfus Affair and the threat of nationalism and anti-Semitism, student socialism was a constant and lively presence in Paris. It also received some encouragement from left-wing academics, and the librarian of the École Normale, Lucien Herr, was reputed to have a particular influence in spreading socialism there at the time of the Dreyfus Affair.[34]

Despite these socialist activities, the internationalism characteristic of 1848 was no longer a marked feature of student movements. Nationalists, logically enough, did not go in for international fraternity, and they came to form the strongest, or at least the noisiest, political tendency in both France and Germany. In Germany the rise of 'academic illiberalism' among students has been traced in the broader context of university life in an authoritative book by Konrad Jarausch, who concludes that despite some countervailing tendencies, the 'cumulative effect' by the 1900s of the 'gradual politicization of German universities was the transformation of instinctive patriotism into self-conscious modern nationalism. Although the degree of involvement and particular accent differed widely among individuals, the student majority was unquestionably monarchist, anti-Semitic, anti-Socialist, and

[31] W. Van Rooy, 'L'agitation étudiante et la fondation de l'Université Nouvelle en 1894', *Revue Belge d'Histoire Contemporaine*, 7 (1976), 209–10.

[32] Y. Cohen, 'Avoir vingt ans en 1900: à la recherche d'un nouveau socialisme', *Le Mouvement Social*, 120 (1982), 11–29.

[33] C. Prochasson, 'Histoire intellectuelle/histoire des intellectuels: le socialisme français au début du XXe siècle', *Revue d'Histoire Moderne et Contemporaine*, 39 (1992), 432.

[34] R. J. Smith, *The École Normale Supérieure and the Third Republic* (Albany, NY, 1982), 87–97; C. Charle, *Paris fin de siècle: culture et politique* (Paris, 1998), 227–74.

imperialist.'[35] The students shared the rightward evolution of the professors, but whereas the latter were restrained by residual liberalism, their sense of professional responsibility as teachers of youth and public servants, and the ideal of objective scholarship, students had fewer such inhibitions, and corps and *Burschenschaften* were particularly ready to embrace anti-Semitism and *völkisch* nationalism, confining membership to those of 'Aryan' stock.[36] As with the professors, the reasons lay partly in the general political evolution of Germany after 1871, and partly in factors specific to the universities such as the 'enrolment explosion' (Jarausch), the threat which an intellectual proletariat posed to career opportunities, competition from women students, and xenophobia towards foreign ones, especially Russians.[37] The pervasiveness of extreme nationalism and anti-Semitism among students before 1914 unquestionably paved the way for the acceptance of Nazism by much of the bourgeois elite, though as with Ringer's mandarin thesis one should not read the post-war conditions of national humiliation and economic crisis back into the pre-war years.[38] Recent scholarship has tended to emphasize the optimism, modernism, and diversity of Wilhelmine society. The willingness of Jewish students to form their own student societies, for example, can be seen as a sign of growing confidence in their distinctive identity rather than a response to anti-Semitic threats, and those who argued that 'we can be Jews and good Germans at the same time' (as a student fraternity at Breslau put it in 1886) continued to predominate even when Zionist student organizations spread after 1900.[39] Still, as the history of socialism also showed, Germany before 1914 was a compartmented or imperfectly integrated society rather than a truly pluralist one, and nationalists occupied the largest and most powerful compartments.

In France, where the orientation of forces favoured the left, student nationalism was part of the attack on the 'new Sorbonne', directed against the liberal establishment in university and state. The 'Agathon' authors went on from that attack to publish *Les Jeunes Gens d'aujourd'hui* (1912), a portrait of the new generation based on a (highly selective) survey of student opinion which claimed that the younger generation had been captured for nationalism and longed secretly for war.[40] This mood was exploited by the Action française, whose 'programme of intellectual reconquest' especially targeted students.[41] Maurras's movement combined

[35] Jarausch, *Students, society and politics*, 388. For a critique see G. Eley, 'Educating the bourgeoisie: students and the culture of "illiberalism" in Imperial Germany', *History of Education Quarterly*, 26 (1986), 287–300.

[36] G. L. Mosse, *The crisis of German ideology: intellectual origins of the Third Reich* (New York, 1964), 190–203; P. G. J. Pulzer, *The rise of political anti-semitism in Germany and Austria* (New York, 1964), 251–6.

[37] C. Weill, 'La "question des étrangers": les étudiants russes en Allemagne 1900–1914', *Le Mouvement Social*, 120 (1982), 79–80.

[38] Kampe, *Studenten und 'Judenfrage'*, 205–12.

[39] Pickus, *Constructing modern identities*, 13, 81–3, 95 (for quotation); J. Borut, 'Jewish politics and generational change in Wilhelmine Germany', in M. Roseman (ed.), *Generations in conflict: youth revolt and generation formation in Germany 1770–1968* (Cambridge, 1995), 105–20.

[40] R. Wohl, *The generation of 1914* (Cambridge, Mass., 1979), 5–9, 16; P. Bénéton, 'La génération de 1912–1914: image, mythe et réalité?', *Revue Française de Science Politique*, 21 (1971), 981–1009.

[41] C. F. Bompaire-Evesque, *Un Débat sur l'Université au temps de la Troisième République: la lutte contre la Nouvelle Sorbonne* (Paris, 1988), 38.

intellectual rigour with a taste for violence, and it specialized in attacks, verbal and physical, on professors of whom it disapproved. The most famous case was that in 1908 of Amédée Thalamas, a lycée professor whose lectures in the Sorbonne were judged to have insulted the nationalist icon Joan of Arc. In Germany political views were expressed in violent words and parades of strength, but less commonly in riots or strikes. In France, violence in the streets and disruption of classes had long been a customary aspect of student discontent, and much of it had little to do with politics. There was a long series of protests in the Paris medical faculty in the 1900s, resulting in regular suspension of lectures by the authorities, and although students in medicine as in law tended to be conservative, the ostensible motives were not political but grievances over the organization of examinations, the unpopularity of certain professors, and difficult access to hospital wards. Deeper reasons were overcrowding of the lecture-halls and the medical profession, resentment at the increased competition caused by the baccalaureate reforms of 1902, and hostility to foreign students.[42] European universities generally were experiencing a period when enrolments were rising fast without a corresponding expansion in the posts to which a university education led. The serious student riots in Italy in the 1890s and 1900s had similar causes, and in the 1900s the futurist movement, which combined aesthetic revolt, nationalism, and a cult of violence, stirred up student discontents in much the same way as Maurras.

There were also more idealistic roots of discontent, and a generational factor which separated students from professors. It has been said that the attack on the new Sorbonne resonated with 'the generous aspirations of a generation which was turning away from dehumanized erudition and seeking in the classical humanities a source of elevated sentiments and noble ideas', which included patriotism.[43] This was expressed on the left as well as the right, and in a turning to Catholicism as well as nationalism. Students were prominent in the democratic Catholic movement Sillon, founded by Marc Sangnier in the 1890s but condemned by the pope in 1910. The complex spirit of the younger generation was also expressed by the *normalien* poet and pamphleteer Charles Péguy, who started as a supporter of Dreyfus before turning to a mystical blend of Catholicism and patriotism, then becoming an early casualty of the trenches. In his *Notre jeunesse* (1910) he launched his own attack on the socialists of the École Normale for having (in a celebrated formula) turned the idealist *mystique* of the Dreyfusard cause into a self-interested *politique*.[44]

Historians customarily speak of a 'generation of 1914', meaning those whose lives were shaped by the experience of the war, but the experiences and values of the pre-war generation of upper- and middle-class youth also help to explain the 'spirit of 1914' and many aspects of post-war politics. The heightened international tension of these years, and the rhetoric of national missions and destinies characteristic of

[42] G. Weisz, 'Reform and conflict in French medical education 1870–1914', in R. Fox and G. Weisz (eds.), *The organization of science and technology in France 1808–1914* (Cambridge, 1980), 84–9; A. Tuilier, *Histoire de l'Université de Paris et de la Sorbonne. II. De Louis XIV à la crise de 1968* (Paris, 1994), 459–64.

[43] Bompaire-Evesque, *Un Débat sur l'Université*, 230, and cf. 115.

[44] C. Péguy, *Notre jeunesse* (Paris, 1933), 43–7.

the age, inevitably shaped those who thought of themselves as future leaders. It was patriotic idealism, rather than nationalist extremism, which made so many of them welcome the war as an exalted experience and sustained the spirit of sacrifice thereafter. In Germany, the spirit of 1914 was perhaps at its most intense in the universities, among professors as well as students. Meinecke later recalled 1914 as 'one of the great moments of my life which suddenly filled my soul with the deepest confidence in our people and the profoundest joy'.[45] But this was hardly less the case in Britain. Pre-war Cambridge 'had been converted to the religion of nationalism', said the Bloomsbury writer Quentin Bell.[46] The values of the public schools and the universities, reinforced by the voluntary Officers' Training Corps to which so many students belonged, fed straight into the trenches.

The complex of cultural and intellectual changes often defined as a 'revolt against reason' had its roots in social Darwinism, the influence of Nietzsche, disillusion with the liberal vision of progress, and romantic impatience with the material comforts of a philistine, bourgeois civilization. This spirit made a special appeal to youth, for whom the university establishment was a natural target. Scandinavian students were enthused by the Danish Nietzschean Georg Brandes, who was refused a chair at Copenhagen, and whose *Aristocratic radicalism* (1889) preached the vocation of the intellectual 'to lead society out of the morass of mediocrity and complacency into which it [had] sunk'.[47] For 'Agathon', it was the role of intellectuals to 'orient the civic spirit'.[48] Alienation, a yearning for spiritual renewal, and a sense of the duties of leadership were combined. Since students were mostly members of the bourgeoisie, middle-class versions of this combination such as nationalism and cultural elitism had the greatest appeal. But the tensions within universities also reflected the rise of class conflicts in the world outside, and a feeling that universities needed to respond creatively to the needs of democracy.

[45] Cited in J. B. Joll, *Intellectuals in politics: three biographical essays* (London, 1960), 90.

[46] Cited (1974) in R. N. Stromberg, *Redemption by war: the intellectuals and 1914* (Lawrence, Kan., 1982), 32.

[47] N. Kent, *The soul of the north: a social, architectural and cultural history of the Nordic countries 1700–1940* (London, 2000), 61.

[48] Wohl, *Generation of 1914*, 40.

19
Mission to the People?

In 1900 Émile Durkheim addressed an international congress on 'the role of universities in the social education of the country'. The universities should emerge from isolation and expand their sphere of influence by helping to form citizens. 'Higher education is hardly an unnecessary luxury for democracies. It is precisely democratic societies which, in reality, have the greatest need for a higher scientific culture.' Being 'recruited from all classes', universities 'are sufficiently above class conflicts to enable them to gain the confidence of the working population'. He concluded that

> however essential the scientific and scholarly work of universities, they must never lose sight of the fact that they are also, and above all, educational institutions. They have therefore to play a role in the moral life of the country and they must not try to avoid it. Just as the universities of Germany contributed to the formation of German unity, the universities of France must strive to form French moral beliefs.... This is also the best way to demonstrate clearly their utility to the mass of the population. For if the ordinary people have constant dealings with universities, they will not even dream of asking themselves what purpose they serve and whether they are not a sort of luxury with which, if necessary, it is possible to dispense.[1]

In 1899 Ernest Lavisse had republished a set of lectures given by Michelet in 1847–8, calling on students to reach out to the people. It was, said Lavisse, Michelet's message to the 'intellectuals of his time', and he returned to the theme when opening the new premises of the Paris Students' Association in the same year: Michelet had seen students as the mediators between two nations—the small one of the intellectuals, and the great one formed by the mass of the people; it was they who would perfect the unity of France.[2] The congress addressed by Durkheim was organized by the 'solidarist' tendency in Republican politics, which argued that economic individualism needed to give way to social reform if the workers were not to be driven into the arms of socialism, and the idea that education created social solidarity was at the centre of Durkheim's pedagogic thought. The issue was given a special edge in France by the Dreyfus Affair and the need to rally popular opinion to the Republic, but similar ideas were to be found in all countries. Belgian observers had said of the English extension movement in 1895 that its purpose was 'to defend the ancient conservative universities against the prejudices of democracy.... To that

[1] 'Émile Durkheim on the French universities', *Minerva*, 14 (1976), 380, 387–8.

[2] J. Michelet, *L'Étudiant* (Paris, 1899), 12; Y. Cohen, 'Avoir vingt ans en 1900: à la recherche d'un nouveau socialisme', *Le Mouvement Social*, 120 (1982), 11.

end, it was necessary to make them known to the masses, to go to the people, to show them the life of the members of the universities, and to make them participate in that life by interesting them in science.'[3] Even the Workers' Educational Association was closer to the 'new liberalism' of the 1900s than to socialism, and there were rival organizations supported by the trade-union movement which claimed to serve working-class interests more directly.[4]

In Germany these issues was taken up by members of the Verein für Sozialpolitik. In 1897, Lujo Brentano called in a lecture to students for a regeneration of liberalism so that it would again attract the masses and inspire the idealism of youth.[5] In the 1900s the Verein debated at length the relations between intellect (*Geist*) and the masses, coming to the characteristically cautious and elitist conclusion that intellectuals should act as a 'spiritual aristocracy', giving independent cultural leadership rather than working through the state.[6] But even some marxist socialists adopted Durkheim's argument that universities could act as a focus of social conciliation because their members stood above class. In Austria Max Adler, himself a former student activist at Vienna University, argued in his *Socialism and the intellectuals* (1910) that students should be part of a progressive coalition of intellectuals working for the popular cause and combating the anti-Semitic and nationalist right.[7]

It was perhaps in Italy that the relationship between socialists and university intellectuals was closest, not surprisingly when in 1904 twenty-two of the twenty-eight socialist deputies were university graduates, and nine were university teachers (in France in 1910 there were eight professors among seventy-six deputies). Michels, with some exaggeration, described the Italian socialist party as the 'party of university teachers'.[8] One who was certainly prominent was Antonio Labriola, a professor of philosophy who was converted to marxism (and retained his chair—something unthinkable in Germany). In 1896 there was a scandal when he opened the session at Rome University with a speech on 'the university and the liberty of science', in the presence of the minister of education and in the context of recent political disputes; the minister was hissed by the students, and Labriola was reprimanded. In this speech, Labriola conceded that universities would never be the cultural instruments of the peasants, artisans, or proletariat. But they should be as accessible, communicative, and democratic as possible. The English had used university extension to adapt their old-fashioned universities to more modern cultural ends. In Italy,

[3] A. Hirsch and M. Huisman, *L'Extension universitaire belge: ce qu'elle devrait être, ce qu'elle est* (Brussels, 1895), 3.

[4] B. Simon, *Education and the labour movement 1870–1920* (London, 1965), 296–342.

[5] J. J. Sheehan, *The career of Lujo Brentano: a study of liberalism and social reform in Imperial Germany* (Chicago, 1966), 138.

[6] R. vom Bruch, *Wissenschaft, Politik und öffentliche Meinung: Gelehrtenpolitik im Wilhelminischen Deutschland (1890–1914)* (Husum, 1980), 278–93.

[7] L. Olausson, 'Socialism and intellectuals in fin-de-siècle Vienna: Max Adler on the relationship between socialism and intellectuals', in R. Eyerman and others, *Intellectuals, universities and the state in western modern societies* (Berkeley, 1987), 205–6.

[8] M. Clark, *Modern Italy 1871–1982* (London, 1984), 143–4; R. Michels, *Political parties: a sociological study of the oligarchical tendencies of modern democracy* (New York, 1959), 257.

this should be an 'organic condition' of university life, and professors should use their freedom to spread knowledge and make it an everyday thing rather than a mystery for privileged initiates.[9] In their belief in science and university autonomy, Labriola and the intellectual journal of Italian socialism, *Critica Sociale*, were in many respects simply continuing the standard radical critique of centralization, and owed more to old-fashioned positivism than to marxism, though with the proviso that scientific autonomy would be fruitless if it remained in the hands of the old university hierarchy.[10]

The aim of such intellectuals was to 'link higher education with the social life of the country as a function of its democratic growth'.[11] But how was the university to carry out this wider social mission? To open university study more widely to the working class encountered the barrier of privileged secondary education. But there was another way of reaching the workers: English university extension, which *Critica Sociale* saw as a 'university of labour', recruiting the intelligentsia for the task of guiding the masses.[12] In Italy as in some other countries, extension classes were called 'popular universities'. The movement appeared in the university cities in 1900–1, then spread to smaller towns with the blessing of university and political authorities. A national congress was held at Florence in 1904, leading to the first international congress on 'popular education' at Milan in 1906 (there was to be a second at Paris in 1908, a third at Brussels in 1910). But by then popular universities were already in decline.[13] This chronology was common to Italy, Spain, and France, as were the general features of the movement: lectures on a wide variety of literary, scientific, historical, or cultural subjects, given sometimes by professors and junior university staff, but also by schoolteachers, professional men, writers, and assorted local intellectuals and experts. The work also attracted idealistic students, and could be an outlet for socialist impulses.

In France, the Société des Universités Populaires founded in 1899 was part of a range of solidarist initiatives aimed at the workers, which formed 'a kind of laboratory for experiments in class collaboration'.[14] Leading figures included university professors such as Charles Gide (economics) and Gabriel Séailles (philosophy), as well as Lavisse and other spokesmen for governmental republicanism. By 1901 there were 124 *universités populaires* throughout France, with 50,000 members.[15] Most local courses had no direct connection with universities, though university

[9] A. Labriola, *Scritti pedagogici* (Turin, 1981), 596–7.

[10] G. Genovesi, '"Critica Sociale" e questione universitaria', in T. Tomasi and others, *Scuola e società nel socialismo riformista (1891–1926)* (Florence, 1982), 154 ff.; T. Tomasi and L. Bellatalla, *L'università italiana nell'età liberale (1861–1923)* (Naples, 1988), 50–2.

[11] L. Berlinguer, 'L'autonomia universitaria tra legge Casati e riforma Gentile: prime considerazioni', in M. Ascheri (ed.), *Scritti di storia del diritto offerti dagli allievi a Domenico Maffei* (Padua, 1991), 567–8.

[12] Genovesi, '"Critica Sociale" e questione universitaria', 165–6.

[13] M. G. Rosada, *Le università popolari in Italia 1900–1918* (Rome, 1975), *passim*.

[14] S. Elwitt, 'Education and the social questions: the *universités populaires* in late nineteenth century France', *History of Education Quarterly*, 22 (1982), 57.

[15] L. Mercier, *Les Universités populaires 1899–1914: éducation populaire et mouvement ouvrier au début du siècle* (Paris, 1986), 47, and *passim* for this section; G. Weisz, *The emergence of modern universities in France 1863–1914* (Princeton, 1983), 310–14; F. Mayeur, *De la Révolution à l'école républicaine*, Histoire générale de l'enseignement et de l'éducation en France, ed. L. H. Parias, vol. 3 (Paris, 1981), 272–81.

professors led the movement at Rennes and Montpellier,[16] and students were often involved. A notable example was the Fondation Universitaire de Belleville in Paris, which was officially supported by the University of Paris and combined educational activities with another import from Britain, the residential university 'settlement' planted in a slum area and staffed by students or young graduates. (The most famous of these was Toynbee Hall, in the east end of London, founded in 1884 and connected with Balliol College.) The Paris settlement was short-lived, but the foundation itself lasted from 1899 to 1909. Another Parisian example was the Union Mouffetard, which was supported by students at the neighbouring École Normale, and attracted a galaxy of university talent. But this collapsed in 1906: enthusiasm was at its height in the early years, while the Dreyfus crisis was still alive, and then fell off fairly rapidly. After the early period, the courses attracted rather more socialist support, though they were denounced by marxists as instruments of bourgeois ideology, and suffered from the rivalry of the worker-run *bourses du travail*, which combined adult education, recreation, and political agitation. Other problems included Catholic competition, failure to address the problem of communicating elite culture to the masses, and the absence of the tutorials and essays used by the British WEA to give continuity to the lectures. By 1914 only about twenty *universités populaires* were left, but while they lasted, they did provide a genuine forum for the meeting of workers and middle-class intellectuals, and they had made university intellectuals 'reflect on their real social function and the injustices of the educational system', with consequences for the future.[17]

In Spain this movement was yet another activity of the circles connected with the Institución Libre de Enseñanza and the Madrid Ateneo. The British extension and settlement movements were discussed at a pedagogic congress at Madrid in 1892, and courses started at Zaragoza, Barcelona, and elsewhere in the 1890s. They were more directly connected with the universities than in France, being seized on by academics who despaired of other means of 'regenerating' Spain's sclerotic universities, and the term 'university extension' was adopted from English. The most successful courses were at Oviedo, the smallest Spanish university, but situated in the mining area of Asturias, and home of the 'Oviedo group' of intellectuals led by the writer and university professor Clarín (Leopoldo Alas). The movement was at its height around 1902–3, but then declined, partly because the working class developed its own schemes.[18]

Extension-type activities, including settlements and other attempts to reach out to the working class, were common in Scandinavia, Belgium, and Holland. In Belgium, the New University of Brussels which started in 1894 had strong socialist links—one of the reasons for its breakaway from the Free University was the latter's withdrawal of a lecture invitation to the French geographer and anarchist Élisée

[16] C. H. Johnson, *The life and death of industrial Languedoc 1700–1920* (New York, 1995), 248–50; Mercier, *Les Universités populaires*, 33–4.

[17] C. Charle, *Les Intellectuels en Europe au XIXe siècle: essai d'histoire comparée* (Paris, 1996), 264–5.

[18] J. L. Guereña, 'Les institutions du culturel: politiques éducatives', in C. Serrano and S. Salaün (eds.), *1900 en Espagne (essai d'histoire culturelle)* (Bordeaux, 1988), 63–5; Y. Turin, *L'Éducation et l'école en Espagne de 1874 à 1902: libéralisme et tradition* (Paris, 1959), 281–9.

Reclus.[19] In Russia, 'people's universities' inevitably multiplied after the 1905 revolution.[20] But in many cases extension movements followed the early British model in aiming at middle-class audiences, without radical aspirations. In Germany, where Scandinavian precedents were as influential as British ones, numerous political and religious bodies were already engaged in adult education. The students at the Berlin Technical High School ran courses for workers, but the proletarian nature of the German SPD, and its own extensive educational efforts, limited the scope for popular universities.[21] It was much the same in Austria, where Vienna University's extensive scheme started in 1894, followed by the other universities. Graz began in 1898, and reached thirty-eight towns, including Trieste, where James Joyce was one of the lecturers.[22] At Cracow, a similar scheme starting in 1901 reached most of the towns of western Galicia.[23] All these efforts had full official approval—on condition, of course, that they avoided controversial questions, which in Austria included national ones.

'The peasants, the workers, the economic and intellectual proletariat . . . do not have the time or means to gain access to higher education, however free or eclectic it may resolve to become', wrote the socialist leader Filippo Turati in *Critica Sociale* in 1898. Therefore reforming it was an unnecessary diversion of energy, especially in a country still grappling with mass illiteracy.[24] Until secondary education became more democratic, it was impossible for European universities to open themselves to the masses. University extension was both an attempt to palliate this situation, and a way of avoiding a more radical democratization which would change the nature of university education and challenge the privileges of high culture. But it was none the less one of many signs that universities before 1914 were far from being ivory towers set apart from the social currents of the age.

[19] E. H. Kossmann, *The Low Countries 1780–1940* (Oxford, 1978), 321–2.

[20] D. Wartenweiler, *Civil society and academic debate in Russia 1905–1914* (Oxford, 1999), 166–89.

[21] Bruch, *Wissenschaft, Politik und öffentliche Meinung*, 262–4.

[22] W. Höflechner, *Die Baumeister des künftigen Glücks: Fragment einer Geschichte des Hochschulwesens in Österreich vom Ausgang des 19. Jahrhunderts bis in das Jahr 1938* (Graz, 1988), 82–3.

[23] E. Sapia-Drewniak, 'La participation des professeurs de l'Université Jagellonne aux travaux de l'instruction publique à la fin du XIXe et au début du XXe siècle', in *L'Université et l'enseignement extra-universitaire XVIe–XIXe siècles. IIe Session Scientifique Internationale Cracovie, 11–12 mai 1979* (Cracow, 1983), 177–82.

[24] Genovesi, '"Critica Sociale" e questione universitaria', 145–6.

20

Conclusion: European Universities in 1914

Introducing the translation of Paulsen's book on German universities in 1906, the English educationist Michael Sadler said that 'international relationships in university study are closer to-day than at any previous time since the beginning of the sixteenth century'.[1] There were indeed more international conferences and scientific associations, and more exchanges of students and professors, which were now extending across the Atlantic as Europeans became aware of the vigour of American university life.[2] Innovations like the Nobel prizes testified to a new internationalism in science, though like the revived Olympic games of the same era they encouraged national competition as much as harmony. Röntgen was the first winner of the Nobel physics prize, but when his discovery of X-rays was announced in 1896, the Kaiser had telegraphed to him, 'I thank God who has reserved for our German fatherland this new triumph of science.'[3] French attempts to reply in kind led to an embarrassing fiasco when the discovery of 'N-rays' at the University of Nancy in 1903 proved bogus.[4] Franco-German intellectual rivalries seemed to run in parallel with the rise of extreme nationalism and chauvinism among students, and to foreshadow the conflict of 1914.

Few institutions were as directly affected by the war as universities, as most male students were recalled to their units or volunteered for service. Norman Davies has evoked 'the scenes at the Jagiellonian University [of Cracow] at the end of the summer term in July 1914, when many of the students, who were reserve officers in the Russian, German, or Austrian Army, took their leave of each other under the shadow of impending war'.[5] Universities in the war zones, in Belgium or Poland, closed down, and when the conflagration was over many found themselves in new countries. Casualties were severe among both professors and students. In Britain, where up to 20 per cent of those who served were killed, they gave rise to the myth of a 'lost generation'. In France, it has been estimated that 260 university professors were killed, out of a total of less than a thousand; at the École Normale,

[1] F. Paulsen, *The German universities and university study* (London, 1906), p. vii.

[2] C. Charle, *La République des universitaires 1870–1940* (Paris, 1994), 343–96.

[3] P. Schiera, 'Scienza e politica in Germania da Bismarck a Guglielmo II', in G. Corni and P. Schiera (eds.), *Cultura politica e società borghese in Germania fra otto e novecento* (Bologna, 1986), 34.

[4] M. Hanna, *The mobilization of intellect: French scholars and writers during the Great War* (Cambridge, Mass., 1996), 204.

[5] N. Davies, *Heart of Europe: a short history of Poland* (Oxford, 1986), 264.

28 per cent of those who served died, including 107 of the 211 current students in 1914.[6]

The prestige of the German universities was another casualty. The outbreak of war was a profound shock for British and French academics who had admired Germany as the homeland of science and scholarship, and painful mental adjustments were needed.[7] The willingness of German academics to justify their country's policies as a defence of 'culture', notably in the manifesto of ninety-three professors issued in October 1914, began a propaganda war into which French and British professors threw themselves with equal zeal, exploiting events such as the burning of the Louvain University library in the course of German reprisals against civilians. The French pacifist Romain Rolland denounced this surrender to nationalism in September 1914, but few were listening then; after the war, revulsion against the partisanship of intellectuals was to be expressed in Julien Benda's thoughts on the 'treason of the clerks', and in the search of sociologists like Karl Mannheim (following Alfred Weber) for a new independent basis for 'free-floating' intellectuals.[8] French-led boycotts of the German universities in the 1920s, and the disappearance of the Russian ones into the new Soviet state, meant that the unity of European universities around a set of common academic values was not restored.

It was easy to cultivate nostalgia for a golden age of university leisure and privilege, and to see the ideal of disinterested scholarship as an aspect of the liberal civilization which had been irrevocably destroyed. But on the eve of 1914 universities were not untroubled havens of the elite, or remote from the concerns of the age. Students in France, Italy, Austria, and Russia were likely to have their studies disrupted by violent demonstrations and university closures, and the expansion of enrolments was causing social tensions, actual and potential. In Spain and Italy, numbers were not expanding in the 1900s, but in other countries they seemed to be on an upward curve. This included the enrolment of women, and during the war women were often able to move into the places vacated by men, paving the way for further advances after it. Changes in secondary education were increasing the presence of lower-middle-class students, and even of working-class ones. Despite the real increase in enrolments by two or three times since the 1870s, university education in 1914 was still overwhelmingly associated with a limited social elite, but if peace had lasted it is likely that pressures for greater democratization, including some lowering of the barriers between mass and elite education, would have continued.

The German classical scholar Ludwig Curtius, recalling the days before 1914 (and 1933), thought few professional lives more satisfying than that of the German professor, 'alternating between the contemplative pleasure of his individual research and his active collaborative work with young people, between the often hectic

[6] P. Ory and J. F. Sirinelli, *Les Intellectuels en France, de l'Affaire Dreyfus à nos jours* (Paris, 1986), 62–3.

[7] S. Wallace, *War and the image of Germany: British academics 1914–1918* (Edinburgh, 1988), 1–42; Hanna, *Mobilization of intellect, passim.*

[8] Ibid. 98; R. Eyerman and others, *Intellectuals, universities and the state in western modern societies* (Berkeley, 1987), 2.

bustle of the semester and the reflectiveness of the long holidays'.[9] For many, the Humboldtian ideal seemed intact, even if the battle against specialization had been lost and disciplinary research was now the centre of the university teacher's activity. For most scholars and scientists, research remained an individual task, driven by their own choice of subject and sustained by their sense of professional duty and responsibility. If original research had become the distinctive function of universities in official rhetoric and in academic aspirations, it was still closely coupled with the teaching and professional training which had historically always been their dominant function and the reason why they were supported by the state. This balance was now threatened by 'big science', as was most clearly demonstrated in Germany, though the result might be the growth of research outside the university framework, as with the Kaiser-Wilhelm-Gesellschaft, rather than a change in the universities' internal priorities.

By the 1900s governments recognized, even in Britain, that state support for science and technology was an essential element in military and industrial power, but they were happy to share the cost with industrial interests or with individual 'Maecenas' figures. Plurality of funding could increase academic freedom, but could also mean serving the needs and the whims of the donors. Some, like Andrew Carnegie in Scotland, did not try to control the detailed use of their gifts. A rather different attitude was taken by Ernest Solvay, who had made a fortune as a chemical manufacturer and joined the council of the Free University at Brussels in the 1890s. With his brother Alfred, he financed a series of new institutes, some connected with the Free University, others remaining under Solvay's personal control. They included an Institute of Sociology, which concentrated on empirical social studies inspired by Solvay's own views rather than the theoretical approaches of Weber or Durkheim. In 1903–4 Solvay financed the creation of a School of Commerce. He took a leaf out of Althoff's book by situating most of his foundations on a campus in the Brussels suburbs, the Parc Léopold, conceived as a 'scientific city'.[10] Solvay was also a generous patron of science and medicine, founding an Institute of Physiology, and organizing international scientific encounters. The first of these in 1911, attended by Einstein, Max Planck, Ernest Rutherford, Marie Curie, and others, was an important landmark in the history of theoretical physics, and was followed by the creation of Solvay Institutes of Physics and Chemistry in 1912 and 1913 respectively.

Solvay's creations illustrate both the internationalism of this period, and the growing differentiation of higher education. Business schools and social science often accompanied each other, as in such initiatives as the London School of Economics, the Bocconi University at Milan, or the new University of Frankfurt. They was beginning to form a private or semi-private third sector, alongside the existing second sector of Technical High Schools in Germany and elsewhere, which were mainly state-financed. The contribution of these sectors to economic development continues to be debated. From one point of view, they were a symptom that the

[9] L. Curtius, *Deutsche und antike Welt: Lebenserinnerungen* (Stuttgart, 1952), 321.

[10] A. Despy-Mayer and D. Devriese (eds.), *Ernest Solvay et son temps* (Brussels, 1997), *passim*.

classic university was failing to adapt to new needs; from another, they showed that higher education as a whole was developing in a flexible, pragmatic, and diversified way, and one can argue, as Sanderson does for Britain, that such limited needs as industry or commerce felt in this period for higher training and research were being quite adequately met.

The prime responsibility for universities in Europe still lay with the state, and Britain was coming into line in that respect. During the nineteenth century, national uniformity had replaced local diversity, professorates had become bureaucratic hierarchies, and universities had lost whatever financial independence had survived from the *ancien régime*. While the power of the state grew, liberal politics and the secularization of thought pushed religious influences to the margin. After 1870, within state-dominated university systems, academic freedom seemed to be guaranteed by the Humboldtian tradition of self-government, by constitutional provisions for freedom of teaching and learning, and by the professional ideal of disinterested science and scholarship as an apolitical criterion of judgement and a protection against arbitrary interference. The Arons case showed that these freedoms could be overridden, but in the *Rechtsstaat* not without controversy and opposition.

Perhaps the best guarantee of freedom was harmony of values between the university world and the governing elite, but this had drawbacks too. It depended on the universities subscribing to and legitimizing the existing social order, and sharing the conventional political ideas of the establishment, which meant in Germany the exclusion of any socialist tendencies, and in most countries an identification with the supposed cultural mission and the great-power interests of the nation. Most professors made this identification as a natural result of their background and training. But if the nature of the governing elite changed, universities could be left stranded, and as 1933 was to prove in Germany, constitutional guarantees meant nothing if liberty itself was destroyed. In that sense, nostalgia apart, the universities of pre-1914 Europe and their intellectual freedom were indeed an achievement of liberal, bourgeois culture, and their fate was tied up with its future.

Bibliography

This bibliography, although long, is selective, and does not include all the works cited in footnotes. The main aim is to guide the reader to the scholarly work which has developed since the 1960s, and for this reason some important review articles have been included. I have also tried in the text footnotes to flag up important contributions in collective volumes. Older books are cited only when they still contain indispensable information, and general historical works only when they have significant relevant sections. No attempt is made to cover the history of science, medicine, or other disciplines, and institutional histories and biographies are listed very sparingly.

Current work in university history was listed in J. M. Fletcher (ed.), *The history of European universities: work in progress and publications*, 5 vols. (Birmingham, 1978–82). Since 1988, these listings have been continued in the journal *History of Universities*, which started in 1981. This is the main specialized journal. Italy is served by *Annali di Storia delle Università Italiane* since 1997, and Germany by the *Jahrbuch für Universitätsgeschichte* since 1998. *Minerva*, devoted since 1962 to general questions of science and higher education, has regular historical articles. Also valuable are the main history of education journals: *Paedagogica Historica* (international), *History of Education* (Britain), *History of Education Quarterly* (USA), and *Histoire de l'Éducation* (France, with an annual bibliography of recent work).

GENERAL AND COMPARATIVE

Ahlström, G., *Engineers and industrial growth: higher technical education and the engineering profession during the nineteenth and early twentieth centuries. France, Germany, Sweden and England* (London, 1982).

Albisetti, J., 'The feminization of teaching in the nineteenth century: a comparative perspective', *History of Education*, 22 (1993), 253–63.

Anderson, C. A., 'The social composition of university student bodies: the recruitment of nineteenth-century élites in four nations, a historical case study', *The Year Book of Education*, 1959, 502–6.

Anderson, R. D., 'Nationalism and internationalism: European universities before 1914', *Aberdeen University Review*, 54 (1992), 334–45.

—— 'Before and after Humboldt: European universities between the eighteenth and the nineteenth centuries', *History of Higher Education Annual*, 20 (2000), 5–14.

Ben-David, J., 'The scientific role: the conditions of its establishment in Europe', *Minerva*, 4 (1965–6), 15–54.

—— 'The growth of the professions and the class system', in R. Bendix and S. M. Lipset (eds.), *Class, status, and power: social stratification in comparative perspective*, 2nd edn. (London, 1967), 459–72.

—— *The scientist's role in society: a comparative study* (Englewood Cliffs, NJ, 1971).

—— *Centers of learning: Britain, France, Germany, United States* (New York, 1977).

—— and Zloczower, A., 'The idea of the university and the academic market place', *Archives Européennes de Sociologie*, 2 (1961), 303–14.

—— and —— 'Universities and academic systems in modern societies', *Archives Européennes de Sociologie*, 3 (1962), 45–84.

Bender, T. (ed.), *The university and the city: from medieval origins to the present* (New York, 1988).

Bollack, M. and Wismann, H. (eds.), *Philologie und Hermeneutik im 19. Jahrhundert. II* (Göttingen, 1983).

Bonner, T. N., *To the ends of the earth: women's search for education in medicine* (Cambridge, Mass., 1992).

—— *Becoming a physician: medical education in Britain, France, Germany and the United States 1750–1945* (New York, 1995).

Bourdieu, P. and Passeron, J. C., *Reproduction in education, society and culture* (London, 1977). [orig. French 1970]

Brehmer, I. and others, *Frauen in der Geschichte IV. 'Wissen heisst leben . . .': Beiträge zur Bildungsgeschichte von Frauen im 18. und 19. Jahrhundert* (Düsseldorf, 1983).

Brizzi, G. P. and Verger, J. (eds.), *Le Università dell'Europa: dal rinnovamento scientifico all'età dei Lumi* (n.p., 1992).

—— and —— (eds.), *Le Università dell'Europa: le scuole e i maestri: l'età moderna* (n.p., 1995).

Brocke, B. vom, '"Die Gelehrten": Auf dem Weg zu einer vergleichenden Sozialgeschichte europäischer Bildungssysteme und Bildungseliten im Industriezeitalter', *Annali dell'Istituto Storico Italo-Germanico in Trento*, 10 (1984), 389–401.

Brockliss, L., 'Gown and town: the university and the city in Europe 1200–2000', *Minerva*, 38 (2000), 147–70.

Calì, V. and others, *Gli intellettuali e la Grande Guerra* (Bologna, 1998).

Cardwell, D. S. L., 'The development of scientific research in modern universities: a comparative study of motives and opportunities', in A. C. Crombie (ed.), *Scientific change: historical studies in the intellectual, social and technical conditions for scientific discovery and technical innovation, from antiquity to the present* (London, 1963), 661–77.

Charle, C., 'A la recherche des bourgeoisies européennes', *Le Mouvement Social*, 153 (1990), 91–7.

—— *Les Intellectuels en Europe au XIXe siècle: essai d'histoire comparée* (Paris, 1996).

—— and Verger, J., *Histoire des universités* (Paris, 1994).

Charrier, E., *L'Évolution intellectuelle féminine* (Paris, 1931).

Chartier, R., 'Student populations in the eighteenth century', *British Journal for Eighteenth-Century Studies*, 2 (1979), 150–62.

—— and Revel, J., 'Université et société dans l'Europe moderne: position des problèmes', *Revue d'Histoire Moderne et Contemporaine*, 25 (1978), 353–74.

Compère, M. M., *L'Histoire de l'éducation en Europe: essai comparatif sur la façon dont elle s'écrit* (Bern, 1995).

Conze, W. and Kocka, J. (eds.), *Bildungsbürgertum im 19. Jahrhundert. Teil I. Bildungssystem und Professionalisierung in internationalen Vergleichen* (Stuttgart, 1985).

Crawford, E., 'Competition and centralisation in German and French science in the nineteenth and early twentieth centuries: the theses of Joseph Ben-David', *Minerva*, 26 (1988), 618–26.

Crosland, M. (ed.), *The emergence of science in western Europe* (New York, 1976).

Denley, P., 'University records, social history, and the creation of large databases', *History of Universities*, 8 (1989), 219–29.

Eyerman, R., *Between culture and politics: intellectuals in modern society* (Cambridge, 1994).

—— and others, *Intellectuals, universities and the state in western modern societies* (Berkeley, 1987).

Fraisse, G. and Perrot, M. (eds.), *A history of women in the west. IV. Emerging feminism from revolution to world war* (Cambridge, Mass., 1993).

Frijhoff, W., 'Sur l'utilité d'une histoire comparée des systèmes éducatifs nationaux', *Histoire de l'Éducation*, 13 (1981), 29–44.

—— 'Universities: 1500–1900', in B. R. Clark and G. R. Neave (eds.), *The encyclopedia of higher education* (Oxford, 1992), 1251–9.

Gellner, E., *Nations and nationalism* (Oxford, 1983).

Gieysztor, A. and Koczerska, M. (eds.), *Universitates studiorum saec. XVIII et XIX: études présentées par la Commission Internationale pour l'Histoire des Universités en 1977* (Warsaw, 1982).

Hammerstein, N., 'University development in the seventeenth and eighteenth centuries: a comparative study', *CRE-Information*, 62 (1983), 81–8.

—— 'The modern world, sciences, medicine, and universities', *History of Universities*, 8 (1989), 151–78.

Harvey, A. D., 'European universities in a period of change 1789–1815', *Higher Education Review*, 23/3 (1991), 41–9.

Higher education and society: historical perspectives. Educación superior y sociedad: perspectivas históricas (Salamanca, 1985).

Hobsbawm, E. J., *Nations and nationalism since 1870: programme, myth, reality*, 2nd edn. (Cambridge, 1992).

Hofstetter, M., *The romantic idea of a university: England and Germany 1770–1850* (Basingstoke, 2001).

Hroch, M., *Social preconditions of national revival in Europe: a comparative analysis of the social composition of patriotic groups among the smaller European nations*, 2nd edn. (New York, 2000). [orig. edn. 1985]

Irsay, S. d', *Histoire des universités françaises et étrangères. II. Du XVIe siècle à 1860* (Paris, 1935).

Jarausch, K. H. (ed.), *The transformation of higher learning 1860–1930: expansion, diversification, social opening, and professionalization in England, Germany, Russia, and the United States* (Chicago, 1983).

Jílek, L. (ed.), *Historical compendium of European universities. Répertoire historique des universités européennes* (Geneva, 1984).

Jones, H. S., 'Student life and sociability 1860–1930: comparative reflections', *History of Universities*, 14 (1995–6), 225–46.

Julia, D., Revel, J., and Chartier, R. (eds.), *Les Universités européennes du XVIe au XVIIIe siècle: histoire sociale des populations étudiantes. I. Bohème, Espagne, États italiens, Pays Germaniques, Pologne, Provinces-Unies* (Paris, 1986).

Kaelble, H., 'Long-term changes in the recruitment of the business elite: Germany compared to the US, Great Britain and France since the industrial revolution', *Journal of Social History*, 13 (1979–80), 404–23.

—— 'Educational opportunities and government policies in Europe in the period of industrialization', in P. Flora and A. J. Heidenheimer (eds.), *The development of welfare states in Europe and America* (New Brunswick, 1981).

Klingenstein, G. and others (eds.), *Bildung, Politik und Gesellschaft: Studien zur Geschichte des europäischen Bildungswesens vom 16. bis zum 20. Jahrhundert* (Vienna, 1978).

Kocka, J. (ed.), *Bürgertum im 19. Jahrhundert: Deutschland im europäischen Vergleich*, 3 vols. (Munich, 1988).
—— 'The middle classes in Europe', *Journal of Modern History*, 67 (1995), 783–806.
—— and Mitchell, A. (eds.), *Bourgeois society in nineteenth-century Europe* (Oxford, 1993).
Kulczykowski, M. (ed.), *Les Grandes Réformes des universités européennes du XVIe au XXe siècles: IIIème session scientifique internationale, Cracovie 15–17 mai 1980* (Cracow, 1985).
—— (ed.), *Les Étudiants: liens sociaux, culture, moeurs du moyen-âge jusqu'au 19e siècle: Vème session scientifique internationale, Cracovie 28–30 mai 1987* (Warsaw, 1991).
Langewiesche, D., 'Studenten in den europäischen Revolutionen von 1848', *Jahrbuch für Universitätsgeschichte*, 2 (1999), 38–57.
Le Goff, J. and Köpeczi, B. (eds.), *Objet et méthodes de l'histoire de la culture* (Paris, 1982).
Lieven, D., *The aristocracy in Europe 1815–1914* (New York, 1993).
Locke, R. R., 'Industrialisierung und Erziehungssystem in Frankreich und Deutschland vor dem 1. Weltkrieg', *Historische Zeitschrift*, 225 (1977), 265–96.
—— *The end of the practical man: entrepreneurship and higher education in Germany, France, and Great Britain 1880–1940* (Greenwich, Conn., 1984).
Lundgreen, P., 'Bildung und Besitz—Einheit oder Inkongruenz in der europäischen Sozialgeschichte? Kritische Auseinandersetzung mit einer These von Fritz Ringer', *Geschichte und Gesellschaft*, 7 (1981), 262–75.
—— (ed.) *Sozial- und Kulturgeschichte des Bürgertums: Eine Bilanz des Bielefelder Sonderforschungsbereichs (1986–1997)* (Göttingen, 2000).
McClelland, C. E., 'A step forward in the study of universities', *Minerva*, 14 (1976), 150–61.
Maffei, D. and Ridder-Symoens, H. de (eds.), *I collegi universitari in Europa tra il XIV e il XVIII secolo* (Milan, 1991).
Mazzacane, A. and Vano, C. (eds.), *Università e professioni giuridiche in Europa nell'età liberale* (Naples, 1994).
Meriggi, M. and Schiera, P. (eds.), *Dalla città alla nazione: borghesie ottocentesche in Italia e in Germania* (Bologna, 1992).
Müller, D. K., Ringer, F., and Simon, B. (eds.), *The rise of the modern educational system: structural change and social reproduction 1870–1920* (Cambridge, 1987).
Musatti, M. P. (ed.), *Università e collegi: storia e futuro* (Bologna, 1994).
Norrback, M. and Ranki, K. (eds.), *University and nation: the university and the making of the nation in northern Europe in the 19th and 20th centuries* (Helsinki, 1996).
O'Boyle, L., 'The problem of an excess of educated men in western Europe 1800–1850', *Journal of Modern History*, 42 (1970), 471–95.
—— 'Education and social structure: the humanist tradition reexamined', *Internationales Archiv für Sozialgeschichte der Deutschen Literatur*, 1 (1976), 246–57.
Perkin, H., 'The changing social function of the university: a historical retrospect', *CRE-Information*, 62 (1983), 117–31.
—— 'The historical perspective', in B. R. Clark (ed.), *Perspectives on higher education: eight disciplinary and comparative views* (Berkeley, 1984), 17–55.
Pilbeam, P., *The middle classes in Europe 1789–1914: France, Germany, Italy and Russia* (Basingstoke, 1990).
Porciani, I. (ed.), *L'università tra Otto e Novecento: i modelli europei e il caso italiano* (Naples, 1994).
Prahl, H. W. and Schmidt-Harzbach, I. *Die Universität: Eine Kultur- und Sozialgeschichte* (Munich, 1981).

Problèmes d'histoire de l'éducation: actes des séminaires organisés par l'École française de Rome et l'Université de Roma-La Sapienza (Rome, 1988).

Ridder-Symoens, H. de, 'Universiteitsgeschiedenis als bron voor sociale geschiedenis', *Tijdschrift voor Sociale Geschiedenis*, 4 (1978), 87–115.

—— (ed.), *A history of the university in Europe. II. Universities in early modern Europe (1500–1800)* (Cambridge, 1996).

Ringer, F., 'Problems in the history of higher education: a review article', *Comparative Studies in Society and History*, 19 (1977), 239–58.

—— 'The education of elites in modern Europe', *History of Education Quarterly*, 18 (1978), 159–72.

—— *Education and society in modern Europe* (London, 1979).

—— 'Differences and cross-national similarities among mandarins', *Comparative Studies in Society and History*, 28 (1986), 145–68.

—— 'Patterns of access to the modern European universities: rates of enrollment', *History of Higher Education Annual*, 14 (1994), 101–25.

—— 'Patterns of access to the modern European universities: the social origins of students', *History of Higher Education Annual*, 15 (1995), 127–42.

Robinson-Hammerstein, H. (ed.), *European universities in the age of Reformation and Counter-Reformation* (1997).

Romano, A. (ed.), *Università in Europa. Le istituzioni universitarie dal medio evo ai nostri giorni: strutture, organizzazione, funzionamento* (Messina, 1995).

—— and Verger, J. (eds.), *I poteri politici e il mondo universitario (XIII–XX secolo)* (Messina, 1994).

Rothblatt, S., 'Historical and comparative remarks on the federal principle in higher education', *History of Education*, 16 (1987), 151–80.

—— 'The writing of university history at the end of another century', *Oxford Review of Education*, 23 (1997), 151–67.

—— and Wittrock, B. (eds.), *The European and American university since 1800: historical and sociological essays* (Cambridge, 1993).

Rudy, W., *The universities of Europe 1100–1914: a history* (London, 1984).

—— *Total war and twentieth-century higher learning: universities of the western world in the First and Second World Wars* (Cranbury, NJ, 1991).

Schalenberg, M., 'Neuere Synthesen zur Geschichte westeuropäischer Universitäten', *Jahrbuch für Universitätsgeschichte*, 3 (2000), 253–9.

—— *Humboldt auf Reisen? Die Rezeption des 'deutschen Universitätsmodells' in den französischen und britischen Reformdiskursen (1810–1870)* (Basel, 2002).

Schriewer, J., Keiner, E., and Charle, C. (eds.), *Sozialer Raum und akademische Kulturen: A la recherche de l'espace universitaire européen. Studien zur europäischen Hochschul- und Wissenschaftsgeschichte im 19. und 20. Jahrhundert: Études sur l'enseignement supérieur aux XIXe et XXe siècles* (Frankfurt, 1993).

Schubring, G. (ed.), *'Einsamkeit und Freiheit' neu besichtigt: Universitätsreformen und Disziplinenbildung in Preussen als Modell für Wissenschaftspolitik im Europa des 19. Jahrhunderts* (Stuttgart, 1991).

Schwinges, R. C. (ed.), *Humboldt International: Der Export des deutschen Universitätsmodells im 19. und 20. Jahrhundert* (Basel, 2001).

Scott, H. M. (ed.), *Enlightened absolutism: reform and reformers in later eighteenth-century Europe* (Basingstoke, 1990).

Siegrist, H. (ed.), *Bürgerliche Berufe: Zur Sozialgeschichte der freien und akademischen Berufe*

im internationalen Vergleich (Göttingen, 1988).
Stone, L. (ed.), *The university in society. II. Europe, Scotland, and the United States from the 16th to the 20th century* (Princeton, 1974).
—— (ed.) *Schooling and society: studies in the history of education* (Baltimore, 1976).
Stromberg, R. N., *Redemption by war: the intellectuals and 1914* (Lawrence, Kan., 1982).
Tournier, M., 'Women and access to university in France and Germany (1861–1967)', *Comparative Education*, 9 (1973), 107–17.
Trebitsch, M. and Granjon, M. C. (eds.), *Pour une histoire comparée des intellectuels* (Brussels, 1998).
L'Université et l'enseignement extra-universitaire XVIe–XIXe siècles. IIe Session Scientifique Internationale Cracovie, 11–12 mai 1979 (Cracow, 1983).
Les Universités européennes du XIVe au XVIIIe siècle: aspects et problèmes (Geneva, 1967).
Wawrykowa, M., *'Für eure und unsere Freiheit': Studentenschaft und junge Intelligenz in Ost- und Mitteleuropa in der ersten Hälfte des 19. Jahrhunderts* (Stuttgart, 1985).
Wohl, R., *The generation of 1914* (Cambridge, Mass., 1979).

AUSTRIA-HUNGARY AND SOUTH-EASTERN EUROPE

Beller, S., *Vienna and the Jews 1867–1938: a cultural history* (Cambridge, 1989).
Boyadjieva, P., 'The social legitimization of an "untimely" institution: the case of the first Bulgarian university', *History of Universities*, 16/1 (2000), 179–96.
Cohen, G. B., *Education and middle-class society in Imperial Austria 1848–1918* (West Lafayette, Ind., 1996).
Derwissis, S. N., *Die Geschichte des griechischen Bildungswesens in der neueren Zeit mit besonderer Berücksichtigung der Einflüsse der deutschen Pädagogik* (Frankfurt, 1976).
Donoghue, E. F., 'Brief tenure but lasting influence: Baron Roland Eotvos and the Budapest Collegium', *History of Education Society Bulletin*, 63 (1999), 35–9.
Ducreux, M. E., 'Nation, état, éducation: l'enseignement de l'histoire en Europe centrale et orientale', *Histoire de l'Éducation*, 86 (2000), 5–36.
Ebert, K., *Die Grazer Juristenfakultät im Vormärz: Rechtswissenschaft und Rechtslehre an der Grazer Hochschule zwischen 1810 und 1848* (Graz, 1969).
Engelbrecht, H., *Geschichte des österreichischen Bildungswesens*, vols. 3–4 (Vienna, 1984–6).
Forkl, M. and Koffmahn, E. (eds.), *Frauenstudium und akademische Frauenarbeit in Österreich* (Vienna, 1968).
Freisitzer, K. and others, *Tradition und Herausforderung: 400 Jahre Universität Graz* (Graz, 1985).
Gall, F., *Alma Mater Rudolphina 1365–1965: Die Wiener Universität und ihre Studenten*, 3rd edn. (Vienna, 1965).
Haag, J., 'Students at the University of Vienna in the First World War', *Central European History*, 17 (1984), 299–309.
Heindl, W. and Tichy, M. (eds.), *'Durch Erkenntnis zu Freiheit und Gluck . . .': Frauen an der Universität Wien (ab 1897)* (Vienna, 1990).
Henderson, G. P., *The Ionian Academy* (Edinburgh, 1988).
Hitchins, K., *Rumania 1866–1947* (Oxford, 1994).
Hochgerner, J., *Studium und Wissenschaftsentwicklung im Habsburgerreich: Studentengeschichte seit der Gründung der Universität Wien bis zum Ersten Weltkrieg* (Vienna, 1983).

Höflechner, W., *Die Baumeister des künftigen Glücks: Fragment einer Geschichte des Hochschulwesens in Österreich vom Ausgang des 19. Jahrhunderts bis in das Jahr 1938* (Graz, 1988).

Kann, R. A., 'Higher education and politics in the Austrian constitutional monarchy (1867–1918)', in R. A. Kann, *Dynasty, politics, and culture: selected essays* (Highland Lakes, NJ, 1991), 311–32.

Karady, V., 'Assimilation and schooling: national and denominational minorities in the universities of Budapest around 1900', in G. Ránki (ed.), *Hungary and European civilization* (Budapest, 1989), 285–319.

——and Kulczykowski, M. (eds.), *L'Enseignement des élites en Europe centrale (19–20e siècles)* (Cracow, 1999).

——and Mitter, W. (eds.), *Bildungswesen und Sozialstruktur in Mitteleuropa im 19. und 20. Jahrhundert. Education and social structure in Central Europe in the 19th and 20th centuries* (Cologne, 1990).

Kernbauer, A. and Schmidlechner-Lienhart, K. (eds.), *Frauenstudium und Frauenkarrieren an der Universität Graz* (Graz, 1996).

Klingenstein, G., 'Despotismus und Wissenschaft: Zur Kritik norddeutscher Aufklärer an der österreichischen Universität 1750–1790', in F. Engel-Janosi, G. Klingenstein, and H. Lutz (eds.), *Formen der europäischen Aufklärung: Untersuchungen zur Situation von Christentum, Bildung und Wissenschaft im 18. Jahrhundert* (Vienna, 1976), 126–57.

——'Bildungskrise: Gymnasien und Universitäten im Spannungsfeld theresianischer Aufklärung', in W. Koschatzky (ed.), *Maria Theresia und ihre Zeit* (Salzburg, 1979), 213–23.

Krause, P., *'O alte Burschenherrlichkeit': Die Studenten und ihr Brauchtum* (Graz, 1980).

Le Goff, J. and Köpeczi, B. (eds.), *Intellectuels français, intellectuels hongrois, XIIIe–XXe siècles* (Budapest, 1985).

Lemberg, H. and others, *Bildungsgeschichte, Bevölkerungsgeschichte, Gesellschaftsgeschichte in den Böhmischen Ländern und in Europa: Festschrift für Jan Havránek zum 60. Geburtstag* (Vienna, 1988).

Lentze, H., *Die Universitätsreform des Ministers Graf Leo Thun-Hohenstein* (Vienna, 1962).

Louros, N. C., 'L'Université Nationale d'Athènes (1837–1937): repères d'histoire', *CRE-Information*, 68 (1984), 13–18.

Maisel, T., *Alma Mater auf den Barrikaden* (Vienna, 1998).

Mazsu, J., *The social history of the Hungarian intelligentsia 1825–1914* (Boulder, Colo., 1997).

Meister, R., *Entwicklung und Reformen des österreichischen Studienwesens* (Vienna, 1963).

Oberkofler, G. and Goller, P., *Geschichte der Universität Innsbruck (1669–1945)*, 2nd edn. (Frankfurt, 1996).

Okey, R., *The Habsburg Monarchy, c. 1765–1918: from enlightenment to eclipse* (London, 2001).

Plaschka, R. G. and Klingenstein, G. (eds.), *Österreich im Europa der Aufklärung: Kontinuität und Zäsur in Europa zur Zeit Maria Theresias und Josephs II.* (Vienna, 1985).

——and Mack, K. (eds.), *Wegenetz europäischen Geistes: Wissenschaftszentren und geistige Wechselbeziehungen zwischen Mittel- und Südosteuropa vom Ende des 18. Jahrhunderts bis zum Ersten Weltkrieg* (Vienna, 1983).

——and ——(eds.), *Wegenetz europäischen Geistes. II. Universitäten und Studenten: Die Bedeutung studentischer Migrationen in Mittel- und Südosteuropa vom 18. bis zum 20. Jahrhundert* (Munich, 1987).

Preglau-Hämmerle, S., *Die politische und soziale Funktion der österreichischen Universität: Von den Anfängen bis zur Gegenwart* (Innsbruck, 1986).

Sadlak, J., 'The use and abuse of the university: higher education in Romania 1860–1990', *Minerva*, 29 (1991), 195–225.

Skilling, H. J., *T. G. Masaryk: against the current 1882–1914* (Basingstoke, 1994).
Slavinski, I. and Strelka, J. P. (eds.), *Glanz und Elend der Peripherie: 120 Jahre Universität Czernowitz* (Bern, 1998).
Sphiroéras, B., 'La présence de l'Université d'Athènes dans l'histoire de l'État grec', *CRE-Information*, 68 (1984), 5–11.
Student und Hochschule im 19. Jahrhundert: Studien und Materialen (Göttingen, 1975).
Szögi, L., 'Zur Geschichte des Universitätsbesuchs innerhalb der Habsburger-Monarchie 1790–1850', in K. Mühlberger and T. Maisel (eds.), *Aspekte der Bildungs- und Universitätsgeschichte, 16. bis 19. Jahrhundert* (Vienna, 1993), 361–98.
—— and Varga, J. (eds.), *Universitas Budensis 1395–1995* (Budapest, 1995).
Wangermann, E., *Aufklärung und staatsbürgerliche Erziehung: Gottfried van Swieten als Reformator des österreichischen Unterrichtswesens 1781–1791* (Vienna, 1978).

BELGIUM AND HOLLAND

Art, J., 'Les *Rapports triennaux sur l'état de l'enseignement supérieur*: un arrière-fond pour des recherches ultérieures sur l'histoire des élites belges entre 1814 et 1914', *Revue Belge d'Histoire Contemporaine*, 17 (1986), 187–224.
Baggen, P. A. M., *Vorming door Wetenschap: universitair onderwijs in Nederland 1815–1960* (Delft, 1998).
Bartier, J., *Libéralisme et socialisme au XIXe siècle: études rassemblées et publiées par Guy Cambier* (Brussels, 1981).
Bosch, M., *Het geslacht van de wetenschap: vrouwen en hoger onderwijs in Nederland 1878–1948* (Amsterdam, 1994).
Braive, G., *Histoire des Facultés Universitaires Saint-Louis: des origines à 1918* (Brussels, 1985).
Clough, S. B., *A history of the Flemish movement in Belgium: a study in nationalism* (New York, 1968).
Davis, W. W., *Joseph II: an imperial reformer for the Austrian Netherlands* (The Hague, 1974).
De Clerck, K. and others, *Kroniek van de strijd voor de vernederlandsing van de Gentse universiteit* (Antwerp 1980).
Despy-Meyer, A. and Becquevort, J., *Les Femmes et l'enseignement supérieur: l'Université Libre de Bruxelles de 1880 à 1914* (Brussels, 1980).
—— and Devriese, D. (eds.), *Ernest Solvay et son temps* (Brussels, 1997).
Disco, C., 'Making the grade in Dutch civil engineering 1780–1920', *Paedagogica Historica*, 30 (1994), 371–410.
Dodde, N. L., *Het Nederlandse onderwijs verandert* (Muiderberg, 1983).
Frijhoff, W., *La Société néerlandaise et ses gradués 1575–1814: une recherche sérielle sur le statut des intellectuels à partir des registres universitaires* (Amsterdam, 1981).
Halkin, L. E., 'Documents et notes sur le Congrès International des Étudiants réuni à Liège en 1865', *Annales d'Histoire Liégoise*, 8 (1964–5), 119–226.
Hasquin, H. (ed.), *Histoire de la laïcité, principalement en Belgique et en France* (Brussels, 1979).
Henssen, E. W. A. (ed.), *Het Corps als Koninkrijk: 150 jaar Delftsch Studenten Corps* (Hilversum, 1998).
Huizinga, J., *Verzamelde werken. VIII. Universiteit, wetenschap en kunst* (Haarlem, 1951).
Kingma, J. and others, *Universitair leven in Groningen 1614–1989* (Groningen, 1989).

Kossmann, E. H., *The Low Countries 1780–1940* (Oxford, 1978).
Kurgan-Van Hentenryk, G. (ed.), *Laboratoires et réseaux de diffusion des idées en Belgique (XIXe–XXe siècles)* (Brussels, 1994).
Lacomble-Masereel, B., *Les Premières Étudiantes à l'Université de Liège: années académiques 1881–1882 à 1919–1920* (Liège, 1980).
Lejeune, R. and Stiennon, J. (eds.), *La Wallonie, le pays et les hommes: lettres—arts—culture. IV. Compléments* (Brussels, 1981).
Mallinson, V., *Power and politics in Belgian education, 1815 to 1961* (London, 1963).
Massaux, G., 'L'Université de Louvain dans la société et dans l'Église d'hier et de demain', *CRE-Information*, 39 (1977), 27–40.
Otterspeer, W., *De wiekslag van hun geest: de Leidse Universiteit in de negentiende eeuw* (The Hague, 1992).
Reynebeau, M., *De Gentse Universiteit als katalysator in het politieke groeiproces (1846–1870)* (Ghent, 1979).
Simon-Van der Meersch, A. M., *De eerste generaties meisjesstudenten aan de Rijksuniversiteit te Gent (1882/1883 tot 1929/1930)* (Ghent, 1982).
Tamse, C. A. and Witte, E. (eds.), *Staats- en Natievorming in Willem I's Koninkrijk (1815–1830)* (Brussels, 1992).
Uyttebrouck, A. and Despy-Meyer, A., *Les cent cinquante ans de l'Université Libre de Bruxelles* (Brussels, 1984).
Van Rooy, W., 'L'agitation étudiante et la fondation de l'Université Nouvelle en 1894', *Revue Belge d'Histoire Contemporaine*, 7 (1976), 197–241.
Vrankrijker, A. C., *Vier eeuwen nederlandsch studentenleven* (Voorburg, n.d. [*c.*1939]).
Vroede, M. de, 'Hogeschooluitbreidingen en Volksuniversiteiten', *Revue Belge d'Histoire Contemporaine*, 10 (1979), 255–78.
Wachelder, J. C. M., *Universiteit tussen vorming en opleiding: de modernisering van de nederlandse universiteiten in de negentiende eeuw* (Hilversum, 1992).

BRITISH ISLES

Alexander, W., *First ladies of medicine: the origins, education and destination of early women medical graduates of Glasgow University* (Glasgow, 1987).
Alter, P., 'Staat und Wissenschaft in Grossbritannien vor 1914', in H. Berding and others (eds.), *Vom Staat des Ancien Regime zum modernen Parteienstaat: Festschrift für Theodor Schieder* (Munich, 1978), 369–83.
—— *The reluctant patron: science and the state in Britain 1850–1920* (Oxford, 1987). [orig. German 1982]
Anderson, R. D., *Education and opportunity in Victorian Scotland: schools and universities* (Oxford, 1983).
—— 'Education and society in modern Scotland: a comparative perspective', *History of Education Quarterly*, 25 (1985), 459–81.
—— 'Scottish university professors 1800–1939: profile of an elite', *Scottish Economic and Social History*, 7 (1987), 27–54.
—— *The student community at Aberdeen 1860–1939* (Aberdeen, 1988).
—— 'Universities and elites in modern Britain', *History of Universities*, 10 (1991), 225–50.
—— *Universities and elites in Britain since 1800* (London, 1992).

Annan, N., *The dons: mentors, eccentrics and geniuses* (London, 1999).
Argles, M., *South Kensington to Robbins: an account of English technical and scientific education since 1851* (London, 1964).
Armytage, W. H. G., *Civic universities: aspects of a British tradition* (London, 1955).
Ashby, E., *Technology and the academics: an essay on universities and the scientific revolution* (London, 1958).
—— 'The future of the nineteenth century idea of a university', *Minerva*, 6 (1967–8), 3–17.
—— and Anderson, M., *Portrait of Haldane at work on education* (London, 1974).
Barnes, S. V., 'England's civic universities and the triumph of the Oxbridge ideal', *History of Education Quarterly*, 36 (1996), 271–305.
Bebbington, D., 'The secularization of British universities since the mid-nineteenth century', in G. M. Marsden and B. J. Longfield (eds.), *The secularization of the academy* (New York, 1992), 259–77.
Becher, H. W., 'The social origins and post-graduate careers of a Cambridge intellectual elite 1830–1860', *Victorian Studies*, 28 (1984–5), 97–127.
Bennett, D., *Emily Davies and the liberation of women 1830–1921* (London, 1990).
Brock, M. G. and Curthoys, M. C. (eds.), *The history of the University of Oxford. VI. Nineteenth-century Oxford, Part 1* (Oxford, 1997).
—— and —— (eds.) *The history of the University of Oxford. VII. Nineteenth-century Oxford, Part 2* (Oxford, 2000).
Brooke, C. N. L., *A history of the University of Cambridge. IV. 1870–1990* (Cambridge, 1993).
Brown, A. L. and Moss, M., *The University of Glasgow 1451–1996* (Edinburgh, 1996).
Cant, R. G., 'The Scottish universities and Scottish society in the eighteenth century', *Studies on Voltaire and the Eighteenth Century*, 58 (1967), 1953–66.
—— *The University of St Andrews: a short history*, 3rd edn. (St Andrews, 1992).
Cardwell, D. S. L., *The organisation of science in England*, 2nd edn. (London, 1972).
Carter, J. J. and McLaren, C. A., *Crown and gown 1495–1995: an illustrated history of the University of Aberdeen* (Aberdeen, 1994).
—— and Withrington, D. J. (eds.), *Scottish universities: distinctiveness and diversity* (Edinburgh, 1992).
Chapman, A. W., *The story of a modern university: a history of the University of Sheffield* (London, 1955).
Culler, A. D., *The imperial intellect: a study of Newman's educational ideal* (New Haven, 1955).
Curthoys, M. C. and Jones, H. S., 'Oxford athleticism 1850–1914: a reappraisal', *History of Education*, 24 (1995), 305–17.
Dahrendorf, R., *LSE: a history of the London School of Economics and Political Science 1895–1995* (Oxford, 1995).
Davie, G. E., *The democratic intellect: Scotland and her universities in the nineteenth century*, 2nd edn. (Edinburgh, 1964).
Deslandes, P. R., 'Competitive examinations and the culture of masculinity in Oxbridge undergraduate life 1850–1920', *History of Education Quarterly*, 42 (2002), 544–78.
Donnelly, J. F., 'Getting technical: the vicissitudes of academic industrial chemistry in nineteenth-century Britain', *History of Education*, 26 (1997), 125–43.
Dyhouse, C., *No distinction of sex? Women in British universities 1870–1939* (London, 1995).
Ellis, E. L., *The University College of Wales Aberystwyth 1872–1972* (Cardiff, 1972).
Emerson, R. L., 'Scottish universities in the eighteenth century 1690–1800', *Studies on Voltaire and the Eighteenth Century*, 167 (1977), 453–74.

Emerson, R. L., *Professors, patronage and politics: the Aberdeen universities in the eighteenth century* (Aberdeen, 1992).

Engel, A. J., *From clergyman to don: the rise of the academic profession in nineteenth-century Oxford* (Oxford, 1983).

Foley, T. (ed.), *From Queen's College to National University: essays on the academic history of QUC/UCG/NUI Galway* (Dublin, 1999).

Garland, M. M., *Cambridge before Darwin: the ideal of a liberal education 1800–1860* (Cambridge, 1980).

Gascoigne, J., *Science, politics and universities in Europe 1600–1800* (Aldershot, 1998).

Gibert, J. S., 'Women students and student life at England's civic universities before the First World War', *History of Education*, 23 (1994), 405–22.

Gillispie, C. C., 'English ideas of the university in the nineteenth century', in M. Clapp (ed.), *The modern university* (Ithaca, 1950).

Goldman, L., *Dons and workers: Oxford and adult education since 1850* (Oxford, 1995).

Green, V. H. H., *British institutions: the universities* (Harmondsworth, 1969).

Haig, A. G. L., 'The church, the universities and learning in later Victorian England', *Historical Journal*, 29 (1986), 187–201.

Halsey, A. H. and Trow, M. A., *The British academics* (London, 1971).

—— Floud, J., and Anderson, C. A. (eds.), *Education, economy and society: a reader in the sociology of education* (London, 1961).

Hammerstein, N., 'Matthew Arnolds Vorschlag einer Reform der englischen Universitäten', in L. Kettenacker and others (eds.), *Studien zur Geschichte Englands und der deutsch-britischen Beziehungen: Festschrift für Paul Kluke* (Munich, 1981), 103–29.

Hargreaves, J. D., *Academe and empire: some overseas connections of Aberdeen University 1860–1970* (Aberdeen, 1994).

Harrison, B. (ed.), *The history of the University of Oxford. VIII. The twentieth century* (Oxford, 1994).

Harte, N., *The University of London 1836–1986: an illustrated history* (London, 1986).

Harvie, C., *The lights of liberalism: university liberals and the challenge of democracy 1860–86* (London, 1976).

Hennock, E. P., 'Technological education in England 1850–1926: the uses of a German model', *History of Education*, 19 (1990), 299–331.

Hewitt, M. (ed.), *Scholarship in Victorian Britain* (Leeds, 1998).

Heyck, T. W., *The transformation of intellectual life in Victorian England* (London, 1982).

—— 'The idea of a university in Britain 1870–1970', *History of European Ideas*, 8 (1987), 205–19.

Horn, D. B., *A short history of the University of Edinburgh 1556–1889* (Edinburgh, 1967).

Howarth, J., 'Science education in late-Victorian Oxford: a curious case of failure?', *English Historical Review*, 102 (1987), 334–71.

—— and Curthoys, M. C., 'The political economy of women's higher education in late nineteenth and early twentieth-century Britain', *Historical Research*, 60 (1987), 208–31.

Hutchison, I. G. C., *The university and the state: the case of Aberdeen 1860–1963* (Aberdeen, 1993).

Ives, E., Drummond, D., and Schwarz, L., *The first civic university: Birmingham 1880–1980. An introductory history* (Birmingham, 2000).

Jenkins, H. and Jones, D. C., 'Social class of Cambridge University alumni of the 18th and 19th centuries', *British Journal of Sociology*, 1 (1950), 93–116.

Jones, D. R., *The origins of civic universities: Manchester, Leeds and Liverpool* (London, 1988).

Kelly, T., *For advancement of learning: the University of Liverpool 1881–1981* (Liverpool, 1981).

Kendall, C. M., 'Higher education and the emergence of the professional woman in Glasgow, *c.* 1890–1914', *History of Universities*, 10 (1991), 199–223.

Kinzer, B. L., 'John Stuart Mill and the Irish university question', *Victorian Studies*, 31 (1987–8), 59–77.

Knights, B., *The idea of the clerisy in the nineteenth century* (Cambridge, 1978).

Lynch, M., Phillipson, N. T., and Anderson, R. D., *The University of Edinburgh: an illustrated history* (Edinburgh, 2003).

McClelland, V. A., *English Roman Catholics and higher education 1830–1903* (Oxford, 1973).

McDowell, R. B. and Webb, D. A., *Trinity College Dublin 1592–1952: an academic history* (Cambridge, 1982).

McGrath, F., *Newman's university: idea and reality* (London, 1951).

McWilliams-Tullberg, R., *Women at Cambridge*, 2nd edn. (Cambridge, 1998).

Mathew, W. M., 'The origins and occupations of Glasgow students 1740–1839', *Past and Present*, 33 (1966), 74–94.

Matthew, H. C. G., 'Noetics, Tractarians and the reform of the University of Oxford in the nineteenth century', *History of Universities*, 9 (1990), 195–225.

Moody, T. W., 'The Irish university question of the nineteenth century', *History*, 43 (1958), 90–109.

—— and Beckett, J. C., *Queen's, Belfast 1845–1949: the history of a university* (London, 1959).

Moore, L., *Bajanellas and semilinas: Aberdeen University and the education of women 1860–1920* (Aberdeen, 1991).

Morrell, J., *Science, culture and politics in Britain 1750–1870* (Aldershot, 1997).

Morse, E. J., 'English civic universities and the myth of decline', *History of Universities*, 11 (1992), 177–204.

Moss, M., Munro, J. F., and Trainor, R. H., *University, city and state: the University of Glasgow since 1870* (Edinburgh, 2000).

Muhs, R., Paulmann, J., and Steinmetz, W. (eds.), *Aneignung und Abwehr: Interkultureller Transfer zwischen Deutschland und Grossbritannien im 19. Jahrhundert* (Bodenheim, 1998).

Nockles, P. B., 'An academic counter-revolution: Newman and Tractarian Oxford's idea of a university', *History of Universities*, 10 (1991), 137–97.

Parkes, S. M., 'Higher education 1793–1908', in W. E. Vaughan (ed.), *A new history of Ireland. VI. Ireland under the Union: II, 1870–1921* (Oxford, 1996), 539–70.

Paseta, S., 'The Catholic hierarchy and the Irish university question 1880–1908', *History*, 85 (2000), 268–84.

Pedersen, J. S., 'The reform of women's secondary and higher education: institutional change and social values in mid and late Victorian England', *History of Education Quarterly*, 19 (1979), 61–91.

—— 'Enchanting modernity: the invention of tradition at two women's colleges in late nineteenth- and early twentieth-century Cambridge', *History of Universities*, 17 (2001–2), 162–91.

Perkin, H., 'The recruitment of elites in British society since 1800', *Journal of Social History*, 12 (1978–9), 222–34.

—— *The rise of professional society: England since 1880* (London, 1989).

Perrone, F., 'Women academics in England 1870–1930', *History of Universities*, 12 (1993), 339–67.

Phillipson, N. (ed.), *Universities, society and the future* (Edinburgh, 1983).
Powell, J. P., 'Some nineteenth-century views on the university curriculum', *History of Education Quarterly*, 5 (1965), 97–109.
Prest, J. (ed.), *The illustrated history of Oxford University* (Oxford, 1993).
Rapple, B. A., 'Matthew Arnold on the Irish university question', *History of Education*, 23 (1994), 1–15.
Roach, J. P. C., 'Victorian universities and the national intelligentsia', *Victorian Studies*, 3 (1959–60), 131–50.
Robbins, K., *Nineteenth-century Britain: integration and diversity* (Oxford, 1988).
Robertson, P., 'Scottish universities and Scottish industry 1860–1914', *Scottish Economic and Social History*, 4 (1984), 39–54.
—— 'The development of an urban university: Glasgow 1860–1914', *History of Education Quarterly*, 30 (1990), 47–78.
Roderick, G. W. and Allsobrook, D. A., 'Welsh society and university funding 1860–1914', *Welsh History Review*, 20 (2000), 34–61.
—— and Stephens, M. D., 'The higher education of engineers in England in the nineteenth century, with observations on engineering training on the Continent and in America', *Paedagogica Historica*, 16 (1976), 362–86.
—— and —— 'Scientific studies at Oxford and Cambridge 1850–1914', *British Journal of Educational Studies*, 24 (1976), 49–65.
—— and —— (eds.), *Where did we go wrong? Industrial performance, education and the economy in Victorian Britain* (Lewes, 1981).
Rothblatt, S., *The revolution of the dons: Cambridge and society in Victorian England* (London, 1968).
—— *Tradition and change in English liberal education: an essay in history and culture* (London, 1976).
—— 'Supply and demand: the "two histories" of English education', *History of Education Quarterly*, 28 (1988), 627–44.
—— *The modern university and its discontents: the fate of Newman's legacies in Britain and America* (Cambridge, 1997).
—— 'State and market in British university history', in S. Collini and others (eds.), *Economy, polity and society: British intellectual history 1750–1950* (Cambridge, 2000), 224–42.
—— and Trow, M., 'Government policies and higher education: a comparison of Britain and the United States 1630–1860', in C. Crouch and A. Heath (eds.), *Social research and social reform: essays in honour of A. H. Halsey* (Oxford, 1992), 173–215.
Rubinstein, W. D., 'Education and the social origins of British elites 1880–1970', *Past and Present*, 112 (1986), 163–207.
Sanderson, M., *The universities and British industry 1850–1970* (London, 1972).
—— *The universities in the nineteenth century* (London, 1975).
—— 'The English civic universities and the "industrial spirit" 1870–1914', *Historical Research*, 61 (1988), 90–104.
Searby, P., *A history of the University of Cambridge. III. 1750–1870* (Cambridge, 1997).
Sher, R. B., *Church and university in the Scottish Enlightenment: the moderate literati of Edinburgh* (Edinburgh, 1985).
Slee, P., *Learning and a liberal education: the study of modern history in the universities of Oxford, Cambridge and Manchester 1800–1914* (Manchester, 1986).
—— 'The Oxford idea of a liberal education 1800–1860: the invention of tradition and the manufacture of practice', *History of Universities*, 7 (1988), 61–87.

Smith, J. and Stray, C. (eds.), *Teaching and learning in nineteenth-century Cambridge* (Woodbridge, 2001).

Soffer, R. N., 'The modern university and national values 1850–1930', *Historical Research*, 60 (1987), 166–87.

—— 'Nation, duty, character and confidence: history at Oxford 1850–1914', *Historical Journal*, 30 (1987), 77–104.

—— 'The development of disciplines in the modern English university', *Historical Journal*, 31 (1988), 933–46.

—— 'Authority in the university: Balliol, Newnham and the new mythology', in R. Porter (ed.), *Myths of the English* (Cambridge, 1992), 192–215.

—— *Discipline and power: the university, history, and the making of an English elite 1870–1930* (Stanford, 1994).

Sparrow, J., *Mark Pattison and the idea of a university* (Cambridge, 1967).

Stephens, W. B., *Education in Britain 1750–1914* (Basingstoke, 1998).

Stone, L. (ed.), *The university in society. I. Oxford and Cambridge from the 14th to the early 19th Century* (Princeton, 1975).

Stray, C., 'Curriculum and style in the collegiate university: classics in nineteenth-century Oxbridge', *History of Universities*, 16/2 (2000), 183–218.

Sutherland, G., 'The movement for the higher education of women: its social and intellectual context in England c.1840–80', in P. J. Waller (ed.), *Politics and social change in modern Britain: essays presented to A. F. Thompson* (Brighton, 1987), 91–116.

—— 'Education', in F. M. L. Thompson (ed.), *The Cambridge social history of Britain 1750–1950. III. Social agencies and institutions* (Cambridge, 1990), 119–69.

Sutherland, L. S. and Mitchell, L. G. (eds.), *The history of the University of Oxford. V. The eighteenth century* (Oxford, 1986).

Symonds, R., *Oxford and empire: the last lost cause?* (Oxford, 1986).

Thompson, F. M. L. (ed.), *The University of London and the world of learning 1836–1986* (London, 1990).

Vernon, K., 'Calling the tune: British universities and the state 1880–1914', *History of Education*, 30 (2001), 251–71.

Vicinus, M., *Independent women: work and community for single women 1850–1920* (London, 1985).

Wallace, S., *War and the image of Germany: British academics 1914–1918* (Edinburgh, 1988).

—— ' "The first blast of the trumpet": John Stuart Blackie and the struggle against university tests in Scotland 1839–53', *History of Universities*, 16/1 (2000), 155–78.

Ward, W. R., *Victorian Oxford* (London, 1965).

White, R., 'The anatomy of a Victorian debate: an essay in the history of liberal education', *British Journal of Educational Studies*, 34 (1986), 38–65.

Williams, J. G., *The University College of North Wales: foundations 1884–1927* (Cardiff, 1985).

—— *A history of the University of Wales. I. The university movement in Wales* (Cardiff, 1993).

—— *A history of the University of Wales. II. The University of Wales, 1893–1939* (Cardiff, 1997).

Williams, P., 'Passing on the torch: Whewell's philosophy and the principles of English university education', in M. Fisch and S. Schaffer (eds.), *William Whewell: a composite portrait* (Oxford, 1991), 117–47.

Willson, F. M. G., *Our Minerva: the men and politics of the University of London 1836–1858* (London, 1995).

Wood, P., *The Aberdeen Enlightenment: the arts curriculum in the eighteenth century* (Aberdeen, 1993).

—— 'Science, the universities, and the public sphere in eighteenth-century Scotland', *History of Universities*, 13 (1994), 99–135.

FRANCE

Anderson, R. D., *Education in France 1848–1870* (Oxford, 1975).
Aulard, A., *Napoléon Ier et le monopole universitaire: origines et fonctionnement de l'Université Impériale* (Paris, 1911).
Baker, D. N. and Harrigan, P. J. (eds.), *The making of Frenchmen: current directions in the history of education in France 1679–1979* (Waterloo, Ont., 1980).
Belhoste, B., 'Les origines de l'École polytechnique: des anciennes écoles d'ingénieurs à l'École centrale des travaux publics', *Histoire de l'Éducation*, 42 (1989), 13–53.
—— and others (eds.), *La Formation polytechnicienne 1794–1994* (Paris, 1994).
Ben-David, J., 'The rise and decline of France as a scientific centre', *Minerva*, 8 (1970), 160–79.
Bénéton, P., 'La génération de 1912–1914: image, mythe et réalité?', *Revue Française de Science Politique*, 21 (1971), 981–1009.
Bompaire-Evesque, C. F., *Un Débat sur l'Université au temps de la Troisième République: la lutte contre la Nouvelle Sorbonne* (Paris, 1988).
Bonnerot, J., *La Sorbonne: sa vie, son rôle, son œuvre à travers les siècles* (Paris, 1927).
Bourdieu, P., *La Noblesse d'État: grandes écoles et esprit de corps* (Paris, 1989).
Bradley, M., 'Scientific education for a new society: the École Polytechnique 1795–1830', *History of Education*, 5 (1976), 11–24.
Brockliss, L. W. B., 'Patterns of attendance at the University of Paris 1400–1800', *Historical Journal*, 21 (1978), 503–44.
—— *French higher education in the seventeenth and eighteenth centuries: a cultural history* (Oxford, 1987).
—— 'L'enseignement médical et la révolution: essai de réévaluation', *Histoire de l'Éducation*, 42 (1989), 79–110.
Burney, J. M., 'Student organization in nineteenth-century France: the example of Toulouse', *History of Education Quarterly*, 25 (1985), 303–23.
—— *Toulouse et son université: facultés et étudiants dans la France provinciale du 19e siècle* (Paris, 1988).
Caron, J. C., *Générations romantiques: les étudiants de Paris et le Quartier Latin (1814–1851)* (Paris, 1991).
Charle, C., 'Le champ universitaire parisien à la fin du 19e siècle', *Actes de la Recherche en Sciences Sociales*, 47–8 (1983), 77–89.
—— *Les Élites de la République (1880–1900)* (Paris, 1987).
—— *Naissance des 'intellectuels' 1880–1900* (Paris, 1990).
—— 'The present state of research on the social history of elites and the bourgeoisie: a critical assessment', *Contemporary European History*, 1 (1992), 99–112.
—— *La République des universitaires 1870–1940* (Paris, 1994).
—— *A social history of France in the nineteenth century* (Oxford, 1994). [orig. French 1991]
—— *Paris fin de siècle: culture et politique* (Paris, 1998).
—— and Ferré, R. (eds.), *Le Personnel de l'enseignement supérieur en France aux XIXe et XXe siècles* (Paris, 1985).

Chartier, R., *The cultural origins of the French revolution* (Durham, NC, 1991). [orig. French 1990]
—— Compère, M. M., and Julia, D. *L'Éducation en France du XVIe au XVIIIe siècle* (Paris, 1976).
Chervel, A., *Histoire de l'agrégation: contribution à l'histoire de la culture scolaire* (Paris, 1993).
Chevalier, J. C., 'Victor Cousin et l'enseignement supérieur', in *Au bonheur des mots: mélanges en l'honneur de Gérald Antoine* (Nancy, 1984).
Cholvy, G. (ed.), *Histoire de Montpellier* (Toulouse, 1984).
Clark, T. N., 'Émile Durkheim and the institutionalization of sociology in the French university system', *Archives Européennes de Sociologie*, 9 (1968), 37–71.
—— *Prophets and patrons: the French University and the emergence of the social sciences* (Cambridge, Mass., 1973).
Cocard, H., 'Professeurs et étudiants de la Faculté des droits d'Angers au XVIIIe siècle', *Annales de Bretagne et des Pays de l'Ouest*, 86 (1979), 39–43.
Cohen, P., 'Les élèves catholiques de l'École Normale Supérieure 1906–1914', *Cahiers d'Histoire*, 29 (1984), 33–46.
Cohen, Y., 'Avoir vingt ans en 1900: à la recherche d'un nouveau socialisme', *Le Mouvement Social*, 120 (1982), 11–29.
—— and Weill, C., 'Les mouvements étudiants: une histoire en miettes?', *Le Mouvement Social*, 120 (1982), 3–10.
Costabel, P. (ed.), *L'Enseignement classique au XVIIIe siècle: collèges et universités* (Paris, 1986).
Coutin, A., *Huit siècles de violence au Quartier Latin* (Paris, 1969).
Crosland, M., *The Society of Arcueil: a view of French science at the time of Napoleon I* (London, 1967).
—— *Studies in the culture of science in France and Britain since the Enlightenment* (Aldershot, 1995).
Damamme, D., 'Genèse sociale d'une institution scolaire: l'École Libre des Sciences Politiques', *Actes de la Recherche en Sciences Sociales*, 70 (1987), 31–46.
Danguy des Déserts, P., 'Origines et destins des étudiants en droit inscrits à la faculté de Rennes à la fin de l'ancien régime', in M. Morabito (ed.), *La Révolution et les juristes à Rennes* (Paris, 1989), 159–217.
Daumard, A., 'Les élèves de l'École Polytechnique de 1815 à 1848', *Revue d'Histoire Moderne et Contemporaine*, 5 (1958), 226–34.
Day, C. R., 'Science, applied science and higher education in France 1870–1945: an historiographical survey since the 1950s', *Journal of Social History*, 26 (1992–3), 367–84.
Denis, M., 'Mgr Freppel, Mgr Sauvé et l'Université catholique d'Angers', *Annales de Bretagne*, 78 (1971), 423–49.
Dhombres, N. and Dhombres, J., *Naissance d'un pouvoir: sciences et savants en France (1793–1824)* (Paris, 1989).
Digeon, C., *La Crise allemande de la pensée française (1870–1914)* (Paris, 1959).
Dintzer, L., 'Le mouvement des universités populaires', *Le Mouvement Social*, 35 (1961), 3–17.
Durkheim, É., 'Émile Durkheim on the French universities', *Minerva*, 14 (1976), 377–88.
Elwitt, S., 'Education and the social questions: the *universités populaires* in late nineteenth century France', *History of Education Quarterly*, 22 (1982), 55–71.
Espagne, M. and Werner, M., 'La construction d'une référence culturelle allemande en France: genèse et histoire (1750–1914)', *Annales*, 42 (1987), 969–92.

Espagne, M. and Werner, M. (eds.), *Transferts: les relations interculturelles dans l'espace franco-allemand (XVIIIe et XIXe siècle)* (Paris, 1988).

Fabiani, J. L., *Les Philosophes de la République* (Paris, 1988).

Favre, P., 'Les sciences d'État entre déterminisme et libéralisme: Émile Boutmy et la création de l'École libre des sciences politiques', *Revue Française de Sociologie*, 22 (1981), 429–65.

Fayolle, R., 'Sainte-Beuve et l'École Normale: l'affaire de 1867', *Revue d'Histoire Littéraire de la France*, 67 (1967), 557–76.

Fox, R., 'Scientific enterprise and the patronage of research in France', *Minerva*, 11 (1973), 442–73.

—— 'Science, the university, and the state in nineteenth-century France', in G. L. Geison (ed.), *Professions and the French state 1700–1900* (Philadelphia, 1984), 66–145.

Fox, R. and Weisz, G. (eds.), *The organization of science and technology in France 1808–1914* (Cambridge, 1980).

Gallaher, J. G., *The students of Paris and the revolution of 1848* (Carbondale, Ill., 1980).

Gelfand, T., *Professionalizing modern medicine: Paris surgeons and medical science and institutions in the 18th century* (Westport, Conn., 1980).

Gerbod, P., *La Condition universitaire en France au XIXe siècle* (Paris, 1965).

—— 'Les étudiants et leurs études en France depuis 1870', *Revue Française de Pédagogie*, 52 (1980), 47–55.

—— 'La catégorie étudiante en France depuis 1870', *Paedagogica Historica*, 21 (1981), 93–110.

Greenberg, L., 'Architects of the new Sorbonne: Liard's purpose and Durkheim's role', *History of Education Quarterly*, 21 (1981), 77–94.

Grevet, R., 'La réforme des études en France au siècle des Lumières', *Revue Historique*, 297 (1997), 85–123.

Guenée, S., *Les Universités françaises, des origines à la Révolution: notices historiques sur les universités, studia et académies protestantes* (Paris, 1982).

Hanna, M., *The mobilization of intellect: French scholars and writers during the Great War* (Cambridge, Mass., 1996).

Hartog, F., *Le XIXe siècle et l'histoire: le cas Fustel de Coulanges* (Paris, 1988).

Horvath-Peterson, S., *Victor Duruy and French education: liberal reform in the Second Empire* (Baton Rouge, La., 1984).

Hummel, P., *Humanités normaliennes: l'enseignement classique et l'érudition philologique dans l'École normale supérieure du XIXe siècle* (Paris, 1995).

Institut Catholique de Paris: le livre du centenaire 1875–1975 (Paris, 1975).

Jewsbury, G. F., 'Russian students in Nancy, France 1905–1914: a case study', *Jahrbücher für Geschichte Osteuropas*, NS 23 (1975), 225–8.

Julia, D., 'Une réforme impossible: le changement de cursus dans la France du 18e siècle', *Actes de la Recherche en Sciences Sociales*, 47–8 (1983), 53–76.

—— (ed.), *Atlas de la Révolution française. II. l'enseignement 1760–1815* (Paris, 1987).

—— 'Le choix des professeurs en France: vocation ou concours? 1700–1850', *Paedagogica Historica*, 30 (1994), 175–205.

—— and Revel, J. (eds.), *Les Universités européennes du XVIe au XVIIIe siècle: histoire sociale des populations étudiantes. II. France* (Paris, 1989).

Kagan, R. L., 'Law students and legal careers in eighteenth-century France', *Past and Present*, 68 (1975), 38–72.

Karady, V., 'Normaliens et autres enseignants à la Belle Époque: note sur l'origine sociale et la réussite dans une profession intellectuelle', *Revue Française de Sociologie*, 13 (1972), 35–58.

—— 'L'expansion universitaire et l'évolution des inégalités devant la carrière d'enseignant

au début de la IIIe République', *Revue Française de Sociologie*, 14 (1973), 443–70.
—— 'Durkheim, les sciences sociales et l'Université: bilan d'un semi-échec', *Revue Française de Sociologie*, 17 (1976), 267–311.
—— 'Recherches sur la morphologie du corps universitaire littéraire sous la Troisième République', *Le Mouvement Social*, 96 (1976), 47–79.
—— 'Forces of innovation and inertia in the late 19th century French university system (with special reference to the academic institutionalisation of the social sciences)', *Westminster Studies in Education*, 2 (1979), 75–97.
—— 'Scientists and class structure: social recruitment of students at the Parisian Ecole Normale Superieure in the nineteenth century', *History of Education*, 8 (1979), 99–108.
—— 'Stratégies de réussite et modes de faire-valoir de la sociologie chez les durkheimiens', *Revue Française de Sociologie*, 20 (1979), 49–82.
Keylor, W. R., *Academy and community: the foundation of the French historical profession* (Cambridge, Mass., 1975).
Legrand, L., *L'Influence du positivisme dans l'œuvre scolaire de Jules Ferry: les origines de la laïcité* (Paris, 1961).
Léonard, J. 'Les études médicales en France entre 1815 et 1848', *Revue d'Histoire Moderne et Contemporaine*, 13 (1966), 87–94.
—— *La Médecine entre les savoirs et les pouvoirs: histoire intellectuelle et politique de la médecine française au XIXe siècle* (Paris, 1981).
Liard, L., *L'Enseignement supérieur en France 1789–1893* (Paris, 1888–94).
Ligou, D., 'The University of Dijon in the eighteenth century', *British Journal for Eighteenth-Century Studies*, 3 (1980), 47–58.
Livet, G., *L'Université de Strasbourg de la Révolution française à la guerre de 1870: 'la rencontre avec l'histoire'* (Strasbourg, 1996).
Logette, A., *Histoire de la Faculté de Droit de Nancy (1768–1864–1914)* (Nancy, 1964).
Lukes, S., *Émile Durkheim, his life and work: a historical and critical study* (Harmondsworth, 1975).
Machin, H. and Wright, V., 'Les élèves de l'École nationale d'administration de 1848–1849', *Revue d'Histoire Moderne et Contemporaine*, 36 (1989), 605–39.
Margadant, J. B., *Madame le professeur: women educators in the Third Republic* (Princeton, 1990).
Mayeur, F., *L'Enseignement secondaire des jeunes filles sous la Troisième République* (Paris, 1977).
—— *De la Révolution à l'école républicaine*, Histoire générale de l'enseignement et de l'éducation en France, ed. L. H. Parias, vol. 3 (Paris, 1981).
—— 'Une réforme réussie de l'enseignement supérieur en France', *Histoire de l'Éducation*, 22 (1984), 3–19.
—— 'Fustel de Coulanges et les questions d'enseignement supérieur', *Revue Historique*, 274 (1985), 387–408.
Mercier, L., *Les Universités populaires 1899–1914: éducation populaire et mouvement ouvrier au début du siècle* (Paris, 1986).
Meuleau, M., *Histoire d'une grande école* [Hautes Études Commerciales] (Jouy-en-Josas, 1981).
Minot, J., *Histoire des universités françaises* (Paris, 1991).
Morange, J. and Chassaing, J. F., *Le Mouvement de réforme de l'enseignement en France 1760–1798* (Paris, 1974).
Mouton, M. R., 'L'enseignement supérieur en France de 1890 à nos jours (étude statistique)',

in P. Chevallier (ed.), *La Scolarisation en France depuis un siècle* (Paris, 1974), 175–202.

Nancy: 'Centenaire de la Faculté des Lettres de Nancy', special no. of *Annales de l'Est*, 5th ser., 5 (1954).

Niklaus, R., 'Le *Plan d'une université* de Diderot et le plan d'instruction publique de Condorcet mis en regard', *Diderot Studies*, 24 (1991), 105–19.

Nye, M. J., 'The scientific periphery in France: the Faculty of Sciences at Toulouse (1880–1930)', *Minerva*, 13 (1975), 374–403.

Ory, P. and Sirinelli, J. F., *Les Intellectuels en France, de l'Affaire Dreyfus à nos jours* (Paris, 1986).

Osborne, T. R., *A grande école for the grands corps: the recruitment and training of the French administrative élite in the nineteenth century* (New York, 1983).

Outram, D., 'Politics and vocation: French science 1793–1830', *British Journal for the History of Science*, 13 (1980), 27–43.

Palmer, R. R., 'The old regime origins of the Napoleonic educational structure', in E. Hinrichs and others, *Vom Ancien Régime zur Französischen Revolution: Forschungen und Perspektiven* (Göttingen, 1978), 318–33.

—— *The improvement of humanity: education and the French Revolution* (Princeton, 1985).

Paul, H. W., *From knowledge to power: the rise of the science empire in France 1860–1939* (Cambridge, 1985).

Ponteil, F., *Histoire de l'enseignement en France: les grandes étapes 1789–1964* (Paris, 1966).

Prelot, P. H., *Naissance de l'enseignement supérieur libre: la loi du 12 juillet 1875* (Paris, n.d.).

Prochasson, C., 'Histoire intellectuelle/histoire des intellectuels: le socialisme français au début du XXe siècle', *Revue d'Histoire Moderne et Contemporaine*, 39 (1992), 423–48.

—— and Rasmussen, A., *Au nom de la patrie: les intellectuels et la première guerre mondiale (1910–1919)* (Paris, 1996).

Prost, A., *Histoire de l'enseignement en France 1800–1967* (Paris, 1968).

Raphael, P. and Gontard, M., *Un Ministre de l'instruction publique sous l'Empire autoritaire: Hippolyte Fortoul 1851–1856* (Paris, 1975).

Ringer, F., *Fields of knowledge: French academic culture in comparative perspective 1890–1920* (Cambridge, 1992).

Rivé, P., *La Sorbonne et sa reconstruction* (Lyons, 1987).

Roche, D. *Les Républicains des lettres: gens de culture et Lumières au XVIIIe siècle* (Paris, 1988).

—— *La France des Lumières* (Paris, 1993).

Rohr, J., *Victor Duruy, ministre de Napoléon III: essai sur la politique de l'instruction publique au temps de l'Empire libéral* (Paris, 1967).

Shinn, T., 'Des corps de l'État au secteur industriel: genèse de la profession d'ingénieur 1750–1920', *Revue Française de Sociologie*, 19 (1978), 39–71.

—— 'The French science faculty system 1808–1914: institutional change and research potential in mathematics and the physical sciences', *Historical Studies in the Physical Sciences*, 10 (1979), 271–332.

—— *Savoir scientifique et pouvoir social: l'École polytechnique 1794–1914* (Paris, 1980).

—— 'Des sciences industrielles aux sciences fondamentales: la mutation de l'École supérieure de physique et de chimie 1882–1970', *Revue Française de Sociologie*, 22 (1981), 167–82.

—— 'Reactionary technologists: the struggle over the École polytechnique 1880–1914', *Minerva*, 22 (1984), 329–45.

Singer, B., 'The ascendancy of the Sorbonne: the relations between centre and periphery in the academic order of the Third Republic', *Minerva*, 20 (1982), 269–300.

Smith, R. J., 'L'atmosphère politique a l'École Normale Supérieure à la fin du XIXe siècle', *Revue d'Histoire Moderne et Contemporaine*, 20 (1973), 248–68.

—— *The École Normale Supérieure and the Third Republic* (Albany, NY, 1982).

—— 'The students of the École d'Administration 1848–9', *History of Education*, 16 (1987), 245–58.

—— 'The social origins of students of the École Libre and the Institut d'Études Politiques 1885–1970', *History of Education*, 17 (1988), 229–38.

Spitzer, A. B., *The French generation of 1820* (Princeton, 1987).

Stock, P., 'Students versus the university in pre-world war Paris', *French Historical Studies*, 7 (1971), 93–110.

Trénard, L., 'Les facultés des lettres sous la monarchie de juillet', in *Actes du 89e Congrès National des Sociétés Savantes. Lyon 1964. Section d'histoire moderne et contemporaine* (Paris, 1965), vol. 2, 669–715.

—— *De Douai à Lille . . .: une université et son histoire* (Lille, 1978).

Tuilier, A., *Histoire de l'Université de Paris et de la Sorbonne. II. De Louis XIV à la crise de 1968* (Paris, 1994).

Verger, J. (ed.), *Histoire des universités en France* (Toulouse, 1986).

Viguerie, J. de, 'Quelques remarques sur les universités françaises au dix-huitième siècle', *Revue Historique*, 262 (1979), 29–49.

Weiss, J. H., *The making of technological man: the social origins of French engineering education* (Cambridge, Mass., 1982).

Weisz, G., 'Le corps professoral de l'enseignement supérieur et l'idéologie de la réforme universitaire en France 1860–1885', *Revue Française de Sociologie*, 18 (1977), 201–32.

—— 'The French universities and education for the new professions 1885–1914', *Minerva*, 17 (1979), 98–128.

—— 'L'idéologie républicaine et les sciences sociales: les durkheimiens et la chaire d'histoire d'économie sociale à la Sorbonne', *Revue Française de Sociologie*, 20 (1979), 83–112.

—— 'Associations et manifestations: les étudiants français de la Belle Époque', *Le Mouvement Social*, 120 (1982), 31–44.

—— *The emergence of modern universities in France 1863–1914* (Princeton, 1983).

Wright, V., 'L'École nationale d'administration de 1848–1849: un échec révélateur', *Revue Historique*, 255 (1976), 21–42.

Zeldin, T., 'Higher education in France 1848–1940', *Journal of Contemporary History*, 2/3 (1967), 53–80.

—— *France 1848–1945. II. Intellect, taste and anxiety* (Oxford, 1977).

GERMANY

Ackerknecht, E. H., *Rudolf Virchow: doctor, statesman, anthropologist* (Madison , Wis., 1953).

Albisetti, J., 'The fight for female physicians in Imperial Germany', *Central European History*, 15 (1982), 99–123.

—— *Secondary school reform in Imperial Germany* (Princeton, 1983).

—— 'Women and the professions in Imperial Germany', in R. E. Joeres and M. J. Maynes (eds.), *German women in the eighteenth and nineteenth centuries: a social and literary history* (Bloomington, Ind., 1986), 94–109.

—— *Schooling German girls and women: secondary and higher education in the nineteenth century* (Princeton, 1988).

Albisetti, J., '*The decline of the German mandarins* after twenty-five years', *History of Education Quarterly*, 34 (1994), 453–65.

Andernach, N., *Der Einfluss der Parteien auf das Hochschulwesen in Preussen 1848–1918* (Göttingen, 1972).

Anrich, E., *Die Idee der deutschen Universität: Die fünf Grundschriften aus der Zeit ihrer Neubegründung durch klassischen Idealismus und romantischen Realismus* (Darmstadt, 1956).

Ascher, A., 'Professors as propagandists: the politics of the Kathedersozialisten', *Journal of Central European Affairs*, 23 (1963), 282–302.

Ash, M. G. (ed.), *Mythos Humboldt: Vergangenheit und Zukunft der deutschen Universitäten* (Vienna, 1999). [orig. English 1997]

Barkin, K. D., 'Fritz K. Ringer's *The decline of the mandarins*', *Journal of Modern History*, 43 (1971), 276–86.

Bartol, G., *Ideologie und studentischer Protest: Untersuchungen zur Entstehung deutscher Studentenbewegungen im 19. und 20. Jahrhundert* (Munich, 1978).

Baum, R. J. (ed.), *'Wir wollen Männer, wir wollen Taten!' Deutsche Corpsstudenten 1848 bis heute* (Berlin, 1998).

—— and others, *1582–1982. Studentenschaft und Korporationswesen an der Universität Würzburg* (Würzburg, 1982).

Baumgart, P. (ed.), *Bildungspolitik in Preussen zur Zeit des Kaiserreichs* (Stuttgart, 1980).

—— (ed.) *Vierhundert Jahre Universität Würzburg: Eine Festschrift* (Neustadt an der Aisch, 1982).

—— and others, *Wider Zopf und Philisterey: Deutsche Studenten zwischen Reformzeit und Revolution (1800–1850)* (Würzburg, 1985).

—— and Hammerstein, N. (eds.), *Beiträge zu Problemen deutscher Universitätsgründungen der frühen Neuzeit* (Nendeln/Liechtenstein, 1978).

Baumgarten, M., *Vom Gelehrten zum Wissenschaftler: Studien zum Lehrkörper einer kleinen Universität am Beispiel der Ludoviciana Giessen (1815–1914)* (Giessen, 1988).

—— *Professoren und Universitäten im 19. Jahrhundert: Zur Sozialgeschichte deutscher Geistes- und Naturwissenschaftler* (Göttingen, 1997).

Ben-David, J., 'The universities and the growth of science in Germany and the United States', *Minerva*, 7 (1968–9), 1–35.

Berg, C. (ed.), *Handbuch der deutschen Bildungsgeschichte. IV. 1870–1918: Von der Reichsgründung bis zum Ende des Ersten Weltkriegs* (Munich, 1991).

Biastoch, M., *Tübinger Studenten im Kaiserreich: Eine sozialgeschichtliche Untersuchung* (Sigmaringen, 1996).

Bien, G., 'Kants Theorie der Universität und ihr geschichtlicher Ort', *Historische Zeitschrift*, 219 (1974), 551–77.

Blanning, T., *Reform and revolution in Mainz 1743–1803* (Cambridge, 1974).

Boehm, L., 'Wilhelm von Humboldt (1767–1835) and the university: idea and implementation', *CRE-Information*, 62 (1983), 89–105.

—— *Geschichtsdenken, Bildungsgeschichte, Wissenschaftsorganisation: Ausgewählte Aufsätze von Laetitia Boehm anlässlich ihres 65. Geburtstages* (Berlin, 1996).

—— and Müller, R. A., *Universitäten und Hochschulen in Deutschland, Österreich und der Schweiz: Eine Universitätsgeschichte in Einzeldarstellungen* (Düsseldorf, 1983).

Boockman, H., *Wissen und Widerstand: Geschichte der deutschen Universität* (Berlin, 1999).

Borscheid, P., *Naturwissenschaft, Staat und Industrie in Baden (1848–1914)* (Stuttgart, 1976).

Boyd, B. A., *Rudolf Virchow: the scientist as citizen* (New York, 1991).

Braubach, M., *Bonner Professoren und Studenten in den Revolutionsjahren 1848/49* (Cologne, 1967).

Brocke, B. vom, 'Friedrich Althoff: a great figure in higher education policy in Germany', *Minerva*, 29 (1991), 269–93.

—— *Wissenschaftsgeschichte und Wissenschaftspolitik im Industriezeitalter: Das 'System Althoff' in historischer Perspektive* (Hildesheim, 1991).

—— and Krüger, P. (eds.), *Hochschulpolitik im Föderalismus: Die Protokolle der Hochschulkonferenzen der deutschen Bundesstaaten und Österreich 1898 bis 1918* (Berlin, 1994).

—— and Laitko, H. (eds.), *Die Kaiser-Wilhelm-/Max-Planck-Gesellschaft und ihre Institute. Studien zu ihrer Geschichte: Das Harnack-Prinzip* (Berlin, 1996).

Bruch, R. vom, *Wissenschaft, Politik und öffentliche Meinung: Gelehrtenpolitik im Wilhelminischen Deutschland (1890–1914)* (Husum, 1980).

—— *Weltpolitik als Kulturmission: Auswärtige Kulturpolitik und Bildungsbürgertum in Deutschland am Vorabend des Ersten Weltkrieges* (Paderborn, 1982).

—— 'Universitätsreform als soziale Bewegung: Zur Nicht-Ordinarienfrage im späten deutschen Kaiserreich', *Geschichte und Gesellschaft*, 10 (1984), 72–91.

—— and Müller, R. A. (eds.), *Erlebte und gelebte Universität: Die Universität München im 19. und 20. Jahrhundert* (Pfaffenhofen, 1986).

—— and —— (eds.), *Formen ausserstaatlicher Wissenschaftsförderung im 19. und 20. Jahrhundert: Deutschland im europäischen Vergleich* (Stuttgart, 1990).

—— and others, *Kultur und Kulturwissenschaften um 1900. II. Idealismus und Positivismus* (Stuttgart, 1997).

Bruford, W. H., *The German tradition of self-cultivation: 'Bildung' from Humboldt to Thomas Mann* (Cambridge, 1975).

Brümmer, M., *Staat kontra Universität: Die Universität Halle-Wittenberg und die Karlsbader Beschlüsse 1819–1848* (Weimar, 1991).

Burchardt, A., *Blaustrumpf—Modestudentin—Anarchistin? Deutsche und russische Medizinstudentinnen in Berlin 1896–1918* (Stuttgart, 1997).

Burchardt, L., *Wissenschaftspolitik im Wilhelminischen Deutschland: Vorgeschichte, Gründung und Aufbau der Kaiser-Wilhelm-Gesellschaft zur Förderung der Wissenschaften* (Göttingen, 1975).

Burger, P., 'Magnet für werdende Geister? Die sozialwissenschaftlichen Studentenvereinigungen und der Sozialliberalismus der Jahrhundertwende', *Jahrbuch zur Liberalismus-Forschung*, 3 (1991), 113–29.

Busch, A., *Die Geschichte der Privatdozenten: Eine soziologische Studie zur grossbetrieblichen Entwicklung der deutschen Universitäten* (Stuttgart, 1959).

—— 'The vicissitudes of the *Privatdozent*: breakdown and adaptation in the recruitment of the German university teacher', *Minerva*, 1 (1962–3), 319–41.

Cahan, D., *An Institute for an Empire: the Physikalisch-Technische Reichsanstalt 1871–1918* (Cambridge, 1989).

Charle, C. (ed.), *Les Universités germaniques, XIXe–XXe siècles*, special no. of *Histoire de l'Éducation*, 62 (1994).

Chickering, R., *Karl Lamprecht: a German academic life (1856–1915)* (Atlantic Highlands, NJ, 1993).

Classen, P., 'Zur Geschichte der "Akademischen Freiheit", vornehmlich im Mittelalter', *Historische Zeitschrift*, 232 (1981), 529–53.

Cocks, G. and Jarausch, K. (eds.), *German professions 1800–1950* (New York, 1990).

Corni, G. and Schiera, P. (eds.), *Cultura politica e società borghese in Germania fra otto e novecento* (Bologna, 1986).

Craig, G. A., 'Engagement and neutrality in Germany: the case of Georg Forster 1754–94', *Journal of Modern History*, 41 (1969), 1–16.

Craig, J. E., *Scholarship and nation building: the universities of Strasbourg and Alsatian society 1870–1939* (Chicago, 1984).

Dickerhof, H., 'Bildung und Ausbildung im Programm der bayerischen Universitäten im 19. Jahrhundert', *Historisches Jahrbuch*, 95 (1975), 142–69.

—— 'Staatliches Bildungsmonopol: Die Idee einer katholischen Universität und die Schulen der katholischen Theologie im 19. Jahrhundert', *Archiv fur Kulturgeschichte*, 66 (1984), 175–214.

Dickmann, E. and Schöck-Quinteros, E. (eds.), *Barrieren und Karrieren: Die Anfänge des Frauenstudiums in Deutschland* (Berlin, 2000).

Doerr, W. (ed.), *Semper apertus: Sechshundert Jahre Ruprecht-Karls-Universität Heidelberg 1386–1986 . . . II. Das neunzehnte Jahrhundert* (Berlin, 1985).

Droz, J., 'Libéralisme et bourgeoisie dans le "Vormärz" (1830–1848)', *Le Mouvement Social*, 136 (1986), 29–52.

Düwell, K., 'Konstitution, Maschine und Schule: Zur preussischen Hochschulpolitik im Rheinland vor der Reichsgründung', in K. Kluxen and W. J. Mommsen (eds.), *Politische Ideologien und nationalstaatliche Ordnung: Studien zur Geschichte des 19. und 20. Jahrhunderts* (Munich, 1968), 273–95.

Eley, G., 'Educating the bourgeoisie: students and the culture of "illiberalism" in Imperial Germany', *History of Education Quarterly*, 26 (1986), 287–300.

Ellwein, T., *Die deutsche Universität: Vom Mittelalter bis zur Gegenwart*, 2nd edn. (Frankfurt, 1992).

Emundts-Trill, P., *Die Privatdozenten und Extraordinarien der Universität Heidelberg 1803–1860* (Frankfurt, 1997).

Ferber, C. von, *Die Entwicklung des Lehrkörpers der deutschen Universitäten und Hochschulen 1864–1954* (Göttingen, 1956).

Ferry, L. and others (eds.), *Philosophies de l'université: l'idéalisme allemand et la question de l'université. Textes de Schelling, Fichte, Schleiermacher, Humboldt, Hegel* (Paris, 1979).

Fiedler, G. and Pollmann, K. E., 'Engineering students at Brunswick Institute of Technology during the period of industrial expansion 1862–1914', *History of Universities*, 13 (1994), 251–70.

Fischer, T. E., *Die Anfänge des Frauenstudiums in Deutschland: Das Beispiel der Universität Kiel* (Trier, 1996).

Fläschendräger, W. and Steiger, G. (eds.), *Magister und Scholaren, Professoren und Studenten: Geschichte deutscher Universitäten und Hochschulen im Überblick* (Leipzig, 1981).

Fricke, D., 'Zur Militarisierung des deutschen Geisteslebens im wilhelminischen Kaiserreich: Der Fall Leo Arons', *Zeitschrift für Geschichtswissenschaft*, 8 (1960), 1069–107.

Gilbert, F., 'Political power and academic responsibility: reflections on Friedrich Meinecke's *Drei Generationen Deutscher Gelehrtenpolitik*', in L. Krieger and F. Stern (eds.), *The responsibility of power: historical essays in honor of Hajo Holborn* (London, 1968), 402–15.

Gillot, G., 'Les corporations étudiantes: un archaïsme plein d'avenir (Allemagne-Autriche, 1880–1914)', *Le Mouvement Social*, 120 (1982), 45–75.

Glaser, E., *Hindernisse, Umwege, Sackgassen: Die Anfänge des Frauenstudiums an der Universität Tübingen (1904–1934)* (Weinheim, 1992).

—— and Herrmann, U., 'Konkurrenz und Dankbarkeit: Die ersten drei Jahrzehnte des

Frauenstudiums im Spiegel von Lebenserinnerungen—am Beispiel der Universität Tübingen', *Zeitschrift für Padagogik*, 34 (1988), 205–26.
Grün, B. and others, *Zwischen Korporation und Konfrontation: Beiträge zur Würzburger Universitäts- und Studentengeschichte* (Cologne, 1999).
Hahn, E. J. C., 'The junior faculty in "revolt": reform plans for Berlin University in 1848', *American Historical Review*, 82 (1977), 875–95.
Hammerstein, N., *Ius und Historie: Ein Beitrag zur Geschichte des historischen Denkens an deutschen Universitäten im späten 17. und im 18. Jahrhundert* (Göttingen, 1972).
—— *Aufklärung und katholisches Reich: Untersuchungen zur Universitätsreform und Politik katholischer Territorien des Heiligen Römischen Reichs deutscher Nation im 18. Jahrhundert* (Berlin, 1977).
—— 'Jubiläumsschrift und Alltagsarbeit: Tendenzen bildungsgeschichtlicher Literatur', *Historische Zeitschrift*, 236 (1983), 601–33.
—— 'Zur Geschichte und Bedeutung der Universitäten im Heiligen Römischen Reich deutscher Nation', *Historische Zeitschrift*, 241 (1985), 287–328.
—— 'Die Moderne in der deutschen Wissenschaft im 19. Jahrhundert: Zum Wandel einer Vorstellung', *Annali dell'Istituto Storico Italo-Germanico in Trento*, 16 (1990), 9–42.
—— *Antisemitismus und deutsche Universitäten 1871–1933* (Frankfurt, 1995).
—— (ed.), *Universitäten und Aufklärung* (Göttingen, 1995).
—— 'Professoren in Kaiserreich und Weimarer Republik und der Antisemitismus', in P. Alter and others (eds.), *Die Konstruktion der Nation gegen die Juden* (Munich, 1999).
—— *Res publica litteraria: Ausgewählte Aufsätze zur frühneuzeitlichen Bildungs-, Wissenschafts- und Universitätsgeschichte* (Berlin, 2000).
Hardtwig, W., 'Krise der Universität, studentische Reformbewegung (1750–1819) und die Sozialisation der jugendlichen deutschen Bildungsschicht: Aufriss eines Forschungsproblems', *Geschichte und Gesellschaft*, 11 (1985), 155–76.
—— 'Protestformen und Organisationsstrukturen der deutschen Burschenschaft 1815–1833', in H. Reinalter (ed.), *Demokratische und soziale Protestbewegungen in Mitteleuropa 1815–1848/49* (Frankfurt, 1986), 37–76.
—— 'Sozialverhalten und Wertwandel der jugendlichen Bildungsschicht im Übergang zur bürgerlichen Gesellschaft (17.–19. Jahrhundert)', *Vierteljahrschrift für Sozial- und Wirtschaftsgeschichte*, 73 (1986), 305–35.
—— 'Studentenschaft und Aufklärung: Landsmannschaften und Studentenorden in Deutschland im 18. Jahrhundert', in É. François (ed.), *Sociabilité et société bourgeoise en France, en Allemagne et en Suisse 1750–1850* (Paris, 1986), 239–60.
—— 'Studentische Mentalität—Politische Jugendbewegung—Nationalismus: Die Anfänge der deutschen Burschenschaft', *Historische Zeitschrift*, 242 (1986), 581–628.
—— and Brandt, H. H., *Deutschlands Weg in die Moderne: Politik, Gesellschaft und Kultur im 19. Jahrhundert* (Munich, 1993).
Hartke, W. and Maskolat, H. (eds.), *Wilhelm von Humboldt: Erbe—Gegenwart—Zukunft* (Halle, 1967).
Harwood, J., 'Mandarins and outsiders in the German professoriate 1890–1933: a study of the genetics community', *European History Quarterly*, 23 (1993), 485–511.
Herrmann, D. P., 'Wirtschaft, Staat und Wissenschaft: Der Ausbau der privaten Hochschul- und Wissenschaftsförderung im Kaiserreich', *Vierteljahrschrift für Sozial- und Wirtschaftsgeschichte*, 77 (1990), 350–68.
Herrmann, U. (ed.), *'Die Bildung des Bürgers': Die Formierung der bürgerlichen Gesellschaft und die Gebildeten im 18. Jahrhundert* (Weinheim, 1982).

Herzig, A., 'Der Primat der Politik in der Hochschulbildung des 18. und beginnenden 19. Jahrhunderts', *Jahrbuch des Instituts für Deutsche Geschichte*, 7 (1978), 71–109.

Jarausch, K., 'Studenten, Gesellschaft und Politik im Kaiserreich: Ein Versuch', *Informationen zur Erziehungs- und Bildungshistorischen Forschung*, 3 (1976), 61–90.

—— 'Liberal education as illiberal socialization: the case of students in Imperial Germany', *Journal of Modern History*, 50 (1978), 609–30.

—— 'The social transformation of the university: the case of Prussia 1865–1914', *Journal of Social History*, 12 (1978–9), 609–36.

—— 'Die neuhumanistische Universität und die bürgerliche Gesellschaft 1800–1870: Eine quantitative Untersuchung zur Sozialstruktur der Studentenschaften deutscher Universitäten', *Darstellungen und Quellen zur Geschichte der deutschen Einheitsbewegung im neunzehnten und zwanzigsten Jahrhundert*, 11 (1981), 11–58.

—— 'Students, sex and politics in Imperial Germany', *Journal of Contemporary History*, 17 (1982), 285–303.

—— *Students, society and politics in Imperial Germany: the rise of academic illiberalism* (Princeton, 1982).

—— *Deutsche Studenten 1800–1970* (Frankfurt, 1984).

Jeismann, K. E., 'Preussische Bildungspolitik vom ausgehenden 18. bis zur Mitte des 19. Jahrhunderts: Thesen und Probleme', in U. Arnold (ed.), *Zur Bildungs- und Schulgeschichte Preussens* (Lüneburg, 1988), 9–37.

Johnson, J. A., *The Kaiser's chemists: science and modernization in Imperial Germany* (Chapel Hill, NC, 1990).

Kampe, N., 'Jews and antisemites at universities in Imperial Germany. (I). Jewish students: social history and social conflict', *Leo Baeck Institute Yearbook*, 30 (1985), 357–94.

—— 'Jews and antisemites at universities in Imperial Germany. (II). The Friedrich-Wilhelms-Universität of Berlin: a case study on the students' "Jewish question"', *Leo Baeck Institute Yearbook*, 32 (1987), 43–101.

—— *Studenten und 'Judenfrage' im Deutschen Kaiserreich: Die Entstehung einer akademischen Trägerschicht des Antisemitismus* (Göttingen, 1988).

Kertz, W. (ed.), *Technische Universität Braunschweig: Vom Collegium Carolinum zur Technischen Universität 1745–1995* (Hildesheim, 1995).

Kocka, J., 'La bourgeoisie dans l'histoire moderne et contemporaine de l'Allemagne: recherches et débats récents', *Le Mouvement Social*, 136 (1986), 5–27.

König, C. and Lämmert, E. (eds.), *Konkurrenten in der Fakultät: Kultur, Wissen und Universität um 1900* (Frankfurt, 1999).

Krause-Vilmar, D., 'Die zeitgenössische marxistische Diskussion der "Überfüllung" akademischer Berufe am Ende des 19. Jahrhundert', *Zeitschrift für Pädagogik*, 14. Beiheft (1977), 99–106.

Kück, H., *Die Göttinger Sieben: Ihre Protestation und ihre Entlassung im Jahre 1837* (Aachen, 1987).

La Vopa, A. J., 'Vocations, careers and talent: Lutheran pietism and sponsored mobility in eighteenth-century Germany', *Comparative Studies in Society and History*, 28 (1986), 255–86.

—— *Grace, talent and merit: poor students, clerical careers and professional ideology in eighteenth-century Germany* (Cambridge, 1988).

Liedman, S. E., 'Institutions and ideas: mandarins and non-mandarins in the German academic intelligentsia', *Comparative Studies in Society and History*, 28 (1986), 119–44.

Lundgreen, P., 'Education for the science-based industrial state? The case for nineteenth-century Germany', *History of Education*, 13 (1984), 59–67.

—— 'Akademiker und "Professionen" in Deutschland', *Historische Zeitschrift*, 254 (1992), 657–70.

Lutz, R. R., 'The German revolutionary student movement 1819–1833', *Central European History*, 4 (1971), 215–41.

McClelland, C. E., 'German universities in the eighteenth century: crisis and renewal', *Studies on Voltaire and the Eighteenth Century*, 167 (1977), 169–89.

—— *State, society and university in Germany 1700–1914* (Cambridge, 1980).

—— 'The wise man's burden: the role of academicians in Imperial German culture', in D. B. King and others, *Essays on culture and society in modern Germany* (College Station, Tex., 1982), 45–69.

—— 'Structural change and social reproduction in German universities 1870–1920', *History of Education*, 15 (1986), 177–93.

Machinek, A. (ed.), *Dann wird Gehorsam zum Verbrechen: Die Göttinger Sieben, ein Konflikt um Obrigkeitswillkür und Zivilcourage* (Göttingen, 1989).

Maier, H., 'Aufklärung, Pietismus, Staatswissenschaft: Die Universität Halle nach 300 Jahren', *Historische Zeitschrift*, 261 (1995), 769–91.

Malettke, K. (ed.), *175 Jahre Wartburgfest, 18. Oktober 1817–18. Oktober 1992: Studien zur politischen Bedeutung und zum Zeithintergrund der Wartburgfeier* (Heidelberg, 1992).

Manegold, K. H., *Universität, Technische Hochschule und Industrie: Ein Beitrag zur Emanzipation der Technik im 19. Jahrhundert unter besonderer Berücksichtigung der Bestrebungen Felix Kleins* (Berlin, 1970).

Marchand, S. L., *Down from Olympus: archaeology and philhellenism in Germany 1750–1970* (Princeton, 1996).

Maschke, E. and Sydow, J. (eds.), *Stadt und Hochschule im 19. und 20. Jahrhundert* (Sigmaringen, 1979).

Mazón, P., 'Die Auswahl der "besseren Elemente": Ausländische und jüdische Studentinnen und die Zulassung von Frauen an deutschen Universitäten 1890–1919', *Jahrbuch für Universitätsgeschichte*, 5 (2002), 185–98.

Mechow, M., *Berliner Studenten 1810–1914* (Berlin, 1975).

Menze, C., *Die Bildungsreform Wilhelm von Humboldts* (Hanover, 1975).

Michalski, G., *Der Antisemitismus im deutschen akademischen Leben in der Zeit nach dem I. Weltkrieg* (Frankfurt, 1980).

Mitgau, H., 'Soziale Herkunft der deutschen Studenten bis 1900', in H. Rössler and G. Franz (eds.), *Universität und Gelehrtenstand 1400–1800: Büdinger Vorträge 1966* (Limburg/Lahn, 1970).

Möller, S., *Zwischen Wissenschaft und 'Burschenherrlichkeit': Studentische Sozialisation im Deutschen Kaiserreich 1871–1914* (Stuttgart, 2001).

Mommsen, W. J., *Bürgerliche Kultur und künstlerische Avantgarde: Kultur und Politik im deutschen Kaiserreich 1870 bis 1918* (Frankfurt, 1994).

Moraw, P., 'Humboldt in Giessen: Zur Professorenberufung an einer deutschen Universität des 19. Jahrhunderts', *Geschichte und Gesellschaft*, 10 (1984), 47–71.

—— and Press, V. (eds.), *Academia Gissensis: Beiträge zur älteren Giessener Universitätsgeschichte* (Marburg, 1982).

Mosse, G. L., *The crisis of German ideology: intellectual origins of the Third Reich* (New York, 1964).

Müller, D., 'The qualifications crisis and school reform in late nineteenth-century Germany', *History of Education*, 9 (1980), 315–31.

Müller, G. and others, *Die Universität Jena: Tradition und Innovation um 1800* (Stuttgart, 2001).

Müller, R., *Ideal und Leidenschaft: Sexuelle Sozialisation der akademischen Jugend im Biedermeier* (Berlin, 1999).

Müller, R. A., *Akademische Ausbildung zwischen Staat und Kirche: Das bayerische Lyzealwesen 1773–1849* (Paderborn, 1986).

Müth, R., *Studentische Emanzipation und staatliche Repression: Die politische Bewegung der Tübinger Studenten im Vormärz, insbesonders von 1825 bis 1837* (Tübingen, 1977).

Nipperdey, T., *Deutsche Geschichte 1866–1918. I. Arbeitswelt und Bürgergeist* (Munich, 1990).

—— *Germany from Napoleon to Bismarck 1800–1866* (Dublin, 1996). [orig. German 1983]

O'Boyle, L., 'Klassische Bildung und soziale Struktur in Deutschland zwischen 1800 und 1848', *Historische Zeitschrift*, 207 (1968), 584–608.

—— 'Learning for its own sake: the German university as nineteenth-century model', *Comparative Studies in Society and History*, 25 (1983), 3–25.

—— 'Judgments of German society: the history of higher education in nineteenth-century Germany', *Internationales Archiv für Sozialgeschichte der Deutschen Literatur*, 13 (1988), 140–57.

Oelschlägel, T., *Hochschulpolitik in Württemberg 1819–25: Die Auswirkungen der Karlsbader Beschlüsse auf die Universität Tübingen* (Sigmaringen, 1995).

Paletschek, S., *Die permanente Erfindung einer Tradition: Die Universität Tübingen im Kaiserreich und in der Weimarer Republik* (Stuttgart, 2001).

Paulsen, F., *The German universities and university study* (London, 1906). [trans. of German edn. 1902]

Pester, T., *Zwischen Autonomie und Staatsräson: Studien und Beiträge zur allgemeinen deutschen und Jenaer Universitätsgeschichte im Übergang vom 18. zum 19. Jahrhundert* (Jena, 1992).

Petry, L., 'Die Gründung der drei Friedrich-Wilhelms-Universitäten Berlin, Breslau und Bonn', in O. Brunner and others (eds.), *Festschrift Hermann Aubin zum 80. Geburtstag* (Wiesbaden, 1965), 687–709.

Pfetsch, F. R., 'Scientific organization and science policy in Imperial Germany 1871–1914: the foundation of the Imperial Institute of Physics and Technology', *Minerva*, 8 (1970), 557–80.

—— *Zur Entwicklung der Wissenschaftspolitik in Deutschland 1750–1914* (Berlin, 1974).

Pickus, K. H., *Constructing modern identities: Jewish university students in Germany 1815–1914* (Detroit, 1999).

Polster, G., *Politische Studentenbewegung und bürgerliche Gesellschaft: Die Würzburger Burschenschaft im Kräftefeld von Staat, Universität und Stadt 1814–1850* (Heidelberg, 1989).

Pozzo, R., 'Kant's *Streit der Fakultäten* and conditions in Königsberg', *History of Universities*, 16/2 (2000), 96–128.

Prahl, H. W., *Sozialgeschichte des Hochschulwesens* (Munich, 1978).

Pulzer, P. G. J., *The rise of political anti-semitism in Germany and Austria* (New York, 1964).

Richarz, M., *Der Eintritt der Juden in die akademischen Berufe: Jüdische Studenten und Akademiker in Deutschland 1678–1848* (Tübingen, 1974).

Riedel, M., 'Wilhelm von Humboldts Begründung der "Einheit von Forschung und Lehre" als Leitidee der Universität', *Zeitschrift für Pädagogik*, 14. Beiheft (1977), 231–47.

Riese, R., *Die Hochschule auf dem Wege zum wissenschaftlichen Grossbetrieb: Die Universität Heidelberg und das badische Hochschulwesen 1860–1914* (Stuttgart, 1977).

Ringer, F., 'Higher education in Germany in the nineteenth century', *Journal of Contemporary History*, 2/3 (1967), 123–38.

—— *The decline of the German mandarins: the German academic community 1890–1933* (Cambridge, Mass., 1969).

—— 'The German academic community 1870–1920', *Internationales Archiv für Sozialgeschichte der Deutschen Literatur*, 3 (1978), 108–29.

—— 'Bildung, Wirtschaft und Gesellschaft in Deutschland 1800–1960', *Geschichte und Gesellschaft*, 6 (1980), 5–35.

—— 'Academics in Germany: German and Jew, some preliminary remarks', *Leo Baeck Institute Year Book*, 36 (1991), 207–12.

—— 'A sociography of German academics 1863–1938', *Central European History*, 25 (1992), 251–80.

Roseman, M. (ed.), *Generations in conflict: youth revolt and generation formation in Germany 1770–1968* (Cambridge, 1995).

Rösener, W., 'Das katholische Bildungsdefizit im Deutschen Kaiserreich: ein Erbe der Säkularisation von 1803?', *Historisches Jahrbuch*, 112 (1992), 104–27.

Rupp, E., *Der Beginn des Frauenstudiums an der Universität Tübingen* (Tübingen, 1978).

Schelsky, H., *Einsamkeit und Freiheit: Idee und Gestalt der deutschen Universität und ihrer Reformen* (Reinbek bei Hamburg, 1963).

Schiera, P., *Laboratorium der bürgerlichen Welt: Deutsche Wissenschaft im 19. Jahrhundert* (Frankfurt, 1992).

Schindling, A., *Bildung und Wissenschaft in der frühen Neuzeit 1650–1800* (Munich, 1994).

Schlüter, A. (ed.), *Pionierinnen, Feministinnen, Karrierefrauen? Zur Geschichte des Frauenstudiums in Deutschland* (Pfaffenweiler, 1992).

Schmeiser, M., *Akademischer Hasard: Das Berufsschicksal des Professors und das Schicksal der deutschen Universität 1870–1920. Eine verstehende soziologische Untersuchung* (Stuttgart, 1994).

Schneider, U. J., 'The teaching of philosophy at German universities in the nineteenth century', *History of Universities*, 12 (1993), 197–338.

See, K. von, *Die Göttinger Sieben: Kritik einer Legende*, 2nd edn. (Heidelberg, 1997).

Sheehan, J. J., *The career of Lujo Brentano: a study of liberalism and social reform in Imperial Germany* (Chicago, 1966).

—— *German history 1770–1866* (Oxford, 1989).

Shils, E. (ed.), 'Academic freedom then and now: the dismissal of Leo Arons from the University of Berlin', *Minerva*, 18 (1980), 499–520.

Siemann, W., 'Chancen und Schranken von Wissenschaftsfreiheit im deutschen Konstitutionalismus 1815–1918', *Historisches Jahrbuch*, 107 (1987), 315–48.

Sing, A., *Die Wissenschaftspolitik Maximilians II. von Bayern (1848–1864): Nordlichterstreit und gelehrtes Leben in München* (Berlin, 1996).

Speitkamp, W., 'Staat und Bildung in Deutschland unter dem Einfluss der französischen Revolution', *Historische Zeitschrift*, 250 (1990), 549–78.

Sperber, J., '*Bürger, Bürgertum, Bürgerlichkeit, Bürgerliche Gesellschaft*: studies of the German (upper) middle class and its sociocultural world', *Journal of Modern History*, 69 (1997), 271–97.

Steiger, G., *Aufbruch: Urburschenschaft und Wartburgfest* (Leipzig, 1967).

Steinhilber, H., *Von der Tugend zur Freiheit. Studentische Mentalitäten an deutschen Universitäten 1740–1800* (Hildesheim, 1995).

Stickler, M., 'Neuerscheinungen zur Studentengeschichte seit 1994: Ein Forschungsbericht über ein bisweilen unterschätztes Arbeitsfeld der Universitätsgeschichte', *Jahrbuch für Universitätsgeschichte*, 4 (2001), 262–70.

Sweet, P. R., *Wilhelm von Humboldt: a biography*, 2 vols. (Columbus, Ohio, 1978–80).

Thielbeer, H., *Universität und Politik in der deutschen Revolution von 1848* (Bonn, 1983).

Titze, H., 'Überfüllungskrisen in akademischen Karrieren: eine Zyklustheorie', *Zeitschrift für Pädagogik*, 27 (1981), 187–224.

—— 'Die zyklische Überproduktion von Akademikern im 19. und 20. Jahrhundert', *Geschichte und Gesellschaft*, 10 (1984), 92–121.

—— *Datenhandbuch zur deutschen Bildungsgeschichte. I. Hochschulen. 1. Teil: Das Hochschulstudium in Preussen und Deutschland 1820–1944. 2. Teil: Wachstum und Differenzierung der deutschen Universitäten 1830–1945*, 2 vols. (Göttingen, 1987–95).

Tribe, K., 'Business education at the Mannheim Handelshochschule 1907–1933', *Minerva*, 32 (1994), 158–85.

Tuchman, A., *Science, medicine and the state in Germany: the case of Baden 1815–1871* (New York, 1993).

—— 'Institutions and disciplines: recent work in the history of German science', *Journal of Modern History*, 69 (1997), 298–319.

Turner, R. S., 'The growth of professorial research in Prussia 1818 to 1848: causes and context', *Historical Studies in the Physical Sciences*, 3 (1971), 137–82.

—— 'The *Bildungsbürgertum* and the learned professions in Prussia 1770–1830: the origins of a class', *Histoire Sociale-Social History*, 13 (1980), 105–35.

—— 'The Prussian universities and the concept of research', *Internationales Archiv für Sozialgeschichte der Deutschen Literatur*, 5 (1980), 68–93.

—— 'The Prussian professoriate and the research imperative 1790–1840', in H. N. Jahnke and M. Otte (eds.), *Epistemological and social problems of the sciences in the early nineteenth century* (Dordrecht, 1981), 109–21.

—— 'The great transition and the social patterns of German science', *Minerva*, 25 (1987), 56–76.

—— 'Universitäten', in K. E. Jeismann and P. Lundgreen (eds.), *Handbuch der deutschen Bildungsgeschichte. III. 1800–1870: Von der Neuordnung Deutschlands bis zur Gründung des Deutschen Reiches* (Munich, 1987), 221–49.

Volkov, S., 'Soziale Ursachen des Erfolgs in der Wissenschaft: Juden im Kaiserreich', *Historische Zeitschrift*, 245 (1987), 315–42.

Weber, C., *Der 'Fall Spahn' (1901): Ein Beitrag zur Wissenschafts- und Kulturdiskussion im ausgehenden 19. Jahrhundert* (Rome, 1980).

Weber, Marianne, *Max Weber: a biography* (New York, 1974).

Weber, M. 'The power of the state and the dignity of the academic calling in Imperial Germany: the writings of Max Weber on university problems', *Minerva*, 11 (1973), 571–632.

Wehler, H. U., *Deutsche Gesellschaftsgeschichte. III. Von der 'Deutschen Doppelrevolution' bis zum Beginn des Ersten Weltkrieges 1849–1914* (Munich, 1995).

Weill, C., 'La "question des étrangers": les étudiants russes en Allemagne 1900–1914', *Le Mouvement Social*, 120 (1982), 77–94.

Weischedel, W. (ed.), *Idee und Wirklichkeit einer Universität: Dokumente zur Geschichte der Friedrich-Wilhelms-Universität zu Berlin* (Berlin, 1960).

Wiener, P. B., 'German universities in the age of nationalism', *University of Birmingham Historical Journal*, 12 (1969–70), 100–27.

Willett, O., *Sozialgeschichte Erlanger Professoren 1743–1933* (Göttingen, 2001).

Windolf, P., *Expansion and structural change: higher education in Germany, the United States, and Japan 1870–1990* (Boulder, Colo., 1997).

ITALY

Barbagli, M., *Educating for unemployment: politics, labor markets, and the school system—Italy 1859–1973* (New York, 1982). [orig. Italian 1974].

Berlinguer, L., 'L'autonomia universitaria tra legge Casati e riforma Gentile: prime considerazioni', in M. Ascheri (ed.), *Scritti di storia del diritto offerti dagli allievi a Domenico Maffei* (Padua, 1991), 557–76.

Bologna: *Università di Bologna. Gaudeamus Igitur: studenti e goliardia 1888–1923* (Bologna, 1995).

Boudard, R., *L'Organisation de l'université et de l'enseignement secondaire dans l'Académie impériale de Gênes entre 1805 et 1814* (Paris, 1962).

Boyer, F., 'Les institutions universitaires en Piémont de 1800 a 1802', *Revue d'Histoire Moderne et Contemporaine*, 17 (1970), 913–17.

Brizzi, G. P. and Varni, A. (eds.), *L'università in Italia fra età moderna e contemporanea: aspetti e momenti* (Bologna, 1991).

Broccoli, A., *Educazione e politica nel mezzogiorno d'Italia (1767–1860)* (Florence, 1968).

Bucci, S., *La scuola italiana nell'età napoleonica: il sistema educativo e scolastico francese nel Regno d'Italia* (Rome, 1976).

Carpanetto, D. and Ricuperati, G., *Italy in the age of reason 1685–1789* (London, 1987).

Ciprandi, I. and others, *Problemi scolastici ed educativi nella Lombardia del primo ottocento. 2. L'istruzione superiore* (Milan, 1978).

Colao, F., *La libertà di insegnamento e l'autonomia nell'università liberale: norme e progetti per l'istruzione superiore in Italia (1848–1923)* (Milan, 1995).

Ermini, G., *Storia della Università di Perugia* (Bologna, 1947).

Guagnini, A., 'Higher education and the engineering profession in Italy: the *Scuole* of Milan and Turin 1859–1914', *Minerva*, 26 (1988), 512–48.

Laven, D., 'Liberals or libertines? Staff, students, and government policy at the University of Padua 1814–1835', *History of Universities*, 11 (1992), 123–64.

Malatesta, M. (ed.), *Society and the professions in Italy 1860–1914* (Cambridge, 1995).

Mazzotti, M., 'The making of the modern engineer: analytic rationality and social change in the kingdom of Naples', *History of Universities*, 17 (2002), 121–61.

Milan: *Il centenario del Politecnico di Milano 1863–1963* (Milan, 1964).

Milan: *Il Politecnico di Milano: una scuola nella formazione della società industriale 1863–1914* (Milan, 1981).

Montaldo, S., 'Università, professioni, pubblico impiego (1814–1859)', *Annali di Storia delle Università Italiane*, 5 (2001), 117–38.

Mor, C. G. and Di Pietro, P., *Storia dell'Università di Modena* (Florence, 1975).

Moretti, M. and Porciani, I., 'Il reclutamento accademico in Italia: uno sguardo retrospettivo', *Annali di Storia delle Università Italiane*, 1 (1997), 11–39.

Musiedlak, D., *Université privée et formation de la classe dirigeante: l'exemple de l'Université L. Bocconi de Milan (1902–1925)* (Rome, 1990).

Outram, D., 'Education and politics in Piedmont 1796–1814', *Historical Journal*, 19 (1976), 611–33.

—— 'Military empire, political collaboration, and cultural consensus: the *Université Impériale* reappraised, the case of the University of Turin', *History of Universities*, 7 (1988), 287–303.

Polenghi, S., *La politica universitaria italiana nell'età della destra storica (1848–1876)* (Brescia, 1993).

Porciani, I., 'L'università dell'Italia unita', *Passato e Presente*, 29 (1993), 123–35.

Raicich, M., *Scuola, cultura e politica da De Sanctis a Gentile* (Pisa, 1981).

Ricuperati, G., 'L'Università di Torino nel Settecento: ipotesi di ricerca e primi risultati', *Quaderni Storici*, 8 (1973), 575–98.

—— and Roggero, M., 'Educational policies in eighteenth-century Italy', *Studies on Voltaire and the Eighteenth Century*, 167 (1977), 223–69.

Roggero, M., *Il sapere e la virtù: stato, università e professioni nel Piemonte tra settecento ed ottocento* (Turin, 1987).

Rosada, M. G., *Le università popolari in Italia 1900–1918* (Rome, 1975).

Rossi, M., *Università e società in Italia alla fine dell'800* (Florence, 1976).

Santoni Rugiu, A., *Chiarissimi e magnifici: il professore nell'università italiana (dal 1700 al 2000)* (Scandicci, 1991).

Soldani, S. (ed.), *L'educazione delle donne: scuole e modelli di vita femminile nell'Italia dell'Ottocento* (Milan, 1989).

—— and Turi, G. (eds.), *Fare gli italiani: scuola e cultura nell'Italia contemporanea. I. La nascita dello stato nazionale* (Bologna, 1993).

Tomasi, T. and Bellatalla, L., *L'università italiana nell'età liberale (1861–1923)* (Naples, 1988).

—— and others, *Scuola e società nel socialismo riformista (1891–1926)* (Florence, 1982).

Torraca, F. and others, *Storia della Università di Napoli* (Naples, 1924).

Weiss, O., 'La "scienza tedesca" e l'Italia nell'Ottocento', *Annali dell'Istituto Storico Italo-Germanico in Trento*, 9 (1983), 9–85.

RUSSIA AND POLAND

Alston, P. L., *Education and the state in Tsarist Russia* (Stanford, 1969).

—— 'Two centuries of higher education in Russia: reflections on recent books and articles', *Paedagogica Historica*, 27 (1991), 261–9.

Bailes, K. E., *Science and Russian culture in an age of revolutions: V. I. Vernadsky and his scientific school 1863–1945* (Bloomington, Ind., 1990).

Beauvois, D., *Lumières et société en Europe de l'Est: l'Université de Vilna et les écoles polonaises de l'Empire russe (1803–32)* (Lille, 1977).

Besançon, A., *Éducation et société en Russie dans le second tiers du XIXe siècle* (Paris, 1974).

Brim, S., *Universität und Studentenbewegung in Russland im Zeitalter der Grossen Reformen 1855–1881* (Frankfurt, 1985).

Brower, D. R., 'Student political attitudes and social origins: the Technological Institute of Saint Petersburg', *Journal of Social History*, 6 (1972–3), 202–13.

—— *Training the nihilists: education and radicalism in Tsarist Russia* (Ithaca, 1975).

Clay, C. B., 'Le rôle de l'ethnologie universitaire dans le développement d'une nation ukrainienne dans l'Empire russe 1830–1850', *Histoire de l'Éducation*, 86 (2000), 61–82.

Engel, B. A., 'Women medical students in Russia 1872–1882: reformers or rebels?', *Journal of Social History*, 12 (1978–9), 394–414.

—— *Mothers and daughters: women of the intelligentsia in nineteenth-century Russia* (Cambridge, 1983).

Flynn, J. T. 'Russia's "university question": origins to great reforms 1802–1863', *History of Universities*, 7 (1988), 1–35.

—— *The university reform of Tsar Alexander I 1802–1835* (Washington, DC, 1988).

Hajdukiewicz, L. and Karas, M., *The Jagiellonian University: traditions—the present—the future* (Cracow, 1978).
Hamm, M. F., *Kiev: a portrait 1800–1917* (Princeton, NJ, 1993).
Hans, N., 'Educational reform in Poland in the eighteenth century', *Journal of Central European Affairs*, 13 (1954), 301–10.
Hausmann, G., *Universität und städtische Gesellschaft in Odessa 1865–1917: Soziale und nationale Selsbstorganisation an der Peripherie des Zarenreiches* (Stuttgart, 1998).
Hosking, G., *Russia: people and empire 1552–1917* (London, 1997).
Johanson, C., *Women's struggle for higher education in Russia 1855–1900* (Kingston, Ont., 1987).
Kassow, S. D., *Students, professors, and the state in Tsarist Russia* (Berkeley, 1989).
—— 'Professionalism among university professors', in H. D. Balzer (ed.), *Russia's missing middle class: the professions in Russian history* (Armonk, NY, 1996), 197–221.
McClelland, J. C., *Autocrats and academics: education, culture, and society in Tsarist Russia* (Chicago, 1979).
Mathes, W. L., 'N. I. Pirogov and the reform of university government 1856–1866', *Slavic Review*, 31 (1972), 29–51.
—— 'N. I. Pirogov and the university question in the era of the great reform', *Jahrbücher für Geschichte Osteuropas*, NS 36 (1988), 1–14.
Pushkin, M., 'The professions and the intelligentsia in nineteenth-century Russia', *University of Birmingham Historical Journal*, 12 (1969–70), 72–99.
Siilivask, K. (ed.), *History of Tartu University 1632–1982* (Tallinn, 1985).
Wartenweiler, D., *Civil society and academic debate in Russia 1905–1914* (Oxford, 1999).
Whittaker, C. H., 'From promise to purge: the first years of St. Petersburg University', *Paedagogica Historica*, 18 (1978), 148–67.
—— *The origins of modern Russian education: an intellectual biography of count Sergei Uvarov, 1786–1855* (De Kalb, Ill., 1984).

SCANDINAVIA

Blomqvist, G., 'State, university and academic freedom in Sweden: the Universities of Uppsala and Lund between 1820 and 1920', *Minerva*, 35 (1997), 171–94.
Johannisson, K., *A life of learning: Uppsala University during five centuries* (Uppsala, 1989).
Kent, N., *The soul of the north: a social, architectural and cultural history of the Nordic countries 1700–1940* (London, 2000).
Klinge, M., *Eine nordische Universität: die Universität Helsinki 1640–1990* (Helsinki, 1992).
Kolbe, L., 'The university town as a *lieu de mémoire*: student identity and manifestations at the University of Helsinki 1828–1990', *History of Universities*, 14 (1995–6), 181–200.
Lindroth, S., *A history of Uppsala University 1477–1977* (Stockholm, 1976).
Stybe, S. E., *Copenhagen University: 500 years of science and scholarship* (Copenhagen, 1979).

SPAIN AND PORTUGAL

Addy, G. M., 'The first generation of academic reform in Spanish universities 1760–1789', *Studies on Voltaire and the Eighteenth Century*, 167 (1977), 475–89.
Aguilar Piñal, F., *Los comienzos de la crisis universitaria en España: antología de textos del siglo XVIII* (Madrid, 1967).

Aguilar Piñal, F., *La Universidad de Sevilla en el siglo XVIII: estudio sobre la primera reforma universitaria moderna* (Seville, 1969).

Álvarez de Morales, A., *La ilustración y la reforma de la universidad en la España del siglo XVIII*, 2nd edn. (Madrid, 1979).

Baldó Lacomba, M., 'La Universidad de València bajo el signo del absolutismo (1814–33)', *Estudis d'Història Contemporània del País Valencià*, 2 (1981), 163–213.

Baratas Díaz, L. A., 'La influencia francesa en el proyecto de reforma universitaria español de principios del siglo XX: una analogía incompleta', *Hispania*, 55 (1995), 645–72.

Claustros y estudiantes: Congreso internacional de historia de las universidades americanos y españolas en la edad moderna (Valencia, 1989).

Delgado, B., *La Institución Libre de Enseñanza en Catalunya* (Barcelona, 2000).

Delgado Criado, B. (ed.), *Historia de la educación en España y América. III. La educación en la España contemporánea (1789–1975)* (Madrid, 1994).

Doctores y escolares: II Congreso internacional de historia de las universidades hispánicas (Valencia, 1998).

Ferreira Carrato, J., 'The Enlightenment in Portugal and the educational reforms of the marquis of Pombal', *Studies on Voltaire and the Eighteenth Century*, 167 (1977), 359–93.

Guereña, L. L. and Fell, E. M. (eds.), *L'Université en Espagne et en Amérique latine du moyen âge a nos jours. II. Enjeux, contenus, images* (Tours, 1998).

Hernández Díaz, J. M., 'L'Université dans l'Espagne contemporaine (1812–1983)', *Histoire de l'Éducation*, 78 (1998), 31–56.

Herr, R., *The eighteenth-century revolution in Spain* (Princeton, 1958).

Historia de la educación en España. II. De las Cortes de Cádiz a la revolución de 1868, 2nd edn. (Madrid, 1985).

Jiménez García, A., *El krausismo y la Institución Libre de Enseñanza* (Madrid, 1985).

Kagan, R. L., *Students and society in early modern Spain* (Baltimore, 1974).

O liberalísmo na peninsula ibérica na primeira metade do século XIX (Lisbon, 1982).

Maxwell, K., *Pombal, paradox of the Enlightenment* (Cambridge, 1995).

Molero Pintado, A., *La Institución Libre de Enseñanza: un proyecto español de renovación pedagógica* (Madrid, 1985).

Peset, J. L. and Peset, M., *Carlos IV y la Universidad de Salamanca* (Madrid, 1983).

Peset, M., 'La monarchie absolue et les universités espagnoles', *CRE-Information*, 72 (1985), 75–104.

—— and Peset, J. L., *La universidad española (siglos XVIII y XIX): despotismo ilustrado y revolución liberal* (Madrid, 1974).

——, ——, and Mancebo, M. F., 'La población universitaria de Valencia durante el siglo XVIII', *Estudis d'Història Contemporània del País Valencià*, 1 (1979), 7–42.

—— and others, *Historia de las universidades valencianas* (Alicante, 1993).

Puelles Benítez, M. de, 'The influence of political factors on the formation of the Spanish educational system 1809–1814', *Paedagogica Historica*, 28 (1992), 485–510.

Rodriguez, M. A., *A Universidade de Coimbra e os seus reitores: para uma história da instituição* (Coimbra, 1990).

Rodríguez-San Pedro Bezares, L. E., 'Les universités espagnoles à l'époque moderne', *Histoire de l'Éducation*, 78 (1998), 11–29.

—— (ed.), *Las universidades hispánicas: de la monarquía de los Austrias al centralismo liberal*, 2 vols. (Salamanca, 2000).

Salamanca: *Actas I Congreso Historia de Salamanca* (Salamanca, 1992).

Sarrailh, J., *L'Espagne éclairée de la seconde moitié du XVIIIe siècle* (Paris, 1954).

Sauter, G. O. and Puelles Benítez, M. de (eds.), *La revolución francesa y su influencia en la educación en España* (Madrid, 1990).

Serrano, C. and Salaün, S. (eds.), *1900 en Espagne (essai d'histoire culturelle)* (Bordeaux, 1988).

Shubert, A., *A social history of modern Spain* (London, 1990).

Turin, Y., *L'Éducation et l'école en Espagne de 1874 à 1902: libéralisme et tradition* (Paris, 1959).

—— *Miguel de Unamuno universitaire* (Paris, 1962).

—— 'Le problème universitaire et la révolution de 1868 en Espagne', *Revue d'Histoire Moderne et Contemporaine*, 18 (1971), 282–95.

Villacorta Baños, F., *Burguesia y cultura: los intelectuales españoles en la sociedad liberal* (Madrid, 1980).

—— *El Ateneo Cientifico, Literario y Artistico de Madrid (1885–1912)* (Madrid, 1985).

Viñao Frago, A., 'Les origines du corps professoral en Espagne: les Reales Estudios de San Isidro 1770–1808', *Paedagogica Historica*, 30 (1994), 119–74.

SWITZERLAND

Bonjour, E., *Die Universität Basel von den Anfängen bis zur Gegenwart 1460–1960* (Basel, 1960).

Borgeaud, C., *Histoire de l'Universite de Genève: l'Académie de Calvin dans l'Université de Napoléon 1798–1814* (Geneva, 1909).

Bouvier, N., Craig, G. A., and Gossman, L., *Geneva, Zurich, Basel: history, culture and national identity* (Princeton, 1994).

Delessert, A., *L'Université au défi: une histoire sociale de l'Université de Lausanne* (Lausanne, 1991).

Erb, H., *Geschichte der Studentenschaft an der Universität Zürich 1833–1936* (Zurich, 1937).

Feller, R., *Die Universität Bern 1834–1934* (Bern, 1935).

Gagliardi, E. and others, *Die Universität Zürich 1833–1933 und ihre Vorläufer* (Zurich, 1938).

Geisendorf, P. F., *L'Université de Genève 1559–1959: quatre siècles d'histoire* (Geneva, 1959).

Geneva: *Histoire de l'Université de Genève: l'Académie et l'Université au XIXe siècle* (Geneva, 1934).

Gossman, L., *Basel in the age of Burckhardt: a study in unseasonable ideas* (Chicago, 2000).

Im Hof, U., 'Die schweizerischen Varianten der kleindeutschen Universität: Zum Problem der ausländischen Einflüsse auf das schweizerische Hochschulwesens im 19. Jahrhundert', in *Festgabe Hans von Greyerz zum sechzigsten Geburtstag* (Bern, 1969), 593–623.

Marcacci, M., *Histoire de l'Université de Genève 1559–1986* (Geneva, 1987).

Meuwly, O., *Histoire des sociétés d'étudiants à Lausanne* (Lausanne, 1987).

Neumann, D., *Studentinnen aus dem Russischen Reich in der Schweiz (1867–1914)* (Zurich, 1987).

Scandola, P. (ed.), *Hochschulgeschichte Berns 1528–1984: Zur 150-Jahr-Feier der Universität Bern 1984* (Bern, 1984).

Staehelin, A., *Geschichte der Universität Basel 1632–1818* (Basel, 1957).

—— *Geschichte der Universität Basel 1818–1835* (Basel, 1959).

Tissot, L. and Wisard, F., 'L'Université de Lausanne et l'État de Vaud: la question de l'autonomie (1890–1945)', *Schweizerische Zeitschrift für Geschichte*, 43 (1993), 341–74.

Index